Medieval Learning and
Literature

R. W. HUNT

Medieval Learning and Literature

Essays presented to
RICHARD WILLIAM HUNT

Edited by
J. J. G. ALEXANDER
and
M. T. GIBSON

OXFORD
AT THE CLARENDON PRESS
1976

Oxford University Press, Ely House, London W. 1

GLASGOW NEW YORK TORONTO MELBOURNE WELLINGTON
CAPE TOWN IBADAN NAIROBI DAR ES SALAAM LUSAKA ADDIS ABABA
DELHI BOMBAY CALCUTTA MADRAS KARACHI DACCA
KUALA LUMPUR SINGAPORE HONG KONG TOKYO

ISBN 0 19 822402 8

© *Oxford University Press 1976*

*Printed in Great Britain
at the University Press, Oxford
by Vivian Ridler
Printer to the University*

FOREWORD

In the language of the medieval courts, this volume is a recognizance. It is an acknowledgement of an immense debt, and it is offered to Richard Hunt on the occasion of his retirement from the Keepership of Western Manuscripts at the Bodleian. He has held this position for just thirty years, and during this long period he has had a unique place in medieval studies as the guide and friend of hundreds of scholars of all ages and countries. He has done for them far more than it would be reasonable to expect from the busy guardian of one of the world's great manuscript collections. He has always been accessible to help research, to draw attention to unnoticed materials, to point out manuscripts and published work which would have escaped any but the most vigilant eye. And if he has done all this for the annual stream of correspondents and scholarly visitors to Oxford, what shall we say of his help to those who have had the good fortune to live here, his pupils, colleagues, friends, and fellow students?

Only those who have benefited from the liberal outpouring of his learning can say how much they owe to him. Speaking for myself, I have never willingly made up my mind on any important medieval issue until I have heard what he has to say about it. His comments have been the surest guide to the direction in which the truth will in the end be found to lie. Over the widest range of subjects he has the most accurately balanced judgement of anyone I have known. His is the rarest combination of gifts: a widely ranging learning combined with a most acute perception of what is important, a most decisive judgement without a particle of rancour. It is a combination of extraordinary power, and we have all drawn on his resources. There can be no question of repayment. So this volume is only a token; but besides being an expression of gratitude, it may serve to illustrate some of the areas in which his influence has been most strongly felt.

This is not the place to speak in detail of his own writings. There is a list of them at the end of this volume, and I suspect that it will be the most frequently consulted part of the book. It will seldom be consulted without making new discoveries. In reading it, there are two impressions which it leaves most vividly on my mind. The first is how often he has written on some topic which seemed austerely remote at the time of writing, but which has become increasingly central in the course of time. Consider the articles on the grammatical doctrines of the twelfth and thirteenth centuries. Who could have predicted, at the time when the material for the *Studies on Priscian* was collected, that grammatical doctrines would come to have so large a place in philosophical discussions, and that medieval doctrines long forgotten would re-emerge in the teachings of modern philosophical gurus? Or, to speak only of medieval scholarship, who would have foreseen the extent to which students of Anselm, Abelard, and Gilbert of Poitiers would have found themselves driven back to the study of grammar in order to understand their subjects? This auspicious foresight is to be found everywhere in the writings listed here. It may be said of many of the subjects with which they deal, as Stubbs said of Constitutional History, that they cannot be approached without an effort. But they contain the key to understanding the systematic thought of the western world.

The other impression which the list of writings at the end of this volume leaves on my mind is the importance of that twilight period forty years ago before the second World War. It was the period in medieval studies in Oxford when the influence of Professor Powicke was at its height. He exercised a liberating and expansive influence, and, like all great teachers, he pointed the way to areas beyond those in which he was himself engaged. He made the works of Denifle, Ehrle, Grabmann, Pelzer, and Wilmart, as well as the new writers of the recently founded *Recherches de théologie ancienne et médiévale*, which he at once introduced into the History Faculty Library, thoroughly at home among Oxford medievalists. Under these influences it is not surprising that medieval studies began to open out in new ways, and ambitious plans were made for the future. Among the young of those days, Richard Hunt was the best equipped for the task of mastering the great flood of new material and new ideas, and he was a natural leader in pressing forward along new lines of research.

One of the projects which emerged from the discussions of those years was the new periodical *Mediaeval and Renaissance Studies*, familiarly known at the time, in anticipation of the likely conditions of its birth, as MARS. I mention it here not only because

Richard Hunt was one of the editors from the beginning and several of his most perceptive articles are to be found in its pages, but also because it recalls the freshness and adventure, too easily forgotten, of those darkening days. The fact that it appeared at all, after being destroyed in Belgium in 1940 and (incredibly enough) reprinted in England in 1941, is also a hopeful sign in days scarcely more propitious for medieval studies than 1940.

These distant events linger pleasantly in the memory. Much more was planned than could be achieved. The promise of the spring was blighted by the war. But the Keeper of Western Manuscripts, who took up his duties when the war ended, has continued steadfastly on his course. In the Bodleian and at his home, he has fostered research, illuminated old and new problems, encouraged beginners, and helped everyone who needed help. In his own work, and in that of others, he has kept medieval scholarship moving along the lines which he was largely responsible for identifying forty years ago.

May he long continue, in his new freedom from the strain of administration, to be what he has always been. In making our recognizance, we express this hope and offer this volume as a token of gratitude and affection.

R. W. SOUTHERN

THE Editors would like to record their gratitude to Mrs. Susan Hall for her unfailing help at every stage in the preparation of this volume.

CONTENTS

List of Illustrations   xi

Abbreviations   xiii

I. MEDIEVAL LIBRARIES

1. Die Hofbibliothek unter Ludwig dem Frommen, *by*
   BERNHARD BISCHOFF   3

2. The Beginnings of Salisbury Cathedral Library, *by*
   NEIL RIPLEY KER   23

3. Describing Medieval Bookbindings, *by*
   GRAHAM POLLARD   50

4. The *Florilegium Angelicum*: its Origin, Content, and
   Influence, *by* RICHARD HUNTER ROUSE and MARY
   AMES ROUSE   66

5. The Influence of the Concepts of *Ordinatio* and
   Compilatio on the Development of the Book, *by*
   MALCOLM BECKWITH PARKES   115

II. HISTORY OF TEXTS

6. A Ninth-century Manuscript from Fleury: *Cato de
   senectute cum Macrobio, by*
   BRUCE CHARLES BARKER-BENFIELD   145

7. The Graz and Zürich Apocalypse of Saint Paul: An
   Independent Medieval Witness to the Greek, *by*
   THEODORE SILVERSTEIN   166

8. Some Poems Attributed to Richard of Cluny, *by*
   ALEXANDER BRIAN SCOTT   181

9.   La Tradition manuscrite des 'Quaestiones Nicolai peripatetici', *Anonymous*   200

10.   The Return of Petronius to Italy, *by*
ALBINIA CATHERINE DE LA MARE   220

III. SCHOOLS AND SCHOLARSHIP

11.   Master Vacarius and the Beginning of an English Academic Tradition, *by*
RICHARD WILLIAM SOUTHERN   257

12.   Peter of Corbeil in an English Setting, *by*
ELEANOR RATHBONE   287

13.   Oxford University Sermons, 1290–1293, *by*
BERYL SMALLEY   307

14.   Nicholas Trevet, Historian, *by*
RUTH JOSEPHINE DEAN   328

15.   Oxford Academical Halls in the Later Middle Ages, *by*
ALFRED BROTHERSTON EMDEN   353

16.   An Unnoticed Letter from Bessarion to Lorenzo Valla, *by* LOTTE MINNE LABOWSKY   366

IV. THE LAITY

17.   *E cathena et carcere*: The Imprisonment of Amaury de Montfort, 1276, *by* LEONARD EUGENE BOYLE, O.P.   379

18.   Instructions for a Devout and Literate Layman, *by*
WILLIAM ABEL PANTIN †   398

A Bibliography of the Published Writings of R. W. Hunt, *by* SUSAN PENELOPE HALL   423

Indices

     Manuscripts   431

     Personal Names   441

     Place-names   452

LIST OF ILLUSTRATIONS

PLATES

R. W. Hunt. *Frontispiece*

I   Bamberg, Staatsbibliothek, Class. 46, fol. 64. See pp. 3–22

II   Bamberg, Staatsbibliothek, Class. 42, fol. 49ᵛ

III   (*a*) Exeter Cathedral 3500. Exon Domesday, fol. 9. See pp. 23–49

        (*b*) London, British Library, Cotton Tiberius C. 1, fol. 112ᵛ

IV   Oxford, Bodleian Library, MS. Bodley 765

        (*a*) Fol. 1

        (*b*) Fol. 18

        (*c*) Fol. 51

V   Oxford, Keble College, MS. 22, fol. 6

VI   (*a*) Aberdeen, University Library, MS. 216, fol. 36

        (*b*) Oxford, Bodleian Library, MS. Bodley 756, fol. 1

VII   Vatican City, Biblioteca Apostolica Vaticana, Pal. lat. 957, fol. 97. See pp. 66–114

VIII   Rome, Biblioteca Angelica, MS. 1895, fol. 1

IX   Oxford, Bodleian Library, MS. Auct. D. 2. 8, fol. 105. See pp. 115–41

X   Oxford, St. John's College, MS. 49, fol. 12ᵛ

XI   Paris, Bibliothèque Nationale, lat. 3050, fol. 76

XII   Oxford, Bodleian Library, MS. Bodley 287, fol. 74ᵛ

XIII   Oxford, Keble College, MS. 26, fol. 17ᵛ

XIV   Oxford, New College, MS. 98, fol. 138

XV   Oxford, University College, MS. 67, fol. 52ᵛ

XVI   Oxford, Bodleian Library, MS. Bodley 568, fol. 242ᵛ

XVII   Oxford, Bodleian Library, MS. Auct. D. 4. 13, fol. 218. See pp. 379–97

XVIII   Paris, Bibliothèque Nationale, lat. 16677, fol. 9ᵛ. See pp. 145–65

XIX   Paris, Bibliothèque Nationale, lat. 7299, fol. 33

XX   Paris, Bibliothèque Nationale, lat. 6842D. See pp. 220–54

        (*a*) Fol. 1

        (*b*) Fol. 12ᵛ

        (*c*) Fol. 4

        (*d*) Fol. 75ᵛ

XXI (*a*) Vatican City, Biblioteca Apostolica Vaticana, Vat. lat.
      3403, fol. 31ᵛ
      (*b*) Vienna, Nationalbibliothek, 3198, fol. 63ᵛ
XXII Florence, Biblioteca Laurenziana, 47, 31, fol. 1
XXIII Vienna, Nationalbibliothek, s.n. 4755, fol. 1
XXIV Florence, Biblioteca Laurenziana, 37, 25
      (*a*) Fol. 8
      (*b*) Fol. 9
XXV   Florence, Biblioteca Laurenziana, 37, 25
      (*a*) Fol. 35
      (*b*) Fol. 24
      (*c*) Fol. 62ᵛ
XXVI Paris, Bibliothèque Nationale, lat. 7989
      (*a*) p. 188
      (*b*) p. 193
      (*c*) p. 188
      (*d*) p. 193
XXVII Paris, Bibliothèque Nationale, lat. 6106
      (*a*) Fol. 102ᵛ
      (*b*) Fol. 93
XXVIII Paris, Bibliothèque Nationale, lat. 7989, p. 233

Photographs are reproduced here by kind permission of the following:

Aberdeen, University Library. Pl. VI*a*
Bamberg, Staatsbibliothek. Pls. I, II
Exeter Cathedral, The Dean and Chapter. Pl. III*a*
Florence, Biblioteca Laurenziana. Pls. XXII, XXIV, XXV
London, British Library Board. Pl. III*b*
Oxford, Bodleian Library. Pls. IV, VI*b*, IX, XII, XVI, XVII
Oxford, Keble College, The Warden and Fellows. Pls. V, XIII
Oxford, New College, The Warden and Fellows. Pl. XIV
Oxford, University College, The Master and Fellows. Pl. XV
Oxford, St. John's College, The President and Fellows. Pl. X
Paris, Bibliothèque Nationale. Pls. XI, XVIII, XIX, XX, XXVI,
    XXVII, XXVIII
Rome, Biblioteca Angelica. Pl. VIII
Vatican City, Biblioteca Apostolica Vaticana. Pls. VII, XXI*a*
Vienna, Nationalbibliothek. Pls. XXI*b*, XXIII

ABBREVIATIONS

A.L.K.G.	*Archiv für Literatur- und Kirchengeschichte des Mittelalters*
Archives	*Archives d'histoire doctrinale et littéraire du moyen âge*
Beiträge	*Beiträge zur Geschichte der Philosophie (und Theologie) des Mittelalters*
B.L. [London]	British Library (formerly British Museum)
B.N. [Paris]	Bibliothèque Nationale
B.R. [Brussels]	Bibliothèque Royale
B.R.U.O.	A. B. Emden, *Biographical Register of the University of Oxford to A.D. 1500*, 3 vols., Oxford, 1957–9
Bodl. L.R.	*Bodleian Library Record*
C.L.A.	*Codices Latini Antiquiores*
C.S.E.L.	*Corpus Scriptorum Ecclesiasticorum Latinorum*
C.P.L.	*Calendar of Entries in the Papal Registers: Letters*
D.N.B.	*Dictionary of National Biography*
E.E.T.S., o.s./e.s.	Early English Text Society, Original Series/Extra Series
E.H.R.	*English Historical Review*
J.-L.	Ph. Jaffé, G. Wattenbach, &c., *Regesta Pontificum Romanorum ad annum 1196* (Leipzig, 1885–8)
M.A.R.S.	*Medieval and Renaissance Studies*
M.G.H.	*Monumenta Germaniae Historica*
O.H.S.	Oxford Historical Society
O.U.A.	Oxford University Archives
P.L.	Migne, *Patrologia Latina*
R.S.	Rolls Series
S.T.C.	A. W. Pollard and G. R. Redgrave, *A Short-title Catalogue of Books printed 1475–1640*, 2 vols., London, 1926
T.R.H.S.	*Transactions of the Royal Historical Society*
V.C.H.	*The Victoria History of the Counties of England*

I
MEDIEVAL LIBRARIES

1

Die Hofbibliothek unter Ludwig dem Frommen

'AUCH hinsichtlich der Bücher, von denen er in seiner Bibliothek eine große Menge zusammenbrachte, bestimmte er, daß sie von den Interessenten für einen angemessenen Preis erworben werden könnten und der Erlös den Armen zugutekommen sollte.' Diese Worte Einhards, die er nach dem Testament Karls des Großen in seiner Vita des Kaisers überliefert, sind der Grabgesang auf die erste große Bibliothek des Frankenreichs. Um 780 wurde sie durch den Willen des Herrschers begründet, und was wir darüber noch wissen können,[1] zeigt, daß nunmehr weitherzig und umsichtig Bewährtes und Vergessenes, erst jetzt von neuem Beachtetes gesammelt wurde. Daß die Bibliothek z. B. eine Anzahl von wertvollen und seltenen Klassikertexten besaß, läßt ein Verzeichnis erkennen, das mit größter Wahrscheinlichkeit ihr zugeschrieben werden kann.[2] Nicht bloß sich selbst genug, strahlte diese Bibliothek Wirkungen aus, indem sie Vorbild für andere wurde und diesen zugleich Texte vermittelte; so hat sie entscheidend zur Sicherung und Verbreitung der klassischen und patristischen Überlieferung und der darauf gegründeten neuen Bildung beigetragen.

Während die Hofbibliothek wuchs, brachten die Werkstätten der Kalligraphen und Buchmaler am Hofe, der schließlich in Aachen seine feste Residenz fand, jene kostbaren Handschriften hervor, die durch Wilhelm Koehler in zwei Bänden der 'Karolingischen Miniaturen' eine monumentale Veröffentlichung erfahren

---

[1] Vgl. B. Bischoff in *Karl der Große*, 2, *Das geistige Leben* (Düsseldorf, 1965), 42 ff.

[2] ebd., S. 59 ff. mit Abb. 6. Vgl. ferner die Einführung der von mir herausgegebenen Faksimileausgabe *Sammelhandschrift Diez.B Sant. 66* (*Codices selecti phototypice impressi*, 42; Graz, 1973), 21 ff. und 38 f.

haben.[1] Hier arbeitete jene Gruppe von Kräften, die mit dem Kalligraphen Godescalc beginnt und, sich allmählich verjüngend, die großen Prachthandschriften bis hin zum 'Lorscher Evangeliar' geschaffen hat. Ebenso, und nicht ohne Fühlung mit denLeistungen der 'Hofschule'[2] waren nach Koehler seit den letzten Jahren des VIII. Jahrhunderts auch die Künstler und Schreiber — unter ihnen Fremde[3] — am Hofe tätig, von denen die Evangeliare der viel weniger zusammengeschlossenen 'Gruppe des Wiener Krönungsevangeliars' hergestellt wurden.

Mit Recht sah Koehler die Entstehung und die Pflege dieser höfischen Buchkunst, ja die Möglichkeit ihrer Existenz stark an die Persönlichkeit des Herrschers gebunden; mit dieser Anschauung steht bei ihm als Ergebnis seiner Forschung im Einklang, daß die 'Hofschule' mit Karls Tode, 'wenn nicht schon früher' ihr Ende fand[4] und auch das Wirken der 'Gruppe des Krönungsevangeliars' nicht über 810 hinausgeht.[5] Zusammengesehen mit der Auflösung der Bibliothek Karls hinterläßt ein solches Abbrechen der damals vornehmsten Buchkunst am Hofe den Eindruck eines schicksalhaften Niedergangs, der 814 mit dem Thronwechsel unausweichlich eintreten mußte.[6] Das zwiespältige Bild, das die Geschichtsschreibung von Ludwig dem Frommen entwickelt hat, könnte der Meinung Vorschub leisten, daß die führende kulturelle Rolle des Hofes ausgespielt war.[7]

[1] W. Koehler, *Die Hofschule Karls des Großen* (*Die karolingischen Miniaturen*, 2; Berlin, 1958) und *Die Gruppe des Wiener Krönungs-Evangeliars*; *Metzer Handschriften* (dass., 3; Berlin, 1960). Zitiert als: Koehler 2 bzw. 3.

[2] Vgl. besonders Koehler 3, 25 ff. über die Initialen des Wiener Evangeliars; ferner S. 32 und 48. Die Lokalisierung dieser Gruppe am Hofe ist ein besonderes Verdienst Koehlers.

[3] Koehler (3, 51 Anm.) hielt es für möglich, daß einer von diesen mit dem Eintrag 'DEMETRIOS PR(ES)B(YTER)' (in Goldschrift auf fol. 118 des Wiener Codex) seinen Namen verewigt habe. Nach meinem Eindruck paßt der Charakter der Rustica jedoch sehr viel besser in ottonische Zeit; vgl. auch *C.L.A.* x. 1469.

[4] Koehler 2, 11.   [5] ebd. 3, 53.

[6] Die ausschließliche Bindung dieser Kunst an die Gestalt des großen Kaisers, der ihr höchste Ziele gesetzt hatte, klingt dort an, wo flüchtig des Nachfolgers und seiner neuen Männer gedacht wird (Koehler 2, 12). Über Ludwigs Persönlichkeit vgl. B. Simson, *Jahrbücher des Fränkischen Reiches unter Ludwig dem Frommen*, 1 (Leipzig, 1874), 33, über seine Bildung besonders, 38 f.; R. R. Bezzola, *Les Origines et la formation de la littérature courtoise en Occident*, 1 (Paris, 1958), 147 ff. Thegan, c. 19 (*M.G.H. Scriptores*, 2. 594) bezeugt seine Abneigung gegen die 'poetica carmina gentilia', deren Lektüre zu seiner Erziehung gehört hatte.

[7] Die Kontinuität nach 814 unterstreicht J. Fleckenstein, *Die Hofkapelle der deutschen Könige*, 1 (*Schriften der M.G.H.* 16. 1, Stuttgart, 1959), 231 ff.

Ich glaube jedoch, daß diese düstere Perspektive einer gewissen Revision bedarf. Zunächst ist nichts darüber bekannt, ob tatsächlich die Bibliothek Karls vollständig aufgelöst wurde;[1] da nachweislich Texte, die sich in ihr befunden hatten, im Umkreis des Hofes in Ludwigs Zeit benützt wurden, ist es recht unwahrscheinlich.[2] Es sind auch einige Handschriften erhalten, die selbst die Bestimmung für Ludwig bezeugen oder als sein Besitz angesprochen werden können. Noch als König erhielt er von Angilbert von Saint-Riquier ein Exemplar von Augustins 'De doctrina christiana' mit zwei Begleitgedichten.[3] Unter den Geschenken, die 827 eine Gesandtschaft des griechischen Kaisers Michael überbrachte, befand sich die schöne Handschrift der Werke des Pseudo-Dionysius, nach der die karolingischen Übersetzungen geschaffen wurden.[4] Diesen bekannten Stücken kann die von Theodulf mit einer persönlichen Widmung an Ludwig noch als König versehene Abschrift seines Werkes 'De spiritu sancto' hinzugefügt werden.[5]

Wie seinem Vater sind auch Ludwig literarische Werke von den Autoren gewidmet worden,[6] und nicht nur an den Kaiser, sondern auch an seine zweite Gemahlin, die schöne und ungewöhnlich gebildete Judith, die seit 819 die Physiognomie des Hofes mitbestimmte, wurden sowohl Gedichte wie Erklärungen biblischer Bücher gerichtet.[7] Vom Aussehen des von Hraban

---

[1] Vermutungen darüber, welche Bücher zu den verkauften gehört haben könnten, in *Karl der Große*, 2 (wie S. 3, Anm. 1), 61 f.

[2] ebd., S. 61 (Libri Carolini; Mensuratio orbis; 'authentischer Text' der Regula S. Benedicti; der von Walahfrid erwähnte 'Liber Albini magistri').

[3] P. E. Schramm–F. Mütherich, *Denkmale der deutschen Könige und Kaiser* (München, 1962), 121 und 225 (Abb.).

[4] ebd., S. 120 f. und 224 (Abb.).

[5] London B.L. Harley 3024. Die von mehreren Händen des für Theodulf arbeitenden Skriptoriums in Orléans geschriebene Handschrift erhielt auf dem sonst leeren Bl. 2ᵛ von einer weiteren Hand die zweite Widmung (*Poetae*, 1, 528, v. 37 ff.); der 'rex' kann nur Ludwig sein. — Die von P. Lehmann, *Mitteilungen aus Handschriften*, 2 (*Sitzungsber. d. Bayer. Akad. d. Wiss., Phil.-hist. Kl.* 1930), 27 ff., angenommene Entstehung im mittleren Westdeutschland trifft nicht zu.

[6] Sich ergänzende Aufzählungen bei E. Lesne, *Les Livres, 'scriptoria' et bibliothèques du commencement du VIIIᵉ à la fin du XIᵉ siècle* (*Histoire de la propriété ecclésiastique en France*, 4; Lille, 1938), 447 f., und Bezzola (wie S. 4, Anm. 6), 151 ff. Die für Ludwig angefertigte Kopie von Dungals 'Responsa adversus perversas Claudii Taurinensis sententias' liegt vielleicht im Vaticanus Reg. Lat. 200 vor; vgl. M. Ferrari, *Italia medioevale e umanistica*, 15 (1972), 15. Unsicher ist die Beurteilung der bei Lesne, S. 447 genannten Vita S. Maximini.

[7] Über Judith vgl. E. Dümmler, *Geschichte des ostfränkischen Reiches*, 1, 2. Aufl. (Leipzig, 1887), 41, Anm. 3; Bezzola (wie S. 4, Anm. 6), S. 162 f.; F. von Bezold, *Historische Zeitschrift*, 130 (1924), 377 ff.

überreichten Exemplars von 'De laudibus sanctae crucis' kann
man sich nach anderen Fuldaer Abschriften mit dem Figuren-
gedicht, in das die Darstellung des Kaisers eingeschlossen ist, eine
Vorstellung bilden,[1] von jenem des Widmungsexemplars der für
Judith verfaßten Kommentare zu den Büchern Judith und Esther
nach einer jetzt in Genf befindlichen Kopie.[2]

Schließlich übte der Lorscher Mönch Gerward, der bereits 814
zum Personal des Hofes gehörte, schon längere Zeit vor 828 das
Amt des 'palatii bibliothecarius' aus.[3] Aus Versen Gerwards, die
in einigen Codices von Einhards 'Vita Karoli' stehen, ist, wie es
scheint, auf eine Abschrift dieses Werkes zu schließen, die Ludwig überreicht wurde.[4]

So ungleich diese Zeugnisse sind, und obwohl gewiß manche
der späten Widmungen mehr das Unglück als den Glanz der
Regierung Ludwigs zum Anlaß haben, sprechen sie doch im
ganzen dafür, daß Buch und Bibliothek von der Kultur auch dieses Hofes untrennbar waren. Ludwig selbst schenkte eines der
Glanzstücke, die aus der älteren 'Hofschule' hervorgegangen
waren, ein etwa um 800 entstandenes Evangeliar, im Jahre 827
dem Kloster Saint-Médard in Soissons.[5]

Wie oben bemerkt,[6] hat Koehler für den Ablauf und Ausgang
der beiden von ihm dargestellten Werkgruppen bestimmte enge
zeitliche Grenzen angegeben, obwohl über 795, den Terminus
ad quem für den Dagulf-Psalter, hinaus keinerlei brauchbarer
Fixpunkt bekannt war. Angesichts der großen Unterschiede
im Schriftbild der mittleren und der späten Handschriften muß

---

[1] S. Schramm–Mütherich (wie S. 5, Anm. 3), S. 121 f. und 227 (Abb.).

[2] ebd., S. 121 und 226 (Abb).

[3] Über ihn s. H. Löwe, *Deutsches Archiv*, 8 (1950), 88 f.; J. Fleckenstein (wie
S. 4, Anm. 7), S. 66 (hier auch die Namen von Lehrern der Hofschule); K. Hampe
in *Neues Archiv*, 21 (1896), 611. Über ältere Handschriften, die mehr oder weniger
sicher aus der Hofbibliothek stammen und später auf dem Umweg über Gerwards Büchersammlung in Gannita bei Nymwegen nach Lorsch gelangt sind,
vgl. vorläufig *Karl der Große*, 2 (wie S. 3, Anm. 1), 61 Anm. 75. Es handelt sich
um: Vatic. Pal. lat. 210 (Augustinus, Opuscula; Nicetas; in Unziale saec. VI–VII;
C.L.A. i. 84), das jetzt verschollene älteste Fragment des Justinus (angel-
sächsisch saec. VIII; *C.L.A.* ix. 1370), Pal. lat. 189 (Augustinus, De doctrina
christiana, saec. VIII–IX) und — freilich mit sehr geringer Wahrscheinlichkeit —
den Vergilius Palatinus, Pal. lat. 1631 (*C.L.A.* i. 99).

[4] *Poetae*, 2, 126; *Einhardi Vita Karoli Magni* rec. G. Waitz, ed. sexta (Han-
nover, 1911), S. xxix und vgl. S. xvii. Die überschwengliche Huldigung des
'supplex famulus' kann schwerlich an einen anderen als Ludwig gerichtet sein.

[5] Koehler 2, 70.

[6] S. oben S. 4.

die Frage gestellt werden, ob die von ihm zugrundegelegten Datierungen sich halten lassen.

Nach der ikonographisch-stilistischen Entwicklung ergab sich ihm für die letzten Vertreter der 'Hofschule' zwingend die Reihenfolge: Evangeliar von Saint-Médard, jüngere Teile der Trierer Ada-Handschrift ('Ada II'), Lorscher Evangeliar; die damit erreichte Chronologie ist zwar nur eine relative, doch war sie durch 'paläographische und textkritische Argumente kontrolliert und gestützt', und wenigsten die letzteren hat Koehler summarisch dargeboten.[1] Die 'paläographische Nachprüfung', für die er durch wohlbedachte Abbildung aller in den Handschriften enthaltenen Schriftarten die Möglichkeit geschaffen hatte, hat noch nicht stattgefunden; doch hat er selbst bei der Behandlung der 'Gruppe des Wiener Krönungsevangeliars' im dritten Band der 'Karolingischen Miniaturen' auf einige Elemente zurückgegriffen.

Die methodischen Grundlagen für Koehlers Beurteilung dieser jüngeren am Hofe gepflegten Stilrichtung sind die gleichen: kunsthistorische, textliche und paläographische Untersuchung, jedoch war die Auswertung der uneinheitlichen Befunde bei dieser Gruppe schwieriger.

Ihrem äußeren Bilde nach stehen sich das eine in goldener Rustica und Unziale geschriebene Wiener Purpurevangeliar und drei in schlichter Minuskel geschriebene Codices, die näher verwandten Evangeliare von Aachen und Brescia und das Brüsseler Evangeliar, gegenüber. Der kunstgeschichtliche Zusammenhang manifestiert sich in der antikischen Stilisierung der Evangelistenbilder und in den von großartig einfachen klassischen Architekturen eingefaßten Kanontafeln, ferner, im Negativen, in der Abwendung von dem reichen Initial- und Rahmenschmuck der 'Hofschule'; nur in den Initialen des Wiener Evangeliars war noch eine Kompromißlösung versucht worden. In allen zeigen sich die Wirkungen einer entschiedenen Orientierung an älteren Vorbildern; Koehler sprach sogar die Vermutung aus, der Urheber des 'retrospektiven' Stiles sei Einhard gewesen.[2]

Nach den textlichen Erhebungen sind das Wiener Evangeliar und die drei anderen in der Textgeschichte, wie sie sich nach Koehler

---

[1] Zum Vorhergehenden: Koehler 2, 13 ff.

[2] Koehler 3, 55. Auch in dem spätesten erhaltenen Codex der 'Hofschule', dem Lorscher Evangeliar, erfolgt nach der Initialseite zu Matthäus die entschiedenste Abkehr von dem üppigen und schweren Dekor der Evangelienanfänge.

am Hofe abgespielt hat, verwurzelt, doch in verschiedener Weise.[1] Das Wiener Evangeliar ist mit jenem von Abbeville verknüpft, das innerhalb der 'Hofschule' in mehrfacher Beziehung eine Sonderstellung einnimmt; dagegen steht der Text der Minuskelhandschriften dem des Soissons-Evangeliars und nicht etwa dem der jüngsten Handschriften der 'Hofschule' am nächsten.

Koehler, der wertvolle Anregungen zur Verfeinerung der paläographischen Methode gegeben hat,[2] hat im Zusammenhang der Untersuchung der Gruppe des Krönungsevangeliars auch zur Schrift eingehend Stellung genommen und dabei alle vier vorkommenden Schriftarten berücksichtigt: die monumentale Capitalis ('Quadrata'), die Capitalis rustica, die Unziale und die Minuskel, die bildsamste, die für die paläographische Beurteilung am dankbarsten ist.

Die monumentale Capitalis ist schon in der 'Hofschule' auf der Stufe der Evangeliare von Soissons und Abbeville über eine noch etwas willkürliche, auch durch ihre kleinen Zierformen unklassische Form hinausgelangt.[3] Dadurch sind dieser Stufe die Capitalis-Zeilen in den Handschriften der 'Gruppe des Wiener Evangeliars' vergleichbar.

Die Capitalis rustica findet sich als zusammenhängend gebrauchte Schriftart nur in den Vorstücken des in Unziale geschriebenen Wiener Evangeliars, nach älteren Vorlagen gestaltet, wie Koehler betont.[4] Immerhin löst sie auch in der 'Hofschule' in zunehmendem Maße die 'Quadrata' in den oft beengten Beischriften der Kanontafeln ab, und im Lorscher Evangeliar ist die Rustica im allgemeinen gut proportioniert. Mit besonders eleganter Natürlichkeit, die auch die Schrift des Wiener Evangeliars weit übertrifft, ist sie als Auszeichnungsschrift in den Evangeliaren von Aachen und Brescia ausgeführt. Im Brüsseler Codex ist einige Rustica bemerkenswert gut,[5] andere schlecht.

[1] Koehler 3, 33 ff., besonders 40 f. Die obigen Bemerkungen beziehen sich nur auf den Evangelientext, nicht auf Vorstücke und Capitularia.

[2] In seiner Anzeige von Rand's *Script of Tours*, 1 in *Göttinger Gelehrte Anzeigen*, 193 (1931), 332 ff.

[3] Koehler, 3, 28 f. Im Abbeville-Codex wird außerdem die Benützung einer neuen vortrefflichen Vorlage sichtbar. Es ist jedoch noch nicht das Musteralphabet des 'scriptor regius' Bertcaudus, das die Handschrift Bern 250 überliefert hat (vgl. die Abbildung in *Karl der Große, Werk und Wirkung, Katalog der Ausstellung*, Aachen, 1965, Abb. 36, dazu S. 222 f.).

[4] Koehler 3, 24.

[5] ebd. 3, Taf. 46 *b, d.*

Diese Schriftart war nach fast völligem Aussterben in den festländischen Schriftgebieten — vielleicht mit Ausnahme Spaniens — durch die Angelsachsen als Auszeichnungschrift und zur Differenzierung von Texten wiederaufgenommen und danach in der karolingischen Schriftreform zu einem festen Bestandteil der Hierarchie der Schriftarten geworden. Man wahrte zwar das Alphabet, aber eine kräftige, dichte, nicht manierierte Rustica, die einer antiken Schrift nachgeschrieben oder nachempfunden war, ist im Mittelalter selten zu beobachten. Wo sie begegnet, mag man sie geradezu als einen Gradmesser des Verständnisses für antike Form ansehen.[1] Unter diesem Aspekt verdient die Rustica der jüngeren Handschriften der 'Gruppe des Krönungsevangeliars' hervorgehoben zu werden.

Koehler hat eine ähnliche Beobachtung für die Unziale ausgesprochen, wenn er der 'Unziale des VIII. Jahrhunderts', die in der 'Hofschule' im späten Lorscher Codex noch einmal aufgenommen wurde,[2] sehr pointiert die Unziale des Wiener Evangeliars gegenüberstellte, die nach ihm ihre Qualität der Nachahmung italienischer Schrift des VI. Jahrhunderts verdankt.[3] In den Minuskelhandschriften der zweiten Gruppe kommt Unziale auffälligerweise nicht einmal als Auszeichungsschrift vor.

Bei der Minuskel ist es notwendig, bis zu den Anfängen der 'Hofschule' zurückzugehen, ohne daß damit das Problem der jüngsten am Hofe entstandenen Prachthandschriften aus den Augen verloren würde. Die Minuskel läßt sich in der 'Hofschule' von etwa 780 an verfolgen, da sie für ganze Codices oder, in den Unzialhandschriften, in Beigaben, besonders in den Capitularia evangeliorum, verwendet ist.[4] Die Schrift zeigt zwischen der schweren und schwungvollen Minuskel Godescalcs, die sich mit anderen 'austrasischen' Schriften vergleichen läßt,[5] und der streng gebundenen des Lorscher Evangeliars mehrfach ein anderes Gesicht. Die Gruppierung der 'jüngeren' Minuskelhandschriften: Aachen und Brescia gegenüber Brüssel gilt auch für die Schrift.

Überraschenderweise hat Koehler bei den Minuskelschriften

---

[1] Noch die Form und der Duktus, die Lupus von Ferrières und seine Schüler der Rustica geben, lassen sich für diese Behauptung ins Feld führen. Lupus hat in den letzten Jahren Ludwigs des Frommen am Hofe gelebt, wahrscheinlich als Mitglied der Hofkapelle; vgl. Fleckenstein (wie S. 4, Anm. 7), S. 72.

[2] Koehler 2, 24.   [3] ebd. 3, 24 f.   [4] ebd. 3, 24.

[5] Vgl. B. Bischoff in: *Karl der Große*, 2 (wie S. 3, Anm. 1), 234.

das Wagnis unternommen, die Schrift beider Gruppen, der 'Hofschule' wie der von ihr etwas abgesetzten 'Gruppe des Krönungsevangeliars',[1] in eine Art Stammbaum zusammenzuführen.[2] Er entwirft das Bild einer Entwicklung, deren Ausgangspunkt bei der als monumental empfundenen Schrift der ersten Anlage des Ada-Codex (Abb.: Koehler 2, Taf. 29 f.), d. h. im Formenbestand bei der Godescalc-Stufe (2, Taf. 7) liegt; den zweiten Höhepunkt erreicht sie in der gleichfalls 'monumentalen' Schrift des Aachener Evangeliars (3, Taf. 29 und 36). Ein formaler Fortschritt wird — immer nach Koehler — durch die Einführung des Sechsliniensystems erzielt, das im Abbeville-Evangeliar (2, Taf. 33) und im Harley-Evangeliar (2, Taf. 66) greifbar wird.[3] Vervollkommnet und 'verbunden mit einer entschiedenen Vertikaltendenz erscheint es zuerst im Soissons-Evangeliar (2, Taf. 93), dessen Minuskel die größte Verwandschaft mit der des Evangeliars in Brescia (3, Taf. 39) hat'. Koehler hat hier die Konsequenz gezogen, daß die beiden Handschriften und dazu das Aachener Evangeliar (3, Taf. 29 und 36) als praktisch gleichzeitig entstanden angesehen werden müßten. In der Reihe der Minuskelschriften der 'Hofschule' stellt jene des Soissons-Evangeliars 'die klarste Formulierung ihrer Eigenart' dar. Mit ihr verglichen, fallen 'Ada II' (2, Taf. 98) und das Lorscher Capitulare (2, Taf. 111*b*) ab, auch infolge geringerer Regelmäßigkeit. Noch krasser stellt sich die parallel laufende Entwicklung innerhalb der anderen Gruppe dar. Denn im Brüsseler Evangeliar (3, Taf. 49 und 46 f.), das mit den letzten 'Hofschul'-Handschriften etwa gleichzeitig angesetzt wird, ist 'der Schrifttypus der Evangeliare in Aachen und Brescia in Auflösung begriffen'.

Wenn diese Ausführungen Koehlers zutreffen, die zwar kein neues absolutes Datum zutage fördern konnten, aber von ihm in die Begründung der oben zitierten Begrenzung: 'spätestens 814, wenn nicht früher' bzw. 'nicht nach 810' eingebaut sind, müßte die Datierung der spätesten Handschriften paläographisch verbindlich sein können. Das erscheint mir nicht möglich.

Koehler scheint bei der Beurteilung der Schriften der kunsthistorisch so eng zusammengehörigen 'Hofschul'-Codices von

---

[1] Die Schreiber der Minuskelhandschriften nennt Koehler (3, 52) 'Einheimische'.

[2] Koehler, 3, 30 f.

[3] Über dieses 'System', dessen Definition und Gültigkeit sehr problematisch wird, wenn man es an den Denkmälern mißt, s. Koehler 3, 30 Anm. 19.

Maßstäben auszugehen, wie sie für ein geschlossenes Skriptorium gelten, bei dem schon der Schreibunterrrricht am Ort als erste Voraussetzung künftiger Teilnahme an der Tätigkeit der Schreiber angenommen werden kann. Für solche bildet die klösterliche Welt den idealen Rahmen;[1] dort kann durch mehrere Generationen der gleiche Stil gepflegt werden, wobei er sich allmählich verändert. Aber viel häufiger sind auch unter den großen karolingischen Klosterschulen, die einen hohen Schriftstandard bewahren, jene, die im Laufe des IX. Jahrhunderts mehrere Male zu einem neugeprägten Stil übergegangen sind, meistens wahrscheinlich bei einem Wechsel des Schreiblehrers. Dabei kann der neue Stil aus einer Reform des alten hervorgegangen sein oder auch garnicht in einem erkennbaren Zusammenhang mit ihm stehen. Aber der Fortschritt der sich oft kaum merklich vollziehenden Entwicklung der Schrift kann darin ruckartig sichtbar werden.

In dem besonderen Falle der Schreiber der 'Hofschule', eines an einem Hofe mit beträchtlicher Fluktuation tätigen, nicht monastischen Skriptoriums, ist über dessen Einheit, über seine Rekrutierung und über den Schreibunterricht kaum etwas festzustellen. Während die Anwendung der besonderen Schriftarten und die Wahl ihrer Typen für die Prachthandschriften der Koordinierung in höherem Grade unterliegen mußte und auch der sparsame Gebrauch von Abkürzungen eine Norm des Skriptoriums sein konnte, brauchte für die Form der Minuskel ein Zwang nicht zu bestehen, sofern sie nur 'karolingisches Niveau' hatte. Noch weniger ist bezüglich der Schreiber der jüngeren Minuskelhandschriften von Aachen und Brescia einerseits, von Brüssel andererseits über die Schultradition am Hofe[2] oder die Bindung ihrer Stilideale an diese eine Aussage möglich; die drei Kriterien, die die Minuskel des Aachener Evangeliars mit den ältesten 'Hofschul'-Handschriften verknüpfen sollen,[3] sind nicht spezifisch genug, um eine Einheitlichkeit eines Skriptoriums, die über mehrere Jahrzehnte angehalten hätte, zu beweisen.

Anstelle zusammenhängender Entwicklung sehe ich in den Minuskelschriften dieser Codices einen Wechsel von kleinen Gruppen und einzelnen Händen, die mit einem anderen, anderswo

---

[1] Ähnlich Koehler in der Besprechung von Rand (wie S. 8, Anm. 2), S. 335.
[2] S. oben S. 10, Anm. 1.
[3] Koehler 3, 29 f. Über den vierten Punkt, das 'Sechsliniensystem', müßten weitere Beobachtungen gesammelt werden.

erlernten Stil auftreten. Gruppen bilden: Godescalc, das Arsenal-Evangeliar und 'Ada I'; Dagulf und der neben ihm an dem Psalter beteiligte Schreiber; höchst wahrscheinlich das Evangeliar von Abbeville und 'Ada II'. Als einzeln auftretende Hände sind dagegen zu bezeichnen: jene des Cotton Fragments;[1] die Minuskel des Harley-Evangeliars. Bei der eigenartigen Hand des Evangeliars von Soissons kann noch ein Nachklang insularer Schreibtradition im Spiele sein, wobei das *t* besonders verräterisch ist.

Aber von all diesen Händen und ihrer Freiheit ist die nachdrücklich disziplinierte Schrift des Lorscher Capitulares sehr verschieden;[2] sie ist von einem neuen Prinzip beherrscht: einer strengen Bindung aller Elemente mit der Wirkung harmonischer Dichte — einem Prinzip, das ich mir selbst am Ende von Karls Regierungszeit noch nicht als wirksam vorstellen kann. Die wichtigsten, das Erscheinungsbild mitbestimmenden Einzelmomente sind: das niedrige runde *d* neben langem *d*, seltenes Majuskel-*N*, seltenes nach unten verlängertes *i* nach *l* und *t* am Wortende; *a* mit schmalem, fast spitzem Bogen; *g* mit geschlossenem, meist etwas zusammengedrücktem unterem Bogen; *x* mit einwärts gekrümmtem linkem unterem Strich; als Ligaturen *et*, selten *NT*, *st* und, mit kurzem *r*: *re* und selten *ra* (mit geschlossenem *a*); unter den Kürzungen -*q*, und selten -*b*;.

Von Wesen und Form her ist das völlige Gegenbild zu dieser Schrift die Minuskel, die in zahlreichen Lorscher Codices, z. B. in fünf Evangeliaren,[3] vorliegt.[4] Das eine von diesen ist auf einen Zeitraum von 12–13 Jahren datierbar: die aus der Phillipps-Sammlung (Nr. 3015) stammende Handschrift, die vorübergehend zur Bibliothek Dr. Martin Bodmer, Cologny, gehörte und sich jetzt im Besitz von H. P. Kraus, New York, befindet. Sie ist für den Wormser Bischof Folcwich geschrieben, der 825 oder 826 sein Amt antrat. Die Schrift hat auch in Lorsch starke Veränderungen durchgemacht, ehe diese magistrale Form ausgebildet und rezipiert war. Aber, dem dritten Jahrzehnt des IX.

---

[1] Koehler 2, Taf. 32*c*; vgl. *Karl der Große*, 2 (wie S. 3, Anm. 1), 55 und Taf. 2.

[2] Neben Koehler 2, Taf. 111*b* muß das Vollfaksimile: *Das Lorscher Evangeliar*, Einleitung von W. Braunfels (München, 1965), herangezogen werden.

[3] Bamberg, Bibl. 95; ehemals Cologny, s. unten; Darmstadt 1957; Manchester, Rylands Library, Latin 9; Orléans 20 (17).

[4] Über den 'jüngeren Lorscher Stil' s. B. Bischoff, *Lorsch im Spiegel seiner Handschriften* (Sonderausgabe aus der Festschrift *Die Reichsabtei Lorsch 764–1964*, Band 2; München 1974), S. 35 ff., vgl. Taf. 12.

Jahrhunderts voll angemessen, ist diese meiner Meinung nach im ersten Jahrzehnt undenkbar, was, wie ich glaube, ebenso für die Minuskel des Capitulare evangeliorum im Lorscher Codex gilt. Zwei Möglichkeiten der Erklärung für die Übereinstimmung der Schrift desselben mit den anderen Lorscher Schriften scheinen sich anzubieten: entweder kam der Schreiber, der in Lorsch die Schrift reformierte, vom Hofe,[1] oder das Prachtevangeliar wurde erst in Lorsch durch das Capitulare ergänzt.[2]

Wie besonders beim Vergleich mit der Freiheit der älteren Schriften der 'Hofschule' deutlich wird, unterliegen auch die unter sich verwandten Hände des Evangeliars von Aachen und jenes von Brescia, das von mehreren Schreibern geschrieben ist,[3] einem Prinzip strenger Regulierung und Geschlossenheit, mit dem meines Erachtens eine Datierung ins erste Jahrzehnt nach 800 unvereinbar ist und das diese Handschriften, die auch eine treffliche Rustica auszeichnet,[4] in Ludwigs Zeit verweist.[5]

Die Hände des Brüsseler Evangeliars[6] — es sind wenigstens vier — sind in sich sicher, schräg, und z. T. mit einem etwas breiteren weichen Duktus geschrieben; sie sind in einer anderen Schule ausgebildet, wenn nicht in zwei verschiedenen Schulen.[7]

---

[1] In Anbetracht dessen, daß der 'Hofschule' ja auch verlorene Prachthandschriften in unbekannter Zahl zugeschrieben werden müssen, von denen nur einzelne aus ihren Nachwirkungen erschlossen werden können (vgl. F. Mütherich in: *Karl der Große, Lebenswerk und Nachleben*, 3, Düsseldorf, 1965, 39 ff.), ist vielleicht auch die Zeitspanne für die Aktivität der 'Hofschule' etwas länger als im äußersten Falle bis 814 anzusetzen.

[2] Die Untersuchung der Capitularia erlaubt vielleicht eine Entscheidung.

[3] Koehler, 3, Taf. 29 and 36 (Aachen) bzw. 39 (Brescia); auch nur eine stilistische Parallele zwischen letzterem und der Schrift des Soissons-Codex vermag ich gegenüber Koehler (3, 31) nicht zu erkennen.

[4] S. oben S. 8.

[5] Koehler sah eine Rechtfertigung seiner Datierung der Minuskelcodices in der Schrift des 811/812 entstandenen Sakramentars des Bischofs Hildoard von Cambrai, Cambrai Ms. 164. Vgl. Koehler, *Buchmalerei des frühen Mittelalters* (München, 1972), S. 136 f.; eine Abbildung bei E. K. Rand, *Studies in the Script of Tours*, 2 (Cambridge, Mass., 1934), Taf. 38, 2, dazu S. 92 (Rand seinerseits erklärte aus einem Vorurteil die Handschrift für eine Kopie aus dem zweiten Viertel des IX. Jahrhunderts und die Datierung für eine Übernahme aus dem Original). Die Schrift von Cambrai 164 ist aber nicht streng gebunden wie jene der Evangeliare von Lorsch und Aachen; sie gehört einem auch sonst in Nordostfrankreich anzutreffenden schmalen, schrägen Stil mit gewissen älteren Freiheiten an, ohne die kleine kanonische Gruppe von Ligaturen.

[6] Drei davon auf den Tafeln 40, 46, 47 bei Koehler 3.

[7] Koehler (3, 24 und 31) wollte in dieser Schrift die Auflösung des Schrifttypus der Evangeliare von Aachen und Brescia erkennen, die angesichts seiner Datierung in unwahrscheinlich kurzer Zeit erfolgt sein müßte.

In der Ausführung dieser Handschrift hat eine gewisse Nachlässigkeit geherrscht, aber wenigstens am Anfang des Matthäus-Evangeliums ist in der monumentalen Capitalis und der Rustica die Hand eines Meisters sichtbar, die den Zusammenhang mit dem Hofe bestätigt.[1] Die Minuskel des Codex dürfte einer Datierung in das erste Viertel des IX. Jahrhunderts nicht im Wege stehen; das Auftreten der stilvollen Rustica spricht nach den vorangegangenen Ausführungen über die Evangeliare von Aachen und Brescia für eine Entstehung in der Zeit Ludwigs.

Mit Hilfe paläographischer Feststellungen und zwar gerade durch den Vergleich mit diesem trotz seiner Mängel höfischen Brüsseler Evangeliar lassen sich weitere Handschriften in die Betrachtung einer Schreibtätigkeit im Umkreis Ludwigs und seines Hofes einbeziehen. Es gibt unter den karolingischen Handschriften der Volksrechte, die im allgemeinen eher ein kleines Format einhalten,[2] einen Riesen, den Parisinus lat. 4418. Der Codex mißt 42·7 × ca. 30 cm (34–35·5 × 22–22·5 cm), in 2 Kolumnen zu 39–40 Zeilen (fols. 38–48 in Langzeilen). Auf 294 Blättern enthält er die Epitome Aegidiana, Julians Epitome und folgende Leges: L. Ribuaria, L. Salica emendata, L. Burgundionum, L. Visigothorum. Die Handschrift ist von mehreren ähnlichen Händen hergestellt, unter denen eine vorherrschende in demselben eigentümlich weichen Duktus wie die erwähnte Hand des Bruxellensis schreibt, mit der sie wahrscheinlich identisch ist. Die Vergleichbarkeit der Handschriften erstreckt sich bis in die gelegentlich recht ungeschickte Form der Satzinitiale A und die Form der Sporen bei dem vergrößerten einfachen N als Initiale. Von Ligaturen (selbst *st* und *ra* mit geschlossenem *a*) ist die Schrift fast frei, ebenso von Abkürzungen (außer -*b*, und seltenem -*b*;, -*q*', ferner Rechtstermini in der Lex Salica). Ein solches Corpus konnte nicht für den gewöhnlichen Richter bestimmt sein. Um so mehr aber kann es der Rechtsprechung und Rechtsfindung am Hofe gedient haben, wo es vielleicht durch ein Exemplar der süddeutschen Volksrechte vervollständigt wurde.[3]

[1] Koehler 3, Taf. 46*b*. S. oben S. 8.
[2] Auffällige Schriftverwandtschaft einer Anzahl von Legeshandschriften aus der ersten Hälfte des IX. Jahrhunderts macht es geradezu wahrscheinlich, daß sie serienmäßig in einem Skriptorium, in dem französischer Stil herrschte, geschrieben wurden.
[3] Wegen der Zusammensetzung der Handschrift dachte R. Buchner, *Textkritische Untersuchungen zur Lex Ribvaria (Schriften des Reichsinstituts für ältere*

Daß in der Umgebung Ludwigs ein solches Corpus entstand, mag sogar durch ein persönliches Interesse des Herrschers veranlaßt worden sein, der nach dem Zeugnis Thegans[1] in der Kenntnis der weltlichen Gesetze ausgebildet war.

Diesen zwei Handschriften, der Evangelien und der Leges, ist auch ein Klassikercodex zuzuordnen. Die Bamberger Handschrift Class. 46 (M. V. 14) mit Senecas Epistulae morales, lib. XIV–XX: ep. 89–124 (21·5 × 18 cm (15·5 × 11·7 cm), 21 Z.) ist von mehreren ähnlichen Händen geschrieben, die auch an dem etwas breiteren, weichen Duktus, der in dem Brüsseler Evangeliar vorkommt, teilhaben (s. Tafel 1); nur die Schrift von fols. 52^v–53 oben fällt durch dünnere und steilere Formen heraus. Während die Auszeichnungsschrift ungleichwertig ist, greift stellenweise ein Rubrikator mit einer kräftigen, etwas scharfen Rustica in die Arbeit ein.[2] Die textlich besonders wertvolle Handschrift ist aus einem Unzialcodex kopiert worden.[3] Die Vermutung, daß dies am Hofe geschah, wird auch dadurch gestützt, daß der als Erzieher des Kaisersohnes Karl in Aachen weilende Walahfrid einen dem Bambergensis engst verwandten Text von ep. 120 in sein Vademecum aufnehmen konnte.[4]

Daß am Hofe Ludwigs sowohl Prachthandschriften, die für Pfalzkapellen und Kirchen des Reiches bestimmt sein konnten, wie Texthandschriften verschiedener Kategorien hergestellt wurden, für die die Hofbibliothek der gegebene Aufbewahrungsort war, kann wohl als erwiesen gelten. Aber auch bei anderen 'anonymen' Handschriften darf unter Abwägung alles Für und Wider auf Grund ihrer künstlerischen, kalligraphischen und textlichen Qualität Entstehung am Hofe oder im Auftrag mit ihm eng

---

deutsche Geschichtskunde, 5, Leipzig, 1940), S. 80 f., an südfranzösische Herkunft. Obwohl Ludwigs Herrschaft in Aquitanien damit in Einklang zu bringen wäre, scheint mir die Nähe zum Brüsseler Evangeliar (und dem Seneca, s. unten) den Ausschlag für die Entstehung am Aachener Hofe zu geben.

[1] Kap. 2 (*M.G.H. Scriptores*, 2, 591).

[2] Vgl. auf der Tafel 173*a* bei E. Chatelain, *Paléographie des classiques latins* (Paris, 1884–92), das Explicit and Incipit mit 'VALE' und 'SENECA...SALVTEM'. — Über die Schrift des nach F. Bücheler, *Senecae epistulae aliquot ex Bambergensi et Argentoratensi codicibus* (Bonn, 1879), S. vi, aus dem ersteren abgeschriebenen, 1870 zugrundegegangenen Straßburger Codex ist nach Büchelers Abbildung ein Urteil nicht möglich.

[3] Vgl. L. D. Reynolds, *The Medieval Tradition of Seneca's Letters* (Oxford, 1965), 55 ff.

[4] Vgl. B. Bischoff, *Mittelalterliche Studien*, 2 (Stuttgart, 1967), 47 Anm. 38; Reynolds, S. 92 f.

verbundener Persönlichkeiten zum mindesten in Betracht gezogen werden. Das gilt von drei illustrierten Handschriften antiker Texte, die zu den hervorragendsten Denkmälern karolingischer Buchmalerei aus der Zeit zwischen 820 und der Mitte des Jahrhunderts zählen: dem vatikanischen Terenz, dem Londoner und dem Leidener Aratus.[1] Sie sind in dem später Lotharingien genannten Gebiet zwischen Ost und West entstanden 'für hochstehende Empfänger oder Auftraggeber in humanistisch interessierten und gebildeten Kreisen', an Stellen, die über antike Codices und über ausgezeichnete Künstler verfügt haben müssen.[2] Von dem prächtigen Leidener Arat, der eine leider namenlose persönliche Widmung 'Vale fidens in Domino Christi vestitus amore' enthält, läßt sich zudem stilistisch eine Verbindungslinie zu dem letzten karolingischen Atelier in Aachen, der 'Hofschule' Lothars, ziehen.[3]

Ich glaube, daß auch für eine nicht beschriebene Gruppe von schmucklosen Handschriften antiker und patristischer Texte, die noch in der Zeit Ludwigs, im ersten Drittel des IX. Jahrhunderts, ihren Schwerpunkt hat, die Entstehung an seinem Hofe wahrscheinlich gemacht werden kann.[4] Sie sind ausgezeichnet durch die Wahl der Texte, die über den schlichten Durchschnitt hinausgeht, durch die Disziplin und Ökonomie der Schrift, die jener der Evangeliare von Aachen und Brescia sehr nahekommt, durch die Anlage des Buches nach dem Muster spätantiker Vorbilder, vielleicht der jeweiligen direkten Vorlage, und schließlich durch

---

[1] W. Koehler–F. Mütherich, *Die Hofschule Kaiser Lothars, Einzelhandschriften aus Lotharingien* (*Die karolingischen Miniaturen*, 4, Berlin, 1971), 73 ff. — In den drei Handschriften ist auch die Rustica (s. oben S. 8 f.) in verschiedener Gestaltung, aber z. T. mit verständnisvoller Beobachtung antiker Modelle verwendet; vgl. Koehler 4, Taf. 28 ff.; 62 ff. (besonders z.B. 65b, 72a); 96.

[2] Koehler 4, 74.

[3] Koehler 4, 82 f.; vgl. S. 32. Da in diesem Codex die Monatsbilder des Kalenders von 354 benützt sind (ebd., S. 81), verstärkt sich die Wahrscheinlichkeit, daß auch dieser im Original oder in einer karolingischen Kopie am Hofe zugänglich war und daß Walahfrid ihn hier benützen konnte; s. Bischoff (wie S. 15 Anm. 4), S. 43 f. — Weitere Rückschlüsse für die Buchmalerei am Hofe unter Ludwig dem Frommen sind von Untersuchungen über die in der späteren karolingischen Kunst gebräuchlichen Evangelistentypen zu erwarten. Vgl. F. Mütherich in *Intuition und Kunstwissenschaft, Festschrift für Hanns Swarzenski* (Berlin, 1973), 77.

[4] Hinweise darauf habe ich in *La scuola nell' Occidente latino nell' alto Medioevo* (*Settimane di studio del Centro Italiano di studi sull' alto Medioevo*, xix, 1, Spoleto, 1972), 392, und in *Die Reichsabtei Lorsch* (wie S. 12, Anm. 4) gegeben. Sie werden hier etwas modifiziert.

die hohe textliche Qualität. Der in den Haupthandschriften bestimmende unverkennbare Schrifttyp kann nicht aus einer bekannten Schule abgeleitet werden und mündet auch nicht in eine solche ein; in einigen Codices sind die Hände dieses Typs von sehr andersartigen Schriften umgeben. Diese verschiedenen Momente lassen sich etwa in folgender Weise einheitlich interpretieren: in den Haupthandschriften wird die intensive, anscheinend auf eine kurze Zeit beschränkte Tätigkeit einer wohlgeschulten Gruppe von Schreibern sichtbar, die zur Herstellung von stilvollen Abschriften sorgfältig gewählter Texte herangezogen wurde. Es will mir scheinen, daß die Entstehung dieser Handschriften mit der Lokalisierung an einem Orte, an dem eine retrospektive Schriftkultur und Buckkunst gepflegt wurde und wo es Kenner der Literatur wie Einhard und Gerward gab, die ungezwungenste Erklärung fände. Auch der Besitzgang der Handschriften ist dieser Annahme günstig: denn eine gelangte nach Lorsch, das durch Gerward einige Bücher erhielt, die teils sicher teils wahrscheinlich auf die Hofbibliothek zurückgeführt werden können,[1] und zwei andere gehörten zur Mitgift des Bamberger Domstiftes, in der sich unter anderem einstiger Besitz Karls des Kahlen befindet.

Als Kerngruppe möchte ich die folgenden fünf Codices bezeichnen, die ganz oder in wesentlichen Teilen in dem Typ geschrieben sind.

1. Bamberg, Class. 42 (M. V. 10), Plinius, Naturalis historia, lib. 32–37; 26×21·8 cm (18×14·5 cm), 2 Kol. zu 26 Z. Vielleicht von einer einzigen Hand (s. Tafel II).

2. Bamberg, Patr. 113 (B. IV. 27), Origenes, Peri archon, interpr. Rufino; 29·8×22·5 cm (23·7×14·5 cm), 31 Z. Recht einheitliche Minuskel von mehr als einer Hand. Eine etwas derbere Schrift — z. B. auf fol. 136 — bedient sich zur Auszeichnung einer eigenartig formlosen Unziale.

3. Oxford, Bodl. Libr., Laud. Misc. 105, Cyprianus, Tractatus; 29×24 cm (19·8×15·3 mm), 31 Z.; aus Lorsch nach Eberbach gelangt. Recht einheitliche Schrift von mehreren Händen. Die Handschrift hat textlich ein genaues Gegenstück im Vatic. Reg. lat. 118, vgl. M. Bévenot, *The Tradition of Manuscripts. A Study in the Transmission of St. Cyprian's Treatises* (Oxford, 1961), 137; dieser auffallend große Codex (36·5×28·6 cm (25·7×20·2 cm), 2

---

[1] S. oben S. 6 und in *Die Reichsabtei Lorsch* (wie S. 12 Anm. 4), 56 f.

Kol. zu 36 Z.) ist im zweiten Viertel des IX. Jahrhunderts sicher in Lorsch geschrieben, aber schon um die Mitte desselben als Geschenk nach Frankreich gekommen. S. *Die Reichsabtei Lorsch* (wie S. 12, Anm. 4).

4. Berlin, Deutsche Staatsbibliothek, Phill. 1651, Augustinus, De genesi ad litteram; $30 \cdot 5 \times 25 \cdot 8$ cm ($21 \cdot 3 \times 16 \cdot 5 - 17 \cdot 2$ cm), 27 Z.; im X. Jahrhundert in Metz, S. Vincenz. Wohl von zwei häufig wechselnden Händen, von denen die eine der folgenden Beschreibung genau entspricht, während die andere, ihr ähnliche, gleichmäßig leicht schräg schreibt.

5. München, Clm 3824, Augustinus, De doctrina christiana, u. a.; $30 \cdot 5 \times 23 \cdot 5$ cm ($21 \times 14 \cdot 5$ cm), 25 Z.; im Spätmittelalter in der Augsburger Dombibliothek. In dieser Handschrift findet auf fols. 73–78 mehrfach ein Wechsel von zwei den Händen von Berlin, Phill. 1651 ganz ähnlichen Schriften statt; die leicht schräge Hand, die hier zuerst auf fol. 17ᵛ erscheint, ist mit der entsprechenden des Berliner Codex wahrscheinlich identisch. Im Gegensatz zu diesen beiden Händen ist die sonstige Schrift, die stellenweise (z. B. auf fol. 111) an den reichbelegten Mainzer Stil erinnert, wenig diszipliniert. Die Buchtitel sind in wuchtiger monumentaler Capitalis geschrieben. Vgl. B. Bischoff, *Die südostdeutschen Schreibschulen und Bibliotheken in der Karolingerzeit*, 1, 2. Aufl. (Wiesbaden, 1960), 12 f.

Die Schrift, die diese Handschriften verbindet, wirkt im ganzen aufrecht, da zur leichten Neigung der Mittelschäfte die Senkrechtstellung der verhältnismäßig kurzen Oberlängen im Wechselspiel steht. Die Oberlängen beginnen mit einer kleinen dreieckigen zahnförmigen oder unregelmäßigen Verstärkung nach links, dem insularen 'Spachtel' ähnlich, aber ohne besondere Hervorhebung (sie sind nicht keulenförmig). Auch der Ansatz der mittellangen Schäfte und der *s*, *f* und *p*, kann eine deutlich dreieckige Form annehmen. Nur karolingisches *a* wird gebraucht; der untere Bogen des *g* ist beinahe nur ebenso groß wie der obere, nach links oft eckig, meist nicht ganz geschlossen; am Wortanfang kommt gelegentlich Majuskel-*N* vor; *s* und *f* stoßen nur wenig unter die Zeile; auch der linke Fuß des *x* geht oft nicht über die Zeile hinaus. Die Ligaturen sind auf *et*, *NT* (am Wort- oder Zeilenende), *ra* (auch *rra*, mit geschlossenem *a*), *re* (auch *rre*), *rt* (oft besonders spitz), *st* (gern etwas schräg) beschränkt. Die Kürzungen gehen nur ganz selten über -*b*, (mit sehr kurzem Komma) und -*q·*

hinaus.[1] Ein winziges Detail ist oft zu beobachten, das offenbar in
karolingischen Schriften garnicht sehr verbreitet ist: die Zunge
des am Wortende und vor allem des am Zeilenende stehenden *e* ist
häufig nicht nur etwas angehoben und verlängert, sondern auch
mit einer kleinen Verdickung abgeschlossen. Das Schriftbild der
Minuskel kann eine ausgesprochene Schärfe annehmen, was wohl
durch eine leichte Federdrehung erreicht wird. Es zeigt ferner ein
im ganzen erfolgreiches Bemühen um eine sehr deutliche weite
Worttrennung. Die Rustica ist kräftig, kommt aber nur gelegentlich antikem Stil nahe (z. B. in Bamberg, Patr. 113, fol. 1). Alle
diese Handschriften besitzen keine Initialen, sondern begnügen
sich mit bescheidenen vergrößerten Capitalen.

In einzelnen Details ist noch die Einwirkung antiker Vorlagen
spürbar. Sowohl der Bamberger Plinius wie der Oxforder Cyprian
weisen Seitentitel in winziger Minuskel auf. Alte Marginalien
wurden in kleiner Schrift sowohl in den Bamberger Origenes wie
in den Augustinus Phill. 1651 übernommen. Wunschformeln für
das Heil des Lesers, die ursprünglich sogar individuell dem
Besteller des Buches gegolten haben können, haben sich in letzterem wie im Cyprian erhalten; Phill. 1651, fol. 100 'IN DEO VIVAS.
LEGE FELICITER' und Laud. Misc. 105, fol. 65 'LEGE FELICITER'.

Es gibt weitere Codices derselben Zeit, deren in Ligaturen und
Abkürzungen sparsame Schrift ohne volle Übereinstimmung mit dem
Stil der hier beschriebenen Handschriften mehrere oder einzelne
Merkmale derselben teilt, und die auch keinem anderen bekannten
Skriptorium zugewiesen werden können. Da sich vielleicht aus künfti-
gen Untersuchungen größere Klarheit über die Umgebung der 'Gruppe
des Wiener Evangeliars' und der 'Gruppe des Bamberger Plinius'
ergibt, seien sie aufgezählt, zumal sie in der Überlieferung der betreffen-
den Texte eine wichtige Stellung einnehmen.

1. Oxford, Bodl. Libr., Laud. Lat. 104 + Erlangen, Univ.-Bibl.
2112, Nr. 7, Apollinaris Sidonius (der Laudianus ist am Ende, fol. 102ᵛ,
unvollständig, wie Richard Hunt hilfsbereit bestätigte; das fragmen-
tarische Doppelblatt in Erlangen enthält Carm. 7, 554–601; 9, 284–331);
25·5 × 18·3 cm (18 × 14·4 cm), 24 Z.; der Laudianus ist aus Lorsch
nach Eberbach gelangt. In dieser Handschrift scheint die erste Hand
(fols. 2–58) trotz steilerer und runderer, etwas knotiger Formen nur
eine Variante des Typs zu sein. Aber auch die ungefällige Hand, die

---

[1] In typischer Form, aber in dünnem, unscharfem und eher etwas faserigem
Duktus begegnet die Minuskel für wenige Zeilen in Paris B.N. lat. 1912 (Augustinus, Confessiones) auf fol. 31, Z. 1–15; sie steht zwischen schrägen, scharf-
geschnittenen Schriften.

auf fols. 99–102^v die Briefe IX, 2 ff. und danach auch noch Gedichte hinzufügte, kann an ihm orientiert sein, auch wenn z. B. das *g* seine besondere Form verloren hat. Für Überschriften ist schwarze, ziegelrote oder blaustichig rote Unziale oder Rustica gebraucht. Der in antiker Manier weit über fol. 1^v verteilte Titel ist in sorgfältiger vergrößerter Rustica geschrieben. Nach diesem Codex muß das Fuldaer Exemplar abgeschrieben worden sein, das noch im XVI. Jahrhundert existierte und mit den gleichen Worten endete wie jetzt der Laudianus auf fol. 102^v (vgl. K. Christ, *Die Bibliothek des Klosters Fulda im 16. Jahrhundert* (Leipzig, 1933), S. 125); ein Fragment des Sidonius in Fuldaer Schrift des zweiten Viertels des IX. Jahrhunderts im Staatsarchiv Marburg (Hr 4, 15) kann als Überrest desselben angesehen werden. Rätselhaft ist, wie fast unmittelbar nach der Herstellung des Oxforder Codex die Fortsetzung abgetrennt werden und doch ein Fragment davon (jetzt in Erlangen) erhalten bleiben konnte.

2. Berlin, Deutsche Staatsbibliothek, Phill. 1684, die älteste und wichtigste Handschrift der dogmatischen Werke des Marius Victorinus; 27·2 × 22·5 cm (19·5 × 14·5 cm), 27 Z.; im XII. Jahrhundert in Saint-Denis. Neben Übereinstimmungen mit der Schrift des Evangeliars von Brescia und der Gruppe des Plinius findet sich häufig ein offenes *a* mit zwei Spitzen. Teilweise sehr gute schwarze oder blaustichig rote Rustica. Kritische Marginalien in kleiner Schrift aus einer alten Vorlage.

3. Köln, Erzbischöfliches Archiv, Pfarrarchiv S. Maria im Kapitol, Capsula 34, 1; ein Blatt (34 Z.) der 'Annales Einhardi'. Die im Gegensatz zur Schrägrichtung der regelmäßigen, sorgfältigen Schrift senkrechten Oberlängen haben zahnförmige Ansätze; das etwas unter die Zeile reichende *r*, das unligiert bleibt, schwingt etwas nach links.

4. Florenz, Laur. pl. 76. 40, Seneca, Epistulae morales, lib. I–VI. 3 (Nr. 1–65); 28·8 × 22·7 cm (21 × 15 cm), 28 Z. Vgl. Chatelain (wie S. 15, Anm. 2), Taf. 170*d*; Reynolds (wie S. 15, Anm. 3), Taf. 3. Die im ganzen recht gleichmäßige, gelegentlich zur Schärfe der Formen neigende Schrift scheint mir eher lotharingisch oder westdeutsch als französisch zu sein. Die blaustichig rote Rustica der Rubriken verrät gute Übung. Daß die Überlieferung der ersten Hälfte der Briefe nicht so einseitig französisch ist, wie es nach Reynolds, S. 95 den Anschein hat, ergibt sich aus einer Anspielung bei Einhard (*M.G.H. Epistolae*, 5, 147, 39 f.) auf Seneca, Ep. 87, 38; vgl. S. Hellmann, *Ausgewählte Abhandlungen* (Darmstadt, 1961), S. 212 Anm. (vorher *Historische Vierteljahrsschrift*, 27, 1932, 93 Anm.).

5. Vatic. Pal. lat. 1564, Agrimensores, mit farbigen Autorenbildern; ca. 28 × 19·5 cm (21 × 13 cm), 26 Z.; von Johannes Sichardus in Fulda entdeckt. Kleine Proben der Schrift bei C. Thulin, *Die Handschriften des Corpus agrimensorum Romanorum* (Berlin, 1911), Taf. 7, 1 und 2. Die mäßig schräge, etwas scharfe, kalligraphische Hand trägt west-

deutschen Charakter. Die sorgfältig ausgeführten, wenn auch nicht ganz festen Auszeichnungsschriften, darunter Rustica, sind in blaustichigem Rot geschrieben; das Pergament ist ungewöhnlich gut präpariert. 6. Karlsruhe, Aug. LXXIII, der beste Textzeuge des Martianus Capella; ca. 31·5×20·5–21·5 cm (25·5×14·7 cm), 40 Z. Die gleichmäßige, meist etwas schräge Schrift dürfte ebenfalls westdeutsch sein. Die Carmina sind in gewandter, doch nicht stilechter Rustica geschrieben. Das Rot ist z. T. stark blaustichig.

Unter besonderen Verhältnissen ist Florenz, Laur. pl. 49. 9, der führende Codex von Ciceros Epistulae ad familiares, geschrieben; 24×20·8 cm (15·8×12·8 cm), 23 Z. Vgl. Chatelain, Taf. 34*a*. Hier begegnen sich eine französische Hand (etwa aus dem Loire-Gebiet?; fol. 1 ff.), eine offenbar in Fulda geschulte (fol. 64^v usw.) und eine an Mainzer Stil erinnernde Hand (fols. 171^{rv}, 182^{rv}, 241 ff.); der Besuch einer auswärtigen Schule könnte sie zusammengeführt haben. In den Indices der Bücher sind zwei recht bemerkenswert eigenwillig gestaltete Formen von Rustica angewendet. Die Handschrift war später in den Händen des Bischofs Leo von Vercelli (um 1000).

Stärker von der Gruppe des Plinius abzuheben ist (gegenüber *Settimane*, 19, 392; s. S. 16, Anm. 4) Brüssel 10054–6, die wertvollste Handschrift der philosophischen Werke des Apuleius, mit ihrer dichten, geneigten, ohne Worttrennung geschriebenen Minuskel. Eine Rustica-Überschrift in blaustichigem Rot auf fol. 38^v ist freilich von besonderer Qualität. Auch den an derselben Stelle genannten Priscian (Zürich C 49) möchte ich nicht mehr mit gleicher Bestimmtheit in den Umkreis der Gruppe einbeziehen.

Nur sehr unvollkommen und nach Umwegen ist es möglich, am Hofe Ludwigs des Frommen Umrisse einer Büchersammlung sich abzeichnen zu sehen, die wie andere bedeutende Bibliotheken der Zeit alte und zeitgenössische Theologie, seltenere Klassiker und illustrierte Bücher besaß, für die aber auch eine des Kaiserhofes würdige Gesetzessammlung geschrieben worden war. Immerhin kann auf die Hofbibliothek bezogen werden, was Hraban 829 an den Erzkaplan Hilduin schrieb: 'vos . . . apud quem librorum maxima copia est'.[1]

Über das Ende der neuen kaiserlichen Sammlung sind wir wieder auf Vermutungen angewiesen; denn unter den 'libri', die Ludwig auf dem Sterbebett seinem Halbbruder Drogo zusammen mit den Kronen und Waffen, Gefäßen und priesterlichen Gewändern zu verzeichnen und aufzuteilen befahl,[2] können nur liturgische Codices mit ihren kostbaren Einbänden verstanden werden.

---

[1] *M.G.H. Epistolae*, 5, 402, 16; vgl. Lesne (wie S. 5, Anm. 6), S. 447 f.
[2] Nach dem 'Astronomus', Kap. 63 (*M.G.H. Scriptores*, 2, 647).

Wenn jedoch die oben vorgetragenen Zuweisungen erhaltener Texthandschriften an den Hof begründet sind, so scheinen sie nach Ost und West zerstreut worden zu sein, nachdem die unter Karl verwirklichte Idee der Hofbibliothek sich trotz der ganz anderen Sinnesart seines Nachfolgers noch einmal als lebenskräftig erwiesen hatte.

B. BISCHOFF

2

The Beginnings of Salisbury Cathedral Library

WITHIN half a century of the foundation of the cathedral at Salisbury[1] in 1075 the bishop, dean, and canons possessed a library of some size. William of Malmesbury tells us so and we can infer as much from the existing books. A score of them are 'old', books written on the Continent or in England in or before the middle of the eleventh century and therefore, necessarily, imports to Salisbury. The rest, about eighty, are 'new', books written in the late eleventh century or the early twelfth. New and old are without history, apart from what we can tell from their script, decoration, and contents: the earliest *ex libris* inscriptions are of the thirteenth century and they are few. The 'new' books are the largest group of this date in England and it is with them that we are nearest to the beginnings of a scriptorium, if we can answer 'Yes' to one fundamental question, 'Is there any reason to suppose that these books originated at Salisbury?' A superficial view suggests that many of them did so: one would not expect to find such untidy writing, such poor parchment—holes abound—and such faulty ruling in books commissioned or given. Examination shows that thirty-seven books contain the writing of five co-operating scribes. At least the majority of these books, if not all of them, must be the products of one scriptorium. My impression is that this scriptorium was very active over a short period—the late eighties and the nineties seems a likely time—and that it consisted of one principal scribe (scribe A) whose hand occurs in Exon Domesday and who may have been a professional, any number of helpers, presumably in most cases canons of the cathedral, and a director (scribe C). Some of the copying was done in a hurry,

---

[1] The site was at Old Sarum two miles to the north of the present cathedral.

perhaps because an exemplar had to go back on a fixed date: when one scribe was unable to continue, another took his place, often only for the time it took to write a page or less. Some copies were bad, because the exemplars were bad: if a better exemplar was procured, the first copy was scrapped or corrected.[1] A little later, after scribes A and C were no longer active, some manuscripts of good quality were produced, probably with help from professional scribes.

The earlier manuscripts fall into five groups, according to whether they contain (groups I–IV) or do not contain (group V) the writing of scribes A and C and the small number of helpers whose hands I have been able to recognize as yet in more than one manuscript (scribes B1–B3). In time it should be possible to extend group II considerably and to reduce group V. The probably later manuscripts form group VI. Most of them are the work of scribes whose hands occur in more than one manuscript (scribes D1–D3).

The manuscripts of groups I–IV and group VI are set out on pp. 34–49. In the following summary list bold type shows that a book belongs to groups I–IV and italic type that it belongs to group VI. The rest form group V. The list includes four books not in my *Medieval Libraries of Great Britain*,[2] Cotton Vitellius A. xii and Royal 6 B. xv, for which I thought the Salisbury evidence insufficient in 1964,[3] not knowing about the script, Keble College 22, a recent discovery by Mr. Malcolm Parkes, and Salisbury Cathedral 198, which was not known until 1970. Exon Domesday, not, of course, a Salisbury book, is included because it contains writing by scribe A. The interesting manuscript, Salisbury Cathedral 157, is omitted because it seems to have been in Normandy in the early thirteenth century.[4]

Aberdeen, University, **216.**
Cambridge, Trinity College, 982.
Dublin, Trinity College, 174.
Exeter, Cathedral, **3500.**

[1] See below, pp. 31–2.   [2] Second edition, 1964; subsequently *M.L.G.B.*
[3] Cf. N. R. Ker, 'Salisbury Cathedral Manuscripts and Patrick Young's Catalogue', *Wiltshire Archaeological and Natural History Magazine*, liii (1949), 156, 172, 178.
[4] Some of the hands seem to be English and probably of the mid 11th century. Others are of s. xi ex. In the earlier part there are many insular (Irish?) abbreviations.

London, British Library, Cotton **Tiberius C. 1, Vitellius A. XII**, Royal 5 E. XVI, **5 E. XIX**, *6 B. XV*, 15 C. II.

Oxford, Bodleian, Bodley *392*, 444, fols. 1–27, 698, **756, 765, 768, 835**, Fell **1**, **3**, **4**, Rawlinson C. **723**.

Oxford, Keble College, **22**.

Salisbury Cathedral, *4*, *5*, **6**, **7**, 9, **10**, 11, *12*, **24**, **25**, **33**, 35, **37**, 37 (flyleaves), 57, 58, 59, *61*, 63, *64*, *65*, **67**, **78**, **88**, **106**, *109*, 110, 112, **114**, 115+B.L. Royal 15 B. XIX, fols. 200–5,[1] *116*, 118, **119**, 120, 124, 125, **128**, **128 (flyleaves)+114 (flyleaves)+109 (flyleaves)**, **129**, 130, *131*, **135**, *136*, 137, **138**, 138 (flyleaves), *139*, **140**, **140 (flyleaves)**, **154**, **159**, 160, 162, 164, fols. 64–129, **165**, fols. 23–87, 165, fols. 1–22 and 88–177,[2] **168**, *169*, **179**, *197*+B.L. Royal *App. 1*, *198*.

In view of the importance of scribes A and C we should expect to find the principal books of the new collection in groups I–IV and this is, in fact, where we do find them. I. 5, 6 and III. 18[3] are three of the four passionals and homiliaries for reading during the year, IV. 18 is the great collection of church law introduced into England by Lanfranc, I. 15 is Amalarius, *Liber officialis*, I. 7 is Cassian, *Collationes Patrum*, IV. 19 is the collection of short texts centring on the *Institutiones* of Cassiodorus, IV. 27 is a volume of Origen in translation, and most of the rest are copies of works of the four great Latin Fathers. The patristica include Augustine, *Confessiones* and on St. John, Jerome on Isaiah and Ezekiel, and Gregory's *Moralia on Job* (IV. 12, IIc. 2, IIa. 5, IIb. 3, I. 8). Accidental loss and deliberate replacement may account for the absence of other fundamental books. There is no copy of Augustine's letters or of *De Civitate Dei* now, and the extant copy of *De Trinitate* is thirteenth-century. Gregory's and Jerome's letters are twelfth century. Augustine on the Psalms, Jerome on Matthew, and Isidore, *Etymologiae*, are group V books (Sal. 57, 58, 137, 112). A fragment of a discarded copy of Jerome on Minor Prophets in the binding of MS. 138 (group V) is evidence for the existence once of the copy which replaced it. So few books of secondary importance are in groups I–IV that one wonders about those there are.

---

[1] The question mark in *M.L.G.B.* can be removed. A pattern of wormholes is common to Royal and the last leaf of 115.

[2] See below, III. 16.

[3] References in this form are to the list of MSS. on pp. 34–49.

Why did scribe C spend time on III. 3 and copy there the whole of an otherwise unknown sermon? Apart from the four books just mentioned there is not much of importance in group V. On the whole they are not the sort of books in which we should expect to find hands A and C. Some probably were not made at Salisbury. One group VI book, Salisbury 65, is not the first Salisbury copy of two works of Augustine, but an improvement on the copy in group I, Salisbury 138. Others in this group are second copies also. I shall return later to this question of second copies.

At an early date someone went through the principal books of the new collection and marked noteworthy passages in at least twenty-seven of them with the letters 'D.M.' in the margins, a 'nota bene' sign meaning, probably 'Dignum Memoria'.[1] Twenty-three of the twenty-seven are in groups I–IV. The others are Bodley 444 and Salisbury 112 (group V) and Bodley 392 and Salisbury 198 (group VI). It is likely that the annotation was done before most of the books in groups VI were written. MS. 65 (group VI) and not MS. 138 (group I) would have been marked, if it had existed.

There are a few fine books in groups I–V, but on the whole they are not much to look at. This is partly because the great advances of the twelfth century had hardly begun. Scribes still wrote even quite large books in a single column, with lines too long for the reader's convenience.[2] The writing tends to be small and the unused space between the ruled lines wide: one line of writing does not lead on easily to the next. Line endings are ragged: scribes preferred to write beyond the bounding line, instead of breaking a word with a hyphen at or near it. Word division is not attended to carefully. These are common faults of layout at this

---

[1] *Cf.* Ker, 'Salisbury Cathedral MSS. . . ', pl. opp. p. 168 showing Bodley 756, fol. 72. Royal 5 E. xix (fol. 50ᵛ) and Sal. 198 can be added to the list in *M.L.G.B.*, p. 171. Some other Salisbury MSS. have 'D.M.' or 'D'M'' in other hands, among them Royal 6 B. xv which has 'Dign' M'' once (fol. 19ᵛ). In Exon Domesday this marking occurs only in the margins of the Wiltshire Geld Account A (see *V.C.H. Wilts.* ii, pl. opposite p. 180) and—but much less often—Geld Account B (pl. opposite p. 181). 'Dignum memoria' is in full in University College, Oxford, 191, fols. 115, 121, a twelfth-century English MS. with an erased *ex libris*, '[Liber] Sancte Marie de [. . . . . .] anathema sit amen'.

[2] For example, Fell 1, Fell 4, and Salisbury 179. The only two-column books are Bodley 698, Fell 3, fols. 102–17, Salisbury 33, 35, 57, 58, 59, 67, 137, and the flyleaves of 138. These are all from group V, except 33 and 67. 59, Cassiodorus, has an almost square written space at first, 245 × 210 mm. By the end it has become 270 × 180 mm.

time. So too is the making of books smaller than their contents warrant. The passionals and homiliaries are big books for reading aloud (Fell 1, Fell 4, Salisbury 179), but the copies of Augustine on the Psalms and St. John, Cassiodorus on the Psalms, Gregory's *Moralia*, and Jerome on Isaiah have a written space only about 250 mm high and 170 mm wide. It is a common enough size for the time; indeed, the Salisbury *Moralia* has a bigger page than the Durham and Lanthony copies contemporary with it.[1] On the other hand, the holes within the written space and the irregularities of the ruling seem more conspicuous in Salisbury manuscripts than in most. Even good scribes spoiled their pages by spacing the horizontal lines unequally and failing to draw the vertical bounding lines in the outer margin parallel with the lines in the inner margin. When looking at these manuscripts one realizes that ruling with a hard point was not an easy thing to do. Manuscripts in two columns were especially troublesome, because there were more vertical lines to keep parallel and one had to take care to make the second column the same width as the first. Untidiness is another feature, caused partly by the corrections in the margins and between the lines and partly by the frequent changes of hand on a single page or double opening. Even if two good scribes are at work the result is bad if their hands clash, as happened when scribe A or scribe B2 was co-operating with scribe C: I. 3, I. 12, and III. 8 are good examples.

The script is often quite good. Scribes A, B1, C, D1, and D3 had been taught in good schools. They wrote clearly and regularly and avoided ligatures and abbreviations which were already going out of use before the end of the eleventh century. Scribe A, indeed, by avoiding the *ct* ligature is in line with the best practice of the late eleventh century, but not with later practice: the attempt to remove this form from the repertory of scribes failed.[2]

The good scribes are a minority, however. Many Salisbury scribes, whether their writing looks English or Norman, are behind the times, uncertain about what they ought to do, and careless about what they did. An up-to-date teacher would have faulted

---

[1] Durham Cathedral B. III. 10 and Trinity College, Oxford, 39. The latter was found to be unsatisfactory in the 12th century when a new copy, now Lambeth Palace 56, was made.

[2] The Bec (?) scribe of Trinity College, Cambridge, 405 does not use the *ct* ligature: Ker, *English Manuscripts in the century after the Norman Conquest*, 1960, pl. 4.

them on these points: writing a hyphen at the beginning of a line as well as at the end; making an *rt* ligature; making the *et* ligature in the middle or at the beginning of a word; using rounded *d* as an alternative to upright *d*, not solely in order to save space;[1] writing *ae* or *æ* instead of *ę*; allowing *f*, *r*, and *s*, one, two, or three of them, to fall below the line; using round *s*; making a special form of *a* after *r*; using peculiar forms of abbreviation for *autem* and *enim*; finishing minims with horizontal feet or serifs. Not that all inferior scribes do all these things, of course—the three last are characteristic of older English not older Norman script[2]—but all do some of them, and all share a slackness which allows them to make one letter-form or one form of a mark of abbreviation in one place and another form in another place, without reason, and endless little variations in the shape of letters, especially compli-cated ones like *g* and the ampersand. In this respect they compare badly with the Augustinian canons of Cirencester half a century later.[3]

Eleven of these manuscripts are now in the Bodleian Library and qualify, therefore, for a place in the great repertory made by Otto Pächt and J. J. G. Alexander, *Illuminated Manuscripts in the Bodleian Library*. In fact, only two of the eleven are there, Bodley 698 ('Good and other initials') and Bodley 768 ('Initials'). This makes the point that the majority have no illumination to speak of, which is not the same thing as to say that they have no pleasing decoration. Small well-drawn initials in the ink of the text, often a warm purplish black, are a feature of the better Salisbury books, and similar initials in brick-red occur often.[4] A few are in green or

---

[1] Some good scribes use rounded *d* in any position, scribe A among them in some of his work, but it is on the whole a mark of the inferior scribe, as one can see from the amount of it in patches of poor writing in otherwise well-written books: Salisbury 12, fols. 56–60ᵛ; 139, fols. 94–103ᵛ; 169, fols. 77ᵛ–91ᵛ; 197, fols. 55ᵛ–56.

[2] Examples of the special *a* after *r* are in Sal. 25, fol. 140, Sal. 138, fol. 64ᵛ, Sal. 140, fol. 2 (flyleaf), of the H-like sign for *enim* in Sal. 35 and in Sal. 59, fol. 164, and of the spurred *h* for *autem* in Sal. 37, fol. 131, Sal. 59, fol. 198, Sal. 109, fols. 3ᵛ, 5 (flyleaves), Sal. 135, fol. 9, Sal. 165, fol. 86. Minims terminating in horizontal feet or serifs are a feature of Sal. 37, fols. 5–100, Sal. 120, fols. 36–38ᵛ, Sal. 135, fols. 1–9ᵛ/11 and the writing of scribe D2.

[3] Cf. Ker, *English Manuscripts* . . ., pl. 20.

[4] For example, Sal. 63, 78, 168, 179. Scribe C's initials are always in the ink of the text. Initials like this are common in earlier MSS: for some examples from England, 10th and 11th centuries, see N. R. Ker, *Catalogue of Manuscripts containing Anglo-Saxon*, 1957, pp. xxxvii-xxxix.

blue.[1] More than one colour in one initial is rare.[2] More elaborate
and possibly distinctive initials occur in Salisbury 128, after art. 1,
and in manuscripts of group VI.[3] Initials made up of elements that
are not obviously letters of the alphabet are rare.[4] Since there was
no convention that initials had to be in colour the spaces for them
were seldom left blank.[5]

The first words or even the whole line following an initial, as
well as explicits and headings, are commonly in rustic capitals,
sometimes filled with red. The writing is often competent and the
capitals are a good feature in many books. Scribe C's are untidy
and distinctive.

Many quire signatures have probably been cut off, but enough
remain to show that there was not as yet a settled way of making
them. A number on the last verso became normal in the twelfth
century and is already the common mark, but we find also a
number on the first recto, a letter on the last verso, and a letter on
the first recto. In five manuscripts written by scribe A, Bodley
765, Fell 4, Salisbury 106, 140, 154, the last versos are numbered
and in one, Salisbury 10, the first rectos. The idea of writing catchwords was beginning to spread from Spain at this time[6] and a few
catchwords are to be found in these books: Bodley 392, fol. 38ᵛ;
Bodley 756, fol. 8ᵛ; Fell 4, quires 3–8; Salisbury 9, fols. 16ᵛ, 24ᵛ,
44ᵛ, 52ᵛ; Salisbury 169, fol. 20ᵛ; also in Salisbury 33, fols. 265ᵛ,
273ᵛ, where the catchwords consist of the last word of one quire
and the first two words of the next quire.

The marks of punctuation vary also. The mark at the end of a
sentence is not always the simple point, as it was later, but often
the punctus versus (;). Scribe A used the punctus versus almost
always. A few scribes were indifferent whether they used it or the
point and some seem to have been making a deliberate effort not

---

[1] Fell 4, fol. 1 (blue). Sal. 57 and 78 (green alternating with red). Sal. 139, fol.
1ᵛ (blue).

[2] Bodley 698, fol. 1 and Bodley 768, fol. 1 (green, red, and blue). Sal. 57, fol.
39, etc. and Sal. 78, fol. 68ᵛ (green and red). Sal. 116, fol. 188 (purple and red).

[3] Sal. 61, 64, 65, 116, 131.

[4] Sal. 10, fol. 3 (knotwork). Sal. 33, fol. 442ᵛ (whale swallowing Jonah?: bk.
32). Sal. 78, fol. 1 (dragon). Sal. 131, fol. 15ᵛ (dragon). Sal. 139, fol. 36 (dragon?).
In Sal. 33, fol. 486 the O beginning bk. 35 contains a head.

[5] Blank in Sal. 25 sometimes and in Sal. 110. In Sal. 57 a large space for an
initial B on fol. 1 was left unfilled.

[6] J. Vezin, 'Observations sur l'emploi des réclames dans les manuscrits
latins', *Bibliothèque de l'École des Chartes*, cxxv (1967), 5–33.

to use it.[1] The mark within the sentence, the punctus elevatus (ᵛ), does not always have a tick as its upper member, but sometimes a mark rather like a tick facing the other way. Scribe B1's punctus elevatus always looked like this (pl. IV*a*). On the other hand, the hyphen varies very little. It is a horizontal, or nearly horizontal line, not a diagonal, as later.

Where did the authorities at Salisbury find the books from which to copy? Two exemplars have been pointed out, but neither is localizable: Hereford Cathedral O. iii. 2 is the exemplar of Salisbury 88 and London B.L. Add. 23944 the exemplar of Salisbury 138. Both are ninth-century continental books which were in England early and may have been for a time at Canterbury.[2] For the rest we can as yet only suggest probable places and possible manuscripts. Winchester is less than twenty-five miles and Glastonbury, Malmesbury, Sherborne, and Wells not more than forty miles from Salisbury in a direct line. We are ill informed about the book collections in all these places. One Winchester manuscript of the eleventh century, Trinity College, Oxford, 28, contains the same text, Bede on the Tabernacle, as Salisbury 165, and a manuscript written by the same hand as the Sherborne Pontifical, Paris B.N. lat. 943, contains all but three of the texts in Vitellius A. XII.[3] At Exeter, about ninety miles from Salisbury, the books bequeathed by Bishop Leofric in 1072 included Bede on the Apocalypse and Augustine, *De adulterinis conjugiis* in Lambeth Palace 149, Amalarius, *Liber officialis*, in Trinity College, Cambridge, 241, and Isidore, *De miraculis Christi*, in Bodley 319: they may be worth comparing with the Salisbury copies now in Aberdeen 216, Salisbury 128, Salisbury 154, and Royal 5 E. XVI respectively.[4] Canterbury is over 100 miles from Salisbury. The cathedral had the first English exemplar of Lanfranc's collection of decretals, now Trinity College, Cambridge, 405, but it does not seem to have been the immediate source of Salisbury 78.[5] St. Augustine's had, *inter alia*, Freculphus, now Corpus Christi College, Cambridge,

---

[1] It must have been an objection to the punctus versus that it is the same as the mark of abbreviation for -*us* in the ending -*bus*: 'manifestationib;;' (Sal. 106, fol. 72ᵛ/6) does not look good.

[2] R. A. B. Mynors, *Cassiodori Institutiones*, 1937, pp. xv, xliv. Ker, *English Manuscripts . . .*, pp. 13, 57.

[3] See below, group IIa. 1.

[4] For 128 see below, p. 35.

[5] Z. N. Brooke, *The English Church and the Papacy*, 1931, pp. 231–5.

267: the two early copies at Salisbury are MSS. 119, 120. For some works, for example Augustine, *Speculum*, pseudo-Augustine (Ambrosiaster), *Quaestiones* 127, and Pelagius on the Pauline Epistles, no earlier manuscripts than the ones at Salisbury are known in England.[1]

Some books in groups I–VI and some later books may exist because there was money available for 'correctio librorum'. An income for this purpose had long existed when, in the late twelfth century, Bishop Jocelin granted a virgate of land 'que ab antiquo pertinere solet ad correctionem librorum ecclesie Sar'' to one of the canons, Philip of St. Edward, 'ut idem Philippus operam et diligentiam adhibeat ad eorundem librorum correctionem'.[2] It may have been started very early in the cathedral's history to assist the chancellor in the duty defined in Saint Osmund's *Institutio* of 1091, 'Thesaurarius in conservandis thesauris ... præeminet. Similiter cancellarius in scholis regendis et in libris corrigendis.'[3] One thinks of correction as the sort of thing scribe C and other scribes did in the margins of books of groups I–V and the more elaborate and skilled work by erasure and rewriting common in the better twelfth-century manuscripts.[4] The former could hardly be a source of expense and the latter was not done at Salisbury apparently. There is, however, a third and more considerable operation which could, I think, properly be called correction, the renewing of books and parts of books which were considered unsatisfactory, because the text was bad or because it was not easy to read—heavily corrected, perhaps, in the margins and between the lines. Renewing is easily seen if a scribe only got part of the way. At Salisbury, the first quires of MS. 33 (I. 8) were renewed in the twelfth century and the first quires and last leaves of MS. 67 (IIc. 2) in the thirteenth. Renewal is impossible to detect, except by luck, if a whole new manuscript was made and the old one scrapped. At Salisbury, MSS. 14 (s. XII[1], the winter part of the

---

[1] F. Römer, *Die handschriftliche Überlieferung der Werke des heiligen Augustinus*, ii. 1 (Österreichische Akademie der Wissenschaften, Phil.-hist. Kl., Sitzungsberichte, cclxxxi, 1972), pp. 173, 154. For the Pelagius, Salisbury 5, and its insular exemplar, see A. Souter in *Texts and Studies*, ix (1922–6), i. 283–6.

[2] *Register of St Osmund* (R.S., 1883–4), i. 224.

[3] Op. cit. i. 214; Frere, *Use of Sarum*, i. 260. The surviving copies are later than Osmund's time and 'cancellarius' is unlikely to be the word he used: cf. Kathleen Edwards in *V.C.H. Wilts*. iii. 158.

[4] Ker, *English Manuscripts* ..., p. 50 and pls. 24, 25, and in *Studies in London History presented to Philip E. Jones*, 1969, pl. 3.

homiliary of Paul the Deacon) and 22 (s. XII[1], Augustine on Psalms 101–50) may be renewals of this sort: all we can see is that they are very different from what should be their companions, MSS. 179 (III. 18) and 57, 58 (group V: Augustine on Psalms 1–100). On the other hand Sal. 114 (I. 11) and Sal. 129 (IV. 23) can be shown to be renewals, because the old bad manuscripts were not completely destroyed, but survive in part as flyleaves in bindings, in one case actually in the binding of the manuscript by which it was superseded. Enough survives of the 'old' manuscript of *De Genesi ad litteram* (III. 10) for us to see that the text is so bad that scribe A cannot have made Sal. 114 (I. 11) directly from it[1] and enough of the 'old' manuscript of *Quaestiones* 127 to suggest that Sal. 129 may have been copied from it directly.[2] Renewal is or may be detectable if an 'old' manuscript was thought to be worth keeping as a spare. Sal. 138 (I. 13) was kept, although its lines were too long, after the making of a handsome copy, Sal. 65.[3] Whether other doubles have this relationship, exemplar and copy, remains to be discovered. There are surprisingly many of them and each pair needs individual study. The business of getting better texts, in the sense of better looking, more legible texts, seems to have begun early and continued into the thirteenth century. The following, among others, are in question.

Salisbury Cathedral 120, Freculphus (group V). Sal. 119 (III. 9) is of about the same date.

Salisbury Cathedral 61, art. 10, Augustine, *De natura boni*, by scribe D1. The older copies are Sal. 63 and 106 (III. 8, I, 10).

Salisbury Cathedral 197+Royal App. 1, pseudo-Augustine, *Hypognesticon*, by scribe D1. The older copy is Sal. 35.

Salisbury Cathedral 169, arts. 1–7, Augustine, by scribe D3. The older copies are: art. 1, *De penitentia* in Bodley 765 (I. 4);

---

[1] The 'old' MS. may not have been completed, like III. 13. We have remains of the first three quires only. Examples of its readings are: MS. 128, fol. 1/37 in uerbia eternitate; MS. 128, fol. 1ᵛ/3 Quo deus ita; MS. 128, fol. 1ᵛ/5 quo perdidis creature; MS. 109, fol. 8ᵛ/35 ut omni non nature. MS. 114 has the *P.L.* reading in each place: *P.L.* xxxiv. 248/4, 13, 17–18, 305/14.

[2] MS. 37, fols. 1, 2, 165, 166, 3, 4 are three bifolia from the beginning of the text and correspond to fols. 1ᵛ–6ᵛ of MS. 129. Bad division of the words 'quae reseruata', MS. 37, fol. 4/29, may have caused the misreading 'quaere seruata', MS. 129, fol. 6/21.

[3] Ker, *English Manuscripts . . .*, p. 13. In *M.L.G.B.* (1964 edn.) I stated the relationship the wrong way round in footnote 3 on p. 173 and footnote 6 on p. 175.

art. 2, *Quaestiones* 65 in Sal. 115 (group V); art. 3, *Contra Felicianum* in Sal. 35 (group V) and Sal. 165 (III. 16); art. 4, *De disciplina Christiana* in Sal. 63 and Sal. 106 (III. 8, I. 10); arts. 5–7, *De muliere forti*, two sermons, and *Ad Dulcitium de 8 quaestionibus* in Sal. 106 (I. 10).

Salisbury Cathedral 142, Isidore, *Etymologiae*, s. xii ex. The older copy is Sal. 112 (group V).

Salisbury Cathedral 164, fols. 1–63ᵛ, Sermons of Ivo of Chartres in a fine hand, s. xii¹. The older and defective copy is Sal. 164, fols. 64–129 (group V).

Salisbury Cathedral 100, fols. 89–141, eight works of Augustine, s. xiii.¹ The older copy is Sal. 117, s. x.

Saint Osmund was bishop of Salisbury from 1078 until his death in 1099. During that time most of the manuscripts in groups I–V were probably written. Did Osmund take part in their copying? He did so, according to William of Malmesbury who was writing twenty-five years later: 'Librorum copia conquisita cum episcopus ipse nec scribere nec scriptos ligare fastidiret'.² The *Institutio* of 1091 shows Osmund's interest in the correction of books and the fund to pay for their correction may date from his time. *Possibly* scribe C, who was above all a corrector, is Osmund: his work in these manuscripts is not more than we might expect from an active bishop one of whose most urgent duties was to make a collection of books. I doubt we can go further than that at present. We might do so, if scribe C had left more traces of his own interests in the margins. So far as I know, the only place where he writes in the first person is on a page of the Amalarius (I. 15, IV. 26) to make the point that he had not found the next ten pages about the offices of Maundy Thursday in another copy. Perhaps he *has* left more traces. Give and take, the books with 'D.M.' in the margins are the books in which he wrote and the *D* of 'D.M.' has the same shape as his *D*, narrowing to a point at the base. Two letters are not enough to go on, however, nor the three words in IIa. 1 written by someone with a special interest in Saint Wulfran (of Sens and St. Wandrille), which look like scribe C's writing, but are without distinctive letter forms. Until more evidence turns up,

---

¹ MS. 100 is an expertly written book, with a contemporary cathedral *ex libris*, which suggests that it is more likely to have been made for Salisbury than to have been a gift.

² *Gesta Pontificum* (R. S., 1870), p. 184.

it seems better to suppose that Osmund appointed a competent person, scribe C, to look after the books, and did some copying himself under his direction.[1]

I add to this brief account of the early Salisbury scriptorium a description of the work done by eight scribes who appear to have written in more than one extant book. Scribe A wrote in fourteen Salisbury books and Exon Domesday. These form group I. Scribe B1 wrote in six books, scribe B2 in six and scribe B3 in three. These form group II: all but two of them occur in groups I, III, or IV. Scribe C wrote in thirty-three books. These form groups III and IV: eighteen of them have already occurred in groups I and II. Scribe D1 wrote in eight books, scribe D2 in four, and scribe D3 in two or three. These form nearly all of group VI. The books forming group V are not itemized, but may be found by reference to the list on pp. 24–5.

GROUP I. *Books containing writing by Scribe A*

Scribe A seems to have been the principal scribe employed in making the new collection of books at Salisbury. He wrote a total of nearly 1,000 leaves in an admirably steady, regular hand which suggests an English rather than a continental training. The *-rum* abbreviation is perhaps his most distinctive letter form. His *g* is almost always of the English form, an *o* with a stroke like a reversed *c* attached to the base of it. The placing of this stroke so that the head of the reversed *c* just touches the *o* was not too easy. Scribes who used this form of *g* and wrote less expertly than scribe A tend to leave a small gap between the *o* and the reversed *c*. Others, scribe B2 and William of Malmesbury among them, approached the base of the *o* with a rising stroke from the left. Others make a short joining stroke between the base of the *o* and the reversed *c*. Our scribe avoided these varieties and always placed his reversed *c* very exactly. *a* is one of the few letters he varies. It tends to have a head in careful writing and to be without a head in less formal or hurried or informal writing, except when it follows letters like *f*, *r*, and *t* which end in a stroke from which the head of *a* can conveniently be begun. The headed *a* is regular in I. 2 (pl. III*b*), the headless *a* regular in the specimen from I. 4 shown in pl. IV*b* (but cf. *fa*

---

[1] It may be worth considering whether either Salisbury 154 or 135 (IV. 26, 24) had any influence on the consuetudinary in the Register of St. Osmund.

and *ta*, lines 5, 6). Except in I. 2, I. 3, and after fol. 41 in I. 9 he
writes the punctus versus at the end of a sentence. Often it is not
a point and comma, but two commas one above the other. The
tailed *e* (pl. III*b*, line 4) and the stiff straight strokes over double *i* are
also distinctive. A capital letter at the beginning of a line is not put
outside the written space. The ampersand is used sometimes for
-*et*, but not for -*et*-. *s* descends a little below the line sometimes,
but not *f* or *r*. The *ct* ligature does not occur. Scribe A fails to make
a good effect when he has to write a longer line or more closely than
suited him: I. 9, 13. His work was not much corrected as a rule, but
there are many corrections and much evidence of what appears to
be carelessness in I. 12, where corrections by scribe C of errors due
to homoioteleuton are about one to each page. In fact, however,
I. 12 is, so far as I have collated it, a very faithful copy, errors and
all, of Lambeth Palace 149, one of Bishop Leofric's gifts to Exeter
Cathedral. Scribe C had access to a better copy by which to
correct it.

I. 1. Exeter Cathedral 3500 (Exon Domesday), fols. 7^v/2–31,
8/12–30, 9/7–40, 9^v/1–10, 13/1–14/20, 14^v/1–16/26. Fols. 13–16
(formerly 276–279) contain the Wiltshire Geld Account C,
printed in *V.C.H. Wiltshire*, ii. 178–215. Scribe A wrote nearly
all of it. Fols. 7–9^v (formerly 288–290) contain the Wiltshire
Geld Account B, collated ibid. Scribe A wrote most of it, but he
did not begin either fol. 8 or fol. 9. Facsimiles ibid., opposite
pp. 181, 216, show fols. 8 (B) and 14 (C). Pl. III*a* is from fol. 9.

The Geld Accounts are datable in or about 1086.[1] Account C occupies a quire of four leaves. Account B is on the first three leaves of a
six-leaf quire, which was at one time folded down the middle length-
ways: no other quire shows the mark of a crease in this position except,
perhaps, that containing Geld Account A. Account B ends on fol. 9^v/24.
The next leaf is blank on both sides. Fols. 11–12^v are partly filled with
Dorset geld entries in a hand which occurs often in Exon Domesday.
There is a presumption that scribe A wrote before fols. 11, 12 were
written on, but he need not have done so. Whenever he wrote, it was
after this quire and fols. 13–16 were ruled like the rest of the volume
(except fols. 1–6 (Geld Account A) and fols. 526–529) with twenty
widely spaced lines. The scribes of Accounts B and C did not follow
this ruling. The number of lines they wrote varies from page to page
and rises to 42 on fol. 8. Scribe A kept an admirably straight course.

---

[1] V. H. Galbraith, 'The date of the Geld Rolls in Exon Domesday', *E.H.R.*
lxv (1950), 1–17.

I. 2. London, British Library, Cotton Tiberius C. i, fols. 112ᵛ/11–116ᵛ/11. See III. 2, IV. 2 and pl. III*b*.

Three orders, the blessing of an abbot (fols. 112ᵛ–113ᵛ), the consecration of a virgin, and the blessing of an abbess in a pontifical which seems to have accompanied the bishop when the see was moved from Sherborne to Salisbury in 1075; cf. N. R. Ker, 'Three Old English Texts in Cotton Tiberius C. i', *Studies presented to Bruce Dickens*, 1959, pp. 262–79. The three texts are those edited by H. A. Wilson, *The Pontifical of Magdalen College*, Henry Bradshaw Society, xxxix (1910), 81–9, from manuscripts half a century or more later than Tib., which he did not use. They are thought to have been introduced into England by Lanfranc.

I. 3. London, British Library, Royal 5 E. xix, fol. 6/4–37. See IIb. 1, III. 3, IV. 3.

Scribe A suited his hand to Scribe B2's and wrote smaller than usual.

I. 4. Oxford, Bodleian, Bodley 765, fols. 1–81, the whole of a manuscript of opuscula of Augustine and Ambrose, except seven short passages, fols. 1/16–19, 38/12–19, 46/1–27, 46ᵛ/7–10, 47/14–25, 48/1–21, 49/5–13. See IIa. 2, IV. 5 and pl. IV.

I. 5. Oxford, Bodleian, Fell 1, fol. 288ʳᵛ. See IV. 8.

Fell I is the second of two volumes of lives of saints: cf. I. 6. The lives are numbered 63–118 and run from 15 June to 9 October. The original intention seems to have been to begin a third volume at 1 October (fol. 184), where there is a table of contents numbered from 112 to 161. Only seven of these fifty lives occur and they are bound in with the lives for 15 June to 30 September. No. 118, the *Vita Sancti Richarii*, begins at fol. 283ᵛ. A fairly good scribe wrote as far as fol. 286ᵛ/4, after which three pages are in a poor hand. Scribe A made a good ending.

I. 6. Oxford, Bodleian, Fell 4, fols. 1–223/2. See III. 5, IV. 9.

Fell 4 is the first of two volumes of lives of saints: cf. I. 5.[1] The lives are numbered 1–60 and run from 1 January to 9 June. Nos. 61, 62, Getulius, 10 June, and Basilides, 12 June, are missing at the end. Scribe A began by writing 33 lines to the page with a space of about 9 mm between the ruled lines. On fol. 89, the first leaf of quire 9, he changed to 36 lines and a space of about 7 mm between the ruled lines. He wrote nearly to the end of the life of Saint Mark, no. 41. After this a life of

---

[1] The slightly earlier Worcester Cathedral copy of this same collection is now partly in London B.L., Cotton Nero E. i, and partly in Corpus Christi College, Cambridge, 9.

Blasius has been squeezed in by another hand in space left blank at the end of quire 28. A new scribe begins with Vitalis, no. 42, on the first leaf of quire 29 and continues to the end, fol. 277^v, where the life of Primus and Felicianus ends imperfectly. Probably he was working at the same time as scribe A.[1]

I. 7. Salisbury Cathedral 10, fols. 3–113, the whole of a copy of Cassian, *Collationes Patrum*, except for twenty-three short passages: fols. 6^v/1–7/14; 8^v/9–31; 14/1–7; 21/12–18; 22/17–32; 22^v/26–32; 23/18–23; 24/1–18; 25/23–32; 25^v/8–32; 27^v/13–20; 29/1–15; 30/21–30^v/4; 34/4–8; 49/9–12; 60/28–60^v/6; 81^v/1–3; 83/1–85^v/23; 102/11–15; 104^v/24–33; 108/19–33; 110/4–23; 111/2–33. See IIa. 4, III. 7, IV. 13.

I. 8. Salisbury Cathedral 33, fols. 274–380ra/17 (except 313va/4–41, 377ra/37–377va/12, 378va/6–378vb/41, 379va/22–379vb/41) and fols. 453–97, in all about one-third of a massive copy of Gregory's *Moralia* on 497 leaves. See IIc. 1.

This copy of the *Moralia* is divisible into two after bk. 18 and may once have been in two volumes: if so, scribe A's work was entirely in vol. 2, fols. 258–497. His part makes a fine book on good parchment. Fols. 1–66, bks. 1–4 and part of bk. 5, were supplied on 8 quires in s. XII.

I. 9. Salisbury Cathedral 63, fols. 24^v/5–24, 25^v/32–45, 26^v/1–15, 32^v/1–13, 38/1–17, 41^v/1–14, 45/32–45^v/6, 50^v/1–16. See IIb. 5, III. 8 (scribe C is the main scribe), IV. 16.

I. 10. Salisbury Cathedral 106, fols. 1–72^v, the first five of nine opuscula of Augustine, as the quires are now arranged. An old quire numbering shows that arts. 6–9 came first originally. See IV. 20.

Scribe A wrote larger towards the end and changed from 41 to 40 lines to the page.

I. 11. Salisbury Cathedral 114, fols. 6–122, the whole of a copy of Augustine, *De Genesi ad litteram*.

On fols. 30–37, quire 4, scribe A wrote 40 lines to the page, instead of 36. The smaller number suits his writing better.

I. 12. Salisbury Cathedral 128, ten passages comprising most of the first piece, *De adulterinis conjugiis*, in a volume of Augustine's opuscula: fols. 5–16/16; 16/19–33; 16^v/1–4; 16^v/18, 19;

---

[1] Saint Matthew, fol. 278, is an addition in another hand.

17/1–17^v/18 (except 17^v/1); 18/1–18^v/5; 18^v/21–19/33; 19^v/11–21^v/14; 22/1–24/33; 24^v/15–25/27. See IIa. 6, III. 11, IV. 22, and above, p. 30.

I. 13. Salisbury Cathedral 138, fols. 3^v/6–32^v/36 (except 16^v/43–48 and 21^v/19–34), Augustine, *De nuptiis*, and the first nineteen leaves of Augustine, *Contra Julianum*. See IIb. 6, III. 12.

The format set by scribe C, with lines 165 mm long and 48 of them to the page, did not suit scribe A's writing.

I. 14. Salisbury Cathedral 140, fols. 3/15–96^v (end), Ambrose, *De Spiritu Sancto*. See III. 14, IV. 25.

I. 15. Salisbury Cathedral 154, the whole of Amalarius, *Liber officialis*, (pp. 5–157), except pp. 39/5–16, 50/15–19. See III. 15, IV. 26.

The type of text here is noticed at IV. 26. Pp. 2–4, 158–62 are additions in other hands.

GROUP II. *Books containing writing by scribes who were co-operating with Scribes A and C and whose work occurs in more than one manuscript*[1]

Scribe B1's admirable hand is of Norman type, very stable, small, and upright, distinguished by the small head of *g*, the rather clumsy two-tier *s*, the big wavy nota for *et*, common only in IIa. 1, the ampersand with final stroke curving high to the left or, in IIa. 5, 6, crossed at the top by a nearly flat curve, and the shape of the upper stroke of the punctus elevatus. His special peculiarity is to save space by writing *a* in an open-headed form above the line (pls. IV*a*, V; also, for example, IIa. 1, fol. 55, IIa. 2, fol. 1/16). The point, not the punctus versus, is used at the end of a sentence. If a capital letter comes at the beginning of a line it is placed outside the written space and between the two vertical bounding lines. The lines of writing appear widely spaced, because the ruled lines are 6 or 7 mm apart and the minims not much more than 1 mm high.

IIa. 1. London, British Library, Cotton Vitellius A. XII, fols. 4^v–71, Rabanus Maurus, *De computo*, and other texts.

The texts on fols. 10^v–65 appear to be derived, but not immediately, from Exeter Cathedral 3507. The others are: fols. 4^v–8, *Dialogus*

---

[1] My B1, B2, B3 is evidently only a beginning. Other scribes are there for the finding.

Ecgberhti;[1] fols. 8ᵛ–10ᵛ, Abbo of Fleury, *De differentia circuli et sperae*;[2] fols. 65ᵛ–71, a calendar, no. 7 in Wormald's *English Kalendars before A.D.* 1100 (Henry Bradshaw Society, lxxii, 1934). For the first four months the calendar agrees almost letter for letter with the Glastonbury calendar in the Leofric Missal, as originally written (op. cit., no. 4), except for the omission of eleven feasts: 'Translatio Sancti Wlfranni' was added early at 20 March, perhaps by scribe C. Later both calendars share the odd mistake 'Maia Generoi' in the verse heading May and have VII instead of VIII for the hours of daylight in November, but the selection of saints is different. None of the other nineteen calendars printed by Wormald has Monulf and Gundulf, bishops (of Utrecht), at 16 July, Evortius, bishop (of Orléans) and confessor, at 7 September, Cunibert, bishop (archbishop of Cologne) and confessor, at 12 November, Otmar, abbot (of St. Gallen), at 16 November, Barbara, virgin, at 16 December, and Victoria, virgin and martyr, at 23 December. In the names Ælfg(y)fe, Æþelburge and Æþeldriðe, insular or semi-insular letter-forms are used for *d, e, f, g*, and *r*. Leland saw Rabanus and the Dialogue at Salisbury, presumably in this copy.[3]

IIa. 2. Oxford, Bodleian, Bodley 765, fol. 1/16–19, thirty-six words in a manuscript written by scribe A. See I. 4, IV. 5 and pl. IVa.

IIa. 3. Oxford, Keble College. 22, fols. 3/21–4ᵛ/3 (extracts on the eucharist added in a blank space), 5ᵛ/1–7/1 morte, 10/1–13 fidem, of a copy of Pauline Epistles, with marginal and interlinear glosses.[4] Scribe B did no glossing. See III. 6, IV. 11 and pl. V.

IIa. 4. Salisbury Cathedral 10, fols. 21/12–18, 22/17–32, 22ᵛ/26–32, 23/18–23, 24/1–18, 25/23–32. See I. 7, III. 7, IV. 13.

IIa. 5. Salisbury Cathedral 25, fols. 176ᵛ–203, the last 28 leaves of Jerome on Isaiah. See IV. 14.

IIa. 6. Salisbury Cathedral 128, fols. 25/27–116 (end) of a copy of works of Augustine. See I. 12, III. 11, IV. 22.

Scribe B2 wrote a distinctive hand of markedly English type.

---

[1] A. W. Haddan and W. Stubbs, *Councils and Ecclesiastical Documents*, iii (1871), 403–13.

[2] Noticed by A. van de Vyver in *Revue Bénédictine*, xlvii (1935), 141.

[3] *Itinerary*, ed. L. Toulmin Smith, i. 263.

[4] I owe my knowledge of the Keble MS. to Mr. M. B. Parkes who found scribe B1's hand in Salisbury 25. It may be the 'Epistolae Pauli cum comment. 4ᵗᵒ', no. 135 in Patrick Young's catalogue (Ker, 'Salisbury Cathedral Manuscripts . . .', p. 171).

An easily seen feature is the punctus versus with its comma not directly below the point, but a little to the left.

IIb. 1. London, British Library, Royal 5 E. XIX, fols. 1–6/4, 6^v/1–18^v/10, 21/1–34, 23/18–25/29, 26^v/1–28^v/17, 29/1–34/14, 35/20–36^v/26 (end), that is to say most of art. 1, Isidore, *Synonyma*, and most of art. 2c–m, Homilies, in a manuscript containing also Alcuin on Song of Songs. See I. 3, III. 3, IV. 3.

The homilies are nos. 76, 1, 2; 77, 29, 34, 36, 37, 52, 53 of the 'Homéliaire de Saint-Père de Chartres' to which Dom Morin drew attention in 1913, as listed by H. Barré, *Les Homéliaires carolingiens de l'école d'Auxerre* (Studi e Testi, ccxxv, 1962), pp. 18–24. As Barré noted, his no. 29 still has its old number 'xxviii' attached to it here. Leaves are missing after no. 2, which ends imperfectly, fol. 28^v.

IIb. 2. Oxford, Bodleian, Bodley 756, fols. 88–90^v of a copy of Ambrosiaster on the Pauline Epistles. See III. 4, IV. 4.

In Royal and Rawlinson scribe B2 set his own spacing: in Rawlinson it is 34 lines in 220 mm. In Bodley 756 he was forced by scribe C to write 48 lines in 225 mm. Collisions resulted, for example between the tail of *g* in one line and the ascender of *h* in the next, fol. 89/19, 20. The main scribe, writing in a small hand of Norman type, did not have trouble of this kind.

IIb. 3. Oxford, Bodleian, Rawlinson C. 723, Jerome on Ezekiel. See IV. 10.

IIb. 4. Salisbury Cathedral 24, fol. 58^v/18–41 of a copy of Jerome on Jeremiah.

Once a handsome book by a very good scribe.

IIb. 5. Salisbury Cathedral 63, fol. 10^v/1–12. See I. 9, III. 8, IV. 16.

IIb. 6. Salisbury Cathedral 138, fol. 16^v/43–48. See I. 13, III. 12.

Scribe B3 did not write very well, but his hand is easily distinguished by the punctus versus, ' . , ', instead of ' ; ' : the comma is angular. In Sal. 88 he sometimes wrote ' . , ' and sometimes ' ; '.

IIc. 1. Salisbury Cathedral 33, fols. 67–196. See I. 8.

IIc. 2. Salisbury Cathedral 67, fols. 1–179^v of a copy of Augustine on St. John. See IV. 17.

IIc. 3. Salisbury Cathedral 88, Cassiodorus, *Institutiones*, and other texts. See IV. 19.

GROUP III. *Books containing writing by Scribe C in the text*

The nature of scribe C's interventions suggests that he was in some sense the director of the scriptorium. His hand occurs in the text of eighteen books, but he did not copy much in any of them, and even in III. 8, where he is the main scribe, he wrote only about thirty leaves: his *forte* was correction. In six books, III. 4, 9, 12, 13, 14, 17, he set the format and the spacing of the lines, that is to say he began the copying and gave place to another scribe after writing at most just over one page. In III. 1 he finished the text. In these and other manuscripts he came in also for short periods, writing often a double opening or finishing a leaf. His hand is Norman, very regular, with distinctive features, particularly the up-down-up form of the common mark of abbreviation, the ampersand with straight final stroke, running steeply up so that the right-hand side looks like a *v*, the tailed *e*, the *g* with long open tail, the final round *s* made tall and linked to the preceding letter and the final *e* with tongue curved to the right. *f* is a descender and *s* tends to be one, but shorter. Hair lines are sometimes attached to descenders. A point, not the punctus versus, is used at the end of a sentence. If the capital letter beginning a sentence comes at the beginning of a line, it is put outside the written space. Long-tailed *r* is used in marginalia sometimes. The hand can look well as a text hand (pl. VI*a*), but often it looks crowded and confused and is uneven, especially when the lines are long: the tendency to an upward slope conflicts with keeping on the ruled lines. It is better in corrections, where it gives an impression of expert work.

III. 1. Aberdeen University 216, fol. 36/1–11, the last eleven lines of Victorinus on the Apocalypse in Jerome's recension (*C.S.E.L.* xlix. 151/5–153/3),[1] which follows after Bede on the Apocalypse. Shown in pl. VI*a*. See IV. 1.

III. 2. London, British Library, Cotton Tiberius C. 1, parts of fols. 112ᵛ–113ᵛ. See I. 2, IV. 2.

---

[1] This MS. was not used by the editor, J. Haussleiter, who refers to the readings of three later English MSS. on pp. lxix-lxxii. The Aberdeen copy seems to be, like them, of the CB text.

Scribe C put in the heading, fol. 112ᵛ/8–10, and directions for the dialogue and actions of bishop and abbot, fols. 112ᵛ/13, 15, 17, 18, 19, 21, 22–24, 113/5, 8, 11, 22, 113/ᵛ17, in spaces left blank by scribe A.¹ These spaces are sometimes too long and sometimes too short, as though scribe A did not quite know how much text was to go in them. Another scribe put in headings and directions on fols. 113ᵛ/21–23 and 114ᵛ–116ᵛ.

III. 3. London, British Library, Royal 5 E. xix, fols. 19/31–38, 19ᵛ/34–20ᵛ/22, 21ᵛ/1–23/17, 25ᵛ/1–26/33, 28ᵛ/18–32, 34/15–35/ 20, that is to say part of art. 2a, all art. 2b, and parts of art. 2c-m. See I. 3, IIb. 1, IV. 3.

Art. 2a, b are independent of c-m (see IIb. 1) on the last two leaves, fols. 19, 20, of the quire on which art. 1, Isidore, ends, and appear to be quire fillers. Art. 2a, 'Non est graue Theodore cadere luctantem . . .', is known in seven other manuscripts, which Dr. Richard Rouse has kindly listed for me, Conches 7, fol. 112ᵛ, Douai 392, fol. 105, London B.L., Royal 8 F. v, fol. 149ᵛ, Metz 223, fol. 137ᵛ, Rouen 488, fol. 141, Troyes 239, Troyes 710. Art. 2b, 'Fratres karissimi habemus a Domino nostro exemplum . . .', is a Palm Sunday sermon: scribe C's copy of it here seems to be the only one known.

III. 4. Oxford, Bodleian, Bodley 756, fol. 1/1–4, the title and the first forty-six words. See IIb. 2, IV. 4, and pl. VIb.

III. 5. Oxford, Bodleian, Fell 4, fol. 223/2–16, completing the life of Saint Mark from the point where scribe A ceased. See I. 6, IV. 9.

III. 6. Oxford, Keble College 22, fols. 45ᵛ–46 (text) and fols. 5ᵛ–6, 29–32, 42ᵛ, 75, 110ᵛ–112 (all or part of the gloss). See IIa. 3, IV. 11.

Pl. V shows fol. 6, where scribe C wrote all the interlinear glosses and all the glosses in the margins, except the last one from the word 'statum'. The first word of the text on fol. 6 'Reuelatur', is glossed by scribe C, but he fitted the gloss in at the foot of fol. 5ᵛ, not on fol. 6.

III. 7. Salisbury Cathedral 10, fols. 7/7–14, 8ᵛ/28–31, 14/1–7, 49/9– 12, 81ᵛ/1–3, 83ᵛ1–84/32. See I. 7, IIa. 4, IV. 13.

III. 8. Salisbury Cathedral 63, fols. 10ᵛ/37–19ᵛ/21, 20/1–24/32, 24ᵛ/1–5, 24ᵛ/25–25ᵛ/32, 26/1–45, 26ᵛ/15–28/45, 28ᵛ/23–45, 29/30– 31/12, 31ᵛ/11–32/23, 32ᵛ/14–33ᵛ/13, 33ᵛ/30–37ᵛ/24, 38/18–39ᵛ/45,

¹ In 'Three Old English Texts . . .', p. 269, this scribe is scribe XII. I said, wrongly, that he wrote three prayers and a blessing on fols. 116ᵛ–117.

40ᵛ/1–41/45, 41ᵛ/14–45/31, 46/1–50/21, 50/32–45, 50ᵛ/17–52/32 (end), that is to say, the greater part of arts. 4–8, 'Liber Athanasii de processione Spiritus Sancti'[1] and the four opuscula of Augustine which follow it. See I. 9, IIb. 5, IV. 16.

Scribes A and C did the whole of three double openings between them, fols. 24ᵛ–27.

III. 9. Salisbury Cathedral 119, fols. 1/1–6, 1ᵛ/7–33, 5/17–34 of Freculphus, *Chronicon*. See IV. 21.

The six lines on fol. 1 are the beginning of the preface and the 27 lines on fol. 1ᵛ are the first 24 entries in the table of contents of bk. 1.

III. 10. Salisbury Cathedral 128, fol. 4ᵛ/1–5.

Fols. 1–4 are the two outer bifolia of the first quire of a copy of Augustine, *De Genesi ad litteram*, used as waste (in s. XII?). The two outer bifolia of quire 2 are now flyleaves in MS. 114 (fols. 2–5) and all eight leaves of quire 3 are flyleaves in MS. 109 (fols. 1–8). The remaining text corresponds to *P.L.* xxxiv. 245–252/45, 264/18–274/39, 283/10–305/22. See above, p. 32.

III. 11. Salisbury Cathedral 128, fols. 16ᵛ/20–17/1, 17ᵛ/1, 18ᵛ/6–20, 19ᵛ/1–10, 21ᵛ/15–33, 24ᵛ/1–14. See I. 12, IIa. 6, IV. 22.

At all these points scribe C either precedes or follows scribe A.

III. 12. Salisbury Cathedral 138, fols. 3ᵛ/1–5, 34/6–14. See I. 13, IIb. 6.

III. 13. Salisbury Cathedral 140, fol. 1/1–6 and half line 7.

Fols. 1, 2 are the beginning of a copy of Berengaudus on the Apocalypse. It was abandoned in the thirtieth line on fol. 2ᵛ. The leaves were used in binding by s. XII, when a stylish title for the main text, Ambrose, *De Spiritu Sancto*, was written on fol. 2ᵛ.

III. 14. Salisbury Cathedral 140, fol. 3/1–14 and some headings. See I. 14, IV. 25.

III. 15. Salisbury Cathedral 154, p. 39/5–16 and headings on p. 5. See I. 15, IV. 26.

III. 16. Salisbury Cathedral 165, fol. 23/1–5 and the first three

---

[1] The text begins 'Athanasius. Quod spiritus sanctus . . .', and is a string of excerpts about the Third Person of the Trinity ascribed to Athanasius, Cyril, Hilary, Ambrose, Jerome, Augustine, Fulgentius, 'Ormisda' (Hormisdas), Leo, Gregory, Isidore, and Prosper, in that order.

words in line 6, beginning a copy of Bede, *De tabernaculo.*[1] See IV. 28.

III. 17. Salisbury Cathedral 168, fols. 2/1–2ᵛ/4, 62ᵛ/1–63/27, 65ᵛ/1–15, 66/1–13, 67ᵛ/1–68/11, 68ᵛ/1–77/26, that is to say the beginning, the end, and four other passages of Augustine, *Quaestiones* 83, and the beginning of pseudo-Augustine, *De duodecim abusivis*: the latter occupies fols. 76–85ᵛ.

III. 18. Salisbury Cathedral 179, fols. 53ᵛ/10–55/41, 73ᵛ/31–74/19, 74ᵛ/1–26, 94/34–94ᵛ/49 (end) of the summer part of a homiliary containing mainly homilies found in the Homiliary of Paul the Deacon.

The text is imperfect at beginning and end and lacks six quires after fol. 27.

GROUP IV. *Books containing writing by Scribe C in corrections and annotations*

Scribe C's hand occurs in the margins of twenty-seven manuscripts, usually in corrections, but occasionally in headings and directions which help the reader to find his way (IV. 15, 18, 26). Omissions are supplied in three ways. If short, a dozen words or less, they are between the lines: a comma is at the point of insertion and a corresponding comma before the first supplied word. If long, they are in the margin, preceded either by a sign like a theta or the sign shown in pl. III*b*: the same sign is at the point of insertion.[2] And whether short or long, they are fitted in by running on into the margin, if they come at the end of a line or so near the end of a line that only a word or two has to be erased. Since homoioteleuton is the main cause of scribal error, most errors are repaired in these ways. Small corrections are made in the line, but

[1] MS. 165 consists of six separable pieces, fols. 1–10, 11–22, 23–87, 88–107, 108–21, 122–77. Scribe C's hand is only in the third piece and the marking with 'D.M.' in the margins occurs only here.
[2] These are two out of some thirty different *signes de renvoi* used in these MSS. The sign in the text is always the same as the sign in the margin, except in two places, so far as I know, Sal. 78, fol. 106ᵛ and Sal. 179, fol. 81ᵛ, where 'h' in the margin answers 'ð' in the text. This pair of signs occurs in two mid-11th-century English MSS., London B.L., Royal 5 F. XIII, fol. 46, and Harley 3080, fol. 30. There and in Sal. 106, 179 they are a hangover from Anglo-Saxon usage: cf. E. A. Lowe in *Miscellanea Giovanni Mercati*, vi (Studi e Testi, cxxvi, 1946), p. 76.

they can only be attributed with certainty to scribe C if one of his distinctive letter-forms appears.

Scribe C emended his own work very little and no one else emended it.

Some books have a good many corrections, some very few. I have tried to note one example of correction in the margin, (*m*), and one of interlinear correction, (*i*).

IV. 1. Aberdeen University 216. Fol. 30*m*. See III. 1.

IV. 2. London, British Library, Cotton Tiberius C. 1. See I. 2, III. 2.

On fol. 112ᵛ scribe A missed the question 'Vis sanctę matri ęcclesię seriberiensi canonicam per omnia subiectionem exhibere?' and the answer to it 'Volo', after 'Volo' in line 19. Scribe C added the question in the margin, but forgot to add the final 'Volo' (pl. III*b*).

IV. 3. London, British Library, Royal 5 E. xix. Fols. 37*m*, 41*i*. Art. 3, Alcuin on the Song of Songs, was much corrected. See I. 3, IIb. 1, III. 3.

IV. 4. Oxford, Bodleian, Bodley 756. Fols. 27ᵛ*m*, 29ᵛ*i*. See III. 4.

IV. 5. Oxford, Bodleian, Bodley 765. Fol. 18*m*. See I. 4, IIa. 2.

IV. 6. Oxford, Bodleian, Bodley 768, Ambrose, *De virginitate*, etc. Fols. 34ᵛ*i*, 48ᵛ–49*m*.

IV. 7. Oxford, Bodleian, Bodley 835, Ambrose, *De Ioseph patriarcha*, etc. Fols. 7ᵛ*m*, 38*i*.

IV. 8. Oxford, Bodleian, Fell 1. Fol. 95*m*. See I. 5.

IV. 9. Oxford, Bodleian, Fell 4. Fol. 113ᵛ*m*, See I. 6, III. 5.

IV. 10. Oxford, Bodleian, Rawlinson C. 723. Fols. 22ᵛ*m*, 31ᵛ*i*. See IIb. 3.

IV. 11. Oxford, Keble College 22. Fol. 111*m*. See IIa. 3, III. 6.

IV. 12. Salisbury Cathedral 6, Augustine, *Confessiones*. Fols. 6*m*, 34*i*.

IV. 13. Salisbury Cathedral 10. Fol. 60ᵛ*i*. See I. 7, IIa. 4, III. 7.

IV. 14. Salisbury Cathedral 25. Fol. 54ᵛ*m*. See IIa. 5.

IV. 15. Salisbury Cathedral 37, Bede on Luke. Fols. 41m, 68^vi; also, in the margins, the first words of gospel texts.

IV. 16. Salisbury Cathedral 63. Fol. 7m. See I. 9, IIb. 5, III. 8.

IV. 17. Salisbury Cathedral 67. Fols. 44^vm. 215i. See IIc. 2.

IV. 18. Salisbury Cathedral 78, 'Excerpta ex decretis Romanorum pontificum.' Fols. 51m, 88i; also, in the margins, many headings.

IV. 19. Salisbury Cathedral 88. Fols. 25i, 46m. See IIc. 3.

IV. 20. Salisbury Cathedral 106. Fols. 17^vm, 23i; also 'Explicit . . .', fols. 29, 41^v, and 'Incipit . . .', fol. 20. See I. 10.

IV. 21. Salisbury Cathedral 119. Fols. 56m, 62i. See III. 9.

IV. 22. Salisbury Cathedral 128. Fols. 5i, 6m. Art. 1, Augustine, *De adulterinis conjugiis*, was much corrected. See I. 12, IIa. 6, III. 11.

IV. 23. Salisbury Cathedral 129, pseudo-Augustine, *Quaestiones 127 Veteris et Novi Testamenti.* Fols. 14m, 63^vi.

IV. 24. Salisbury Cathedral 135, a treatise or treatises on the significance of rites and observances of the Church, etc.[1] fol. 20^vm.

IV. 25. Salisbury Cathedral 140. Fol. 35^vm. See I. 14, III. 14.

IV. 26. Salisbury Cathedral 154. Pp. 55m, 78i; also some headings, titles, and notes. See I. 15, III. 15.

MS. 154 is an aberrant version of 'Retractatio I' of the *Liber officialis* not referred to by J. M. Hanssens, *Amalarii episcopi opera liturgica omnia* (Studi e Testi, cxxxviii–cxl, 1948–50). The differences from 'Retractatio I' as set out by Hanssens, i. 163–8, consist in additions and changes of order, the absence of the preface *Postquam scripsi* and some other passages and the absence of any division into books or chapters. The place of *Postquam scripsi* is taken by a short preface beginning '[S]cribimus namque nostris consimilibus puerulis causa pulsandi et quaˊeˊreˋnˊ-di de officio continuato quod agitur in nostra ęcclesia ut pulsent et quęrant. si forte dominus aperiat eis'. 'Retractatio I', ii. 33, 'In antiquis libris . . .', follows the preface immediately, and ii. 34–36 are also taken

---

[1] Partly also in Exeter Cathedral 3525, s. XII, and other MSS: see E. G. W. Bill, *A Catalogue of Manuscripts in Lambeth Palace Library, MSS. 1222–1860*, 1972, p. 59.

before i. 2–12, which occupy pp. 9/21–18/6. At this point ten pages on the offices of Holy Thursday, 'Eadem uero nocte . . .', come in place of i. 13–17, and scribe C wrote in the margin 'Hic superest quod in alio non inueni usque parasceue'. At p. 28/2 text agreeing with i. 18, 'De parasceue', begins. Corrections by scribe C are not many, except perhaps small ones in the line. He added words on p. 90, 'id est usque ad omen consilium tuum confirmet', to come after the sentence 'Mittat . . . sequentes' (ed., ii. 322) and, I think, a gloss on p. 30, 'id est odorifera' above 'emorousa' (ed., ii. 104, the line numbered 12).

IV. 27. Salisbury Cathedral 159, Origen on Exodus and Leviticus. Fols. 23*m*, 112ᵛ*i*.

IV. 28. Salisbury Cathedral 165. Fol. 29ᵛ*m*. See III. 16.

GROUP V. *Books likely to be coeval with those of Groups I–IV*

This is a not fully explored rag-bag. Some of it will go into group II and perhaps other groups when more work has been done on Salisbury scribes. Some books are more or less like books in groups I–IV. Some may not originate in Salisbury. Six, Royal 5 E. xvi, Salisbury 7, 9, 35, 115, 130, are notably poor looking.

GROUP VI. *Books likely to be rather later than those of Groups I–V*

These books are tidier and better written than most of the books in groups I–V and, to my eye, they look rather later in date. Not many scribes were concerned in making them.

Scribe D1 may have had the same sort of leading position as scribe A seems to have occupied a little earlier. He wrote a total of over 700 leaves: fols. 2–122ᵛ, all but the last thirty leaves, of Royal 6 B. xv, Cyprian, perhaps the best-looking early Salisbury manuscript now extant;[1] Salisbury 61, fols. 1–10ᵛ, 21–43ᵛ/7, most of a miscellany of works by Augustine and others, of which fols. 21–30,

---

[1] Royal 6 B. xv and seven other MSS., all English and all but one 12th century, form Maurice Bévenot's 5B family, a distinct English tradition going back possibly to the late-4th-century copy, London B.L. Add. 40165A (*C.L.A.* 179). It is probably the earliest of the family. Bévenot collated it as 'e' and noted its superiority (*The Tradition of Manuscripts*, 1961, pp. 79, 83).

De natura boni, form an independent quire in shorter lines than the rest; Sal. 64, fols. 1–80, works of Augustine;[1] Sal. 116, Augustine, *Contra Faustum*, on—for Salisbury—unusually good parchment; Sal. 131, fols. 1–8^v (quire 1), 17–20^v (quire 3, leaves 1–4) and 25 (quire 4, leaf 1) of 'Libri beati effrem diaconi';[2] Sal. 139, Eusebius, *Historia ecclesiastica*, except fols. 88–89^v, 94–103^v, 106^{rv}; Sal. 197+Royal App. 1, works of Augustine, and Jerome against Lucifer, except fols. 14/1–12 and 55–56; Sal. 198, works of Augustine.[3] The hand is of Norman type with prominent long-backed *g* and an attractive and distinctive form of the ampersand which is not always used, probably because it wastes space: the final projecting stroke is long and turns over to the right at the end. This spreading ampersand is the common form in some manuscripts, for example Sal. 198. In others it is rare and used mainly near the end, where the scribe would be in a position to know that he had room to spare. Probably manuscripts in which the spreading form is common throughout are early works.[4]

Scribe D2, not a distinguished scribe, wrote the whole of Salisbury 4 (Hilary), 109, flyleaves apart (Augustine, Ambrose, etc.), and 136 (Bede on Samuel), and seventy leaves of Sal. 64, where he co-operated with scribe D1.

Scribe D3 wrote Salisbury 12 (Smaragdus), except fols. 56/15–60^v, and Sal. 169, arts. 1–8 (fols. 1–77^v), works of Augustine, except fol. 54/12–30. The writing looks very trim, with low minims and, for the size of the script, wide spacing between the ruled lines. D3 perhaps wrote Bodley 392 (Sermons).

Scribes who make only a single appearance, so far as I know, and

[1] These were originally the last ten quires. At some later date, before the table of contents was added in the thirteenth century, they were put in front of quires 11–19 (fols. 81–150^v, by scribe D2).

[2] He co-operated with another scribe who wrote fols. 9–16^v (quire 2), as appears from the inexact join between quires 2 and 3: fol. 16^v was left blank. On fol. 3 scribe D1 wrote in the margin the English words 'ofer þæt oðer hus'. I can only suppose that they were scribbled in the margin of the exemplar. There is nothing in the text to account for them.

[3] Bought from Lancing College who withdrew it from Sotheby's, 16 December 1970, lot 25. 107 leaves. A reduced facsimile of fol. 83 is in the sale catalogue. The size of the written space is 195 × 115 mm. The contents are listed by Römer, op. cit. ii. 2 (*Sitzungsberichte* cclxxvi, 1972), p. 321.

[4] Two other points suggest that Sal. 198 may be an early work of scribe D1. One is that the vertical bounders are single instead of double on fols. 17–107: single bounders are seldom used in the MSS. of groups I–VI and never elsewhere by scribe D1. The other is that this is the only MS. by scribe D1 which has marking with 'D.M.' in the common hand: see above, p. 26.

wrote well, were responsible for Salisbury 5 (Pelagius) and 65 (Augustine).[1]

N. R. KER

NOTES TO THE PLATES

PL. III

(*a*) Exeter Cathedral 3500, Exon Domesday fol. 9. Shows scribe A and a scribe who worked with him on Geld Account B. Group I. 1.

(*b*) London, British Library, Cotton Tiberius C I, fol. 112ᵛ. Shows scribe A; also scribe C in directions in the text and in the addition in the margin. Group I. 2.

PL. IV

(*a*) Oxford, Bodleian Library, Bodley 765, fol. 1. Shows scribe A interrupted by scribe B1 for thirty-six words. The eighth word by B1 has his open *a* in *-tate*. Group I. 4.

(*b*) Oxford, Bodleian Library, Bodley 765, fol. 18. Shows scribe A and also scribe C making a running-on correction. Group I. 4.

(*c*) Oxford, Bodleian Library, Bodley 765, fol. 51. Shows scribe A's typical *-rum* abbreviation, which appears in pl. III *a* and *b*, but not in pl. IV *a* or *b*. Group I. 4.

PL. V

Oxford, Keble College, 22, fol. 6. Shows scribe B1 in the text (including open *a* in line 18) and scribe C in the glosses (see p. 42). Group IIa. 3.

PL. VI

(*a*) Aberdeen, University Library, 216, fol. 36. Scribe C. A good specimen of his hand and shows his capitals. Group III. 1.

(*b*) Oxford, Bodleian Library, Bodley 756, fol. 1. Shows scribe C writing the title in capitals and the first three lines of the text which was continued by a scribe with an English-type hand. In line 7 *deo* is a correction by scribe C. Group III. 4.

---

[1] See above, p. 26.

3

Describing Medieval Bookbindings

1. *The Lack of Description in Catalogues*

THE study of medieval binding does not owe as much as it should
to catalogues of manuscripts. We still depend on catalogues of the
late eigtheenth and nineteenth centuries for our knowledge of
what there is in many of the most important collections; and these
catalogues normally omit information about the bindings. From
1895 to 1934 M. R. James described the medieval manuscripts of
at least thirty libraries. He noticed the occasional stamped binding
and sometimes the brilliant hue of the leather on a manuscript in
pristine state; but his descriptions, so helpful in other respects,
never include anything about the construction of the binding.
Falconer Madan's formulary for *A Summary Catalogue of Western
Manuscripts in the Bodleian Library* specified as the eighth and last
item in a description 'Binding, if remarkable'.[1] Madan and his
collaborators considered a larger proportion of medieval bindings
remarkable than M. R. James did; but their descriptions are
briefer, and include some attributions of date which later research
has not confirmed.

2. *The Vicious Circle*

Some years ago I grumbled at a cataloguer who had described
a binding as fifteenth century, whereas I thought it was twelfth
century and contemporary with the manuscript which it covered.
His reply was both civil and embarrassing. 'If you would direct
me to anything in print about this, I will certainly read it and cite
it.' Embarrassing, because there is very little in print about the
construction or development of medieval binding;[2] and for two

---

[1] Vol. iii (1895), p. [x]. Repeated in the preliminaries of the later volumes.
[2] Except Berthe Van Regemorter's essay in *Scriptorium*, ii. 2 (1948),
275–85, but this does not go beyond 1200.

sufficient reasons. First, because they cannot be found in existing catalogues; and secondly, because their plain exteriors[1] do not provoke curiosity about how or why or when they differ from one another. Thus we are in a vicious circle. Cataloguers cannot describe these bindings properly because there are no printed studies to tell them how; and printed studies cannot be produced because students of medieval bookbinding cannot find the books to study.

What the cataloguer needs to know is the technical changes in the construction of bindings which may indicate place or date. So it occurred to me that it might go a little way towards breaking the vicious circle if I tried to set down, and classify under easily recognizable features, how the construction of English bindings changed over the four centuries from 1100 to 1500. It must be clear from the outset that what I have to say is not based on any systematic survey. Friends have drawn my attention to many bindings; some I have noticed as they were issued to other readers across the counter in Duke Humphrey's Library; more still have been discovered on privileged visits to the stacks in several important collections. In the last fifteen years I suppose I have seen more than a thousand medieval bindings; but I cannot claim that the bindings which I have noticed are representative. In one respect my sample is certainly biased because, working almost entirely in English libraries, I have not seen enough continental bindings to identify the characteristics which may distinguish them from English work.

My information is unsystematic in another way. One of the features which I used to note when I started was the different colour combinations in silk sewn headbands; but I gave this up because it did not seem to yield any significant pattern of time or place. On the other hand, it was only recently that I realized that adhesive,[2] though of very ancient origin, was not at first used in

---

[1] Bindings decorated with blind stamps have been studied: The romanesque bindings of the 12th and 13th centuries (106 of them, only 8 certainly English) by G. D. Hobson, *English Binding before 1500* (Cambridge, 1929); additions and corrections in *The Library*, 4th ser. xv (Sept. 1934), 161–211 and xix (Sept. 1938), 202–49. Much has been written on blind-stamped bindings after 1450, conveniently listed by A. R. A. Hobson, *The Literature of Bookbinding*, London, The National Book League, 1954, pp. 4–5, 10–11, to which add J. B. Oldham, *Blind Panels of English Binders*, Cambridge, 1958), and G. Pollard, 'The Names of some English Fifteenth-century Binders', *The Library*, 5th Ser. xxv (Sept. 1970), 193–218.

[2] Paste made with flour and water or glue made by boiling down bones, horns,

bookbinding, and may thus be a criterion of date. Consequently in my earlier notes I have omitted to record whether the leather cover is attached to the boards by pasting down the turn-ins or by sewing their mitres together. There are likely to be other features of which I have failed to discern the significance, and still more which I have not noticed at all.

3. *The Size and Content of the Entry*

Students of bookbinding must not be unreasonable in their demands on the cataloguer. He has other matters to record, text, palaeography, illumination, provenance, some of them more important than the binding. Medieval manuscripts offer such fascinating problems that it is all too easy for a cataloguer to be sidetracked into research about particular books at the expense of never finishing his catalogue. Madan estimated half an hour as the average time required for cataloguing a manuscript. He catalogued upwards of 30,000 manuscripts in twenty years; and *A Summary Catalogue* is one of the very few catalogues of a large collection of manuscripts which has ever been finished. The function of a cataloguer is to alert scholars to the special features of the manuscripts he describes; and we ought not to expect more than perhaps a couple of dozen words devoted to the binding.

In this small compass the catalogue will have to include; (*a*) a brief description of the exterior (e.g. white leather over oak boards); (*b*) sewing (original or resewn or unascertainable. See below, par. 5); (*c*) approximate date with a minimum of supporting evidence (e.g. about 1200, with tabs); (*d*) any repairs, if possible with an approximate date (e.g. rebacked in late nineteenth century). It is more helpful to say 'nineteenth-century half morocco, re-sewn' than to omit all reference to the binding. It may eventually be possible to date most medieval bindings within half a century or so, as the palaeographers date a script; but in the meantime it does not help to be more precise than the evidence warrants; 'probably

and hooves. Both are very ancient; but glue was hardly used at all in binding during the Middle Ages. The only instance I know is the autograph MS. of Higden's *Policronicon* from St. Werburg's, Chester about 1352 (now San Marino, Huntington MS. HM. 132). The volume is in its original sewing, and has on the recto of the last leaf a note of the materials used by the binder with their cost. He paid a halfpenny for glue which he used in the grooves and spine of the book.

XIV² ' is often more accurate than 'XIV² ' without qualification. But even 'medieval binding' is better than complete silence.

4. *Medieval Bindings are Not of One Making*

Nowadays we are accustomed to think of the hard cover as an integral part of a modern book produced by the publisher along with the printed text. Medieval books are more often like an old house in which parts have been demolished, parts altered, and parts added. Although a surprising number of medieval bindings have survived unaltered in their original state, these are nevertheless only a small proportion of the extant total. We must not assume that all the parts of an old binding were made at one time. Lincoln Cathedral MS. 174 is a twelfth-century glossed psalter. Its sewing and thongs are original, but the thongs have been pulled through strawboards which have been covered in modern polished half calf within the last 100 years. The sewing is 700 years older than the cover. No doubt this is an extreme example. But it shows that each part of a binding has to be separately considered before describing the binding as a whole.

5. *The Sewing*

Sewing is the basic operation in all bookbinding.[1] A sewing frame[2] is set up vertically on the edge of a table; it is rectangular, and thongs—generally double thongs—are attached to its top bar, stretched tight over the table edge, and secured to a bar below. The quires to be bound are then placed on the table with their fold flush with the table edge and resting against the thongs. A thread is tied to the end thong, pierces with a needle the hinge of the first quire, runs up the central gutter of the quire until it is opposite the second thong, then pierces the hinge outwards, is wound round the second thong, then back through the hinge into the gutter of the quire, and so on. The process is repeated in each quire for each thong until the whole book is firmly attached to the

---

[1] I have not here considered Coptic binding where the quires are sewn to each other, and not on thongs. This covers Greece, the Near East, and North Africa. It is probably the origin of the method used in the Stonyhurst Gospel (Northumbrian; late 7th century). But this method was not used in England 1000–1500. There are a few freaks without sewing (e.g. Corpus Christi College, Oxford, MS. 220).

[2] Van Regemorter (op. cit., pl. 19, second roundel on the right) reproduces a 12th-century picture of one.

thongs, leaving a length of each thong loose at both sides of the book.

For the purpose of dating the binding it is important to discover whether the sewing is original or whether the book has been resewn. There are two methods of ascertaining this: (*a*) if the spine is defective or sufficiently loose to examine the back of the quires, it can be seen whether there is any horizontal line of punctures in addition to those now in use for attaching the quires to the thongs. It is not necessary to examine the whole length of the spine: half-way from the top or the tail is enough to show whether there has been an earlier sewing. Or (*b*) open the volume in the middle of a quire in the middle of the book. There is a thin thread running down the gutter, attached through the hinge at intervals corresponding to the thongs. Take a pointed but not sharp bone paper-knife, and lift the thread a couple of millimetres gradually throughout its length. If you can see any punctures beneath the thread, then the book has been resewn. It is best to take a check about a quarter and three-quarters of the way through the book to see whether there are unused punctures at corresponding points throughout, and that you have not been deceived by a speck of dust in the first instance. If there is a regular line of unused punctures in the hinge of the quires throughout the book, it has been resewn. If the binding is too tight to allow either method of examination, all that can be done is to record that the binding is too tight to show the sewing; but you may privately suspect (as I do) that in such cases the binding has been sophisticated since it was first bound.

If there is no line of unused punctures across the hinges of the quires, then the book has never been resewn,[1] and the present sewing is original. The sewing fixes the thongs in position, so that the present thongs must also be original; and, if their position fits the only grooves for fixing them to the boards, then the boards must likewise be original.

6. *Attaching the Boards*

The long loose ends of the thongs were threaded into wooden boards; and the different patterns of their attachment provide the

---

[1] It is technically possible to re-sew a book using the old holes; but I know of no evidence that this was done before the late eighteenth century.

simplest way of recognizing the approximate date of a binding.
I have set out the main patterns in figures 1–6 on page 57.

Figure 1 shows an eleventh-century pattern. Its noticeable
feature is that the head and tail bands are secured in triangular
grooves. The double thong enters a short tunnel set at an angle of
forty-five degrees in the inner corners of the board. The two
strands emerge on the outside of the board separated in two arms
of a V-shaped groove; they are pulled through two holes at the end
of the V; twisted together in a groove on the inside of the board;
and pegged in the two holes. This arrangement is found in Bodley
MS. 775 (*The Winchester Troper*, mid eleventh century); British
Library, Additional MS. 37517 (*The Bosworth Psalter* from St.
Augustine's, Canterbury, about 1000); Bodley MS. 97 (*Prudentius* from Christ Church, Canterbury, early eleventh century);
Bodleian MS. Auct. F. 1. 15 (*Boethius*, written at Canterbury
about 1000, but probably bound at Exeter shortly after the death
of Bishop Leofric in 1072). *The Winchester Troper* has its sewing
and boards in their original state; but the others have all been
resewn, probably in the fourteenth century, and the boards
turned round to make room for the slots of the new thongs. These
pre-conquest bindings are less standardized than the sets of the
Early Fathers bound for the Norman abbots[1] shewn in figure 2.
The few early bindings which survive seem to combine grooves on
the outside as well as the inside of the boards; and the triangle
with its sides on the inside and its base on the outside is probably
the simplest and latest form of the practice. All the bindings
in which I have noticed it are eleventh-century work; and we
may provisionally regard the presence of original grooves on both
sides of the boards as an indication that these boards were made
before 1100.

Figure 2 shows the style from about 1100 to about 1240. The
thongs enter through a tunnel in the thickness of the board, and
emerge on the inside into a groove which extends nearly half-way
across the board before being pegged. The number of thongs
(excluding the head and tail bands) is usually two: as many as
four is unusual even on large folios. The thongs from the head and
tail bands normally have a straight groove at forty-five degrees

---

[1] See N. R. Ker, *English Manuscripts in the Century after the Norman Conquest* (Oxford, 1960), pp. 4–9.

from the corner; but I have seen one or two manuscripts[1] where these grooves take a sharp turn. This may indicate that the binding is not English, and it therefore deserves mention.

Figure 3 is not as common as figures 2, 4, and 6. It occurs sporadically, but mainly in the second half of the thirteenth century. The thongs now enter the board, not through a tunnel in its thickness, but by a short groove on the outside, then through the board into a groove on the inside which is not as long as those in figure 2.

The weakest part of the bindings shown in figures 2 and 3 was the hinge where the thong receives its greatest degree of wear, and must often have broken. Probably taking the thong round the outside of the inner edge of the board instead of through a tunnel in the thickness of the boards increased the exposure of the thong to wear at this point. To avoid breakage at the hinge the number of thongs was increased (figs. 3, 4, and 5). Whereas there would normally be only two thongs on a binding of about 1200, there might be as many as eight on a book of the same size in 1400. The number of thongs (=bands) increases from about 1250 until about 1400 when it begins to decline. The maximum number of bands that I have noticed is eleven on a not very large folio of about 1400 (Bodley MS. 250), and ten on the large folio volume of the accounts for the city of Canterbury for 1393.[2]

The number of bands increased and they were not stretched so far across the inside of the board. This meant that an increasing number of holes had to be bored closer together in a vertical line (fig. 3), so that the board tended to split along that line. This was countered in the fourteenth century or perhaps a little earlier by staggering the line of holes (figs. 4 and 5), so that they did not lie in one vertical line, and the board was less likely to split. Finally about the middle of the fourteenth century to about the middle of the fifteenth they reduced the number of holes required by plugging two thongs in one hole, thus producing the V I V I pattern shown in figure 6.

7. *The Material and Shape of the Boards*

The boards of English bindings are usually made of oak, so it is probably not necessary to mention this detail. But if the wood is not

---

[1] e.g. Bodleian MS. Lyell 3.

[2] Nine on Bodleian MS. Auct. D. 1. 19. (sc. 2335) from Reading.

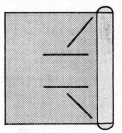

Fig. 1. Before 1100. The thongs across the bases of the triangles are twisted on the side of the board, shewn here by dotted lines

Fig. 2. About 1100 to about 1240. The thongs enter through a tunnel, usually tabs of thicker leather at top and tail

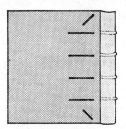

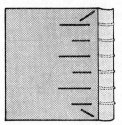

Fig. 3. Second half of 13th century. Thongs enter by a groove on the outside of the board

Fig. 4. The thongs are pegged to a staggered pattern. 14th century

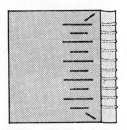

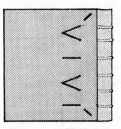

Fig. 5. The number of thongs is increased. Second half of 14th century

Fig. 6. 1350–1459. Two thongs are pegged in one hole

oak (beech, lime, chestnut, sycamore, etc.) it should perhaps be mentioned and the possibility considered that the book was not bound in England.

The edges of the boards in the early twelfth century are uncompromisingly square (e.g. Bodley MS. 835 from Salisbury); but the boards soon begin to acquire a bevel on the outer edges, which grow more rounded as time goes on. I have not been able to discern any chronological or local pattern in this, for some early thirteenth-century bindings have hardly any bevel, while some late twelfth-century ones have the outer edge of the board well rounded. But there is one feature of the boards which is characteristic of the fourteenth century. This is what I have called elsewhere the cushion bevel. The curve from the outer edge of the board starts sharply and decreases all the way over towards the centre, so that no part of the side of the book is absolutely flat. This is in marked contrast to the earlier bindings as well as to those of the fifteenth century where most of the side is quite flat and the bevel is less than an inch wide. Boards with a cushion bevel are, even in the centre, noticeably thinner than those of earlier date.

8. *The Material of the Cover*

The skin of practically every mammal including man can be made into leather suitable for binding a book.[1] In describing the leather of a medieval binding the process of cure is generally more useful than the species of animal used. Sheep and calf were commonly available; goat sometimes. Seal is not common; but the four bindings on which I have noticed it all come from Lincoln Cathedral and Fountains Abbey,[2] places near the east coast, where seals are still plentiful.

There are two methods of curing the skin: tanning with oak bark, and curing with alum and salt (whittawing). Both methods of cure may have either a smooth polish or a rough, suede-like finish. The polished brown surface of tanned calf was necessary for bindings decorated with blind stamps; and so it was used for the 'romanesque' bindings of the twelfth to thirteenth centuries

---

[1] H. T. Riley, *Memorials of London*, 1868, p. 234; *The Coventry Leet Book* (E.E.T.S. O.S. cxxxv, 1908), p. 401.

[2] Queens' College, Cambridge, MSS. 5 and 6; Lincoln Cathedral MS. 31 (all from Lincoln); Corpus Christi College, Oxford MS. D. 209 (from Fountains Abbey).

and very widely after 1450. Tanned leather is apt to stain contiguous sheets of vellum. Possibly for this reason it was not often used for binding books (except for 'romanesque' bindings) before the middle of the fifteenth century.

Whittawed leather for binding books was dyed red or white or green. Where the skin was highly polished, it has retained its brilliant reddish puce tint (e.g. Hereford Cathedral MS. O. 8. ix and Princeton University, Scheide Collection MS. 22); but when it had a suede finish the colour has usually faded to a dirty white, and is now only discernible on the turn-ins.

9. *Putting the Cover on the Boards*

There are two ways of fixing the leather cover over the boards: the turn-in; and the chemise. In both methods a cured skin is taken, considerably larger than the book when opened out; and any projections are trimmed away to leave a rough rectangle. In the turn-in method a triangular piece is cut from the four corners of the skin to make mitres over the four outer corners of the boards. The skin is then folded round the edge of the boards and secured either by sewing across the mitres or by pasting the whole of the turn-in to the inside of the board.[1] A further and later refinement is to leave a thin strip in the middle of the mitre (I call them third mitres) to ensure that in pasting down the mitres the leather lies taut against the outside of the board.[2] In the chemise method two additional rectangles of leather, longer but narrower than the boards, are sewn to the inside of the main skin along their three outer edges so that they form two large pockets. The boards are folded right back and inserted in these pockets. When the boards are brought back to their normal position, the leather is stretched firmly round the whole volume, leaving a wide frill which can be wrapped round the whole book. A well-known example in original state is the Ormesby Psalter (Bodleian, Douce MS. 366); but the frill was often cut away. Bosses have sometimes been added and fixed right through the outside of the chemise, the board, and the inner pocket, so that the chemise is now immovable. Indeed in a

---

[1] There is a diagram of this in *The Library*, 5th ser. xvii (1962), 15.

[2] e.g. Pembroke Coll. Cambridge MSS. 61 and 100; Bodleian MS. Laud Misc. 371; Bodley MS. 86; and see the diagram in [Sir Hilary Jenkinson], *Domesday Rebound*, London, Public Record Office, 1954, p. 39, fig. 6.

worn example without its frill it may not be at all obvious that the cover is a chemise. A finger run gently along the outer edges of the board may feel a regular series of tiny bumps. These are remains of the stitches by which the pocket was originally sewn to the outer cover, and are sure evidence that the present cover is really a chemise. The earliest chemise that I have noticed is Bodleian MS. Laud Misc. 546 which was given to Durham by William de St. Carilef who died in 1096. The latest is a Roger Bacon of the early fifteenth century (Bodleian MS. e Mus. 153); but earlier and later examples doubtless exist.

11. *The Use of Adhesive*

These observations prompt the question whether there is any significance, chronological or local, in the use of paste in book-binding.[1] For the turned-in covers one might suppose that the mitres sewn across preceded those pasted down, and perhaps with more confidence that those with 'third mitres' are later than those without. Sewing across the mitres certainly occurs early: Bodleian MS. Laud Misc. 118 from Blois about 1100, Bodley MS. 672 from Chester, and Pembroke College, Cambridge, MSS. 12 and 15, both from Bury St. Edmunds, all before 1200, have this feature. But books of the middle of the twelfth century from Salisbury (Bodley MS. 835) and Cirencester (Jesus College, Oxford, MS. 3) apparently had their turn-ins pasted down (though not very neatly mitred) from the beginning. It seems therefore that in the twelfth century the use of paste may be evidence of location, but is not evidence of date. The chemise, of course, requires no paste.

12. *The Bands across the Spine*

I would not have given space to this small problem of the mitres, if it had not been relevant to the more important question of when the horizontal bands across the spine begin to be made prominent. To make the bands stand out from the spine, it is necessary to apply paste to the back of the quires and the thongs before the leather spine is put on. Strings must then be tied tightly round the outside of the book above and below each band, and removed when the paste has set. These bands have been the most

See above, p. 51 n. 2.

prominent feature of a binding from the middle of the thirteenth century down to the present day.

The earliest binding that I know with projecting bands is Bodley MS. 477, which was given to Oseney Abbey by Richard Wurth who died in 1236. The bands still enter the thickness of the board, but it never had any tabs at the top and tail of the spine. Paste was used to make the spine stick to the backs of the quires between the bands, and traces can still be seen of the strings tied round the book above and below each band. Hereford Cathedral MS. P. 2. xiii (mid thirteenth century) has bands treated in the same way except that they enter the boards in grooves on the outside instead of through tunnels in the thickness of the board.

13. *Projecting Squares*

The last constructional change that I have to record is the projection of the squares, that is the boards are made wider and taller than the leaves of the book. They are no longer flush with the edges of the leaves, but project beyond them. This begins just before the middle of the fifteenth century. Before then it is probable that the book with its boards attached but without the cover was put in a vice; and the edges of the leaves and the boards were trimmed in one operation with a hammer and chisel or more probably a plane.[1] The leather cover was put on later, and the effect is that the edges of the leaves are flush with the edges of the boards. We do not know when the bookbinders' plough was invented: the earliest picture of it is given by Jost Amman in 1568.[2] But it seems to have come into use just after 1440. Bodley MS. 52 written by John Mainsforth about this date is entirely in the old style. Lincoln College, Oxford, MS. lat. 101 written by John Malberthorp about the same time has projecting squares. This change of construction was quickly followed by a change to tanned leather decorated with blind stamps. This fashion seems to have started in Germany not long before the invention of printing. But it spread more quickly for books were being bound in this style at London, Oxford, and Salisbury by 1460.

[1] Traces of this operation (i.e. slight skids by the plane or chisel) can be seen on the edges of Bodleian MS. Laud Misc. 460 and Hereford Cathedral MS. p. 2. xiii.

[2] Hartman Schopper, Πανοπλια *Omnium liberalium mechanicarum et sedentarium artium genera continens* (Frankfort, 1568), sig. C 5.

14. *Tabs; Bookmarkers; Bosses; Clasps; Chain Staples*

None of these features are a necessary part of the construction of a medieval binding. They are nevertheless parts of the binding which have to be described.

TABS project beyond the head and tail of the spine, and are sometimes of different leather from the cover. They are semi-circular or square, often whipped round the edges with different coloured silks and occasionally lined with colour-woven cloth. They occur as early as the ninth century on two bindings at Autun,[1] and the latest example known is Wisbech Museum MS. 5 from Ramsey Abbey. One of the tracts in that volume is Robert Grosseteste's *Templum Domini* which was not put into circulation before he became a bishop in 1235. The only purpose served by these tabs seems to have been to pull the volume out of a row of similar books placed fore-edge downwards in a chest. Later when the books were put on shelves, the tabs were in the way, and so were cut off. When there appear to be two layers of leather in the spine, it is worth looking to see whether the inner layer was originally a tab. The tab cannot be added once the cover has been put on; so that the presence of a tab is a useful guide for dating a binding before 1240 at the latest.

The upper tab sometimes has a hole in the centre which may be sewn round with coloured silk. This was for the BOOKMARKER, which was secured through the hole with a knot. One still survives like this on Jesus College, Oxford MS. 93, from Evesham. But the bookmarkers, sometimes as many as four of them for one volume, are more often sewn to the headband or the edge of the tab.[2]

Even when BOSSES are part of the original design, they had to be the last thing added by the binder. Thus it is always difficult to tell when they were added. They go back to very early times; and were

[1] Autun, Bibliothèque de la Ville, MSS. 5 and 19, reproduced by Van Rege-morter, op. cit. pl. 20 (b and c).

[2] Jean Destrez, 'L'outillage des copistes du XIIIe et du XIVe siècles' in *Aus der Geisteswelt des Mittelalters. Studien und Texte Martin Grabmann zur Vollendung des 60. Lebensjahres gewidmet* (Münster, 1935), pp. 19–35; Wordsworth and Littlehale, *The Old Service-books of the English Church*, 1904, p. 280; M. R. James on Corpus Christi College, Cambridge, MS. 49. The more elaborate types of bookmarker in which there is a rotating disc to indicate which of the four columns in an opening is required, and which can be moved up and down the marker to show which line in the column is wanted, are probably French, not English.

for lectern books used in church or refectory. They should properly appear on only one cover. Occasionally they can be seen to be later than the rest of the binding because the bolt which secures them has intruded into writing on a pastedown inside the cover. In the fourteenth and fifteenth centuries they may have been added for decorative rather than functional purposes. An unusual form of boss may sometimes indicate provenance; a truncated cone with fluted sides is characteristic of books from Holme Cultram.[1]

CLASPS were often added to the binding later. The earliest form is a single narrow strap on the edge of the upper cover, stretched across the fore-edge of the leaves, and fitted over a pin set in the middle of the lower cover. This begins about 1200, and dies out about 1300. Two straps of this kind must be close to 1300, but examples are not common. Two clasps are perhaps earlier on service books than others. In the Exhibition of 'Opus Anglicanum' at the Victoria and Albert Museum in 1965 there was a long series of splendid copes loaned by cathedrals on the Continent. The traditional decoration of a cope includes the figure of Saint Peter with a book in the crook of his arm. It was noticeable that in all the copes dated before 1300, this book had no clasps; but in those dated from about 1320 onwards the book always had two clasps. It is doubtful if two clasps were in general use before the fourteenth century; and some are additions of much later date. The pewter catches hammered into the width of the fore-edge of the lower board in twelfth-century bindings from Bury St. Edmunds now at Pembroke College, Cambridge, were added as late as the early seventeenth century. J. B. Oldham observed[2] of late fifteenth-century stamped bindings that in England and France the clasps were put on the upper cover and the catches on the lower cover, whereas in Holland and Germany the reverse was the case. The normal position of the clasps on fourteenth- and fifteenth-century English bindings certainly conforms to Oldham's suggestion.

CHAIN STAPLES, or more often the marks which show that they have been removed, ought to be mentioned because they sometimes provide evidence of provenance. But this mention is much more useful if it includes the precise position of the mark on the binding: upper or lower cover, top edge, fore-edge, or bottom edge

---

[1] e.g. Bodleian MS. Lyell 2; San Marino, Huntington 19915.
[2] *English Blind Stamped Bindings*, 1952, p. 8.

with the distance of their position along the edge. The earliest known reference to chaining books is in Archbishop Peckham's injunctions to Merton College Oxford in 1284; but he only specified three grammatical works, Papias, Hugutio, and the Summa Britonis.[1] These books were for reference rather than reading. The first mention of chaining books for reading seems to be the intention of Thomas de Cobham, who died in 1327, to have chains put on the books which he left to found a library for the University of Oxford.[2] Chaining a whole library can hardly have become a common practice before the second half of the fourteenth century. It continued for some three hundred years, for the library at Wimborne Minster, where the books are still chained, was not founded until 1686.[3] A considerable proportion of staple marks must thus be post-medieval.

15. *Chronological Summary*

Over the four centuries from A.D. 1100 to 1500 there are two main changes in the technique of bookbinding with consequent changes in the appearance of the book. The flat spines, tabs, and thongs going into a tunnel in the thickness of the board all disappear in the second quarter of the thirteenth century. This change coincides with the earliest records of lay bookbinders at London and Oxford. The horizontal bands prominent across the spine begin about 1250, and increase in number until about 1400 after which they decrease. The second important change is the projection of the boards beyond the edge of the leaves which starts just before 1450, and is quickly followed by the general use of tanned leather and its decoration with small blind Stamps. Panel stamps begin to be used in England on small books about 1490. The next important change is from wood to pasteboard as the material for the boards. This was in use at Paris by 1508, and came to England about 1520, which is outside the period of this essay.

1000–1100. Head and tail bands secured in triangular grooves. Grooves on the outside as well as the inside of the boards. Tabs. Thongs enter a tunnel in the thickness of the board.

---

[1] *Statutes of the Colleges of Oxford . . . Merton College*, 1853, p. 41.
[2] *Oriel College Records*, edd. C. L. Shadwell and H. E. Salter (O.H.S. lxxxv, 1926), p. 22.
[3] See also J. N. L. Myres in *The English Library before 1700*, edd. F. Wormald and C. E. Wright, 1958, pp. 236–7.

1100–1230/50. Tabs, flat spines, thongs enter a tunnel in thickness of the board. Not more than four thongs, which extend half-way across the board.

1230/50–1450. More bands (see figs. 3–5). Bands project. They enter the board round the outside of its inner edge. Cushion bevel.

1450–1500– . Squares project. Tanned leather, blind stamps.

I have here tried to describe some of the ways in which plain English bookbindings differ; and to propound some hypotheses about why and when these differences occur. But they are hypotheses, not definitive rules; and will doubtless have to be modified in the light of further information. In the meantime I hope that they may draw some points which may indicate date in the construction of bindings to the attention of those who have to describe medieval manuscripts.

GRAHAM POLLARD

4

The Florilegium Angelicum: *its Origin, Content, and Influence*[1]

THE *Florilegium Angelicum* is a collection of extracts from ancient and patristic orations and epistles compiled in France during the second half of the twelfth century. It takes its name from Rome, Biblioteca Angelica MS. 1895. The *florilegium* contains extensive extracts from a number of rare works, such as the younger Pliny's letters, Cicero's Verrine orations, the works of Ennodius, and the pseudo-Plautine *Querolus*. For these in particular, it was a significant vehicle of dissemination in the twelfth and thirteenth centuries. Surviving wholly or in part in at least seventeen manuscripts the *Florilegium Angelicum* thus achieved a far larger circulation than its more famous contemporary, the *Florilegium Gallicum*. Yet for all practical purposes this book is still unknown. We wish to excavate this *florilegium* in specific, and, in the process, to illustrate through it some aspects of what can be gained from the study of *florilegia* in general.

The whole *florilegium* or substantial portions of it are found in nine manuscripts: Rome, Bibl. Angelica 1895, fols. 1–79^v, s. XII^2, France (A), incomplete; Vatican, Pal. lat. 957, fols. 97–184^v, s. XII^2, France (P), incomplete; Florence, Bibl. Laurenziana, Strozzi 75, s. XII^2, France (F); Vatican, Reg. lat. 1575, fols. 63–100^v, s. XII–XIII, France (R), rearranged; Sydney, University Libr., Nicholson 2, s. XIII^2, France (N), extracts; Vatican, Vat. lat. 3087, fols. 23–68^v, s. XIII^2, S. France or Italy (V); Paris, Bibl. de l'Arsenal

[1] We are grateful to M.-Th. d'Alverny, Bernard Bischoff, Élisabeth Pellegrin, and Jean Vezin for their considerate help on numerous details in the preparation of this paper. We wish in particular to thank Birger Munk Olsen for sharing with us his extensive knowledge of pre-13th-century MSS. of Latin classical authors. Thanks are also due to the curators of Latin MSS. at the Bibliothèque Nationale and the staff of the Institut de Recherche et d'histoire des textes, Paris. This study was carried out with the support of the American Council of Learned Societies.

1116 E, fols. 128–142ᵛ, s. xiii¹, France, St. Victor (S), extracts;
Évreux, Bibl. Municipale 1 fols. 64–114ᵛ, s. xiii med., France,
Lyre (E), incomplete; and London, British Libr. Add. 25104, s.
xv, Italy (L). To these should be added the description of a copy
now lost, item 84 in the *Biblionomia* of Richard de Fournival (d.
1260).[1] Of them, Angelica 1895 (A), which alone contains a
prologue, is the dedication copy. Selections or brief extracts from
the *florilegium* are found in six manuscripts: Auxerre, Bibl. Municipale 234, s. xiv², France (x); Brussels, Bibl. Royale 10098–10105,
s. xiii¹; France (b), Cicero orations and Jerome only; Leyden,
Universiteitsbibl. B.P.L. 191B, s. xiii² (l); London, Brit. Libr.,
Royal 11 A.v., s. xii–xiii (r), Jerome only; Paris, Bibl. Nationale,
lat. 15172, s. xiii, France, St. Victor (s); and Vatican, Reg. lat.
358, s. xv, France, Tours (v). Complete reorganizations of the
florilegium in which the extracts are arranged by subject are known
in two manuscripts, Rome, Bibl. Angelica 720, s. xiii, France (a)
and Paris, Bibl. Nationale, lat. 1860, s. xiii med., S. France (p).
Since many of these are uncatalogued, a description of each is
given in Appendix III. For three further manuscripts see p. xxx.

The manuscripts of the *florilegium* can be grouped as follows, on
the basis of a collation of the extracts from Pliny's letters and from
Seneca's *De beneficiis* and through a comparison of their contents.
The two oldest manuscripts, A and Pal. lat. 957 (P), are sufficiently
similar in physical appearance to have been written in the same
scriptorium. This must in fact have been the case, because A is a
direct copy of P, scrupulously corrected from the archetype. This
is evident from the following readings, in which errors unique
to P have been corrected: Pliny's letters, 1. 13. 5 *desideria* PA,
desidia A corr., cett.; 4. 9. 8 *Iugulari* PA, *Iugulat* A corr., cett.;
Seneca, *De beneficiis* 1. 5. 2 *materiam et* PA, *materiam beneficii et*

---

[1] Published in L. Delisle, *Le Cabinet des manuscrits de la Bibliothèque nationale*,
ii (Paris, 1874), pp. 518–35; item 84, p. 529, and Appendix III below. In addition to Fournival's library, MSS. of the *Florilegium Angelicum* were known in
two other medieval libraries, Cluny and Notre-Dame in Paris: item 224, *Flores
philosophorum excerpti ex libri Saturnalium Macrobii*, in a catalogue of the books
at Cluny made in 1800 (L. Delisle, *Inventaire des manuscrits de la Bibliothèque
nationale: Fonds de Cluni* [Paris, 1884], pp. 397–404); and item 47, *Flores
philosophorum, excerpti de libro Macrobii Saturnaliorum*, among the books left to
Notre-Dame in 1296 by Pierre de Joigny, canon of Rouen and master of theology
in Paris (Delisle, *Cabinet*, iii. 5; and P. Glorieux, *Répertoire des Maîtres en
théologie de Paris au XIIIᵉ siècle*, i [Paris, 1933], no. 183). We are unable to
identify either of these among the surviving MSS. For the Cluny reference we
are indebted to B. Barker-Benfield, the Bodleian Library, Oxford.

A corr., cett.; 1. 8. 2 *gravius* **PA**, *gratius* **A** corr., cett.; 2. 16. 1
amicosa vox **PA**, *animosa vox* **A** corr., cett. The affiliation of **P** and
A is further apparent in the errors which they share against the
rest of the tradition, which the scribe of **A** failed to rectify. For
example, in Pliny's letters 1. 20. 11, where the others rightly read
prestare dicentibus brevitas, both **P** and **A** omit *dicentibus*. In the
extracts from *De beneficiis* 1. 1. 7, both **P** and **A** place the phrase
Errat qui sperat . . . torsit before two other phrases from the same
paragraph, while the other manuscripts concur in placing this
phrase after the others, following the order of Seneca's text.
Two extracts from *De ben.* 1. 4. 3 and 4. 4, *Qui referre gratiam
debet . . .* and *Honestissima contentio est beneficiis . . .*, found in the
others, are lacking in **P** and **A**. One cannot postulate that **P** is a
copy of **A** made before correction, firstly because the corrections
are made in the hand of the manuscript and thus without significant
time lapse; and secondly, because of the unique readings in **A** not
found in **P**: Pliny 1. 16. 8, *floruisset in primis* **A**, *floruisset in precio*
P cett. (wording not in Pliny text); 5. 5. 4 *finivit* **A**, *finunt* **P**,
finiunt cett. (recte); *De ben.* 1. 1. 1 *fero* **A**, *sero* **P** cett. (recte); 1. 6.
3 *optime* **A**, *opime* **P** cett. (recte). Another indication is found
in the extract from *De ben.* 2. 11. 1; the passage, as rephrased in
the *florilegium*, begins *Quidam tibi proscriptione servatus . . .* In **P**
there is an erasure between the words *tibi* and *proscriptione*,
although nothing is missing. (The length of the erasure suggests
that it may have been *proscriptione* written twice.) **A** reproduces
the meaningless blank. Finally, there is the fact that **P** does not
present the extracts from Gregory's letters following the extracts
from Jerome, a sequence found only in **A**. **P** hence emerges as a
fair copy of the archetype, almost certainly the compiler's fair copy.

A evidently produced one descendant, that being the collection
of extracts from the *florilegium* in Arsenal 1116 E (**S**). **S** agrees in
error with **AP** against the rest of the tradition at Pliny 1. 20. 11,
with **A** and the rest against **P** in error at 3. 3. 7, and it includes
extracts from Gregory's letters. **P** produced, apart from **A**, only
the partial text in Auxerre 234 (**x**). It is obviously related to **P**
because it is the only other manuscript of the *florilegium* to include
the extracts from Julius Paris. Three manuscripts which contain
the complete *Florilegium Angelicum*, Strozzi 75 (**F**), Reg. lat. 1575
(**R**) and Vat. lat. 3087 (**V**), descend independently from the archetype. While they may be at some remove from it, the three share

no errors in common against **P** and **A** and hence do not descend from a single intermediate parent. Each of the three contains errors and omissions not reproduced in the others. **F**, oldest of the three, thus cannot be an ancestor of either of the other two; apart from its unique errors, it has numerous *lacunae* of one or more words. In evidence, one need cite only the most glaring example, its omission of three successive extracts from Pliny's letters, 1. 17. 2, 17. 3, 18. 5, which appear in the other two. **R** cannot be an ancestor of **V**, not only because of unique errors and *lacunae*, such as the omission of an entire extract from Pliny 1. 12. 3, but also because **R**, as we shall see, represents a rearranged order while **V** presents the original sequence. **V** is late in date (fourteenth century) and replete with independent errors. Despite the possible distance from the archetype of **F**, **R**, and **V**, there is no pattern of common errors that pair any two against the third, and hence no indication of a common ancestor intermediate between two of them and the archetype. The remaining manuscript of the whole text, London B.L. Add. 25104 (**L**) of the fifteenth century, seemingly shares a common ancestor (γ) with **F**, as these readings suggest: Pliny 1. 7. 3 *qui* **FL**, *quid* rem.; 2. 4. 3 *liberalitas* **FL**, *liberalitas tua* rem.: 2. 6. 5 *aliquanto* **FL**, *aliquando* rem.; 3. 21. 3 *putamus* **APFL**, *putavimus* **RV**. Moreover, only **F** and **L** conclude with the brief *Alexander Atheniensibus* which must have been in γ. Évreux 1 (**E**), Leyden B.P.L. 191 B (**l**), and **R** constitute another sub-family, descending from a manuscript (β) in which the works were grouped by author, with the Christian authors (Gregory, Jerome, Sidonius, and Ennodius) preceding the classical authors and, among the latter, with the 'proverb' material concluding the collection. This order is reflected in **E** and **R**.[1] The extracts in **l** are few and dispersed among other texts, but shared readings show its affiliation: for example, Pliny 1. 3. 5 *ipse tibi* **REl**, *tibi ipse* rem.; 1. 20. 12 *varie sunt voluntates* **REl**, *varie voluntates* rem.; 2. 3. 5 *milicie* **REl**, *malicie* rem. Although Sydney Nicholson 2 (**N**) contains selections from virtually every text in the *florilegium*, the extracts are too few and the manuscript too badly effaced to permit a precise affiliation. **N** does not reflect the *lacunae* of **AP** (*De ben.*

---

[1] **R** and **E** each has errors not found in the other. For example, the extract from Pliny 1. 12. 3 omitted in **R** is found in **E**. And in many instances **E** differs, in error, from **R**; for example, Pliny 1. 4. 4 *dicimus* **E**, *dominis* **R** recte; 1. 5. 17 *etiam verum* **E**, *verum etiam* **R** recte; 1. 9. 8 *Tullius* **E**, *Attilius* **R** recte.

1. 4. 4) or **F** (Pliny 3. 9. 8), nor the revised order of β, and hence it appears to derive independently from the archetype. The six remaining manuscripts, those which are rearranged topically and those which contain only a handful of extracts from the *florilegium*, we have not attempted to place on the stemma.

Having established the relative authority of the manuscripts of the *Florilegium Angelicum*, we are now equipped to settle a number of problems regarding the arrangement and actual contents of the archetype. The two most authoritative manuscripts, **A** and **P**, are both unfortunately incomplete. **A** breaks at the end of quire 10 in the middle of extracts from Aulus Gellius, indicating that it once contained more, and is now lacking its final quire or quires. **P** has quires numbered i–x; quire x breaks in the midst of extracts from Ennodius, indicating a missing quire or quires. It is followed by a quire numbered i, containing extracts from Gregory's letters and from Julius Paris' Epitome of Valerius Maximus. The text of the Epitome breaks at mid-sentence at the end of the quire, indicating that another quire or more are lacking here as well. One must hence turn to the later copies in order to determine what the *florilegium* actually contained. Where the manuscripts containing the full text or large portions of it, **APFNVLRES**, concur, we have the contents of the *florilegium*. With the exception of the prologue, which appears in **A** alone, and of the extracts from Gregory's letters, which are a separate question, the nine agree upon the following content and (saving **RE**) sequence: Macrobius, *Saturnalia*; *Proverbia philosophorum*; Jerome, epistles; Apuleius, *De deo Socratis*; Pliny the Younger, epistles; Cicero, orations; Sidonius, epistles; Seneca, *De beneficiis*; Seneca, *Epistulae ad Lucilium*; *Sententiae philosophorum*; *Praecepta Pithagorae*; *Ænigmata Aristotilis*; Cicero, Tusculan Disputations; Aulus Gellius, *Noctes Atticae*. At this point **A** breaks off. But the other manuscripts, including **A**'s exemplar **P** and its descendant **S**, continue with extracts from Cicero's Verrine orations and the works of Ennodius. Here the extracts in **S** cease, and the text in **P** is broken. However, the remaining manuscripts, including **P**'s descendant, **x**, continue with extracts from Martin of Braga, *De formula honestae vitae*; *Querolus*; and Censorinus, *De die natali*.

The extracts from Censorinus mark the limit of reliable consensus and thus presumably the end of the archetype. However, there remains one problem concerning the sequence of works in the *florilegium*, the extracts from the letters of Gregory the Great. Extracts from Gregory's letters were clearly a part of the archetype of the *Florilegium Angelicum* since the Gregory extracts in **A**, copied from the added quire in **P**, are corrected from the archetype and since they appear in other manuscripts of the *florilegium*—though not in the same place in the order, and not in all manuscripts. The Gregory extracts may have been an afterthought—a tactful addition to a *florilegium* dedicated to a pope. In making his fair copy, the compiler added them on a separate quire numbered i, along with extracts from Julius Paris. In making the presentation copy, he entered the Gregory extracts where they might most appropriately appear, following the extracts from the letters of Jerome. That the Gregory extracts remained unattached to the archetype, perhaps in the form of a loose quire, is also suggested by their treatment in the later manuscripts. The manuscripts which include them follow the suggestion of **P**, presumably reflecting that of the archetype, that they precede the collection because the quire that contains them bears the signature i. β must have contained the Gregory extracts at the beginning, since both **R** and **E** do. The writer of **S** placed the extracts from Gregory and those from Jerome as well at the head of the collection. In **x** the Gregory extracts appear instead as the final section, following the example rather than the precept of **P**, **N**, **V**, γ, and Fournival's manuscript omit the extracts from Gregory's letters entirely and proceed in the order described above.

What disposition the compiler made of the extracts from Julius Paris we cannot know, because of the incomplete state of **A**. The fact that these extracts appear in only two manuscripts, **P** and the partial text in **P**'s descendant **x**, suggests that they were an addition to **P** which did not exist in the archetype.

Extracts from three other works are found in more than one manuscript. At an early stage in the transmission, extracts from the oration of the Scythian legates to Alexander, from Quintus Curtius 7. 8. 12–30, were added to the *florilegium* following the extracts from Censorinus. These appear in four manuscripts: **FL** (γ), **N**, and **V**. Moreover, the writer of β included longer extracts from Quintus Curtius, an addition probably inspired by his having seen the *Oratio Scytharum*. Since a sample collation indicates that β, γ, **N**, and **V** descend independently from the archetype, the extracts thus must represent an addition to the archetype itself. The absence of these extracts from x indicates that this addition was made after the presentation copy was written; and the description of Fournival's manuscript of the *Florilegium Angelicum* also suggests that the Censorinus extracts, not Quintus Curtius, originally marked the end of the *florilegium*. Extracts called *Alexander Atheniensibus*, three sentences from Julius Valerius (ed. Keubler, p. 46. 20–8), follow the *Oratio ad Alexandrum* in **F** and **L**. This represents an individual addition by the writer of γ, one obviously suggested to him by the subject-matter of the preceding extracts. Finally, there are lengthy extracts from Ps.-Quintilian's *Declamationes maiores* in two manuscripts, **R** and x, and a shorter series from the collection in Paris B.N. lat. 15172 (**s**). Quotations from Quintilian in the topically arranged Paris B.N. lat. 1860 (**p**) perhaps derive from this same collection. As with the *Alexander Atheniensibus*, these were obviously not part of the archetype; but their independent addition to the *Florilegium Angelicum*, based on orations and epistles, is wholly understandable.

An examination of the transmission of the more unusual texts included in the *Florilegium Angelicum* has permitted the identification of two manuscripts, Vat. lat. 4929 and Berne 136, from which the compiler drew his extracts. The appearance in the *florilegium* of extracts from the *Querolus*, from Censorinus' *De die natali*, and, in two manuscripts, extracts from Julius Paris's Epitome of Valerius Maximus, reveals the presence of Vat. lat. 4929, assembled by Heiric of Auxerre. Vat. lat. 4929, discovered by Barlow and Billanovich,[1] was probably put together by Heiric toward the mid ninth century from a number of older books, among which was a collection of three texts which had been edited in the sixth century at Ravenna by Rusticius Helpidius Domnulus: the Epitome of Valerius Maximus, Pomponius Mela's *De chorographia*, and Vibius Sequester's *De fluminibus*. For these it is the sole remaining authority.[2]

---

[1] C. Barlow, 'Codex Vaticanus latinus 4929', *Memoirs of the American Academy in Rome*, xv (1938), 87–124 and plates 11–18; G. Billanovich, 'Dall'antica Ravenna alle biblioteche umanistiche', *Aevum*, xxx (1956), 319–53.

[2] Vat. lat. 4929 (V) was annotated around 1100 by a grammar master who added extensive scholia to the *Querolus*. In the mid 12th century a copy of V was made which included the scholia, but it is now lost. It in turn produced Vatican Reg. lat. 314 pt. VI, fols. 112–16, s. xii² (S), which survives in a collection of fragments assembled by Paul Petau. Barlow, p. 100, and G. Ranstrand, *Querolus-studien* (Stockholm, 1951), pp. 26–7, assign this MS. to Micy St. Mesmin; how-

Of the texts[1] contained in Vat. lat. 4929, extracts from the
Querolus and Censorinus follow one another at the end of the
Florilegium Angelicum; and extracts from Julius Paris appear in
the odd last quire of P (fol. 184^{rv}), and immediately following the
Querolus and Censorinus in x (fols. 156^v–169^v).[2] While there are
other manuscripts of the *Querolus* and Censorinus upon which our
compiler might have drawn, Vat. lat. 4929 is the only complete
manuscript of the Epitome. That the *Florilegium Angelicum* drew
on Vat. lat. 4929 was first noticed inadvertently by Ranstrand; he
recognized the influence of readings in Vat. lat. 4929 on the extracts from the *Querolus* in Paris, B.N. lat. 15172 (s) fol. 126^v.
(He and Gagnér, who had also examined it, considered s to be a
variant version of the extracts from the *Querolus* in the *Florilegium
Gallicum*.[3]) A collation of the extracts from the *Querolus* shows that
the text of the *Florilegium Angelicum* shares five readings with
Vat. lat. 4929 (V) against the other manuscripts of the *Querolus*;
three of these are from the text of V, and two derive from the late-
eleventh- or early-twelfth-century glosses on the text. From Ranstrand's edition of the *Querolus*,[4] the five readings are: p. 11. 22
peierat: perierat V, florilegium; p. 13. 12 *dibacchationes: debaccha-
tiones* VR, flor.; p. 20. 15 *inesse felicem sinunt: esse felicem non
sinunt* V, flor.; p. 9. 21–2 *satis aliis multis defensorum: satis tibi
aliisque multis defensorum* V (*tibi* add. interlin.), flor.; p. 20. 12

ever, Reg. lat. 314 is made up of eight or nine fragments of varying dates, only
the first of which bears the Micy ex libris. The lost MS. (copy of V, parent of S)
moved south at some date and was acquired by Petrarch at Avignon in 1335; a
copy, incorporating Petrarch's notes, survives as Milan, Bibl. Ambrosiana H 14
inf. (s. xv). Cf. Billanovich, op. cit.

[1] Vat. lat. 4929 contains, fol. 1^{rv}, a fragment of the Greek alphabet (s. xi);
fols. 2–34, Censorinus, *De die natali*; fol. 34^v, blank; fols. 35–50, an epitome of
Augustine's *De musica*; fols. 50^v–54, four anonymous sermons (s. ix-x); fol. 54^v,
blank; fols. 55–77, *Querolus*, with commentary added s. xi ex. or s. xii in.; fol.
77^v, three concentric circles; fol. 78, labyrinth; fols. 78^v–148, Julius Paris, Epitome of Valerius Maximus; fols. 148^v–149, blank; fol. 149^v, verses beg. *Septem
mira* . . .; fols. 149^v–188, Pomponius Mela, *De chorographia*; fols. 188–95, Vibius
Sequester, *De fluminibus*; fols. 195^v–196, blank; fol. 196^v, list of churches (s. xi;
Barlow, s. x); fol. 197^{rv}, blank except for pen trials. Taken from Barlow, pp.
87–8.

[2] The initial survey of the extracts from Vat. lat. 4929 was carried out by
Edward Weeden.

[3] Ranstrand, op. cit., pp. 69–72; A. Gagnér, *Florilegium Gallicum. Untersuchungen und Texte zur Geschichte der mittellateinischen Florilegienliteratur*,
Skrifter utgivna av Vetenskaps-Societeten, xviii (Lund, 1936), p. 212.

[4] G. Ranstrand, ed., *Querolus sive Aulularia incerti auctoris comoedia*, Göte-
borgs Högskolas Årsskrift, lvii (1951).

corpora videntur quantum animus: *corpora videntur sed quantum animus* V (*sed* add. interlin.), flor.

The extracts from the Epitome of Julius Paris in **P** contain four readings which tie them to Vat. lat. 4929. The most significant is Kempf 476. 16,[1] where V and **P** give the dative singular *Locri*, and the later manuscripts as well as Valerius Maximus offer the correct genitive singular *Locris*. Three readings in **P** derive from corrections made in the text of V by the above-mentioned glossator: 476. 22 *Epidauriae Scolapio*, corr. to *Epidauri Aescolapio*; 476. 23 *turpei dei* corr. to *turpe id ei*; [13. 15] *ignorares eandi* corr. to *ignorare se an di*. The readings in the Epitome, as well as those in the *Querolus*, which derive from corrections made by the glossator, represent his invention rather than the readings of another manuscript. The two extracts from Censorinus in the *Florilegium Angelicum* contain no significant variants.

The *Florilegium Angelicum* contains, in sequence, extracts from Apuleius called *De deo Socratis* (but including as well his *Asclepius*, *De Platone*, and *De mundo*); from the younger Pliny's letters; and from the following orations of Cicero: (Pseudo-Cicero) *Pridie quam in exilium iret, Post reditum in senatu, Post reditum ad Quirites, De domo sua, Pro Sestio, In Vatinium, De provinciis consularibus, De haruspicum responsis, Pro Balbo*, and *Pro Caelio*. The last two texts, Pliny's letters and this group of orations, were not easily found in twelfth-century France. Fortunately, the manuscript from which the extracts were taken can be identified as Berne, Burgerbibliothek 136 s. XII[2], which contains Gregory, *In Ezechielem*; Apuleius, *De deo Socratis, Asclepius, De Platone, De mundo*; Pliny's epistles bks. 1. 1–5. 6; and Cicero's orations (in the number and order given above). It is a well-known manuscript and has been collated and classified for its texts of Pliny and Cicero.

For its text of Pliny (and Apuleius as well) Berne 136 descends from Florence, Bibl. Laurenziana, S. Marco 284, s. XI (F), of the ten-book family.[2] Berne 136 contains the same works of Apuleius

---

[1] C. Kempf, ed., *Valerius Maximus* (Stuttgart, 1966), pp. 472–591.

[2] The transmission of the younger Pliny's letters is set forth in R. A. B. Mynors, *C. Plini Caecili Secundi epistularum libri decem* (Oxford, 1963), pp. v–xxii. Concerning the direct dependence of Berne 136 on F, see E. T. Merrill, *C. Plinii Caecili Secundi epistolarum libri decem* (Leipzig, 1922), p. xi n. 23. The initial survey of the extracts from Pliny in the *Florilegium Angelicum* was carried out by William Patt.

and the same text of the letters as are found in S. Marco 284, i.e. that ending at bk. 5. 6. The editors of Pliny's letters have long known of the existence of the extracts in the *Florilegium Angelicum* and that they belong to the ten-book family; but the editors knew them in only five manuscripts, **F, R, V, S**, and Angelica 720 (a)[1] and, since they contribute nothing toward establishing the text of the letters, they received little attention. It is clear on the basis of the readings that the compiler of the *florilegium* used an F text as his source. However, because Berne 136 is so faithful a copy of F, we cannot prove from readings alone that Berne 136 rather than F is the source of the extracts. The proof rests in the fact that excerpts from Apuleius, Pliny, and Cicero all three appear in the *florilegium* consecutively and in the same order as in Berne 136.

The collection of Cicero's orations in Berne 136 is quite as rare as Pliny's letters.[2] These orations are known in only five manuscripts which date from before 1200, all descending from a common archetype: Paris, Bibl. Nationale, lat. 7794, s. ix, France (P);[3] London, British Libr., Harley 4927, s. xii[2], France (H); Brussels, Bibl. Royale 5345, s. xii, ascribed to Gembloux (G);[4] Berlin, Staatsbibl. Preussischer Kulturbesitz lat. fol. 252, s. xii, Corvey, presumably assembled by Wibald of Corvey (E); and Berne 136.[5]

---

[1] D. Johnson, 'The manuscripts of Pliny's Letters', *Classical Philology*, vii (1912), 70.

[2] Concerning the transmission of this group of Cicero's orations see A. C. Clark, 'The Vetus Cluniacensis of Poggio', *Anecdota Oxoniensia*, Classical Series pt. 10 (Oxford, 1905); W. Peterson, 'Cicero's *Post reditum* and Other Speeches', *Classical Quarterly*, iv (1910), 167–77; Clark, *The Descent of Manuscripts* (Oxford, 1918), pp. 266–80; J. Cousin, ed., *Cicéron: Discours Pour Caelius, Sur les provinces consulaires, Pour Balbus*, Collection Budé (Paris, 1962), pp. 58–74; idem, *Cicéron: Discours Pour Sestius, Contre Vatinius*, Collection Budé (Paris, 1965), pp. 91–103. The initial survey of the extracts from these orations in the *Florilegium Angelicum* was carried out by Joyce Segor.

[3] The MS. written by several Tour hands, had probably come to Paris by the late 14th or the 15th century, for it bears an erased note of that date on fol. 32[v] upper marg.: *A frere Joachim Perion estudiant a Montagu a Paris en crestiente*, referring to the Collège de Montagu (1314–1792). On fol. 1 top left, it bears the unidentified pressmark: O. lx. xxix (similar to, but not that of, St. Denis). Few books survive from the college, making it difficult to determine whether or not this is the college pressmark. The MS. was part of the Royal Library by 1622 (Rigault CCCVII).

[4] The ascription stems from the presence of a 12th-century leaf from Gembloux in its binding.

[5] Besides these five, extracts from this collection of orations appear in the *Florilegium Gallicum*, compiled in France toward the middle of the 12th century; two leaves of a mid-9th-century (*c.* 860) MS. written in the area of the Loire,

For the orations Berne 136 is a direct copy of the ninth-century P made after the latter was corrected and punctuated in the early twelfth century, apparently from the parent of G and E. The writer of Berne 136 followed the system of punctuation and was influenced by the manner in which P² broke the text into sentences by the use of capital letters.[1] As in the case of Pliny's letters, Berne 136 reads so close to its exemplar that one cannot tell on the basis of readings alone from which the extracts in the *Florilegium Angelicum* derive. That the extracts come from Berne 136 is again proven by the fact that the latter also contains Apuleius and Pliny's letters.

One wonders, of course, where the compiler of the *Florilegium Angelicum* found these two important manuscripts. He was obviously working at a place where interesting classical texts were available, including a number that were rare in twelfth-century Europe. (To those already mentioned, one would want to add in particular the Verrine orations of Cicero.) As we shall see later, the compiler's purpose was to provide a collection of eloquent quotations, from which one might draw apt and stylish phrases for the composition of public pronouncements and official letters. In the second half of the twelfth century this combination of interests, in the classical authors and in the *ars dictaminis*, immediately suggests Orléans as a possible home for the *Florilegium Angelicum*. While present knowledge of the curriculum at Orléans is slight, its position as the centre for classical studies is clearly established in the well-known statements of such contemporaries and near-contemporaries as Matthew of Vendôme, Geoffrey of Vinsauf,

---

containing the *Pro Sestio* 41. 88–46. 99 are found in Leyden Voss. lat. F. 67, fols. 1–2ᵛ; the Ps.-Ciceronian *Pridie* is known in Rouen MS. 1040, fol. 11 (s. xii; Lyre); and Berne, Burgerbibliothek, MS. 395, fols. 1–15 (s. xiii med.) contains the *Pridie, Post reditum in senatu,* and *Post reditum ad Quirites.* The 13th-century extracts from the orations in Brussels Bibl. Royale, MS. 10098–10105 (Van den Gheyn 1334) come from the *Florilegium Angelicum.* The 10th-century text in Paris B.N. nouv. acq. lat. 340, fol. 107 (Cluny), said by Hauréau (*Notices et Extraits,* vi (Paris, 1893), pp. 260–1) and Manitius (*Geschichte der lateinischen Literatur,* ii (Munich, 1911), p. 482) to be an introduction to the *De haruspicum responsis,* is a fragment of Grillius on Cicero's *De inventione*; see E. Courtney, 'Ignis fatuus extinguitur', *Scriptorium,* xv (1961), 114–15. Thus far no effort has been made to classify the extracts in the *Florilegium Angelicum* or the *Florilegium Gallicum,* or the texts in the Leyden MS. or Berne 395.

[1] Peterson, op. cit.

Helinand of Froidmont, Alexander Neckham, and John of Garland, and is celebrated posthumously, so to speak, in Henri
d'Andeli's *Battle of the Seven Liberal Arts* in the middle of the
thirteenth century. And Orléans seems to have been famous across
Europe for teaching the *ars dictaminis*.[1] We can, therefore, accept
as a hypothesis that the *Florilegium Angelicum* was compiled at
Orléans. To make this more than an assumption, one must
consider the external evidence.

The information one can glean from Vat. lat. 4929, one of the
manuscripts used by the compiler of the *Florilegium Angelicum*,
goes far toward confirming our assumption. The transmission of
individual works in Vat. lat. 4929 offers supporting evidence at
least. For its text of the *Querolus*, one can localize its sister manuscript (Leyden Voss. lat. Qu. 83, s. ix[1]) at Fleury,[2] whence it
passed to Pierre Daniel. The *De fluminibus* of Vibius Sequester
was copied from Vat. lat. 4929 at least once, producing Vatican
MS. Reg. lat. 1561, fols. 11^v–15^v, (s. xii[2]);[3] this also belonged to
Pierre Daniel. More telling as to its whereabouts in the eleventh
and twelfth centuries is the physical evidence in Vat. lat. 4929
itself. The earliest evidence is the appearance on fol. 196^v of a late-
tenth- or early-eleventh-century list of thirty-six parishes and the
tithes they paid under the administration of one Arnulf. Delisle
identified the parishes with villages in the area of Pithiviers, which
lies in the diocese of Orléans.[4] Barlow suggested that the writer of

---

[1] Concerning the schools at Orléans see L. Delisle, 'Les écoles d'Orléans au
xiie et au xiiie siècle', *Annuaire: Bulletin de la Société de l'histoire de France*, vii
(1869), 139–54; L. J. Paetow, *The Arts Course at Medieval Universities . . .*,
University Studies, iii (Urbana, 1910), pp. 503–9, 575–81; E. Faral, *Les Arts
poétiques du XIIe et du XIIIe siècle* (Paris, 1924); B. Marti, *Arnulfi Aurelianen-
sis Glosule super Lucanum . . .*, Papers and Monographs of the American Academy
in Rome, xviii (1958), Introduction. Besides the bibliography given in these, see
S. Guenée, 'Université d'Orléans', *Bibliographie d'histoire des universités françaises des origines à la Révolution*, Institut de Recherches et d'histoire des textes
et Commission internationale d'histoire des universités (Paris, 1970). The best
survey of medieval letter collections with full bibliography is the introduction
to *The Letters of Peter the Venerable*, ed. Giles Constable, ii (Cambridge, 1967),
pp. 1–44.

[2] Ranstrand, op. cit., p. 24, description (incorrectly dated s. x); 37–41, ana-
lysis; 59, stemma.

[3] Incorrectly dated s. xiii in R. Gelsomino, ed., *Vibius Sequester* (Leipzig,
1967), p. xx.

[4] The list is printed by L. Delisle, 'Notice sur vingt manuscrits du Vatican',
Bibliothèque de l'École des Chartes, xxxvii (1876), 487–8. It was also published by
A. Reifferscheid, *Bibliotheca patrum latinorum italica*, i (Vienna, 1870), 445–6.

the list might be identified with Arnulf, bishop of Orléans 973–1003.[1] This would suggest that Vat. lat. 4929 belonged to the library of the Cathedral of Orléans or to some member of the chapter. It almost certainly remained at Orléans, to judge from the glosses of the late-eleventh- or early-twelfth-century scholar or scholars who annotated the manuscript. Among the glosses and additions are two concerning the Loire. Finding the *De fluminibus* deficient in its knowledge of his home, he adds: *Liger* [Loire], *Gallie, dividens aquitanos et celtas, in oceanum brittannicum evolvi-tur.*[2] Noting the appearance of *Liger* in the *Querolus* (16. 22), he reminds readers that Tibullus knew of his river, with the gloss: *Ligerem*] *Ligerem dicit a nominativo Liger, quem ponit Albius Tibullus, carnutis et flavi cerula limpha Liger* (Tibullus 1. 7. 12).[3]

The writer's corrections, glosses, and his commentary on the *Querolus* show that he was learned, and suggest that he was a master at the schools in Orléans. Like Heiric, who had corrected the manuscript before him, he was concerned about correct divisions between words and the proper use of capital letters. He knew Greek well, according to Barlow. In the scholia to the *Querolus* he gives extensive verbatim quotations from Firmicus Maternus, *Mathesis*; Fulgentius, *Mythologia*; and Justinian's *Institutes*.[4] Both Fulgentius and Firmicus, neither of whom was common *c.* 1100, were known at Fleury, not twenty miles from Orléans.[5]

Berne 136 bears no *ex libris*. Soon after it was written it was used by the compiler of the *Florilegium Angelicum*. Paris B.N. lat. 14749, fols. 22–121ᵛ, containing Cicero's orations, was copied from Berne 136 in the fifteenth century.[6] It has recently been discovered that B.N. lat. 14749 was in large part written by the French humanist Nicolas de Clémanges;[7] however, we do not know where Clémanges copied Berne 136, save to suppose that—as did the compiler of the *florilegium*—he found it at some centre of learning. In the middle of the sixteenth century, Berne 136

---

[1] Barlow (p. 72 n. 1 above), pp. 99–100.   [2] Ibid., p. 123, and pl. 18.
[3] Ibid., pp. 106, 109.   [4] See ibid., pp. 105–7.
[5] Fulgentius appears in the 11th-century booklist of the abbey, and Firmicus is cited in the catalogue of 1552; G. Becker, *Catalogi bibliothecarum antiqui* (Bonn, 1885), p. 147, item 62. III; *Catalogue général des manuscrits des bibliothèques publiques de France*, xii (Paris, 1889), p. 52.
[6] Peterson (p. 75 n. 2 above).
[7] The discovery was made by Gilbert Ouy, whose discussion in detail of Nicolas's hand is still awaited; see Ouy's report in the *Annuaire de l'École des Hautes études* (1965–6), p. 259.

belonged to Pierre Daniel, who wrote the table of contents on fol.
1. Daniel crops up yet again, in connection with one of the earliest
known excerpts from the *Florilegium Angelicum*. At the top of the
second column of the last page (fol. 34ᵛ) of Berne 633 (s. xii²;
France), the hand of the manuscript has copied the first of the
florilegium's extracts from Aulus Gellius, leaving the rest of the
column blank. The reproduction of the passage as it appears in
the *Florilegium Angelicum*, in which the wording of the original has
been altered in a distinctive fashion, proves that the latter and not
a text of Gellius was the writer's source. This manuscript belonged
to Daniel in the sixteenth century.

Pierre Daniel was a lawyer at Orléans and sometime *bailli* of the
abbey of Fleury. Although he acquired a number of books from
other scholars and libraries, notably Pierre Pithou and St. Victor,
the greater part of his library was assembled from ecclesiastical
collections in and around Orléans. Therefore, when one is faced,
as in this case, with a group of manuscripts that belonged to
Daniel and that are known to emanate from a common centre, it is
reasonable to assume that it was in the Orléanais.[1]

In sum, when one considers jointly the nature and purpose of
the *Florilegium Angelicum*; the indications of place afforded by
Vat. lat. 4929; and the omnipresence of Pierre Daniel in the later
life of manuscripts related to the *florilegium*, one has a strong case
for Orléans as the home of the *Florilegium Angelicum*.

Although one has references to Orléans as a centre of classical
studies, and one knows the names of a few individuals associated
with the schools there, actual physical remains are few—works
known to have been composed there, texts known to have been
available there, manuscripts with an undisputed Orléans provenance. Therefore, to establish Orléans as the probable home of
the *Florilegium Angelicum* has implications extending beyond the
work itself. It is self-evident that if the *florilegium* was compiled at
Orléans, the texts used by its compiler must also have been available there. Let us examine briefly some specific applications of
this fact. MS. Berne 136 was used above to provide evidence of
a possible home for the *Florilegium Angelicum*; one can now, with

---

[1] Regarding Daniel see É. Pellegrin, 'Membra disiecta floriacensia', *Bibliothèque de l'École des Chartes*, cxvii (1959), 1–56, esp. 1–9; and A. Vidier, *L'Historiographie à Saint-Benoît-sur-Loire et les miracles de Saint Benoît* (Paris, 1965²),
pp. 30–3.

greater justification, use the cumulative evidence concerning the latter to localize Berne 136 at Orléans. Moreover, since Berne 136 was itself written only shortly before our compiler used it, one is provided as well with a strong suggestion that the two important older codices from which it was copied—the eleventh-century S. Marco 284 (Pliny's letters and Apuleius) and the ninth-century Paris B.N. lat. 7794 (Cicero's orations)—were both in Orléans in the mid twelfth century.[1]

The *Florilegium Angelicum* contains extracts from many works that were widely available, and there is no point in labouring the fact that a text of each was probably at Orléans. But the localization is important as it applies to two rare texts, Cicero's Verrine orations and the works of Ennodius. The northern or X family of the Verrines[2] emerged in the late eighth century among the books of the palace library of Charlemagne, as described in Berlin Diez B.

[1] While B.N. lat. 7794 produced no descendants save Berne 136, S. Marco 284 apparently produced a family of MSS. presumably disseminating from Orléans. Among these was a MS. of the letters and Apuleius given to Bec by Philip of Bayeux in 1164, which may in turn have been the parent of Rouen 1111 (s. XIII; Lyre OSB), containing the F text, and of a MS. now lost but once at Mont-Saint-Michel; and Leyden Universiteitsbibl. B.P.L. 199 (s. XIII; N. France) which also contains the F text, as do a group of hitherto unnoticed extracts in Paris B.N. lat. 18104, pt. III fols. 160ᵛ–161 (s. XIII). The letters and Apuleius are also found together in a codex described in the late-12th-century catalogue of St. Martial of Limoges by Bernard Itier. The letters alone appear in the 12th-century catalogue of St. Aubin at Angers, but there is no way of telling its parentage. See the appropriate sections of G. Nortier, *Les Bibliothèques médiévales des abbayes bénédictines de Normandie*, edn. 2 (Caen, 1971), and M. Manitius, 'Handschriften antiker Autoren in mittelalterlichen Bibliothekskatalogen', *Zentralblatt für Bibliothekswesen*, Beiheft lxvii (Leipzig, 1935), 141. The MS. of the letters at St. Martial is incorrectly entered in Manitius (121) under Pliny the elder.

[2] At the head of the Italian or Y family stand Paris B.N. lat. 7776, s. XI; Paris B.N. lat. 4588A fols. 66–91, s. XIII; Florence, Laurenziana, pl. 48. 29, s. XV; British Libr. Harley 2687, s. XV; and a bi-folium of the 12th century written in a Caroline hand, in Monte Cassino 361 P, pp. 219–22. Paris B.N. lat. 7776, written in Italy, bears the following notes of ownership: fol. 174ᵛ: *In reversione mea de curia. Ego istud proposui facere et ducere ad effectum et firmavi cum ⟨sten?⟩. In dominica ii de mense septembri. In segnoria. Ingh. de ⟨manga ponti?⟩ 1226* [The date may be a later addition]. fol. 1 bottom, erased (s. XIV–XV): *per Stephanum presbiterum de ecclesia...Jacobi monachi remisi Solinum.* Centre partially covered by arms of the Cittadini family of Siena. MS. bears notes by Celso Cittadini, 1553–1627 (concerning his books, see M. Cl. Di Franco Lilli, *La biblioteca manoscritta di Celso Cittadini* (Studi e Testi, cclix, 1970). Sent to Paris with other MSS. for the Royal Library by Mabillon, 8 July 1686; see P. Gasnault, 'Manuscrits envoyés d'Italie à la Bibliothèque du roi par Mabillon', *Bibliothèque de l'École des Chartes*, cxxix (1971), 411–20.

Sant. 66;[1] and the text dispersed in the course of the ninth century from Tours. The oldest manuscript, British Libr. Add. 47678 (formerly Holkham Hall 387) s. IX[1] (C), containing 2 Act. II–III, was written in the script of Tours and passed to Cluny, where it is described in the twelfth-century catalogue of the abbey's books.[2] (A single leaf from this mutilated manuscript is now Geneva, Bibliothèque publique et universitaire MS. lat. 169.[3]) From the Cluny catalogue one can see that C once contained the same works as the codex described from the palace library. Another spur from Tours appears at Cologne in the form of the extracts from the Verrines in British Libr. Harley 2682 s. XI (H) and the direct copy of these in Berlin lat. fol. 252 s. XII, Corvey (E), made by Wibald of Corvey.[4] A third line is seen in Paris B.N. lat. 7774A (2 Act. IV–V) s. IX[1] (R), also written at Tours. This manuscript may have passed to Lupus of Ferrières, since he is known to have had a manuscript of the Verrines and since he annotated the second manuscript now in MS. lat. 7774A (fols. 103–184ᵛ), Cicero's *De inventione*.[5] A second witness to the parent of R survives in Paris B.N. lat. 7775 (2 Act. I paragraphs 90–111, IV, V) s. XII (S), which belonged to Richard de Fournival in the first half of the thirteenth century and passed with his books via Gerard of Abbeville to the Sorbonne library.[6] Both R and S are incomplete today, but fortunately a copy was made of S by Nicolas de Clémanges in the early fifteenth century when it was still whole. The latter volume is Paris B.N. lat. 7823 (D), which was left to St. Victor (pressmark HHH 8) by Simon de Plumetot.[7]

[1] B. Bischoff, 'Die Hofbibliothek Karls des Grossen', in *Karl der Grosse, 2 Das geistige Leben* (Düsseldorf, 1965), pp. 42–62.

[2] Ed. Delisle (p. 67 n. 1 above), pp. 458–81, item 498. In the early 15th century the MS. was taken to Italy by Poggio. The history of the Vetus Cluniacensis was reconstructed largely by A. C. Clark; see his *Descent of Manuscripts*, pp. 281–323, and the other works in p. 75 n. 2 above.

[3] G. Vaucher, 'Un fragment de MS. de Cicéron aux Archives de Genève', *Bulletin du Musée de Genève* (1931), pp. 120–4. The identification with London, B.L. Add. 47678 we owe to Professor Bischoff.

[4] A. C. Clark, 'Excerpts from the Verrines in the Harleian MS. 2682 . . .', *Journal of Philology*, xviii (1890), 69–87.

[5] Lupus requests (*c.* 856–8) a MS. of the Verrines in ep. 101 to Reg.; ed., trans. G. W. Regenos, *The Letters of Lupus of Ferrières* (The Hague, 1966). There is of course no way of telling how long the two parts of Paris B.N. Lat. 7774A have been together.

[6] See R. H. Rouse, 'Manuscripts belonging to Richard de Fournival', *Revue d'histoire des textes*, iii (1973), 259.

[7] The hand of Nicolas de Clémanges and the donation of Simon de Plumetot

It requires no stretch of the imagination to assume that the Verrines, disseminated from Tours, might find their way to Orléans. However, on the basis of the quite limited amount of text we have to deal with, it is difficult to ascertain whether the *florilegium*'s source was one of the surviving manuscripts, or another no longer extant. The *Florilegium Angelicum* contains eighteen extracts from Actio II, books IV and V of the Verrines. One would naturally assume that they come from a text of the northern European family. The reading at V. 71 *inducte* with R and S against *indictae*, of the Italian or Y family, indicates as much; but at IV. 105, the extracts read *perstringere* with the Y family against R, *praestringere*. S reads *perstringere*, corrected to *prestringere*. The correction cannot be dated, save to say that it appears to be medieval; if it occurred after the *Florilegium Angelicum* was compiled, then S could have been the source of the extracts. Henceforth, in dealing with Paris B.N. lat. 7775, one should at least consider the possibility that it was either written at Orléans or carried there within a relatively short time after it was written.

Of the Christian authors represented in the *florilegium*, Ennodius is surely the rarest. Vogel knew of eighteen manuscripts, only four of which antedate the *Florilegium Angelicum*—and two of these are English.[1] He noticed none of the twelve manuscripts of the *florilegium* which contain extracts from Ennodius.[2] The manuscripts of Ennodius emerge in northern Europe in two classes. The first of these is represented by a single manuscript from Lorsch,[3] now Brussels Bibl. Royale, 9845-8 (Van den Gheyn 1218), s. IX¹ (B); it produced no known descendants. The surviving manuscripts of the second class disseminate from Corbie. Ennodius was known to Radbert of Corbie (d. *c*. 850).[4] The oldest manuscript of the second class, Vat. lat. 3803 s. IX² (V), is written in a good Corbie hand of the second half of the ninth century, and is probably to

were kindly confirmed by Gilbert Ouy, who has long studied these two individuals and who is editing the St. Victor catalogue of Claude de Grandrue; see his 'Les manuscrits autographes du chancelier Gerson', *Scriptorium*, xvi(1962), 293–7.

[1] The transmission of the Ennodius corpus is set forth by F. Vogel, *Magni Felicis Ennodi Opera*, M.G.H. *Auct. ant.*, vol. vii (Berlin, 1885), pp. xxix-xlviii.

[2] Brussels B.R. 10098–10105, the Ennodius *florilegium* cited by Vogel, does not come from the *Florilegium Angelicum*, despite the fact that portions of two selections (Jerome and Cicero's orations) from the latter appear in 10098–10105.

[3] B. Bischoff, *Lorsch im Spiegel seiner Handschriften*. Münchener Beiträge zur Mediävistik und Renaissance-Forschung, Beiheft. (Munich, 1974), pp. 39, 67, 85.   [4] Manitius (p. 75 n. 5 above), pp. 407, 411.

be identified with the Ennodius in the twelfth-century catalogue of the abbey.[1] A direct copy of this manuscript, Lambeth Palace 325 s. IX^2 (L), also written in Corbie script,[2] was taken to England and came to rest at Durham Cathedral, where it was copied in the twelfth century producing Berlin, Deutsche Staatsbibl. Phill. MS. 1715 (Rose 172), Fountains Abbey, O. Cist. Ennodius continued to circulate through English houses, but our concern is with the continental circulation.

Of the surviving continental manuscripts, even the oldest of V's descendants is too late to have served as source for the *Florilegium Angelicum*; this is the late-twelfth- or early-thirteenth-century text contained in Troyes MSS. 658, 461, 469 (Clairvaux E. 45, I. 22, I. 23). Vogel thought that the Clairvaux text derived from a now-missing apograph of V, and this manuscript is of course a potential source of our extracts. The Pseudo-Isidorian *Decretals*, written *c*. 850 perhaps at Reims,[3] afford evidence of yet another potential source. They contain (under specious attributions) four works of Ennodius, taken from a text of the second class older than V, ancestor or sister of the latter.[4] In addition, Philip of Bayeux owned a manuscript of Ennodius which passed with his books to Bec in 1164.[5] The twelfth century witnessed an effort to produce a compendium or abbreviation of Ennodius, since the whole text was long and cumbersome. This abbreviation is found in two manuscripts, Bourges 400, fols. $126^v–133$, (s. XII^2; St. Sulpice) and British Libr. Royal 8 E. IV(*c*. 1200; Rievaulx?). Vogel presumed the first of these to have been lost and did not know of the second. There is no way to determine whether or not the manuscript from Bourges was written in that area. But it permits the supposition that a manuscript of the second class no longer

---

[1] Ed. Delisle (p. 67 n. 1 above), p. 239, item 343 *Ennodius, Exameron Basilii*; and p. 430, item 128 *Ennodii liber*.

[2] We are grateful to Professor Bischoff for identifying the script of V and L.

[3] W. Goffart, *The Le Mans Forgeries*, Harvard Historical Studies, lxxvi; (Cambridge, Mass. 1966), pp. 66–7: and H. Fuhrmann, *Einfluss und Verbreitung der pseudoisidorischen Fälschungen*, Schriften der M.G.H. 24. 1 (Stuttgart, 1972), pp. 191–4.

[4] There is no way of comparing the text of Ennodius used for the *Florilegium Angelicum* with that used by Pseudo-Isidore. For the four works which the *Decretals* reproduce, there are no extracts from XLVIII or CLXXIV; and there are no variant readings recorded from the *Decretals* for those passages in the *Florilegium Angelicum* which comprise the two extracts from CCXIV and the sixteen from IL.

[5] Becker (p. 78 n. 5 above), p. 201, item, 86: 55.

extant was available in the Loire region in the twelfth century, to be copied for Philip of Bayeux and to be used both in the making of the abbreviation and in the compilation of the *Florilegium Angelicum*.

The localization at Orléans of the *Florilegium Angelicum* and Vat. lat. 4929 has wider implications concerning Orléans as a cross-roads in the dissemination of classical texts in central France. The *Florilegium Gallicum* also drew on Vat. lat. 4929,[1] and hence its contents probably also reflect the libraries of mid-twelfth-century Orléans. Of the two oldest surviving manuscripts of the *Florilegium Gallicum*, Paris, Bibl. de l'Arsenal 711 (s. XII; St. Victor) once concluded with extracts from Pomponius Mela,[2] of which Vat. lat. 4929 contains the archetype; and Paris, Bibl. Nationale, lat. 7647 was evidently owned by Pierre Daniel.[3] Similarly, portions of the

[1] The *Florilegium Gallicum*'s *Querolus* extracts contain readings which derive from glosses in Vat. lat. 4929; see Ranstrand (p. 72 n. 2 above), pp. 67–9. Concerning the *Florilegium Gallicum* see Gagnér (p. 73 n. 3 above), and the bibliography in R. H. Rouse, 'The *A* Text of Seneca's Tragedies . . .', *Revue d'histoire des textes*, i (1971), 103 n. 1.

[2] The later folios of the MS. are now missing save for fols. 244–7, which R. Rouse recently identified with Hamburg Staats- und Universitätsbibl. MS. 53c in scrin. (formerly belonging to Friedrich Lindenbrog [1573–1648] who had business offices in Paris). However, the original contents of MS. 711 were recorded by Claude de Grandrue; see H. Martin, ed., *Catalogue des manuscrits de la Bibliothèque de l'Arsenal*, ii (Paris, 1886), 52. The *De chorographia* of Pomponius Mela moved in the 12th century to three important French libraries. It appears among the books which Philip of Bayeux left to Bec in 1164, *Pomponius Mela de cosmographia et Tullius . . . et Hilarius de sinodis et eiusdem liber contra Valentem et Auxencium*; Becker (p. 78 n. 5 above), p. 201, item 86: 64. A brief portion of the *De chorographia* (lib. I cc. 1–7) appears in a 12th-century MS. of the works of St. Hilary of Poitiers, following Hilary's *Adversus Arrianum Auxencium*; the MS., bearing the 17th-century ex-libris of Mont-Saint-Michel, is now Vendôme MS. 189, fols. 65–9. The volume is almost certainly a copy of that which belonged to Philip of Bayeux; besides the association with Hilary, a substantial number of Mont-Saint-Michel's books were copied from Bec exemplars (see Nortier [p. 80 n. 1 above] pp. 45, 69). Another copy is recorded in the late 12th-century catalogue of St. Martial of Limoges by Bernard Itier; ed. Delisle (p. 67 n. 1 above), p. 497, item 3: 48. Significantly, this is the same dissemination one has for the younger Pliny's letters which, starting from the Orléanais, are owned by Philip of Bayeux, Mont-Saint-Michel, and St. Martial of Limoges; see above, p. 80 n. 1.

[3] Two leaves from the first part of Paris B.N. lat. 7647 containing the *Distinctiones monasticae* were recently found in Leyden Voss. lat. Qu. 2, fols. 57–8 (Paul Petau), by É. Pellegrin (p. 79 n. 1 above), p. 52. It should also be remembered that Gagnér (p. 73 n. 3 above), pp. 211–12, noted that one of four variant readings recorded by Daniel from a MS. at Saints-Gervais-et-Protais compared favourably with MS. 7647. Ranstrand (p. 72 n. 2 above), p. 75, however, disagreed and concluded that the *Florilegium Gallicum* from Saints-Gervais-et-Protais is now lost.

library of Richard de Fournival may have come from Orléans.
Fournival, the *Florilegium Gallicum*, and the twelfth-century
annotator of Vat. lat. 4929 probably drew on a common source for
their knowledge of Tibullus: the annotator quotes Tibullus in
glossing the word 'Loire', the *Florilegium Gallicum* contains
lengthy extracts from Tibullus, and Fournival owned the manuscript of the whole text from which all surviving copies of Tibullus
descend.[1] Fournival also owned a manuscript of the Verrines,
possibly that used by the compiler of the *Florilegium Angelicum*,[2]
as well as a manuscript of the *florilegium* itself. Finally, four rare
texts connected with the *Florilegium Angelicum* or with Vat. lat.
4929—the Ps.-Ciceronian oration *Pridie quam in exilium iret*,
Pliny's letters, Ennodius, and Pomponius Mela—appear in the
collection left to Bec by Philip of Bayeux in 1164, suggesting that
the libraries of Orléans also supplied him with books.[3]

Having localized the *Florilegium Angelicum*, we may now take
up the question of its date and authorship. To judge from the hand
and the decoration of P and A, the *florilegium* was compiled in the
third quarter of the twelfth century. Neither manuscript contains
letter unions, save for pp. Ampersands, the tironian seven un-
crossed and *et* written out are used interchangeably. The cedilla is
still found frequently, and A preserves an occasional *ae*, but as an
archaism, as is the occasional appearance of the N̄ ligature in P.
These features tend to date the manuscripts toward the middle
rather than toward the end of the century. On the other hand, the
appearance of the ȝ ligature in P would not permit the manuscript to date earlier than the middle of the century; here,

---

[1] The extracts in the *Florilegium Gallicum* are discussed in B. L. Ullman,
'Tibullus in Medieval *Florilegia*', *Classical Philology*, xxiii (1928), 128–74. Barlow (p. 72 n. 1 above), p. 106, felt that the line from Tibullus in Vat. lat. 4929
came from a *florilegium*, and pointed to its existence in Clm 6929 as evidence. In
1100, however, that *florilegium* was at Freising, and the only other contemporary
collection of Tibullus extracts was at Monte Cassino; see F. Newton, 'Tibullus
in Two Grammatical *Florilegia* of the Middle Ages', *Transactions of the American
Philological Association*, xciii (1962), 253–86. The fact that the compiler of the
Florilegium Gallicum drew on a complete MS. of Tibullus suggests instead that
the Orléans annotator may have known a MS. of the whole text.
[2] Paris B.N. lat. 7775; see above, p. 81.
[3] Concerning Philip of Bayeux, see V. Bourrienne, *Un Grand Bâtisseur:
Philippe de Harcourt, évêque de Bayeux* (Paris, 1930); S. E. Gleason, *An Eccle-
siastical Barony of the Middle Ages. The Bishopric of Bayeux 1066–1204*,
Harvard Historical Monographs, 10 (Cambridge, Mass. 1936), pp. 28–9; and
Nortier (p. 80 n. 1 above), pp. 42–5.

paleographic evidence is confirmed by the compiler's reliance upon
Berne 136, written at or after mid century. The decoration of the
two manuscripts, in particular of A which, as the presentation copy,
is the more elaborate, also merits attention (see pls. VII–VIII). The
section initials contain a stylized stem-and-leaf design, geometric
and two-dimensional. Red, purple, yellow, green, and blue are
used. The backs of upright letters are outlined with thick line or
tendril, scalloped at times but never extending beyond the end of
the letter as tendrils will begin to do toward the end of the century.
A good example of decoration of this style is seen in Brussels,
Bibl. Royale, MS. II 1635, dated 1156.[1]

The prologue in A dedicates the *Florilegium Angelicum* to a pope,
who, 'enmeshed in the business of the world, with a ready response
judges the intricacies of causes [*involucra causarum determines*] in
such fashion that all marvel' at his eloquence. The approximate
dates of P and A exclude Innocent III (1198–1215) as too late.
The hands of the two are not sufficiently early for Eugene III
(1145–53), nor would the inflated language of the prologue very
likely have been addressed to the protégé of Saint Bernard. This
leaves Adrian IV (1154–9), Alexander III (1159–81), and the five
popes whose brief tenures bring one to the end of the century. Of
them, the canon lawyer Alexander III best fits the dedicatee of the
prologue and the dates of P and A. Moreover, Alexander III (as
well as his successor) employed masters from Orléans in the papal
chancery.[2]

Nothing can be said about the author of the *Florilegium Angelicum*, save that he was someone at Orléans in the third quarter of the
twelfth century who was interested in epistolary style, knowledge-
able in the classics and, no doubt, desirous of papal preferment.
One can, however, lay to rest a troublesome ghost, emanating from
the attribution of the *florilegium* to Censorinus in the *Biblionomia*
of Richard de Fournival. Manitius, Beeson, and Ullman, in their

---

[1] See M. Wittek, ed., *Manuscrits datés conservés en Belgique*, i. *819–1400*
(Brussels, 1968), p. 20, item 7, pls. 27–9.

[2] John, Robert, and William; see letters 65 and 85 of Stephen of Tournai, *P.L.*
ccxi. 356–7, 380–1. It is interesting to note that in 1177 John of Cornwall also
praises Alexander III for his ability to see through intricate language, 'que contra
obici possunt dissoluuntur et Iohannis Damasceni involucrum enodatur';
Eulogium ad Alexandrum papam III, ed. N. M. Haring, *Mediaeval Studies*, xiii
(1951), 276. Concerning the meaning and use of the esoteric term *involucrum* see
M. D. Chenu, '*Involucrum*: le mythe selon les théologiens médiévaux', *Archives*,
xxii (1955), 75–9.

efforts to identify the Censorinus mentioned by Hadoard in the poem prefaced to his *florilegium*, seized upon the *florilegium* attributed to Censorinus in the *Biblionomia* and noticed other similarities, real or presumed, between the two *florilegia*, namely, that each quoted from Sidonius' letters and from the *Sententiae philosophorum*; they also found it significant that Fournival's manuscripts of Cicero's philosophical works (*Biblionomia* 73–6) were arranged in the rare order of the Leyden corpus, as were the extracts in Hadoard's *florilegium*. They concluded that Fournival's *florilegium*—i.e. the *Florilegium Angelicum*—must therefore have already been in existence in the ninth century.[1] Because of Fournival's attribution, Censorinus not only became the author of the *florilegium* but was also made the author of an anonymous collection of aphorisms called *Sententiae philosophorum*, since it appears in both Hadoard's and Fournival's *florilegia* associated with the name Censorinus.

In actuality there is no connection between the two *florilegia*. They do not contain extracts from the same collection of *sententiae philosophorum*. Hadoard's are drawn from Publilius Syrus,[2] and those in Fournival's *florilegium* are the anonymous collection erroneously attributed to Caecilius Balbus.[3] The attribution to Censorinus in the *Biblionomia* is the result of an easily understandable muddle. In the *Florilegium Angelicum*, the extracts from the *Querolus* are followed by extracts from Censorinus' *De die natali*. The change is marked by the rubric, *Explicit. Censorinus.*, meaning *Explicit Querolus. Incipit Censorinus.* The description in the *Biblionomia* shows that Fournival's manuscript ended with the *Querolus*, doubtless concluding with the ambiguously worded rubric. On that basis, Fournival simply took the little-known author of the *De die natali* and made him author of the twelfth-century *Florilegium Angelicum*. In our ignorance of the actual compiler's identity, we must take what comfort we can from the elimination of one well-known but ill-suited candidate.

The compiler, while preserving his anonymity, at least displays his literary style for us in the prologue or dedicatory epistle

---

[1] Manitius (p. 75 n. 5 above), p. 480; C. H. Beeson, 'The Collectaneum of Hadoard', *Classical Philology*, xi (1945), 205–6; B. L. Ullman, 'A List of Classical Manuscripts perhaps from Corbie', *Scriptorium*, viii (1954), 24–37.

[2] W. Meyer, ed., *Publilii Syri Mimi Sententiae* (Leipzig, 1880).

[3] E. Woelfflin, ed., *Caecilii Balbi De nugis philosophorum quae supersunt* (Basle, 1855), pp. 37–43.

contained in **A**.[1] At the same time, he reveals his concept of the purpose and value of the *florilegium*. The prologue falls into three parts: (1) a commendation of the book, calling attention to its merit and to the labour involved in its creation; (2) a flattering statement of the book's appropriateness to its papal dedicatee; and (3) a request for (continued?) papal favour and protection. The writer briefly indulges in an initial flourish of rhymed pairs of parallel verbs ('compactus et redactus'..., 'elegi et collegi...', etc.), then abandons the device. Under the circumstances, his classical quotations are quite restrained in number, though aptly chosen— a snippet from Quintilian, a longer segment from one letter of Seneca. The vast majority of his quotations are scriptural; these include allusions, which may or may not be conscious (such as the echo of Matthew 4: 4, 'in verbis gratie que procedent de ore tuo'). Although one should allow for the role played by convention, it is also probable that intentional flattery is implied by his application to the pope of language which, in its biblical context, referred to God (such passages as 'quid a te volui...', 'O custos hominum...', 'Sub umbra alarum tuarum ...', and so on).

The *Florilegium Angelicum* is a book of maxims or aphorisms, sententious statements of universal truths eloquently expressed. However, it is quite evident, from the emphasis of the prologue, that the compiler gave greater consideration to beauty of expression than to ethical content. The book contains 'brief passages remarkable for their memorable words..., profound meaning clad in the most attractive language'. He tells his recipient that, unable to include everything, he has rather 'chosen and collected together those passages in which your spirit might delight and take pleasure'. There is no hint of a pious hope that the contents might lead to salvation or even to edification. As the compiler makes clear in the prologue, the *florilegium* is a reference book for discourse, for the writers of business letters. He has written the work, he tells the pope, 'so that you may have always at hand [a source] from which to fit your speech appropriately to person and place and occasion'. The *florilegium* permits one to give advice, support arguments, state conclusions, in the eloquent language of famous men of letters.

The compiler's manner of working is easy to discern. He nor-

---

[1] Edited by B. Munk Olsen, 'Note sur quelques préfaces de florilèges latins du XIIᵉ siècle', *Revue romane*, viii (1973), 185–91; and below, Appendix I.

mally selects brief passages, often mere parts of sentences in his exemplar. He alters them as much as is necessary to make a coherent free-standing statement out of context. In order to do this, (1) he changes verb-forms and cases of nouns so as to have the proper grammatical components to form a sentence; (2) as frequently as possible he eliminates references to specific persons, substituting a noun of general or universal application; (3) he naturally omits words and phrases that refer by implication to preceding or subsequent passages which are not included in his extract; (4) when the meaning of a passage is obscure without its context, he supplies his own word or phrase which epitomizes the author's meaning. Two examples from Pliny's letters will illustrate the changes:

> *Pliny, Ep.* 1. 6. 2. Iam undique siluae et solitudo ipsumque illud silentium quod uenationi datur, magna cogitationis incitamenta sunt.
>
> *Florilegium Angelicum.* Silentium maximum cogitationis incitamentum est.
>
> *Pliny, Ep.* 3. 16. 6. (Describing the admirable behaviour of Arria, a Roman matron): Sed tamen ista facienti, ista dicenti, gloria et aeternitas ante oculos erant.
>
> *Florilegium Angelicum.* Quicquid facias, gloria sit tibi ante oculos et eternitas.

Amusingly enough, as the latter example shows, the compiler was not averse to an occasional slight improvement of the word order found in his models of eloquence. The total effect of his method is that scarcely a passage escapes without some mark of its having gone through his hands.

Normally, it is not easy to trace the use made of a *florilegium*, because of the difficulty of determining with certainty the immediate source of classical quotations which float freely about, entirely detached from their matrix. We can show, however, in this case that the *Florilegium Angelicum* was extensively used by Gerald of Wales in the later years of his life.[1] He used it in a number of works written after 1198, the most important of which are the *De principis instructione* and the collection of letters included in the

---

[1] Gerald's quotations from ancient Latin prose texts are identified and extracted in Edward E. Best Jr., 'Classical Latin Prose Writers quoted by Giraldus Cambrensis', unpubl. Ph.D. diss. (University of North Carolina, 1957). For his citations from verse see G. J. E. Sullivan, 'Pagan Latin Poets in Giraldus Cambrensis', unpubl. Ph.D. diss. (University of Cincinnati, 1950).

Symbolum electorum.[1] The latter work provides a good example of how such a *florilegium* might be used. Take for example epistle 24, addressed to Walter Map. Gerald's theme is that the mature man turns his intellectual efforts to study of the divine, and abandons the frivolous classical literary studies of his youth. In support of this he cites not only the story of Saint Jerome's fear of being judged 'Ciceronianus, non Christianus', but also a passage from Cicero himself. The irony is more apparent than real, for Gerald's view is the traditional Christian attitude toward the pagan past: studying the pagans for one's own enjoyment is a misuse of time and effort, but it is legitimate and even laudable to 'spoil the Egyptians', taking truth where one finds it from the 'dicta poetarum moralia et philosophorum'. He adduces a lengthy string of patristic and scriptural quotations intertwined to prove that one should devote oneself to serious study and abhor the frivolous, and adds, 'Hear the concurring testimony of the Gentiles.' Thereupon he produces eight successive passages from the ancients, six of which are taken from the *Florilegium Angelicum*, namely four extracts from Pliny's letters and one each from Cicero's Tusculans and Sidonius' letters. Proof that these quotations are drawn from the *florilegium* rather than from the respective whole texts is provided by the wording of the quotations, which in each case agrees with the revised form imposed by the florilegist.

For example, Gerald's epistle 24 and the *Florilegium Angelicum* read, 'Dulce honestumque ocium ac pene omni negotio pulchrius est studere', for Pliny 1. 9. 6, 'O dulce otium honestumque ac paene omni negotio pulchrius!' Epistle 24 includes consecutively two sentences which are treated as one extract in the *florilegium* (i.e. the second has no paragraph mark of its own): 'Nulla tibi temporis asperitas studii tempus eripiat. Nam perit omne tempus quod studiis non impertitur.' These come from two paragraphs in Pliny, 3. 5. 15, 16, with some twenty words intervening: '. . . ut ne caeli quidem asperitas ullum studii tempus eriperet . . . Nam perire omne tempus arbitrabatur, quod studiis non impenderetur.' And in his *De principis instructione* 1. 15 Gerald repeats, with only one variant, the *florilegium*'s extract from Pliny 3. 16. 6 noted

[1] Gerald's works are published in the Rolls Series: *Symbolus electorum*, ed. J. S. Brewer, i (1861), pp. 199–395; *De principis instructione*, ed. G. F. Warner, viii (1891). Concerning the latter work see K. Schnith, 'Betrachtungen zum Spätwerk des Giraldus Cambrensis: De principis instructione', *Festiva Lanx, Festgabe Johannes Spörl* (Munich, 1966), pp. 53–66.

above, beginning 'Quicquid agas [facias: *Florilegium Angelicum*] gloria sit . . .'. In all, the *Florilegium Angelicum* accounts for the whole of Gerald's knowledge of Pliny's letters and of Cicero's orations and the Tusculans, and for at least a portion of his quotations from Seneca's letters, the *De beneficiis*, Macrobius, Aulus Gellius bks. 10–20, and the letters of Sidonius.[1]

Gerald probably used a manuscript of the β family of the *Florilegium Angelicum*. This is suggested by the fact that he quotes four passages from the letters of Symmachus. He is again using a collection of extracts,[2] one that was popular in France in the twelfth century, rather than the letters themselves; he shares the reading 'supervacanei' (*Vita Remigii* 27) with the Symmachus *florilegium*, against 'superforanei' in the text of the letters (ep. 3. 48). The Symmachus *florilegium* precedes the *Florilegium Angelicum*, written in the hand of the latter, in R. The Symmachus collection also appears in E, but in a different hand and in a separate manuscript bound with the text of the *Florilegium Angelicum*. Unlike E, R is perhaps old enough to have been the manuscript which Gerald used. However, the presence of Symmachus in E, even as an addition, raises the possibility that the Symmachus *florilegium* appeared in β, common parent of R and E. The most one can say is that Gerald of Wales probably used the *Florilegium Angelicum* in R, in β, or in some late-twelfth-century copy of the latter now lost. Gerald used the *Florilegium Angelicum* only in works written

---

[1] Gerald was an avid user of intermediate sources, among them Petrus Cantor's *Verbum abbreviatum* and perhaps the *Moralium dogma philosophorum*; see E. M. Sanford, 'Giraldus Cambrensis' Debt to Petrus Cantor', *Medievalia et Humanistica*, iii (1945), 16–32; and W. Berges, *Die Fürstenspiegel des hohen und späten Mittelalters*, Schriften des Reichsinstituts für ältere deutsche Geschichtskunde, ii (Leipzig, 1938), pp. 145. To these one should also add the *Florilegium Gallicum*. It is, for example, the source for most of Gerald's knowledge of Seneca's *De clementia*, cited seven times in the *De principis instructione* and elsewhere. In two instances Gerald and the *Florilegium Gallicum* (cited from Paris B.N. lat. 17903, fol. 128ᵛ) agree in readings against the established text: *De clem.* 1. 1. 7, *conplectuntur: amplectuntur* Flor. Gal., Prin. inst. 1. 7, Symbolum ep. 31, Spec. eccles. intro.; and *De clem.* 1. 9. 11, *advocatum: advotum* Flor. Gal., Prin. inst. 1. 7, Top. Hib. 3. 48. Nothdurft, unaware of his use of a *florilegium*, remarks that Gerald was the only person besides Hildebert at the beginning of the century to draw on the *De clementia* in any substantial fashion; see K. D. Nothdurft, *Studien zum Einfluss Senecas auf die Philosophie und Theologie des zwölften Jahrhunderts* (Leyden, 1963), pp. 119–20.

[2] Best (p. 89 n. 1 above), pp. 131–2, 141. Thirty-eight collections of extracts from the letters of Symmachus are listed by J. P. Callu, *Symmaque: Lettres, Livres I–II*, Collection Budé (Paris, 1972).

after 1198, indicating that he did not know of it in England or in his earlier school-days in Paris. He probably found the *florilegium* in the course of his trips to Rome, *c.* 1197–1214, to argue his claim to St. Davids.[1]

As a witness to changing interests in classical authors, it is instructive to observe how long into the thirteenth century the *Florilegium Angelicum* continued to be copied, and what happened to it toward the middle of the century. At most, four of the seventeen surviving manuscripts date from the twelfth century. The thirteenth century saw ten copies of this collection or parts of it written in France. The last copy was made in the mid fifteenth century, when the winds blew from the south. A similar pattern is seen in the *Florilegium Gallicum* of which two manuscripts were written in the twelfth century and eight in the thirteenth, fourteenth, and fifteenth centuries. These texts well indicate by their survival that the interest of twelfth-century humanists in classical authors did not pass away with Peter of Blois, Gerald of Wales, and Walter Map.[2] The *florilegia* of the twelfth century did not disappear; instead, they were appropriated, absorbed, and eventually recast as preachers' tools.

We can see both the *Florilegium Angelicum* and the *Florilegium Gallicum* changing form before our eyes. In Brussels, Bibl. Royale, 10030–2 (Van den Gheyn 1508), the greater part of the *Florilegium Gallicum* has been absorbed into the *Flores paradysi* B, a Cistercian *florilegium* compiled at the abbey of Villers-en-Brabant in the second quarter of the thirteenth century. The *florilegium* is equipped with an extensive subject index of twenty-three folios and was intended, according to its compiler, to aid in the composition of sermons.[3] On two different occasions in the mid thirteenth century the *Florilegium Angelicum* was totally rearranged by broad topic.

[1] Concerning Gerald see D. Knowles, *The Monastic Order in England* (Cambridge, 1950), pp. 662–77; R. B. C. Huygens, 'Une lettre de Giraud le Cambrien à propos de ses ouvrages historiques', *Latomus*, xxiv (1965), 90–100.

[2] Concerning this question see Paetow (p. 77 n. 1 above); E. K. Rand, 'The Classics in the Thirteenth Century', *Speculum*, iv (1929), 249–69; H. Wieruszowski, 'Arezzo as a Center of Learning and Letters in the Thirteenth Century', *Traditio*, ix (1953), 321–91, and in particular her 'Rhetoric and the Classics in Italian Education of the Thirteenth Century', *Studia Gratiana*, xi (1967), 169–208; these two articles are conveniently found in Wieruszowski's collected studies *Politics and Culture in Medieval Spain and Italy*, Storia e letteratura, Studi e Testi, 121 (Rome, 1971), pp. 387–474, 589–627.

[3] Concerning the *Flores paradysi* see R. H. Rouse, 'Cistercian Aids to Study in the Thirteenth Century', *Studies in Cistercian History*, forthcoming.

The first rearrangement survives in Rome, Bibl. Angelica 720 (**a**), a small handbook of the thirteenth century. In it the extracts have been arranged under subject headings, often virtues and vices: *De commendatione ieiunii, De iusticia, De humilitate quod non debet esse nimia,* and so on. A far more elaborate example of such restructuring is seen in Paris B.N. lat. 1860, fols. 75–153^v (**p**), of the mid thirteenth century. In **p**, the text of the *Florilegium Angelicum* has been supplemented with additional material from Terence, Sallust, Cicero (*De officiis, De senectute, De paradoxis, De amicitia*), and Boethius. The extracts from Christian authors Gregory, Jerome, and Ennodius have been dropped. The *florilegium* is arranged under 299 chapter-headings. At the head of the text stands a subject index of *c*. 330 entries in triple columns, referring to the 299 chapters. Attention is called to the *exempla* occurring in the text itself by marginal rubrics. This is only the prose portion of the new *florilegium*; it is followed on fols. 153^v–216 by a parallel collection of verse extracts from the poets, namely the authors of the *Liber Catonis* (Cato, Avian, Theophilus, Claudian, Statius, Maximianus, Pamphilianus), Horace, Virgil, Persius, Juvenal, and Prudentius. The extracts are again arranged by subject, under 231 chapter-headings, but without a subject index. Finally, in the opening years of the fourteenth century portions of the *Florilegium Angelicum*, taken from Fournival's copy, were absorbed into the *Manipulus florum* written by Thomas of Ireland at the Sorbonne. This *florilegium* is topically organized and alphabetically arranged. In the *Manipulus*, which survives in some 200 copies, classical aphorisms from the *Florilegium Angelicum* were given renewed currency among preachers and writers of the fourteenth and succeeding centuries.

The *Florilegium Angelicum* is a window through which we can observe a stage in the transmission of several classical texts. It documents the influence of ninth-century Carolingian libraries on a twelfth-century cathedral school. It illustrates how certain twelfth-century humanists' *florilegia* were transformed into thirteenth-century preachers' tools. It accounts in part for at least one medieval author's glittering knowledge of classical texts. And it reminds us once again of the significant role played by *florilegia* in the medieval dissemination of ancient thought and letters.

R. H. ROUSE AND M. A. ROUSE

APPENDIX I

Dedicatory epistle affixed to the *Florilegium Angelicum* (Rome, Bibl. Angelica MS. 1895, fol. 1ʳᵛ)

Suo domino suus servus sedulam in omnibus servitutem. Et hunc librum tibi offero, sedis apostolice gloria, qui et sentenciarum maiestate scintillet et eloquii prefulgeat claritate. Clausule breves sunt et verbis memorabilibus insignite. Ediderunt eas veteris eloquencie viri et cum summo eloquutionis ornatu posteris reliquerunt. In unum corpus meo labore liber iste compactus est et redactus in formam. Et quia omnes mittere non potui, elegi et collegi de omnibus in quibus letaretur et delectaretur anima tua. Et ut commendem ministerium meum in hac parte, non parvum putes vel reputes hunc laborem. Vigilanti quippe oculo[1] opus fuit ad cernendum et discernendum tot et tantorum sentencias oratorum. Cum philosophus dicat, Non habetur admirationi una arbor ubi in eandem altitudinem tota silva surrexit. Totus contextus illorum virilis est et eminerent singula nisi inter paria legerentur.[2] Defloravi tamen flosculos digniores et candidiores manipulos tuis oculis presentavi. Patet ibi tam philosophorum quam divinorum numerosa facundia et profundi sensus venustissimis sermonibus vestiuntur. Et hoc multum credidi illi tue singulari excellencie convenire ut semper ad manum habeas unde possis et personis et locis et temporibus aptare[3] sermones. Nichil [fol. 1ᵛ] quippe tam cognatum sapiencie, nichil eloquencie tam innatum, quam singula verba suis librare ponderibus et quid cuique conveniat invenire. Accedit ad hec quod iuxta prophetam dedit tibi dominus linguam eruditam[4] ut noveris quando debeas proferre sermonem, eruditam plane et lucidissimo sermonum flore vernantem que speciali dulcedine mulceat auditores. In miraculum vertitur et stuporem quod tocius mundi negociis intricatus repentinis responsionibus involucra causarum determines ut mirentur omnes in verbis gracie que procedunt de ore tuo.[5] Ego, ut verum fatear, sepius admiratus sum et plerumque nichil aliud timebam nisi ne desineres cum cepisses. Sed parco verbis ne adulationis notam incurram. Testes michi sunt qui audierunt verba oris tui, si tamen intelligere potuerunt. Et nunc, domine pater, quid a te volui super terram[6] nisi dignantissimam graciam tuam que me prevenit in benedictionibus dulcedinis.[7] O custos hominum,[8] illa michi custos sit et custodem alium non requiro. Ecce non dormit neque dormitat[9] invidia, virtutum virus, caritatis exclusio, tinea sanctitatis. Sub umbra alarum tuarum protege me[10] ne quando dicat inimicus meus, Prevalui adversus eum.[11] Scio, dulcissime pater, quia in me perficies quod cepisti et quem recepisti ad graciam in graciam conservabis, ut tibi semper illum versiculum et memoriter teneam et ore decantem,[12] Quoniam ex omni tribulatione eripuisti me et super inimicos meos d[espexit] o[culus]

---

[1] *oculo*: superscript, in original hand.
[2] Seneca, *ep.* 33. 1, 4.
[3] Quintilian, *Institutiones* 6. 5. 11.
[4] Is. 50. 4.
[5] Cf. Matth. 4: 4.
[6] Ps. 72: 25.
[7] Ps. 20: 4.
[8] Job 7: 20.
[9] Cf. Ps. 120: 4.
[10] Ps. 16: 8.
[11] Ps. 12: 5.
[12] Cf. Deut. 31: 19.

meus.[1] Filius virginis qui te fecit sacerdotem magnum et excelsum in
verbo glorie incolumem te conservet ecclesie sue, sibi ad honorem, tibi ad
virtutem, orbi ad salutem in longitudinem dierum.

APPENDIX II

Contents of the *Florilegium Angelicum*

Dedicatory epistle

In Rome, Bibl. Angelica MS. 1895, fol. 1ʳᵛ, only.
Beg. *Suo domino suus servus sedulam in omnibus servitutem. Et hunc
librum tibi offero sedis . . .*, ends *. . . tibi ad virtutem orbi ad salutem in
longitudinem dierum.*

Macrobius, *Saturnalia*

Extracts from books I–II only.
Beg. *Animo melius distincta servantur* (Praef. 6). *¶Oportet versari . . .*,
ends *. . . ibi saltem timeat. ¶Vivebat enim in eo excedens iocus et seria
mordacitas* (II. 3. 13).

Versus Ciceronis (among the extracts from Macrobius)

Anthologia Latina 268 (Riese).
> *Crede ratem ventis animum ne crede puellis*
> *Namque est feminea tutior unda fide*
> *Femina nulla bona vel si bona contigit ulla*
> *Nescio quo fato res mala facta bona est.*

Proverbia philosophorum

Corresponds to the text edited by Woelfflin under the name of Caecilius
Balbus (Basle, 1855), 18–35, items I. 1–XLVIII. 3.
Beg. *Cum quidam stolidus audiente Pitagora . . . ¶Socrates: Que facere
turpe . . .*, ends *. . . cotidie se punit consciencia. ¶ Verbosa lingua indicium
est malicie.*

Jerome, epistles

Beg. *Studio legendi quasi cotidiano cibo alitur et pinguescit oratio* (ep. 35.
1). *¶Libenter accipitur ab . . .*, ends *. . . libidinosa coinquinacione violarint.
¶Cuius corpus integrum est sit et inviolabilis conversacio.* Continues without rubric:
[*Adversus Jovinianum*] Beg. *Difficile est ab experte quondam voluptatis
illecebras abstinere* (I. 3). *¶Quando minora maioribus . . .*, ends *. . . libi-
dinem quam excercent. ¶Virtus excelsum te faciat, non voluptas humilem*
(II. 38).

---

[1] Ps. 53: 9.

Gregory the Great, epistles

Extracts from the first nine books only.
Beg. *Ubi presentes esse non possumus nostra per eum cui precipimus . . .*
(I. 1), ends . . . *Opinionem male agentium ex indiscrete defensionis ausu in nos nullo modo transferamus* (IX. 79).

Apuleius

Taken from Berne, Burgerbibl. MS. 136, fols. 7–23.
De deo Socratis. Beg. *Quorumdam imperitorum hominum turbav ana . . .*
(III). ¶*Plerique se incuria discipline . . .*, ends . . . *indoctus et incultus existit.* ¶*In emendis equis . . . parentes pepererunt et fortuna largita est* (XXIII). Continues without rubric:
[*Asclepius*]. Beg. *Tractatum numinis maiestate plenissimum . . .* (I).
¶*A divine cognacionis partibus . . .*, ends . . . *et agitacione vegetatur.* ¶*Summe incensiones dei sunt cum gracie referuntur a mortalibus* (XLI). Continues without rubric:
[*De Platone*]. Beg. *Egritudo mentis est stulticia cuius partes . . .* (I.
xviii). ¶*Insania ex pessima consuetudine . . .*, ends . . . *turbidi violentique sunt.* ¶*Confunditur dignitas cum regendi potestatem non mores boni sed opulencia consecuta est* (II. xxviii). Continues without rubric:
[*De mundo*]. Beg. *Phylosophya est virtutis indagatrix expultrix . . .* (I).
¶*Nebula constat aut . . .*, ends . . . *posteriora videtur ostendere.* ¶*Deum ultrix necessitas . . . se totum dedit atque permisit* (XXXVIII).

Pliny the Younger, epistles

Taken from Berne, Burgerbibl. MS. 136, fols. 42–73, of the ten-book family.
Beg. *Numquam te obsequii peniteat* (I. 1. 2). ¶*Humiles et sordidas . . .*,
ends . . . *causas cotidie finiunt.* ¶*Acerba semper et immatura mors eorum qui immortale aliquid parant* (5. 5. 4).

Cicero, orations

Taken from Berne, Burgerbibl. MS. 136, fols. 74–154^v.
Extracts from the following orations:
Ps.-Cicero, *Pridie quam in exilium iret.* Beg. *Liberale officium est serere beneficium* (I. 2). ¶*Ut metere possis . . .*, ends . . . *fortune poscit libido.* ¶*Nemo generis antiquitate sed virtutis ornamentis summam laudem consequitur.*
Cum senatui gracias egit. Beg. *Numquam in nobis beneficiorum memoria moriatur* (3). ¶*Quis ullam ulli . . .*, ends . . . *improbos bonos excites.* ¶*Cui amicissimus . . . necessarios tuos amicos reddere elabora* (29).
Cum populo gracias egit. Beg. *Nichil est in presenti magis . . .* (2).
¶*Nichil dulcius hominum . . .*, ends . . . *et qui habet solvit.* ¶*Memoriam beneficii . . . eius monimenta in te permaneant ad graciam referendam* (24).
De domo sua. Beg. *Exercitacionem mali et petulancia . . .* (3). ¶*In imperita multitudine . . .*, ends . . . *ante quam ipse didicerit.* ¶*Virtutis ingenii fortune . . . et carendo impaciencia* (146).

Pro P. Sestio. Beg. *Plus miramur hoc tempore siquem* . . . (1). *¶Pio dolori et iuste* . . ., ends . . . *acciderit feramus. ¶Cogitemus corpus esse mortale animi vero motus et virtutis gloriam sempiternam* (143).

In P. Vatinium testem. Beg. *Melius est plerumque scelus et* . . . (6). *¶Quid quisque nostrum* . . ., ends . . . *non suo defendat. ¶Quos crimine coniungis testimonio disiungere non potes* (41).

In senatum de provinciis consularibus. Beg. *In sentencia dicenda non pareas dolori* . . . (2). *¶Indignissimum est ut scelus* . . ., ends . . . *perditis non exquirant. ¶Cum sedate fuerint* . . . *numquam beneficio sit extincta* (47).

De haruspicum responsis. Beg. *Nichil facias iratus nichil impotenti* . . . (3). *¶Iniquum valde est* . . ., ends . . . *concordia retinere possumus. ¶Faciles sunt apud eos* . . . *unam salutis ostendunt* (63).

Pro Cornelio Balbo. Beg. *Patronorum auctoritates multum in iudiciis valent* (1). *¶Cum maximis rei publice negociis* . . ., ends . . . *particeps et commodorum. ¶Perversum est cum non de viciorum pena sed de virtutis premio in iudicium quis vocatur* (65).

Pro Caelio. Beg. *Multis etiam in communi ocio esse* . . . (1). *¶Aliud est maledicere aliud accusare* . . . ends, . . . *industrie sint future. ¶Conservande* [sic] *sunt cives bonarum artium, bonarum partium, bonorum hominum* (77).

Sidonius, epistles

Extracts from books 1–9.
Beg. *Audias plurima pauca respondeas* (1. 2. 4). *¶In convivio aut nulla* . . ., ends . . . *est durius agitur. ¶Res in scribendo discrepantissime sunt maturitas et celeritas* (9. 16. 3).

Seneca, *De beneficiis*

Extracts from books 1–2 only.
Beg. *Beneficia male collata male debentur de quibus non redditis sero querimur* (1. 1. 1). *¶Inter plurima maximaque* . . ., ends . . . *relicta eloquencia. ¶Ac inter alia hoc quoque* . . . *sed non patitur aviditas quemquam esse gratum* (2. 27. 3).

Seneca, *Epistulae ad Lucilium*

Extracts from letters 1–52 only.
The coincidence in the number of letters suggests that the compiler drew on a manuscript of the Beta family.
Beg. *Turpissima est iactura que per negligenciam fit* (ep. 1. 1). *¶Omnes horas complectere* . . . *¶Non puto pauperem* . . ., ends . . . *quemadmodum laudet aspexeris. ¶Dampnum facere philosophiam non dubium erit postquam prostituta est* (ep. 52. 15).

Sententiae philosophorum

Corresponds to the text edited by Woelfflin under the name of Caecilius Balbus (Basle, 1855), pp. 37–43, items 1–83.

Beg. *Nulle sunt occultiores insidie quam hee . . .*, ends . . . *Hactenus preteriti temporis infamia migrat.*

Praecepta Pithagorae

Items 144–5 of Ps.-Seneca *Liber de moribus*; ed. Haase, Seneca *Opera*, suppl. (Leipzig, 1869).
Beg. *Fugienda sunt omnibus modis et abscidenda igni ac ferro . . .*, ends . . . *veritas colenda est que sola homines proximos deo facit.*

Ænigmata Aristotilis

Ed. B. Hauréau, *Notices et Extraits des manuscrits de la Bibliothèque nationale*, xxxiii. 1 (Paris, 1890), pp. 227–8. In manuscripts of the *Florilegium Angelicum* the sentence beg. *Nemo alieno peccato punitur . . .* is frequently given the rubric 'Galienus'.
Beg. *Stateram ne transilias id est ne pretergrediaris iusticiam. ¶Ignem gladio . . .*, ends . . . *excesserit vicium est. ¶Nichil facias quod fecisse peniteat.*

Cicero, Tusculan disputations

Extracts from books I–V.
Beg. *Honos alit artes omnesque inceduntur ad studia gloria* (I. 2. 4) *¶Iacent ea semper que . . .*, ends . . . *Epitaphium Sardanapalli regis Sirie: Hec habeo que edi queque exsaturata libido hausit at illa iacent multa et preclara relicta* (V. 35. 101).

Aulus Gellius

Extracts from books IX–XX only.
Beg. *Herodes consularis Atticus vir ingenio ameno et greca facundia . . .* (IX. 2. 1). *¶Video inquit Herodes . . .*, ends . . . *vivendi disciplina est. ¶Ne imperium sit . . . si qua scimus omnibus aliis fient communia* (XX. 5. 8).

Cicero, Verrine orations

Extracts from Actio II books iv–v only.
Beg. *Abducuntur non numquam a iure homines et ab institutis suis magnitudine pecunie* (II. iv. 12). *¶In rebus venalibus . . .*, ends . . . *et inclinacio temporum. ¶Tacite magis et occulte inimicicie sunt timende quam inducte atque aperte* (II. v. 182).

Ennodius

Extracts from nearly all Ennodius' works, save the *carmina*.
Beg. *Usu rerum inter homines evenit ut quantum . . .* (1) *¶Superflua scribere res . . .*, ends . . . *morbis prestat obsequia. ¶Debit humiliare potentissimos optata sublimitas* (468).

Martin of Braga, *Formula honestae vitae*

Extracts from paragraphs 2–5.
Beg. *Prudentis animi est examinare consilia et non . . .* (2) *¶Crebro*

speciem . . ., ends . . . *prodesse nulli nocere.* ¶*Nichil tibi intersit an iures an firmes* (5).

Querolus (rubr.: *Plautus in Aulularia*)

Taken from MS. Vat. lat. 4929, fols. 55–77.
Beg. *Pecunia est rerum ac sollicitudinum causa et caput*(prologue). ¶*Quod pro meritis* . . ., ends . . . *totum ille qui potest.* ¶*Tres edaces domus una non capit* (V. 4).

Censorinus, *De die natali*

Two sentences taken from MS. Vat. lat. 4929, fols. 2–34.
    Non quanto quisque plura possidet sed quanto pauciora optat tanto est locupletior. Nichil egere deorum est quam minime autem proximum a diis (1. 4). Followed without rubric by four unidentified sentences:
    Ea est consuetudinis vis ut ea inveterata etsi falsa opinione genita est nichil inimicius sit veritati. Pudet imbecillitatis cum rationis et veritatis auctoritate. Quem profecto homine melior est nichil prestantius esse deberet. Quicquid difficile est in precepto leve est amanti.

Addenda to the *Florilegium Angelicum*

Quintus Curtius Rufus, *Oratio Scytharum ad Alexandrum*

Ed. E. Hedicke, *Historiae Alexandri Magni* (Leipzig, 1908), 7. 8.12–30.
Found in F, L, N, V.
Beg. *Si dii habitum corporis tui aviditati animi parem esse* . . . ¶*Quid tu ignoras* . . ., ends . . . *benivolencia dubites.* ¶*Imperio tuo hostes an amicos nos velis esse considera.*

Alexander Atheniensibus

Ed. B. Keubler, Julius Valerius' *Res gestae Alexandri* (Leipzig, 1888), p. 46, lines 20–8.
Found in F, L.
Beg. *Imperiale siquidem videbatur cum armis et iusticia me vestre urbi* . . ., ends . . . *Non enim valebitis si in his perseveratis.*

Ps. Quintilian, *Declamationes maiores*

Extracts from Bks. 2, 1, 3–8, 11–19.
Found in s (partial), x, R.
Beg. *Non est simplicis innocencie negare facinus* (2. 4). ¶*Uxor est quam iungit* . . ., ends . . . *cui potest credi.* ¶*Quisquis in tormentis occiditur ideo tortus est ut occideretur* (19. 12).

Julius Paris, Epitome of Valerius Maximus' *Factorum ac dictorum memorabilium libri IX.*

Found in P, x.
Beg. *Decem principum filii senatus auctoritate* . . . (1. 1) ¶*E mille virginis vestalis* . . ., ends . . . *se canum vallavit.* ¶*Dyonisius tyrannus metu tonsorum* . . . *barbaros et servos habebat* (9 Ext. 2. 4).

CONTENTS BY MANUSCRIPT[1]

	P	A	F	N	V	L	Fournival	R	E	S	x	a	p	s	l	v	b	r
Dedicatory epistle		o																
Macrobius	1	1	1	1	1	1	1	16		3	x	x						
Proverbia philosophorum	2	2	2	2	2	2	2	17		4	x	x			3			
Jerome	3	3	3	3		3	3	2	2	1	x						1	1
Gregory	17	4						1	1	2	14	x						
Apuleius	4	5	4	4	3	4	4	12		5	x	x						
Pliny	5	6	5	5	4	5	5	5	5	6	x	x			3	2		
Cicero, orations	6	7	6	6	5	6	6	9	9	7	x	x					2	
Sidonius	7	8	7	7	6	7	7	3	3	8	x	x			4	4		
Seneca, *De beneficiis*	8	9	8	9	7	8	8	7	7	9	x	x	2					
Seneca, epistles	9	10	9	8	8	9	9	6	6	10	8	x	5	1				
Sententiae philosophorum	10	11	10	10	9	10	10	18		11	1	?	?	1	1			
Praecepta Pithagorae	11	12	11	?	10	11	?	19		12	2	?	?	2				
Ænigma Aristotilis	12	13	12	?	11	12	?	20		13	3	x	?	3				
Cicero, Tusculans	13	14	13	11	12	13	11	8	8	14	4	x	x					
Aulus Gellius	14	15	14	12	13	14	12	13		15	5	x						
Cicero, Verrines	15		15	13	14	15		10		16	6	?	x					
Ennodius	16		16	14	15	16		4	4	17	7	x					5	5
Martin of Braga			17	15	16	17		11			9	x	7					
Querolus			18	16	17	18	13	14			10	x	4					
Censorinus			19	17	18	19	14	15			11	x	6					
Quintus Curtius			20	18	19	20	22											
Alexander Atheniensibus			21		21													
Quintilian										21	13	?	8					
Julius Paris	18										12							

[1] The numbers represent the relative order of a given work within each manuscript. (Manuscripts **a** and **p** are arranged by topic rather than by author.)

APPENDIX III
The Manuscripts

THE following manuscripts contain the text of the *Florilegium Angelicum*; selections (i.e. entire sections) from it; and extracts (i.e. excerpts from sections) from the *florilegium*. Titles in square brackets indicate that the manuscript has no rubric nor other physical indication to mark the beginning of a given section. An asterisk denotes material which is not part of the *Florilegium Angelicum*.

x Auxerre, Bibl. Municipale, 234 (s. XIV²; France). Selections from the *Florilegium Angelicum*.

*fols. 1–140 Giles of Rome, *De regimine principum*; beginning lacking.

fols. 141–142 *Sententiae philosophorum.*

fol. 142 *Praecepta Pithagorae.*

fol. 142 *Ænigmata Aristotilis.*

fols. 142–146 Cicero, Tusculans.

fols. 146–148ᵛ Aulus Gellius.

fols. 148ᵛ–149 Cicero, Verrine orations.

fols. 149–152 Ennodius.

fols. 152–156 Seneca, *Epistulae ad Lucilium.*

fol. 156 Martin of Braga, *Formula honestae vitae.*

fol. 156ʳᵛ *Querolus.*

fol. 156ᵛ Censorinus, *De die natali.*

fols. 156ᵛ–169ᵛ Julius Paris.

fols. 169ᵛ–173 Quintilian, *Declamationes.*

*fols. 173–174 Jerome, epistles; extracts from epp. 64, 55, 123, 54, beg. *Quod pectore concepimus ore probemus* . . ., ends . . . *Quod luxurie parabatur virtus insumat.*

fols. 174–178 Gregory, epistles.

*fols. 178–179 Ps.-Hegesippus, extracts from books 1–4 of the Histories, beg. *Nemo clarior sit splendore generis quam munere religionis* . . ., ends . . . *potuerunt cavere quod divinitus decernebatur.*

*fols. 180–242 Praises of the Virgin, beg. *Sicud sol oriens mundo in altissimis dei* . . .; text breaks, incomplete, at the end of the quire.

Written by one or two hands in two columns of 41–3 lines each, on parchment and paper. Parchment ruled with lead point; paper not ruled. Sexterns. 292 × 205 mm (215 × 150). Belonged to Pontigny in 1778, no. 276 in catalogue of that date; not in the revolutionary commission's list of 1794; cf. Talbot, 'Notes on the Library of Pontigny', *Analecta sacri ordinis Cisterciensis*, x (1954), 165. Described in *Catalogue général des manuscrits des Bibliothèques publiques de France*, vi (Paris, 1887), p. 81. Manuscript seen.

b Brussels, Bibl. Royale MS. 10098–10105 (Van den Gheyn 1334)
(s. XIII[1]; France). Selections (Jerome and Cicero's orations) from the
Florilegium Angelicum.

I. *fols. 1–9   Solinus, *Collectanea rerum memorabilium*; extracts.

 *fols. 10–15   Fulgentius, extracts.

 fols. 15–18   Jerome, epistles; extracts. Only the extracts on fol. 15
are taken from the *Florilegium Angelicum.*

 *fols. 19–20   Cicero, *De senectute*; extracts.

 *fol. 20ᵛ   Cicero, *De amicitia*; extracts.

 *fols. 21–28ᵛ   Cicero, *De officiis*; extracts.

 fol. 28ᵛ   Cicero, orations (*De domo*, [*Pro Sestio*], *In Vat.*, *De
prov. cons.*, *De harusp.*, *Pro Balbo*, *Pro Caelio*); added
in a different hand.

 *fols. 29–37   Ennodius.

 fol. 37ᵛ   Cicero, orations (*Pridie*, *Cum senatui gracias egit*, *Cum
populi gracias egit*); added in a different hand.

 *fols. 38–41   Claudian. Brief extracts from the following in this
order: *Panegyricus de tertio consulatu Honorii Augusti*;
Pan. de quarto cons. H. A.; *Pan. dictus Manlio Theo-
doro consuli*; *De consulatu Stilichonis*; *Pan. de sexto
cons. H. A.*; *De bello Getico*; *Carmina minora*; *In
Rufinum*; *De bello Gildonico*; *In Eutropium*; *Fescennina
de nuptiis Honorii*; *Epithalamium de nupt. Hon.*; *Carmina minora xxxii.*

 *fols. 41–42ᵛ   Horace, *Carmina* and *De arte poetica*; extracts.

II. *fols. 43–88ᵛ   Isidore, *Quaestiones in Vetus Testamentum.*

Two manuscripts, already bound together by the fifteenth century.

I. Written by several hands in two columns (fols. 38–42, 3 cols.) of 40–50
lines each.

Ruled with ink and lead point. 220 × 145 mm. Modern binding. fol. 1
(s. XV), *Liber carthusiensium prope Leodium* (Carthusians of Liège, est.
1390); fol. 1 (s. XVII), *Coll. societatis Iesus Lovanii* (repeated). The manuscript passed to the Bibl. Royale in 1838. According to the fifteenth-
century table of contents describing I and II on fol. 1, portions of the
manuscript are missing. Described in J. Van den Gheyn, *Catalogue des
manuscrits de la Bibliothèque royale de Belgique*, ii (Brussels, 1902), pp.
280–1; and P. Thomas, *Catalogue des manuscrits de classiques latins de la
Bibliothèque royale de Bruxelles* (Ghent, 1896), p. 63, nos. 198–201.
Manuscript seen on film.

E Évreux, Bibl. Municipale, 1 (s. XIII med.; France). *Florilegium
Angelicum.*

*I. fol. 1   lacking.

 fols. 2–31   Seneca, *De beneficiis*, epitome. fol. 2 beg. . . . *bene
posito beneficio multorum amissorum dampna solatur* . . .,
ends . . . *dare et perdere. Hoc est magni animi perdere et
dare.*

	fols. 31ᵛ–32ᵛ	blank.
*II.	fols. 33–62	Symmachus, epistles; extracts. Beg. *Frivolis meis litterata potius curiositate quam iusta . . .*, ends *. . . mundum epistolis saltem nuntiis erigatur.*
	fols. 62ᵛ–63ᵛ	blank.
III.	fols. 64–69ᵛ	Gregory, epistles.
	fols. 69ᵛ–79ᵛ	Jerome, epistles, [*Adversus Jovinianum*]. End of quire ii. fol. 79ᵛ bottom, note: *Tercius quaternus et proximus sequens debent hic intrare. .ii.* [catchword:] *pulchrum et affirmare.* [Cf. fol. 98 below.]
	fols. 80–81ᵛ	Ennodius.
	fols. 81ᵛ–85ᵛ	Pliny, epistles.
	fols. 85ᵛ–90ᵛ	Seneca, *Epistulae ad Lucilium.*
	fols. 90ᵛ–93ᵛ	Seneca, *De beneficiis.*
	fols. 93ᵛ–97	Cicero, Tusculans.
	fol. 97ʳᵛ	Cicero, orations. Text breaks, incomplete, with end of quire; catchword, *delectionem que versari,* indicates a missing quire or quires. fols. 98–114ᵛ, comprising two quires, are misplaced and should follow fol. 79ᵛ.
	fols. 98–104	Jerome (concluded).
	fols. 104ᵛ–112	Sidonius, epistles.
	fols. 112–114ᵛ	Ennodius; completed fols. 80–81ᵛ above.
*IV.	fols. 115–119ᵛ	Cyprian, epistles; moral extracts. Beg. *Ne eloquium nostrum arbiter prophanus inpediat aut clamor . . .*, ends *. . . munimentum spei tutela fidei medela peccati.*
	fols. 119ᵛ–122ᵛ	Cassiodorus, epistles; moral extracts. Beg. *Dictio semper agrestis est que aut . . .*, ends *. . . iudicem dehonestat cum more vestium verba suspensa venduntur.* Quire ends here without catchword; text may be incomplete.
*V.	fols. 123–138ᵛ	Jerome, epistles; moral extracts. Beg. *In epistola prima Damasus papa Jeronimo. Capitulo, Dormientum te etc. Lectione veluti cotidiano cibo aliter et* [ep. 35] *. . .*, ends *. . . quis iste dolor qui nec tempore ratione curatur* [ep. 97]. Quire ends here; text may be incomplete.
*VI.	fols. 139–157	Solinus, extracts. Beg. *Cum et aurum clementia et optimarum artium . . .*, ends *. . . non obscure iam pridem lacedemoniorum fedo exitu.*
	fols. 157ᵛ–158ᵛ	blank save for ex-libris.
*VII.	fols. 159–168	*Moralium dogma philosophorum.*
	fol. 168	Publilius Syrus, *Sententiae* A–F.
	fol. 168ᵛ	Ten legal formulas (see Évreux catalogue for bibliography).

fol. 169 pastedown. Hymn to St. Nicholas and various brief notes by different hands.

Seven individual manuscripts already bound together by the fifteenth century. III. Written in long lines, 28–32 per page. Ruled with lead point. 1⁴ sig. i., 2⁴ sig. ii. (at end in a contemporary hand: *Tercius quaternus et proximus sequens debent hic intrare*), 3⁵, 4⁴, 5⁴ sig. iii (misplaced), 6⁴⁺¹. 176 × 130 mm (127 × 97). Plain initials in green, blue, red. Original binding, oak board, bevelled edges, bare; front cover lacking. fol. 158ᵛ, *Iste unus librorum est cenobii Lirensis ordinis sancti Benedicti Ebroicensis dyoceseos. Alecis* (and monogram, s. xv) = Lyre OSB. Described in *Catalogue général des manuscrits des Bibliothèques publiques de France*, ii (Paris, 1888), pp. 401–2. Manuscript seen.

F Florence, Bibl. Laurenziana, Strozzi 75 (s. xii²; France). *Florilegium Angelicum.*

*fol. iʳᵛ	Notes in French hand, s. xiv–xv.
fols. 1–5ᵛ	Macrobius, *Saturnalia*; with *Versus Ciceronis.*
fols. 5ᵛ–8ᵛ	*Proverbia philosophorum.*
fols. 8ᵛ–23	Jerome, epistles, [*Adversus Jovinianum*].
fols. 23–25ᵛ	Apuleius, *De deo Socratis*, [*Asclepius, De Platone, De mundo*].
fols. 25ᵛ–28ᵛ	Pliny, epistles.
fols. 28ᵛ–33ᵛ	Cicero, orations.
fols. 33ᵛ–40ᵛ	Sidonius, epistles.
fols. 40ᵛ–43ᵛ	Seneca, *De beneficiis.*
fols. 43ᵛ–48	Seneca, *Epistulae ad Lucilium.*
fols. 48–49ᵛ	*Sententiae philosophorum.*
fol. 49ᵛ	*Praecepta Pithagorae.*
fols. 49ᵛ–50	*Ænigmata Aristotilis.*
fols. 50–54ᵛ	Cicero, Tusculans.
fols. 54ᵛ–57ᵛ	Aulus Gellius.
fols. 57ᵛ–58	Cicero, Verrine orations.
fols. 58–62	Ennodius.
fol. 62ʳᵛ	Martin of Braga, *Formula honestae vitae.*
fols. 62ᵛ–63	*Querolus.*
fol. 63	Censorinus, *De die natali.*
fol. 63ʳᵛ	Quintus Curtius, *Oratio Scytharum.*
fol. 63ᵛ	*Alexander Atheniensibus.*
*fols. 63ᵛ–72ᵛ	Valerius Maximus, *Facta et dicta memorabilia*; extracts. Beg. *Sulpicio sacerdoti inter sacrificandum . . .*, ends . . . *taurus ad amorem Enee vacce immugiit.*
*fols. 72ᵛ–74	Notes by various Italian hands, s. xvi.

Written by one hand in long lines, 32 per page. Quaternions, signed in Roman numerals; catchwords. First initial decorated, vine stems in gold, short tendrils terminating in scallops outline major letters. Front pastedown: *Comprato da me Carlo di Tommaso Strozzi l'anno 1616 in Spoleto.*

Described in A. M. Bandini, *Biblioteca Leopoldina Laurentiana* . . ., ii (Florence, 1792), cols. 408–9. Manuscript seen on film.

1 Leyden, Universiteitsbibl., B.P.L. 191 B (s. XIII²). Extracts from Seneca's letters and *De beneficiis*, Pliny, Sidonius, and Ennodius, taken from the *Florilegium Angelicum.*

*I. fols. 1–42ᵛ Augustine, *De catechizandis rudibus.*

*II. fols. 43–135ᵛ A collection of texts on the monastic life: *Instructio pie vivendi et superna meditandi*; Hugh of St. Victor, *De institutione noviciorum*; Martin of Braga, *Formula honestae vitae*; Arnulfus, *Speculum monachorum* (*P.L.* clxxxiv. 1175); *Sermo de b. Arsenio anachoreta* (*Acta Sanctorum, Iulii,* IV, p. 617).

III. fols. 136–142ᵛ Seneca, *Epistulae ad Lucilium*; extracts from epp. 1–88; only the extracts on fols. 141ᵛᵇ–142ᵛ are taken from the *Florilegium Angelicum.*

 fols. 142ᵛ–144 Seneca, *De beneficiis.*

*fols. 144ᵛ–145ᵛ Seneca, *De remediis fortuitorum*; extracts.

*fol. 145ᵛ Jerome, *De viris illustribus* c. 12, *Seneca.*

*fols. 146–148ᵛ Martin of Braga, *Formula honestae vitae.*

*fols. 149–153ᵛ Seneca, *Epistulae ad Lucilium*; extracts from epp. 1–47.

*fols. 153ᵛ–155 Correspondence of 'Seneca' and 'Paul'; followed, bottom of the page, by *Epithaphium Senece.*

*fols. 155–159 Seneca, tragedies; extracts.

 fols. 159ᵛ–161 Pliny, epistles.

 fols. 161–163 Sidonius, epistles.

 fol. 163ʳᵛ Ennodius.

*fols. 163ᵛ–167 Cicero, *De senectute*; extracts.

*fol. 167ʳᵛ Sallust, *Bellum Catilinae*, cc. 1–4; text breaks incomplete with the end of the quire.

*IV. fols. 168–183 Guillelmus de Boldensele, *Peregrinatio ad terram sanctam.*

A composite manuscript in four parts. They were bound together in the fourteenth or early fifteenth century (after 1351) when the volume was foliated in Roman numerals and described on a slip of parchment now bound in the volume. It belonged to the abbey of St. James OSB in Liège.

 I. fols. 1–42ᵛ (s. XII); II. fols. 43–135ᵛ (s. XIV); IV. fols. 168–183ᵛ (A.D. 1351). III. fols. 136–167ᵛ (s. XIII²). Written by one hand in two columns of 31 lines each. 1–4⁴, catchwords. (150 × 115 mm). fol. 136, *Liber sancti Iacobi in Leodio.* Described in *Bibliotheca Universitatis Leidensis, Codices manuscripti,* iii, *Codices Bibliothecae Publicae Latini* (Leyden, 1912), pp. 94–5; and G. I. Lieftinck, *Manuscrits datés conservés dans les Pays-Bas,* i (Amsterdam, 1964), p. 81, and ii, pl. 144 (of fol. 170). Manuscript seen.

r London, British Libr., Royal 11 A.v (s. XII–XIII; Merton Priory, Surrey). Extracts from Jerome's epistles, taken from the *Florilegium Angelicum* (fols. 69–72ᵛ).

*fols. 1–3	Notes headed *De ecclesiastica correctione.*
*fols. 3–30	Collection of anonymous *sententiae* arranged by subject. Beg. *De divina natura. Principium et causa omnium deus* . . .
*fols. 30–32ᵛ	Additional *sententiae* arranged by subject. Beg. *Ecclesia dicitur fidelium conventus* . . .
*fols. 33–68ᵛ	Isidore, *Expositio in Genesim et Exodum.*
fols. 69–72ᵛ	Jerome, epistles. Beg. *Studio legendi* . . ., ends incomplete, . . . *quod si negaverit terra consumptum est.*
*fols. 73–98ᵛ	Abelard, *Sic et non;* mutilated.
*fols. 99–109ᵛ	*Dialogus inter philosophum Iudaeum et Christianum;* fragment.
*fols. 110–112ᵛ	Fourteen excerpts primarily on religious life attributed in the rubric to St. Bernard.

Written by one hand in two columns (fols. 1–98). ex libris, *Liber sancte Marie Merton.* Described in G. F. Warner and J. P. Gilson, *Catalogue of Western Manuscripts in the Old Royal and Kings Collections,* i (London, 1921), p. 337.

L London, British Libr., Add. 25104 (s. xv, Italy). *Florilegium Angelicum.*

fols. 1–8	Macrobius, *Saturnalia;* with *Versus Ciceronis.*
fols. 8–14	*Proverbia philosophorum.*
fols. 14–40ᵛ	Jerome, epistles, [*Adversus Jovinianum*].
fols. 40ᵛ–44	Apuleius, *De deo Socratis,* [*Asclepius, De Platone, De mundo*].
fols. 44–50	Pliny, epistles.
fols. 50–58ᵛ	Cicero, orations.
fols. 58ᵛ–70	Sidonius, epistles.
fols. 70–75ᵛ	Seneca, *De beneficiis.*
fols. 75ᵛ–83ᵛ	Seneca, *Epistulae ad Lucilium.*
fols. 83ᵛ–85ᵛ	*Sententiae philosophorum.*
fols. 85ᵛ–86	*Praecepta Pithagorae.*
fol. 86ʳᵛ	*Ænigmata Aristotilis.*
fols. 86ᵛ–94ᵛ	Cicero, Tusculans.
fols. 94ᵛ–101ᵛ	Aulus Gellius.
fols. 101ᵛ–102	Cicero, Verrine orations.
fols. 102–109	Ennodius.
fols. 109–110	Martin of Braga, *Formula honestae vitae.*
fols. 110–111	*Querolus.*
fol. 111	Censorinus, *De die natali.*
fols. 111–112	Quintus Curtius, *Oratio Scytharum.*
fol. 112ʳᵛ	*Alexander Atheniensibus.*

Written by one hand in long lines, 28 per page. Parchment ruled in ink. Eleven alternating sexternions and quaternions. 180 × 114 mm (134 × 68). Humanist hand, titles and paragraph marks in red. Described briefly in *Catalogue of Additions to the Manuscripts in the British Museum in the Years 1854–1875,* ii (London, 1877), p. 155. Manuscript seen.

S   Paris, Bibl. de l'Arsenal, 1116E (fols. 128–142ᵛ) (s. XIII¹; France; St. Victor). Extracts from the *Florilegium Angelicum*.

fols. 128–133   Jerome, epistles, [*Adversus Jovinianum*].
fols. 133–135   Gregory, epistles.
fol. 135ʳᵛ   Macrobius, *Saturnalia*; with *Versus Ciceronis*.
fol. 135ᵛ–136   *Proverbia philosophorum.*
fol. 136ʳᵛ   Apuleius, De deo Socratis, [*Asclepius, De Platone, De mundo*].
fols. 136ᵛ–137   Pliny, epistles.
fol. 137ʳᵛ   Cicero, orations.
fols. 137ᵛ–138ᵛ   Sidonius, epistles.
fols. 138ᵛ–139   Seneca, *De beneficiis.*
fols. 139–140   Seneca, *Epistulae ad Lucilium.*
fol. 140ʳᵛ   *Sententiae philosophorum.*
fol. 140ᵛ   *Praecepta Pithagorae.*
fol. 140ᵛ   *Ænigmata Aristotilis.*
fols. 140ᵛ–141ᵛ   Cicero, Tusculans.
fol. 141ᵛ   Aulus Gellius.
fol. 141ᵛ   Cicero, Verrine orations.
fols. 141ᵛ–142   Ennodius.
*fol. 142   *Sententiae* from Gregory, Jerome, Augustine, Seneca, Rabanus, Ambrose, and the Scriptures. Beg. *Pollutus nigritie viciorum non cessat . . .*, ends *. . . non solum non proficit sed etiam lapsum incurrit.*
fol. 142ᵛ   blank.

Written by one hand in two columns of *c.* 50 lines each. Parchment pricked but not ruled. 1⁴, 2⁴⁽⁻¹⁾; catchwords. 206 × 150 mm (148 × 115). Capitals in red; rubricated. Arsenal 1116 is a composite manuscript in 12 parts dating from the twelfth to the fifteenth centuries. They appear as one volume with the pressmark PP 14 in the catalogue of St. Victor by Claude de Grandrue (A.D. 1514). Described in H. Martin, *Catalogue des manuscrits de la Bibliothèque de l'Arsenal,* ii (Paris, 1886), 286–9. Manuscript seen.

p   Paris, Bibl. Nationale, lat. 1860 (s. XIII med.; S. France). *Florilegium Angelicum* arranged by subject.

I.   *fols. 1–56ᵛ   *Interpretationes nominum hebraicorum.*
*fols. 57–59   Alan of Lille, *De sex alis cherubim*; lacks beginning.
*fols. 59–60   Brief extracts from patristic texts on penitence.
*fols. 60ᵛ–72ᵛ   *Moralium dogma philosophorum.*
*fols. 72ᵛ–74ᵛ   Martin of Braga, *Formula honestae vitae.*
fols. 75–153ᵛ   *Florilegium* of classical prose, being the classical texts (only) from the *Florilegium Angelicum*, enlarged and arranged by subject under 299 headings, and preceded by a subject index A–V on fols. 75–7. Beg. fol 77, c. I. *De proposito et deliberatione alicuius rei faciende. Tullius de officiis primo. Efficiendum est*

ut rationi appetitus obediant eamque neque . . ., ends
*c. CCXC. Quorum virtus est placitis abstinere vel
modum tenere . . . Ennodius in epistola: Gravius est
calcasse degustata dulcia quam intacta.*

*fols. 153ᵛ–216   *Florilegium* of classical verse arranged in 231 chap-
ters, preceded by a table of chapters, fols. 153ᵛ–155.
Beg. fol. 155, *c. I. De novo inceptore alicuius rei . . .
Et labor est unus tempora prima pati . . .*, ends *c.
CCXXXI. De consumacione alicuius operis . . .
Anchora de prora iacitur stant littore puppes.*

    fol. 216ᵛ   blank.

*II. fols. 217–246ᵛ Summary of the O.T., with marginal concordance.
Beg. *Inter varia nature et gratie dona . . . Quattuor
sunt regule scripture, istoria . . .*, ends *. . . fiant opera
sicut Cornelius faciebat.*

Comprises two manuscripts.

I. (s. XIII med., S. France). Written by one hand in two columns of *c.*
50 lines each. Ruled with lead point. 1–27⁴; catchwords. 335 × 220 mm
(210 × 97). Initials orange-red, occasionally blue; short single tendrils
terminating in scallops.

II. (s. XIII in., N. France). Written in two columns of 55 lines each. fol.
246ᵛ (s. XV): *Liber sancti Marie de Mortuimaris* (Abbey of Mortemer OSB
in the diocese of Rouen).

The whole is identified with item 15 in the catalogue of books taken by
M. de Mareste from the Abbey of Mortemer in 1677; ed. L. Delisle,
Cabinet des manuscrits, i (Paris, 1868), p. 525. Colbert 959, Regius 3758¹⁰.
Described in Ph. Lauer, *Catalogue général des manuscrits latins*, ii (Paris,
1940), pp. 200–1. Manuscript seen.

s   Paris, Bibl. Nationale, lat. 15172, fols. 122–40 (s. XIII¹; France; St.
Victor). Selections from the *Florilegium Angelicum*.

*fols. 122ᵛ–125ᵛ Ps. Seneca, Proverbs. Beg. *Alienum est omne quicquid
. . .*, ends *. . . zelum autem hominibus viciosum est.*

fols. 125ᵛ–126 *Sententiae philosophorum.*

fol. 126ʳᵛ *Praecepta Pithagorae.*

fol. 126ᵛ *Ænigmata Aristotilis.*

fol. 126ᵛ *Querolus.*

fols. 127–130ᵛ *Seneca, Epistulae ad Lucilium.*

fol. 130ᵛ *Censorinus, De die natali.*

fol. 131 *Martin of Braga, Formula honestae vitae.*

fols. 131–134ᵛ *Quintilian, Declamationes, beg. *Incipit mathematicus.
Mors est laudanda . . .*, ends incomplete, *. . . Affirma-
tionem sumit ex veritate quicquid non habet ex homine.
Ex hoc iniquissimum.*

*fol. 134ᵛ Sequence, beg. *In affectu cordis puri assurgamus . . .*,
ends *. . . mente loco imitari petrum tot . . .* [illeg.].

*fols. 135–137ᵛ (misnumbered 131–133ᵛ) Jerome, epistles; extracts.

Beg. *Libenter accipio ab offerente* . . ., ends . . . *Vinctum me tenet affectio tui. Verba concessi.*

*fol. 137ᵛ (133ᵛ) Vegetius, *De re militari*; extracts. Beg., *Nemo metuit facere* . . ., ends . . . *etiam si honerosa gestaverit.*

*fol. 138ʳᵛ (134ʳᵛ)Unidentified extracts, beg. *Sancta et apostolica romana ecclesia que tanquam pia mater ad sublevandos gemitus et labores* . . .

*fol. 138ᵛ (134ᵛ) Unidentified extracts, beg. *Bone mentis intentio semper in opere pietatis elucet et in religionis amore atque defensione iusticie* . . .

fols. 139–140ᵛ (135–136ᵛ) blank, except for pen essays and the note: *Obiit frater Andreas.*

Two quires written by one hand in two columns of 35 lines each. Ruled with dry point and lead point. 1^{4+2}, 2^{3+3}. 175×120 mm (140×90). fol. 122 s. XIII, ex libris and anathema of St. Victor. By the end of the fifteenth century the two quires had been bound together with a number of twelfth- and thirteenth-century manuscripts and formed item FFF 22 in the catalogue of St. Victor by Claude de Grandrue (A.D. 1514). Manuscript seen.

a Rome, Bibl. Angelica 720 (s. XIII; France). *Florilegium Angelicum* arranged by subject.

fols. 1–106ᵛ *Florilegium* in 105 chapters. Mutilated. The first 10 chapters are missing; the text begins in the middle of chapter 11. A quire containing chapters 73–86 is missing between fols. 86ᵛ and 87, and another containing chapters 102–3 is lacking between fols. 103ᵛ and 104. Beg. . . . *sed secundum famem restringere. Idem. Ubi aqua et panis est ibi nature satisfactum* . . . [ch. 12] *De commendatione ieiunii* . . ., ends [ch. 105] *De ingratitudine et inuriis irrogatis* . . . *Iniurias vero dilatat atque auget quod autem et amplius.*

fol. 107ʳᵛ Miscellaneous notes; s. XIV–XV, Italy.
fol. 108ʳᵛ Subject index, letters A–E; s. XIV–XV.

Written by one hand in long lines, 17–19 per page. Ruled with lead point. 1^{4+1}, 2^4, 3^{4+1}, 4^{4+1}, 5–8^5, 9^{5+1}, quire missing, 11^4, 12^{4+1}, quire missing, 14^4; catchwords. 147×105 mm (111×70). Initial letters slashed in red. Described briefly in H. Narducci, *Catalogus codicum manuscriptorum* . . . *in Bibliotheca Angelica* . . . (Rome, 1893), pp. 301–2. Manuscript seen.

A Rome, Bibl. Angelica, 1895 (s. XII²; France). *Florilegium Angelicum.*

I. fol. i blank.
fol. 1ʳᵛ Dedicatory epistle.
fols. 2–8 Macrobius, *Saturnalia*; with *Versus Ciceronis.*
fols. 8–12ᵛ *Proverbia philosophorum.*
fols. 12ᵛ–31 Jerome, epistles, [*Adversus Jovinianum*].
fols. 31–37 Gregory, epistles.
fols. 37–40 Apuleius, *De deo Socratis*, [*Asclepius, De Platone, De mundo*].

fols. 40–44ᵛ   Pliny, epistles.
fols. 44ᵛ–51   Cicero, orations.
fols. 51–59   Sidonius, epistles.
fols. 59–63   Seneca, *De beneficiis.*
fols. 63–69   Seneca, *Epistulae ad Lucilium.*
fols. 69–70ᵛ   *Sententiae philosophorum.*
fol. 70ᵛ   *Praecepta Pithagorae.*
fol. 71ʳᵛ   *Ænigmata Aristotilis.*
fols. 71ᵛ–77   Cicero, Tusculans.
fols. 77–79ᵛ   Aulus Gellius; text breaks, incomplete, with the end of quire ten.
*II.   fols. 80–81   Grammatical rules.
*III.   fols. 81ᵛ–96   Prudentius, *Psychomachia.*
*IV.   fols. 97–105   Horace, *Epistola ad Pisones.*
*V.   fols. 105–133   Horace, *Epistolarum libri duo.*
*VI.   fols. 133ᵛ–137   Grammatical rules and a Latin–Italian glossary.

A composite manuscript in six parts.

I. Written by one hand in long lines, 27 per page. Ruled with lead point. 1–10⁴, 185 × 117 mm (143 × 94). Large section initials coloured dusty blue, red, and gold. Described in A. Sorbelli, *Inventari dei manoscritti delle biblioteche d'Italia,* lvi (Florence, 1934), pp. 82–3. Manuscript seen.

N Sydney, University Lib., Nicholson 2 (s. XIII¹; France). Extracts from the *Florilegium Angelicum.*

fols. 1–2   Macrobius, *Saturnalia;* with *Versus Ciceronis.*
fols. 2–3ᵛ   [*Proverbia philosophorum*].
fols. 3ᵛ–11ᵛ   Jerome, epistles [*Adversus Jovinianum*].
fols. 11ᵛ–13   Apuleius, *De deo Socratis,* [*Asclepius, De Platone, De mundo*].
fols. 13–15ᵛ   [Pliny, epistles.]
fols. 15ᵛ–22   Cicero, orations.
fol. 22   Seneca, *Epistulae ad Lucilium.*
*fols. 22ᵛ–24   Boethius, *De consolatione philosophiae,* extracts.
fols. 24ᵛ–25   Seneca, *De beneficiis.*
*fols. 25–26   Unidentified extracts, illegible.
fols. 26–27   *Sententiae philosophorum.*
fol. 27   Cicero, Tusculans.
fol. 27ʳᵛ   [Aulus Gellius.]
fol. 27ᵛ   [Cicero, Verrine orations.]
fols. 27ᵛ–29ᵛ   [Ennodius.]
fols. 29ᵛ–30   Martin of Braga, *Formula honestae vitae.*
fol. 30   [*Querolus.*]
fol. 30   [Censorinus, *De die natali.*]
fol. 30   [Quintus Curtius, *Oratio Scytharum.*]
*fols. 30–31ᵛ   Unidentified extracts, beg. *Qui descendet a superis sola hymnorum licet mercede . . .*

*fol. 31ᵛ   In lower margin, verses beg. *In coitu sex dampna luo nam*
             denarium do . . . (Walther no. 8864).
*fols. 31ᵛ– Brief extracts from Seneca, Jerome, Ambrose, Aristotle,
  32ᵛ   and the Scriptures, beg. *Fastidientis stomachi est multa*
             degustare . . .

Written by one hand in long lines, 28 per page. Ruled in ink. 1–8². 158 ×
130 mm. First and second initials blue and red, with red and blue pen-
work; remaining ten initials in red. Fol. 32ᵛ erased: *Iste liber est ad usum*
fratris Laurentii; given to the University of Sydney from the estate of
Sir Charles Nicholson in 1924. Described in K. V. Sinclair, *Descriptive*
Catalogue of Medieval and Renaissance Western Manuscripts in Australia
(Sydney, 1969), pp. 175–8. Manuscript seen on film.

P   Vatican City, Bibl. Apostolica, Pal. lat. 957 (s. xii²; France). *Flori-*
    legium Angelicum.

*I.   fols. 1–60   Walter Burleigh, *De vita et moribus philosophorum.*
      fols. 61–84ᵛ   Theobald, *Pharetra fidei contra iudeos.*
      fols. 85–92   Guido Aretinus (?), *Regulae rhythmicae.*
      fols. 92ᵛ–95   Thomas Colete, *Ars notaria.*
      fols. 95ᵛ–96ᵛ   *Obiectiones contra iudeos*, beg. *Mota dicit dominus*
                        in evangelio . . .
 II. fols. 97–102   Macrobius, *Saturnalia*; with *Versus Ciceronis.*
      fols. 102–107   *Proverbia philosophorum.*
      fols. 107–125ᵛ   Jerome, epistles [*Adversus Jovinianum*].
      fols. 125ᵛ–128ᵛ   Apuleius, *De deo Socratis*, [*Asclepius, De Platone,*
                        De mundo].
      fols. 128ᵛ–132ᵛ   Pliny, epistles.
      fols. 132ᵛ–139   Cicero, orations.
      fols. 139–147ᵛ   Sidonius, epistles.
      fols. 147ᵛ–151ᵛ   Seneca, *De beneficiis.*
      fols. 151ᵛ–158   Seneca, *Epistulae ad Lucilium.*
      fols. 158–159ᵛ   *Sententiae philosophorum.*
      fol. 159ᵛ   *Praecepta Pithagorae.*
      fols. 159ᵛ–160ᵛ   *Ænigmata Aristotilis.*
      fols. 160ᵛ–166ᵛ   Cicero, *Tusculans.*
      fols. 166ᵛ–171ᵛ   Aulus Gellius.
      fols. 171ᵛ–172   Cicero, Verrine orations.
      fols. 172–176ᵛ   Ennodius. Text breaks incomplete with the end
                        of quire ten, . . . *dampna sermonis. Mater bonorum*
      fols. 177–184   . . . Gregory, epistles.
      fol. 184ʳᵛ   Julius Paris. Text breaks incomplete with the end
                        of the quire, . . . *trahebat ab ea se que nam aut*
                        agenda aut intan . . .

Composed of two manuscripts probably joined in Heidelberg.
    I. (s. xiv.) fol. 92, *Explicit summa magistri Gwidonis anno domini 1368*
in octava epiphanie domini.
    II. Written by two hands: (1) fols. 97–176ᵛ, (2) fols. 177–184ᵛ, in long

lines, 28 per page. Ruled with lead point. 1–10⁴ (sig. i-x), 11⁴ (sig. i). 207 ×
133 mm (160 × 90). Initials coloured red, yellow, and blue; titles in semi-
rustic capitals. Manuscript seen.

v Vatican City, Bibl. Apostolica, Reg. lat. 358 (s. xv; France; Tours).
    Extracts from the *Florilegium Angelicum.*

> fols. 1–108ᵛ A collection of extracts from Scripture and from medieval
> and ancient authors; beg. *Incipit hic series descripta para-*
> *bolarum Flosculus* . . . [Proverbia Salomonis:] *Audiens*
> *sapiens sapiencior erit* . . ., ends [John of Salisbury, *Policra-*
> *ticus:*] . . . *dampnum nobis in curia detur. Liber ad eos etc.*
> The collection includes a block of extracts from the *Flori-*
> *legium Angelicum*:
>
> fols. 74–75 *Sententiae philosophorum*; twenty-four sentences.
> fol. 75 Pliny, epistles; seven sentences.
> fol. 75ʳᵛ *Proverbia philosophorum*; twenty-seven sentences.
> fol. 75ᵛ Sidonius, epistles; eleven sentences.
> fols. 75ᵛ–76 Ennodius: seventeen sentences.

Parchment. ex libris note, s. xvi: *Ce livre est a Lucas Fumee chanoine de*
Tours. Paul and Alexander Petau. There is no reason to repeat a description of the whole manuscript since it is fully described in A. Wilmart,
Codices Reginenses Latini, ii (Vatican, 1945), pp. 331–40. Manuscript
seen.

R Vatican City, Bibl. Apostolica, Reg. lat. 1575 (s. xii/xiii; France).
    Florilegium Angelicum.

> *fols. 1–24 Council of Aachen 816, *Regula canonicorum.*
> *fols. 34–40ᵛ *Epistola beati Jeronimi de vita et exitu sancti Pauli.*
> *fols. 41–59 Symmachus, epistles; extracts. Beg. *Ne michi vicio*
> *vertatur intermissio litterarum* . . ., ends . . . *studium*
> *meum incitamento religionis acuetur.*
> *fol. 59ᵛ–61ᵛ Epistles of 'Alexander and Dindimus'.
> *fol. 62 Sermon, beg. *Miserere mei deus* . . . *Triplex est divina*
> *misericordia, parva, mediocris et magna* . . .
> *fol. 62ᵛ Augustine, *Sermo de trinitate,* beg. *Audio fratres quod*
> *quidam inter se disputant* . . ., followed by a fragment of
> a poem: . . . *pauperibus placuit pro condicione/* . . . *pro sola*
> *po–itate chorus/* . . . *humili paupertas provida passu/* . . .
> *piti copia rapta gradu/* . . . g̅r̅i̅ *terrici/* . . . *ius cognomine*
> *non quia durus/* . . . *lor ferebat honus/* . . . *francie ludovici/*
> . . . *ut rex hec loca regi/* . . . *homo deteriore domo.*
> fols. 63–65ᵛ Gregory, epistles.
> fols. 65–72ᵛ [Jerome, epistles, *Adversus Jovinianum.*]
> fols. 72ᵛ–75ᵛ Sidonius, epistles.
> fols. 76–78 Ennodius.
> fols. 78–79ᵛ Pliny, epistles.
> fols. 79ᵛ–82 Seneca, *Epistulae ad Lucilium.*
> fols. 82–83ᵛ Seneca, *De beneficiis.*
> *fols. 83ᵛ–85 Seneca, *De remediis fortuitorum.*

fols. 85–87   Cicero, Tusculans.
fols. 87–89ᵛ   Cicero, orations.
fol. 89ᵛ   Cicero, Verrine orations.
fol. 90   Martin of Braga, *Formula honestae vitae.*
fols. 90–91   Apuleius, *De deo Socratis*, [*Asclepius, De Platone, De mundo*].
fol. 91–92ᵛ   Aulus Gellius.
fol. 92ᵛ–93   *Querolus.*
fol. 93   Censorinus, *De die natali.*
fols. 93–94ᵛ   Macrobius, *Saturnalia*; with *Versus Ciceronis.*
fols. 94ᵛ–96ᵛ   *Proverbia philosophorum.*
fols. 96ᵛ–97   [*Sententiae philosophorum.*]
fol. 97   *Praecepta Pithagore.*
fol. 97   *Ænigmata Aristotilis.*
fols. 97–99ᵛ   Quintilian, *Declamationes.*
fols. 99ᵛ–100ᵛ   Quintus Curtius, *Historiae Alexandri*; extracts, includ-
                  ing the *Oratio Scytharum.* Beg. *Ingenium plerumque et
                  naturam fortuna corrumpit* . . ., ends . . . *moribus quam
                  insignibus estimari.*
*fol. 101   Jerome, *De viris illustribus* c. 80, Methodius.
*fols. 101–105   Methodius, *De consummatione seculi.*
*fols. 105ᵛ–106   Ivo of Chartres, ep. 63, beg. *Post multam oblivionem* . . .

Written in three hands in two columns of 46–50 lines each. Ruled with
lead point. Quires of 4 leaves signed vi, vii, viii, viiii, x, xxii, xxv, mutilated
quire of 3 leaves, quire of 4 leaves unsigned, xxviii, xxviiii, xxx, quire of
4 leaves signed xxxii; inserts on slips of parchment. 230 × 153 mm. Plain
initials without tendrils. fol. 40ᵛ (s. XIII–XIV), *Universis presentes litteras
visuris, dominus Guillelmus miles de Villañ.* Fol. 106ᵛ, medieval ex libris note
erased: *Iste* . . . Fol. i, table of contents by Alexander Petau. Manuscript
seen.

V   Vatican City, Bibl. Apostolica, Vat. lat. 3087 (s. XIII²; S. France or
    Italy). *Florilegium Angelicum.*

I. *fols. 1–18ᵛ   Moral exempla drawn largely from Scripture and
                     arranged by subject (*De caritate, De patientia, De
                     dilectione seu amore* . . .). Table of chapters, f. 1. Text,
                     f. 1ᵛ, beg. *De caritate. Dominus dicit in evangelio,
                     Maiorem caritatem nemo habet* . . ., ends . . . *ut non
                     cum hoc mundo damnemur cui est honor et gloria in
                     secula seculorum amen.*
    *fols. 19–22ᵛ   Sixteen *carmina* in honour of the Virgin, among which
                     are two by Adam of St. Victor and one by Peter
                     Abelard.
    fols. 23–27   Macrobius, *Saturnalia*; with *Versus Ciceronis.*
    fols. 27–31   *Proverbia philosophorum.*
    fols. 31–33   Apuleius, *De deo Socratis*, [*Asclepius, De Platone, De
                     mundo*].
    fols. 33–36ᵛ   Pliny, epistles.

fols. 36ᵛ–41ᵛ　Cicero, orations.
fols. 41ᵛ–48　Sidonius, epistles.
fols. 48–51　Seneca, *De beneficiis.*
fols. 51–55　Seneca, *Epistulae ad Lucilium.*
fols. 55–56　*Sententiae philosophorum.*
fol. 56　*Praecepta Pithagorae.*
fol. 56ʳᵛ　*Ænigmata Aristotilis.*
fols. 56ᵛ–60　Cicero, Tusculans.
fols. 60–63ᵛ　Aulus Gellius.
fol. 63ᵛ　Cicero, Verrine orations.
fols. 63ᵛ–67ᵛ　Ennodius.
fols. 67ᵛ–68　Martin of Braga, *Formula honestae vitae.*
fol. 68　[*Querolus*].
fol. 68　Censorinus, *De die natali.*
fol. 68ʳᵛ　Quintus Curtius, *Oratio Scytharum.*
*II　fols. 69–85　Seneca, *De beneficiis*; extracts.
fols. 85–87　Martin of Braga, *Formula honestae vitae.*
fols. 87–88ᵛ　Seneca, *De remediis fortuitorum.*
fols. 88ᵛ–89ᵛ　Ps.-Seneca, *De moribus.*
fols. 89ᵛ–90ᵛ　Seneca, *De clementia*; extracts.
fols. 90ᵛ–91ᵛ　Seneca, *Epistulae ad Lucilium*; extracts.
fol. 92ʳᵛ　Johannes Belvantessis, *Summa grammaticalis.* Beg. *Multis modis dicitur sciencia, una plurimum . . .*; followed by a song in praise of the Virgin, beg. *Salve mater salvatoris, missus Gabriel de celis . . .*
fol. 93　table of contents, ex-libris note, erased.

In two parts which were together soon after pt. I was completed, since a hand of pt. I reappears in a song added to pt. II, fol. 92ᵛ.

I. Written by three hands: (1) fols. 1–18ᵛ, (2) fols. 19–22ᵛ, (3) fols. 23–68ᵛ, in long lines, 35 per page. Ruled with lead point. 1⁶, 2–3⁵, 4–5⁴, 6–7⁵; catchwords. 222 × 158 mm (168 × 100).

II. fols. 69–91ᵛ, s. XIII¹, France; fol. 92ʳᵛ, s. XIII/XIV. Manuscript seen.

Richard de Fournival, *Bib8lionomia,* item 84.

Taken from L. Delisle, *Le Cabinet des manuscrits de la Bibliothèque nationale,* ii (Paris, 1874), p. 529.

Censorini exceptiones florum ex operibus quorumdam sanctorum et phylosophorum moralium: primo quidem de libro Machrobii Saturnariorum vel Saturnarium. Secundo proverbia quorumdam philosophorum. Tercio de epystolis beati Jheronimi. Quarto de libro Epuleii Madaurensis de Deo Socratis. Quinto de epystolis Plinii secundi. Sexto de harenga Tullii pridie quam in exilium iret. Septimo cum senatui gratias egit. Octavo de epystolis Sidonii. Nono de libro Senece de beneficiis. Decimo de epystolis eiusdem ad Lucilium. Undecimo sententie quorumdam philosophorum. Duodecimo de libro Tullii Tusculanarum. Tercio decimo de libro Agellii noctium Atticarum. Quarto decimo de comedia Plauti que dicitur Allularia. In uno volumine cuius signum est littera [K].

5

The Influence of the Concepts of Ordinatio *and* Compilatio *on the Development of the Book*[1]

IT is a truism of palaeography that most works copied in and before the twelfth century were better organized in copies produced in the thirteenth century, and even better organized in those produced in the fourteenth. During the course of the twelfth century the monastic culture gave way to the culture of the schools. There were new kinds of books—a more technical literature—and new kinds of readers. The monastic *lectio* was a spiritual exercise which involved steady reading to oneself, interspersed by prayer, and pausing for rumination on the text as a basis for *meditatio*.[2] The scholastic *lectio* was a process of study which involved a more ratiocinative scrutiny of the text and consultation for reference purposes.[3] The two kinds of reading required different kinds of presentation of the texts, and this is reflected in changes in features of layout and in the provision of apparatus for the academic reader. For this reason it seems to me that from the twelfth century onwards developments in the *mise-en-page* of texts were bound up with developments in methods of scholarship

---

[1] I am grateful to Dr. N. R. Ker, Mr. A. J. Piper, and Dr. B. Smalley who read various drafts of this paper and who contributed valuable criticisms and suggested various references. I am also grateful to my pupil A. J. Minnis for valuable discussion. References innocently suggested by Dr. R. W. Hunt have also found their way into this paper. The errors, omissions, and the views expressed are entirely my own.

[2] For a contemporary description of the monastic *lectio* see the account given in the *Life of Christina of Markyate*, ed. C. H. Talbot (Oxford, 1959), pp. 92–3, of Christina's reading of the psalter when she finally achieved religious solitude. For a modern account see J. Leclercq, *The Love of Learning and the Desire for God* (New York, 1961), pp. 19 and 89.

[3] For a contemporary description of the scholastic *lectio* see the prologue to Abelard's *Sic et Non* (printed *P.L.* clxxviii. 1339); cf. M.-D. Chenu, *Introduction à l'étude de S. Thomas d'Aquin* (Paris, 1954), pp. 118–19.

and changes in attitude to study. What follows is speculation on the nature of some of the influences at work, and an attempt with the aid of a few illustrations to explain how some of the changes took place in the physical appearance of books.

In the twelfth century the principal apparatus for the academic reader was the gloss, and the principal developments in the *mise-en-page* of the book in the twelfth century centred on the presentation of the gloss. Inherited material—the *auctoritates*[1]—was organized in such a way as to make it accessible alongside the text to be studied. During the course of the twelfth century the content of the gloss to the Bible became stabilized and producers of books introduced refinements of presentation culminating in the layout of copies of what are probably the most highly developed of glossed books, the commentaries of Peter Lombard on the Psalter and the Pauline Epistles (cf. pl. IX). The whole process of indicating text, commentary, and sources was incorporated into the design of the page, presumably by a process of careful alignment worked out beforehand in the exemplar. The full text of the Psalter or Epistles was disposed in a larger, more formal version of twelfth-century script in conveniently sited columns, and the size of the columns was determined by the length of the commentary on that particular part of the text. In the commentary itself the *lemmata* were underlined in red. Each of the *auctores* quoted in the commentary was identified by name in the margin, again in red, and the extent of the quotation was also marked. As the final refinement each of the *auctores* was given a symbol consisting of dots or lines and dots which was placed both against the name in the margin, and against the beginning of the *auctoritas* or quotation in the body of the commentary.[2] The practice of indicating sources in the margin derived from earlier manuscripts[3] is here systemat-

---

[1] *Auctoritates* were texts rather than persons. They are *sententiae* or ideas excerpted from their immediate context in a work and divorced from the wider context of the writings of an *auctor*. 'Auctoritas: id est sententia digna imitatione' (Hugutius Pisanus, *Magnae deriuationes*, s.v. *augeo*). Cf. Chenu, op. cit., pp. 109–13.

[2] On the system of indicating sources and the use of *puncti*, see *Petri Lombardi Sententiae in IV libris distinctae, Spicilegium Bonaventurianum*, iv (Rome, 1971), prolegomena, 68* and 138*.

[3] For illustrations of the practice in 9th-century manuscripts see New Palaeographical Society, *Facsimiles of Ancient MSS &c*, 1st ser. (London, 1903–12), pl. 236 of Cambridge, Pembroke Coll., MS. 308 (given to St. Remi by Archbishop Hincmar, 845–82); and 2nd ser. (London, 1913–30), pl. 120 of Paris B.N. MS. lat. 9575, dated 811.

ized, and becomes the ancestor of the modern scholarly apparatus of footnotes.

The *mise-en-page* of such copies of the Lombard's commentaries is one of the major achievements of twelfth-century book production. It reflects in practical and visual terms a dominant attitude to the ordering of studies found in the first half of the twelfth century, and expressed in statements like the following from the prologue to the *De sacramentis* of Hugh of St. Victor: 'omnes artes naturales divinae scientiae famulantur, et inferior sapientia recte ordinata ad superiorem conducit.'[1] In the commentary each phrase of scripture was expounded in the order in which it occurred in the Bible text. The *ordo* followed in the gloss was the *ordo narracionis* of the text, and within this framework the *auctoritates* were subordinated to the study of the sacred page. The Bible text was sufficiently familiar to the reader so that no further ostensible guide to the arrangement of the material was required, and in such circumstances no further developments were stimulated.

The opportunity for further developments in the presentation of texts came as a result of the drive to reorganize inherited material in a new, systematic way, to make *auctoritates* not only accessible but accessible in terms of new ways of thinking. By the mid twelfth century scholasticism had developed new techniques for the handling of *auctoritates*, which were employed in texts like the *Quatuor libri sententiarum* of Peter Lombard and the *Concordia discordantium canonum* of Gratian. To think became a craft. The application of scholastic method demanded closer scrutiny of the arguments, and the reorganization of the material according to topics produced the need for more ostensible guides to the new organization to facilitate reference. The shape of *mises-en-page* to come is foreshadowed in the experiments seen in early copies of the *Sentences*, and in the apparatus introduced into copies of Gratian in the second half of the twelfth century.

In early copies of the *Sentences* (like that in pl. X, produced before 1169) not only are the sources indicated in red in the margin, as in the glossed books, but there are also some attempts to indicate and emphasize the organization of the subject-matter inherent in the text, a groping towards the clearer definition of what came to be known as the *ordinatio* of the work. Rubrics at the

[1] *De sacramentis Christianae fidei*, prol. cap vi (printed *P.L.* clxxvi. 185).

beginning of each chapter define the topic under discussion, but in this early copy there are also other rubrics placed in the margin at certain points, sub-headings like 'prima causa', 'secunda', 'tercia', 'obiectio', 'responsio', which serve to identify stages in the argument within the chapter, and sometimes even within a quotation from one of the sources. Whether Peter Lombard was himself responsible for all these rubrics[1] or whether some were added by commentators[2] is not important in the context of my argument. The *ad hoc* nature of these devices in these early surviving copies[3] demonstrates first that readers felt the need for more ostensible help in finding their way about in a highly sophisticated and technical argument, and secondly that the producers of books had not yet developed a recognized procedure for coping with this problem.

Twelfth-century copies of Gratian illustrate how the commentators set about producing an apparatus designed to make the work easier to consult. Gratian appears to have divided his work into three parts, and the second (dealing with judgements) into *causae*.[4] In the surviving twelfth-century manuscripts each of these parts was indicated by a number carried in a running-title.[5] By the second half of the twelfth century the first and last parts had been further divided by commentators into *distinctiones*.[6] Each of these new subdivisions was numbered and to facilitate reference the numbers were inserted in the margin at the appropriate point. Within the text the *dicta* of Gratian were distinguished from the

---

[1] Cf. I. Brady, 'The Rubrics of Peter Lombard's Sentences', *Pier Lombardo*, vi (1962), 5–25; and the prolegomena to the edition of the *Sentences* previously cited, pp. 138*–41*.

[2] Cf. *Opera omnia S. Bonaventurae* (Quaracchi edn.), i (1882), lxxxiii.

[3] In Bristol, City Libr., MS. 4, a copy of the *Sentences* made in the second half of the 12th century, the rubrics (including those at the beginning of each chapter) were omitted by the copyist. He has subsequently inserted them all in the margins. See the illustration (of II, cap. 23–4) in N. Mathews, *Early Printed Books and MSS in the City Reference Library Bristol* (Bristol, 1899), p. 65 and pl. 11. A comparable practice occurs in a late-12th-century copy of Langton's commentary on the Pentateuch (Bodleian Libr., MS. Canon. Pat. Lat. 186) in which contemporary hands have entered the headings 'moraliter', 'allegorice', and 'mystice' in the margins to indicate the stages in the commentary.

[4] Cf. A. van Hove, *Prolegomena* (Antwerp, 1945), 344.

[5] For a typical first page see R. A. B. Mynors, *Durham Cathedral Manuscripts to the End of the Twelfth Century* (Oxford, 1939), pl. 47 (no. 134).

[6] F. Gillman, 'Rührt die Distinktioneneinteilung des ersten und des dritten Dekretteils von Gratian selbst her?' *Archiv für katholisches Kirchenrecht*, cxii (1932), 504–33.

texts of the *auctoritates* by means of *paragraphi*.[1] Also by the second half of the twelfth century the work was preceded by a *materia operis* which acted as a kind of synoptic introduction and which indicated the topics dealt with in each section.[2] Such copies demonstrate the value of ostensible guides in such a work, and indicate that the academic reader was becoming more demanding.

The turning-point in the history of the presentation of a text for the academic reader came in the thirteenth century when the rediscovered Aristotelian logic and the consequent interest in more rigorous philosophical procedures entailed the adoption of principles which demanded a more precise method of dissecting and defining human knowledge. The thirteenth-century position is spelt out in the *Summa* attributed to Alexander of Hales: '. . . modus definitivus debet esse, divisivus, collectivus, et talis modus debet esse in humanis scientiis, quia apprehensio veritatis secundum humanam rationem explicatur per divisiones, definitiones, et ratiocinationes.'[3] The change from the early twelfth-century attitude is reflected in general discussions about the structure of knowledge and the subordination of the sciences to the study of theology, and can be seen by comparing the statement from Hugh of St. Victor quoted above[4] with the following statement by Bonaventura: 'Sunt ergo quatuor genera scripturarum, circa quae oportet ordinate procedere et exerceri. Primi libri sunt sacrae scripturae, secundi libri sunt originalia sanctorum, tertii sententiae magistrorum, quarti doctrinarum mundialium sive philosophorum.'[5] Bonaventura takes a comparable view of the hierarchy of studies, but he specifies the studies he is referring to—he is more *definitivus*. However, what is important is the shift of

---

[1] *Paragraphi* occur in the earliest surviving copy in England (Cambridge, Gonville and Caius Coll., MS. 6), and they can be seen in the plates of the late-12th-century Danzig MS. from Bologna reproduced in *Studia Gratiana*, i (1953), tavv. xx, xxvii, and xxxv. The tradition that the practice goes back to Gratian himself has been questioned by A. Vetulani, 'Le Décret de Gratien et les premiers décrétistes', *Studia Gratiana*, vii (1959), 318–19.

[2] The text (beginning *In prima parte agitur*) has been printed in *Bibliotheca Casinensis*, ii (1875), 171–96. See J. Rambaud-Buhot, 'L'Étude des manuscrits du Décret de Gratien', *Studia Gratiana*, i (1953), 124. On the term *materia* see H. Kantorowicz, *Studies in the Glossators of the Roman Law* (Cambridge, 1938), p. 38.

[3] *Summa theologiae* (Quaracchi edn., 1924), Tractatus introductorius, quaestio i, art. 1, cap. 4, ad secundum.

[4] p. 117.

[5] *Collatio xix in Hexaemeron*, in *Opera* (Quaracchi edn.), v (1891), 421.

emphasis. Whereas Hugh's use of the terms 'recte ordinata' emphasizes the ordering of studies within the structure of knowledge, Bonaventura's use of the terms 'ordinate procedere et exerceri' emphasizes the need to recognize the principles of order inherent in each branch of knowledge and to follow the appropriate procedure. The procedure to be followed is dictated by the nature of the subject to be studied: 'Ordo diversimode traditur a diversis, sed oportet ordinate procedere ne de primo faciant posterius.'[1] Thirteenth-century scholars saw different fields of study as autonomous branches of knowledge, each with its own appropriate mode of procedure, and they insisted upon organization and method in the various procedures.[2]

With the recognition of the principle that different kinds of *ordo* were appropriate in different kinds of study, the organization of an individual work came under closer scrutiny. For the first time scholars formulated a definition which included the disposition of material within a text into books and chapters. This is found in commentaries in which the work of an author, and in particular his way of handling material, was defined more precisely according to a revised technical vocabulary based on the Aristotelian notion of the four causes. In Jordan of Saxony's commentary on *Priscianus minor* (*c*. 1220) Priscian's mode of procedure and the form in which his work was arranged were described for the first time as two aspects of a single thing, the formal cause:

> Causa formalis huius scientie est forma tractandi et forma tractatus. Forma tractandi est modus agendi qui est principaliter diffinitivus, divisivus, probativus, improbativus et exemplorum suppositivus; forma tractatus est forma rei tradite que consistit in separatione librorum et capitulorum et ordine eorundem.[3]

The *forma tractandi* is here reduced to the terms of the *modus definitivus*, and the *forma tractatus*—the disposition of the material into books and chapters—is defined as the physical manifestation of that mode of procedure. In Kilwardby's *Notule super Priscianum minorem* the relationship between mode of procedure and disposi-

---

[1] *Opera*, v, 421.

[2] Cf. S. Thomas Aquinas, *Summa theologiae*, I, Quaestio i, art. 1, ad secundum.

[3] Quoted from Leipzig Univ. Libr. MS. lat. 1291 by M. Grabmann, *Mittelalterliches Geistesleben*, iii (Munich, 1956), 234. On Jordan as the first commentator to employ this kind of terminology see J. Pinborg, *Die Entwicklung der Sprachtheorie im Mittelalter*, Beiträge, xlii (1967), 25.

tion of material is maintained, but the term *ordinatio* is introduced
to convey the notion described by Jordan of Saxony as *forma
tractatus*: 'Causa formalis consistit in modo agendi et in ordinatione partium doctrine.'[1] A generation later Nicholas of Paris
tidied up the terminology in his commentary on Aristotle's
Perihermeneias: '. . . causa formalis tractatus que est ordinatio
librorum partialium et capitulorum.'[2] Academic discussion bent
on more precise definition focused on the ostensible arrangement
of a work and formulated the concept of *ordinatio*, thus providing
a theoretical foundation for attempts to meet the readers' practical
needs.

In such circumstances the structure of reasoning came to be
reflected in the physical appearance of books. There was more
ostensible 'packaging' of the text, and in copies of the works of
thirteenth-century writers the *ordinatio* of the work was more
clearly defined. The rubricator inserted the number of the relevant
quaestio, *distinctio*, or chapter in the margin at the appropriate
point, and the stages in the argument were carefully indicated by
means of *litterae notabiliores* and paraph marks. *Lemmata* were
underlined. The scribes would mark the divisions by inserting
one or two parallel diagonal lines as a guide to the rubricators. A
typical *mise-en-page* of the text of a commentary on the *Sentences*
would follow something like the following pattern:

Ad intelligentiam huius partis duo principaliter queruntur ¶ primo
. . . ¶ secundo. . . ¶ circa primum queruntur tria ¶ primo. . . ¶ secundo
. . . ¶ tercio . . . Circa primum . . . ¶ item . . . ¶ item . . . ¶ contra . . .
¶ contra . . . ¶ responsio . . .

and so on (pl. XI).[3] Moreover, new aids to reference were introduced which helped to identify the disposition of the material. In

---

[1] Quoted from Oxford, C.C.C. MS. 119, and Paris B.N. MS. lat. 16221 by
R. W. Hunt, 'The Introductions to the "Artes" in the Twelfth Century', *Studia
mediaevalia in honorem R. J. Martin* (Bruges, 1948), p. 107. Compare the use of
similar terminology in the commentary of Elias Brunetti on the *Topics* of
Aristotle (1248–56) printed by Grabmann, *Mittelalterliches Geistesleben*, iii. 147.

[2] Quoted from Munich Clm. 14460 by B. Sandkühler, *Die frühen Dante-
kommentare und ihr Verhältnis zur mittelalterlichen Kommentartradition*, Münchener romantische Arbeiten, xix (Munich, 1967), 41.

[3] My examination of a random selection of copies of works by Alexander of
Hales, William of Auxerre, and Bonaventura surviving in French and English
libraries supports the impression given in J. Destrez, *La Pecia dans les manuscrits universitaires du XIIIe et du XIVe siècle* (Paris, 1935), p. 46 and plates, that
the practice seems to have become standard by the mid 13th century.

addition to marginal numbers thirteenth-century scribes and rubricators developed and extended the use of running-titles, and introduced the analytic table of contents as a guide to the *ordinatio* and to facilitate the readers' access to component parts of a work.

The use of running-titles was an ancient practice[1] which had been somewhat neglected, perhaps because in the process of the monastic *lectio* they had become redundant. In the twelfth century we find them used again, particularly in the systematically arranged collections of canon law, like the *Panormia* of Ivo of Chartres,[2] and later in copies of Gratian.[3] But in the first half of the twelfth century they were used somewhat *ad hoc*, and neither the form nor the placing of the running-titles was consistent. During the thirteenth century the potential of running-titles was explored and realized. They were used frequently in all kinds of texts, and were often made conspicuous by the use of the colours red and blue, and occasionally emphasized further by the addition of flourishes. In Reims MS. 864 (s. XIII), a copy of the *Libri naturales* of Aristotle, each letter of the running-titles has been adorned with flourishes.[4] The form of the titles became more consistent, they became more informative and were placed in such a way that they gave a more precise indication of the beginning of a new division of the text. In early copies of the *summae* of Thomas Aquinas (like Troyes MS. 982, s. XIII ex.) the running-titles consist not merely of the number but also the *titulus* of each *quaestio*, and whenever a new division occurs in the text the new running-title is carefully placed over the appropriate column (cf. pl. XVI). In plate XI, a copy of a commentary on the *Sentences*, the roman numeral in the centre of the top margin indicates the number of the book. The abbreviated title for *Distinctio* is placed over the first column, and the number of the *Distinctio* is placed over the second column,

---

[1] See E. A. Lowe, *Palaeographical Papers*, i (Oxford, 1972), 199.

[2] In Troyes MS. 480, an early-12th-century copy of the *Panormia*, the running-titles lack consistency. Occasionally the number of the division is written out in full (e.g. 'secunda pars'), sometimes either word or both words have been abbreviated, and sometimes the words have been replaced by a number. Sometimes the running-titles occur on the recto only, sometimes (e.g. at the beginning of a new division) on both pages of the opening. The running-titles cease after the beginning of the last division. In Troyes MS. 1519, a late-12th-century copy of the same work, the running-titles have been written out in full on the recto of the first dozen or so leaves of the text, after which a numeral has been used consistently throughout the rest of the volume.

[3] See above, p. 118.

[4] *Aristoteles Latinus, Codices*, i (Rome, 1938), no. 735.

thus indicating that both columns contain the commentary on this section of the text.

The analytical table of contents listed the major topics discussed, in the order in which they occurred in the text. The placing of chapter-headings before each book of the text was an ancient practice;[1] but in the thirteenth century they were brought together in one place and arranged in tabular form. The scheme of the table was often emphasized by the use of red ink for the major headings and black for the subheadings as in Troyes MS. 820, a copy of Bonaventura on the *Sentences*. In many thirteenth-century manuscripts the table of contents occurs in a separate booklet which has been added to the beginning or end of a book some time after it had been written,[2] but by the beginning of the fourteenth century the table was copied by the scribe as part of the book, as in Troyes MSS. 161, 187, and 624, copies of the *Summa Theologiae* of Thomas Aquinas. In Reims MS. 680, a thirteenth-century copy of Gratian preceded by the usual *materia* or synoptic introduction, an analytical table of contents has been added at the end and headed 'Incipit ordinatio vera omnium capitulorum et palearum et paragraphum in libro decretorum.' The twelfth-century apparatus has been reinforced by a more up-to-date guide to Gratian's *ordinatio*.

The new interest in the organization and procedure within an individual work—the concern to study an argument from beginning to end, which led to the formulation of the concept of *ordinatio*—also stimulated a desire to see the *auctoritates*, the individual *sententiae*, in their full context. There was a return to the *originalia*, the works of the *auctores in toto*.[3] New copies were made, fat volumes embracing as many as possible of the writings of a single *auctor*, and constructed from independent 'booklets' or units, each of which contained a complete long work or a group of shorter works. Precedent for such collections was perhaps provided by the copies of the *Corpus vetustius* of Aristotle's *Libri naturales* which

---

[1] It occurs, for example, in the late-6th-century copy of Gregory the Great's *Cura pastoralis*, copied at Rome in the lifetime of the author, and now Troyes MS. 504 (*C.L.A.* 838). Cf. B. Bischoff, *Mittelalterliche Studien*, ii (Stuttgart, 1967), 319.

[2] For example as in Laon MS. 141, Nijmegen, Univ. Lib. MS. 61, and Troyes MS. 982.

[3] Cf. J. de Ghellinck, '"Originale" et "Originalia"', *Bulletin Du Cange*, xiv (1939), 95.

circulated in the schools by the mid thirteenth century.[1] The necessary compression of a large work into a 'booklet' was achieved by the adoption of very small handwriting and the copious use of abbreviations. The process can be illustrated from manuscripts containing the works of Augustine. Oxford, Bodleian Library, MS. Bodley 568 comprises eight booklets: one containing the *De trinitate* with its list of capitula, Epistle 174, and the relevant passages from the *Retractationes*; another booklet containing the *Super Genesim* together with a list of the *quaestiones* and the relevant passages from the *Retractationes*; a third booklet containing the whole of the *Retractationes*, and five booklets containing shorter works. Gonville and Caius College, Cambridge, MS. 108 comprises four booklets: one containing the *Enchiridion* and Epistle 137, another containing the *De doctrina Christiana* together with sixteen of Augustine's letters, a third containing the *Super Genesim* and other works, and a fourth containing the *De trinitate*.[2] In such volumes running-titles assume greater importance, and in copies of the *Libri naturales* of Aristotle (for example, Bordeaux MS. 421, Cambridge, University Library, MS. Ee. 2. 31, and Reims MS. 864)[3] elaborate decorated or historiated initials help the reader to locate the different works in the corpus.

However, earlier texts had not been written according to thirteenth-century principles, therefore thirteenth-century readers required thirteenth-century guides to the *ordinatio*. More often than not this involved a redefinition of the *ordinatio* to make it accessible to the reader in thirteenth-century terms. Although earlier divisions (like the chapter-headings or *Breviculi* to the *De civitate Dei* and the *De trinitate* of Augustine)[4] were resurrected, scholars also produced independent means of access in accordance

---

[1] Cf. G. Lacombe in *Aristoteles Latinus, Codices*, i. 49; Rashdall's *Universities of Europe in the Middle Ages*, ed. F. M. Powicke and A. B. Emden (Oxford, 1936), i. 442–3, iii. 480–2.

[2] Further examples of 13th- and 14th-century collections of works by Augustine which were built up in this way include Cambridge, Corpus Christi Coll., MS. 34, Gonville and Caius Coll., MS. 100, Oxford, Merton Coll., MS. 55, and Troyes MS. 860.

[3] *Aristoteles Latinus, Codices*, i, nos. 453, 260, and 735.

[4] The *breviculi* are printed in *De civitate Dei* ed. B. Dombart and A. Kalb, Corpus Christianorum (Series Latina), xlvii-xlviii (1955); and *De trinitate* ed. W. J. Mountain, Corpus Christianorum, l (1968). Cf. C. Lambot, 'Lettre inédite de S. Augustin relative au *De Civitate Dei*', *Revue Bénédictine*, li (1939), 109–21; H.- I. Marrou, 'La Division en chapitres des livres de la cité de Dieu', *Mélanges J. de Ghellinck* (1951), pp. 235–49; R. W. Hunt, 'Manuscripts containing the

with new ways of thinking. Grosseteste produced a set of *tituli* to the *Ethics* of Aristotle.[1] Robert Kilwardby produced a series of synopses of works of the Fathers variously called *intenciones*, *capitula*, or *conclusiones*.[2] They kept to the order of the existing *ordinatio* but they divided each chapter into smaller sections and analysed and summarized the contents of each section. The summaries were designed to bring out the distinctive qualities of each book by dividing up the material according to a mode of procedure which was in line with current notions of the dissection of knowledge. As Kilwardby himself said in another context, 'ordinatio partium doctrine in divisione patebit'.[3] In addition to these synopses certain commentaries were also influential. Whereas commentators on the Bible depended on existing divisions of the text, commentators on other texts had to divide and subdivide the text in order to expound it. Some commentators, like Averroes on Aristotle and Alexander of Hales on the *Sentences*, were regarded with special respect and their divisions of the texts came to be regarded as standard.[4]

Once an apparatus has been produced for a text it is inevitable that copies of that text will be produced or adapted for use alongside the apparatus. New divisions were introduced into old books. The precedent was undoubtedly provided by the 'Parisian' division of the Bible into standard chapters for convenience of reference. Troyes MS. 1046 indicates that this was known in France in 1203, but the commentaries of Peter Comestor and Peter the Chanter, as well as those of Langton, indicate that it had its predecessors.[5] In the thirteenth century the scholars of St.

Indexing Symbols of Robert Grosseteste', *Bodl. L.R.* iv (1953), 241–55; idem, 'Chapter Headings of Augustine *De Trinitate* ascribed to Adam Marsh', *Bodl. L.R.* v (1954), 63.

[1] Cf. *Robert Grosseteste, Scholar and Bishop*, ed. D. A. Callus (Oxford, 1955), p. 64.

[2] Cf. D. A. Callus, 'The "Tabulae super Originalia Patrum" of Robert Kilwardby O.P.', *Studia mediaevalia in honorem R. J. Martin* (Bruges, 1948), pp. 243–70; idem, *Dominican Studies*, ii (1949), 38–45; idem, 'The Contribution to the Study of the Fathers made by the Thirteenth-Century Oxford Schools', *Journal of Ecclesiastical History*, v (1954), 139–48.

[3] Quoted by R. W. Hunt, 'Introductions to the "Artes" in the Twelfth Century', p. 107.

[4] On the influence of Alexander of Hales's commentary on the division of the text of the *Sentences* see I. Brady, 'The *Distinctiones* of Lombard's Book of Sentences and Alexander of Hales', *Franciscan Studies*, xxv (1965), 90.

[5] B. Smalley, *The Study of the Bible in the Middle Ages*, 2nd edn. (Oxford, 1952), pp. 222 ff.

Jacques produced a *Concordantia*, and further subdivided the chapters of the Bible into equal parts indicated by letters of the alphabet for use alongside this reference work.[1] However, this subdivision is rarely found in manuscripts: the principle on which it was based was simple enough to be applied *ad hoc* by readers who used the concordance alongside an unmarked text.[2] In copies of the *Sentences* the Lombard's own division of the text into chapters was supplemented by a new division into *distinctiones*, a practice attributed to the influence of the commentary of Alexander of Hales.[3] In the earliest copies (cf. pl. X) these have been inserted by thirteenth- and fourteenth-century hands, often in arabic numerals.[4] Similar developments can be seen in copies of Aristotle. Taking the *De anima* as an example, Avranches MS. 221 (s. XII) is free of apparatus and no divisions have been inserted. In Douai MS. 698 (s. XIII) the text has been divided into smaller units by means of layers of paraphs inserted by successive rubricators and readers. In Cambridge, University Library, MS. Ee. 2. 31 (s. XIII–XIV) paraphs inserted in the text are accompanied in the margin by numbers preceded by the word 'commentum', which relate the text to sections of the commentary of Averroes.[5] In copies of the Fathers we find various systems of chapter division,[6] and numerous copies have been provided with marginal numbers which relate to the various kinds of apparatus prepared by Robert Kilwardby.[7] In some copies we find line numbers and column numbers.[8] In Keble College, Oxford, MS. 26 (cf. pl. XIII), a copy of

---

[1] Cf. the article by E. Mangenot, *Dictionnaire de la Bible*, s.v. *Concordances.*

[2] In Oxford, Oriel Coll. MS. 77, for example, it is used in the first ten folios only.   [3] I. Brady, loc. cit.

[4] For example, as in Bodleian Libr. MSS. Barlow 15 and Laud Misc. 695 and 746.

[5] *Aristoteles Latinus, Codices*, i, nos. 401, 479, and 260. For an illustration of the practice of numbering sections of the commentaries see the reproduction from Cesena, Bibl. Malatestiana, Cod. lato destro xxiii. 6 (containing commentaries by Avicenna, Averroes, and Albertus Magnus, copied by Bartholomaeus de Ledula at Évreux and Paris in 1320–1) in New Palaeographical Society *Facsimiles*, 2nd ser., pl. 21.

[6] See the references cited above, p. 124 n. 4; p. 125 nn. 1 and 2; and N. R. Ker, 'The English Manuscripts of the *Moralia* of Gregory the Great', *Kunsthistorische Forschungen Otto Pächt zu Ehren*, ed. A. Rosenauer and G. Weber (Salzburg, 1973), p. 82.

[7] See below, p. 132 n. 1 and pl. XVI.

[8] Continental scholars have stated that all MSS. containing numbering of lines were certainly written in England, and probably in Oxford; see P. Lehmann, *Erforschung des Mittelalters*, iii (Stuttgart, 1960), 58.

the *Sentences* produced in the second half of the thirteenth century, the *distinctio* numbers have been furnished by the rubricator, and a professional scribe has added the commentary of Peter of Tarentaise. In at least one booklet of MS. Bodley 568 (Augustine, s. xiv) the Kilwardby numbers were copied by the scribe. In Peterhouse, Cambridge, MS. 56 (*De anima*, s. xiv) text and commentary were copied alternately by the scribe who numbered each section of the commentary. In each case the apparatus had been supplied before the book came into the hands of the reader.

Thirteenth-century scholars paid close attention to the development of good working tools based on scientific principles. The drive to make inherited material available in a condensed or more convenient form led them to recognize the desirability of imposing a new *ordinatio* on the material for this purpose. In the thirteenth century this led to the development of the notion of *compilatio* both as a form of writing and as a means of making material easily accessible. Compilation was not new (it is implicit in the work of Gratian and Peter Lombard);[1] what was new was the amount of thought and industry that was put into it, and the refinement that this thought and industry produced. The transmission of these refinements on to the page led to greater sophistication in the presentation of texts.

The role of the compiler was defined by Bonaventura alongside those of the scribe, the commentator, and the author:

. . . quadruplex est modus faciendi librum. Aliquis enim scribit aliena, nihil addendo vel mutando; et iste mere dicitur scriptor. Aliquis scribit aliena addendo, sed non de suo; et iste compilator dicitur. Aliquis scribit et aliena et sua, sed aliena tamquam principalia, et sua tamquam annexa ad evidentiam; et iste dicitur commentator non auctor. Aliquis scribit et sua et aliena, sed sua tamquam

---

[1] However, the term *compilator* was not applied to either writer in the 12th century. Gratian was seen by 12th-century commentators as a *compositor* (see the quotation in J. F. Schulte, *Die Geschichte der Quellen und Literatur des canonischen Rechts*, i (Stuttgart, 1875), p. 254). In the prologue to the *Sentences* Peter Lombard describes his literary activity as follows '. . . hoc volumen . . . compegimus ex testimoniis veritatis . . . in quatuor libros distinctum'. For another example of a 12th-century antecedent to the notion of *compilatio* see B. Smalley, *The Becket Conflict and the Schools* (Oxford, 1973), pp. 232–3. The title *Compilatio* in the new sense seems to have been applied first to the systematic collections of decretal letters produced at Bologna at the end of the 12th century, see van Hove, *Prolegomena*, 356.

principalia, aliena tamquam annexa ad confirmationem et debet dici auctor.[1]

The compiler adds no matter of his own by way of exposition (unlike the commentator) but compared with the scribe he is free to rearrange (*mutando*). What he imposed was a new *ordinatio* on the materials he extracted from others. In the words of Vincent of Beauvais: 'Nam ex meo pauca, vel quasi nulla addidi. Ipsorum igitur est auctoritate, nostrum autem sola partium ordinatione.'[2] The *compilatio* derives its value from the authenticity of the *auctoritates* employed, but it derives its usefulness from the *ordo* in which the *auctoritates* were arranged.[3]

Vincent of Beauvais elevated *compilatio* into a literary form[4] which served as a vehicle for others. He was the most ambitious of compilers, but he was also the most articulate about his mode of procedure, and for this reason he is a good example. In the *Speculum maius* the *ordinatio* operates at two levels: at one level it involves the adoption of a general scheme or structure in which the compiler can incorporate most conveniently the particular materials he has selected; at another level it involves the choice of a critical procedure by which the diverse *auctoritates* can be divided up and redeployed according to the nature of the subject-matter. At the higher level of *ordinatio* Vincent sought to enclose natural science, Christian doctrine, and the history and achievements of the human race within the general framework of a 'speculum', or mirror of the universe. The scheme of his book was

---

[1] *In primum librum sententiarum*, proem, quaest. iv. Printed *Opera* (Quaracchi ed.), i (1882), 14, col. 2.

[2] *Speculum maius*, apologia actoris (first recension), cap. iii (cf. edition pr. Venice 1591, General Prologue, cap. iv). All my quotations from Vincent of Beauvais are printed from the text of the first recension as preserved in Dijon MS. 568 (329). In the text printed at Venice 1591 the 'apologia actoris' is printed as a General Prologue but the version on which it is based is post-Vincent.

[3] The significance of the notion of *compilatio* in the preparation of books for use in the liturgy is suggested by the Dominican lectionary, and the incipit which occurs in the MS. Archetype (Santa Sabina, Rome, MS. xiv L 1, fol. 142) 'Iste est liber lectionarius ordinis fratrum predicatorum diligenter compilatus et correctus et punctatus et versiculatus.' Cf. L. E. Boyle, 'Dominican Lectionaries and Leo of Ostia's *Translatio S. Clementis*', *Archivum Fratrum Praedicatorum*, xxviii (1958), 371.

[4] The novelty of this literary form may be inferred from the fact that Hugh of St. Cher and Nicholas of Lyra describe II Maccabees as a *compilacio*, whereas Peter Comestor and Stephen Langton had previously described it as a *recapitulatio* of I Maccabees.

intended to mirror the scheme of reality. In working out his scheme, with commendable humility he followed the example of the Almighty ' . . . ut iuxta ordinem sacrae scripturae, primo de creatore, postea de creaturis, postea quoque de lapsu et reparatione hominis, deinde vero de rebus gestis iuxta seriem temporum suorum, et tandem etiam de iis que in fine temporum futura sunt, ordinate disserem.'[1] In the *Speculum naturale* he follows the chronological order of the six days of creation given in the Book of Genesis. At the lower level of *ordinatio* his procedure was influenced by the *modus definitivus* of his own age. Since, according to Alexander of Hales, '. . . apprehensio veritatis secundum humanam rationem explicatur per divisiones, definitiones, et ratiocinationes',[2] Vincent achieves the subordination of his material by dissecting his *auctoritates* and redeploying the diverse materials into discrete, self-contained chapters. In the *Speculum naturale* the third, fourth, and fifth days of creation give him the opportunity to review all that was then thought about minerals, vegetables, and animals. By dividing his work into books and chapters he is able to include as many as 171 chapters on herbs, 134 chapters on seeds and grains, 161 chapters on birds, and 46 chapters on fishes. In the *Speculum historiale* by the same process of redeployment into discrete units he includes such material as the account of the ancient gods, and the 'biographies of leading authors'[3] of antiquity accompanied by extracts from their works—all subordinated within the framework of universal history. In all, the *Speculum maius* is divided into 80 books and 9,885 chapters: it is the classic example of the principle of *compilatio* which emerged in the thirteenth century, 'divide and subordinate'.

The age of the compiler had arrived. The term *compilatio* becomes more frequent in the titles of works produced from the thirteenth century onwards,[4] although not all compilations were so called. The works range from the highly ambitious and sophisticated works of Vincent of Beauvais, Bartholomaeus Anglicus,

---

[1] *Speculum maius*, apologia actoris (Dijon MS.), cap. iii.

[2] See above, p. 119. On the possible dependence of Vincent on Alexander of Hales for some of his ideas see L. Lieser, *Vincenz von Beauvais als Kompilator und Philosoph* (Leipzig, 1928); and M. Gorce, 'La Somme théologique de Alexandre de Hales, est-elle authentique?', *The New Scholasticism*, v (1931), 62.

[3] B. Ullman, 'A Project for a New Edition of Vincent of Beauvais', *Speculum*, viii (1933), 321.

[4] P. Lehmann, 'Mittelalterliche Büchertitel', *Erforschung des Mittelalters*, v (Stuttgart, 1962), 21.

and Brunetto Latini on the one hand, to much humbler works like the Franciscan compilation in Durham, Cathedral Library, MS. B. IV. 19 on the other.[1] From the thirteenth century onwards all the compilations which follow this literary form operate by the same method: by disposing the material into clearly defined books and chapters, or other recognizable divisions based on the nature of the subject-matter, as in the following examples selected at random. John Ashenden begins his *Summa judicialis de accidentibus mundi*: 'Intencio mea in hoc libro est compilare sentencias astrologorum de accidencium prognosticacione que accidunt in hoc mundo ex corporum superiorium volubilitate.'[2] He arranges his *auctoritates* according to the nature of the material into two books, each of which is divided into twelve *distinctiones* which in turn are further subdivided into chapters. The *Compendium morale* of Roger of Waltham is compiled 'de virtuosis dictis et factis exemplaribus antiquorum' disposed in thirteen *rubricae* relating to government and political virtues.[3] Even the *florilegium*, the collection of excerpts from the Fathers, was made to conform to this new logical arrangement. The 'liber qui vocatur Flores Bernardi' is a collection of excerpts from a single *auctor* redistributed according to the nature of the subject-matter: '. . . quia de diversis rebus mentionem facit, secundum diversitatem rerum quibus loquitur libros in diversos distinguitur et decem librorum tractatibus concluditur.'[4] As a literary form *compilatio* influenced works in vernacular literature. The process of *ordinatio* at the higher level may be detected in the general schemes of the *Decamerone*, the *Confessio amantis*, *Les Cent Balades* and the incomplete *Canterbury Tales*. The *Canterbury Tales* is divided according to pilgrims rather than into books and chapters, yet the attitude of compiler seems to lie behind Chaucer's words in the General Prologue:

> Thogh that I pleynly speke in this mateere,
> To telle yow hir wordes and hir cheere,
> Ne thogh I speke hir wordes proprely.
> For this ye knowen al so wel as I,
> Whoso shal telle a tale after a man,
> He moot reherce as ny as evere he kan

---

[1] Cf. A. G. Little, *Liber Exemplorum ad usum praedicantium*, British Society of Franciscan Studies, i (1908).
[2] Bodleian Lib., MS. Digby 225.
[3] London, British Lib., MS. Royal 7 E. VII.
[4] Lincoln Coll., Oxford, MS. lat. 29.

Everich a word, if it be in his charge,
Al speke he never so rudeliche and large,
Or ellis he moot telle his tale untrewe
Or feyne thyng, or fynde wordes newe.[1]

In the context of the structure of the work these words seem to parallel those of Vincent of Beauvais, 'Nam ex meo pauca, vel quasi nulla addidi. Ipsorum igitur est auctoritate, nostrum autem sola partium ordinatione.'[2] In both cases the writer claims to be adding nothing of his own, but Vincent of Beauvais's scholarly reticence has become a constituent device of a literary form which enables a writer to disclaim responsibility for the statements he records.

The notion of *compilatio* not only gave rise to a sophisticated literary form but also promoted the development of a new kind of apparatus for use alongside existing texts: the *tabula* or alphabetical index. By employing a new *ordinatio* the *tabula* provided a means of access to subordinate topics within the existing *ordinatio* of a work. These were extracted and defined, thus being made available for use in the context of different arguments. The range of *tabulae* was wide: there were standard *tabulae* (like those prepared by Robert Kilwardby on the Fathers and the *Sentences*)[3] and those prepared by individuals for their own use. They were a most convenient form of quick reference work, and the practices of compiling and collecting *tabulae* became popular in the fourteenth and fifteenth centuries. In many manuscripts subordinate topics in the text were entered as sub-headings in the margins. Sometimes a *tabula* was bound up with the work it refers to: Oriel College, Oxford, MS. 43 (s. xiv in.) contains a copy of Fishacre on the *Sentences* accompanied by a comprehensive *tabula*, and in Merton College, Oxford, MS. 55 a *tabula* has been added to the booklet containing the *De civitate Dei*. More frequently we find collections of different *tabulae* bound together: Peterhouse, Cambridge, MS. 147 (s. xiii–xiv) comprises nine booklets containing *tabulae* on works by Augustine, Anselm, and Chrysostom; Durham, Cathedral Library, MSS. B. iii. 27 and 28 (s. xiv) are

---

[1] *The Canterbury Tales*, General Prologue, lines 727–36. Mr. A. J. Minnis has discussed applications of the notion of *compilatio* in vernacular literature in his forthcoming Ph.D. Thesis for the Queen's University of Belfast, 'Medieval Discussions of the Rôle of the Author.'

[2] See above, p. 128.

[3] Cf. Callus, 'The "Tabulae super Originalia Patrum" of Robert Kilwardby O.P.'

two collections of booklets which between them contain *tabulae* to works by Gregory, Anselm, Isidore, Augustine, and Bernard; Peterhouse, Cambridge, MS. 184 (s. xv) includes *tabulae* on Aristotle's *Libri naturales* and *Ethics*.

A *tabula* easily 'slides into' a more sophisticated compilation. It can be produced as a simple concordance related to copies of the *originalia* by a system of numbered divisions,[1] or less conveniently to a particular copy by references to folio and column.[2] The entries can be amplified into a series of definitions in alphabetical order, or further supported by extracts from the *originalia*, thus becoming independent of the copies of the texts. In the late twelfth century William de Montibus had recognized the value of alphabetical order as a means of making material easily available to the preacher, and had experimented with this order in his collections of *distinctiones* and in his *Proverbia*.[3] In the late thirteenth century a new kind of compilation begins to appear, influenced by the more sophisticated arrangement of the scholarly *tabulae* and promoted by the new accessibility of the material. The *Alphabetum auctoritatum* of Arnulph of Liège appeared in 1276, the *Tabula exemplorum secundum ordinem alphabeti* in 1277, the *Speculum laicorum* between 1279 and 1292, and the *Alphabetum narrationum* in 1296.[4] These were the first of many, and their content ranges from collections of *flores patrum* like the *Manipulus florum* of Thomas of Ireland[4] to the digests of Aristotle's *Libri naturales* and *Ethics*.[5] They represent one of the end products of the complex interaction between the applications of the notions of *ordinatio* and *compilatio* in the fourteenth and fifteenth centuries.

Because a *compilatio* is essentially a rearrangement, the new *ordinatio* employed by the compiler must be clearly defined and the new division of the material made obvious to the reader.

---

[1] See pl. XVI. A list of copies of the *De trinitate* with the Kilwardby numbers in the margins is given by R. W. Hunt in *Bodl. L.R.* v (1954), 68 n. 2.

[2] Cf. the example cited by N. R. Ker, 'The English Manuscripts of the *Moralia* of Gregory the Great', p. 83; and p. 136 n. 2 below.

[3] Cf. H. MacKinnon, 'William de Montibus: a Medieval Teacher', *Essays in Medieval History presented to Bertie Wilkinson*, ed. T. A. Sandquist and M. R. Powicke (Toronto, 1969), p. 37.

[4] Cf. M. A. and R. H. Rouse, 'The Texts called *Lumen Anime*', *Archivum Fratrum Praedicatorum*, xli (1971), 14; H. G. Pfander, 'The Medieval Friars and some Alphabetical Reference-books for Sermons', *Medium Aevum*, iii (1934), 19.

[5] See M. Grabmann, *Methoden und Hilfsmittel des Aristotelesstudiums im Mittelalter*, Sitzungsberichte der Bayerischen Akademie der Wissenschaften, Phil.-hist. Abt. 5 (Munich, 1939).

Nobody was more aware of this than Vincent of Beauvais. He tells us in the *apologia* to the *Speculum* that he has divided his work into books and chapters to make it easier for the reader: 'Ut huius operis partes singulae lectori facilius elucescant, ipsum totum opus per libros, et libros per capitula distinguere volui.'[1] These divisions had to be carefully and clearly labelled: '... quia multorum librorum florem quendam, atque medullam in unum volumen compegi; totum sub certis titulis ordine congruo redegi.'[2] He improves the usefulness of the work by prefixing to each book a detailed table of the *tituli* of each chapter. He gave considerable thought to the method of indicating his sources. He considered as precedents the practices developed in copies of the works of the Lombard and Gratian. He decided to follow the practice he found in the latter, to place the names in the body of the text rather than in the margins lest they be misplaced by a careless scribe: 'nequaquam in margine sicut sit in psalterio glosato et epistolis pauli vel in sentenciis, sed inter lineas ipsas sicut in decretis ea inserui.'[3] If, as seems likely, the Dijon copy of the first recension of the *Speculum maius* was a presentation copy to Louis IX,[4] then not only were all these features employed in this copy, but it is also one of the earliest manuscripts I have seen which exploits to the full the potential of running-titles discussed above.[5] The *Speculum* survives in a large number of copies most of which follow this pattern (pl. XII) and its impact on the standard of presenting texts should not be under-estimated. Compilations were handy books. The notion of *ordinatio* developed by the commentators was realized, the disposition of material into books and chapters was made manifest in the lay-out of these books, and the concomitant apparatus of headings, running-titles, *tabulae*, and other devices was disseminated along with the compilations.

The dissemination of this apparatus for indicating the *ordinatio* led to much greater sophistication in the production of books. Features of the apparatus can be found even in well-produced copies of vernacular texts which do not presuppose an academic readership. The indication of proper names, by underlining them or placing them in boxes, can be found in manuscripts of *Piers*

---

[1] *Speculum maius*, apologia (Dijon MS.), cap. ii.

[2] Ibid., cap. iii.   [3] Ibid., cap. ii.

[4] Cf. C. Oursel, 'Un Exemplaire du *Speculum maius* de Vincent de Beauvais' *Bibliothèque de l'École des Chartes*, lxxxv (1924), 251; also Ullman, loc. cit.

[5] p. 122.

Plowman and the English *Brut*.[1] The most spectacular example is
the Ellesmere manuscript of the *Canterbury Tales*. Here we find
almost all the trappings of *ordinatio*: sources and topics are indicated in the margins, and the word '*auctor*' is placed alongside
a sententious statement. The text is well disposed in its sections,
and each section is carefully labelled by means of full rubrics.
There are running-titles, and the final touch is the introduction of
pictures of each of the pilgrims (the basis of the division of the
work) in order to assist the reader to identify them with the General
Prologue. Last but not least is the way in which *Sir Thopas* has
been laid out: the bracketing serves to emphasize the 'drasty'
rhymes and the stanza division is carefully followed.

Perhaps the best way to demonstrate the increasing sophistication introduced by the interaction between *ordinatio* and *compilatio* is to compare the way in which an early thirteenth-century
scribe and an early fifteenth-century scribe treated two different
kinds of alphabetical compilation. New College, Oxford, MS. 98
is an early thirteenth-century copy of the *Proverbia* of William
de Montibus and an anonymous collection of *narrationes*, late
twelfth-century compilations disposed in alphabetical order (pl.
XIV). The 'key' alphabetical words, often preceded by the preposi-
tion 'de', are placed in red at the end of the last line of the preceding entry, in script of the same size as the rest of the text. The
large coloured initials at the beginning of each entry do not form
part of the alphabetical sequence. The reader has to find his way
about the compilation by means of the rubrics. By contrast, in
University College, Oxford, MS. 67, an early fifteenth-century
copy of the *Alphabetum narrationum* of Arnulph of Liège (pl.
XV), the first word of each entry is the alphabetical 'key' word: it
begins with a *littera notabilior* in blue occupying two lines, and the
rest of the word or phrase is underlined in red. At the beginning
of a new section of the alphabet, the initial occupies three or four
lines, and there is another *littera notabilior* in the top margin. A
further refinement is the introduction of cross-references. In
these the first letter is preceded by a paraph, but occupies only
one line and is in the same ink as the rest of the entry. To distinguish it as a separate entry, the letter is splashed with red. Fol-

---

[1] Cf. W. W. Greg, *Facsimiles of Twelve Early English Manuscripts in the
Library of Trinity College Cambridge* (Oxford, 1913), pl. vii; M. B. Parkes, *English
Cursive Book Hands 1250–1500* (Oxford, 1969), pl. 21.

lowing the *Alphabetum narrationum* in this manuscript there is an 'opusculum narrationum' in which the stories are disposed under headings or sections. In the list of titles which precedes it, each section is numbered, and in the body of the text the beginning of each section is further emphasized by means of numerals added in the margin.

The late medieval book differs more from its early medieval predecessors than it does from the printed books of our own day. The scholarly apparatus which we take for granted—analytical table of contents, text disposed into books, chapters, and paragraphs, and accompanied by footnotes and index—originated in the applications of the notions of *ordinatio* and *compilatio* by writers, scribes, and rubricators of the thirteenth, fourteenth, and fifteenth centuries. By the fourteenth century the reader had come to expect some of these features, and if they had not been supplied by scribe or rubricator the reader himself supplied the ones he wanted on the pages of his working copy. Troyes MS. 718 is a very roughly made copy of Ockham's commentary on the second book of the *Sentences*. A reader has subsequently worked through the manuscript inserting his own paragraph marks in the text with corresponding marks in the margins accompanied by numerals, and headings like 'contra' and 'responsio' to indicate the stages in the argument. Readers have also added two sets of running titles: the first set placed in the centre of the top margin refers to the *Distinctio* of the *Sentences* being commented upon, the second set placed in the top right-hand corner refers to Ockham's *quaestio* number. Citations in the text have been underlined. Peterhouse, Cambridge, MS. 89 (s. XIII) is a copy of Gregory's *Moralia in Job* which was assigned to Friar William de Tatewic who 'manu sua a principio usque ad finem diligenter correxit et notabilia specialia in marginibus titulauit et per decursum alphabeti in separatis quaterniis per modum tabulae designauit.'[1] In some late thirteenth- and fourteenth-century manuscripts scribes or readers have copied in the margins the indexing symbols of Robert Grosseteste.[2] In

---

[1] Cf. M. R. James, *A Descriptive Catalogue of Manuscripts in the Library of Peterhouse* (Cambridge, 1899), p. 106.

[2] R. W. Hunt, *Bodl. L.R.* iv (1953), 241–55. Some of the apparatus and notes on patristic texts which Grosseteste prepared for his own use were later copied and prefixed to Bodleian Lib., MS. Bodley 785, see R. W. Hunt, 'The Library of Robert Grosseteste', *Robert Grosseteste Scholar and Bishop*, ed. D. A. Callus (Oxford, 1955), pp. 122–3.

Durham, Cathedral Library, MS. B. II. 22, an eleventh-century copy of the *De civitate Dei*, a fourteenth-century hand has divided the text into chapters, and indicated subordinate topics in the margin. When this manuscript served as an exemplar for Durham MSS. B. II. 23 and 24 this apparatus was copied along with the text.[1] In Oriel College, Oxford, MS. 31 (fols. 191–193) we can see someone compiling his own *tabula* on some *quodlibet*s of Henry of Ghent. What appears to be another example of a first draft of a *tabula* survives at Durham on the dorse of an *obit* roll of Bishop Hatfield (d. 1381).[2]

Librarians and others responsible for the custody of books also introduced features of the new apparatus. In the mid fourteenth century Bishop Grandisson worked his way through books in Exeter Cathedral Library inserting inscriptions of ownership, guides to the *ordinatio*, and comments of his own. Bodleian Library, MS. Bodley 691, is a twelfth-century copy of Augustine's *De civitate Dei*. At the beginning of the volume Grandisson inserted a small quire containing a fourteenth-century synoptic table of contents. He numbered each entry in this table then worked through the manuscript dividing the text into books and chapters to agree with the divisions in the table, and finally added running-titles. In MS. Bodley 732, a twelfth-century copy of Bede's commentary on Luke, he divided up the text indicating the chapter numbers in the margins and adding running-titles in pencil. Later he replaced the pencilled running-titles with ones in ink. He inserted headings in MSS. Bodley 94, 230, and 377, and paragraph marks in MSS. Bodley 132 and 230. Later in the fourteenth century Henry Kirkstede was engaged in a similar kind of activity at Bury St. Edmunds.[3] At Durham *tabulae* and *compendia* were acquired for the convent in 1390 by William Appleby.[4] A fifteenth-century librarian of Gunville Hall bound a booklet containing Kilwardby's *Intenciones* along with copies of the texts

---

[1] Cf. R. A. B. Mynors, *Durham Cathedral Manuscripts to the end of the Twelfth Century*, no. 33.

[2] Durham, Dean and Chapter Muniments, Loc. i: 2. The references seem to be to folio and column, and therefore the *tabula* seems to have been drawn up for use alongside a particular MS. Directions found in Oxford, New Coll. MS. 112 for the use of such a *tabula* are printed by Lehmann, *Erforschung*, iii. 45.

[3] See further R. H. Rouse, 'Bostonius Buriensis and the Author of the *Catalogus Scriptorum Ecclesie*', *Speculum*, xli (1966), 490–1.

[4] Cf. R. B. Dobson, *Durham Priory 1400–1450* (Cambridge, 1973), p. 370 n. 4.

of Augustine to which they relate (Gonville and Caius College, Cambridge, MS. 108). William Seton had *Tabulae alphabeticae in varios auctores* copied for him when he was Bursar of Durham College, Oxford, in 1438, and the volume subsequently passed into the Cathedral Library (MS. B. III. 29).[1]

Why were these academic notions of *ordinatio* and *compilatio* translated so rapidly into practical terms in the thirteenth and fourteenth centuries? First, by the thirteenth century an organized book trade existed to cater for academic needs in Paris and elsewhere. The members of this trade consciously strove to achieve uniformity in matters of format and features of layout,[2] adopting and developing new ideas in response to new demands from the readers. Secondly, the orders of friars were founded in the thirteenth century to manifest a new conception of the apostolic life, and (especially in the case of the Dominicans) to preach against heresy. They formed the personnel for an essentially orthodox evangelical activity which of necessity had to pay close attention to good working tools, and to develop still further the craft of establishing and utilizing the processes of discussion based upon texts which were regarded as *auctoritates*. All the scholarly activity in the convents situated at the universities was directed towards making material available in easily accessible form to the preacher in the field. The title of Aquinas's *Summa contra gentiles* speaks for itself, and elsewhere he elaborates upon his intentions in phrases like 'scripta componere quidam modus docendi est.'[3] The search for *originalia*,[4] the production of new copies, and the collection of these ideas into new compendia to make them more readily accessible to the student and the preacher were essential to the fulfilment of the evangelical purpose of the new orders. In this context the definition of *ordinatio* led to the development of the notion of *compilatio* both as a form of writing and as a means of making material easily accessible. The orders of friars provided the institutional framework in which such an activity could evolve

---

[1] *B.R.U.O.* iii. 1671–2.

[2] J. Destrez, *La Pecia dans les manuscrits universitaires du XIIIe et du XIVe siècle*, p. 46.   [3] *Supplementum*, quaestio 96, art. 11.

[4] On the preparation of the *Registrum Anglie de libris doctorum et auctorum veterum* and the *Tabula Septem Custodiarum super Bibliam*, two of the earliest 'union catalogues', see M. R. James, 'The List of Libraries Prefixed to the Catalogue of John Boston and Kindred Documents', *Collectanea Franciscana* (British Society of Franciscan Studies, x, 1922), 37; R. H. Rouse, *Speculum*, xli (1966), 471.

rapidly: the big compilers like Vincent of Beauvais and Hugh of St. Cher had smaller compilers to help them. Compiling became an industry. Richard de Bury comments on the activity of the members of the two orders ' . . . qui diversorum voluminum correctionibus, expositionibus, tabulationibus ac compilationibus indefessis studiis incumbebant'.[1] In this kind of situation a scholar of very humble talents could be given a task in which he could feel that he was contributing to something of importance. The compilations produced were both autonomous compilations and apparatuses designed to be used alongside a text. With the dissemination of the compilations, the notion of *compilatio* both as a form of writing and as a kind of book was disseminated too. We find writers both in academic circles and outside adopting and adapting the form to suit their own academic or artistic purposes. The expectation of readers was changed, and this is reflected in changes in the physical appearance of books. A writer organized his work for publication,[2] and if he did not do so then a scribe would, for inside many a scribe there lurked a compiler struggling to get out. The production of books became more sophisticated, and the increasing number of books and the increasing demand for readily accessible information led scholarly librarians to provide yet more bibliographical aids, in the form of tables of contents, and *tabulae*; for of the making of books there is no end.

M. B. PARKES

NOTES TO PLATES IX–XVI

PLATE IX

Oxford, Bodleian Library, MS. Auct. D. 2. 8 (S.C. 2337), fol. 105 (scale 2:3). Peter Lombard, *Commentarii super Psalmos* (Ps. 45: 12–Ps. 46: 1–6). Copied in England in the late twelfth century. O. Pächt and J. J. G. Alexander, *Illuminated Manuscripts in the Bodleian Library*, iii (Oxford, 1973), no. 231. Compare the layout of text and commentary and the method of indicating sources here (discussed above, p. 116) with the *ad hoc* layout of the early glossed book illustrated in pl. V. The Bodleian manuscript belonged to Exeter Cathedral Library.

---

[1] *Philobiblon*, ed. M. Maclagan (Oxford, 1969), p. 92.
[2] As, for example, John Capgrave (cf. P. J. Lucas, 'John Capgrave, O.S.A. (1393–1464), Scribe and Publisher', *Transactions of the Cambridge Bibliographical Society*, v (1969), 1–35).

PLATE X

Oxford, St. John's College, MS. 49, fol. 12ᵛ (scale 7:10). Peter Lombard, *Sententiae in Quatuor libris distinctae* (Book I, Dist. x, cap. ii, 3–Dist. xi, cap. i, 4). Copied in France early in the second half of the twelfth century. An inscription on fol. 2 records that the volume belonged to Hilary, bishop of Chichester 1147–69 (see the catalogue of *Archbishop Laud Commemorative Exhibition*, Bodleian Library, Oxford, 1973, no. 4). Note the rubrics in the text to indicate the beginning of each chapter, and (in the left-hand margin) the indication of sources and compare with pl. IX. Rubrics in the right-hand margin 'prima causa', 'secunda', 'tercia' which indicate stages in the argument are discussed above, p. 118. The *distinctio* number has been added by a late thirteenth-century hand (see above, p. 126).

PLATE XI

Paris, Bibliothèque Nationale, MS. lat. 3050, fol. 76 (scale 2:3). Peter of Tarentaise, *In primum librum Sententiarum* (I, Dist. xxi). Copied in Paris in the second half of the thirteenth century (see J. Destrez, *La Pecia dans les manuscripts universitaires du xiiiᵉ et du xivᵉ siècle* (Paris, 1935), p. 90). Note the pecia mark in the right-hand margin. Compare with the previous plates and note here the use of *litterae notabiliores* and paraphs to indicate stages in the argument (discussed above, p. 121) and the running-titles (discussed above, p. 122).

PLATE XII

Oxford, Bodleian Library, MS. Bodley 287 (S.C. 2435), fol. 74ᵛ (scale 9:16). Vincent of Beauvais, *Speculum historiale* (V, caps. xvii–xx). A fourteenth-century copy, chosen at random, which illustrates the layout typical of well-produced manuscripts of this work including Dijon MS. 568 (329), the thirteenth-century copy which was probably made for presentation to Louis IX. Note the use of titles in red at the beginning of each chapter, the indication of sources in red in the body of the text, and the use of running-titles (here 'tempora ptholomei') which follow the principle of Vincent's own rearrangement 'iuxta seriem temporum' (see above, pp. 129 and 133).

PLATE XIII

Oxford, Keble College, MS. 26, fol. 17ᵛ (scale 2:3). Peter Lombard, *Sententiae in quatuor libris distinctae*, Book I, Dist. x, cap. ii. 5–Dist. xi, cap. i. 3. Copied in France (Paris?) in the second half of the thirteenth century. Compare with pl. X (an earlier copy of the same text) and note here the running-title and the *distinctio* number inserted by the rubricator, and the various kinds of apparatus added for and by readers.

Exact references to passages of the Bible cited as authorities in the text have been added in a very small hand close to the boundaries of the written space; extracts from the commentary of Peter of Tarentaise (F. Stegmüller, *Repertorium commentariorum in sententias Petri Lombardi* (Würzburg, 1947), no. 690) added in the margins in a formal book hand of the early fourteenth century. In the bottom margin a single four-teenth-century cursive hand has added a series of glosses and, in the bottom left-hand corner of the page, a verse summary of the contents of the book (Stegmüller, op. cit., no. 14), see J. de Ghellinck, 'Medieval Theology in Verse', *Irish Theological Quarterly*, ix (1914), 336–54; idem, *Le Mouvement théologique du xii⁰ siècle* (Bruges, 1948), pp. 272–273. Note also the paragraph marks inserted in the text in the second column.

The addition of the commentaries and the verse summary, and the omission of the twelfth-century system of indicating the sources of the *auctoritates* in the margin with corresponding *puncti* in the text, probab-ly reflect a change in the way in which the *Sentences* was read. By this date it was no longer regarded primarily as a harmony of *auctoritates* but as a textbook in its own right.

PLATE XIV

Oxford, New College, MS. 98, fol. 138 (scale 7:8). 'Anonymi cuiusdam narrationes alphabeticae.' Copied at the beginning of the thirteenth century. Compare the layout of this alphabetical compilation with that of the next plate, and see the discussion above, p. 134. From the library of Ely Cathedral Priory.

PLATE XV

Oxford, University College, MS. 67, fol. 52ᵛ (actual size). Arnulph of Liège, *Alphabetum narrationum.* Copied at the beginning of the fifteenth century. Compare with previous plate and see the discussion above, p. 134. Formerly in the possession of the Dominicans at Beverley.

PLATE XVI

Oxford, Bodleian Library, MS. Bodley 568 (S.C. 2008), fol. 242ᵛ (scale 13:20). A collection of works by Augustine copied in England at the be-ginning of the fourteenth century. The plate illustrates the end of the *De videndo deo* and the beginning of *Epistola* 152. The text of the *De videndo deo* has been divided into sections by means of red paragraph marks, and each new division is indicated by a number in the margin (the Kilward-by divisions). The *Epistola* follows the previous text without interrup-tion and is marked only by a rubric and a comparatively undistinguished initial. However, the new running-title is placed directly over the column in which the new text occurs, and not centrally as in the rest of the text. On fol. iii of the volume there is a table of contents in a fourteenth-century hand, and a fifteenth-century inscription 'pertinet conventui'. It has been suggested by M. Grabmann, *Mittelalterliches Geistesleben*, i (Munich, 1926), pp. 23–5, that the utilitarian appearance of such copies is typical of manuscripts which belonged to the mendicant orders (cf. the remarks of Humbert of Romans, *Opera de vita regulari*, ed. J. J. Berthier (Rome, 1888–9), i, p. 448).

II
HISTORY OF TEXTS

6

A Ninth-century Manuscript from Fleury: Cato de senectute cum Macrobio[1]

VATICAN Reg. lat. 1587, fols. 65–80 (s. IX), is an important manuscript of Cicero's *De senectute*, which the editors have designated D.[2] The front flyleaf bears the following inscription, added in bold capitals probably in the tenth century (fol. 65^v): *Cato de senectute cum Macrobio.* The promised Macrobius is missing. Only a title and a short introduction to the Commentary on the *Somnium Scipionis* survive, after the end of the *De senectute* (fol. 80^v). The lost Macrobius is now in the Bibliothèque Nationale at Paris: lat. 16677. Script, measurements, and quality of parchment are identical, and the matter is clinched by the surviving quire-signatures.[3]

I believe that the reconstructed volume belonged to the great Benedictine abbey of Fleury(Saint-Benoît)-sur-Loire, and was probably written there. Many manuscripts from that library have suffered dismemberment at one period or another, down to the

---

[1] I should like to thank the following especially for their help during the preparation of this article: Professor B. Bischoff, Dr. A. C. de la Mare, Dr. M. Gibson, Sir Roger Mynors, Mlle É. Pellegrin, Flight Lieutenant R. S. N. Perry, Miss C. Starks.

[2] I shall refer to the MS. as D throughout, although the Macrobius in Paris B.N. lat. 16677 is MS. E in the Teubner edition of J. Willis (*Macrobius*, ii. 1963). I hope later to publish a full description of D with the bulk of my work on the MSS. of Macrobius's Commentary. A list of the sigla I have used is printed at the end of the article.

[3] Quire-signatures, probably by the scribe: I (Reg., fol. 73^v)–X (Paris, fol. 65^v), surrounded by patterns of dots, in the centre lower margin of the last verso of each quire; II and IX now lost. Original collation i–xi^8, with later changes: q. ii, leaf 8, is now lost after Reg., fol. 80; q. iii (Paris, fols. 1–8) now has its bifolia misbound, 3, 4, 1, 2, 7, 8, 5, 6; q. xi, leaf 8, perhaps blank, is now lost after fol. 72. The following leaves were probably all added at the same time in the 10th century: flyleaf (Reg., fol. 65) before q. i; Paris, fols. 56–7, now between qq. ix and x; Paris, fols. 73–5, at the end.

time of Guglielmo Libri. We owe a great debt to many scholars, and recently in particular to Mlle É. Pellegrin, for reuniting so many *membra disiecta Floriacensia*. Such work often throws light on the activities of the sixteenth-century humanists, as well as leading us back to the intellectual life of medieval Fleury.

To prove that the manuscript belonged to Fleury, I shall have to discuss the history of the two parts in detail. Later I shall attempt to show that the interesting combination of Cicero's *De senectute* with Macrobius' Commentary on Cicero's *Somnium Scipionis* appears also in other centres in France, and had crossed to southern Germany by the end of the tenth century.

Later History of D

The *De senectute* in Reg. lat. 1587 was first noticed by A. Barriera, who published his discovery in 1920 in an article entitled 'L'*alter codex vetus Danielis* del *Cato Maior*'.[1] He claimed that the manuscript had belonged to Pierre Daniel of Orléans (*c.* 1530–1603 or 1604). I think that he is right, although his two arguments are inadequate. The title of his article refers to the note on *De senectute* § 8 in Gruter's 1618 edition,[2] 'quod non fuisset uox *ignobilis* in uno ueteri codice Danielis nisi a manu recenti, in altero uero nihil illius loco'. W. Gemoll recognized that the condition for the first *codex Danielis* was fulfilled by Mommsen's discovery, L,[3] and Barriera claimed the second as his new find, D. However, Gruter's characterization of the second manuscript is far too slight to allow identification with D or any other specific manuscript. D does not contain the reading *ignobilis*, but nor do three of the other six ninth-century manuscripts;[4] and Pierre Daniel may well have owned more than two manuscripts of the *De senectute*.[5] Barriera's second argument for Daniel's ownership was the presence of his ex-libris in Reg. lat. 1587, fols. 1 and 50[v]. But

[1] *Athenaeum: Studi Periodici di Letteratura e Storia*, 1st ser. viii (1920), 174–176; see also Barriera's edition in *Corpus Scriptorum Latinorum Paravianum*, n.d. (?1921, reprinted 1937).

[2] J. Gruterus, *M. Tullii Ciceronis opera omnia* (1618), iv. 442. The information is given on the authority of Puteanus.

[3] For L see below, pp. 157–9. W. Gemoll, 'Zwei neue Handschriften zu Ciceros Cato maior', *Hermes*, xx (1885), 332.

[4] V, b, and A in the edition of C. Simbeck, Teubner, 1st edn., 1912, apparatus for p. 22 l. 13.

[5] H. Hagen, *Catalogus codicum Bernensium* (1875), p. 154, describes a 13th-century fragment from the *De senectute* in a volume which *fuit P. Danielis*

these both fall in the first of the four separate manuscripts which form the volume, the *De senectute* being the last. Evidence of ownership in one part must not be applied to another unless it can be established that they were together at the time.

When were the four manuscripts bound together? The library of Queen Christina of Sweden (1626–89) passed into the Vatican Library in 1690. Reg. lat. 1587 now wears the usual *Reginensis* binding of red leather, which can be precisely dated from the arms on the spine: those of Enrico Noris, cardinal librarian 1700–4, with the emblems of Clement XI (1700–21). But the four items in Reg. lat. 1587 were once part of a larger collection of fragments, no. 1732 in the catalogue of the Queen's manuscripts made by the Maurists of Rome in the 1680s[1] and printed by Montfaucon in 1739.[2] This collection contained nine separate fragments, of which all but one have now been identified:[3]

1. *Albini Magistri carmina. Martialis Carmina quaedam. Maximus Victorius de re Grammatica. Sergius de arte Grammatica. Bedae Orthographia.* Now Reg. lat. 1587, fols. 1–50.
2. *Cassiodorus de anima.* Now Reg. lat. 54, fols. 1–42.
3. *Ovidii liber Tristium.* Unidentified.
4. *Glossae Veteris et Novi Testamenti.* Now Reg. lat. 1587, fols. 51–6.
5. *Joannis cujusdam carmina ad Carolum Calvum.* Now Reg. lat. 1587, fols. 57–64 [? + Reg. lat. 1709, fols. 16–23].
6. *Cicero de Senectute.* Now Reg. lat. 1587, fols. 65–80.
7. *Palladius de Agricultura.* Now Reg. lat. 2120, fols. 1–10.
8. *Excerpta varia ex Tibullo, Boëtio, Anticlaudiano, Sedulio, Matthaeo Vindocinensi, Ovidio et Horatio.* Now Reg. lat. 2120, fols. 11–35.

(Berne 104, fols. 56–7); however, it does not contain the relevant part of the text.

[1] Now Paris B.N. lat. 13076, fols. 7–223. Although the MS. bears an ex-libris dated 1691 (fol. 7), which has sometimes been cited as the date of the catalogue itself, it describes the collection as it was before the changes initiated in 1690. See J. Sparrow, 'A Manuscript from Queen Christina's Library: The *Amores* of Sigismondo Boldoni', *The Library*, 5th ser., xvii (1962), 297–304.

[2] B. de Montfaucon, *Bibliotheca bibliothecarum manuscriptorum nova* (1739), i, p. 53, col. I B–C.

[3] See D. M. Robathan, 'The Missing Folios of the Paris Florilegium 15155', *Classical Philology*, xxxiii (1938), 188–97 (on item 8); [F. De Marco], 'Les manuscrits de la Reine de Suède au Vatican: réédition du catalogue de Montfaucon et cotes actuelles', *Studi e Testi*, ccxxxviii (1964), 97.

9. *Vibius Sequester de fluminibus. Sententiarum excerpta varia.*
Now Reg. lat. 1561, fols. 1–22.

The first leaf of item 1 bears the inscription *nunc Nicolai Heinsii*. Nicholas Heinsius (1620–81) had belonged to Queen Christina's circle of manuscript enthusiasts, and provided several of her manuscripts.[1] The volume, or at least items 1 and 3, had passed into the Queen's collection by 1655, when the following entry appears in the Antwerp catalogue: *Albini, Martialis, Ovidii, aliorumque scripta.* 4°. The *Librarius Antverpiensis* adds Heinsius's name against the entry as its source.[2]

Heinsius's collations of several items in the volume have survived, and reveal the name of the previous owner. Leyden, Burm. Q. 13,[3] contains among others the following items: 'Vibius Sequester collatus cum manuscripto codice Iacobi Revii . . . Cassiodorus De Anima coll. cum Cod. Reviano — Maximus Victorius coll. cum Cod. Revii — Sergius de Arte Gramm. ex cod. Revii — Beda de Orthogr. ex Cod. Revii.' R. Gelsomino[4] has proved on textual grounds that the *codex Revii* of Vibius Sequester is our item 9. The other items are surely therefore our 2 and 1. East Berlin Diez B 148e, fols. 166–8,[5] contains Heinsius's collation of Ovid *in lib. Tristium ex v. c. Jacobi Revii.* Revius's manuscript only went up to I. 8. 26 (fol. 168), but 'sequebantur in eodem codice, sed longo intervallo, excerpta quaedam ex Ovidianis libris' (fol. 168ᵛ). These excerpts must be those of our item 8, and the manuscript of the *Tristia* must be item 3, which is further described in East Berlin Libri c. not. mss. Diez 4° 1076, p. 160: 'fragmentum, quod librum primum continebat, et penes me est ex dono Cl. V. Jacobi Revii, aliis quibusdam collectaneis annexum. fuerat olim Petri Danielis Aurelii.'[6] The collection of fragments, already bound up, was therefore given to Heinsius by the theologian Jacobus Revius (1586–1658), a friend of his father.

---

[1] See J. Bignami Odier, 'Le fonds de la Reine à la Bibliothèque Vaticane', *Collectanea Vaticana in honorem Anselmi M. card. Albareda*, i (*Studi e Testi,* ccxix, 1962), 165.

[2] Vat. lat. 8171, fol. 155. On the catalogue see Bignami Odier, op. cit., pp. 170–171, 182–3.

[3] See J. Geel, *Catalogus librorum manuscriptorum qui inde ab anno 1741 Bibliothecae Lugduno Batavae accesserunt* (1852), no. 596.

[4] R. Gelsomino, ed., *Vibius Sequester* (Teubner, 1967), pp. xx–xxi.

[5] I am very grateful to Mr. M. D. Reeve for the references to the Ovid material.

[6] Printed by H. Boese, 'Zu den Ovidkollationen des N. Heinsius', *Philologus,* cvi (1962), 167.

Most of the surviving items show signs of having belonged earlier to Pierre Daniel. Items 1, 2, 7, and 9 contain his ex-libris.[1] Item 4 contains a ninth-century excerpt from Petronius (fol. 53ᵛ), from which Daniel quotes readings elsewhere;[2] variants added to it, and the title on fol. 51, seem to be in Daniel's hand. The evidence for Daniel's ownership of five of the nine items in the collection lends some confidence to the identification of his hand in our manuscript of the *De senectute*, item 6: in the title at the top of the front flyleaf (fol. 65), *Cato Maior seu de Senectute*, and the variant *prouidentia* or *prudentia* at § 78 (fol. 79). He also added this variant in L (fol. 23ᵛ). It would seem therefore that the nine items, which have nothing in common except their size and fragmentary condition, were put together by Pierre Daniel or his heirs. It is well known that his collection was shared between Paul Petau and Jacques Bongars (the usual route from Daniel to the *Fondo Reginense* was through Petau rather than through Heinsius). Perhaps some scraps from the collection were acquired by Jacobus Revius when he was studying at Orléans *c.* 1610–12.[3]

The Macrobius, Paris B.N. lat. 16677, cannot be traced back beyond cardinal Richelieu (1585–1642). It is no. 2917 in Blaise's catalogue of 1643 (see fol. (i)), and carries the cardinal's arms stamped in gold on the usual seventeenth-century binding of red leather. The manuscript passed with the Richelieu collection to the Sorbonne in 1660 and thence to the Bibliothèque Nationale in 1795.[4]

Earlier History of D: Fleury

Pierre Daniel obtained many of his manuscripts from the abbey of Fleury, and Barriera argued that D therefore came from that library. Pierre Daniel's manuscripts are often attributed to Fleury solely on the basis of this argument; it is invalid because Daniel certainly had other sources, for example the abbey of St. Victor at Paris, the medieval home of item 8 in the collection discussed above.[5] Again, I believe that Barriera is right, but better evidence for Fleury provenance must be produced.

---

[1] Item 1: Reg. lat. 1587, fols. 1 and 50ᵛ (dated 1560). Item 2: Reg. lat. 54, fol. 1 (1564). Item 7: Reg. lat. 2120, fol. 1. Item 9: Reg. lat. 1561, fol. 22 (1565).

[2] See B. L. Ullman, 'The Text of Petronius in the Sixteenth Century', *Classical Philology*, xxv (1930), 152–3.

[3] See E. J. W. P. Meyjes, *Jacobus Revius, zijn Leven en Werken* (1895), p. 21.

[4] Fonds de la Sorbonne, no. 1563.   [5] See D. M. Robathan, op. cit.

No fewer than three early book-lists have been attributed to Fleury, all on inadequate grounds.[1] The only guide to the collection is the catalogue made in 1552[2] which records one copy of Cicero's *De senectute*: no. 175, *Marci Tulli Cato major*. This is insufficient for identification with an extant manuscript; the entry has sometimes been thought to apply to L (see below, pp. 157–9), but it could equally well be D or another manuscript. The catalogue also lists three copies of Macrobius's Commentary, all with other works which are distinctive enough to identify them with extant manuscripts: no. 84 is Orléans 306 (259), no. 253 is Paris B.N. lat. 7299, and no. 286 is Paris B.N. lat. 6365. However, the 1552 lat. catalogue is certainly far from complete.[3]

Mlle Pellegrin[4] has discovered another piece of evidence for the Fleury library in Berne A 91, no. 24. This is a list of seven manuscripts, with titles, incipits, and explicits carefully given, in the hand of Pierre Daniel. It carries no heading to indicate its purpose. Mlle Pellegrin has identified several of these among the manuscripts now at Orléans, or at the Bibliothèque Nationale in the fonds of Saint-Germain-des-Prés—the present homes of the Fleury manuscripts which escaped the looters of the sixteenth century. She has therefore made the reasonable suggestion that this is a list of manuscripts which Pierre Daniel saw at Fleury but did not add to his collection.

The sixth entry on the list is as follows (punctuation as in the original):

> Macrobius in Somnium Scipionis ut credo sic habet
> in fine. / vere etiam pronunciandum ut nihil hoc opere perfectius
> quo universa philosophiae continetur integritas
> et in subscri   MACROBII ambrosii Commenta ex Cicerone in
> ptione   Somnium Scipionis Explicit de errore emendationis.

We have here the closing words of the text and the final title from

---

[1] See A. Vidier, *L'Historiographie à Saint-Benoît-sur-Loire et les Miracles de Saint Benoît* (1965), pp. 28 n. 4, 38 n. 72, 41 n. 107, 44 n. 116.

[2] Paris B.N. nouv. acq. lat. 137, fols. 9–26 (copy of the seventeenth or eighteenth century) published by Ch. Cuissard in *Catalogue général des manuscrits des bibliothèques publiques de France*, 8° ser., xii, *Orléans* (1889), pp. vii–xviii, and by others.

[3] For example, it only records one work on St. Benedict, although the library certainly possessed others; see Vidier, *L'Historiographie . . .*, p. 30.

[4] É. Pellegrin, 'Essai d'identification de fragments dispersés dans des manuscrits des bibliothèques de Berne et de Paris', *Bulletin d'information de l'Institut de Recherche et d'Histoire des Textes*, ix (1960), 17.

a manuscript of Macrobius's Commentary on the *Somnium Scipionis*. Mlle Pellegrin has tentatively suggested that the entry might refer to Paris B.N. lat. 8663 (see below, p. 155), but this leaves unexplained the last three words, *de errore emendationis*. I think that the entry refers to the Macrobian half of D, Paris B.N. lat. 16677. The end of the text and the closing title in Paris B.N. lat. 16677 (fol. 72ᵛ) correspond exactly to the entry in Daniel's list, and are followed by an apologetic colophon[1] in elegiac couplets:

De errore emendationis.

Da ueniam, lector, si quid male puncta notabunt,
Vel si mendosum pagina texit opus.
Non mens praua mihi sed fallax offuit error,
†Que non sonte subest ūcula [? mihi cul]pe.†

This colophon has long been known from Paris B.N. nouv. acq. lat. 454, fol. 81ᵛ (A, see below, pp. 159–60). A third manuscript in which it appears is Munich Clm 6369, fol. 61ᵛ (F, see below, pp. 160–1). L could well have been a fourth, but the Macrobius in that manuscript had already been dismembered for bindings by the time of Pierre Daniel (see below, pp. 157–9). There are two reasons for believing that the entry in Daniel's list is specifically D, rather than A, F, or another unknown manuscript:

1. *Explicit* occurs only in D. F gives *expliciunt* written out in full, and A gives it as EXPLICĨT, using a strange abbreviation which, in the common ancestor, must have caused D's variant. This is the only significant difference among the three manuscripts in the passage quoted by Daniel.

2. Daniel gives an opening title and/or incipit for all the manuscripts on his list except the Macrobius. The most likely explanation is that the beginning of the manuscript was lost, and the impression is strengthened by Daniel's hesitant *ut credo*. The beginning of the Macrobian half of D, Paris B.N. lat. 16677, is now lost, but A and F remain whole, with their opening titles intact.

If my identification is correct, it follows that in D the *De senectute* had been separated from the Macrobius before Pierre

---

[1] The unintelligible last line has been corrected in erasure by a near-contemporary hand to *Que non sonte subest ucula culpa mihi*, and the gloss *s. relaxa* written over *ucula culpa*; the abbreviation-sign of the mysterious *ūcula* has been erased. The last line in A reads *Quae non sonte subest ūcula mihi culpe* (see K. Strecker, *M.G.H.: Poetae*, VI. i (1951), 169); in F, *Que non sponte subest umcula mihi culpae*. No satisfactory emendation has yet been discovered. Perhaps the line was a hexameter rather than a pentameter.

Daniel's time. Later, he took possession of the *De senectute* part. What happened to the Macrobius? Other manuscripts on the list remained at Fleury; perhaps this did too. At all events, it must have had a peculiar history, for I know of no other manuscript certainly from Fleury in the Richelieu–Sorbonne collection. One other point may be relevant: the entry for the Macrobius, alone of the seven in Daniel's list, has been lightly crossed through, in the same ink as the text.

The second piece of evidence for Fleury provenance takes us back to the eleventh century. It involves the relationship between D and a Macrobius of the early eleventh century, Paris B.N. lat. 7299 (P), and it is therefore first necessary to pin the latter manuscript to Fleury.[1]

On the basis of script and quiring, P falls into three parts. Part I (fols. 3–12) is a computistical compilation of which the principal element is a lunar calendar with the names of saints. Additions made to the calendar, notably *Translatio corporis Sancti PAULI Episcopi et confessoris* on 10 October (fol. 8), and *et Sancti ABBONIS Abbatis* added to the original *Bricii episcopi* on 13 November (fol. 8ᵛ) prove that P was at Fleury in the eleventh century. The additions are made in a script similar to the text-hands of parts II and III. The original, rather sparse, calendar was certainly descended from an English exemplar, for it contains the following: Cuthbert (20 March; *translatio*, 4 September), Augustine (26 May), Alban (22 June), Kenelm (17 July), Oswald (5 August). Indeed, it is just possible that this part of the manuscript, its rounded script contrasting with the more angular hands of parts II and III, was itself written in England, or at least by an English scribe (the parchment, however, is of much the same quality as part II). If so, it must have reached Fleury very soon. The presence of an English calendar at Fleury is not surprising in the context of the well-documented links between Fleury and England around the time of Abbo.[2]

---

[1] P is described in detail in M.-Th. Vernet, 'Notes de Dom André Wilmart sur quelques manuscrits latins anciens de la Bibliothèque nationale de Paris, 2', *Bulletin d'information de l'Institut de Recherche et d'Histoire des Textes*, viii (1959), 21–4, where my parts I and II are conflated.

[2] See Dom L. Gougaud, 'Les relations de l'abbaye de Fleury-sur-Loire avec la Bretagne et les Îles Britanniques (xᵉ et xiᵉ siècles)', *Mémoires de la Société d'Histoire et d'Archéologie de Bretagne*, iv (1923), 3–30.

Part II (fols. 12 *bis*–27) is a continuation of the computistical material of part I. Its principal item is Helpericus' *Liber de computo* (fols. 12 *bis*ᵛ–24; author's name not given). The *annus praesens* at ch. 24, *Qualiter anni ab incarnatione domini inueniantur* (fol. 19), is given as 978, a date which occurs in several manuscripts. A. van de Vyver[1] has suggested that Abbo of Fleury was responsible for the 978 edition of the text. Part III (fols. 28–71) contains only Macrobius's Commentary on the *Somnium Scipionis*. The angular hands of parts II and III, similar to the additions in the calendar, are characteristic of Fleury at the time of Abbo.[2] Similarities in measurements and content suggest that parts II and III were designed to go with I from the start.

Item 253 in the Fleury catalogue of 1552 is as follows: 'Expositio in psalmos cuius principium desideratur, quicum iunctus est liber calculi quem Victorinus composuit; de singulis mensibus qui calendis, nonis et idibus, etiam de diebus consistunt. Item Macrobius in Somnium Scipionis.' This is almost certainly to be identified with P, for part I begins *de singulis mensibus* . . . The *Expositio in psalmos* and the *Liber calculi* of Victorius of Aquitane are now missing. The wording of the catalogue suggests that the *Expositio in psalmos* was an independent item bound up with the rest, whereas the nature of the Victorius indicates a link with the surviving parts. The whole compilation is redolent of Abbo of Fleury, who wrote commentaries on both Victorius's *Liber calculi* and Helpericus' *Liber de computo*.

The main connection between P and D lies in the additions in the two manuscripts to the text of Macrobius's Commentary. In D (Paris B.N. lat. 16677, fol. 9ᵛ), an eleventh-century hand has added a diagram illustrating the passage where Macrobius expounds the union of the four elements (I. 6. 24–33). The script is a very distinctive, rounded hand (see pl. XVIII): *a* is half-uncial with a flat top (a Fleury characteristic); the tail of the *g* is open and pushed to the right; *d* is sometimes rounded. Macrobius's concept is often illustrated by a diagram in the manuscripts, although it is not one of the five standard diagrams which go back to the author. The diagram is usually round, but here the elements and their

---

[1] A. van de Vyver, 'Les œuvres inédites d'Abbon de Fleury', *Revue Bénédictine*, xlvii (1935), 148–9.

[2] See É. Pellegrin, 'Membra disiecta Floriacensia', *Bibliothèque de l'École des Chartes*, cxvii (1959), 14–16.

shared qualities are linked by an angular, continuous line. I have so far found this pattern in only one other manuscript:[1] as an addition on fol. 33 of P. It is unmistakably by the same hand (see pl. XIX).

The hand has also added diagrams in D (Paris B.N. lat. 16677, fols. 9 and 19ᵛ), which do not appear in P. Conversely, the hand is perhaps responsible for diagrams and glosses on fols. 31ᵛ and 32 of P which do not occur in D. But there are other connections between the two manuscripts. Firstly, the texts as they stood before correction belonged to the same family (see below, p. 155). Secondly, the two manuscripts share other additions, though not in the same hand. In P, frequent corrections and a few glosses are added by a single hand of the angular type, similar but not identical to that of the text. This hand echoes additions made in D by two hands: additional hand (2), a clumsy, rounded script in heavy, dark ink, probably tenth-century, and additional hand (3), a smaller, more angular hand of the 'Abbo' type, written with the pen held at a steep angle.[2] Since the shared material seems to be by one hand in P but by two in D, it is more likely that P derives it from D, rather than vice versa or from a common source.

Such connections between P and D, especially the elements diagram in the same hand, must imply that the two manuscripts were being studied in the same centre at the time of the additions (s. XI); and since P was at Fleury almost certainly from the time

---

[1] At the date of writing (October 1973), I have examined about half the extant MSS. of Macrobius's Commentary (total number *c.* 230, including fragments but not excerpts).

[2] The most striking of the shared additions are:

(*a*) The interpolation from I. 12. 1 (Willis 47. 31—48. 5), *Et ita lacteus—numquam relinquit*, added in the margin at I. 15. 7 (Willis 62. 2) *temperaret. | quibus*, in both MSS.: D, Paris B.N. lat. 16677, fol. 26ᵛ, hand (3); P, fol. 43ᵛ. The interpolation is found in several other MSS., sometimes incorporated in the text.

(*b*) The gloss on I. 21. 12 (Willis 87. 10) *clepsydrae.* D, Paris B.N. lat. 16677, fol. 38ᵛ, hand (3)?: *clepsidra est uas unde quasi furando deorsum trahitur aqua.* P, fol. 51 (+ in text, + *gl(o)s(sa)* in margin; variant *clepsidira* for *clepsidra*).

(*c*) The gloss on II. 4. 11 (Willis 109. 5) *netas et hypatas.* D, Paris B.N. lat. 16677, fol. 47ᵛ, hand (2): *Necias prima dicitur extentarum cordarum, hipatas quae est iusta* [sic] *neciam.* P, fol. 57 (as D, but *iuxta*).

(*d*) The gloss on II. 4. 14 (Willis 109. 26) *Catadupa.* D, Paris B.N. lat. 16677, fol. 48, hand (2): *Catadupa proprium nomen montis Aegipti pluraliter dictum de quo Nilus cum magno descendit fragore.* P, fol. 57.

(*e*) The gloss on II. 11. 17 (Willis 130. 17) *Nam* . . . D, Paris B.N. lat. 16677, fol. 61, hand (2): x̄v̄ 𝔪̄𝔵̄ *pars sunt dccL* . . . P, fol. 64. The *signe de renvoi* is the same in both MSS.

when it was written, it follows that the Macrobian part of D was also there in the eleventh century.

I have shown that Paris B.N. lat. 16677 was at Fleury in the eleventh and sixteenth centuries, and in the light of this and of Pierre Daniel's ownership it would be difficult to deny the Fleury provenance of the other part of D, Reg. lat. 1587, fols. 65–80. Where was the manuscript written? I can produce no formal proof for Fleury ownership earlier than the eleventh century. However, there is still the palaeographical evidence. D's script, of which the chief characteristic is a tendency towards pronounced ligatures (*ct, ra, re, rt, st*), suggests that it was written in the ninth century in the area of the Loire valley;[1] if so, why not at Fleury?

Macrobius' Commentary on the Somnium Scipionis *at Fleury*

A number of early copies of Macrobius's Commentary have survived which have connections with Fleury. In addition to D and P, there are two other manuscripts, both dating from around the turn of the tenth and eleventh centuries, which were probably written at Fleury and were certainly there by the eleventh century: (1) Paris B.N. lat. 6365, fols. 1–23[2] (no. 286 in the 1552 catalogue; fol. 2, a copy of the encyclical from the monks of Fleury announcing the death of their prior Andrew, added in the eleventh century);[3] (2) Paris, B.N. lat. 8663 (fol. 58ᵛ, two punning lines, beginning *Florida floriacum* . . . , added by a contemporary hand).[4] Both manuscripts are written in the 'angular' script, found in P and in some of the additions to D, which is beginning to be associated with Fleury at about the time of Abbo (the half-uncial *a*, the prominent ligatures, especially *ct*, and the abbreviation—·for *est* are characteristic features). Paris B.N. lat. 6365 is a member of the

---

[1] I owe this information to the kind help of Professor Bernhard Bischoff. The script is small and neat, by one hand (somewhat larger from Paris B.N. lat. 16677, fol. 52 onwards). *N* in mid-word is frequent.

[2] Detailed description by Wilmart and Vernet, op. cit., pt. 1, *Bulletin*, vi (1957), 33–4.

[3] Published from this MS. by L. Delisle, *Rouleaux des morts du IXᵉ au XVᵉ siècle* (1866), no. XXVIII, pp. 147–50. This prior is perhaps to be identified with the Andrew who wrote the *Vita Gauzlini* and bks. iv–vii of the *Miracula sancti Benedicti* at Fleury in the 1040s: see Vidier, *L'Historiographie* . . . , pp. 52 and n. 163, 121 and n. 55, 123 n. 74, 202 n. 31.

[4] Detailed description by Wilmart and Vernet, op. cit., pt. 2, *Bulletin*, viii (1959), 40–4. For examples of similar verses see Vidier *L'Historiographie* . . . , p. 53 n. 171.

same textual group as D and P. Two further manuscripts can tentatively be attributed to Fleury on the grounds of their affiliation to this group (other firm evidence of ownership is lacking). The first is Paris B.N. lat. 16678, fols. 1–8 + lat. 6620,[1] written probably again at about the time of Abbo, in an exaggerated form of the script. It is a close relative, perhaps a direct descendant, of the second manuscript, L, a ninth-century copy which is closely allied to D (see below, pp. 157–9). All these manuscripts can be distinguished on the basis of both text and appearance from Orléans 306 (259), pp. 1–76, an eleventh-century manuscript with no early indications of provenance which appears in the 1552 catalogue (no. 84); I suspect it is an import.

The identification of the script-type of Fleury in the time of Abbo rests mainly on its presence in the earliest manuscripts of Abbo's own works, some of which may have been executed for the author himself. Extracts from Macrobius' Commentary occur in two of these: East Berlin Phill. 1833 (Rose 138), contains a corpus of Abbo's computistical works, and includes astronomical texts and diagrams from Macrobius on fols. 1, 21^v, 36, 39^v (map). The philosophical corpus reassembled by Mlle Pellegrin,[2] Leyden Voss. Lat. Fol. 70. I, fols. 1–66 + Orléans 277 (233) + Paris B.N. nouv. acq. lat. 1630, fols. 14–16, contains a section of short paraphrases on various subjects from Macrobius's Commentary (nouv. acq. lat. 1630, fols. 14^v–16^v + Voss. Lat. Fol. 70. I, fol. 51). A third manuscript, Orléans 267 (223) + Paris B.N. nouv. acq. lat. 1611, contains philosophical monographs of Boethius and other works including the *Somnium Scipionis* without Macrobius (nouv. acq. lat. 1611, fols. 55^v–57) and an added treatise on logic attributed to Abbo.[3]

From these excerpts, in manuscripts perhaps used by Abbo himself, we can begin to see the importance of Macrobius's Commentary at Fleury in his time. The reduplication of complete texts at Fleury in the same period shows that it must have been one of the major teaching tools. More extant manuscripts of the text were owned by Fleury than by any other medieval centre. However, this may be due to the chances of survival; a parallel is

---

[1] 6620 is described by Wilmart and Vernet, op. cit., pt. 2, *Bulletin*, viii (1959), 8–10. The missing quire at the beginning is certainly 16678, fols. 1–8, since the text fits, and the measurements, etc., are identical.

[2] 'Membra disiecta Floriacensia', pp. 9–16.

[3] van de Vyver, *Revue Bénédictine*, xlvii (1935), 131–2

provided by the library of Christ Church, Canterbury, which in the third quarter of the twelfth century possessed eleven copies of 'Macrobius' and two further commentaries on the author.[1]

Other Manuscripts containing both Cicero's De senectute and Macrobius' Commentary on the Somnium Scipionis

L: Leyden, Voss. Lat. Fol. 12β (= *fols. 15–26*) + *Voss. Lat. Fol. 122* + *London, British Libr., Royal 15 B. xii, fols. 1–2.* The manuscript is French, ninth-century. The *De senectute* survives intact in Voss. Lat. Fol. 12β, fols. 15–24ᵛ. However, the Macrobius was at some time detached and used to provide wrappers or flyleaves for other manuscripts; only the following fragments remain:

(*a*) Voss. Lat. Fol. 12β, fol. 24ᵛ: beginning—*ad corpus* ‖ I. 1. 7 (Willis 3. 6), filling the page at the end of the *De senectute.*

(*b*) Voss. Lat. Fol. 12β, fols. 25–26ᵛ: I. 2. 12 (Willis 6. 15) ‖ *nullam—arescentibus laureis* ‖ I. 4. 2 (Willis 13. 13). Until 1886 the order of the leaves in Voss. Lat. Fol. 12β was 26, 15–24, 25.[2] Two leaves of the Macrobius had been cannibalized to form a wrapper for the *De senectute.* The top margin of fol. 26 (once the front cover) carries the inscription *Ex libb. Petri Danielis Aurelii 1560.*

(*c*) Royal 15 B. xii, fols. 1–2: I. 19. 14 (Willis 75. 26) ‖ *et cur dixerit—lumen in solem* ‖ I. 20. 3 (Willis 78. 31). These are the two halves of one leaf, now bound sideways so that the text runs 1, 2, 1ᵛ, 2ᵛ. They must once have formed the flyleaves or wrapper of the main manuscript, a Juvenal of the tenth century (medieval provenance not known). Warner and Gilson were able to read the ex-libris of Pierre Daniel's brother François at the end of the text (fol. 59ᵛ): *Ex libris Francisci Danielis Aurelii.*[3] The manuscript later passed to Jacques Bongars (fol. 3).

(*d*) Voss. Lat. Fol. 122: II. 1. 13 (Willis 97. 18) ‖ *ex quibus—pari* ‖ II. 2. 11 (Willis 101. 3). This single leaf, folded in two with the edges tucked in and stitched, once formed the cover of Voss. Lat.

---

[1] See the fragmentary catalogue in Cambridge, U.L., MS. Ii. 3. 12, printed by M. R. James, *The Ancient Libraries of Canterbury and Dover*, 1903, pp. 1–12, nos. 54–64, 78–9. Most of these copies probably contained Macrobius's Commentary rather than the *Saturnalia* (still comparatively rare). The many sets of duplicates listed in the catalogue show that this was a teaching library.

[2] See the full description in K. A. de Meyier, *Codices Vossiani Latini*, i (= *Codices Manuscripti*, xiii, 1973), 21–8, esp. 24.

[3] G. F. Warner and J. P. Gilson, *Catalogue of Western Manuscripts in the Old Royal and King's Collections* (1921), iii. 104. Only the final *i* can now be read, owing to the use of a reagent.

Qu. 106, from which it has now been detached. Voss. Lat. Qu. 106 contains the *Enigmata* of Symphosius and Aldhelm, s. ix, and an Anglo-Saxon translation of Aldhelm's Lorica riddle (fol. 25ᵛ) added by a contemporary, continental scribe;[1] it contains no evidence of medieval provenance. Once again, the manuscript shows signs of Pierre Daniel's ownership: Voss. Lat. Fol. 122, fol. 1ᵛ, carries a title for Qu. 106 in his hand, the Aldhelm carries some notes by him, and the book came to Leyden via Daniel's coheir Paul Petau (his number R 37 occurs on Qu. 106, fol. 2).

There is no certain evidence for L's medieval home.[2] The illogical assumption that all manuscripts belonging to Pierre Daniel came ultimately from Fleury has also been applied to Voss. Lat. Fol. 12β. I can produce only vague considerations to strengthen the hypothesis. It seems impossible that Pierre Daniel himself could have used an early classical manuscript for binding purposes, since he hoarded even small scraps. Therefore L, and the two other manuscripts which were bound in its dismembered leaves, came from some library where ancient books were available for disposal, where at some time there was a demand for Cicero's *De senectute* but not for Macrobius's Commentary, and from which books eventually became available to the Daniel brothers. Fleury

[1] See N. R. Ker, *Catalogue of Manuscripts containing Anglo-Saxon* (1957), p. 479.

Since this article was written my attention has been drawn to the work on Voss. Lat. Qu. 106 by M. B. Parkes, 'The Manuscript of the Leiden Riddle', *Anglo-Saxon England*, i (1972), 207–17, pl. I. Parkes shows that neums on fol. 25ᵛ are characteristic of Fleury in the 10th century, and hence that the riddle was added at that date. This is the final piece of evidence needed to show that L belonged to Fleury, for if Voss. Lat. Qu. 106 belonged to Fleury from the 10th century until the time of Pierre Daniel, its wrapper must also have come from Fleury.

[2] De Meyier, op. cit., 23, gives L's date as *c.* 850 and its provenance as 'Gallia (Autissiodurum, teste Bischoff, vel Monasterium S. Benedicti Floriacense)'.

P. E. v. Severus, *Lupus von Ferrières* (*Beiträge zur Geschichte des alten Mönchtums und des Benediktinerordens*, xxi, 1940), pp. 57–8, 102, pl. II, thought that early variants in L's text of the *De senectute* were added directly from Paris B.N. lat. 6332 by Lupus of Ferrières. L and Paris B.N. lat. 6332 are important representatives of the two families of the text, and the correctors of each MS. borrowed readings from the other textual stream (see the stemma of P. Wuilleumier, *Cicéron: Caton l'ancien (de la Vieillesse)*, 3rd edn., Paris, Les Belles Lettres, 1961 [reprinted 1969], p. 65); but it is far too specific to talk of direct borrowing. Von Severus's claim that Lupus used Paris B.N. lat. 6332 is based on insufficient textual arguments. Mlle Pellegrin was unable to identify Lupus's hand either in that MS. or in L ('Les manuscrits de Loup de Ferrières', *Bibliothèque de l'École des Chartes*, cxv (1957), 14–15).

fulfils these conditions, the second of which is proved by the example of D: some one at Fleury before the time of Pierre Daniel divided the *De senectute* of Reg. lat. 1587 from the Macrobius of Paris B.N. lat. 16677, and consequently the inconvenient quiring caused the loss of the first leaf of the Macrobius. It is tempting to suppose that L suffered in the same purge.

A: Paris B.N. nouv. acq. lat. 454. A was written at Corbie, probably in the third quarter of the ninth century. It contains: fols. 1–15, Cicero, *De senectute*; fols. 15–18, Cicero, *Somnium Scipionis*; fols. 18ᵛ–81ᵛ, Macrobius, Commentary, with the colophon *de errore emendationis* at fol. 81ᵛ. The evidence for Corbie origin rests on Bernhard Bischoff's masterly delineation of the ninth-century style of that scriptorium.[1] Another possible manuscript of our group is recorded in the Corbie library catalogue of *c.* 1200:[2] item 282, *arismetica. Tullius de senectute. Macrobius.* There is no sign of *arismetica* in A, and the quire-signatures show that no part of the original manuscript is lost at the beginning. We have therefore three possibilities: (1) the entry refers to A at a time when it was bound with an independent volume of *arismetica*, from which it was later again detached; (2) the entry refers to A, but Delisle is incorrect in giving the three works as a single item; (3) the entry refers to another, related manuscript. A belonged later to St. Martin's, Tours. Delisle identified it as no. 33 in the catalogue made in 1700 and printed by Montfaucon in 1739.[3] The detailed notes made by Bréquigny in 1754 make the identification certain despite Montfaucon's disquieting reference to the *Somnium Scipionis* as *excerptum de libro tertio* [sic] *de Republica Ciceronis*—a mistake which has parallels in other manuscripts[4] but is not present

---

[1] B. Bischoff, 'Hadoard und die Klassikerhandschriften aus Corbie', *Mittelalterliche Studien*, i (1966), 49–63, esp. 53–4, 59 (first published in 1961).

[2] Vatican Reg. lat. 520, fols. 2–5, edited by L. Delisle, *Le Cabinet des Manuscrits*, ii (1874), 432–40.

[3] L. Delisle, 'Notice sur les manuscrits disparus de la Bibliothèque de Tours . . .', *Notices et Extraits des manuscrits*, xxxi, pt. i (1884), pp. 264–6, 354–5; Montfaucon, *Bibliotheca* . . ., ii, p. 1336 col. II c–d.

[4] e.g. Paris, B.N. lat. 5001, fol. 28ʳᵛ (French, s. ix). Besides the excerpt from the *Somnium Scipionis*, this MS. also contains a brief *Cronica regum Francorum* ending in 855 (fols. 17–19ᵛ). The MS. may well be of that date. The text of the chronicle is the same as that of the *Chronica regum Francorum Tiliana* mentioned in *Repertorium fontium historiae medii aevi*, iii *Fontes* C (1970), p. 341, and this is probably the lost MS. of Jean de Tillet. Paris, B.N. lat. 7400B is from the same MS.

in A. There is no evidence to show how or when A reached Tours from Corbie.[1]

It seems to be generally accepted that A, after correction by a contemporary hand or hands, was the manuscript used by Hadoardus for the excerpts from the *De senectute* which appear in his Ciceronian florilegium, Vatican Reg. lat. 1762.[2] This work also contains excerpts from Macrobius's Commentary, of which I expect that A will turn out to be the source.

O: *Oxford, Bodleian, D'Orville 77+95.*[3] Like Hadoardus's excerpts, O's text of the *De senectute* is a descendant of A in its corrected form.[4] The texts of the *Somnium Scipionis* and Macrobius's Commentary in O and A are also very close. The script and decoration of O suggest that it was written in south Germany in the tenth century.

O has links with another German manuscript, Munich Clm 6369 (F), an eleventh-century copy of Macrobius's Commentary and the *Somnium Scipionis* itself, which reached Munich with the Freising collection. F does not contain the *De senectute*, but shares

---

[1] Evidence for a direct connection between the two libraries in the 9th century is provided by three famous copies of the third decade of Livy, the 5th-century uncial MS. Paris B.N. lat. 5730 (*C.L.A.* v. 562, with late evidence for Corbie ownership), and its two descendants: Vatican Reg. lat. 762 (*C.L.A.* i. 109), made at Tours s. VIII–IX, and Florence, Laur. pl. 63. 20, made at Corbie in the same period as A (see Bischoff, op. cit., pp. 54, 58).

[2] Bischoff, op. cit., pp. 53–4. Bischoff has finally established in this article that Hadoardus was a 9th-century librarian of Corbie.

[3] The MS., written in several hands, contains: (1), hand A: Cicero, *Pro Marcello* (MS. 77, fols. 1ᵛ–7); *Pro Ligario* (fol. 7–13); *Pro rege Deiotaro* (fols. 13ᵛ–20). (2), hand B: Cicero, *De amicitia* (fols. 21–34ᵛ); *De senectute* (fols. 34ᵛ–47ᵛ). (3), hand A: [Cicero], *In Sallustium inuectiua* (fols. 48–51); [Sallust], *In Ciceronem inuectiua* (fols. 51–2ᵛ). (4), hand B (+ assistant, fol. 57): Cicero, *Somnium Scipionis* (fols. 53–6); Macrobius, Commentary (fols. 56–111). (5), hand B: items on music (fols. 111ᵛ–114ᵛ), see below, p. 161 n. 1. (6), hands B, C, D: Hyginus, *Astronomica* (MS. 95). The last two quires of the Hyginus (MS. 95, fols. 25–38) are palimpsest. The lower text contained diagrams (fols. 28ᵛ, 31) identical to those found with the astronomical excerpts from Pliny, *Nat. hist.*, bk. ii (see below, p. 161 n. 5). Its format and script suggest that it was waste from the same scriptorium and period as the upper text.
I was led to the reunion of the two parts by the discovery that the early catalogue of the D'Orville collection by J. C. Strackhovius (MS. D'Orville 302) has a code giving the sources of the MSS.; the entries for MSS. 77 and 95 refer to the same lot number (486) in the sale catalogue of the library of Isaac Verburg (Amsterdam, 1746).

[4] See G. S. Vogel, *The Major Manuscripts of Cicero's* De senectute (1939), pp. 46–54.

with O three short items on musical theory.[1] The manuscript was written by two scribes who used two different exemplars; that of the second scribe (fol. 35^v line 16 = Commentary I. 20. 16, Willis 81. 24 || *longitudo* onwards) was textually very close to A and O, and unlike O contained the colophon found in A and D *de errore emendationis* (see above, p. 151).

The existence of two German manuscripts so closely related to the earlier French group means that a copy of *Cato de senectute cum Macrobio* must have passed from France to south Germany by the end of the tenth century. Such a movement of texts has been demonstrated most vividly in Bernhard Bischoff's reconstruction of the activities of Hartwic, pupil of Fulbert of Chartres and monk of St. Emmeram.[2] Macrobius's Commentary on the *Somnium Scipionis* was in fact one of the texts which Hartwic brought back to Germany from France, and the copy still exists in Munich Clm 14436.[3] The earliest part of this manuscript (fols. 34–61), written in northern France, s. x, gives a truncated version of the text, containing the sections on astronomy and musical theory (I. 14. 21–II. 9. 10). This form of text is common in the tenth and eleventh centuries; the oldest surviving copy is French, s. ix ex., perhaps written at Auxerre,[4] but the majority are German.[5] Hartwic added the *Somnium Scipionis* itself and the missing chapters at the

[1] O, fols. 111^v–114^v; F, fols. 63^v–66^v. The items are (1) [Jerome], *Epistula ad Dardanum, de diuersis generibus musicorum*, with diagrams (see B. Lambert, *Bibliotheca Hieronymiana Manuscripta*, iii*A* (1970), no. 323); (2) short excerpts on music from Isidore, *Etymologiae*, iii. xix–xxii, beginning *Ad omnem autem sonum quae materies cantilenarum est*, ending *quae percussa inuicem se tangunt, et sonum faciunt*; (3) *Ambrosii Macrobii de simphoniis musicae. Ex innumera uarietate numerorum . . . epogdous continet tonum*. An extract from Macrobius's Commentary II. 1. 14–25, showing considerable differences from the original, as quoted in the main texts of the MSS.

[2] 'Literarisches und künstlerisches Leben in St. Emmeram . . .', *Mittelalterliche Studien*, ii (1967), 80–4 (first printed in 1933).

[3] Op. cit., p. 82.

[4] It is the first surviving work (Berne 347, fols. 1–22) in the great corpus which includes the earliest copy of Petronius' *excerpta uulgaria*, Berne 347+357+330 + Paris B.N. lat. 7665 + Leyden Voss. Lat. Qu. 30, fols. 57–58.

[5] e.g. Munich Clm 6364, written at Freising, s. x, see below, p. 162; Clm 14353, fols. 94–117 + Clm 29020, fols. (3–4), German, s. x ex.–xi in., medieval home St. Emmeram; Vatican Pal. lat. 1577, German, s. xi; etc. For the characteristics of this group see L. Ianus, ed., *Macrobii . . . opera*, i (1848), pp. lxiv ff., lxxix. The travelling-companion of this form of text is the famous group of astronomical excerpts from Pliny, *Nat. hist.*, bk. ii, for which see V. H. King, 'An Investigation of some Astronomical Excerpts from Pliny's Natural History found in Manuscripts of the Earlier Middle Ages', Oxford B.Litt. thesis, 1969.

beginning of the Commentary in his own hand (fols. 10–32ᵛ), but his copy still lacks the final chapters of book II.

O and F show that the text of Macrobius's Commentary made a second, independent crossing to Germany, this time in the complete form. Judging by the number of extant manuscripts, the truncated form became popular, whereas the form of O and F did not take root. F, indeed, is an example of contamination between the two forms, for the exemplar of the first scribe was, like Hartwic's manuscript, a copy of the truncated version with the earlier chapters added.

For a second example of contamination between the two strains of text, we can return from Germany to France, Fleury, and MS. D. An angular hand of the Fleury type, s. x ex.–xi in. (additional hand (3), see above), has added material to D from a copy of the truncated form, including an introduction before the beginning of the Commentary at Reg. lat. 1587, fol. 80ᵛ:[1]

Macrobius honicretes, id est interpres somniorum. In hoc libro de differentia stellarum et siderum carpso ex ipsius libris prudenter inter Scipionis apocalipsin quam in somniis conspexit interpretari curauit. Ex cuius etiam Scipionis uerbis ad filium somnia narrantis multa inseruit, ut eorum interpretatio adque solutio libere discurrat adque clarescat. Macros grece, longum latine. Bia uia. Inde Macrobius longa uia, utpote de caelo ad terram.

The phrase *libro de differentia stellarum et siderum carpso ex ipsius libris* refers to the title usually found at the beginning of the opening section of the truncated form: *Ex libris Macrobii Ambrosii de differentia stellarum et siderum* (see I. 14. 21). Such a reference is out of place at the beginning of a complete manuscript such as D. The same introduction is found at the beginning of a genuine copy of the truncated form, Munich Clm 6364, written at Freising, s. x.[2] It seems likely, then, that a copy of the truncated version was present at Fleury, again at about the time of Abbo.

---

[1] Other material includes the interpolation from I. 12. 1, *Et ita lacteus* . . . , see above, p. 154 n. 2(a). At fols. 33ᵛ–34, a passage omitted in the truncated form, I. 19. 23 (Willis 77. 18) ‖ *uitam* . . . *et* ‖ 19. 27 (Willis 78. 15), is marked *A* at the beginning and *B* at the end. The same hand also adds material from a complete copy of Macrobius, including the *subscriptio* of Aurelius Memmius Symmachus with the title to bk. II at fol. 41ᵛ.

[2] In the margin of fol. 1ᵛ, in the hand of the main scribe. For a description of the MS. see N. Daniel, *Handschriften des zehnten Jahrhunderts aus der Freisinger Dombibliothek* (*Münchener Beiträge zur Mediävistik und Renaissance-Forschung*, xi, 1973) 152–3.

Cluny. Two further manuscripts containing *Cato de senectute cum Macrobio*, unidentifiable among the extant manuscripts, are recorded in the catalogue of the library of Cluny which was prepared during the reign of abbot Hugo III (1158–61):[1]

Item 477. Volumen in quo continetur Tullius de senectute, et quiddam de sex etatibus, Beda de temporibus, somnium Simeonis [*sic*], commentariumque Macrobii in ipsum somnium, et quedam regule abaci.

Item 518. Volumen in quo continetur Tullius de senectute ad Catonem, et commentum Macrobii in sompnium Scipionis.

The Relationship between the Three Ninth-century Manuscripts, D, L, and A

The stemma produced by P. Wuilleumier[2] for the *De senectute* shows all three as members of his Y family, with A and D as twins, and L descended from an earlier link in the chain. With regard to the Macrobius, I can say no more at this stage of my work on the text than that D, L, and A are very closely connected. There is one striking difference among the three. A contains the text of the *Somnium Scipionis* itself, between the *De senectute* and Macrobius's Commentary, as part of the original make-up of the manuscript. Despite a missing leaf at the crucial place, it is clear that originally D did not contain the *Somnium*; a leaf added at the end of the Macrobius (Paris, B.N. lat. 16677, fol. 73) contains the beginning of the text by two Fleury hands of the second half of the tenth century or first half of the eleventh.[3] Enough survives of L to show that the *Somnium* was never present between the *De senectute* and the Macrobius, as in A, though it may, for all we know, have been at the end. A is in fact the only extant ninth-century manuscript to my knowledge which contains the full text of the *Somnium Scipionis*. It is not present in Paris B.N. lat. 6370, the earliest surviving manuscript of Macrobius's Commentary (French, s. IX[1]), corrected by Lupus of Ferrières;[4] it is an addition of s. X or XI (fols. 71ᵛ–74) in Cologne, Dombibl. 186, a ninth-century manuscript related to the DLA group; there is no sign of

---

[1] Paris B.N. lat. 13108, fols. 236–49, published by L. Delisle, *Inventaire des manuscrits de la Bibliothèque Nationale: Fonds de Cluni* (1884), pp. 337–73.

[2] *Caton l'ancien*, 3rd edn. (1961), 60–7.

[3] The text breaks off at *affricanum* ‖ 3. 3 (Willis 157. 23), at the end of fol. 73ᵛ. The rest of the text, if written, is now lost.

[4] See É. Pellegrin, *Bibliothèque de l'École des Chartes*, cxv (1957), 11.

it, naturally enough, in the truncated form of Macrobius's text in the Berne corpus (see above, p. 161 and n. 4).

If the relationship of A, D, and L as described by Wuilleumier for the *De senectute* holds good for the Macrobius, the absence of the *Somnium Scipionis* in D and L argues that it was included in A or in an immediate ancestor of A from another textual stream. This raises some interesting questions. It had always been accepted as axiomatic that the *Somnium Scipionis* was the only large fragment of Cicero's *De re publica* to survive in the living textual tradition because it descended with the text of Macrobius's Commentary. We have seen that the *Somnium Scipionis* appears as an original part in only one of the six surviving ninth-century manuscripts of Macrobius's Commentary; is this to be explained as an accidental freak of survival? When was the text of the *Somnium Scipionis* extracted from the *De re publica* and added to the Commentary? It may not be without significance that A was written at Corbie, famous as a focus-point for ancient manuscripts and half-forgotten texts.

Cicero's treatise on old age, and the Commentary of Macrobius which preserves the climax of Cicero's *De re publica*, the dream of Scipio on the rewards of the righteous after death, form a logical unit. Indeed, not only is the subject-matter related, but some of the characters in the two dialogues, the *De senectute* and the *De re publica*, are the same; the most notable of these is Scipio Aemilianus himself. The unit *Cato de senectute cum Macrobio* survives in four manuscripts: D, L, and A from ninth-century France (Fleury and Corbie), and O from tenth-century Germany. Two lost manuscripts are recorded in the twelfth century at Cluny, and a possible third at Corbic. I have tried to indicate other, related, manuscripts containing Macrobius's Commentary without Cicero's *De senectute*. The existing manuscripts suggest that despite its vigour at Fleury in the time of Abbo, this family of Macrobius's text had become sterile by the twelfth century.

B. C. BARKER-BENFIELD

SIGLA

A PARIS, Bibl. Nationale, nouv. acq. lat. 454
D VATICAN CITY, Bibl. Apostolica, Reg. lat. 1587, fols. 65–80 +
    PARIS B.N. lat. 16677
F MUNICH, Bayerische Staatsbibl., Clm. 6369
L LEYDEN, Universiteitsbibl., Voss. Lat. Fol. 12β (= fols. 15–26) +
    Voss. Lat. Fol. 122 + LONDON, British Libr., Royal 15 B. XII,
    fols. 1–2
O OXFORD, Bodleian, D'Orville 77+95
P PARIS, Bibl. Nationale, lat. 7299

7

The Graz and Zürich Apocalypse of Saint Paul: an Independent Medieval Witness to the Greek

1. *Two New Texts and their Significance*

THE Western tradition of the Apocalypse of Saint Paul depends mainly on an early Latin version, L^1, of the Greek made in the mid fifth century or soon thereafter and represented in survival by two manuscripts of the eighth and ninth centuries. With but a couple of exceptions, all the known subsequent instances of the work stem directly or indirectly from that version. This includes the forms in the various Western vernaculars, as well as the redactions in Latin. The two exceptions are a brief Latin fragment, *F*, erroneously incorporated in a text of what is otherwise a representative of the main tradition, and an even more fragmentary German version in verse, *K*, found in a manuscript of the late thirteenth century.[1]

The value of these two texts and the original which they evince, L^2, is not only that they demonstrate a further medieval access to the ancient Greek text of the Apocalypse, independent of the main Latin tradition, but also that they offer additional witness both to the nature of that ancient text itself and to the variant forms which it took as copies of it began to multiply and furnish the bases for the many versions, Eastern and Western, by which the Apocalypse came to be known throughout the Mediterranean basin and be-

[1] For a description of these relationships see T. Silverstein, *Visio Sancti Pauli: the History of the Apocalypse in Latin together with Nine Texts* (Studies and Documents, iv, ed. Kirsopp and Silva Lake, London, 1935), esp. chaps. iii and iv and the diagrams on pp. 39 and 60–3; and 'The Vision of St. Paul: New Links and Patterns in the Western Tradition', *Archives*, xxvi (1959), 224–5. As in those accounts, in the present essay *sigla* in roman type represent hypothetical or linking texts or versions, in italic type texts actually extant. For the medieval Latin redactions, which survive generally in more than one manuscript, the *sigla* are unitalicized roman numerals.

yond, from Egypt and Cilicia to Russia and from Armenia to Ireland. It has long been evident that the Greek text, G, discovered
by Constantine Tischendorf, though preserving as a whole the
archetypal language of the Apocalypse, is both abbreviated and in
other ways imperfect. It must be supplemented, if we are to get
some notion of what the archetype was like, by the details of such
fuller and better versions, each going back separately to a Greek
source, as the Syriac, S, the Old Russian, R, the Coptic, C, and
the Long Latin, L^1. But their differences also suggest that the
Greek underwent many changes, of which the Tischendorf text
gives only one group. To the story of those changes the two aberrant Western versions—Latin fragment and fragmentary German
translation—add important complicating particulars.

The existence of the variant Western tradition, L^2, was hypo-
thesized many years ago, on the evidence of the Latin fragment,[1]
but no exemplar of its Latin original was otherwise known to have
survived. It now turns out, however, that two such copies are
extant, both in manuscripts of the fifteenth century: Zürich,
Zentralbibliothek, MS. C 101 (467); and Graz, Universitätsbibliothek, MS. 856. We may here call the former copy Z and the
latter Gz.

The Zürich manuscript, which earlier belonged to the Stiftsbibliothek of St. Gallen and was carried to its present home during
the eighteenth-century wars,[2] has been described on a number of
occasions, most extensively in recent times by Jacob Werner, who
notes the presence there of a text of the *Reuelaciones sancti Pauli*
but is unaware of its nature and special significance.[3] More interesting is the surviving fifteenth-century account by Father Gallus
Kemly, a not unknown and evidently contentious cleric several
times astray from the cloister, who was also himself the scribe of

---

[1] E. Wieber, *De Apocalypsis S. Pauli Codicibus* (Marburg Dissertation, 1904),
pp. 25 ff. Cf. R. P. Casey, 'The Apocalypse of Paul', *Journal of Theological
Studies*, xxxiv (1933), 3; and Silverstein, *Visio Sancti Pauli*, pp. 36–7, 38–9, and
notes.

[2] See F. Weidmann, *Geschichte der Bibliothek von St. Gallen seit ihrer Grün-
dung um das Jahr 830 bis auf 1841* (St. Gallen, 1841), pp. 89–111, and cf. 438.

[3] *Beiträge zur Kunde der lateinischen Literatur des Mittelalters aus Handschriften gesammelt* (Aarau, 1905), pp. 152–83. The account of *Paul* is on p. 159,
with the erroneous note, 'Derselbe Text im Cod. S. Gall. 1050, 248; 1012, 159'.
The latter texts are of Latin redaction IIIc: *Visio Sancti Pauli*, pp. 161 ff. and
220. See also L. C. Mohlberg, *Katalog der Hss. der Zentralbibliothek Zürich*, i
(1952), 52–3.

the manuscript he is describing.[1] Since the description was written about the year 1470, it sets the *terminus ad quem* for the dating of his copy of the Apocalypse. Other items in the manuscript referring to contemporary events bear dates from 1446 to 1457,[2] so that it is fair to assume that the wayward *conventualis* set down his transcript of the Apocalypse of Saint Paul not long after the middle of the century.

The text of the Apocalypse occurs on fols. 70–74ᵛ but neither its immediate setting nor the miscellaneous character of the manuscript as a whole would seem to throw any obvious light on the question as to where Father Kemly got it from. Immediately preceding it are several pieces of what we may call exotic interest: a letter of Prester John to King Manuel of Greece and the Emperor Frederick, a *narracio de sancto Thoma apostolo*, i.e. Thomas of India, and an account *de lacte miraculoso beate Marie virginis* taken from a story of the three magi; but also a contemporary *imprecacio* against thieves of Church property. Following it are a number of works on the Psalms, together with an *Officium ribaldorum*, that is, a parody of the Mass for drinkers. Whether or not this list of texts and their order in the manuscripts were established by an earlier collection which served as Father Kemly's source cannot on present evidence be determined. The codex Vienna 362, which contains the previously known Latin fragment *F* of this version, is otherwise very different in content from his,[3] and this, it will shortly appear, is true also of Graz 856. As for the manuscript of the fragmentary German *K*, if in its original state it had anything similar among its leaves, we can no longer know, since everything

---

[1] Zürich, Zentralbibl. Cod. A 135 (B 240; 785), fols. 2–13: 'Hec est registri pretacti tituli incepcio bibliothece fratris Galli.' Printed by P. Lehmann, *Mittelalterliche Bibliothekskataloge Deutschlands und der Schweiz*, i: *Die Bistümer Konstanz und Chur* (Munich, 1918), pp. 124–35: 'revelaciones sancti Pauli rapti', p. 125. Cf. Mohlberg, item no. 14. For an account of Father Kemly see the *curriculum vitae* in St. Gallen, Stiftsbibliothek Cod. 919, pp. 190–2: G. Scherrer, *Verzeichniss der Handschriften der Stiftsbibliothek von St. Gallen* (Halle, 1875), p. 346; Scherrer's biographical note to Cod. 972ᵇ, *Verzeichniss*, pp. 366–7; and L. Traube in *Abhandlungen der Historischen Klasse der K. bayerischen Akademie*, xxi (1898), 701.

[2] See esp. fols. 143, 144, and 154ᵛ. Following fol. 37ᵛ is a note on a pilgrim's confession dated 1483, but this is in a different hand and was bound in later.

[3] See *Tabulae Codicum Manu Scriptorum . . . in Bibliotheca Palatina Vindobonensi Asservatorum*, i (Vienna, 1864), 54–5. The text of *Paul*, on fols. 7–8ᵛ, is preceded by a *Historia Apollonii Tyrii* and followed by a *Dialogus lucis et tenebrarum*.

but the fragment itself has been lost.[1] The original of Father Kemly's text of the Apocalypse was, however, considerably older than the fifteenth century, when he was engaged in writing it down, as is evident not only from the dates of the manuscripts themselves in which the previously discovered fragments appear, but also from the fact that the German version of that original must first have been made about the year 1150.[2] L[2] is therefore a Latin translation of its Greek source completed, on this evidence, by the middle of the twelfth century at the latest.

The manuscript in which *Gz* occurs came originally from the Cistercian foundation at Neuberg in Austria. Several of its pieces are signed as having been written down by one Brother Henricus Schäbel from Vischach near Wiener Neustadt, *monachus et sacerdos monasterii Novimontensis*, who dates them variously 1428 and 1431, when the scribe was sixty-one and sixty-four years of age, respectively. As these items are the ninth, seventeenth, and twenty-third in a collection of which the first text, occupying fols. 1–6ᵛ, is our copy of L[2], it is likely that *Gz* was written down during or before the earlier of these years.[3] For the rest, Graz 856 contains a miscellany, among which are to be found stories from the *Dialogi monachorum* of Caesarius of Heisterbach; a group of pieces on the Passion, including a version of the *Evangelium Nicodemi*; a commentary on the Eucharist; an exchange of letters attributed to Saints Augustine and Cyril; tales of magnates *qui fuerunt potentes* from the *Gesta romanorum*; a poem of moral precepts; a group of exempla beginning *Secundus phylosophus philosophatus fuit hec sequencia*; and a group of tracts on indulgences, confession, and the imposing of penance. Neither in character nor in order do

[1] Vienna, Nationalbibl. Cod. Ser. N. 338: O. Mazal and F. Unterkircher, *Katalog der abendländischen Handschriften der Österreichischen Nationalbibliothek*, Series Nova, i (Vienna, 1965), 121–2. Text first published by T. G. von Karajan, *Deutsche Sprach-Denkmale des zwölften Jahrhunderts* (Vienna, 1846), pp. 109–10. Republished from Karajan with corrections by C. v. Kraus, *Deutsche Gedichte des zwölften Jahrhunderts* (Halle, 1894), pp. 38–41 and 187 ff. Kraus notes the connection with the Latin in MS. Vienna 362.

[2] See G. Ehrismann, *Geschichte der Deutschen Literatur bis zum Ausgang des Mittelalters*, ii. 1 (Munich, 1922), 161–2, and the literature referred to there.

[3] Anton Kern, *Die Handschriften der Universitätsbibliothek Graz*, ii (Handschriftenverzeichnisse österreichischer Bibliotheken herausgegeben von der Österreichischen Nationalbibliothek, Vienna, 1956), 82–4. It should be observed, however, that near the end of the MS. a tractate on indulgences is dated 1462.

the contents coincide with Father Gallus Kemly's Zürich manuscript or with Vienna 362.

The scope of Z's and Gz's contents makes patent at once that their texts are not further copies of one of the abbreviated Latin redactions normally circulating in the Middle Ages. Though they do not contain the preface of the archetype recounting the discovery of the Apocalypse in the foundations of Paul's house in Tarsus during the year 420, as the story appears in Tischendorf's Greek and, with variations, in James's Long Latin and the Syriac,[1] they nevertheless preserve in somewhat reduced form most of the materials from Sections 3 to 49 of those versions, that is to say, substantially all that the archetypal text contained. Yet they cannot simply be a variant exemplar of the fifth-century Long Latin, L^1, hitherto known to us in James's text from Paris, P, and the imperfect but in some respects superior text from St. Gallen, $St\ G$, published by the present writer.[2] This is plain from the regular deviation of their language from that of P and $St\ G$, both lexically and syntactically, evidence which points to an entirely independent rendering of the Greek original. Moreover, it also happens that Z and Gz differ between themselves in certain minutiae of language and substance, some of which are patently the consequence of scribal error or amendment, but others inherited from previous exemplars of L^2 which were their copy texts. By comparing these variants with the fragmentary F and K we can build a stemma of L^2's textual history having considerable complexity.

Nor is this all in the way of discovery that Z and Gz lead us to. Their common deviations from the texts of L^1, as we very soon become aware, are also in part to be ascribed to their Greek original itself, which in its turn was substantially unlike Tischendorf's G, and in many ways different from the Greek sources of the other major versions. In consequence, we shall now be able to reconstruct, with much greater refinement than previously, the development of the Greek traditions on which all the subsequent texts of the Apocalypse are founded.

[1] C. Tischendorf, *Apocalypses Apocryphae* (Leipzig, 1866), pp. 34–5; M. R. James, *Apocrypha Anecdota*, i (Texts and Studies: Contributions to Biblical and Patristic Literature, ii. 3, Cambridge, 1893), 11; and G. Ricciotti, *L'Apocalisse di Paolo siriaca* (Brescia, 1932), i. 78 ff., §§ 50 ff. Tischendorf and James give the date, respectively, as 380 and 388, but see Silverstein, 'The Date of the "Apocalypse of Paul"', *Mediaeval Studies*, xxiv (1962), 335–48.

[2] *Visio Sancti Pauli*, pp. 131–47.

Extended proof of these statements must await the printing of L² and its commentary. Meanwhile they may be illustrated here by a selection of some key passages from the texts; after which will be given a tentative new stemma of the various versions, based on the distinctions which the illustrations support. That stemma will reassess the relations of all the chief forms, both Eastern and Western, but will be rather more precise for the traditions in Latin and founded on previous reconstructions by the present writer. It will represent, the reader will observe, a conclusion rather than an argument leading to that end; the full display of the evidence being reserved, once again, for the edition now in preparation.

2. *The Independence of L²: its Latinity*

Variations in language between L¹ and L² disclose two different forms of translation. Typical of such difference are the five examples given in the following passages:

(*a*) In a number of places, speaking of the going-out of the souls at death. Thus:

[§ 11][1]

G ἀπέρχονται μετὰ τὴν τελείωσιν αὐτῶν
L¹ cum defuncti fuerint[2]
L² post vite terminum

[§ 13]

G ἐξέρχονται ἐκ τοῦ κόσμου
L¹ exeuntes de mundo
L² de seculo transeuntes

[§ 25]

G ἐξερχόμενος
L¹ cum exierit de mundo
L² post obitum vite

---

[1] Section numbers are those established by Tischendorf and followed for the Long Latin (*P*) by James and the present writer (*St G*). Ricciotti's numbering for *S* varies and *R* and *C* have no numbering in the editions of, respectively, N. Tikhonravov, *Pamyatniki otrechennoi russkoi literatury*, ii (Moscow, 1863), 40–58, and Sir E. A. Wallis Budge, *Miscellaneous Coptic Texts in the Dialect of Upper Egypt* (London, 1915), text pp. 534–74, translation pp. 1043 ff.

[2] In general L¹ is quoted from James (*P*) and L² from *Z*, except where otherwise noted.

(*b*) In the name of an infernal angel:

[§ 34]

G ὁ ἄγγελος ὁ Τεμελοῦχος [*C* Aftemeloukhos, Ethiopic Timliaqos][1]
A rare term, meaning tutelary angel, evidently changed in
L¹'s source to a more familiar term Ταρταροῦχος, i.e. angel
ruling over Tartarus, since we find in

L¹ (*P* and *St G*) angelos tartarucos, angelus tartaruchus
L² princeps tenebrarum [an alternative rendering of Ταρταροῦχος]

(*c*) In the account of sinners tormented by a red-hot razor:

[§ 36]

The passage is missing from *G* but occurs in *S* and *C*. Whatever the word was in the original—ξυστήρ or ξυστήριον =
razor, scraper, tongs—the two Latin texts give clearly variant
renderings of the same Greek phrase:

L¹ (*P* and *St G*) nouaculam grandem ignitam
L² rasorio valde incidente [= incandente?]

(*d*) In the plea of the souls in Hell for mercy:

[§ 43]

G ἐλέησον, κύριε, τοὺς υἱοὺς τῶν ἀνθρώπων, οὓς ἔπλασας κατ'
εἰκόνα σήν
L¹ miserere plasmae tuae [*St G* plasmatio tua] . . . miserere
imagini tue
L² miserere operibus manuum tuarum

(*e*) In the description of angels singing before the Virgin Mary:

[§ 46]

G πλῆθος ἀγγέλων ὑμνούντων αὐτήν
L¹ angelos ante ipsam hymnos dicentes
L² ante quam angelici cetus leti concinerunt coreas

Similar disagreements between the two Latin versions in word,
phrase, and syntax, occurring as they do regularly and throughout
the texts, are evidence of the presence of two translators independently at work on their sources.

[1] For *C*, Budge, pp. 540, fol. 12*a*, and 106*b*. The Ethiopic is in fact an Apocalypse of the Virgin but based very closely on a text of *Paul*: Marius Chaine,
Apocrypha de B. Maria Virgine (Scriptores Aethiopici, Series I, tom. vii, Corpus
Scriptorum Christianorum Orientalium, Rome, 1909), text pp. 53–80, versio
45–68.

3. *The Variant Greek Original of L²*

Though the translator of L² rendered his original idiosyncratically, he also worked from a Greek text which varied in many details from that of L¹. In the illustrations which follow Tischendorf's version is used as the basis for comparison but its own peculiarities are such that it must be supplemented by variant readings from other versions of the Long texts, whose evidence frequently throws light on the special form of L²'s Greek original. A further consequence of the comparison, beyond what it shows of the character of L², is the information it furnishes about the development of the Greek texts themselves and their relations to the non-Greek versions generally.

(*a*) In the City of Christ, St. Paul sees all the prophets:

[§ 25]

G πάντας τοὺς προφήτας

L² omnes prophetas dei; and *S* is the same

L¹ profetas minores et maiores [*St G* maiores et minores]; and *C* corroborates this reading

(*b*) In the same passage is a remarkable crux:

L¹ (*P* and *St G*) Que est uia haec? et dixit mihi: Haec est uia prophetarum; and *C* confirms this reading; but

G αἱ ᾠδαὶ αὗται πασῶν τῶν προφητειῶν

[= these are the songs of all the prophecies]

Z, however, ibi cernebat decorem prophetarum; and L²'s reading is complicated by *Gz*, cernebat delectabilem uiam (though there is some evidence that *Gz* sometimes 'improves' the text when the copyist does not like it as it is). Evidently, therefore, the Greek versions themselves varied here in one of three ways:

ὁδός = road, uia ⎫
⎬ both grammatically feminine
ᾠδή = ode, cantus ⎭

εἴδη or εἶδος = beautiful form, decor; feminine or neuter

(*c*) In the City of Christ, St Paul sees David:

[§ 29]

G ὁ Δαυὶδ ὁ προφήτης

L² Dauit . . . qui fuit rex et propheta; confirmed by *S*

L¹ omits the descriptive phrase altogether, and so does *C*

(*d*) In *infernum* where the sinners beg for mercy:

[§ 43]

G μιᾷ φωνῇ μεγάλη . . . καὶ προσέπεσαν ἐνώπιον τοῦ Θεοῦ

L² ingenti clamore . . . ceciderunt . . . in facies suas proni . . . et clamabant ad deum

L¹, *S*, and *C* all omit these phrases

(*e*) At the beginning of the journey to Paradise Paul meets Enoch and Elijah:

[§ 20]

L² 'Hic', inquit, 'Enoch primus scriba.' Hinc abiit obuiam sanctum vatem Heliiam, qui eum post magne dilectionis oscula compleuit (*Gz* compellauit); *S*, *C*, and the Armenian agree

L¹ (*P* and *St G*), however, gives Enoch and the sun: Et dixit mihi: Hic est Enoc scriba iusticiae. Et ingressus sum interiori loci illius, et statim uidi solem et ueniens salutauit me ilarens et gaudens

G gives Enoch only and *R* substitutes Isaiah for Elijah. Hence the Greek sources must variously have confused *ΗΛΙΑΣ* with *ΗΛΙΟΣ* at this point, and the surviving versions in different ways reflect that confusion, but L²'s original was in this matter correct.

4. *Gz and Z: the Transmission of L²'s Texts*

We have already observed that the Graz and Zürich texts are extensive exemplars of L², but *Gz* is in many respects a better and fuller version than *Z*, which suffers some omissions and abbreviations from either Father Kemly's inadvertence or that of his copy text. The most immediately interesting of the passages are these:

(*a*) Following its title, *Reuelaciones sancti Pauli quando raptus fuit*, *Z* begins at once with the text of the Apocalypse proper: Omnipotentis dei uerbum factum est ad sanctum Paulum dicens, 'O Paule, loquere populo et dic, "Quousque wltis peccatum super peccata operare et temptare deum . . ."' *Gz*, on the contrary, prefaces the text with an elaborate heading:

Incipiunt visiones seu reuelaciones sancti Pauli apostoli de quibus dicitur quod ea in secreto reuelauerit dilectis suis in Xristo, videlicet, Luce euangeliste, Thymotheo et sancto Dyonisio coadiutoribus suis, et dicit sic: 'Scio hominem in Xristo ante annos quatuordecim, siue in

corpore siue extra corpus nescio deus scit, quoniam raptus est in para-
dysum et audiuit archana uerba que non licet homini loqui', et cetera
[2 Corinthians 12:2–5].

Whether or not the opening sentence of the heading itself goes
back to a Greek source, hence to the original text of L², is not
certain, but the quotation from 2 Corinthians surely does, since it
is found in such varied versions as *G*, L¹(*P*), and *R*, and indirectly
S, and Saint Augustine also testifies to its presence in the Apocalypse in the early fifth century even as he condemns the work.[1]

(*b*) In all the full texts which preserve the beginning of his
raptus, that is, *G*, *R*, *S*, L¹(*P*), Saint Paul witnesses the going-out
of three souls at death, one of a just man, the second of an evil, and
the third of an evil man also who seeks to deny his sins (§§ 14–18).
By error *Z* leaves out all but the passage on the first soul, that is, it
omits §§ 15–17 of the text entirely and everything of § 18 but its
last words, which parallel the ending of § 14. *Gz* is complete in
these sections, indeed fuller here than *G* and close throughout to
L¹(*P*), *S*, and *R*.

(*c*) In the sections describing Saint Paul's encounters in the
Earthly Paradise with various of the major and minor prophets,
Gz (§ 49) includes a meeting with Jeremiah, found also in such
other texts as L¹(*P*) and *S*. This is omitted by *Z*.

(*d*) The ending of the Apocalypse is unsatisfactory in all the
surviving Long texts. During Saint Paul's meeting in the Earthly
Paradise with Elijah and Elisha *G*, L¹(*P*), and *R* come to an
abrupt close in the midst of Elijah's speech, and there is no speech
at all for Elisha:

G ἐγώ εἰμι Ἡλίας ὁ προφήτης ὁ προσευξάμενος εἰς τὸν θεόν . . .
πολλάκις γοῦν καὶ οἱ ἄγγελοι παρεκάλεσαν τὸν Θεὸν διὰ τὸν
ὑετόν· καὶ ἤκουσα· μακροθυμήσατε, ἕως ἂν ὁ ἀγαπητός μου Ἡλίας
προσεύξεται [*sic*], κἀγὼ ἀποστείλω τὸν ὑετὸν ἐπὶ τὴν γῆν . . .

L¹(*P*) ego sum Elyas qui horaui, et propter uerbum meum non
  pluit celum annis tribus et mensibus .VI. propter iniusticias
  hominum. Iustus deus et uerax, qui facit uoluntatem famu-
  lorum suorum: sepe etenim angeli deprecati sunt dominum
  propter pluuiam, et dixit: Pacienter agite quoadusque seruus

---

[1] Migne, *P.L.* xxxv. 1885A.

meus Elyas horet et precetur propter hoc, et ego mittam pluuiam super terram;

EXPLICIT VISIO SANCTI PAVLI;

S contains some additional matter. There is still no speech for
Elisha, but Elijah completes his discourse and departs, and the revelation comes to a close swiftly with Saint Paul's return to himself.
Then, perhaps to mask the abruptness of this conclusion, *S* shifts
to the very end the story of the document's discovery in Tarsus,
which occurs as preface in *G* and L¹ (*P*).[1] *C* differs from all the
other versions here. Not only does it add further meetings with
patriarch, prophet, and apostle, but it continues with visits to
other dwellings of the righteous, much of which is patently its
author's own elaboration. The text then concludes with Saint
Paul's being carried back to the Mount of Olives, where he finds
the Apostles assembled and declares to them everything he has
seen; and this may have been the ending of the very earliest,
third-century, form of the Apocalypse.[2] Whatever the case, some
time after the first two or three decades of the fifth century, when
the Greek text was reissued in, as it were, a second edition containing the 'Tarsus preface',[3] a copy may have circulated which
ended the vision swiftly as in *S*, and another followed broken off
in the midst of Elijah's speech, as in *G*, L¹ (*P*), and *R*.

Z ends even more imperfectly than this, omitting as it does
Elijah and Elisha altogether and substituting a general and un-
individualized summary of further beatific encounters: 'Consequenter per omnes gradus prophetarum susceptus et consolatus fuit
Paulus. Et vidit ibi plurima gaudia electorum, qui in ipsis per-
manebunt in secula seculorum. AMEN.' *Gz*, however, gives us at
this point what may be the best surviving version of the fifth-
century text. Rather abbreviated though it is and with some losses
of distinctive phraseology, as is the way with L² throughout—
hence perhaps of L²'s Greek source itself—it yet preserves the
speeches of both Elijah and Elisha and comes to an end, if swiftly
yet completely, with the Apostle's being returned to his starting-
point on earth:

Tunc vidit Helyam et Helyseum. Et Helyas ait Paulo, 'Cum iam

---

[1] Ricciotti, i. 78 ff., §§ 50 ff.

[2] Budge, pp. 1082–3 and 572–3, fols. 36*b*–7*a*. See Casey, pp. 24–5, and *Visio
Sancti Pauli*, pp. 32–3 and 108–9 n. 80.

[3] See Silverstein, *Mediaeval Studies*, xxiv, esp. 336–7 and 347.

homines multum essent peccatores continuit dominus celum ne plueret annos tres et menses sex. Propter sermones meos emendauerunt se et dedit eis pluuiam.' Et dixit Heliseus, 'Et deus fecit vnum hominem per me reuiuiscere sicut tu Paule sepe audisti dicere.' Tunc angelus reduxit sanctum Paulum ad locum ubi invenit eum prius propter ut acciperet ibi honores perpetuales. Amen. Amen.

These then are a few of the differences between Z and Gz, differences which occur everywhere in the narrative, sometimes in the smallest details of word or phrase. And though, where the two copies disagree, Gz on the whole offers superior readings, it also tends occasionally to 'improve' the text. Both, together with F and K, provide a good basis for recovering the original form of L^2, just as they furnish some idea of its development in the course of time from the twelfth to the fifteenth century. As for their relations with the previously known fragments, Gz will generally be found to be closer to F than is Z, though none of the three copies coincide exactly, hence none can be the source of either of the others. With respect to the German fragment K, its early date requires for its source a Latin original different from those texts extant, just as its brevity and its character as a verse translation make difficult the special association of that original with any single one of them.

On the basis of all these observations we may now construct a stemma of L^2. In the previous study of the Western tradition made by the present writer, the relationship of that version to the rest of the texts could, on the evidence of the fragmentary F, only be depicted in simple fashion, with K in an ambiguous connection with the Latin source:

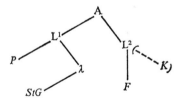

A represents the Greek archetype, fifth-century or later and broken off in the midst of Elijah's speech, which was the source of all the Latin versions. What the new testimony of Z and Gz suggests, since it has wider implication than merely for L^2 itself, will appear in the next section.

5. *The Textual Traditions of the Apocalypse*

The accumulation during the last century and a quarter of copies and of other evidence relating to the development of the Apocalypse of Saint Paul makes possible and necessary a reappraisal of the forms in which it was diffused, as well as of its original form. A minute comparison of the Greek and Latin texts made some years ago by the present writer produced this diagram of their relationships:

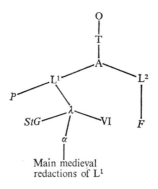

Main medieval
redactions of L¹

Here O stands for the primitive Greek version written, probably in Egypt, in the mid third century. T is the 'Tarsus text', that is, the fifth-century Greek reissue with a new preface describing the discovery of the document during the consulship of Theodosius the Younger and Constantius, i.e. A.D. 420. A is, as we have seen, the Greek archetype of all the Latin texts. It should be emphasized that though other texts have subsequently been discovered, nothing has thus far changed this view of the main development of the medieval Latin, that is, of L¹ and its dependants.[1] L², however, is another matter, and the examination of it both by itself and in comparison with L¹ and all the other, non-Latin, versions, permits a more precise discrimination among the diverging lines of development. In the following new stemma the emphasis and detailed consideration remain, as previously, with the Latin but with rather more concern for the forms in other languages, so as to call attention to the variety of versions of the Greek on which they are founded.

---

[1] See Silverstein, *Archives*, xxvi, 199–248, and especially 224–6.

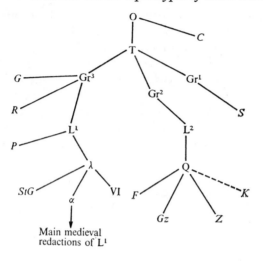

Main medieval
redactions of L¹

O represents the third-century Greek original without the Tarsus
preface and with the Mount of Olives ending as in *C*. T is the
Tarsus text having an abbreviated but complete ending after the
final encounter with Elijah and Elisha and having also an anti-
Nestorian reference to Mary as the Mother of God, which is
preserved in Tischendorf's *G*.[1] Gr¹, Gr², and Gr³ are hypothetical
Greek linking texts: Gr¹ and Gr² come to an end [briefly but
completely] after the final encounter with Elijah and Elisha; and in
addition Gr¹ modifies the anti-Nestorian reference and becomes
the source of those copies which later circulated among the Eastern
Nestorians. Gr³ maintains that reference, confuses $H\Lambda IA\Sigma$ and
$H\Lambda IO\Sigma$ in the account of the City of God, and breaks off incomplete in the midst of Elijah's speech. Q stands for the hypothetical
source common to *F*, *Gz*, and *Z*, to which each is related independently.

Increasingly complicated as the new stemma has become, it
yet presents a simplified view of what must have been the actual
history of the Apocalypse, whose extant manuscripts, including
those of all the translations and adaptations, number perhaps 200.
It is limited to those versions alone which represent the original
work *in extenso* and have been the central concern of the present
study, but even so does not include the various Long forms of the

[1] *Apocalypses Apocryphae*, p. 62, § 41; and see *Mediaeval Studies*, xxiv, especially pp. 345–7.

Syriac beyond *S*, nor the Armenian, nor the several Slavonic versions related to but not necessarily connected with *R* directly, nor any of the Arabic texts, which have yet to find their modern editor. With respect to the reconstruction of the original form of the work, the scholar is evidently faced, not with a lack, but with an embarrassment of riches. And that is also true of the subsequent history during a millennium of changing texts in Greek as well as in translation. The newly available copies of L^2 add substantially to what we know about both aspects of the life of this remarkable apocryphon.

T. SILVERSTEIN

8

Some Poems Attributed to Richard of Cluny

RECENT years have seen a great widening and deepening of our knowledge of that very remarkable medieval institution, the monastic commonwealth of Cluny. Thanks to the work of the archaeologists, headed by K. J. Conant, far more is known about the buildings at Cluny itself. The publication of monographs such as Hallinger's awesome *Gorze-Kluny*,[1] and more recently Guy de Valous's *Le Monachisme clunisien des origines au xve siècle* (Paris, 1970), mean that we have a much more detailed knowledge than formerly of the institutions of Cluny. The spiritual and literary life of the order has not been neglected either. The new edition of Peter the Venerable's letters by Giles Constable, together with the work done by Mlle D'Alverny and J. Kritzeck on the translations of Muslim writings undertaken under Peter's auspices, have shown how the literature which originated in the Cluniac milieu reflects the wide variety of interests and attitudes to be found within the order. These interests included the writing of history, although Cluny itself produced no chronicler until the late Middle Ages. It is questionable whether either Radulfus Glaber or Orderic Vitalis can properly be thought of as Cluniac historians, though Glaber wrote his *Libri quinque historiarum* while at Cluny, and Orderic spent his life at St. Evroul, a house much influenced by Cluniac ideas and ideals.[2]

By contrast the chronicler Richard of Poitou is firmly linked to Cluny.[3] He prefaces the first edition of his chronicle by a dedica-

---

[1] *Gorze-Kluny, Studien zu den monastischen Lebensformen und Gegensätzen in Hochmittelalter, Studia Anselmiana*, xxii–xxv (Rome, 1950).

[2] For an attempt to discover a characteristically Cluniac attitude to the writing of history see P. Lamma, *Momenti di storiografia Cluniacense. Istituto storico Italiano per il medio evo: Studi storici*, xlii–xliv (Rome, 1961).

[3] Incomplete texts of Richard's *Chronicon* were printed by Muratori in his *Antiquitates italicae medii aevi*, iv, cols. 1079–1144, by Martène and Durand in

tory letter to Peter the Venerable,[1] the earliest manuscript of the chronicle (Paris, Bibl. Nationale, lat. 5014) is headed 'Chronica . . . a Richardo Pictaviensi monacho Cluniacensi', and its contents reflect that interest in the Near East which was so characteristic of Cluny while Peter was abbot. Almost all we know about Richard is summed up in these alternative *cognomina*, *Pictaviensis* and *Cluniacensis*. From his detailed descriptions of the region of Poitou known as l'Aunis, and in particular of the island of Aix near La Rochelle, it is clear that he was a native of that area, and almost certainly spent part of his life in the Cluniac monastery of Aix. But Ingeborg Schnack in her monograph on Richard (see p. 181 n. 3) made out a good case for his having spent the middle years of his life at Cluny, until his support of Victor IV in the schism made it difficult for him to remain there any longer, whereupon he retired to his native Poitou some time after 1163. The wide range of sources which he cites at the beginning of his chronicle (Berger, op. cit., p. 122) would certainly not have been available at the remote priory of Aix, and it is noticeable that in the last recension of his chronicle his account of recent events in the wider world beyond Poitou is very sketchy. This does seem to point to his withdrawal back to Aunis in later life. As for the date of his death, Berger (p. 51) suggested 1188, but this is almost certainly too late (see Schnack, p. 17). Schnack has shown that the relationship between the four recensions of the chronicle postulated by Berger is the wrong one (pp. 60–4), but her alternative sequence is not altogether convincing, and the complex relationship of the recensions to each other still needs to be sorted out. As the *terminus post quem* of Richard's death depends on the date of the last event recorded in the last recension of his chronicle which can be shown to be his own work, we are as much in the dark about this as we are about his life as a whole. Even the vague outline suggested above can only be inferred from a close study of his chronicle.

Although it is this chronicle which saves Richard from complete

their *Amplissima . . . collectio*, v, cols. 1159–74, and by the compilers of the *Recueil des historiens . . . de la France*, xii (Paris, 1781), cols. 411–21. Waitz printed a short extract in *M.G.H.*, *Scriptores*, xxvi. 72–84. There are two detailed analyses of the chronicle and its various recensions, by E. Berger, 'Richard le Poitevin, moine de Cluny, historien et pöete', *Bibliothèque des Écoles françaises d'Athènes et de Rome*, vi (1879), 45–138, and by I. Schnack, 'Richard von Cluny, seine Chronik und sein Kloster in den Anfängen der Kirchenspaltung von 1159', *Historische Studien*, cxlvi (Berlin, 1921).

[1] Berger, p. 121.

and utter obscurity, he must also have occasionally experimented in the writing of verse, for he has insinuated some of this into the text of the Chronicon. There is a *planctus* on the death of Raymond of Antioch, in twenty rhythmical lines, printed as prose by Muratori in his edition of recension B of the chronicle (*Antiquitates Italicae*, iv. 1101), but restored to its proper verse form by the compilers of the *Histoire littéraire de la France* (tome xiii (Paris, 1814), p. 536):[1]

> Nostra condolet Asia,
> Tharsus flet cum Cilicia;
> ve! dicit Antiochia
> pro sui morte principis.
>
> Nam luget pre inopia
> Libanus et Apamia,
> necnon et Laodicia
> cum suis appenditiis.
>
> Tyrus stupet metropolis,
> urbs Phenicum mirabilis;
> magnos questus dat Tripolis,
> visis sinistris nuntiis.
>
> Quid dicam de Ierusalem?
> It planctus usque Bethleem;
> clamorque Ptolemäidis
> tangit fines Neapolis.
>
> Urbs fecunda nimis,
> nullis quassata ruinis,
> es privata viro,
> qui te moderamine miro
>   rexit.

The style is naïve, but not ungrammatical, and although it is not a very profound piece of writing one cannot find much fault with it. The rhyme too is simple (AAAB; AAAB; BBBB; CCBB; BBDDE), as is the rhythmical pattern. The first four stanzas consist of lines of eight syllables, of which the last four are always iambic, while the first four vary between ⌣́⌣⌣⌣́, ⌣́⌣⌣́⌣, and the purely iambic ⌣⌣́⌣⌣́. The last verse looks like an attempt at something more ambitious which has not quite succeeded.

---

[1] Printed here from Muratori's text.

There appears to be another attempt at a *planctus* on the return of Louis VII from the second crusade (Muratori, loc. cit.):

Luget Francia, Burgundia, Aquitania de suorum amissione
gaudet Syria, Armenia, Mesopotamia de Christianorum repulsione.

But this is not carried beyond these two lines.

In the first rough draft of his chronicle, which exists in what must have been his working copy, now Paris, Bibl. Nationale, MS. lat. 5014, almost at the end of the text (Martène and Durand, *Amplissima collectio*, tom. v, col. 1173), Richard referred to Abelard's death and added: 'Huius epitaphium huic opusculo inserere volumus', without in fact inserting it. At the end of his life he came back to this early redaction of his work, and used it for the fourth and final version of the chronicle. Only then did he include the epitaph:[1]

Vatum summorum maior Petrus Abaalardus
occidit, immanis factus dolor omnibus unus.
Gallia nil maius habuit vel clarius isto,
nec mors cuiusquam fit tanta ruina Latinis;
in quantum fama Romani nominis exit
illius ingenii studiorum fama volavit.
Nannetis oritur, patre Pictavus et Brito matre,
cum Francis studuit, monachus moritur Cabilonis.

Richard did not expressly acknowledge this unattractive composition as his own, but I believe that we can infer from the way in which he has introduced it into his text that it is in fact his. A certain reticence on his part is understandable, for even judged by the standards of epitaphs it is mediocre. The phrase 'immanis factus dolor', and the 'tanta' of v. 4, taken up by the 'in quantum' of the next verse, are particularly clumsy. At least it is mercifully short. This fourth recension also contains an effusion of some forty lines which Richard tells us he composed on the death of William, duke of Aquitaine, which occurred while that worthy was on pilgrimage to Compostella in 1137. As can be seen from the following extract, the poem scales no heights of literary greatness.[2]

---

[1] Text of the Vatican MS. Ottobon. lat. 750, fol. 73, collated with Berger, p. 135. At v. 4 Berger has emended 'totam' of the MS. to 'tanta'; at v. 7 'ex Brito' to 'et B.', and 'Nam' to 'Nannetis'.

[2] Text of MS. Ottobon. lat. 750, fol. 72, collated with the printed text of *Recueil des historiens*, xii, col. 413. Either a pentameter is missing in the MS. after v. 5, or more likely a hexameter has been added. The editors of the *Recueil* must have regarded v. 5 as an interpolation, for they omit it from their text, but v. 5a is unmetrical (veneranda) and it looks as if it is the intruder.

> Dux Aquitanorum Willelmus morte suprema
> occubuit, Iacobum dum peregrinus adit.
> Discipuli Christi Iacobi sacra limina supplex
> dum peregrinus adit occubuit peregre.
> 5 Occubuit peregre Pirenei monte relicto
> 5a [dum peregrinus adit veneranda pignora sancti]
> pro Christo pauper occubuit peregre.
> Occubuit peregre dux pauper in hospite terra
> exul pro Christo dux venerandus obiit.

After having ploughed through forty lines of this sort of stuff, words like 'feeble' and 'inane' come into one's mind. As verse it is irredeemably bad. Richard may be the author of yet another epitaph. In Vatican MS. Reg. lat. 1911 (Berger's third, Schnack's second recension), in the middle of the list of popes tacked on by Richard to the end of his chronicle, he mentions briefly the murder of Thomas Becket, and follows this up with one verse in accentual metre, obviously part of a *planctus*:

> De profundis clamito,
> nec solito
> luctu se vox exserit,
> nec deserit
> dolorem.
> Fontem fundo lacrimis
> ab intimis;
> cor expavens scaturit,
> et parturit
> merorem.   (Berger, op. cit., p. 128)

The verdict on all these attempts at verse must be that they are no more than passable. There are, however, more ambitious and interesting poems which have been attributed to Richard at various times. In the first volume of *Neues Archiv* (1876, pp. 600–4) W. Wattenbach published seven poems which had been transcribed from an English manuscript by K. Pertz, the son of the illustrious founder of the *Monumenta Germaniae Historica*. Pertz omitted to say in which manuscript he found these poems, but Wattenbach felt that, notwithstanding this, they were worth printing. Of these, the first three are found in a number of manuscripts, but the rest only in one, London, British Library, Add. 11983, which is clearly the source of the text provided for Wattenbach by Pertz. A new text of all seven pieces forms Appendix II of this article. In the *Bibliothèque de l'École des Chartes* for the same year (xxxvii. 443) J. Havet pointed out that the second and third of the poems printed by Wattenbach had been ascribed to Richard of Cluny by the English bibliophile John Bale in his *Scriptorum Illustrium maioris Britanniae catalogus* (cent. xiii, cap. 19, ed. R. L. Poole, p. 342). His entry is as follows (the arabic numerals are my addition):

Ricardus Monachus Cluniacensis, in Anglia scripsisse fertur,

1. Historiam temporum li. i		
2. Epistolas ad diversos li. i		
3. De Cluniacensi monasterio car. i	'Roma secunda vocor, meus'	
4. De Anglia et eius laude car. i	'Anglia terra ferax et fertilis' =Pertz II	
5. De Londonia et eius laude car. i	'Ibis et in nostros dives Londonia'=Pertz III	
6. De transfiguratione Domini car. i	'Letetur hodie matris ecclesie'	
7. De Maria Magdalena car. i	'Procumbit pedibus non lota'	
8. De diva Catherina car. i	'Coelum celibes agit nuptiis'	
9. Alia carmina li. i	'Usus ventilabri quid conferat'	

Claruit A.D. 1140: vide Tritemium.

Did Bale find all these poems in the one manuscript? Many of the entries in his *Catalogus* are in fact based on a single manuscript. He surely cannot have picked on such an obscure person as the author of these poems without some other indication, either from a manuscript or an earlier bibliographer. The beginning of his entry is taken from Trithemius's *De scriptoribus ecclesiasticis liber unus* (Cologne, 1546), p. 163:

> Fertur autem insigne et clarum opus
> Historiarum temporum   lib. i
> Epistolarum ad diversos   lib. i

But Trithemius makes no mention of Richard's talents as a versifier. On the other hand, three of the poems cited by Bale are also found together in the Bodleian MS. Digby 104 (=D), and this suggests that these seven poems all appeared in one manuscript seen by Bale. This does not necessarily mean that all are the work of one versifier, much less that that versifier is Richard. Items 3, 8, and 9 are not known from any other manuscript, nor are they listed in Walther's *Alphabetisches Verzeichnis der Versanfänge mittellateinischer Dichtungen* or Chevalier's *Repertorium*. Item 7 turns up in MS. Digby 104 (=D), at fol. 138, but is separated from the two poems printed by Wattenbach by five other pieces of verse. Item 6, a sequence for the feast of the Transfiguration, was printed by J. M. Neale in *Sequentiae ex missalibus* (London, 1852), p. 147, by P. G. Morel in *Lateinische Hymnen des Mittelalters* (Einsiedeln, 1868), p. 14, and by L. Kehrein in *Lateinische Sequenzen des Mittelalters* (Mainz, 1873), p. 50. No one except Bale has attributed it to Richard. Indeed, in his monograph on the St. Gallen manuscript used by Morel, *Das Sequentiar Cod. 546 der Stiftsbibl. von St. Gallen* (Berne, 1959, p. 144), F. Labhardt suggests that it may have been composed as late as the fourteenth century. Thus, although Bale's entry forces us to consider seriously the possibility that Richard may have written 'Anglia terra ferax' and 'Ibis et in nostros', and perhaps even 'Procumbit pedibus', there is no evidence that any of the other poems in his list are Richard's work. In short Bale's entry is a nuisance. It raises the question of Richard's authorship of at least two of the poems printed by Wattenbach, without offering any help towards a solution.

Before considering further whether all or any of the nine poems printed in *Neues Archiv* are in fact by Richard, we must first decide whether they all come from the same pen, or whether, as seems likely from the manuscript evidence, nos. 1–3 form a group on their own. This is important, for only in nos. 4–7 are there allusions to contemporary persons and events, allusions which have been used to support Richard's claim to be the author of all nine. At this point it may help the reader to see at a glance in which of the manuscripts the poems appear. A brief description of the manuscripts forms Appendix I to this article.

1. Venimus ad naves A D C L;
2. Anglia terra ferax A D C L T Bale (vv. 1–3 also in Oxford, Corpus Christi Coll. 232; vv. 1–2 in Cambridge, Corpus Christi Coll. 371);
3. Ibis et in nostros A D C L La (vv. 13–end) Bale;
4–9. A.

Berger considered that all the poems printed by Wattenbach were Richard's work, naturally enough, for the only manuscript he knew of was A. He was inclined to think that the Henry referred to in 4 could be identified with the great bishop of Winchester, Henry of Blois. Henry was of a 'genus altum', was born in France (cf. v. 3 'Henricus nomen, genus altum, Gallia nutrix'), and was a generous benefactor to Cluny. Henry may also have been the subject of 6. We know that he made at least one visit to Rome, in 1143, and he may well be the personage whose return is celebrated in this poem. But no doubt there were other Cluniac monks who could write verse as well, or as badly, as Richard. Even if we knew for certain that these two poems were composed in honour of Henry of Blois by Richard, this would not prove that all the other poems printed by Wattenbach were by him. Nothing is more likely than that some Cluniac scribe might bring together these two sets of verses, 1–3 and 4–9, which both had a Cluniac background.

An examination of the style of the two groups seems to confirm this, but as the poems in the second add up to only fifty lines, we cannot make a very satisfactory comparison. In both groups we see the sort of rhetorical tricks that one expects to find in verse written in the second half of the twelfth century, for instance the *membrum* in 6 vv. 5, 6:

> quem non detinuit, superavit, terruit, ussit
> accola, predo, labor, semita prava, calor,

and 3 v. 10:

> plena, referta, frequens civibus, ere, foro,

and the typical conceit of *Divitiae* making England her home (2 vv. 13, 14). However, in the poems of the first group the most noticeable feature is the alliteration, mainly in 1 (v. 5 'fidens fide', 7 'celerem per cerula classem', 8 'fugam fingit', 13 'flatus vel fluctus', 46 a completely alliterative line—'mores morales, facta faceta fore'), though there is some in 3 (v. 9 'epulis opulenta', 18 dulces defluus'). Allied to this is the word-play of 1 v. 16 'ratem . . . ratam', 27 'de littore lis', 34 'placuit applicuisse', and 3 v. 26 'dum meat et remeat, dum fugit atque fugat'. Neither alliteration nor word-play is to be found in the poems of the second group. There are, moreover, clear echoes of 1 in 2 (cf. 2. 3 'Anglia dulce solum' and 1. 39; 2. 5 'Anglia plena iocis, gens libera' and 1. 51 'libera gens, cui libera mens . . .'). No such echoes from the earlier group are to be found in Wattenbach's nos. 4–9. It therefore seems clear on stylistic grounds, and in view of the evidence of the manuscripts, that poems 1–3 and 4–9 are the work of different authors. Since even Bale does not ascribe the latter group to Richard, it follows from this that we cannot consider nos. 4–9 as his.

We are still left with the task of discovering the author of the first three of Wattenbach's poems, and unfortunately they provide much less in the way of circumstantial evidence than the other group. All that we can glean from them is that the author was a Frenchman visiting England, probably for the first time, who was impressed with what he saw. This could of course be Richard of Poitou, although there is no evidence from any other source that he made a trip to England. In the manuscripts the poems are generally in a 'British' context, as for instance in C. In A they suffer the common fate of anthology pieces in being used to fill up blank leaves. In no instance are they in a context even remotely connected with Richard, and none of the extant manuscripts as much as mentions his name. In L, on the contrary, 1 and 2 are attributed to Hugh, prior of Montacute (see p. 194). A number of later writers quote from the first and second poems, namely Iacobus de Guisia, *Annales Hanoniae* (ed. *M.G.H., Scriptores*, xxx, pars i, p. 93. He quotes 2 vv. 1, 9, 10, 5), the author of the *Dialogus de scaccario* (I. 11, ed. Johnson, p. 55, quotes 2 v. 14), and Bartholo-maeus Anglicus, *De Proprietatibus Rerum* XV. 14 (ed. Nuremberg 1519, quire qi, quotes 2 vv. 1, 9, 10, 5; 1 vv. 51, 52). Ranulph Hig-den, *Polychronicon*, I. 41 (ed. Babington, vol. ii, (R.S., 1869), p. 18) and Thomas of Otterbourne's Chronicle (ed. T. Hearne, *Duo rerum Anglicarum Scriptores*, Oxford, 1732, pp. 6, 7) quote a curious conflation of verses from 1 and 2 with verse from an unknown source. This was also printed by F. Liebermann in *Neues Archiv*, iv (1878), 25. In Ranulph part of this conflated version is attributed to 'Henricus', perhaps because Henry of Huntingdon had inserted a similar poem in praise of England at chapter six of the first book of his *Historiae Anglorum*, and part to 'Alfridus'. None of these writers cites Richard as the author of the lines they quote.

In the British Library MS. Cotton Julius A. VIII, which is a copy of Thomas of Otterbourne's chronicle, and so contains a quotation of the conflated version just mentioned, a hand other than that of the scribe has written (fol. 6) 'Hos versus fecit Ricardus Cluniacen-sis ordinis Benedicti monachus'. But while the text hand is of the end of the fifteenth century, the hand which has added this mar-ginal note is of the late sixteenth or early seventeenth. The wording is so similar to Bale's entry as to make it seem very likely that the information has come straight from him, or from his partial source Trithemius. Thus, as far as manuscript evidence goes, Richard's claim to be the author of these three poems rests solely on the unknown manuscript seen by Bale, a shaky foundation indeed for any claim.

Yet Richard *did* write verse, and was familiar with a wide range of ancient and contemporary literature. Authors cited by him as sources for his chronicle include Livy, Suetonius, Josephus, and Orosius, as well as Gregory of Tours, Gildas, Paul the Deacon, and Bede. He has an engagingly vague comment on Manegold of Lautenbach (Muratori, col. 1085C): 'His temporibus florere cepit in Theutonica terra Menegaldus philosophus, divinis et secularibus litteris ultra coetaneos suos eruditus.'[1] He pays a fulsome tribute to both Hugh of St. Victor and Abelard—'Hec duo Latinorum luminaria in Francia', as he calls them (Muratori, col. 1098B).[2] It is Richard who identifies Peter of Saintes as the author of the Troy poem 'Viribus, arte, minis'.[3] Richard used to be almost our only source of information about Hugh Primas, before Meyer discovered his poems in the Oxford anthology MS. Rawlinson G. 109.[4] But perhaps the most interesting literary reference for us in the present context is to the poet-bishop Hildebert of Le Mans. Under the year 1124 Richard has the following entry (Muratori, col. 1096E): 'Hac tempestate domnus Hildebertus Cenomannensis episcopus, postea Turonensis archiepiscopus in Andegavensi pago claruit; in metris ita edoctus, ut nulli sit comparandus.' He also pays Hildebert the compliment of quoting from one of his poems, albeit without acknowledgement. In the fourth recension of his chronicle (Berger, p. 130) he introduces as an amusing happening ('tale quid fertur contigisse pago Cenomannico') Hildebert's story of the husband who made a tryst with his woman servant on behalf of his man servant (*Hildeberti Carmina Minora*, ed. Scott, Leipzig, 1969, no. 24), and retells it half in Hildebert's verse and half in his own prose.

Even the most cursory examination of the first three poems printed by Wattenbach shows the influence of Hildebert. The very subjects of the poem—a rough channel crossing and an encomium

---

[1] For similar references to Manegold by other contemporary writers see the first pages of the very thorough article by W. Hartmann, 'Manegold von Lautenbach und die Anfänge der Frühscholastik', *Deutsches Archiv*, xxvi (1970), 47–147.

[2] He mentions four of Hugh's works: the *De sacramentis*, the commentary on Ecclesiastes, the *De archa Noe*, and the *Didascalicon*.

[3] His remarks on Peter are not included in the printed text of the *Chronicon*, as they appear only in the text of Berger's third, Schnack's second recension, at fol. 86 of Vatican MS. Reg. lat. 1911 (see Berger, p. 85).

[4] For the reference to Primas, found only in the first and fourth recensions, see *M.G.H.*, *Scriptores*, xxvi. 81.

of England—are those of two of Hildebert's best-known poems. In the verses on his short 'exile' in England at the court of William Rufus he devotes sixteen lines to a description of the stormy crossing, modelled no doubt on Ovid, *Tristia* I. 2.[1] Our poet's description of his channel crossing is much more developed than Hildebert's, but also one feels more successful. It presents vividly all the miseries suffered by those who cross the English channel on a stormy day. The feeling of dizziness (v. 20), the great longing for the sight of land, the sheer joy of stepping on to that land are all still familiar to us, even though we may make that crossing comparatively quickly in diesel-powered ferries. In comparison with this, Hildebert's account is somewhat academic and unreal, as if he felt that he had to include a storm in this description of his journey into exile, just because Ovid had done so before him. Apart from this theme of stormy weather and the agonies of seasickness, it does not seem as if the writer of this poem has borrowed anything else from Hildebert. The second poem cannot help but recall one of Hildebert's, for their first lines are almost identical, a fact which has confused librarians and bibliographers down to the present time. But Hildebert's poem (ed. cit., no. 37), which begins:

Anglia terra ferax, tibi pax diuturna quietem,

has a different purpose to that of the poem printed by Wattenbach. Hildebert's aim is to say as many flattering things as he can about Henry I of England in the compass of thirty lines, and the opening verses in praise of England form a suitable introduction to this exercise in adulation. But there are some verbal similarities. 'Quicquid letitie, quicquid amoris habet' of our poem (v. 8), recalls Hildebert's 'Quicquid luxus amat, quicquid desiderat usus' (v. 9). Just as here *Divitiae* has made England her home (v. 14), so in Hildebert Nature has chosen her first gifts to bestow on England (vv. 5–7):

Cum pareret Natura parens, varioque favore
　　divideret dotes omnibus una locis,
　　elegit potiora tibi . . .

This then is one further argument, a rather tenuous one as it seems to me, for identifying the writer of these poems with the chronicler Richard of Cluny. We know from his chronicle that

---

[1] *Hildeberti Carmina Minora*, no. 22, vv. 45–60.

Richard admired Hildebert and had read his verse. The author of these poems has also read Hildebert and been influenced by his work. But it must be remembered that Hildebert's verse was very popular, even in his own lifetime, so that there is nothing so very unusual in this coincidence of taste between Richard and our unknown versifier. Richard was clearly someone who had read widely. He wrote passable verse, and was probably quite capable of producing the description of the stormy sea crossing and the poem in praise of England. Like the writer of these poems he knew and was influenced by the poems of Hildebert. But the evidence of the manuscripts is quite against his having written any of the poems printed by Wattenbach. Only the rediscovery of the manuscript used by Bale, or of a similar manuscript, might perhaps alter that.

On the other hand, the mysterious Hugh, prior of the Cluniac house of Montacute, and later abbot of its Benedictine neighbour Muchelney, both in Somerset, might just possibly turn out to be the author when and if more evidence becomes available. The attribution to him in the Longleat manuscript (see p. 194) seems plausible simply because it is so explicit. It would fit in well enough with the general tone of the poems, for Cluny was an essentially French institution. During the twelfth century it seems to have had few Englishmen, or even English-bred Normans, in positions of authority in its English houses.[1] Hugh might well have written these poems just after his arrival in England, perhaps many years before he became prior or abbot.

The only Hugh in the (admittedly incomplete) list of abbots of Muchelney printed in the *Victoria County History of Somerset* (ii. 107) is cited there as having witnessed a charter in 1175. A Hugh, abbot of Muchelney, also witnessed a charter of Roger de Mandeville granted before 1166, while Robert of Lewes was still bishop of Bath and Wells (item 133 in the register of the abbey of Athelney, *Somerset Record Society Publications*, xiv (1899), p. 166). But in between these two dates, the Pipe Roll of 18–19 Henry II (1171, 2) records a vacancy in the abbey which lasted at least until 1175 (see Knowles, Brooke, London, *Heads of religious houses, England and Wales* (Cambridge, 1972), p. 57). So there may have been two abbots Hugh during the last third of the century. In the

[1] See, for instance, Dom David Knowles's remarks on these 'half-alien' Cluniac houses in *The Monastic Orders in England* (Cambridge, 1950), p. 153.

equally incomplete list of priors of Montacute (*V.C.H. Somerset*, ii. 114), the only Hugh cited is identified with Hugh de Noyen in the mid thirteenth century. It is curious that the charter which the editors of the *V.C.H.* used to establish the existence of abbot Hugh of Muchelney is one issued by bishop Reginald FitzJoceline of Bath confirming the grant of certain churches to the monks of Montacute, to which Hugh is a witness.[1] Perhaps this is a sign of continuing interest in the welfare of his former house on the part of the abbot of Muchelney. But the two communities were less than ten miles from each other, and the abbot of one was obviously the most convenient personage available for witnessing documents for the other. Yet only two other documents in the Montacute cartulary (items 49 and 202) are witnessed by abbots of Muchelney. From all of this it must be clear that, though it would be an attractive proposition, we cannot really prove that this very shadowy abbot of Muchelney had been prior of Montacute, or indeed that he wrote these poems.[2] The results of the above inquiry must therefore appear to be somewhat negative. But these are lively and amusing poems, and if this fresh consideration of the problem of their authorship revives interest in them it will have been well worth while. They deserve better than to remain virtually inaccessible in the dusty store-house of *Neues Archiv*.

A. B. SCOTT

APPENDIX I

Manuscripts

A =   London, British Libr., Add. 11983, s. XII[2], containing (fol. 46[v]), after Marbod's *Liber de ornamentis verborum*, poems 1–7 printed from this manuscript by Wattenbach.

---

[1] Montacute cartulary, ed. in *Somerset Record Soc. Publications*, viii (1894), 191, no. 181. As FitzJoceline was consecrated on 23 June 1174, and another witness was Richard who was succeeded as dean of Wells by Alexander in 1180, the charter must have been issued between these dates.

[2] There is an equally explicit attribution to Hugh in the 14th-century Bodleian MS. Digby 166. On fol. 27[v], in the middle of 'Trojan' material, is the well-known poem 'Pergama flere volo' (Walther, op. cit., no 13985, *Carmina Burana*, ed. Hilka–Schumann, no. 101), headed 'Planctus Hugonis prioris de monte acuto ad idem'. Considering the large number of manuscripts in which this poem is anonymous, this attribution in one rather late text can hardly be taken very seriously. The Digby MS. does not seem to be related to the one which Nicholas de Waldey gave to St. Albans, and which is now at Longleat.

D = Oxford, Bodleian, Digby 104, s. XIII[1]. The verse anthology
       begins (fol. 136) with 'Canities etiam mentiri novit et albam'
       (Walther, no. 2360), followed by 1–3, (fol. 136[v]), 'Papa nocens
       quo nemo nocentior' (Walther, no. 13640), 'Celsus ad excelsos'
       (Walther, no. 2604), three poems from Pierre Riga's *Floridus
       Aspectus* and item 7 in Bale's list. This is followed by the *Specu-
       lum monachorum* found also in MS. Bodley 496 (S.C. no. 2159),
       beginning: 'Non tonsura facit monachum' (Walther, no. 12204)
       and nine other short anthology pieces.

C = Cambridge, Corpus Christi Coll. 281. This is made up of three
       MSS. bound together, of which the first, containing Geoffrey of
       Monmouth's *Historia regum Britanniae*, followed (fol. 77[v]) by
       1–3, is of the second half of the twelfth century. The second
       contains some Cluniac material, including the annals of St.
       Andrew's priory, Northampton, but N. R. Ker, *Medieval Lib-
       raries of Great Britain* (2nd edn.), p. 15, thinks that it may be
       from the Benedictine abbey of Burton-upon-Trent, as there is
       a Burton ex-libris of the fifteenth century pasted on to fol. 1.

L = MS. 27 in the library of the Marquess of Bath at Longleat. I
       have been able to use a transcript of the poems in this manuscript,
       and a detailed description of its contents made by Dr. Hunt some
       years ago and given to me, with typical generosity, by him. A
       composite volume made up of six parts written at various times in
       the twelfth and thirteenth centuries. According to an inscription
       in it, it was given to the abbey of St. Albans by Nicholas de
       Waldey. The verse anthology, in a twelfth-century hand, begins
       (p. 114) with extracts from Matthew of Vendôme, and contains
       over thirty items. 'Non tonsura facit monachum', found also in
       D, is here attributed to Anselm of Canterbury. Our poems 1–3
       come towards the end. The first is headed 'Versus Hugonis
       primi [*sic*] prioris de Monte Acuto postea abbatis de Muchele-
       neia'; the second 'Versus eiusdem de Anglia', and the third 'De
       Londonia et de Tamesi flumine'.

The poems in praise of England (2, 3) seem to have had a somewhat
wider circulation independent of 1. Oxford, Bodl. MS. Laud lat. 86,
s. XIII (=La) has (fol. 130) 3, vv. 13–28; Trinity Coll., Cambridge, MS.
895 (R. 14. 22), s. XIII (=T) has (fol. 45[v]) 2, while Corpus Christi Coll.,
Oxford, MS. 232, s. XIV has (fol. 72[v]) 2, vv. 1–3, and Corpus Christi
Coll., Cambridge, MS. 371 has (fol. 1) 2, vv. 1, 2. Even so, there are not
as many manuscripts containing this poem as Walther's entry no. 1021
might suggest, as he has made the usual confusion of this poem with
Hildebert's.

APPENDIX II

I

Venimus ad naves, conscendere me prohibebat
    imperiosa satis causa, timere mori.
Posthabui prohibentia me presagia vana,
    ingrediensque rates aggrediebar aquas.
5   Fidens ergo fide statui mihi corpus in arto,
    sic ut ego navi crederer, illa mari.
Dumque ferunt venti celerem per cerula classem,
    dumque fugam fingit terra, carina facit,
mox animum cure subeunt, incommoda corpus,
10   mox mea pertemptant pectora mille metus.
Oceani spacium vitreamque querebar abissum,
    et solo poteram pene timore mori.
Flatus vel fluctus, si vel dedit aura vel unda,
    et gemuit crebris ictibus icta ratis,
15   tota videbatur laterum compago resolvi,
    pertimuique ratem non satis esse ratam.
Causa timoris ego, pro me de nave timebam,
    sollicitusque mei compatiebar ei.
Hinc me destituit motum mare, prevaluitque
20   debile debilius reddere turbo caput.
Permovit cerebrum permoti vis elementi,
    exegit stomachum nausea crebra nimis.
Inter amara maris discrimina, resque molestas,
    sola mihi terre mentio dulcis erat.
25   Iamque videbantur portus procul ulteriores,
    sed que terra foret lis generalis erat.
Grandis erat de littore lis, nec erat mihi cura,
    quenam terra foret, dummodo terra foret.
Velle solet quodcumque solum, quem territat unda,
30   nec magis hoc illo littore littus amat.
Magne Deus, quam magna dies, quam longa dieta,
    quamque videbatur mors prope, terra procul.
Emenso pelago cum demum Gallus ad Anglos
    applicui, placuit applicuisse mihi.
35   Quivis portus erat gratus mihi, gratior iste,

1 Versus Hugonis primi prioris de Monte Acuto postea abbatis de Mucheleneia L   **1** me] nos D   **10** pertemptat L   mille *omitted* L   **11** vitream] vitam L   querebar] verebar D L   **13** vel[1]] et C   **14** ratis] maris L   **19** hinc] hic D: sic C   **21** permotum D   **29** velle] ville A   **30** illo] ille A   **33** permenso L   Gallos L   **34** applicuit A *Watt.*

quivis dulcis erat, dulcior iste mihi.
Eximios portus pretendens insula Bruti,
    fessis dulce solum, dulcior ipsa dedit.
Dulce solum quod, cum numquam fuerit nisi dulce,
40   tunc mihi precipue post mare dulce fuit.
Processi populique suos advertere ritus,
    post primam curam cura secunda fuit;
cumque hominum cultus adtendere sepe viderer,
    morum precipuus insidiator eram.
45   Perpendens igitur clarum genus indigenarum,
    mores morales, facta faceta fore,
cultus et vultus alacres, et libera corda,
    quasque putes natas ad sua danda manus,
si non mirarer, mirum foret, utpote Gallus,
50   Gallia cui numquam tale videre dedit.
Libera gens, cui libera mens et libera lingua,
    sed lingua melior liberiorque manus.
Libera sunt mens, lingua, manus, tantumque videntur
    libera, quod nequeant liberiora fore.
55   Libera mens, vox liberior, liberrima dextra,
    libertatis opus cogitat, edit, agit.
Ingenii pretium facies promittere leta,
    at monstrare potest officiosa manus.

2

Anglia terra ferax et fertilis angulus orbis,
    fertilior cornu, Copia sacra, tuo!
Anglia, dulce solum, quod non aliena recensque,
    sed sua dulcedo pristina dulce facit.
5   Anglia plena iocis, gens libera, nata iocari,
    tota iocosa, velim dicere tota iocus.
Que nichil a Gallis, sed Gallia mutuat inde,
    quicquid letitie, quicquid amoris habet.
Insula predives, que toto non eget orbe,
10   et cuius totus indiget orbis ope;

---

36 mihi] tamen L: fuit C: fuit vel mihi D   37 Bruti] tecum L   38
dedit] fuit D   39 fuerit numquam L: non umquam fuit A, *altered to* fuerat
Watt.   41, 42 *omitted* A *Watt.*   41 litus D   42 curam] cura L
48 putas L   51 lingua] dextra D   52 melior lingua L   55 vox
l.] et libera vox L   liberrima] celeberrima A *Watt.*   56 cogitat] cogit
C   58 at] quod A *Watt.*
2 Versus eiusdem de Anglia L: Versus de Anglia T   *In* D *the order of vv.*
8–12 *is*: 8, 11, 10, 9, 10 *bis*, 11 *bis*, 12   9 toto que L

insula predives, cuius miretur et optet
delicias Salomon, Octavianus opes;
insula quam quondam fecere sibī specialem
divitieque sinum delicieque larem.

3

Ibis et in nostros, dives Londonia, versus,
    que nos immemores non sinis esse tui.
Quando tuas arces, tua menia, mente retracto,
    que vidi, videor cuncta videre mihi.
5 Fama loquax et nata loqui, moritura silendo,
    laudibus abstinuit cudere falsa tuis.
Non permittit eam mentiri copia rerum;
    sufficit ut dicat materiale bonum.
Urbs locuples, opibus pollens, epulis opulenta,
10   plena, referta, frequens civibus, ere, foro.
Villa frequens, vicus celebris, mirabile castrum,
    quale vel equale non habet orbis opus.
Istic invenies venalia tanta, quod omnes
    expositas merces vix sibi mundus emat.
15 Dicere quid queras tuus est labor, elige quod vis,
    et quod nullus habet, venditor illud habet.
Tamensis fluvius muris allabitur, inde
    in mare fert dulces defluus amnis aquas.
Fit maris excursus, qui dum fluvialibus undis
20   obviat, hospitibus morigeratur aquis.
Fluminis unda fugax, scandens ex inferiori,
    ad superas partes impetuosa redit.
Si mare detumuit seseque coercuit estus,
    mox redit ut currat unda futura mare.
25 Civiles oculos remoratur flumen aberrans,
    dum meat et remeat, dum fugit atque fugat.
Cetera pretereo quia preterit hora diei:
    terminat hora diem, terminat auctor opus.

---

11 T *has* non habuere pares quamvis **predives** uterque   12 Salomo *Watt.*
Octovianus C T   14 sinum] suum D
3 De Londonia et de Tamesi flumine L   C D *have no division between poems*
2 *and* **3.** *The author may well have intended that they should form one poem*
4 timere A   5 flamma A   7 rerum] veri D L   9 pollens opibus
D   polles L   11 vicus] victus A *Watt.*   15 quod] quid D   17
Tamesis L   18 dulcis A *Watt.*   fert *omitted* La   19 excursus] exorsus
A *Watt.* qui] quid La   25 oberrans C D La   27 pretereat L
28 actor A: actor *corr.* auctor C

4

⟨I⟩ stius iste loci prior olim rite peregit,
    Omne prioris opus, gessit honoris onus.
Henricus nomen, genus altum, Gallia nutrix,
    vita fuit virtus, crux via, causa Deus.
5 Et prior et monachus, neutri fur, laus utriusque,
    debitor amborum solvit utrique suum.
Ecclesia grandi loca plenius ista beavit,
    ecclesiam monachis, hos ope, se meritis.

5

Hec duo, carta, salus, mihi, nobis missa fuere,
    Sic commune datum, sic speciale fuit.
Missa mihi socioque salus, res una duobus,
    nos facit esse tuos, res licet una duos.
5 Ambo salutati fuimus, resalutat uterque;
    sic quod utrique dabas nunc ab utroque capis.
Scripta mihi soli misisti, solus habeto,
    solus ego soli scripta remitto tibi.
Sic ego, sic socius, ego carmen, uterque salutem
10   ecce reportamus, debita quisque sua.

6

Exhibet una dies duo gaudia, quando vicissim
    grex de pastore, de grege pastor ovat.
Pastor ovat quod tam feliciter, auspice Christo,
    Romam papam nunc ivit, adivit, adest.
5 Quem non detinuit, superavit, terruit, ussit,
    accola, predo, labor, semita prava, calor.
Prosperitas cum quo pariter pergente profecta,
    cum redeunte redit, cumque manente manet.
Cui valet ad mores, quod semper amavit amari,
10   quod nil plus timuit, quam timor esse suis.
Addidit ad mores Dominus, nunc addat ad annos,
    prebuit esse bonum, prebeat esse diu.

7

Conquereris de nocte tua, quam multa dedisse,
    multa tulisse tibi, nil valuisse doles.

5 1 hec] ut *Watt.*
7 3 in] ad *Watt.*

Ducitur in culpam quasi que tua dona fefellit,
  et que contulerat dona repente tulit.
5 Nox ea, si sapias, nox non fuit. Ergo dies? Non.
  Non hoc, non illud, maius utroque fuit.
Nox ea plena die, penetrans arcana dierum,
  magnum magna fuit vaticinata diem.
Nox ea nocte carens, aliis nox, lux tibi non nox,
10 quod tibi nulla dies, ipsa videre dedit.
Hec tua nox, innoxia nox et nuntia lucis,
  cum reliquis nomen, cetera plus habuit.
Hanc iam causaris sine causa; nil tulit a te,
  si nihil ante dedit. Sed nihil ante dedit,
15 ergo preostendit, nondum pretendit honorem
  et dicto 'presul', non ait 'es' sed 'eris'.

13 hanc] hic A *Watt.*

9

La Tradition manuscrite des '*Quaestiones Nicolai peripatetici*'

Les 'Quaestiones Nicolai peripatetici' paraissent avoir été signalées pour la première fois dans la période moderne par B. Hauréau, dans son ouvrage *De la philosophie scolastique*.[1] Il avait découvert quelques 'Questions naturelles' transcrites dans un manuscrit de la Bibliothèque nationale, fonds de la Sorbonne 841, aujourd'hui lat. 16089, fol. 153ᵛ. Ces questions étaient présentées comme des extraits du livre de 'Nicholaus perypateticus'. Hauréau remarqua que ce personnage, ainsi que le livre mis sous son nom, était cité dans le commentaire d'Albert le Grand sur les *Météores*, et que celui-ci attribuait l'ouvrage à Michel Scot, avec une appréciation péjorative, tant pour le livre que pour l'auteur supposé. C'est donc à propos de Michel Scot que les extraits furent publiés dans l'histoire de la philosophie scolastique. Plus tard, Hauréau revint de nouveau sur cette découverte en publiant une description détaillée du manuscrit composite qui contenait le texte: 'Notice sur le nº 16089 des manuscrits latins de la Bibliothèque nationale.'[2] Le volume est un recueil de cahiers de parchemin renfermant des pièces diverses, de mains variées; la plupart semblent du premier quart du XIVᵉ siècle. Au milieu du recueil se trouvent 18 fols. de papier, fols. 142–159, écrits par des mains cursives de la même époque. Cette partie contient, entre autres, une 'Expositio supra Poeticam' de Barthélemy de Bruges, rédigée en 1307, d'après le colophon (fols. 146–151ᵛ), suivie d'un commentaire sur le 'De inundatione Nili' (fols. 152–153).[3] Au début du fol. 153ᵛ on lit,

---

[1] 1ʳᵉ éd., 1850, i. 470–3.

[2] *Notices et extraits des manuscrits de la Bibliothèque nationale* ... xxxv (1896), 228.

[3] Cf. Ch. Lohr, 'Medieval Latin Aristotle commentaries', *Traditio*, xxiii 1967), 375 et 376–7, sur l'*Expositio brevis* et l'*Expositio in lib.* '*De inundatione Nili*' de Barthélemy.

un opuscule attribué à Thomas d'Aquin: 'Epistola fratris Thome de modo studendi. — Quesiuisti a me qualiter intendere oportet…'. Le scribe a ensuite transcrit plusieurs questions; les premières sont annoncées par un titre marginal: 'Hec sunt extracta de libro Nicholai perypatetici.' Nous reproduisons ces sentences ou notes d'après le manuscrit:

Dico ergo tempus esse mensuram seu quantitatem motus secundum prius et posterius, nam cum motus sit continuorum [Hauréau a écrit: contrariorum] quemadmodum et corpus, necesse est quantitatem inesse motui sicut et corpori, que tempus siue mora appellatur — Item, differunt doctrina Aristotelis et Platonis. Aristoteles enim a debilioribus inchoat ad modum nature tanquam phisicus [philosophicus ms.], Plato a fortioribus inchoat ad modum Dei; theologus enim fuit; imitatur namque Deum qui posuit principium a fortiori et nobiliori creatione, id est angelorum creatione siue intelligentiarum — Item, omne celum est circulare et omne circulare est perfectum; sed nullum perfectum indiget motu; ergo, nullum celum indiget motu; partes autem sui, cum videant bona que non habent, perpendentes se indigere illis bonis, in motum prorumpunt, ut acquirant [acquieunt ms.] sibi bona que non habent, et que est comparatio totius ad totum et partis ad partem; ergo salus nostra est per quietem celi, finis autem per motum partium eius, et hoc est quod dicit Auerozt.

Le dernier extrait attira l'attention d'Ernest Renan, qui nota la trouvaille de son collègue dans le livre *Averroès et l'Averroïsme*.[1]

M. Hauréau a découvert dans le nᵒ 841 de Sorbonne des extraits qui paraissent appartenir à l'un de ses ouvrages … connu jusqu'ici par … Albert. Le fragment exhumé par M. Hauréau … offre la plus frappante analogie avec une digression du commentaire (d'Averroès) sur le XIIᵉ livre de la Métaphysique, digression qui forme souvent dans les manuscrits un opuscule séparé, et dont les premiers mots sont: 'Summa de questionibus quas accepimus a Nicolao; et nos dicemus in hoc secundum nostrum posse.' La doctrine qui y est exposée est d'ailleurs mise expressément sur le compte d'Averroès: 'Omne celum est circulare … et hoc est quod dicit Averozt.'

Les observations de Renan sont fort judicieuses, et l'on n'a pas trouvé mieux, jusqu'ici, au sujet de l'origine probable de l'intitulé: 'Quaestiones Nicolai peripatetici.'

Les *Quaestiones* attribuées par Albert le Grand à Michel Scot passaient pour perdues. Les passages cités dans le commentaire des *Météores* ne correspondaient pas, du reste, aux extraits du ms.

[1] Cf. 2ᵉ éd., pp. 209 sq.

lat. 16089. C'est à propos de l'arc-en-ciel qu'Albert le Grand s'en prend au mystérieux 'Nicolas':[1]

Digressio declarans sententiam Auicenne et Algazelis et Nicolai peripatetici de iride. His quae praedicta sunt fere per omnia concordant Auicenna et Algazel et Nicolaus peripateticus in dictis suis ... Sententia autem Nicolai peripatetici de iride est quod vapor elevatus de terra sit sphaericus, eo quod elevatur de terra sphaerica et sursum frigore coagulatur, cui, cum sol opponitur, iris in eo generatur ... Dicit etiam quod dicitur iris arcus daemonis, eo quod nonnisi a daemone, hoc ⟨est⟩ a sciente et perito scitur, quia daemon graece, latine interpretatur sciens. Duos autem irides dicit fieri ...

Et Albert ajoute sévèrement: 'foeda dicta inveniuntur in libro illo qui dicitur Quaestiones Nicolai peripatetici. Consuevi dicere quod Nicolaus non fecit librum illum, sed Michael Scotus, qui in rei veritate nescivit naturas, nec bene intellexit libros Aristotelis.' Albert cite de nouveau, dans le commentaire des *Météores*, iv. 2:[2] 'Nicolaus peripateticus in Alchimicis' 'Est alius modus mollificationis ... si enim chalybs cavetur ad modum semispherae et fiant pori in chalybe multi ...'

Le mérite de la découverte d'un manuscrit des Questions semble revenir au savant Valentin Rose, qui, ayant eu connaissance d'un manuscrit de la bibliothèque de l'Université de Graz (Graz 482), présentant entre beaucoup d'autres textes une série de questions naturelles précédées du nom de 'Nicolaus peripateticus', en prit une copie qu'il mit en réserve. Un jeune érudit polonais qui travaillait parfois à la bibliothèque de Berlin, Alexandre Birkenmajer, eut communication de cette copie, et alla sur place étudier le précieux manuscrit, dont il releva soigneusement le contenu. Muni de ce témoin, Birkenmajer put s'en servir pour identifier d'autres exemplaires du texte, et les recherches faites pour la préparation de l'Aristote latin lui permirent d'en retrouver un certain nombre. Il avait le dessein d'éditer les *Quaestiones*, dont il avait souligné l'intérêt pour l'histoire de l'aristotélisme dans la première moitié du XIIIe siècle, au cours de la communication faite au VIe congrès international des sciences historiques d'Oslo en 1928:[3] 'Le rôle joué par les médecins et les naturalistes dans la

---

[1] In *Met.* III, c. 25 et 26: éd. Borgnet, iv. 696–7.

[2] Ibid., p. 761.

[3] Réimpr. dans A. Birkenmajer, *Études d'histoire des sciences et de la philosophie du Moyen Age* (Varsovie, 1970), v, 81–2 sur les *Quaestiones Nicolai peripatetici.*

réception d'Aristote au XIIe et au XIIIe siècle' (publié à Varsovie en 1930). Les circonstances l'en empêchèrent, mais ses disciples polonais s'efforcent actuellement d'accomplir son vœu.[1] Laissant aux éditeurs le soin de présenter en détail le contenu des *Quaestiones* et d'indiquer les sources identifiables, nous nous bornerons, comme nous l'avons annoncé, à l'étude de la tradition manuscrite.

Des analyses sommaires des Questions ont été publiées simultanément par M. B. Lawn, dans son intéressante étude sur la littérature des 'Questions naturelles': *The Salernitan Questions, an Introduction to the History of Medieval and Renaissance Problem Literature*,[2] et par L. Thorndike, dans sa monographie *Michael Scot*.[3] Ni l'un ni l'autre ne se prononcent au sujet de l'attribution de l'ouvrage. Les Questions, qui sont en réalité plutôt des notes ou de petits traités sont d'une grande variété et touchent la météorologie, la minéralogie,[4] la médecine et surtout la physiognomie, la botanique et l'alchimie, ainsi que toutes sortes de phénomènes naturels, comme les tremblements de terre. B. Lawn a indiqué que quelques-unes correspondent à des 'Questions salernitaines'. La plupart semblent dépendre de textes arabes ou traduits de l'arabe; l'auteur cite Aristote, Galien, Razi 'in Almansore', c'est-à-dire le traité adressé à Al Mansur traduit par Gérard de Crémone: il s'est aussi inspiré d'Avicenne et d'Averroès. Souvent, il se réfère aux coutumes ou techniques des Maures, et signale en un endroit un phénomène qui se produit dans les environs de Tolède. Il n'ignore pas, malgré tout, les mœurs des pays du Nord, car il décrit l'ébriété du buveur de cervoise. Tout ceci convient à un naturaliste ou médecin voyageur, à l'esprit curieux, en contact probablement avec le monde arabe, du moins par de proches intermédiaires. Nous comprenons

---

[1] Ce sont M. Kurdziałek et S. Wielgus, de l'Université catholique de Lublin.
[2] Oxford, 1963, p. 76 sur les Questions.
[3] London–Edinburgh, 1965, pp. 8–9; analyse et extraits du texte, pp. 126–31.
[4] Un passage sur les propriétés du cristal, considéré comme de l'eau condensée mérite d'être noté comme exemple de l'utilisation du cristal comme loupe: 'neque unquam faceret litteram pergameni fuscam apparere pure nigram, nisi haberet peruiam humiditatem in se, que manifestat littere nigredinem que celabatur per siccitatem incausti existentis in pergameno sicco . . . Littera apparet lata sub cristallo, que apparet coartata per medium aeris . . . Et dico ad hoc quod apparet littera maior sub cristallo quam ipsa sit, hoc est quod cristallus habet in se duriciem resistentem, secundum quam duriciem non de facili penetratur ab immutatione littere; unde illa immutatio inueniens sibi resistens et difficile ad immutandum, non subito transit secundum rectitudinem sed fluit in latum, quare videtur res sub cristallo maior quam sub aere, eo quod aer non resistit aliquo modo immutationem propter sui subtilitatem' (ms. Graz 482, fol. 177).

pourquoi A. Birkenmajer, qui avait dû noter ces détails, a d'abord accepté l'opinion d'Albert le Grand au sujet de Michel Scot. Néanmoins, une bonne partie des questions concernent la physiognomie, et les théories du pseudo-Nicolas ne coïncident pas avec celles qu'a exposées Michel dans sa *Physiognomia* dédiée à Frédéric; c'est sans doute pour ce motif que Birkenmajer a renoncé plus tard à cette hypothèse. Ajoutons que l'auteur des Questions ne paraît pas s'intéresser à l'astrologie. Malgré ces divergences, il est possible qu'il ait été en relations avec l'Écossais, car il semble avoir eu connaissance des traductions d'Averroès dans le premier tiers du XIIIᵉ siècle. M. Kurdziałek, reprenant après Birkenmajer l'étude des Questions[1] a trouvé dans le *Compendium medicinae* de Gilbert l'Anglais,[2] écrit probablement entre 1230 et 1240, une citation de la première question sur l'arc-en-ciel (avec attribution à Averroès), et une large utilisation des passages concernant la physionomie. Nous avons remarqué nous-même que l'auteur inconnu fait volontiers usage du vocabulaire de Michel Scot. A plusieurs reprises, et surtout dans une longue question située vers la fin de la série, dans laquelle la philosophie tient presque autant de place que la physionomie, il traite de la 'virtus informativa', terme employé par Michel Scot dans la traduction du *De animalibus* d'Avicenne, et que l'on rencontre aussi dans la traduction du commentaire d'Averroès sur le *De anima*. A moins de contester les dates proposées par M. Kurdziałek pour le *Compendium medicinae*, il convient donc d'admettre que les Questions du pseudo-Nicolas ont dû circuler avant 1240, et que leur diffusion paraît liée à la première diffusion des traductions d'Averroès. L'appellation 'Nicolaus peripateticus' appliquée par Albert le Grand et par Jean de Secheville, dans son traité *De principiis Naturae*[3] à la collection de questions ne peut du reste provenir que d'une confusion issue des traductions d'Averroès et des formules qui annonçaient l'extrait de la *Métaphysique* signalé par Renan, extrait qui se rencontre dans

---

[1] M. Kurdziałek, 'Les *Quaestiones Nicolai peripatetici*', *Mediaevalia philosophica Polonorum*, ii (1958), 4–5; 'A propos des recherches concernant l'auteur de l'opuscule appelé *Quaestiones Nicolai peripatetici*', ibid. x (1961), 46–9. Dans cet article M. Kurdziałek note l'histoire de la découverte des *Quaestiones* par A. Birkenmajer et les variations de son opinion au sujet de Michel Scot.

[2] *Compendium medicinae Gilberti anglici . . .* Lugduni impressum . . . A.D. MDX . . ., fol. 259 pour la citation attribuée à Averroès et fols. 125 sqq. pour des emprunts à la physionomie.

[3] Jean de Secheville, *De principiis naturae*, texte critique éd. . . . par R. M. Giguère (Montréal–Paris, 1956), p. 178.

un certain nombre de manuscrits du *Corpus aristotelicum*; avec l'incipit: 'Sermo de questionibus secundum quod accepimus a Nicolao.'[1] C'est en effet Averroes qui cite à plusieurs reprises dans ses commentaires le savant Nicolas de Damas[2] avec cette épithète. Ce personnage était d'autre part inconnu des Latins, puisque le *De plantis* circulait sous le patronage d'Aristote, aussi le transfert n'a-t-il pas choqué les lecteurs, malgré les soupçons d'Albert le Grand. Ce transfert n'est du reste pas primitif, et l'on ne doit pas reprocher à l'auteur d'avoir cherché à se dissimuler sous un pseudonyme, car tous les manuscrits que nous allons examiner sont anonymes, à l'exception de deux, et Gilbert l'Anglais, qui semble le plus ancien témoin, ne se réfère qu'à Averroès.

Nous connaissons onze manuscrits des Questions, mettant à part un douzième, le manuscrit latin 16089 de la Bibliothèque nationale, dont nous avons déjà parlé, car il ne contient que des extraits, et ceux-ci ne correspondent pas à ce que l'on peut considérer comme la rédaction commune. Cette rédaction a l'incipit et l'explicit suivants: 'Quoniam terra sperica est, vapor ascendens de ipsa spericus erit . . . − . . . ne possint discernere et odorare vinum potatum ab alio.'

Parmi les six manuscrits qui présentent ce texte complet, quatre méritent une attention particulière en raison de l'encadrement des Questions, soit l'encadrement immédiat, c'est à dire des additions communes, soit l'encadrement général, c'est-à-dire les traités qui les environnent. Cette situation avait déjà attiré l'attention de Birkenmajer: la description de trois manuscrits dans l'*Aristoteles latinus* porte une note signalant la parenté de petits groupes de textes encadrant les Questions.[3]

Le témoin le plus ancien est le ms. Royal 12 C. xv. du British Library. Il a été décrit avec soin dans le catalogue de Warner et Gilson,[4] du moins en ce qui concerne la première partie du recueil, qui contient des traités de médecine, en premier lieu le *Pantegni* de Constantin l'Africain; le *De tempore* d'Alexandre d'Aphrodise,

[1] Les manuscrits sont signalés dans *Aristoteles latinus, Codices*, i, no. 105: Vienne, Nat.bibl. 2302; no. 588: Paris, Nat. lat. 6510; no. 671: Paris, Nat. lat. 16110; no. 952: Würzburg, Univ.bibl. Mp. Med. f. 3.

[2] Cf. H. J. Drossaart-Lulofs, *Nicolaus Damascenus on the Philosophy of Aristotle*, (Leiden, 1965), qui note les citations faites par Averroès.

[3] Description des manuscrits Graz 482 (*Codices*, i, no. 57); London, Brit. Libr. Royal 12Cc. xv (no. 309); Laon 412 (no. 482).

[4] G. F. Warner, J. P. Gilson, *Catalogue of Western Manuscripts in the Old Royal . . . Coll.* ii. 29–31.

attribué par la rubrique à Alpharabi, et la traduction du *De animalibus* d'Aristote par Michel Scot. La seconde partie, qui intéresse directement notre étude, a été traitée plus sommairement, aussi donnons-nous une description complémentaire en Appendice, la notice de l'*Aristoteles latinus* étant, elle aussi, sommaire.[1] Le manuscrit a été transcrit par des scribes anglais dans le second quart du XIIIe siècle; la seconde partie nous paraît contenir des additions d'une main un peu plus récente, vers le milieu du XIIIe siècle. Il serait difficile de prende à la lettre l'indication fournie par une note du fol. 261v: 'Henr. de Charwelton spritsit [*sic*] hoc volumen', car, d'une part, il y a plusieurs scribes, et d'autre part, la mention, comme le remarquent les auteurs du catalogue des Royal manuscripts, est beaucoup plus tardive que le corps du texte. Il convient cependant de retenir que ce personnage est devenu Fellow de Merton College en 1299,[2] et qu'une note de caution au fol. 262v mentionne la 'cista comitisse', fondation de la comtesse de Warwick à Oxford en 1293.[3] Le manuscrit a pu être copié à Oxford ou y séjourner quelque temps avant de passer entre les mains de divers possesseurs anglais, notés dans la description du catalogue.

A partir du fol. 236 de ce recueil, on lit une série de petits textes que nous avons relevés en détail; ils comprennent des notes ou traités brefs de philosophie naturelle mêlée de considérations théologiques et de citations scripturaires, de médecine, d'extraits du *De animalibus* d'Aristote: au milieu de cette collection figure un traité de botanique, qui ne porte pas de titre ici, mais qui dans d'autres témoins a été attribué à un mystérieux 'Moyses Egyptius', celui-ci étant cité dans le texte. Cet opuscule n'est pas sans analogie avec les Questions du pseudo-Nicolas car, bien que rédigé par un occidental, il paraît lié aux collections de traductions arabolatines, et se rencontre toujours dans le voisinage des Questions. Dans l'un des petits traités philosophiques, on remarque une citation de 'Nicolaus peripateticus' qui ne correspond pas au texte des Questions, et dérive sans doute de la lecture d'Averroès; celui-ci est du reste invoqué nommément, ainsi qu'Avicenne. A la suite de cette série est transcrit sans nom d'auteur un petit traité d'Alkindi, *De intellectu*, avec des variantes particulières,[4] puis le *Compendium*

---

[1] *Codices*, i. no. 309. [2] *B.R.U.O.* i. 395.
[3] Cf. *Catalogue* de Warner et Gilson, ad loc.
[4] Cf. A. Nagy, *Die philosophische Abhandlungen des Ja'qub ben Ishaq al-Kindi, Beiträge*, II. 5 (1897), pp. 1–11. A. Nagy n'a pas connu ce manuscrit, ni celui de Laon.

des *Parva naturalia* et le *De substantia orbis* d'Averroès, anonymes; celui-ci s'arrête au cours du livre iii de l'ouvrage. C'est ensuite que se placent les Questions, anonymes et sans titre, fols. 254–260ᵛ. A la suite de l'explicit que nous avons indiqué sont transcrits six petites questions, ou plutôt 'tractaculi' qui s'apparentent à ceux de la série préliminaire, tant par les sujets traités que par le style, fol. 260ᵛ–261ᵛ. Or, c'est dans cette dernière partie que l'on peut reconnaître les extraits contenus dans le manuscrit lat. 16089 de la Bibliothèque nationale,[1] expressément attribués à 'Nicholaus peripateticus'. De fait, cette petite collection de six 'tractaculi' ou notes de philosophie naturelle est annexée aux questions dans trois autres des manuscrits subsistants.

Le manuscrit 412 de Laon,[2] ou du moins sa première partie, fols. 1–15, est très étroitement apparenté au manuscrit Royal 12 C. xv. On y retrouve la même série de textes préliminaires: petits textes de philosophie naturelle, fols. 1–3; opuscule de botanique, anonyme, fols. 3–5: extraits du *De animalibus* d'Aristote et notes de philosophie naturelle entremêlés, fols. 5–7ᵛ; *De intellectu* d'Al-Kindi, anonyme, avec les mêmes variantes, fol. 7ᵛ. Le *Compendium* des *Parva naturalia* manque en cet endroit; il existe cependant dans ce recueil manuscrit, mais dans une autre section, et avec le nom de l'auteur. La suite coïncide de nouveau très exactement: *De substantia orbis*, fols. 7ᵛ–9ᵛ, s'arrêtant au même endroit au milieu du livre iii; Questions du pseudo-Nicolas, anonymes, suivies des six petits traités de philosophie naturelle, fols. 9ᵛ–14ᵛ et 15. Le manuscrit est de la fin du xiiiᵉ siècle et comprend huit parties. D'après les notes marginales, le recueil a dû appartenir à des médecins, bien que le contenu des parties suivantes: œuvres d'Avicenne, d'Averroès, d'Algazel, tables astronomiques, etc., soit beaucoup plus philosophique que celui du manuscrit de Londres. Ce manuscrit a fait partie de la bibliothèque de la cathédrale N.-D. de Laon.

Deux autres manuscrits présentent les Questions suivies des six 'tractaculi', mais non la collection préliminaire. Leur contenu coïncide en partie, mais dans un ordre différent.

Le manuscrit 482 de la Bibliothèque de l'Université de Graz est un remarquable Corpus constitué en majeure partie de traduc-

---

[1] Cf. description du ms. Royal 12 C. xv en Appendice.

[2] Ce manuscrit est décrit dans *Aristoteles latinus, Codices*, i, no. 482: *Avicenna latinus* I. *Archives*, xxviii (1961), 295–301 avec références bibliographiques.

tions d'Alexandre d'Aphrodise, d'Alfarabi, d'Avicenne, d'Algazel et d'Averroès. Il contient aussi le 'Dux neutrorum' de Moïse Maïmonide et, au début, l'*Asclepius* et les œuvres philosophiques d'Apulée. D'après la décoration, il a dû être exécuté à Paris vers l'an 1300, mais une partie des mains paraissent flamandes. Ce manuscrit avait particulièrement attiré l'attention de Birkenmajer: il a été décrit en grand détail dans l'*Aristoteles latinus*.[1] C'est le seul manuscrit qui mette en tête des Questions, fol. 173, le nom de 'Nicolaus peripateticus'. Encore faut-il remarquer qu'il s'agit d'un titre ajouté dans la marge supérieure d'une main cursive.

Le manuscrit de Séville, Colombine 5. 6. 14, provient de Fernando Colón, qui a acheté la plupart des volumes de sa collection hors d'Espagne.[2] De fait, ce manuscrit est écrit par des mains nordiques. Comme le ms. 482 de Graz, il contient le petit traité *De augmento* d'Alexandre d'Aphrodise, suivi de la traduction d'un bref commentaire d'Alfarabi sur la *Physique* d'Aristote (traduction due à Gérard de Crémone, comme celle du texte précédent). Ce commentaire est anonyme dans le ms. de Graz; il est attribué à 'Alexandre' dans celui de Séville. C'est un texte rare; A. Birkenmajer qui l'avait découvert à Graz et dans un manuscrit de Leipzig, probablement aussi d'origine parisienne, l'a publié d'après ces deux témoins en 1935.[3] Le ms. de Séville présente ensuite le traité d'optique de 'Tideus', traduit de l'arabe;[4] ce traité figure également dans le recueil de Graz. Les Questions, anonymes dans le ms. de Séville, suivies des six 'tractaculi', précèdent le traité sur les plantes, qui dans le ms. de Graz était placé immédiatement avant les Questions. Les deux témoins présentent des rubriques analogues: 'Incipit liber Moysi Egyptii de quibusdam plantis tactis a Solone' (Graz, fol. 169ᵛ); 'Incipit Moysi Egyptii de plantis tactis a Solone philosopho' (Séville, fol. 88ᵛ; signalons que le copiste de Séville a omis le début du texte). Quatre autres textes sont communs aux

---

[1] Cf. descriptions dans *Aristoteles latinus, Codices*, i, no. 57: A. Kern, *Die Handschriften der Univ.bibl. Graz*, i (1942), 281–6; *Avicenna latinus* VI, *Archives* xxxiii (1966), 310–17 (avec références bibl.).

[2] Cf. descriptions dans *Aristoteles latinus, Codices*, ii, no. 1181; *Avicenna latinus* VIII, *Archives*, xxxv (1968), 303–6 (avec références bibl.).

[3] A. Birkenmajer, 'Eine wiedergefundene Übersetzung Gerhards von Cremona', *Beiträge*, Suppl. 3 (1935), pp. 475–81; repr. dans *Études d'histoire des sciences* . . ., 22–31.

[4] Sur ce Traité, cf. A. B. Björnbo, 'Alkindi, Tideus und pseudo-Euklid', *Abhandl. z. Gesch. d. math. Wissensch.* xxvi. 3 (1912), 73–82.

deux manuscrits: un 'capitulum de diluviis' d'Avicenne, traduction du dernier chapitre des *Météores* du *Shifa*', qui se présente toujours isolément; (Graz, fols. 241^v–242; Séville, fols. 92^v–93); une petite épître d'optique adressée à un certain 'Constantin' (Graz, fols. 229–230; Séville, fols. 93–94^v); elle est suivie dans les deux manuscrits de la traduction d'un traité de Costa ben Luca, *De physicis ligaturis*, anonyme etanépigrap he dans le ms. de Séville (Graz, fol. 230^{rv}; Séville, fol. 94^v–95^v). Enfin, le *De motu cordis* d'Alfred de Sareshel, anonyme dans Graz (fols. 234^v–241^v) et attribué par une main postérieure à 'Alexandre' dans le ms. de Séville (fols. 95^v–108). Il semble donc que ces deux manuscrits dérivent de recueils apparentés en ce qui concerne plusieurs groupes de textes, en particulier les Questions et le traité des plantes attribué à 'Moyses Egyptius'.

Deux autres manuscrits contiennent les Questions du pseudo-Nicolas avec l'incipit et l'explicit que nous avons indiqué.

Le manuscrit 113 (A. 5. 3.) de la bibliothèque du chapitre de Lincoln,[1] dont nous donnons une description en Appendice, se rapproche sur certains points du ms. Royal 12 C. xv. Il contient au début des textes de médecine, notamment le *Pantegni* de Constantin l'Africain. D'autre part, à la suite des Questions, anonymes, il présente une série de petites questions naturelles ou notes, différentes des 'tractaculi' des manuscrits que nous venons de citer, mais du même genre que les Questions et que certaines notes de la série préliminaire du ms. de Londres et de celui de Laon. Enfin, les Questions précèdent le *Compendium* des *Parva naturalia* d'Averroès, anonyme. Cette partie du manuscrit est écrite par des mains anglaises vers le milieu du XIIIe siècle. Après le *Compendium* d'Averroès, on trouve les gloses d'Alfred de Sareshel sur les *Météores* et le *De plantis*, anonymes. Ces deux gloses se rencontrent dans un manuscrit de la bibliothèque du chapitre de Durham, de date un peu plus tardive (C. III. 15).[2]

Le manuscrit lat. 1870 du fonds Ottoboni de la Bibliothèque vaticane a appartenu au médecin de Laurent le Magnifique, Pier Leoni, qui l'a abondamment annoté. Il a été transcrit par trois

---

[1] La description du manuscrit faite par R. M. Woolley, *Catalogue of the Manuscripts of Lincoln Cathedral Chapter Library* (Oxford, 1927), pp. 79–80, est insuffisante en ce qui concerne la dernière partie du manuscrit, ainsi que l'a indiqué A. Birkenmajer, dans un compte-rendu paru en 1928 dans *Przegląd Biblioteczny*, traduit en français dans *Études d'histoire des sciences . . .*, p. 633.

[2] *Aristoteles latinus, Codices*, i, no. 273.

scribes en élégante écriture humanistique dans la seconde moitié du xvᵉ siècle. Le recueil comprend des traductions arabo-latines de traités d'optique et de mathématiques, deux traductions de traités d'Alkindi, — une traduction de Razi, un traité de Roger Bacon, un opuscule de Robert Grosseteste, le *De motu cordis* d'Alfred de Sareshel, le *De processione mundi* de Gundissalinus. L'Italie est représentée par le traité des songes de Paschalis Romanus, et par un traité anonyme sur le fabrication des statues d'airain et les effets du feu. Enfin, un feuillet contient une note ou dialogue de Nicolas de Cues sur la quadrature du cercle, datée de Brixen en 1457[1]. A l'exception de cet opuscule et du traité sur les statues, tous les textes sont des traductions ou des traités remontant au xiiᵉ et au xiiiᵉ siècle, comme les Questions, anonymes, qui précèdent (fols. 79–97). le traité de Paschalis Romanus: 'Liber thesauri occulti'. L'intérêt de Pier Leoni pour un tel ensemble montre que la curiosité d'esprit des hommes de la Renaissance pouvait encore s'alimenter avec des textes médiévaùx.[2]

Nous devons maintenant examiner les cinq manuscrits incomplets ou fragmentaires des Questions.

Le premier manuscrit incomplet que nous allons citer ne l'est probablement que par accident. C'est le no. 3473 de la Bibliothèque Mazarine qui provient de la bibliothèque des Jacobins.[3] Il a été écrit par des scribes anglais au début du xivᵉ siècle. C'est un recueil de traductions philosophiques. Au début, l'on trouve la 'versio communis' des *Analytica posteriora*, avec le commentaire de Robert Grosseteste, 'Lincolniensis'; puis viennent des commentaires d'Averroès sur le *Physique*, le *De Caelo*, le *De generatione*, ce dernier incomplet, suivi des Questions, anonymes et mutilées, fol. 103ʳᵛ; les quatre feuillets suivants ont été coupés; ils présentaient vraisemblablement le reste de l'ouvrage. Viennent ensuite de nouveau des traités d'Averroès: commentaire du *De Anima*, *Compendium* des *Parva naturalia*, *De substantia orbis*, commentaire de la *Métaphysique*. Un fragment de la traduction du commentaire d'Eustrathe sur le premier livre de l'*Éthique* précède des traduc-

---

[1] Cf. description avec références bibl. dans *Avicenna latinus* X, *Archives*, xxxvii (1970), 354–8.

[2] Cf. J. Ruysschaert, 'Nouvelles recherches au sujet de la bibliothèque de Pier Leoni, médecin de Laurent le Magnifique'. *Acad. royale de Belgique, Bull. Cl. Lettres*, 5ᵉ sér. 46 (1960), 50–1.

[3] Cf. descriptions dans *Aristoteles latinus, Codices*, i, n°. 534; *Avicenna latinus* I, in *Archives*, xxviii (1961), 306–8, avec références bibliographiques.

tions d'Avicenne; *Physique*, pseudo-*De Caelo et mundo* et *Métaphysique*. L'origine anglaise du manuscrit est probable, bien que les Frères Prêcheurs et *scholares* britanniques n'aient pas été rares à Paris à cette époque.

Il n'y a guère de doute au sujet de l'appartenance anglaise du manuscrit Digby 153 de la Bibliothèque Bodléienne.[1] Ce recueil de traités scientifiques, comportant beaucoup d'*experimenta*, a été écrit par des mains anglaises du xive siècle. L'ensemble a appartenu à un Frère Mineur, Johannes Bruyl 'de custodia Londoniensi et de conventu Cantuariensi'[2] qui a indiqué son nom en plusieurs endroits et a écrit de sa main, au début, une table du contenu. Les Questions sont transcrites dans la dernière partie du manuscrit, fols. 148–185, qui nous a paru un peu plus tardive que la partie précédente. Elles suivent, fols. 168–174, un traité intitulé 'Secreta philosophorum', orné de nombreuses figures (fols. 148–167). Les Questions sont anonymes et incomplètes; le Frère Mineur amateur de sciences naturelles en avait conscience. Il a inscrit un titre: Tractatus curiosus de attractione naturali' et, après l'explicit: ' . . . ligna decisa in plenilunio in quo tempore magis est humidum, grossiorem flammam emittunt quam ligna decisa in novilunio [Cf. ms. Graz 482, fol. 176ᵛ]. — Explicit tractatus de attractione naturali', il a noté: 'nunquam vidi plus de illo tractatu, quod doleo; multum concordat cum sententiis Ursonis in Amphorismis.' Les 'Afforismi Ursonis' figurent dans la première partie du manuscrit, fols. 67ᵛ–99.

Deux manuscrits ont été décrits par J. Corbett, dans le *Catalogue des manuscrits alchimiques* du fonds latin de la Bibliothèque nationale.[3] Ils présentent les Questions au milieu de textes de minéralogie, d'astrologie et surtout d'alchimie. Le manuscrit lat.

---

[1] Cf. *Catalogi codicum mss. Bibliothecae Bodleianae pars nona. Codices a viro cl. Kenelm Digby eq. aur. anno 1634 donatos* . . . confecit G. D. Macray (Oxonii, 1883), pp. 152–4.

[2] Sur John Bruyll, cf. Ch. L. Kingsford, *The Grey Friars of London* (British Society of Franciscan Studies, vii, 1915), pp. 56–7 et *passim*. E. B. Fitzmaurice and A. G. Little, *Materials for the History of the Franciscan Province of Ireland A.D. 1230–1450* (British Society of Franciscan Studies, ix, 1920), p. 171. Ce Frère Mineur devint gardien du couvent de Londres en 1397–8, et fut désigné en janvier 1402 comme évêque d'Annaghdown en Irlande.

[3] *Catalogue des manuscrits alchimiques latins. I. Manuscrits des Bibliothèques publiques de Paris* . . . par J. Corbett (Union Académique Internationale, 1939, nº 20, pp. 70–83 = lat. 7156; nº 22, pp. 84–90 = lat. 7158. L'ex-libris: 'Iste est liber domini episcopi Electensis' est du début du xve siècle.

7156 est écrit sur parchemin, par des mains méridionales, dans la première moitié du xive siècle. Il a appartenu à un évêque d'Alet, et porte au fol. 103v une note en provençal. Les Questions, qui ne portaient primitivement pas de titre, sont transcrites fols. 42v–48v:[1] 'Quoniam terra sperica est, vapor ascendens de terra spericus erit . . . – . . . secundum similitudinem picture finestre, cuius oppositum videmus sepe.' — 'Explicit Liber Alpharabii' (en gros caractères). Le traité porte de nombreux titres marginaux qui facilitent la consultation de cet ouvrage composite. C'est ce manuscrit qu'ont utilisé L. Thorndike et B. Lawn pour décrire les Questions. Le traité s'arrête avant la question: *De formatis*, et omet la dernière partie de l'ouvrage (à partir du fol. 177v du ms. de Graz).

Le manuscrit lat. 7158 a été copié sur papier au début du xve siècle pour l'évêque d'Alet, possesseur du manuscrit précédent, mais les mains sont du Nord de la France. Une partie des textes contenus dans le ms. lat. 7156 se retrouvent dans le ms. lat. 7158, mais souvent dans un ordre différent. Le 'Liber Alpharabii' reproduit exactement le texte de son modèle, y compris les titres marginaux, fols. 118–127v.

La question 'De formatis' manque dans les manuscrits alchimiques. Par contre, elle se trouve, isolée, dans un manuscrit du fonds de la Sorbonne, Paris, Nat. lat. 16159. C'est un corpus de textes d'Aristote et d'Averroès exécuté vers la fin du xiiie siècle, à Paris, d'après la décoration. Deux textes ont été ajoutés par une main cursive anglaise: 'Alfarabii de intellectu', fols. 289v–291, et un petit traité portant un titre peint: 'Avicenn. de vi informativa', fols. 368–369v. C'est sous ce titre que le texte est indiqué dans l'*Aristoteles latinus*.[2] Il correspond exactement au traité: 'De virtute informativa' dans la série des Questions: 'De formatis attende quoniam aliqua forma accidit rei formate per intentionem informative et nature in illa re . . . – . . . inconstantia enim pulsus significat inconstantiam cordis in suo motu; inconstantia autem in suo moto significat inconstantiam anime in suis affectibus'; cf. ms. Graz 482, fols. 177v–179.

Tirer des conclusions de cette revue de la tradition manuscrite des Questions au sujet de l'origine du texte serait prématuré. L'on peut seulement faire, avec prudence, quelques constatations.

---

[1] Un titre a été ajouté en marge (fol. 42v): 'Liber Alpharabii.'
[2] Cf. description dans *Aristoteles latinus, Codices*, i. no. 683.

Les questions naturelles sont un type de textes particulièrement variables, sujets à des additions et à des suppressions, selon les besoins et les goûts de l'amateur qui les copie ou les fait copier. Il est presque surprenant, dans ces conditions, que le groupe attribué parfois à 'Nicolas' se présente avec une relative consistance. L'intérêt qu'il paraît avoir suscité, et qui a assuré sa conservation est dû probablement au voisinage des traductions de textes arabes, et surtout des traductions d'Averroès, qu'il accompagne dans la majeure partie des manuscrits. Bien qu'une partie de ceux-ci ait appartenu à des médecins, les Questions sont comprises aussi dans des recueils qui paraissent avoir été exécutés pour des membres des Facultés des Arts, comme le manuscrit de Graz et le manuscrit de Séville. Un autre fait est à noter. Les plus anciens témoins subsistants, Royal 12 C. xv et Lincoln 113 ont été transcrits en Angleterre: ceci semble indiquer que l'intérêt des naturalistes et médecins anglais pour les traductions d'Averroès et les textes qui s'en inspirent a été précoce et durable; rappelons que le manuscrit 3473 de la Mazarine, plus tardif, vient probablement d'Angleterre, et que le franciscain John Bruyll a fait transcrire l'exemplaire incomplet du ms. Digby 153. Il ne faut pas oublier, cependant, que les citations d'Albert le Grand visant la première question, sur l'iris (cf. ms. Graz 482, fol. 173) et la question sur le 'chalybs'[1] (cf. ms. Graz, fols. 175) montrent que les questions étaient connues hors de Grande Bretagne, à l'époque de la rédaction du commentaire des *Météores*, vers 1253–5,[2] et qu'elles étaient déjà attribuées à 'Nicolaus peripateticus'. De même, Jean de Secheville, anglais il est vrai, mais qui a aussi enseigné à Paris, les cite sous ce nom dans un traité rédigé vers 1260–3, d'après son éditeur, R. M. Giguère.[3]

Un point plus important est l'existence d'additions qui paraissent avoir été considérées comme partie intégrante des Questions par le compilateur des extraits du manuscrit lat. 16089. S'agit-il

---

[1] Ce terme grec, qui signifie l'acier, est employé souvent pour désigner le fer au Moyen Age.

[2] Les 'paraphrases' d'Albert le Grand sur les *Libri naturales* d'Aristote datent de l'époque de son enseignement à Cologne, où il est arrivé en 1248. L'éditeur du commentaire sur le *De Caelo* estime qu'il n'a dû commencer que vers 1251 son commentaire sur le *Physique*; le commentaire du *De anima* date des années 1254–7, pendant son provincialat. Ceci permet de dater approximativement les *Météores*, qui se situent entre les deux. Cf. *Alberti Magni . . . De Caelo et mundo . . .* ed. P. Hossfeld, 1971 (*Opera omnia*, v. 1) prolegomena, p. v. cf. aussi prolegomena de l'édition du *De anima* (*Opera omnia*, vii. 1), p. v.

[3] Cf. op. cit., introduction.

d'additions, ou d'une suppression due à d'autres copistes? Rappelons que les six 'tractaculi' dont nous avons parlé suivent les Questions dans quatre manuscrits, dont le ms. Royal 12 C. xv. Notre impression personnelle est que, tant par leur style que par leurs tendances plus théoriques que pratiques, les six petits traités diffèrent un peu des Questions précédentes, bien qu'ils reflètent aussi la première influence d'Averroès dans le milieu des naturalistes.[1] Ceci mérite une étude approfondie de la part des éditeurs.[2] Il faudrait également examiner le cas de l'ensemble de textes englobant les Questions et leurs additions que présentent la dernière partie du manuscrit de Londres et la première partie du manuscrit de Laon. Nous ne pensons pas que le plus récent soit simplement une copie du plus ancien. Ce genre de compilation hétéroclite fait plutôt soupçonner à la source le 'livre de poche' du naturaliste voyageur qui transcrit un choix de textes et l'apporte dans un centre où maîtres et étudiants exploitent le trésor et contribuent à sa diffusion en tout ou partie. Qu'il nous soit permis de terminer cet exposé aride par une hypothèse imaginative qui permettrait de nous représenter les pérégrinations des Questions dans les bagages d'un savant médecin.

APPENDIX

London, British Library, Royal 12 C. xv, usque ad fol. 235ᵛ.

De primis partibus huius codicis cf. descriptionem a cl. viris G. F. Warner et J. P. Gilson editam: *Catalogue of Western Manuscripts in the Old Royal . . . Collections*, ii. 29–31.

(*a*) Tractaculi siue notae de philosophia naturali.

'Considerare animam est dupliciter, aut secundum quod est separata a corpore, aut secundem quod coniuncta est corpori . . . – . . . tres partes philosophie distinguuntur: ab anima, naturalis; a scientia, rationalis; a virtute, moralis; ita quod toti homini tota philosophia et partibus hominis partes ⟨philosophie⟩ appropriantur', fol. 236. — 'Sapiens artifex omnia coadunauit in uno, ut omnium sic constaret tantum esse auctorem . . . – . . . memoria ad sensibile, reminiscentia ad rationale retorquetur', fol. 236ʳᵛ. — 'Licet paralisis sit passio secundum partem . . . – . . . et

---

[1] Nous ne pouvons omettre de rappeler ici les études fondamentales de R. de Vaux, 'La première entrée d'Averroès chez les Latins', *Revue des sciences philosophiques et théol.* xxii (1933), 193–245, et de D. Salman, 'Note sur la première influence d'Averroès', ibid. vi (1937), 203–12.

[2] L'édition vient de paraître. St. Wielgus, Quaestiones Nicolai peripatetici, *Mediaevalia philosophica Polonorum*, xvii (1974), 57–155.

opilationem profundat', fol. 236ᵛ. — 'In opere nature est modus quod natura incoat a perfectiori in actu . . . – . . . recte ergo dixit: Girum celi, etc. et non: in giro celi steti', fol. 236ᵛ. — 'Dicit Auicenna quod iectigatio in facie tantum est signum future paralisis . . . – . . . ab ipso principio, scilicet neruos', fols. 236ᵛ–237. — 'Omne quod prorumpit de terra exit in altum ab imo et intendit ascendere a loco radicis sue . . . – . . . ad cuius cognitionem completam perducat nos Ihesus, qui cum Patre et Spiritu sancto uiuit et regnat Deus per omnia secula seculorum. Amen', fol. 237ᵛ. —'Post hoc superaddidit in verbo suo: Similitudo autem vultus eorum facies hominis . . . [Ezek. i: 10] Et erat questio apud antiquos Caldeos quare duo animalia posuit in una parte et dixit: a dextris, et non a sinistris . . . – . . . et hoc est quod accepi de dictis antiquorum Caldeorum in ista intentione', fols. 237ᵛ–238. — Hi tractaculi eodem ordine leguntur in codice Laudunensi 412, fols. 1–3.

(*b*) Tractatus de plantis.

'Sciendum autem quod cedrus et pinus et terebintus et cipressus et abies omnes communicant in una radice . . . Italici in lingua latina vocant arborem facientem poma maxima crocea habencia grana aquosa cedrum . . . – . . . siliqua autem floris vitis tota est continua, et precipue a superiori parte', fols. 238–240ᵛ. Cf. cod. Laudunensem 412, fols. 3–5; cod. Graecensem 482, fols. 169ᵛ–172ᵛ, ubi tractatus 'Moysi Egyptio' adscribitur; cod. Hispalensem Columb. 5. 6. 14, fols. 88ᵛ–92ᵛ, ubi tractatus incipit: 'Italici in lingua latina . . .' et etiam 'Moysi Egyptio' adscribitur.

(*c*) Excerpta ex libro Aristotelis de Animalibus (iv. 9) secundum translationem Michaelis Scoti, cum glossis nonnullis.

'Vox est secundum quod narrabo. Debemus ergo scire quod ⟨vox⟩ est diuersa a sono . . . – . . . non habet vocem' — 'Strepitus vero siue sibilum [*sic*] . . . – . . . . neque quadrupedia', fol. 241; cf. cod. Laud. 412, fol. 5ʳᵛ.

(*d*) Notae de philosophia naturali.

'Tonitrua fiunt tripliciter . . . – . . . quidam remotiores', fol. 241. — 'Quod terra se habeat ad firmamentum tanquam punctus probat Aristoteles . . . – . . . terra non habet sensibilem quantitatem ad firmamentum', fol. 241. —'R⟨egul⟩a. Si non possumus vadare tanquam elephas, volitabimus super terram tanquam strutio', fol. 241. — 'Nullum animal habens cornua habet dentes in superiori mandibula . . . – . . . contra pinguedinem', fol. 241. — 'Quod apes disciplinantur, patet . . . Quod formice possint disciplinari . . . Si oculi yrundinis extrahantur . . . Talpa non habet oculos . . . Item, nota quod quando aliquis ambulat vel currit

... – ... et non supra terram', fol. 241. — Item, nota quod quedam spe-
culatiua speculatur res prout sunt et utitur de nominibus prout sunt ... –
... sicut curuum et simum', fol. 241ᵛ. — 'Item, nota: ymaginatio anima-
lium vincit rationem ... Item, nota quod duo attribuuntur materie ...
Item, nota quod dum forma rei vincit super materiam, fit augmentum,
et hoc est quod dicit Aristoteles ... – ... propter propagationem indiui-
duorum et saluationem speciei sinper [*sic*]', fol. 241ᵛ. Cf. cod. Laudun.
412, fol. 5ᵛ.

(*e*) Excerpta ex libro Aristotelis de Animalibus (iv. 9).

'Locutio vero non appropriatur soli homini ... conueniens genera-
tioni' fol. 241ᵛ. — 'Vox et sermo diuersificantur secundum regiones et
loca ... – ... voces autem hominum sunt consimiles', fol. 241ᵛ. — 'Animal
non generans habens quatuor pedes habet vocem, non tamen loquitur ...
Modus auium ... Multi vero modi piscium carent voce ... oculi eius
sunt sicut due candele in superficie aque', fol. 242. Cf. cod. Laudun.
412, fol. 6.

(*f*) Notae de philosophia naturali.

'Item, nota quod cum abscindantur cornua capre ... Item, in quibusdam regionibus sunt vacce ... – ... maxime generat odium', fol. 242. —
Item, nota quod equalia sunt spatia a celo ad centrum terre ... Item,
nota quod circa medicinam laxatiuam triplex sit opinio ... – ... et sic
differunt medicus et nigroma⟨n⟩ticus', fol. 242. — 'Motus quatuor elementorum sunt recti et ideo incompleti ... – ... ideo nominant alkami
[*sic*] metalla nomine planetarum', fol. 242ᵛ. — Nota quod bruta differunt
a rationalibus ... – ... et illud est quod narrat Aristoteles in tertio de
Anima, ut in textu patet', fol. 242ᵛ. — 'Nota quod si ponatur nunc sol,
nunc ignis ... – ... nec vermes generat', fols. 242ᵛ–243. — 'Nota quod
quedam corpora reflectunt tantum, ut speculum ... – ... et videtur in
superficie denarius', fol. 243. 'Nota quod speculorum quedam sunt
columpnaria et quedam piramidalia, quedam comburentia, quedam
plana, quedam concaua, quedam conuexa ... Et hoc est quod dicit
Anuerrozech [*sic*] ... – ... sicut aliud est regens', fol. 243. — 'Ad instar
cause primarie plus influentis super causata quam influat aliqua subiec-
tarum causarum ... – ... et illud est quod primus graduum nature cum
suis tribus principiis ... nonus vero hominum', fol. 243. — 'Nota quod
celi dicuntur manus Dei, quia sicut anima agit aliquid per manus mentis ... – ... homo erit animal maxime imperfectum', fol. 243ʳᵛ. — 'Nota
ergo quod in eo quod dicitur granum apud vulgus sunt duo, germen
scilicet et substantia farinosa ... – ... radix in tritico pululat et fructifi-
cat', fol. 243ᵛ. — 'Nota quod si omnis mula sit sterilis ... – ... nusquam
autem melius quam in primo, scilicet mulo', fol. 243ᵛ. — De principiis

senserunt philosophi differenter; alii enim posuerunt unum sicut
Anaxagoras . . . – . . . calidum aut frigidum, humidum et siccum', fols.
243^v–244. Cf. cod. Laudun. 412, fols. 6–7^v.

(*g*) ⟨Al Kindi, De intellectu⟩.

'Sermo de intellectu secundum sententiam Aristotelis et Platonis',
titulus in margine inscriptus, manu currenti. 'Solutio breuis de intellectu secundum sententiam Aristotelis et Platonis. Set sententia eorum
est quod intellectus est secundum quatuor species . . . – . . . et hoc ad
presens sufficiat de diuisione intellectus', fol. 244. Cf. cod. Laudun.
412, fol. 7^v.

(*h*) ⟨Auerroes. Compendium librorum Aristotelis qui Parua Naturalia
vocantur⟩.

De sensu, fols. 244–246; De memoria et reminiscentia, ff. 246^v–247^v;
De somno et vigilia, fols. 247^v–250; De longitudine, fols. 250–251.

(*i*) ⟨De appetitu⟩.

'Continue alterantur sicut resoluunter et eque naturaliter, ergo
naturalis appetitus . . . – . . . nec sunt plante nec animalia, cum organa
non habeant', fol. 251^{rv}. De hoc libello, cf. notam in calce p. 293 Aristotelis Latini, Codices, i.

(*k*) ⟨Auerroes, De substantia orbis⟩.

'De substantia celi et de motibus corporum superiorum et de compositione corporis celestis', titulus in margine inscriptus, manu currenti. 'In hoc tractatu intendimus perscrutari . . . – . . . potest aliquis
estimare in corpore celesti scilicet ipsum habere virtutem finitam et
adquirere', fols. 251^v–254. Desinit imperfectus, tractatu III°, sicut
etiam videtur in codice Laudunensi, fols. 7^v–9^v.

(*l*) ⟨Quaestiones quae dicuntur Nicolai Peripatetici⟩, fols. 254–260^v.

'Quoniam terra sperica est, vapor ascendens de ipsa spericus erit . . .
– . . . et odorare vinum potatum ab alio.'

(*m*) Tractaculi siue Quaestiones de philosophia naturali.

'In sermone nostro de elementis dicendum est quod quatuor sunt
elementa . . . – . . . ut opus proportionetur opifici', fols. 260^v–261. —
'Dicit Aristoteles: Ars ymitatur naturam, cuius ratio hec est . . . – . . . a
forciori et nobiliori creatione, idest angelorum siue intelligentiarum',
fol. 261. — 'Deus prouidit hoc, necessario hoc eueniet . . . – . . . si e
contrario, diuersificantur', fol. 261^{rv}. — 'Cum omnia elementa sint dia-
fona, id est, colore priuata . . . – . . . priuatio omnium colorum in loco non

suo', fol. 261ᵛ. — 'Omne celum est circulare, et omne circulare est perfectum . . . – . . . et hoc est quod dicit Auenrot; vide animal quod vidisti . . .
extra eas', fol. 261ᵛ. — 'In tercio de Anima dicit Aristoteles . . . – . . . sed
nomine elementorum intelligunt elementa elementata non habencia
propositum', fol. 261ᵛ.

Tractatus necnon tractaculi qui a fol. 254 usque ad fol. 261ᵛ exscripti
sunt sunt eodem ordine inueniuntur in codd. MSS. Laudun. 412, fols.
9ᵛ–15; Graecens. 482, fols. 173–180ᵛ; Hispalensi, Columb. 5. 6. 14,
fols. 77–88ᵛ. Codex iste a pluribus librariis anglicis exaratus fuit, saec.
XIIII¹; fols. 146–149ᵛ; 236–240ᵛ, 260ᵛ–261ᵛ exscripta sunt atramento
pallido saec. XIII circa medium, ut opinor. De contentis huius codicis
cf. *Aristotelem latinum, Cod.* i, n⁰ 309.

Lincoln Cathedral Library, 113 (A. 5. 3)

1. Mesue ⟨De medicamentis⟩.

'In nomine Dei misericordis . . . Verborum Iohannis filii Hamet,
filii Helii, filii Abdebla regis Damasceni verbum cecidit inter inquiren-
tes . . . Quoniam de rectificatione medicinarum simplicium . . . – . . . hec
est secunda summa in qua ponit medicinas singulorum membrorum
egritudinibus appropriatas. Explicit Hebenmesue', fols. 3–53ᵛ.

2. Constantinus Africanus, Pantegni.

Domino suo Montis Cassinensis abbati Desiderio . . . Constantinus
Affricanus . . . Con [*sic*] totum patet scientie generalitas . . . – . . . ad
intelligendum. Explicit hic liber 1. Theorica Pantegni. Deo gracias',
fols. 54–108ᵛ. — Fol. 109ʳᵛ. Notae pluribus manibus anglicis saec. XIV
et XV.

3. 'Summa Constantini super Viaticum.'

Titulus in summa pagina inscriptus manu currenti anglica circa
1300. — 'et Passionarius Alexandri'; add. saec. xv. — 'Sicut ab antiquis habemus auctoribus . . . – . . . yliace passiones', fols. 110–145ᵛ.

4. ⟨Quaestiones naturales quae dicuntur Nicolai peripatetici.⟩

'Quoniam terra est sperica vapor ascendens de ipsa spericus erit . . . –
. . . ne possit discernere et odorare vinum potatum ab alio', ff. 146–150ᵛ.
Sequuntur sine intermissione quaestiones naturales nonnullae: 'Attende
quoniam splendor, cum reflectitur ad corpus tersum et lucidum . .
Quedam aues non vidunt nisi in nocte . . . Si autem nullum punctum
videtur nisi in quantum venit ad centrum cristallini per imitationem . . .
Quoniam autem habundantior est humiditas in homine ebrioso . . . – . . .
aquile autem et huismodi debetur lux in habundantia ut ex sublimi

volantes intuentur in inferiora remota ea ex quibus viuendo sustententur', fol. 150ᵛ.

5. ⟨Averroes, Compendia librorum Aristotelis qui Parua Naturalia dicuntur⟩.

(*a*) De sensu et sensato, fols. 151–152ᵛ; (*b*) De memoria et reminiscentia, fols. 152ᵛ–153ᵛ; (*c*) De somno et vigilia, fols. 153ᵛ–155ᵛ; (*d*) De longitudine, fols. 155ᵛ–156.

6. ⟨Alfredus Anglicus⟩ Glossa in Metheora et in librum de Plantis.

'*Postquam precessit rememoratio.* Titulus talis: Liber Aristotelis philosophi sapientis in factura impressionum superiorum que fiunt in alto et inferius. Tractatus primus. Not⟨andum⟩. Alforabius in libro de scientiis, capitulo de naturalibus, ait: inquisitio est de principiis actionum et passionum . . . *Vita in animalibus et plantis inuenta est.* Inferioris mundi IIII. corporum . . . – . . . unde fit amarus', fols. 156–160 (sed notandum quod folia huius partis perperam ligata sunt). Cf. cod. MS. Dunelmensem C. III. 15, fols. 11ᵛ–18 et 115–116ᵛ. — Cf. *Aristot. lat. Codic.* i, nº 273; Ch. H. Lohr, 'Medieval Latin Aristotle Commentaries', *Traditio*, xxiii (1967), 355–6.

7. ⟨Ps. Augustinus. Liber de anima et spiritu⟩. Nota in margine:

'Ag⟨ustinus⟩ de anima.' Initium tantum: 'Quoniam dictum est michi ut me ipsum cognoscam . . . – . . . principium medium et finis assignetur respectu vero incorporee nature / / ', fol. 160ʳᵛ. Desinit mutilus. Codex iste e quatuor partibus constat. Prima pars (fols. 3–53ᵛ) ab uno librario forsan gallico exarata est saec. XIII. circa medium. Litterae initiales vacant; rubricae etiam vacant usque ad fol. 26.—Pars secunda (fols. 54–108ᵛ) ab uno librario forsan gallico exarata est, manu tenuissima saec. XIII². Litterae initiales seu rubrae seu caeruleae alternatim nonnullae, lineis implicatis et elongationibus ornatae. Rubricae. Tituli in summis paginis depicti rubro caeruleoque coloribus fol. 109ʳᵛ–109ᵛ, notae pluribus manibus anglicis, saec. XIV. et XV. — Pars tertia (fols. 110–145ᵛ) a pluribus librariis exarata est, saec. XIII. ex. Litterae initiales miniatae; signa paragraphorum miniata. Rubricae nullae. — Pars quarta (fols. 146–160ᵛ) a duobus librariis anglicis exarata est, saec. XIII. circa medium, quorum secundus (fols. 156–160ᵛ) manu tenuissima scripsit. Litterae initiales miniatae. Rubricae nullae. De ceteris, cf. descriptionem codicis in catalogo impresso: R. M. Woolley, *Catalogue of the Manuscripts of Lincoln Cathedral Chapter Library* (Oxford, 1927), pp. 79–80; cf. etiam emendationem a cl. viro Alexandro Birkenmajer allatam (A.D. 1928), *Études d'histoire des sciences et de la philosophie du Moyen Age* (1970), p. 633.

10

The Return of Petronius to Italy[1]

'PETRONIUS was very little known in Italy throughout the Middle Ages.'[2] This is an unexceptionable statement. Poggio Bracciolini is generally credited with the rediscovery of Petronius for the Italians[3] and it is assumed, surely rightly, to be from the texts discovered by him in the 1420s that all the fifteenth-century manuscripts descend. Yet it seems that Poggio was not the first Italian to bring or send home from abroad a copy of the *excerpta vulgaria* (or O-text) of the *Satyricon*. One of the three extant early manuscripts, Paris, Bibliothèque Nationale, lat. 6842D (R of the editors), containing Petronius and other texts, and copied in France about 1200,[4] has annotations in two fourteenth-century hands which seem to me to be Italian.[5] It may represent yet another of the

[1] Many friends and colleagues have helped in the preparation of this piece, although I am all too conscious that it is a poorer thing for lacking the sobering and enlightening criticism of him for whom it has been written. I am grateful to Bruce Barker-Benfield for the part of mentor that he has played, and for the endless time that he has generously given to discussing the problems that have arisen. I owe a special debt to the Section latine of the Institut de Recherche et d'Histoire des Textes in Paris, who lent me valuable microfilms and photographs without which I could not have made this study. For individual help of many kinds I would like to thank M. François Avril, Mr. John Barr, Dr. Margaret Gibson, Mlle Colette Jeudy, Sir Roger Mynors, Dr. P. F. J. Obbema, Dr. M. B. Parkes, Mlle Élisabeth Pellegrin, Mr. M. D. Reeve, Dr. F. Römer, Mgr. José Ruysschaert, Miss Cornelia Starks, Professor D. F. S. Thomson, and Professor Paola Zambelli.

[2] A. Rini, *Petronius in Italy from the Thirteenth Century to the Present Time* (New York, 1937), p. 1.

[3] They did of course know the few passages cited in florilegia and authors such as Fulgentius.

[4] It has been assigned to various dates between the 11th and 14th centuries; see G. Brugnoli, *Petronius* (Auctores ad stud. paleog. promovenda, ed. E. Paratore, i, Rome, 1961), p. 11. For the text see A. R. Jones, 'Notes on a Paris MS. (6842D) of Petronius', *Trans. Amer. Philol. Soc.* lviii (1927), 63–74.

[5] See pl. XX *b*, *c*. One annotator uses a large, loopy cursive; the hand of the other, small and neat, recalls the annotations attributed by Giuseppe Billanovich to Ser Simone della Tenca of Arezzo (*c.* 1280–1338) who knew Petrarch at Avignon ('Dal Livio di Raterio al Livio del Petrarca', *Italia medioevale e umanistica*, ii (1959), tav. XI, 4–7), although it is probably not the same. However, Ser Simone

discoveries made by Italians visiting or living in France while the Papal court was at Avignon. The manuscript contains Palladius, *De agricultura*, the O-text of Petronius, headed (fol. 74): 'Incipiunt excerta [*sic*] Petronii Satirici' and an extract (fol. 92) 'De differentiis sermonum.'[1] Only one of the fourteenth-century annotations occurs in the Petronius.[2] The manuscript bears the ex-libris of the fifteenth-century Venetian humanist Francesco Barbaro (1390–1454),[3] who was a friend of Poggio, Niccolò Niccoli, and their circle. This interesting fact has long been recorded,[4] but seems to have passed largely unnoticed. Barbaro held a central position among the humanists who were engaged in searching for and

did own a MS. of Palladius (U. Pasqui in *Arch. stor. italiano*, ser. v, iv (1889), 253). The same annotator is probably also responsible for a note in a formal bookhand on fol. 1, *beg.*: 'Agricultura nichil melius' (pl. XX*a*).

[1] Keil, *Grammat. Lat. Suppl.*, ed. H. Hagen (1870), p. 275 l. 12–p. 281 l. 22, *ends*: 'insidiosus. Redibium est quod primo nascitur redivivum quod iterum.' A similar fragment occurs with the earliest surviving copy of the *excerpta* in Berne, Burgerbibl. MS. 330, fol. 45. The manuscript is now in several fragments, and Petronius, which lacks two leaves, is divided between MSS. Berne 357, fols. 34ᵛ–41ᵛ and Leyden Voss. Lat. Q. 30, fols. 57–58 (B to editors of Petronius). For the bibliography on the MS., written in the late 9th century, probably at Auxerre, see O. Homburger, *Die illustr. HSS. der Burgerbibl. Bern. Die vorkarolingischen und karolingischen HSS.* (Berne, 1962), pp. 134–6. The third and last pre-15th-century MS. of the *excerpta* is also French: in Paris B.N. lat. 8049 second section, containing end of Cicero, *De div.* (fol. 17ʳᵛ); Petronius (fols. 17ᵛ–25), and Calpurnius Siculus (P to editors of Petronius). It probably dates from the second half of the 12th century, and has no medieval annotations (reprod. E. Chatelain, *Paléog. des classiques latins,*ii (1894–1900), pl. CI, 1 (fol. 21); Brugnoli, op. cit., Tab. V (fol. 21). Its first part is Berlin Lat. 201 (Phill. 1794), with Cicero, *Phil.* I–IV *De leg.*, and most of *De div.*

[2] Fol. 75ᵛ, at *Sat.* 14. 2 v. 4 *Non numquam nummis*. See pl. XX*d*.

[3] Fol. 1, bottom: 'Palladius de agricultura et Petronius satyricus Francisci Barbari veneti quondam domini Candiani' (the last four words apparently written later than the rest) (pl. XX*a*). Part of the top of fol. 1 has been cut away but there remains an erased 14th-century note, legible under ultra-violet: 'ducat' tres'. The MS. did not later belong to Petau, as the 18th-century catalogue states, but on the binding, Mlle É. Pellegrin has kindly informed me, are the arms of Gaspard Coignet de la Thuilerie (1596–1653), French ambassador in Venice in 1630 (Olivier, Hernal, de Roton, *Manuel de l'amateur de reliures armoriées françaises*, xiv (1928), pl. 1436). I am grateful to Mlle Pellegrin for sending me a description of this MS. Her reference to 'prehumanistic' annotations stimulated me to go and examine it in person.

[4] e.g. by F. Buecheler, introd. to his *editio maior* of Petronius (Berlin, 1862; reprinted 1963), p. xxiii; R. Sabbadini, *Le scoperte dei codici latini e greci ne' secoli XIV e XV*, ii (Florence, 1914; reprinted, with Sabbadini's addenda and corrigenda ed. E. Garin, 1967), p. 240. The MS. is cited, but only for Palladius, by A. Diller, 'The Library of Francesco and Ermolao Barbaro', *Italia med. e um.* vi (1963), 256.

diffusing lost or rare classical texts, and one might expect his ownership of such a manuscript of Petronius to be of considerable significance for the fifteenth-century tradition of the text. However, the manuscript seems to have had little or no influence on this tradition, and though Barbaro annotated the part of the manuscript containing Palladius, there is no trace of his or any other fifteenth-century hand in Petronius. Most fifteenth-century readers were perhaps put off Petronius by the fragmentary nature of the text available to them and the difficulty of its language. There does not seem to have been much demand to read him at this time: only a few of the known fifteenth-century copies of the *Satyricon* were made for rich collectors or the commercial market; it features rarely in fifteenth-century library inventories,[1] and it was printed only twice before 1500.[2]

The fifteenth-century manuscripts of the O-text of Petronius are of scant importance for the text and have attracted little attention from recent editors or students of the tradition of the text.[3]

[1] For the only entries known to me see nos. 8, 11, and p. 238 below.

[2] See L. A. White, 'The Early Editions of the Satiricon of Petronius' (thesis abstract), *University of Pittsburgh Bulletin*, ix (1933) (?), 303–9. The *editio princeps* (Petronius follows the *Panegyrici Latini* and Tacitus, *Agricola*) n.d. (*c.* 1482, see Rini, pp. 20–3), was edited by the Bolognese scholar Franciscus Puteolanus and printed at Milan by Antonius Zarotus (Hain 13119, Proctor 5837; British Museum, *Cat. of Books Printed XVth Cent.* vi (2nd edn., 1963), 718). The second edition, based on the first but with some alterations and corrections (Rini, pp. 25–30), was printed, with Dio Chrysostomus, *Oratio ad Ilienses*, at Venice by Bernardus Venetus de Vitalibus, 23 July 1499 (Hain 6185, Proctor 5533; B.M. *Cat.* cit. v. 549). Both editions have a peculiar lacuna omitting most of 16. 1–25. 2: between *Sat.* 14. 1 v. 6 and 25. 3 *Obstupui ego* they have only 17. 5 *Utique . . . invenire*; 18. 6 v. 1–4; 24. 7 end: *Hodie . . . sumo*; 25. 1 parts of end: *Cur non devirginatur Panichidis nostra?* (In references to the text of the *Satyricon* I use the numbering of the editions by K. Müller, Munich, 1961 and 1965 (revised with German translation by W. Ehlers) in preference to the page- and line-references to Buecheler's 1862 edition which have often been used in the past). The 15th-century editions belong to the α group of Müller's δ family described below, and are closely related to nos. 5 and 6 of the group.

[3] Brugnoli's useful little palaeographical album is an exception but unfortunately his reproductions are of poor quality. C. Beck, *The Manuscripts of the Satyricon of Petronius Arbiter Described and Collated* (Cambridge, Mass., 1863), collated all the 15th-century MSS. known to him (those called A, C, D, F, J, V, W by Müller), with varying degrees of accuracy. Buecheler, 1862 edn. (henceforth referred to as Buecheler), gave readings from A, C, D, F, G, and a few from the first pages of J, derived from Jahn. Both scholars used Jahn's collation of E. Müller (1961 edn., revised edn. 1965) depended on the collations of Beck and Buecheler for the MSS. that they had used but himself collated the more recently discovered K and Q, and looked at V and W. He gives no readings for them, however, apart from one from K cited in his 1965 introduction, p. 390.

Yet they may still be worth considering for the light they may throw on the history of the text, especially in the period immediately following its discovery by Poggio, probably in England in 1420. Thirteen manuscripts are known at present.[1] They were all written in Italy. A fourteenth manuscript, now lost, was probably also written in the fifteenth century. The manuscripts all descend from a lost copy, called δ by Müller, presumed to be the text which Poggio sent back from England. They fall into two groups:[2]

I. Müller's α family[3] (nos. 5 and 6 were not known to him)

MS. A   1. *Paris, Bibl. Nationale, lat.* 7989 (*'Codex Traguriensis'*). (Beck's Trag. 1; A to editors). Described below, p. 240.

MS. F   2. *Leyden, Universiteitsbibl., Voss. Lat. O.* 81 (Beck's Vb; F to

Other editors betray their dependence on Buecheler by citing his wrong or out-of-date shelfmarks (see, e.g., p. 227 n. 5 below). Little or none of the large recent literature on the *Satyricon* concerns the 15th-century MSS. Some useful bibliography can be found in Brugnoli, but the so-much-cited *University of Pittsburgh Bulletin*, vols. iii (1927), vii–ix (1931–3), xi–xii (1935–6), xiv (1938), containing reports on the theses of Sage's pupils, seems almost impossible to find.

[1] The untraced MS. noticed by Rini (pp. 16–17) in the catalogue of the Campori collection is now Modena, Bibl. Estense γ. D. 66 (Campori 41), containing the Ps.-Petronian glossary 'De antiquis dictionibus' (ed. E. Campanile, 'Un glossario medioevale attribuito a Petronio', *Studi urbinati*, xxxv (1961), 118–34. See also M. L. Colker, 'Is there New Evidence of the Survival of a Fuller Petronius?', *Scriptorium*, xxiv (1970), 55–6, who disposes of another false hare).

[2] See Müller's stemma, 1961 edn., p. xiii, revised in 1965 edn., p. 389. The more complicated stemma of the earlier edition agrees with my own theories about the position of J. J is not as close to the rest of the ξ group as his second stemma implies. Undoubtedly contamination makes it difficult clearly to relate the various MSS. I have checked complete sections and crucial passages in complete microfilms of J, Q, O, F, K, S, Barb, and both the 15th-century editions. It can be assumed that readings I cite for these have been checked by me; for the others I have mainly used Beck, and Buecheler where he disagrees with Beck, although I have been able to check some readings (especially in a large section of V) from photographs. Dr. Franz Römer kindly checked a number of crucial readings in V and W for me. Beck's accuracy varies—he is very good, for example, on A, but rather bad on F which uses some misleading abbreviations; he makes a number of mistakes (some serious) on J, V, and W of which his is the only complete printed collation. Many or all of the 'good' readings disagreeing with the rest of the α group which he cites for F do not exist. Buecheler is much more reliable but not infallible. Readings cited for G derive from Buecheler apart from the last page of the MS. I depend on Beck and Buecheler for C and D. Müller prints no list of readings to distinguish the two sub-families of δ. Some examples are: *Sat.* 55. 6 v. 6 *crotalistria*] *e tota listria* (or *lystria*) α; 95. 1 *iac. volutationem*] *volu(p)tationem iac.* α; 129. 5 *homines ambulare posse*] *posse ire* α *homines posse ire* ξ; 130. 2 *hominem*] *homines* α. These readings are unique to the α family. S, a clearly contaminated MS., often disagrees with α, but not here.

[3] Where the MSS. were known to Müller I have used his *sigla*.

editors).[1] *Contents*: (fol. 1) Appendix Vergiliana; (fol. 27) Petronius. *Ends* (fol. 54): 'Petronius Satiricon arbiter finit quom [*sic*] omni diligentia scripture commendavi'; (fol. 54^v) Catullus;[2] (fol. 102^v) Tibullus; (fol. 142^v) Propertius.

Parchment, 226 leaves, 165 × 105 mm. Small, much abbreviated semi-Gothic bookhand, probably written in the mid 15th century or a little later. Carelessly copied. Unusual archaizing pen initials. A few notes in 15th- and 16th-century hands. Remains of ex libris of P. Michon-Bourdelot.[3]

MS. K 3. *Vatican City, Bibl. Apostolica, Vat. lat.* 1671 (not in Beck; U in Milar and Brugnoli; K in Müller).[4] *Contents*: (fol. 1) Petronius; (fol. 38^v) 'Epigramma Julii p. ad eundem' (i.e. Petronius), perhaps by Pomponio Leto;[5] (fol. 38^v) extracts from Sidonius Apollinaris and Propertius.

Paper,[6] i+47 leaves, 214 × 144 mm. Distinctive late 15th-century humanistic cursive. Rome? A few variants by the scribe. Simple illuminated initial, fol. 1. A few annotations, perhaps by Angelo Colocci (1474–1549), who owned the MS.[7]

MS. E 4. Lost 'Codex Messanensis' (Beck's Mess.; E to editors). Formerly in monastery of S. Placidio, Messina, apparently destroyed in 1848.[8] Collated (incompletely) by Jahn in 1839. His collation was used by Beck and Buecheler. The beginning

---

[1] Brugnoli, Tab. IV (fol. 27); W. G. Hale, 'The MSS. of Catullus', *Class. Philol.* iii (1908), 238; M. Zicari, 'Ricerche sulla tradiz. MS. di Catullo', *Bollettino del Comitato per la preparazione dell'Ediz. Naz. dei classici greci e latini*, N.S. vi (1958), 80–8 (MS. Ln); B. L. Ullman, 'The Manuscripts of Propertius', *Class. Philol.* vi (1911), 300–1.

[2] The text belongs to Mynors's η group (introduction to Oxford edn., 1958, p. x). Most of the MSS. in this group were written in NE Italy *c.* 1460 or later.

[3] I am indebted to Dr. P. F. J. Obbema for sending me a copy of the unpublished description of this MS. by Dr. K. A. De Meyier.

[4] Brugnoli, Tabs. VI (fol. 38), VII (fol. 38^v). *Descr.* B. Nogara, *Codd. Vat. Lat.* iii (1912), 155–6. See also H. R. Milar, 'The Interrelations of MSS. AEFU of Petronius' (thesis abstract), *University of Pittsburgh Bulletin*, ix (1933), 189–96; H. R. Milar, N. M. Miller, L. A. White, 'Three New MSS. of Petronius', *Trans. Amer. Philol. Assoc.* lxiv (1933), lxi–lxii; Rini, p. 16 n. 78.

[5] *Beg*: 'Petronii carmen divino pondere currit' (*Anth. Lat.* 890; etc.). See Brugnoli, 26, no. xli, with earlier bibliography.

[6] Watermarks (kindly identified for me by Mgr. José Ruysschaert): a hunting horn, Briquet 7834 (Rome, 1470); letter A, Briquet 7918 (Rome, 1479, also Palermo, Naples, etc.); bird, Briquet 12149 (Rome, 1484).

[7] S. Lattès, 'Recherches sur la bibl. d'Angelo Colocci', *Mélanges d'arch. et d'hist. de l'École française de Rome*, xlviii (1931), 342.

[8] S. Calderone, 'Intorno al Cod. E (Messanensis) di Petronio', *Giornale ital. di filologia*, i (1948), 114–15.

of the MS. was missing; it ended (caps.): 'Petronius Satyricon Arbiter feliciter explicit. *ΤΕΛΟΣ* [*or* τελος].' Ascribed to the 12th century by Jahn but in his edition Müller argues from the collation that it must have been a 15th-century humanistic MS. Apparently contained Petronius only.

Barb 5. *Vatican, Barb. lat.* 4 (not known to the editors; V to Milar, etc., and Brugnoli).[1] *Contents*: (fol. 1) 'Petronii Arbitri satyrici fragmenta quae extant.'[2]

Parchment, iii+30 leaves, 154×97 mm. Skilled near-italic formal humanistic cursive. Marginalia by the scribe and two later hands. Fol. 1, vine-stem border in Ferrarese style of third quarter of 15th century, with Nogarola arms. Original binding in red leather, stamped and gilt.[3] Probably belonged to Isotta Nogarola of Verona (1418–66), who quoted a passage from Petronius in her letters.[4]

MS. S 6. *Belluno, Bibl. del Seminario Gregoriano, Lolli* 25 (not known to the editors; S in Brugnoli).[5] Composite MS.: two items with separate foliation, bound together. 200×180 mm. Paper, no visible watermark:[6] *a* 51 leaves. Ubertinus Pusculus of Brescia, *Constantinopoleos.* Probably written in NE. Italy, 3rd quarter of 15th century, in a good near-italic humanistic cursive.

---

[1] I have called this MS. 'Barb' because Brugnoli's *siglum*, V, is used by Müller for Vienna 179. Brugnoli, Tab. VIII (fol. 13). *Descr.* S. Prete, *Codd. Barberiniani latini. Codd. 1–150* (1968), pp. 6–7. See also White, 'The Early Editions'; Milar, Miller, and White, art. cit., pp. lxi–lxii; Rini, p. 16 n. 78; A. Marucchi, 'Stemmi di possessori di manoscritti conservati nella Bibl. Vat.', *Mélanges Tisserant*, vii (Studi e Testi, ccxxxvii, 1964), 30, no. 1 and Tav. II, 7 (coat of arms).

[2] The text is imperfect, although the collation ($1^8–3^8$, 4^6, with catchwords) shows that no leaves are missing. The scribe left fol. 4ᵛ blank, presumably to indicate a lacuna in his exemplar (from 16. 1 to 25. 6 end: fol. 5 begins -*lum sustulerit*). A slightly later but very similar hand added 16. 1–17. 5 (*Utique nostra regio*) on fol. 4ᵛ. A still later (16th-century) hand supplied an imperfect text, apparently derived from one of the early editions (cf. p. 222 n. 2 above), to bridge the surviving gap (17. 5 *tam presentibus . . . invenire*; 18. 6 vv. 1–4; 24. 7 end (*Hodie . . . sumo*); parts of 25. 1 end as in early editions; 25. 3 mid–25. 6 (*Obstupui ego . . . tollere quae vitu-*).

[3] T. De Marinis, *La legatura artistica in Italia . . .*, i (1960), no. 185 (as Naples).

[4] She cites part of *Sat.* 118. 1 in two letters of 1434 and 1438–9 (*Isotae Nogarolae Veronensis Opera . . .*, ed. E. Abel, i (Vienna, 1886), 6, 187); cit. Rini, p. 118; D. M. Robothan, 'A Fifteenth-Century Bluestocking', *Medievalia et Humanistica*, ii (1944), 109). *Sat.* 118. 1 is one of the passages from Petronius included in the *Florilegium Gallicum* (for which see above p. 73 n. 3), so Isotta may not have known the 'complete' Petronius at this time.

[5] G. Mazzatinti, *Inventari* ii (1892), p. 123; P. O. Kristeller, *Iter Italicum* ii (1967), 495; Rini, p. 16; Brugnoli, p. 11.

[6] As the librarian, Dott. Ottorino Pierobon, kindly informed me.

Vine-stem initial; *b* 37 leaves. Petronius.[1] Untidy humanistic cursive of 15th–16th century, signed at end in Greek: '... διὰ χείρος Ἡρακληάνου περὶ τῶν ἀλβερτῶν ...' The scribe regularly uses 'ω' instead of 'O' for the vocative. Many marginal variants written by the scribe, generally beginning: 'Legitur et.'[2] Additions at the end by the scribe include a copy of the epitaph of Andrea Lampugnano, one of the assassins of Galeazzo Maria Sforza, Duke of Milan, in 1476. Bought in 1527 by the Bellunese humanist Giovanni Persicini.[3]

The two fifteenth-century editions[4] belong to the same sub-group as nos. 5 and 6.

II. Müller's ξ family (no. 12 was not known to him)

MS. J 7. *Florence, Bibl. Laurenziana, pl.* 37, 25 (F1 in Beck; Laur. in Buecheler, Brugnoli, etc.; J in Müller). Begins with Petronius. Described below, p. 236.

MS. Q 8. *Vatican, Vat. lat.* 3403 (N in Goff, etc., and Brugnoli; Q in Müller).[5] *Contents*: (fol. 1) Rutilius Lupus; (fol. 16ᵛ) Aquila Romanus; (fol. 31ᵛ) Petronius; (fol. 62) Apuleius, *Perihermeneias*, ending incomplete in mid sentence but with a full stop at vii. 272. 10: 'Aristotelem commodissime' (fol. 67ᵛ).

Paper, 67 written leaves, *c.* 250×185 mm. Distinctive uncertain early humanistic hand, possibly showing influence of Niccoli (pl. XXI*a*). Simple vine-stem initials in Florentine style of *c.* 1425–40. Variants, marginalia, and corrections by the scribe and several other humanistic hands, some quite early, including notes in Greek by more than one hand. The contents are identical with no. 903 in the catalogue of the library of San

---

[1] The text (though much contaminated) belongs to the same sub-group of the *a* family as Barb, but it is complete.

[2] These variants are derived largely (perhaps entirely) from G (of the ξ family) or a MS. very close to it. See p. 234 n. 1.

[3] Front flyleaf, verso: 'Emptus a me Joanne Persicino Grammatices Professore. Anno domini M.DXXXVII. sol. xii. Joannis Persicini (with notarial sign). τα τῶν φίλων κοινά.' L. Alpago-Novello, *Giov. Persicini, umanista bellunese del secolo XVI* (Venice, 1931), cited by M. E. Cosenza, *Biog. and Bibliog. Dict. of Ital. Humanists*, iii (1962), 2679, has not been available to me.

[4] See p. 222 n. 2 above.

[5] P. de Nolhac, *La Bibl. de Fulvio Orsini* (Bibl. de l'École des hautes études, lxxiv, Paris, 1887), 196; W. Goff, 'A Study of the MSS. NG of Petronius' (thesis abstract), *Univ. of Pittsburgh Bull.* xi (1935), 253–4. Not seen by me but conclusions cited by R. Browning in *Classical Review*, lxxvi N.S. 12 (1962), 220 (review of Müller's first edition); Milar, Miller, and White, 'Three new MSS. ...'; M. Welsh, 'The Transmission of Aquila Romanus', *Classica et Medievalia*, xxviii (1969), 294–6. See also Postscript, p. 252 below.

Marco, Florence, made *c*. 1500.[1] Belonged in 16th century to
Fulvio Orsini (1529–1600), who quite wrongly attributed the
script to Niccolò Perotti. On end flyleaf (late 15th century?):
'V(is)us per me ss. o.'

MS. G   9. *Wolfenbüttel, Herzog August Bibl., Guelf.* 299 *Extrav.* (not
in Beck; G in Buecheler and later editors).[2] *Contents*: (fol. 2)
Seneca, *Apocolocyntosis*; (fol. 17) Petronius; (fol. 59) Ps.-
Aristotle, *Economics* transl. L. Bruni; (fol. 77) [Leonardo
Bruni] *Heliogabali oratio ad meretrices*.[3]

    Probably written in N. Italy (Milan?), late 15th century.
Parchment, 92 leaves. 135×95 mm. Careful formal human-
istic hand. Two small illuminated initials: fol. 2, an epigraphic
'Q' in blue on silver; fol. 59, a rather heavy vine-stem initial.
The text of Petronius was possibly copied from Q.[4]

MS. D   10. *Florence, Laur. pl.* 47, 31 (F2 in Beck; D in editors).[5]
Contents: (fol. 1) Letters of the younger Pliny arranged in
seven books;[6] (fol. 105) Rutilius Lupus; (fol. 116ᵛ) Aquila
Romanus; (fol. 128) Petronius.

    Parchment, 147 written leaves, 268×188 mm. Careful,
rather solid humanistic hand, written by a scribe who was
apparently working for Vespasiano da Bisticci in Florence,
c. 1455–60.[7] Fol. 1, fine Florentine vine-stem border with

---

[1] See below, p. 231.

[2] *Descr.* H. Butzmann, *Die mittelalterlichen HSS. der Gruppen Extravagantes novi und novissimi* (Kataloge der Herzog August Bibl. L, Frankfurt, 1972), pp. 155–7. See also N. M. Miller, 'The Interrelations of MSS. CDGJKQ of Petronius' (thesis abstract), *Univ. of Pittsburgh Bulletin*, ix (1933), 203–9; Goff, art. cit.

[3] *Leonardo Bruni Aretino hum. philos. Schriften*, ed. H. Baron (1928), p. 162.

[4] See Browning, loc. cit., quoting Goff's conclusions. There are certainly remarkable similarities, notably the omission of *Sat.* 124 vv. 282 and 291, omitted in the original text of Q and later supplied in the margin. G, to judge from the readings of Buecheler, reproduces most of the mistakes of Q, and dis- agreements mostly seem to derive from mistakes in G. The few which do not (e.g. *Sat.* 1. 2 *orb. terr.* G and the early MSS. *terr. orb.* Q and all the other later MSS.) may be misreadings by Buecheler.

[5] Wrongly cited as XCVII, 31 by Buecheler, followed by some later editors, e.g. Ernout (Paris, 1958), Castorina (Bologna, 1970). *Descr.* A. M. Bandini, *Cat. Codd. Lat. Bibl. Laur.* ii. 419–21; P. D'Ancona, *La miniatura fiorentina* (Florence, 1914), no. 353. See also Miller, 'The Interrelations . . .'; Rini, p. 13 (discounts a theory that the MS. had belonged to Niccoli, because 'there is not sufficient evidence'. In fact, the MS. must have been copied, many years after his death in 1437); Welsh, 'Transmission', pp. 292–3 (MS. B). See pl. XXII.

[6] For the type of text see Mynors, Oxford edn. (1963), pp. xi–xii.

[7] He also copied Laur. pl. 68, 5, Tacitus with Medici arms; Laur. Fiesole 28,

Medici arms, diamond ring and motto 'SEMPER' in the early style (*c.* 1455–60) of a Florentine illuminator who decorated many of the Fiesole MSS. for Vespasiano in the early 1460s.[1] Perhaps identifiable with 'Epistole di Plinio, scrisse il tedesco', which was among books being sent to Giovanni di Cosimo de' Medici at Cafaggiuolo on 31 August 1457,[2] and almost certainly identifiable in the 1495 inventory of Medici books.[3]

MS. C   11. *Vatican, Urb. lat.* 670 (Vat. in Beck; C to editors).[4]
Contents: (fol. 7) Rutilius Lupus; (fol. 22ᵛ) Aquila Romanus; (fol. 38) Petronius; (fol. 66) Fulgentius, *Mythologiae*; (fol. 114) 'Expositio sermonum antiquorum ad Chalcidium grammaticum.'

Parchment, 122 leaves, 244 × 150 mm. Written in a good formal humanistic hand, ending with a *siglum* which might be read as 'N' or 'LJ' but which has been identified as the notarial sign of Ser Francesco di Ser Bonfiglio de' Contugi of Volterra, a cousin of the famous scribe Matteo de' Contugi.[5] Fol. 6ᵛ, titles framed in a flower-decorated roundel. Fol. 7, Florentine flower border in style of early 1470s, with Montefel-

Jerome with Medici arms; Oxford, Lincoln Coll. Lat. 42, Cicero, *Epist. ad Atticum*, with Greek added by Giorgio Antonio Vespucci, given to the college by Robert Flemmyng, probably in 1465 (A. C. de la Mare, *The Handwriting of Italian Humanists* (Assoc. Internationale de Bibliophilie, 1973), I. i. 137, no. 135 and pl. xxiv; idem, 'Vespasiano da Bisticci and the Florentine Manuscripts of Robert Flemmyng in Lincoln College', *Lincoln College Record* (1962–3), p. 15. I there compared the scribe's hand to that of MSS. signed by Petrus de Middelburch. I am now sure that this comparison was mistaken.

    [1] See A. C. de la Mare, 'Florentine Manuscripts of Livy in the Fifteenth Century', in *Livy*, ed. T. A. Dorey (London, 1971), pl. iii, p. 182 and n. 28, where some dated examples of the artist's work are cited.

    [2] V. Rossi, 'L'indole e gli studi di Giovanni di Cosimo de' Medici', *Rend. Accad. Naz. dei Lincei*, cl. sc. mor. stor. filol., ser. v, 2, part II (1893), 58.

    [3] (no. 159): '440. Plynii epistole in menbranis et Rutilii Lupi Schiemata dyaneas ex greco, latinus codex et rubeus' (E. S. Piccolomini, 'Delle condizioni e delle vicende della libreria medicea privata dal 1494 al 1508', *Arch. stor. ital.* ser. iii, xx (1874), 62).

    [4] Brugnoli, Tab. III (fol. 38). *Descr.* C. Stornajolo, *Codd. Urb. Lat.* ii (1912), p. 178. See also Miller, 'The Interrelations . . .'; Rini, p. 15 n. 76; Welsh, 'Transmission', pp. 273–4 (MS. D).

    [5] By Luigi Michelini Tocci: see introduction to facsimile *Il Dante urbinate della Biblioteca Vaticana* (*Codice Urbinate latino* 365) (Codices e Vaticanis selecti XXIX, Vatican, 1965), p. 28 n. 3. He did not know the present MS., but found the sign in Vatican MSS. Urb. lat. 45, 391, 442 (signed by Francesco at Montecatini in 1462), 462, 890. It is also found in Urb. lat. 1342, 1345, Florence, Laur. S. Croce 20 sin. 7 (signed but undated) and Milan, Bibl. Trivulziana 2151, which contains a translation by Alamanno Rinuccini dated 1471. All these MSS. have Florentine decoration.

tro arms and initials 'C. F.' (i.e. 'Comes Federicus'). Federigo
da Montefeltro was made Duke of Urbino at the end of 1474.
Identifiable as no. 460 in Federigo Veterano's inventory of the
Urbino library, made *c.* 1490.[1]

MS. O   12. *Vienna, Österreichische Nationalbibl. s. n.* 4755 (not known
to editors; O in Brugnoli).[2] *Contents:* (fol. 1) Petronius (no
original heading); (fol. 29) Rutilius Lupus; (fol. 45) Aquila
Romanus.

     Parchment, 59 leaves, 240×156 mm. Written in a good
humanistic cursive bookhand, identifiable as that of the
Florentine humanist Bartolomeo Fonzio (*c.* 1446–1513),
datable to the mid or late 1460s, in which years he seems to
have done some copying for payment.[3] Fol. 1, Florentine vine-
stem border of *c.* 1460–70 with a roundel for a coat of arms,
left blank (pl. XXIII). Original Florentine blind-stamped
binding. Bookplate of Count Franz Joseph Kuenburg
(1716–93).

MS. V   13. *Vienna, Nat.bibl.* 179 (V1 in Beck and Brugnoli; V in
Müller; K in Daschbach, Miller).[4] *Contents:* (fol. 1) Petronius;
(fol. 31) Rutilius Lupus; (fol. 45) Aquila Romanus.[5]

---

[1] Pr. Stornajolo in introduction to catalogue *Codd. Urb. Graeci* (1895),
p. cxvi.

[2] See pl. XXIII. *Descr.* H. J. Hermann, *Illum. HSS. und Inkunabeln der
Nat.bibl. in Wien*, vi. 3 (Beschreibendes Verzeichnis der illum. HSS. in Öster-
reich, ed. F. Wickhoff, viii, Leipzig, 1932), pp. 30–1, no. 24; F. Unterkircher,
Inventar der illum. HSS., Inkunabeln und Frühdrucker der Österr. Nat.bibl. i
(1957), 191. See also Brugnoli, p. 10; Welsh, 'Transmission', p. 294 (MS. O).

[3] The hand is smaller and neater than his later, more familiar bookhand. It is
close in style to his signed Macrobius, Munich, Staatsbibl. Clm 15738, with the
arms of the Hungarian Petrus Garazda, datable to late 1460s (reprod. C. Trinkaus, 'The Unknown Quattrocento Poetics of Bartolomeo della Fonte', *Studies
in the Renaissance*, xiii (1966), 42–3 (fols. 233ᵛ, 117ᵛ), and to Munich Clm 822,
Andrea Fiocchi, *De romanorum magistratibus*, unsigned (my attribution), with
the ex-libris of Gioviano Pontano dated Florence, 1468. On Fonzio see also C.
Marchesi, *Bartolomeo della Fonte* (Catania, 1900); F. Saxl, 'The Classical
Inscription in Art and Politics', *Journal of Warburg and Courtauld Institutes*, iv
(1940–1), 19–46; Trinkaus, 'A Humanist's Image of Humanism: the Inaugural
Orations of B. della Fonte', *Studies in Ren.* vii (1960), 90–147; A. C. de la Mare,
'The Library of Francesco Sassetti' in *Studies in the Italian Renaissance: A collection in honour of P. O. Kristeller*, ed. C. H. Clough, Manchester, 1975. I have
not seen S. Caroti, S. Zamponi, *Lo scrittoio di Bartolomeo Fonzio* (Documenti
sulle arti del libro, x), Milan, 1975.

[4] Brugnoli, Tab. IX (fol. 2ᵛ). *Descr.* Hermann, op. cit., pp. 50–1, no. 44;
Unterkircher, op. cit., p. 9. See also M. Daschbach, 'Sambucus and the text of
Petronius' (thesis abstract), *Univ. of Pittsburgh Bulletin*, vii (1931), 42–4; Miller
'The Interrelations . . .'; Welsh, 'Transmission', pp. 296–7.

[5] A bifolium from Aquila has been misbound in Petronius (fols. 25–26).

Parchment, 47 leaves, 248 × 175 mm. Careful, but rather irregular, formal humanistic hand, identifiable as that of Jacobus Middleburch, who signed Vat. MS. Urb. lat. 64.[1] Written by one scribe, although the quire signatures start afresh at fol. 31. Fol. 1, Florentine vine-stem initial and separate border of *c.* 1460–70. The lower part of the border, which probably included a coat of arms, has been torn roughly away, badly damaging the text. Original Florentine binding of wooden boards covered with dark-brown leather, blind-stamped. Annotations in a semi-humanistic hand, probably German, 15th–16th century. Fols. 1, 57, ex-libris dated 1540 of Johann Faber, bishop of Vienna (d. 1541), bequeathing the MS. after his death to the college of St. Nicholas, Vienna. Hermann suggests that Faber acquired the MS. from the library of the humanist Johannes Cuspinianus (1473–1529), who had contacts with Italy.[2]

MS. W   14. *Vienna, Nat.bibl.* 3198 (V2 in Beck and Brugnoli; Q in Daschbach, Miller; W in Müller).[3] A miscellany of 205 leaves, formed of items in several hands, put together by the Floren-tine humanist and later Dominican friar, Giorgio Antonio Vespucci (*c.* 1434–1514). The first section (fols. 2–62ᵛ), on paper, 220 × 145 mm., was copied by Vespucci himself in his mature hand, hard to date precisely (*c.* 1470–90?). *It contains*: (fol. 2) Catullus; (fol. 42ᵛ) Petronius. On fol. 63ᵛ, following the end of the text, is Vespucci's ex-libris: 'Georgii Antonii Vespuccii.' In the margin has been added: 'MCCCCXL'[4] (pl. XXIb). The MS. may have belonged to Johannes Sam-bucus (1531–84), and may have been used for his edition of Petronius printed in 1565.

---

[1] The MS. has Florentine flower decoration probably of the early 1470s (not later than 1474).

[2] The number '399' on the front flyleaf was perhaps written by Cuspinianus. On his library see H. Ankwicz-Kleehoven, 'Die Bibl. des Dr. Johann Cuspinian', *Oesterr. Nat.bibl. Festschrift Bick* (Vienna, 1948), pp. 208–27.

[3] See pl. XXIb. *Descr.* Endlicher, *Cat. Codd. Phil. Lat.* i (Vienna, 1836), no. cviii; *Tabulae Codd. MSS. Bibl. Palat. Vindob.* ii (1868), 229–30. See also H. Gerstinger, 'Johannes Sambucus als Handschriftensammler', *Festschrift der Nat.bibl. in Wien* (1926), p. 339; Daschbach, 'Sambucus . . .'; Miller, 'The Interrelations . . .'; G. Billanovich, 'Giovanni del Virgilio, Pietro da Moglio, Francesco da Fiano', *Italia med. e um.* vii (1964), 323; de la Mare, *Handwriting*, I. i. 133, no. 184 (on MSS. of Vespucci).

[4] This has led some editors (including Müller) to believe that the MS. was copied in 1440, which is impossible. Brugnoli says (p. 11) that the MS., which he dates to the 16th century, was copied from a MS. dated 1440. This is con-ceivably possible if the addition is in the hand of Vespucci; it is possible that it is.

J (MS. Laur, pl. 37, 25) and the Florentine Manuscripts

We have documentary evidence of two lost manuscripts of the *excerpta*. The first is the manuscript sent by Poggio from England to Niccoli in Florence at some time between 1420 and 1423.[1] It is accepted as the ancestor of all the fifteenth-century manuscripts. In his editions Müller has called it δ. The other manuscript is described in detail as no. 903 in the library catalogue of San Marco, Florence, made *c.* 1500. Its contents are unusual: 'Scemata Publii Rutilii, Romanus Aquila, Petronius Arbiter Satyricon, Apuleius Platonicus peryermenias imperfectus, in volumine parvo in albo in papiro.'[2] We can fairly assume that a manuscript which assembled such a collection of rare texts derived from Niccoli's library which formed the original basis of the San Marco collection.[3]

Müller's work on the text led him to postulate two further lost manuscripts, α and ξ, between δ and the extant manuscripts.[4] The α family includes the text of the *excerpta* in the Codex Traguriensis, a manuscript which had been partly copied by November 1423.[5] The other manuscripts in the family must all have been written much later; one (K) may have been written in Rome, but most of them appear to have come from northern Italy. One of these manuscripts (Barb), made *c.* 1460, probably belonged to Isotta Nogarola of Verona.[6] The descendants of the other lost manuscript, ξ, were almost all copied in Florence.[7] In this family Petronius is usually accompanied by two short rhetorical texts which had apparently been rediscovered at about the same time: Rutilius Lupus (first mentioned in a letter of Ambrogio Traversari to Niccoli datable to 1421)[8] and Aquila Romanus.[9] As we have

---

[1] See below, pp. 247–8. The MS. could have been either the original one that Poggio discovered, or a transcript of it.

[2] B. L. Ullman, P. A. Stadter, *The Public Library of Renaissance Florence* (Padua, 1972), p. 231.

[3] Op. cit., especially pp. 5–15, 59–104.

[4] For all this see his stemmata, p. 223 n. 2 above.

[5] The date comes at the end of Catullus, which precedes Petronius in the MS.: see below, p. 241.

[6] See above, p. 225.   [7] The exception is G.

[8] Ambrogio Traversari, *Epistolae*, ed. P. Cannetus (Florence, 1759), col. 366 (viii. 7): 'Rutilium Lupum cum figuris graecis ad te mitto.'

[9] Aquila is not specifically mentioned at all, but since the text normally circulates with Rutilius it may have been discovered at about the same time (Welsh, 'Transmission', p. 287, assumes that 'cum figuris graecis' in Traversari's letter means Aquila).

just seen, these texts also appeared with Petronius in the lost San Marco manuscript. One of the ξ group, Q, probably written in the 1430s, in fact has contents identical with the San Marco manuscript, down to an incomplete copy of the Apuleius text, but it seems certain that it is not to be identified with the lost manuscript.[1] Q does not have the spelling 'Scemata' for 'Schemata' in the heading to Rutilius Lupus which apparently existed in the San Marco manuscript, but the spelling is found in two other manuscripts of the ξ group: J and D (it was later corrected in the latter).

There would be a strong presumption that the Florentine group of manuscripts derived from Niccoli, the central figure in the diffusion of so many newly discovered or rare texts,[2] even if we did not have the San Marco catalogue entry. Can we assume, however, that the lost San Marco manuscript, probably from Niccoli, is also our lost ξ? The fact that J is the only manuscript to retain the mis-spelt heading 'Scemata' which is there, but corrected, in D, may support such an identification. J, which appears from its script to be the earliest manuscript in the ξ family, stands somewhat apart from the rest of the family, and apparently closer than them to ξ. An intermediate manuscript, such as Müller posited in the stemma to his 1961 edition of Petronius, probably stood between ξ and the rest of the group, including Q. J is separated from the rest of the ξ family in the first place by many mistakes unique to it and one serious lacuna. This lacuna makes it impossible for it to have been the sole ancestor of the rest of the family even if we allow for corrections and emendations by brilliant scholars.[3] Secondly,

---

[1] The text of Apuleius in Q does not look imperfect at first sight, for it ends in the middle of a page, followed by a blank space (see no. 8 above). This suggests that the exemplar was imperfect at this point. It is probable that the S. Marco MS. is to be identified with this exemplar, rather than with Q itself. Q has two serious lacunae in Petronius: it lacks *Sat.* 124 vv. 282, 291 (the missing lines are supplied in the margin in a late 15th-century hand). It also has many mistakes which are not found in the other ξ MSS. with the exception of G, which is later. G is closely related to Q, but does not always follow it. Note, e.g., *Sat.* 6. 1 *hunc*] *hoc* Q Barb S 15th-century eds. L(Scaliger's MS.) *homo* AFKVW(marg. *hoc*)JCDG. See also 17. 5 *Utique* cit. p. 233 n. 3 below.

[2] See B. L. Ullman, *The Origin and Development of Humanistic Script* (Rome, 1960), pp. 61–2, also de la Mare, *Handwriting*, I. i. 46 n. 1, for further references.

[3] *Sat.* 132. 12 *verecundiae . . . contulerim* is omitted. The mistakes unique to J are not as many as one would judge from Beck's collation but there are still plenty, e.g. *Sat.* 88. 4 *coelique*] *celsique* J; 123 v. 242 *Bosphoros*] *bofforas* J; 127. 2 *venio*] *nemo* J; 133. 3 v. 15 *Corniger*] *corriget* J; 135. 5 *sordidissimis*] *sordissimis* J. Interestingly enough, J is separated off from the other MSS also in Aquila, especially by one sentence at the end (Aquila 37. 3): *cum possit . . . voluntaria*

J shares a number of good readings, and a few mistakes, with the α family or most members of it, against its own family. Most of the mistakes could have happened independently, by a slip of the pen in J or a misreading of a word or emendation.[1] In the only case where such an explanation is unlikely, the 'bad' reading could derive from J's exemplar.[2] The good readings are more positive, and suggest that J comes nearer to δ than the other ξ manuscripts.[3] It must be admitted that two of these readings are shared by W,

servitus, also found in the Basle edition of 1521 which was based on a MS., now lost, found at Speyer, but in none of the other MSS. (Welsh, 'Transmission', p. 291). The position is said to be the same too in Rutilius, but even the most recent editors (G. Barabino, Genoa, 1967; E. Brooks, in *Mnemosyne, Suppl.* xi, 1970) use only four of the eleven MSS. known to me: viz. (*a*) eight listed by Welsh because they also included Aquila; (*b*) Florence, Ricc. 153, fols. 114–117 (used by the editors of Rutilius). The fragment of Rutilius is here among excerpts in a notebook copied by Bartolomeo Fonzio; (*c*) London, British Libr., Burney 213, mid 15th century. This is a miscellany on paper, perhaps written in NE. Italy, in which Rutilius and Aquila are found together with a miscellaneous collection of texts, including Pomponius Mela, Solinus, Priscian, *Partitiones XII versuum Aeneidos* and *De figuris numerorum*, and 'Albaldus de minuciis' (i.e. Demetrius Albaldus, see L. Thorndike, P. Kibre, *Cat. of Incipits of Medieval Scientific Writings in Latin*, 2nd edn. (1963), col. 393). Antonio Beccaria (d. 1464), the Veronese humanist, who spent some time in England as secretary to Duke Humfrey of Gloucester, owned a MS. which not only included Rutilius, Aquila, and Albaldus, but also Cicero, *De legibus* (G. P. Marchi, 'L'umanista Antonio Beccaria alla corte di Humphrey di Gloucester e di Ermolao Barbaro', *Univ. di Padova, Fac. di Lingue in Verona. Annali*, ser. II. i (1966–7), 23 of offprint, no. 29); (*d*) S. De Ricci, *Census of Med. and Ren. MSS. in U.S. and Canada*, i, 1935, 499 (Otto H. F. Vollbehr Coll., Washington), no. 1054. Grammatical collection including Rutilius, Aquila. Parchment. Before 1435 (?). From Dominicans of S. Maria de Saxo in Casentino. See also Postscript, p. 252.

[1] The mistakes are: *Sat.* 4. 1 *nolunt*] *volunt* EFKJS Barb (note *not* A); 119 v. 25 *fractique* BR Florilegium Gallicum CDOQLVW *factique* AEFJ (*fáctique*, corrected by scribe)KPS Barb (marg. later *fracti*) 15th century edns. (henceforth cited as edns.); 133. 1 *in* BCDLOQRSVW/om.AEFJKP Barb edns.

[2] 131. 8 v. 2 *damne* for *Daphne*. Similar readings to J's are found in two of the early MSS.: P (Paris, B.N. lat. 8049) and R (Barbaro's MS.). KS Barbedns. have the 'revised' reading *Daphne*.

[3] 2. 4 *lyrici* BKLRSW Barb edns. *lirici* AFJP *lyricis* DOQV *liricis* C; 6. 4 *quocumque* (or *quocunque*) ABEFJKLPRS Barb edns. *quacunque* OW *quaecunque* CDQ(corr. to *quocūque*)V(later corr. to *quocumque*); 17. 5 *Utique* ABEFJKLPRW Barb edns. *utque* DGS *Vitque* OQ (corr. to *fuitque*)V *Viteque* C; 83. 10 v. 4 *nuptas* AEFJKLRS Flor.Gall. Barb edns. *innuptas* P *nupcias* V *muptias* W *muptias* CDGOQ; 88. 5 *plastas* AEFJKLPRS (marg. *plastês*) Flor.Gall. Barb edns. *plastes* CDGOQVW (*plastês*); 110.2 *supercilia* ABEFJKLPRS Barb edns. *supercilio* CDGOQVW (*supercilio̊*); 118. 6 *Deorumque* ABEFJKLPRS Barb edns. *deorum* CDOQVW *derum* G; 124. v. 281 *catervas* ABEFJKLRS (marg. *cathenas*) Barb edns. *quatervos* P *cathenas* CDGOQV(marg. *catervas*)W(marg. *catervas*); 131. 8 v. 2 *tremulaeque* ABEFJKLPRS (marg. *tremulo*) Barb edns. *tremuloque* CDGOQVW.

another member of the ξ family, but as we shall see, W was one of the latest members of the family to be copied, perhaps fifty years after J, and it is a humanist's copy, full of emendations from several sources.

Though our concern is to be chiefly with J, it is worth considering briefly the other manuscripts of the ξ family. G, a late, non-Florentine manuscript, is very closely related to Q and possibly derives directly from it.[1] Q(+G), C, D, and O are all fairly closely related.[2] Q was probably copied in the 1430s and looks like a scholar's copy. It is likely that D (*c.* 1455) and C (*c.* 1470), were both written at the order of the Florentine bookseller Vespasiano da Bisticci, for they were probably made for two of his clients, Giovanni de' Medici and Federigo da Montefeltro,[3] but they are about fifteen years apart in date and Vespasiano need not have used the same exemplar for both. O, which comes between them in date (*c.* 1465), was copied by the Florentine humanist Bartolomeo Fonzio but also appears to have been a commercial copy rather than one made for Fonzio's own use.[4] O has one or two unusual good readings. These are also found in the α family, but O must have been

---

[1] See above, p. 227. Q had apparently left Florence by the later 15th century, so this is possible. For the lacunae in *Sat.* 124 which G shared with the original Q, and for its disagreements with Q, see above p. 232 n. 1. Examples of shared mistakes are: 3. 3 *divitum*] *ad nutum* GQ (and S in marg.); 4. 4 *est*] om. GQ; 89. 2 v. 26 *metu*] *motu* GQ (and S in marg.); 131. 11 *osculis*] *corporis* GQ. S shares a number of mistakes in the original text, as well as marginal variants such as those just cited, e.g. 5 v. 8 *histrionis*] *histrionem* GQS (*hystrionem* marg. *histrionea*); 5 v. 16 *saporem*] *laborem* GQS (marg. *saporem*). S shares with G many mistakes which are not found in Q, e.g. 2. 2 *effecistis*] *efficitis* GS; 88. 2 *homines*] *homines mortales* GS; 88. 3 *hercule*] *hedera* GS (marg. *hercula* and *genera*).

[2] Examples of some shared mistakes: 113. 5 *in gremio*] *ingenio* CDGOQ; 123 v. 199 *iam*] om. CDGOQ; 134. 12 v. 4 *Niliacas*] *Niliadas* CDGOQ.

[3] For Giovanni as Vespasiano's client see Rossi, 'L'indole . . .'. For Federigo there is a great deal of evidence but for brevity we need go no farther than Vespasiano's life of his client (in Vespasiano da Bisticci, *Le Vite*, ed. A. Greco, i (Florence, 1970), 355–416. V (see below) may also have been written for Vespasiano, since its scribe later copied one of the Urbino MSS.

[4] The MS. has a border with a roundel left blank for the coat of arms of a future client, but never filled in (pl. XXIII). There are a few annotations. Fonzio annotated very heavily, with many cross-references, MSS. which actually belonged to him. To illustrate the use of certain words Fonzio copied some short passages from Petronius in one of his notebooks, other parts of which are dated 1476 and 1488: Florence, Ricc. 153 (it is the MS. which contains his incomplete copy of Rutilius on fols. 114–117), fol. 134: 'Ex Petronio arbitro': 7. 4 *Tardet* [sic] . . . *deductum*; 111. 2 *In conditorium . . . cepit*; 112. 5 *Itaque cruciarii unius . . . pendentem*; 122 vv. 144–5. His exemplar may have been similar to W. Caroti/ Zamponi, *Lo scrittoio . . .*, includes a study of Fonzio's notebooks.

written too early to have taken these readings from the 1482(?) printed edition.[1] W, however, which has these and a few other α readings in the original text,[2] may have been copied late enough to derive the readings from the printed text. It is probably the latest of the Florentine manuscripts and was copied by the humanist Giorgio Antonio Vespucci for his own use. It is the only Florentine manuscript where Petronius is not accompanied by Rutilius and Aquila as well. This may be because Vespucci had access to these texts already in another manuscript.[3] The collation of Beck implies that though W has a number of distinctive readings of its own, it is closely related to V, a manuscript copied about 1460–70. VW seem to share a number of good readings not found in the rest of the ξ family. It turns out, however, that all or almost all of the distinctive readings cited by Beck, both for W and VW, are mistaken.[4] A careful, complete collation would probably show that V and W were in origin quite ordinary ξ manuscripts. The distinctive VW readings[5] appear to be the result of later correction from the fifteenth-century editions.[6] While some

[1] e.g. 2. 2 *liceat* ABFKLOPRS(marg. *deceat*)W Barb edns. *diceat* V *diceat* CDJ *deceat* QG; 120 v. 74 *pumice* ABEFKLORSW Barb edns. *spumice* P *punice* CDGJQV. O has a lacuna at 95. 6 *et creberrimis . . . vindicat.*

[2] For additional α readings in W: 2. 4 *lyrici*; 17. 5 *Utique*, see p. 233 n. 3 above. W has other readings which agree with a part only of α and which cannot have come from the editions, though they were later corrected to their reading: 88. 8 *donum* CDEJLOQSV Barb edns. Flor. Gall. *domum* AFKPRW(*domum*); 109. 3 *Encolpion* ELP *encholpion* CDGJOQV *encholpium* R *Eucolpion* AK *eumolpion* FW(*eumolpion*) *eumolpon* S Barb edns.

[3] Florence, Laur. Strozzi 42: Welsh's E ('Transmission', pp. 298–300; see also de la Mare, *Handwriting* I. i. 130, no. 64A). The part containing Rutilius and Aquila is written in a script reminiscent of Giacomo Curlo, with initials in Neapolitan style, mid 15th century.

[4] Dr. F. Römer kindly checked for me in V and W a number of Beck's readings, including those cited above which are correct. Almost all the others that he checked were wrong. It is worth citing some of the corrected W readings: 5 v. 5 *Cliensque*; 17. 4 *haec* om.; 25. 4 *ista* om.; 25. 6 *put. nat. prov.*; 55. 4 *memorata*] *commorata* in W over erasure. For corrections to VW readings see below, n. 6.

[5] They share at least one mistake: 88. 10 *fecerunt*] *fecerant* VW, but this could be a chance coincidence in error. At 113. 5 *interdum*] *modo* W, V reads *interdum*. Each MS. has mistakes not found in the other. Note especially 55. 6 v. 16 *prostare*] *prostrare* W etc. *videre* V.

[6] e.g. 26. 2 *libidine* om. but added in marg. VW; 88. 7 *via*] *viam* corr. to *via* VW; 89 v. 2 *vatis*] *votis* corr. to *vatis* VW; 89 v. 15 *turba*] *turbata* VW; 89 v. 59 *quadrupes*] *quadrupedes* corr. to *quadrupes* VW; 109. 6 *fuscina*] *fuscinas* VW. In each case the usual ξ reading has been corrected to that found in Barb edns. among others. However, at 135. 8 v. 9 *divos* in W was altered to the correct *clavos* apparently found only in P Barb.

but not all, of such corrections in W are by the original scribe, i.e. Vespucci, those in V are later. Similarities in the method of correction suggest that some at least of V's corrections derive from W itself. It is not surprising to find Vespucci emending his manuscript from the early editions.[1] He owned a great many printed books, though Petronius is not known to have been among them, and his identified manuscripts and printed books show that he was an indefatigable emender of texts.[2]

To return to J, can we tell when it was copied and by whom? Maybe we can. I first became interested in the manuscript tradition of Petronius when I saw a photograph of J, which I had ordered because a reference to it by Sabbadini implied that it might be a manuscript close to Niccoli.[3] From the photograph it looked as though J could have been copied by Poggio. It seemed to be written in a gothico-humanistic cursive similar to the hand Poggio used in 1416–17 to make rapid copies of the texts he discovered in France and Germany. I examined the manuscript further. It has other features in common with Poggio's cursive manuscripts: it is written on paper, and ruled in part with a hard point. Like those manuscripts, too, it does not appear to have been written all at the same time.[4] As will be seen from the description below, it falls into distinct sections, each ending with blank leaves, and written with varying degrees of speed.

Description of J (Florence, Biblioteca Laurenziana, pl. 37, 25)[5]

On paper (watermarks: *a* triple mount with cross, not in Briquet, but nearest to 11719, 11722; *b* tower, close to Briquet 15864;

---

[1] The 1499 edition is based on the first, but with corrections and emendations (for distinguishing readings see Rini, *Petronius in Italy*, p. 25). To judge from some of the readings the correctors of W used both editions. Note: 5 v. 13 *mittat*] *imitet* 1482 (?) edn. *immittet* 1499 edn. *mutet* (above *imitet* and *immittat*) W. Many distinctive readings from the editions really derive from the S Barb subgroup of the α family (an example of one found *only* in S Barb edns. is: 2.7 *semelque* all other MSS. including W (marg. *simulatque*) *simul atque* S Barb edns.) but W cites some readings *not* found in S or Barb which are in the editions, e.g. 94. 1 *quae* all MSS. including W (marg. *quam*) *quam* edns.

[2] See de la Mare, *Handwriting*, I. i. 125–36, for a list of Vespucci's known MSS. and printed books, and pl. xxv *b, c, e, g, h,* for examples of his annotations. See also F. Di Benedetto, in *Studi medievali* (1973), 949–50.

[3] *Scoperte*, i (1905), p. 86 n. 9, where the shelfmark is wrongly given as 38. 25.

[4] See de la Mare, *Handwriting*, I. i. 72, 74, 78–9, nos. 14, 16 and esp. pl. xiv *c, d.*

[5] Bandini, *Cat. Codd. Lat. Laur.* ii (1774), cols. 258–9; N. M. Miller, 'The

c triple mount in circle, with and without cross, not in Briquet);[1] 72 leaves; 215 × 142 mm; frame-ruled, fols. 1–32 with a hard point, fols. 33–end in crayon. Plain ink initials. Four distinct sections:

i (fols. 1–22) watermarks type *a* and *b*; collation, 1^{12} (near-central horizontal catchword), 2^{10}; 31–4 lines; fairly formal cursive hand. Fol. 1 (caps.): 'Petronius Arbiter' *beg.*: 'Cum alio genere', *ends* (fol. 18^v): 'archa Iovem. [caps:] Petronius Arbiter. Satiricon' (the last word perhaps added by a different hand). Fols. 19–22^v blank.

ii (fols. 23–32) watermarks *b* and *c*; collation 3^{10}; 28–30 lines; very formal cursive hand. Fol. 23 [caps.]: 'Preexercitamina inc.' *beg.*: 'Fabula est oratio', *ends* (fol. 30^v): 'inglorium est. [caps:] Prisciani Sophiste Ars Preexercitationum Secundum Hermogenem vel Libanium Explicit Feliciter.' Fols. 31–32^v blank.

iii (fols. 33–54) watermarks type *b* and *c*; collation 4^{10}, 5^{12}; fols. 33–34, formal cursive, 28 lines; fols. 35–54, current cursive, with loops, 30–7 lines. *a* (fol. 33, caps.): 'He sunt VII philosophorum sententiae, septenis versibus expedite quorum prior Bias Prieneus sic exorsus est', *beg.*: 'Quenam summi boni? mens que sibi conscia recti', *ends* (fol. 34, Thales Milesius): 'satis est ne sit hoc nimium.'[2] Fol. 34^v blank; *b* (fol. 35, caps.): 'P. Rutilii Lupi Scemata [*sic*] Dianoeas. Ex Greco Vorsa. Gorgia', *beg.*: 'Prosapodosis. Hoc schema duobus modis fieri', *ends* (fol. 42^v): 'causa insexit. FINIT'; (fol. 43, caps.): 'Incipit Romani Aquilae' *beg.*: 'Rhetoricos petis longioris more ac diligentiae', *ends* (fol. 49^v): 'incidamus cavendum est. [caps:] Explicit Aquilae.' Fols. 50–54^v blank.

iv (fols. 55–72) watermark *c*; collation 6^{12} (horizontal catchword near inner margin), 7^6; 32–7 lines; fairly formal cursive hand. Fol. 55 (*Rhetorica ad Herennium* IV. xiii, end § 18) *beg.*: '[D]ignitas est que reddit ornatam . . .' (fol. 62^v, XXX. v, § 47, caps.): 'M.T.C. ad H. Liber V Explicit. Incipit Liber VI', *beg.*: '[D]istributio est cum in plures res', *ends* (fol. 69^v): 'consequemur et exercitatione.

Interrelations of MSS. CDGJKQ of Petronius'; Rini, p. 15 n. 75; M. Welsh, 'Transmission', pp. 290–2 and *passim* (MS. A). See also pls. XXIV–XXV.

[1] A watermark similar to 11719 is also found in Venice, Marcian. lat. cl. XII, 80 (coll. 4167), a Catullus perhaps copied by Poggio *c.* 1400 (A. C. de la Mare, D. F. S. Thomson, 'Poggio's Earliest Manuscript?', *Italia med. e um.* xvi (1973), 179–95. For 11719 Briquet cites Florence, 1403; Siena, 1401–9, 1422–31; Rome, 1427–30; for 11722 Lucca, 1430; Reggio Emilia, 1439–50, etc.: for 15864, Florence, 1422–7; Rome, 1430–2; Lucca, 1419; Pistoia, 1415, etc.

[2] Ed. Schenkl. *M.G.H.: Auct. antiq.* v (1883), 246–50: MS. λ. See also H. Walther, *Initia carminum . . .* (1959), no. 15065.

[caps.:] Explicit Penultimus Liber Rethoricorum [*sic*] M.T.C. Ad Herennium.' Fols. 70–72ᵛ blank.

Some corrections and variants by the scribe in all sections, many in *iv* (pl. XXV*c*). Rutilius and Aquila also have annotations in a different, uncertain, contemporary hand (see pl. XXV*a*). Probably identifiable as no. 191 in the inventory of Medici books made in 1495: 'Petronius Arbiter in papyro sine numero.'[1]

There is no room here adequately to analyse the script of J. I can only reproduce some details and leave readers to judge for themselves (pls. XXIV–XXV). The speed with which the text was written varies considerably from one section to another. The more formal sections recall Poggio's cursive manuscripts of 1416–17[2] but they are more carefully and more regularly written; the more current sections recall the pages of a papal register of 1431 attributed to Poggio by Fink.[3] I must confess that I have doubted the attribution of these pages to Poggio, but I may have been wrong.[4] However, if J turns out not to have been written by Poggio, its resemblance to these pages, whether they were written by Poggio or not, should still be borne in mind, for it suggests a scribe trained in the Papal chancery.[5] Some similarities in the script of J to that of Poggio may be mentioned: the capitals, especially in the incipits and explicits (not those to Petronius which may not be entirely in the scribe's hand)—note, for example, 'G', which is found in both forms favoured by Poggio,[6] and 'P'; in the minuscule, note 'x', 'y', and the '-bus' abbreviation. The similarities are suggestive, but not conclusive. The script, though showing strong humanistic leanings, has a more Gothic duct than any of Poggio's known manuscripts. Could this have been the result of his stay in England?

---

[1] Piccolomini, 'Delle condizioni . . .', *Arch. stor. ital.* ser. III. xx (1874), 62. Poggio's famous transcription of Quintilian, now lost, still belonged to his family after his death but was in the Medici library by 1495 (E. Walser, *Poggius Florentinus*, p. 52 n. 5).

[2] See Ullman, *The Origin . . .*, pl. 27, and p. 236 n. 4 above.

[3] K. A. Fink, 'Poggio Autographen kurialer Herkunft', *Miscellanea archivistica Angelo Mercati* (Studi e Testi, clxv, 1952), Taf. II. 3.

[4] *Handwriting*, I. i. 81, no. v*b*.

[5] Cf. Welsh, 'Transmission', p. 290 n. 24. The script of the transcript of Asconius Pedianus in Oxford, Bodl. MS. Canon. Misc. 217, fols. 69d–98ᵛ, is very close in style to section *i* (Petronius) in J. This is the copy which A. C. Clark considered to be most faithful to Poggio's transcription of the text in Madrid, Bib. Nac. MS. 8514 (x. 81) (Oxford edn. of Asconius, 1907, pp. xxi–xxii).

[6] For these, see Ullman, *The Origin . . .*, p. 56.

If he is the scribe of J I believe that he must have copied it not
long after his return to Italy.[1] The method of correction in J
certainly agrees with Poggio's known habits,[2] and the spelling on the
whole agrees with his preferences.[3]

The Codex Traguriensis

Before we examine the documentary evidence to see whether it
supports an attribution of J to Poggio we must consider the origins
and history of another manuscript: the Codex Traguriensis. This
much discussed manuscript is famous because it contains the only
known copy of the *Cena Trimalchionis* of Petronius, which in the
manuscript follows a copy (belonging to the *a* family) of the
excerpta vulgaria. The other texts in the manuscript are also of
interest. They include one of the earliest dated copies of Catullus,
and one of the earliest known copies of Ovid's *Epistula Saphus ad
Phaonem* (*Heroides* XV), and it is the earliest known manuscript
in which Tibullus, Propertius, and Catullus are brought together.[4]
After being copied, presumably in Italy *c.* 1423–4, the manuscript
disappeared, only to be rediscovered in the mid seventeenth century, at Traù (Trogir) in Dalmatia, in the library of the Cippico
family. It had been there since at least the sixteenth century. Where

[1] See below, p. 250. If he copied it for his own use, it is likely to have been
before about 1425, when he set about writing and commissioning handsome,
formally written texts for his library, apparently in part to replace the cursive
copies he had made earlier. By the late 1420s he had virtually given up copying
himself; see de la Mare, *Handwriting*, pp. 67–8; de la Mare/Thomson, art. cit.,
p. 194.

[2] See A. J. Dunston, 'The Hand of Poggio', *Scriptorium*, xix (1965), 63–70;
C. Questa, *Per la storia del testo di Plauto nell'umanesimo*, i, *La 'recensio' di Poggio
Bracciolini* (Quaderni Athena, vi, 1968), 26–9; de la Mare, *Handwriting*, I. i. 73–4.
J uses frequently, to indicate single variants or corrections, the .. most favoured
by Poggio, and marginal crosses, but in the *Rhetorica ad Herennium* (part *iv* of
MS.), with many more variants to indicate, he uses an elaborate apparatus of
signs (pls. XXIV *a*, *b*, XXV*c*).

[3] For Poggio see Ullman, op. cit., pp. 24–36 *passim*; de la Mare, op. cit., pp.
72–3. J rarely indicates the diphthong for 'ae' except in the *Rhetorica ad Herennium*, where one even gets oddities such as 'ęt' (fol. 69 l. 13). He normally uses *mihi*,
nihil, though there are rare exceptions. However, on the two occasions when he
writes 'Cesar' it is spelt thus (it also appears once in this form in Poggio's
cursive MS. Madrid, Bibl. Nac. 8514 (X. 81), fol. 31), and other words appear
from time to time spelt in the medieval way (e.g. *legittimo* fols. 26, 30ᵛ; *allo-
qutio* fol. 28ᵛ; *posicio* fol. 29ᵛ; *autor* fol. 46, etc.; *apercius* fol. 65ᵛ; etc.). Some of
these spellings may have derived from the exemplars—this is strongly suggested
by the spelling in the *Rhetorica ad Herennium*.

[4] *C. Valerii Catulli Carmina*, ed. R. A. B. Mynors(Oxford, 1958), p. ix.

was it copied and how did it reach Dalmatia and the Cippicos? A facsimile exists of the part containing the *Cena*, but no full description of the whole manuscript is readily available. A detailed examination of it may provide us with clues to its history.

Description of the Codex Traguriensis (Paris, Bibliothèque Nationale, lat. 7989)[1]

On paper of rather poor quality, especially at the beginning (watermarks: *a* (to p. 110) a unicorn's head, fairly close to Briquet 15753, 15759–60, all fourteenth-century types; *b* (pp. 111–208) a hunting horn, fairly close to Briquet 7691 (Padua, 1428) but cf. 7664, 7666, 7692; *c* (pp. 209–48) a triple mount, without cross, cf. Briquet 11652, 11662, 11726 (all found in Florence in the 1430s as well as elsewhere at various dates). 248+2 pages (pp. 249–50 an original parchment flyleaf), 282 × 215 mm, edges badly worn and later repaired; long lines ruled in ink with bounding lines in crayon, writing below top line; 48 written lines up to p. 208 (end of a quire), 41 written lines from p. 209; quires of 12 or 10 (mostly) with central horizontal catchwords. Written by one scribe in a rather fractured but legible semi-Gothic hand, perhaps of Venetian type.[2] No break between the texts except that (apart from the *Moretum*) a new text is normally started on a new page. However, there is a change of ink at the beginning of the *Cena*, and pp. 206–208, to the end of a quire, are written in a smaller hand than the preceding texts. At p. 209 the hand becomes the normal size

[1] Reproduced: E. Chatelain, *Paléog. des classiques latins*, ii, pl. ci. 2 (p. 217 of MS.); S. Gaselee, *A Collotype Reproduction of that Portion of cod. Paris 7989 Commonly Called the Codex Traguriensis* (Cambridge, 1915) (the whole of the *Cena* (pp. 206–29) and pp. 1, 179); Brugnoli, Tab. 1 (p. 217); *Archivio storico per la Dalmazia*, i (1926), 22 (p. 1). Gaselee and the *Archivio* reprint the account of the rediscovery of the MS. by G. Lucio, originally printed in his *Memorie istoriche di Tragurio* (Venice, 1674), pp. 531–5. See also: A. C. Clark, 'The Trau MS. of Petronius', *Classical Review*, xxii (1908), 178–9; Sabbadini, 'Sulla fortuna di alcuni testi latini . . . Petronius', *Rivista di filologia e istruzione classica*, xxxix (1911), 250; idem, 'Per la storia del codex Traurino di Petronio', ibid. xlviii (1920), 27–39; Rini, pp. 59–80; J. A. Foster, 'The Cena Trimalchionis . . .' (thesis abstract), *Univ. of Pittsburgh Bull.* xiv (1938), 86–91; Müller's introductions to his 1961 and 1965 editions of Petronius; Georg Petzl in *Scriptorium* xxvi (1972), 65–6. See also pls. XXVI, XXVIII.

[2] There are similarities to the hand of Francesco Barbaro (cf. pl. XX*a* and exlibris reproduced by A. Diller, 'The Library . . .', *Italia med. e um.* vi, pl. x). Cf. also the hand of the Dalmatian Giorgio Begna, for which see below, p. 245 n. 2. Neither hand, however, appears to be identical with that of the Traguriensis.

again. Except in the *Cena* (which has little verse) the scribe notes the numbers of verses at the end of each poem, and adds up the total at the end of each book. *Contents*: (p. 1) Tibullus. *Ends* p. 43, with epitaph and note on Tibullus; (p. 44) Propertius, preceded by distich of Martial, *ends* p. 131;[1] (p. 132) Catullus, preceded by distich of Martial and the verses *beg.*: 'Ad patriam venio'. *Ends* p. 179. In the lower outer corner of the page is the damaged note, written by the scribe: '1423 d. 20 no.br. per[c . . .] / ep.le 60 versus 22[. .].'[2] The text is related to Zicari's σ group, though not a direct ancestor of it;[3] (p. 180) Ovid, *Epistula Saphus ad Phaonem* (*Heroides* XV), *ends* p. 184. The text belongs to Dörrie's 'q' family;[4] (p. 185) 'Petronius Arbiter. / Petronii Arbitri Satyri fragmenta ex libro quintodecimo et sextodecimo', *ends* (p. 205): 'Petronii Arbitri Satyri Fragmenta expliciunt ex libro quintodecimo et sextodecimo.' The text belongs to Müller's α family of the *excerpta vulgaria*;[5] (pp. 206–29) Petronius, *Cena Trimalchionis*, no heading or explicit; (p. 229 after space) Vergil, *Moretum*, no heading, *ends* (p. 232): 'Moreti liber Virgilii pueri explicit.' Pp. 233–50 were originally blank, but there are two later additions: *a* (pp. 233–7, early sixteenth-cent. (?) italic hand): Claudian, *Phoenix* (Carm. min. xxvii);[6] *b* (p. 249, sixteenth-

---

[1] B. L. Ullman, 'The MSS. of Propertius', *Classical Philology*, vi (1911), 289; A. La Penna, 'Studi sulla tradizione di Properzio', *Studi ital. di filol. classica*, xxv (1951), 197 ff. *passim*. La Penna points out (p. 229) the possible interest of a MS. copied at Traù, 1464, but not seen by him.

[2] Sabbadini first ('Sulla fortuna', p. 250) suggested the reading of the damaged word as 'percensui', but later ('Per la storia', p. 28) changed his mind and thought it read 'peregi'. I believe his first suggestion may have been right. Under ultra-violet light it was clear that the last visible letter is a 'c'.

[3] Zicari, 'Ricerche . . .', *Boll. del Com. per la prep. dell'Ediz. Naz.* . . . (1958), pp. 89 ff, stemma p. 96. See also D. F. S. Thomson, 'A New Look at the Manuscript Tradition of Catullus', *Yale Classical Studies*, xxiii (1973), 126–9 (Appendix II: Codex Parisinus 7989 . . .).

[4] *P. Ovidii Nasonis Epistolae Heroidum*, ed. H. Dörrie (Berlin/New York, 1971), pp. 294, 299.

[5] Müller suggests (introd. to editions) that the scribe wrote the incipit and explicit referring to the fifteenth and sixteenth books after copying the *Cena* (which he assumes had some sort of heading referring to the fifteenth book) and finding from the passages common to both that it belonged in the middle of the *excerpta*. This seems plausible, especially since the *Cena* now has no headings, and the first heading to the *excerpta* (p. 185) is written on two lines, which could easily mean that the phrase 'Petronii . . . sextodecimo' was added. The scribe generally leaves a space of several lines between his heading and the main text. H. Van Thiel ('Sulla tradizione di Petronio', *Maia*, xxii (1970), 257–9) agrees, but thinks the *Cena* probably had an explicit only, which said it was the end of the fifteenth book. [6] See pl. XXVIII.

century) verses 'Ad Leonem ebreum' *beg*: 'Omnia deposui, superest hec sola lacerna'.[1]

Annotations in three hands: *a* the scribe, writing at various dates. He uses a distinctive 'Nota' sign and pointing hands (pl. XXVI *b, c, d*). His additions include verses with note 'Seneca supplevit' or 'Supplevit Seneca' (i.e. Thomas Seneca of Camerino, *c.* 1391–1462)[2] filling gaps in the text of Tibullus[3] and Catullus;[4] *b* a few short notes to the two Petronius texts (pp. 188 (pl. XXVI*a*), 210, 214, 218, 222)[5] in an early humanistic cursive hand; *c* the scribe of the Claudian poem (early sixteenth century?) wrote some notes and variants in all the texts except the *Cena*, and made many additions to Catullus. His annotations show that he knew the commentary on Catullus by Palladio Fosco (pr. Venice, 1496) and perhaps the 1502 Aldine edition.[6] p. 1 (sixteenth century): 'Questo libro sia di me Pola[n]tonio Cipico.' The manuscript was discovered by Marino Statileo in the library of the Cippico family at Traù, *c.* 1650.

It is generally agreed that the Codex Traguriensis was compiled by a careful scholar who continued to add variants and emendations for a while after he had completed his copying. According to Sabbadini, some of his annotations, and his spelling, suggest a man from the Veneto, or even Dalmatia.[7] This may be borne out

---

[1] Pr. Gaselee, p. 9. He suggests that they were addressed to a Jewish pawnbroker.

[2] See Sabbadini in *Giorn. stor. lett. ital.* xviii (1891), 228–30; xlvii (1906), 35–6; A. Zanelli, ibid. xxxiii (1899), 346–53.

[3] Tib. II. 3, between modern verses 14a and 14b (p. 23 in MS.): 'Creditur ad mulcram constituisse prius', and between verses 77 and 78 (p. 24 in MS.): 'Ah pereant artes et mollia iura colendi.' These verses are found in many MSS. (Sabbadini, 'Sulla fortuna', p. 250, points out that not all the supplementary verses attributed to Seneca are included here), and we have Seneca's letter dated Prato, November 1434, sending his edition of Tibullus to his friend the doctor Johannes Ariminensis and mentioning the verses. He says that he has consulted in Florence Serafino of Urbino, Giovanni (Gherardi?) of Prato and Niccolò Niccoli (pr. A. Baehrens, *Albi Tibulli Eleg.* (1878), pp. viii–ix from MS. Vat. lat. 2794, fol. 1). The same letter is in Milan, Bibl. Trivulz., MS. 789, following Tibullus (Sabbadini, *Riv. di filol.* xxvii (1899), 402–3), and Florence, MS. Laur. Ashb. 1702 (1625), fol. 109ᵛ (Kristeller, *Iter Ital.* i. 97).

[4] Cat. lxviii. 47 (p. 170 in MS.): 'Omnibus et triviis vulgetur fabula passim' (apparently first pointed out by Mynors, ed. cit., p. xi, who found this also in Milan, Ambros. H. 46 sup. (attributed to Seneca) and Florence, Bibl. Naz., Magliabecch. VII. 1158 (attributed to Filelfo). His conjecture that Seneca = Thomas Seneca is presumably correct).

[5] The notes to the *Cena* can all be seen in Gaselee's facsimile.

[6] Zicari, 'Ricerche', p. 89, and Professor D. F. S. Thomson (in a letter).

[7] 'Per la storia', pp. 33–5.

by the script that he used.[1] Also, the later fifteenth-century manuscripts textually related to the Traguriensis, at least for Catullus, Propertius, and the Ovid poem, come mainly from north-east Italy,[2] although (with one possible exception),[3] no manuscript of these texts is a direct descendant of it. The verses supplied to Tibullus and Catullus by Thomas Seneca which were later added to our manuscript by the scribe might also have given us a clue, if Seneca had not moved incessantly from place to place. However, he was probably in Florence in 1429,[4] and we do know that he was in touch with Niccoli and others in Florence over his emendations to Tibullus.[5] With the exception of the *Cena Trimalchionis* (followed by the *Moretum*) which may have been copied a little later than the rest of the manuscript, its contents all appear to have been written about the same time. The earlier contents of course include the *excerpta* of Petronius, which about 1423–4 are unlikely to have been readily available for copying outside Florence (where we know them to have been in Niccoli's hands)[6] or, perhaps (as we shall see), Rome. So if our scholar was from the Veneto he is unlikely to have copied his manuscript at home. The exemplar which he used for Catullus appears to have been an early copy of Coluccio Salutati's manuscript,[7] which suggests Florence, and it would probably have been easier for him at this early date to assemble exemplars of Tibullus, Propertius, and Catullus in Florence[8] than elsewhere. His text of Propertius, though apparently much contaminated, or at least conscious of variants from a number of different sources, has variants in his hand deriving from the important twelfth/thirteenth-century manuscript known as N (Wolfen-

---

[1] See p. 240 n. 2 above.

[2] I have seen, or seen photographs of, most of the related MSS. listed by Zicari, La Penna, and Dörrie.

[3] Mons, Bibl. Publ. 218(109) may be a direct descendant of the Traguriensis. It has similar contents, apart from the Petronius texts and the *Moretum*, and the verses are counted up in the same way (Zicari, 'Ricerche', p. 91). It is a 15th-century paper MS. in a current Gothic, perhaps non-Italian hand. I was able to see a microfilm of it in the Bibl. Royale at Brussels.

[4] Sabbadini, *Giorn. stor. lett. ital.* xlvii. 35–6.

[5] See p. 242 n. 3 above.

[6] See below, pp. 248–9.

[7] Thomson, 'A New Look . . .', pp. 126–9.

[8] Coluccio Salutati owned all three texts. His MSS. are now Milan, Ambros. R. 26 sup.; Florence, Laur. pl. 36. 49; Vatican, Ottobon. lat. 1829 (Ullman, *The Humanism of Coluccio Salutati* (Padua, 1963), pp. 178, 144, 193). All three, or copies of them, are likely to have been readily available in Florence. The first two came into the possession of Cosimo de' Medici.

büttel, Gud. Lat. 224). This manuscript probably came from the Rhineland, but appears to have been in Italy by 1421.[1] It has been suggested that Poggio might have discovered it during his searches for texts in France and Germany in 1417, and sent it back to Niccoli. N does not seem to bear any traces of annotation by either Poggio or Niccoli.[2] It is also supposed to have belonged to a collector in Rome in the late fifteenth century,[3] though this does not necessarily mean that it was not in Florence earlier. However, whatever we think about N, Florence, and the *ambiente* of Niccoli, seems to me the most likely birthplace of our manuscript.[4]

The textual links between the Codex Traguriensis and a number of later manuscripts copied in north-east Italy can only be explained by a common ancestor, for it seems itself to have spawned no copies.[5] Why was this? One would have expected the *Cena Trimalchionis*, at least, to have been sought after as a new text.[6] The most likely explanation is that the manuscript was taken to Dalmatia soon after it was written, and so went out of circulation. Sabbadini thought along these lines, and suggested that it might have been taken back to Traù by a member of the Cippico family who had been studying in Italy.[7] The drawback is that we do not know whether any Cippico was in Italy at this time. However, we do know of someone else from Dalmatia who was in Florence at about the time the Codex Traguriensis was being copied, which we can

[1] La Penna, 'Studi sulla tradiz.', pp. 229–30. Traces of N are found in the text of a MS. of this date, Oxford, Bodl. Holkham Misc. 36 (formerly Holkham 333); however, this MS. was probably copied in N. Italy. Ullman had suggested that Poggio might have found N when he passed via Cologne on his return from England in 1423.

[2] I am grateful to the Institut de Recherche et d'Histoire des Textes in Paris for lending me a microfilm of this MS.

[3] Poliziano apparently saw it in the collection of Bernardino Valla (Sabbadini, *Scoperte*, i. 147, 153).

[4] The evidence of the watermarks, as usual, is inconclusive, since none is identical with any in Briquet, but it is interesting: (*a*) that some paper with watermarks of a 14th-century type was used. Most of the MSS. copied by Niccoli are on rather thick paper with watermarks of 14th-century type; (*b*) that one watermark is close to one found in Padua, 1428; (*c*) that the third is similar to several which are all found in Florence as well as elsewhere.

[5] With one possible exception: see p. 243 n. 3 above.

[6] A possible reason for the text's not being copied from the Codex Traguriensis at least is that it has no incipit or explicit there and so might not have been identified for what it was. Müller suggested that Niccoli might have disapproved of the *Cena*, and suppressed it.

[7] 'Per la storia', p. 38.

assume to have been about 1423–5. This is Georgius (or Giorgio) Begna, who finished copying book I of Caesar's *De bello civico* at Florence in August 1425 (having already copied the *De bello Gallico*), in a distinctive humanistic hand (Paris B.N. lat. 6106, fol. 93)[1] (pl. XXVII*b*). The rest of Caesar, which follows in the same manuscript but is not dated, may have been completed by Begna some years later, for it is mostly copied in a hand close in style to the later sections of the manuscript, containing Frontinus and Vegetius. These texts were completed by Begna at Zara in September and November 1435. The last three leaves of Caesar (fols. 141–143) were copied, apparently also by Begna, in a distinctive humanistic cursive hand. This hand is similar to the early humanistic annotations in the Codex Traguriensis,[2] but unfortunately the notes in the latter are too few and too short for an adequate comparison to be made. Begna's hand varies a good deal in the Paris manuscript, but he is clearly not the scribe of the Traguriensis. Further evidence about Begna suggests that he was a keen collector of classical manuscripts and inscriptions—Giuseppe Praga even called him 'almost the Poggio of Dalmatia'.[3] He was a friend of Ciriaco of Ancona, who stayed with him in Zara in November 1435[4] and even more significantly, of Pietro Cippico of Traù,

---

[1] 'Georgius Begna Iadrensis excripsit sibi et cui sors dabit: Florentię iiii idus augusti. MCCCCXXV bene vales qui legis.' For the text, the MS. belongs to a large group of 'deteriores', many of which were written in Florence (see V. Brown, *The Textual Transmission of Caesar's Civil War* (Mnemosyne Suppl. XXIII), Leiden, 1972, p. 58).

[2] The annotations type *b*, on pp. 188, 210, 214, 218, 222. For p. 188 see pl. XXVI*a*. The other notes are reproduced in Gaselee's facsimile. For Paris B.N. lat. 6106 see description in *Catalogue des manuscrits en écriture latine portant des indications de date, de lieu ou de copiste*, ed. C. Samaran, R. Marichal, ii (1962), p. 313. Pl. ci. (fol. 141) shows the cursive hand which resembles the notes in the Traguriensis. Annotations by Begna to the *De bello civico*, in a similar hand, reproduced here (pl. XXVII*a*). I am grateful to M. François Avril both for examining and describing the MS. for me and for much other help.

[3] art. cit. below, or p. 246 n. 2.

[4] E. W. Bodnar, *Ciriaco of Ancona and Athens* (Brussels, 1960), pp. 25–7. According to Scalamonti, Begna was one of the friends to whom Ciriaco wrote (c. Feb. 1431) with the good news that his friend Cardinal Condulmer had been elected pope as Eugenius IV (F. Scalamonti, 'Vita di Ciriaco Anconitano', ed. G. Colucci, *Delle antichità picene*, xv (1792), p. lxxxiv). Some correspondence of Begna in Oxford, Bodl. MS. Canon. Pat. Lat. 223 (copied in Zara in 1489, see fol. 322ᵛ), fols. 304–306ᵛ, suggests that he was living in Venice in 1430, but he was back in Zara by 1432 (an addition at the beginning of Paris B.N. lat. 6106 is signed 'Georgius Begna excripsit Iadrę non. septembr. 1432. Sibi et suis.'). One of Begna's correspondents in the Canonici MS. is Ser Giovanni Tinti,

father of the statesman and historian Coriolano Cippico.[1] In February 1435 he completed Ps.-Pliny, *De viris illustribus*, at Zara 'amico Petro Capioni', and Pietro kept the copy as part of a precious manuscript miscellany, now Venice, Bibl. Marciana Lat. cl. XIV, 124 (coll. 4044), which also contained his own copies of Dalmatian inscriptions and copies of inscriptions from Ciriaco's sylloge.[2] This manuscript belonged by 1457 to the young Bernardo Bembo.

If Begna really acquired the Codex Traguriensis while he was in Florence, as seems possible, it could have passed from him to Pietro Cippico either as a gift during his lifetime or after his death in August 1437.[3] A Bodleian manuscript, MS. Canon. Class. Lat. 224, containing Cicero's *Philippics* and *Topics*, may be significant in this context. It was completed by Pietro Cippico, at Traù, in December 1438, but the first part of the manuscript, containing *Philippics* I–III, is copied in a different, earlier humanistic hand which may be that of Giorgio Begna.[4] If I am right in this attribution, the date of the completion suggests that the manuscript was taken over and finished by Cippico after Begna's death. It should

chancellor of Fabriano, who had earlier been a friend of Coluccio Salutati (Salutati, *Epistolario*, ed. F. Novati, iii (1896), 657–8).

[1] On Coriolano (1425–93) see articles cited below, also D. F. Karaman, 'Cornelio Cippico di Traù', *Annuario dalmatico*, i (1894), 171–82; Iac. Morelli, introd. to edn. of Cippico's *Delle guerre de' Veneziani nell' Asia dal MCCCCLXX al MCCCCLXXIIII* . . . (Venice, 1796). Oxford, Bodl. MS. Canon. Misc. 106, Pompeius Festus, Venice (?), 2nd quarter or mid 15th century, is inscribed 'Quinti Coriolani Cipici sum liber et amicorum' (Pächt and Alexander, *Illuminated MSS. in the Bodleian Library*, ii (1970), no. 538, misread the name as 'Ciprei'). The arms are presumably those of Cippico, though the colours are reversed.

[2] Described (with reproduction of fol. 37) by G. Praga, 'Il codice marciano di Giorgio Begna e Pietro Cippico', *Archivio storico per la Dalmazia*, xiii (Aug. 1932), 210–18. See also *Corpus Inscriptionum Latinarum*, vol. iii, pt. I, p. 272; V. Cian, 'Per Bernardo Bembo le relazioni letterarie, i codici e gli scritti', *Giorn. stor. lett. ital.* xxxi (1898), 71–2; Kristeller, *Iter Ital.* ii. 265; Bodnar, op. cit., pp. 102–3. I am grateful to the Director of the Biblioteca Marciana for sending me a detailed description of the MS. The colophon on fol. 37 reads: 'Georgius Begna excripsit suo optimo et amantissimo amico Petro Capioni Tragurino. Iaderẹ. MCCCCXXXIIII. Kl. Febr.' Praga points out that the 'stile fiorentino', beginning the year on 25 March, was used in Traù, so that the MS. was completed in 1435. I have seen photographs of the MS., and it is clear that Praga's assertion that Pietro Cippico copied all but the first part is correct. See below for a MS. signed by him.

[3] For his death, of the plague, see Praga, art. cit., p. 213 n. 4.

[4] Fols. 1–21^v, the first leaf is missing (collation 1^{14} (1 missing), 2^8). Cippico wrote the rubrics and running headings to this first part.

be noted that in his colophons Cippico used the phrase 'sibi et cui fata dabunt',[1] very close to the phrase 'sibi [*or* mihi] et cui sors dabit [*or* dederit]' used by Begna three times in his manuscript now in Paris.[2] The fact that the early sixteenth-century annotator of the Codex Traguriensis knew the Catullus commentary of Palladio Fosco may also tell us something about the history of the manuscript. For Fosco was a friend of Alvise Cippico, grandson of Pietro, whom he had come to know in Padua in the 1480s, and wrote an 'elegy' celebrating his friend's nomination as bishop in 1489.[3] From 1493 on Fosco actually lived in Dalmatia.[4]

Poggio's letters and the copying of J and the Codex Traguriensis

I have suggested above: (*a*) that J was copied by Poggio; (*b*) (by no means a new idea) that the Codex Traguriensis was copied in Florence. How do these suggestions fit the few references to Petronius that we have in Poggio's letters to Niccoli? Let us examine the evidence (I have given each reference to Petronius a separate minuscule letter).

Poggio to Niccoli, 13 June [1420?]:

De Petronio Arbitrio (*a*) quod scire cupis, quid tractet, lege Macrobii principium super somnio Scipionis, ubi enumerans genera fabularum, dicit, in eis esse argumenta fictis amatorum casibus referta, quibus multum se Arbiter exercuit. Est autem homo gravis versu, et prosa constans, et ut conjicio, paulo post tempora Augusti.[5]

---

[1] Fol. 66ᵛ: 'Petrus Cepio Marci Cepionis filius Dalmatinus ex Tragurio absolvi scribere Philippicas. M. Tullii Ciceronis mihi et cui fata dabunt. Tragurii Nonis Decembris. M:CCCCXXXVIII [*corr. from* M:CCCCXXXIII]. Summus deus tibi qui legis quę bene optas det. Vale.' Fol. 76ᵛ (end of *Topics*): 'Petrus Cepio Marci Cepionis filius Dalmata Tragurinus absolvit Tragurii sibi et cui fata dabunt. Lector vale. M.CCCC.XXX.VIII. Idus decembrias.' Cippico's colophon to the *Philippics* is echoed in its turn in another copy made in Dalmatia, signed: 'Iacobus Naplave scripsit sibi et cui fata dabunt Sibenici pridie Kl. Martias anno d. M.CCCC.LX' (Oxford, Bodl. Canon. Class Lat. 254, fol. 137ᵛ).

[2] See p. 245 n. 1 above. The other colophons (both with 'dederit') are on fols. 163ᵛ and 183ᵛ.

[3] G. Praga, 'Un poemetto di Alvise Cippico sulla guerra di Ferrara del 1482', *Arch. stor. per la Dalmazia*, x (Oct. 1930), 318–19. See this article, and Praga, ibid. xxviii (1939), 218–23 for the bibliography on Alvise (1456–1504), son of Coriolano. He was a doctor in Canon Law at Padua by 1482, bishop of Famagusta from 1489, and was in Rome as an official of the Curia from at least 1489 until his death. He apparently knew Bernardo Bembo in Padua.

[4] From 1493 to 1516 he was in Zara, first teaching and then acting as a civic official; from 1516 to 1520 he taught at Capo d'Istria (Praga, art. cit., p. 319 n. 1).

[5] *Poggii Epistolae*, ed. T. Tonelli, vol. i (Florence, 1832; reprinted in vol. iii of *Poggii Opera Omnia*, ed. R. Fubini, Turin, 1963), p. 38 (i. 8).

Same to same, 28 May 1423:

Allatus est mihi ex Colonia xv liber Petronii Arbitri (*b*) quem curavi transcribendum modo, cum illac iter feci. Mittas ad me oro Bucolicam Calpurnii et particulam Petronii (*c*) quas misi tibi ex Britannia.[1]

Same to same, 11 September 1423:

Petronium (*d*) ad te non misi sperans ipsemet afferre ad te librum.[2] He says that he will send the text if they are unable to meet.

Same to same, 6 November 1423:

Si ibimus ad vos, me conferam subito; et nunc Petronium (*e*) habebitis; hanc enim causam scies fuisse tarditatis; decreveram enim illum afferre mecum; sed pependimus semper . . . Si enim credidissem nos tamdiu hic futuros, jamdudum Petronium ad te misissem, nec nunc quoque illum mitto, illud ipse sperans, me scilicet allaturum, sed infra paucos dies certum quid sciemus.[3]

He then pressingly invites Niccoli, who has never been to Rome, to come and stay with him.[4]

Catullus in the Codex Traguriensis has a note at the end including the date 20 November 1423. This is not necessarily the date of completion of the transcription; but the counting and adding up of the verses in the various poems, to which the date may refer, appears to have been done as an integral part of the copying, so that however the damaged 'per[c . . .]' of the note on p. 179 of the manuscript is interpreted, it still points to November 1423 as the date of the Catullus. The *excerpta* and *Cena* of Petronius come later in the manuscript, and differences in script, ink, and ruling suggest that a certain interval of time may have elapsed between the copying of the two Petronius texts.[5]

Poggio to Niccoli, 13 December 1429. He says that he is sending Niccoli the ancient manuscript of Cicero's speeches (the Cluny manuscript?), and Nonius Marcellus, that he had asked for so insistently, although he knows that Niccoli will keep them for ages without doing anything about them, and deprive him of their use:

Tenuisti iam Lucretium duodecim annis, et item Asconium Pedianum

---

[1] *Paggii Epistolae.*, vol. i, p. 91 (ii. 3).
[2] Ibid., vol. i, p. 93 (ii. 4).
[3] Ibid., vol. i, pp. 98–100 (ii. 7).
[4] Poggio had already invited Niccoli to stay in February, soon after his return from England; ibid., vol. i, pp. 85–6 (ii. 1).
[5] For all these points see description above, pp. 240–1.

et septem annis aut amplius Petronium Arbitrum (*f*) et ut videor templum vestrum citius absolveretur quam abs te ii scribantur libri.[1]

Müller argues, convincingly, that (*a*) and (*c*) are identifiable as a copy (or copies) of the *excerpta vulgaria*, of which (*c*) at least must be δ, the ancestor of all the fifteenth-century manuscripts; (*b*), (*d*), and (*e*) would be the *Cena Trimalchionis*. He further suggests that Poggio wanted the *excerpta* (i.e. (*c*)) to be sent to Rome in May 1423 so that he could bring the two texts together in one manuscript, either for himself or for someone else, and that the result was the Codex Traguriensis. Then, he says, Niccoli could have taken the *Cena* back to Florence with him after his visit in 1424. (*f*) he thinks is also the manuscript of the *Cena* (i.e. (*b*)), which Niccoli had not returned to Poggio perhaps because it had already been stolen or mislaid.[2]

I believe that Müller is correct in his suggestion that Niccoli took (*b*) away from Rome in 1424, and did not return it to Poggio, but I think that its only surviving copy, in the Codex Traguriensis, was made in Florence after Niccoli had brought it there, rather than, as Müller believes, in Rome somewhat earlier. We must now consider the textual evidence. This dictates that two copies (α and ξ) were made of δ at some point.[3] The fate of δ itself is unknown, but it was perhaps lost early on, since it apparently had no further offspring after α and ξ. It seems clear that both α and ξ were early copies. J (ξ's offspring) is certainly early, whoever copied it. α is the exemplar of the *excerpta* in the codex Traguriensis, and so must have been made before this part of the manuscript was copied, probably late in 1423 or early in 1424. Whether, in reply to Poggio's request for the *excerpta* in May 1423, Niccoli sent a copy at once or took one with him later when he visited Poggio in 1424, it is unlikely that he would have relinquished his only copy of the text. Müller's theory means that α must have been in Rome when the Traguriensis was copied from it. But since α must be a copy of δ, the manuscript originally sent by Poggio to Niccoli, it could equally have remained in Florence and have been copied there in the Traguriensis, probably soon after the Catullus was completed in November 1423. The *Cena* would then have been

---

[1] *Epistolae*, vol. i, p. 294 (iv. 2).

[2] Müller, introduction to 1961 edition, pp. viii–xi, xxviii–xxxiii; to 1965 edition, pp. 385–7, 403–11.

[3] See above, p. 223 n. 2.

added to the Traguriensis after Niccoli's return to Florence in the late summer of 1424.[1] This sequence would explain the apparent break in the copying of the manuscript between the *excerpta* and the *Cena*, for which there would have been no obvious reason if the two texts were copied together in Rome.

As we have seen, J is a copy of ξ, the other early transcript of δ. If my suggestion that it is Poggio's copy is correct, it must have been ξ, not a, that was sent or taken to Rome by Niccoli in 1423/4. Niccoli stayed in Rome with Poggio for a period lasting from at least January to June 1424,[1] which would have given Poggio plenty of time to copy any short texts, such as ξ, that Niccoli had brought with him. This would have left Niccoli free, on his departure, to take ξ back to Florence where, probably after further emendation and correction of ξ, another copy of it seems to have been made from which the other 'Florentine' manuscripts of the *excerpta* descend.[2]

I have pointed out above that J falls into several distinct sections.[3] The texts that they contain need not all have derived from manuscripts brought to Rome by Niccoli, but some could have done, i.e. Priscian's *Praeexercitamina* (part *ii* of the manuscript) and Rutilius and Aquila (part *iiib*). The probable connection of the diffusion of Rutilius and Aquila with Niccoli has already been mentioned.[4] Priscian's *Praeexercitamina*[5] was a rare text, though not unknown, in the early fifteenth century.[6] Coluccio Salutati had owned a late fourteenth-century copy (now imperfect),[7] but

---

[1] The evidence for the dates of Niccoli's absence from Florence is summed up by G. Mercati, *Ultimi contributi . . . Traversariana* (Studi e Testi, xc, 1939), pp. 5–6.

[2] See above, pp. 231–4.

[3] See description above, pp. 236–8.

[4] See above, p. 232.

[5] Pr. Keil, *Grammat. Lat.* iii. 430–40.

[6] At least two other early 15th-century copies are known: Milan, Ambros. Q. 35 sup., copied for Giovanni Cornaro, a Venetian pupil of Gasparino Barzizza (this copy is closely related to Salutati's MS., for which see n. 7 below) and Cortona, Bibl. del Comune e Accad. Etrusc. 78, copied by June 1417 when 'Alphonsus G.', signing himself in Greek characters, made a list of the contents in an Italian humanistic hand, at Bruges (MSS. described by G. Billanovich, 'Il Petrarca e i retori latini minori', *Italia med. e um.* v (1962), 135–7). I have seen photographs of the Cortona MS.

[7] Florence, Laur. S. Marco 264, fols. 4ᵛ–8ᵛ (Ullman, *The Humanism of Coluccio Salutati*, p. 154; the MS. came to San Marco from Giorgio Antonio Vespucci, not Niccoli as one might have expected; Ullman/Stadter, *The Public Library*, no. 910).

the transcript in J is not as close to this manuscript as it is to a copy made by Sozomeno of Pistoia, perhaps while he was at Constance in 1417 (Paris, Arsenal 720, fols. 11–15).[1] J and Arsenal 720 are not only textually related but they also share an unusual feature; they both occasionally use a punctuation mark consisting of two points side by side . . (see pl. XXV*b*). Dr. Malcolm Parkes tells me that this is an Irish or Welsh feature, and it can be found in manuscripts from St. Gallen.[2] Is it from such a manuscript that J and Sozomeno's copy descend? It is an attractive possibility, if we remember Poggio's visit to St. Gallen in 1416 and his habit of sending his discoveries, or copies of them, to Niccoli. Sozomeno had access while he was at Constance to a copy of at least one discovery—Asconius Pedianus—that Poggio had made at St. Gallen.[3] It would be interesting to know whether any other fifteenth-century copies of Priscian's *Praeexercitamina* are related to J and the Arsenal manuscript.[4]

I have tried to show that J could have been copied by Poggio. I am still not sure that he was its scribe, but if it was not Poggio, who was it? I am open to suggestions. Meanwhile I hope that my investigations may have shed some light on the diffusion of the *excerpta vulgaria* of Petronius in the fifteenth century and on the history of that mysterious manuscript, the Codex Traguriensis.

A. C. DE LA MARE

[1] See de la Mare, *Handwriting*, I. i. 92, n. 7. Both MSS. include the Greek words, which are mostly latinized in Salutati's copy (Col.). Col. also lacks subheadings found in both the other MSS. (J and Soz.). J and Soz. also share mistakes and some good readings against Col., e.g. Keil, p. 431 l. 1 *affabulationem*] *effabulationem* J Soz.; l. 13, 16 and 22 *Aeetae*] *acete* J Soz.; p. 432 l. 13 *amaram*] *amorem* J Soz. *amarum* Col.; p. 434 l. 9, 10 *arionem* J Soz. *oryonem* Col.; p. 435 l. 19 *ingenuus*] *ingens* J Soz. om. Col.; etc., etc. Keil, p. 438 ll. 13–14 *Andromache . . . potuisset*, omitted in Col., is included in J and Soz., which also agree with Keil at l. 11, where Col. reads: *alloquutiones passionales quedam morales.* However, it is clear that neither J nor Soz. was a copy of the other.

[2] Cf., e.g., St. Gallen 904, reprod. J. Duft, P. Meyer, *The Irish Miniatures in the Abbey Library of St. Gall* (1954), pl. xxxix. The MS. was written at St. Gallen in an Irish minuscule of the mid 9th century.

[3] Sozomeno's copy of Asconius was made at Constance in 1417, but not from Poggio's transcript (A. C. Clark, introd. to edition of Asconius (Oxford, 1907), pp. xix, xxxi–xxxii). See also de la Mare, *Handwriting*, I. i. 92 n. 6, 104 no. 38.

[4] I am grateful to Mlle Colette Jeudy of the Institut de Recherche et d'Histoire des Textes for providing me with a list of the 15th-century MSS. known to her. None of the others appears to be as early in date as our MSS. or those mentioned above, p. 250 n. 6.

POSTSCRIPT

SINCE this article was written some new facts of interest have come to light:

1. Dr. Dieter Harlfinger has told me (in a letter) that some of the Greek annotations in Q (e.g. fol. 2^v, 17, 25^v) are probably in the hand of Francesco Filelfo. If Filelfo was the original owner of the manuscript, it could have been copied for him between 1429 and 1434 when he was in Florence, although he had already asked Traversari in Sept. 1428 to get a copy of Rutilius transcribed for him (Sabbadini, *Scoperte*, i, p. 86 n. 9). The script of other annotations in the manuscript suggests that it had left Florence by the later fifteenth century.

2. Lorenzo Valla (d. 1457) knew a text of the *excerpta vulgaria* of Petronius. In his Quintilian, Paris, B.N. lat. 7723, which he emended in 1444 but apparently annotated over a number of years, he cites (fols. 22^v–23), as a gloss to *Instit. Orat.* 2. 10. 6 *Sed certe sint grandia*, two substantial passages from a text closely related to Q but not identical with it. The passages are 1. 1–6. 1 *fugam* and 118. 1–6: compare, for example, 3. 3 *divitum*] *ad nutum* Val; 4. 4 *est* om. Val; 5 v. 8 *histrionis*] *histrionem* Val; 5 v. 16 *saporem*] *laborem* Val (see p. 234 n. 1 above). Valla's text (Val) generally agrees with Q when G differs from Q: compare, for example, 6. 1 *hunc*] *hoc* Val (see p. 232 n. 1 above). The exception is at 2. 2 *effecistis*] *efficitis* ValGS. Since Valla also cites 'Romanus Aquila' and Rutilius several times (Rutilius is mentioned by Quintilian himself but Aquila is not) the likelihood is that he found all three rare texts in one manuscript (as in JQDCOV and the lost San Marco manuscript). The same passages of Petronius, in the same gloss, are found in at least one of the manuscripts which descend from Valla's Quintilian (see the edition of the *Institutio Oratoria* by M. Winterbottom, Oxford, 1970, i, p. xiii), London B.L. Harley 4995, dated 1470, fols. 22–22^v, and in the glosses attributed to Valla in the Venice, 1494 edition of Quintilian (Hain 13654, Proctor 4865, *B.M. Cat.*, v. 393). In both cases the Petronius text, though showing variants from Val, clearly derives from the same Q-type text.

3. MSS. of Rutilius and Aquila (see p. 232 n. 3). The present whereabouts of the Vollbehr MS. is not known. For yet another MS. which includes Rutilius and Aquila, Florence, Laur. Ashb. 876, see C. Jeudy in *Viator* v (1974), 92–3.

NOTES TO THE PLATES

PLATE XX
Paris, Bibl. Nat., lat. 6842D (MS. R), written *c.* 1200.

(*a*) Fol. 1, detail. Fourteenth-century note on 'Agricultura' and ex-libris of Francesco Barbaro.

(*b*) Fol. 12ᵛ, detail. Fourteenth-century annotations to Palladius.

(*c*) Fol. 4, detail. Fourteenth-century annotations to Palladius, both hands.

(*d*) Fol. 75ᵛ, detail. Fourteenth-century correction to Petronius, *Sat.* 14. 2, v. 4.

PLATE XXI

(*a*) Vatican, Vat. lat. 3403 (MS. Q), fol. 31ᵛ, detail. Opening of Petronius. *c.* 1425–40. Possibly written for Filelfo. Early Florentine vine-stem initial.

(*b*) Vienna, Nationalbibl. 3198 (MS. W), fol. 63ᵛ, detail. End of Petronius. Copied by Giorgio Antonio Vespucci, *c.* 1470–90, with his ex-libris. Date 'MCCCCXL' apparently added.

PLATE XXII
Florence, Laur. 47, 31 (MS. D), fol. 1. Opening of Pliny's Letters. The manuscript also contains Rutilius, Aquila, and Petronius. Mid 1450s? Medici arms. Possibly written for Giovanni di Cosimo de' Medici. Florentine vine-stem border by the 'Fiesole' illuminator. Reduced.

PLATE XXIII
Vienna, Nationalbibl., s.n. 4755 (MS. O), fol. 1. Opening of Petronius. Florentine vine-stem border. Copied by Bartolomeo Fonzio *c.* 1465–70. Heading a later addition. Reduced.

PLATE XXIV
Florence, Laur. 37, 25 (MS. J), perhaps copied by Poggio.

(*a*) Fol. 8, detail. Petronius, *Sat.* 109. 10, v. 2–110. 7.

(*b*) Fol. 9, detail. Petronius, *Sat.* 112. 2–7. Note corrections.

PLATE XXV
Florence, Laur. 37, 25 (MS. J), perhaps copied by Poggio.

(*a*) Fol. 35, detail. Beginning of Rutilius Lupus. Early marginal annotations not by the scribe.

(*b*) Fol. 24, detail. Priscian, *Praeexercitamina*. Note use of punctuation with . . in top line.

(*c*) Fol. 62ᵛ, detail. *Rhetorica ad Herennium*. Explicit and incipit for 'Book V' and 'Book VI'. Note marginal correction and variant by the scribe.

PLATE XXVI

Paris, Bibl. Nat., lat. 7989 (MS. A), 'Codex Traguriensis', written *c.* 1423–4. Marginalia.

(*a*) The early annotator: p. 188, detail. Petronius, *Sat.*, parts of 24. 5–26. 1.

(*b*)–(*d*) Annotations by the scribe: (*b*) p. 193, detail. Parts of *Sat.* 111. 13–112. 7; (*c*) p. 188, detail. Parts of *Sat.* 25. 3–26. 1; (*d*) p. 193, detail. Parts of *Sat.* 111. 6–9.

PLATE XXVII

Paris, Bibl. Nat., lat. 6106, copied by Georgius Begna of Zara.

(*a*) Fol. 102ᵛ, detail, cut at right. Caesar, *Bell. civ.* iii. 3. 1–4. 3. Marginalia also written by Begna.

(*b*) Fol. 93, detail. Colophon to Caesar, *Bell. civ.* i, completed by Begna, Florence, August 1425.

PLATE XXVIII

Paris, Bibl. Nat., lat. 7989, p. 233. Claudian, *Phoenix*, added to the manuscript, probably early sixteenth century. Reduced.

III

SCHOOLS AND SCHOLARSHIP

11

Master Vacarius and the Beginning of an English Academic Tradition[1]

To students of the twelfth century, the name of Master Vacarius conveys a very clear image of an academic man—of the man who brought the renewed study of Roman Law from Bologna to England in about 1149, who lectured on the subject at Oxford, and who wrote the first textbook written in England, the *Liber Pauperum*, which was still in use in the University of Oxford in the early thirteenth century. The outlines of this image were first definitively drawn in Professor Zulueta's edition of Vacarius's textbook in 1927, and this work has provided the basis for the consensus of opinion which has prevailed with minor adjustments ever since.[2]

It is right to begin by recognizing the great attractions of the synthesis which Zulueta made. It embraced a wide variety of evidence, and gave an intelligible account of Vacarius's activity during the long period from his arrival in England to his death about fifty years later. It helped to fill an awkward gap in the development of the schools of Oxford in the twelfth century; and, in doing this, it provided a chronological pattern of academic growth roughly comparable (though at a very much lower level of activity) to that of the great schools of France.

It is only with regret that such a satisfying combination of merits can be abandoned. Yet there are several reasons for thinking that, in its central thesis about Vacarius's place as an academic teacher and in the development of the Oxford schools, it will not do. The doubts which were expressed long ago by R. L. Poole deserved

[1] In offering this tribute to a great scholar and friend of all medievalists, it is a pleasure to associate with it those whose comments and criticisms have improved it: Professor C. R. Cheney, Dr. Christopher Holdsworth, Dr. Margaret Gibson, and Mr. and Mrs. Derek Hall.

[2] F. de Zulueta, *The Liber Pauperum of Vacarius* (Selden Soc. xliv, 1927), pp. xiii–xxiii. A new study of the work will shortly appear: Peter Stein, 'Vacarius and the Civil Law', *Church and Government in the Middle Ages* (*Essays in honour of C. R. Cheney*), ed. C. N. L. Brooke and D. E. Luscombe, Cambridge, 1976.

more attention than they received from Zulueta;[1] and some of the evidence which has become available since 1927 has strengthened these doubts, though not as yet to the extent of seeming to call for any general reconsideration of Vacarius's place in academic history. The doubts may be expressed in three questions:

1. Is the picture of Vacarius's career as a lecturer on Roman Law at Oxford consistent with what we know of his later life and interests?

2. Is it consistent with what we know of the development of the schools at Oxford during the twelfth century?

3. Can the literary evidence, on which Zulueta's reconstruction ultimately depended, support the weight which has been placed upon it?

I will attempt to answer these questions in turn.

I

Apart from the pieces of literary evidence to be examined later, everything that we know of Vacarius's career in England comes either from some brief references in his own works or from charters and official documents. It may be said at once that there is nothing in these sources which suggests that he was engaged in a career of teaching. The details all fit into the well-known pattern of a scholar who, after studying and teaching in a foreign school, came to England and found his employment and rewards in administration and in the duties of a local ecclesiastical dignitary. It is beyond question that Archbishop Theobald brought Vacarius from Bologna to England for the same reason that he brought John of Salisbury from Paris: to help in the work of administering his province. Theobald had many problems on his hands: problems arising from the legatine claims of the powerful bishop of Winchester, Henry of Blois; problems relating to his relations with successive popes; problems, above all, of the enforcement of Canon Law in a country which had so far remained relatively immune from canonical legal processes.[2] John of Salisbury and Vacarius were brought to give expert advice and practical assistance

---

[1] R. L. Poole, 'The Early Lives of Robert Pullen and Nicholas Breakspear', *Essays in Medieval History presented to T. F. Tout* (Manchester, 1925), p. 62 n. (repr. in R. L. Poole, *Studies in Chronology and History* (Oxford, 1934), p. 289 n.).
[2] See A. Saltman, *Theobald, Archbishop of Canterbury* (London, 1956), pp. 12–55.

in the complicated tasks of ecclesiastical government. No doubt, they provided advice and assistance in different ways. John of Salisbury, who was in Theobald's service from 1148 till 1161, was a man of much wider experience and education than Vacarius. Although, as Professor Brooke says, 'he held no title in Theobald's curia and there is nothing to connect him with office routine', he was undoubtedly the mainstay of the archbishop's administration, expecially in matters of high policy, at least from 1154 to 1161.[1] Vacarius's position is more elusive.

We are not clear when he entered the archbishop's service, though as we shall see there is good reason for thinking that it was in 1143.[2] He had certainly left it by 1159 when we find him in the service of Roger, archbishop of York.[3] Roger became archbishop of York in 1154. He had previously been archdeacon of Canterbury and in this position he must have worked closely with Vacarius. Given the dearth of lawyers available for episcopal service at this time, it is understandable that Archbishop Roger should wish to attract Vacarius to his service as quickly as possible. Why Vacarius should have exchanged the service of Theobald for that of the rival archbishop is less clear. The most likely explanation is a simple one that Theobald was either unable or unwilling to reward his servants by giving them benefices, and Vacarius seems to have fared better at the hands of Archbishop Roger. By 1166 he had been rewarded with the best of the prebends in the archbishop's gift in the collegiate church of Southwell, and he never rose higher than this in the ecclesiastical hierarchy. It provided him with a comfortable though not a brilliant position in society, and it may have satisfied all his ambitions.

Vacarius spent nearly fifty years in the province of York, and this long period of time may be divided into two roughly equal parts. The first lasted during the lifetime of archbishop Roger, who died in 1181. During these years the evidence which is collected below shows that he was an important figure in the ecclesiastical

[1] *The Letters of John of Salisbury*, ed. W. J. Millor, H. E. Butler, and C. N. L. Brooke (London, 1955), p. xxix. It is worth noting that nearly all, if not all, the letters written by John of Salisbury on behalf of the archbishop are later than 1154; a fact which could possibly be connected with the departure of Vacarius.

[2] See below, p. 280.

[3] He witnessed Archbishop Roger's confirmation of the possessions of Pontefract Priory in 1159; the text is in *Early Yorkshire Charters*, ed. W. Farrer, iii (1916), 171–3; for the date see W. E. Wightman, *The Lacy Family in England and Normandy* (Oxford, 1966), p. 84.

affairs of the northern province.[1] He travelled with the archbishop to Normandy, acted as his agent in France and in the papal curia, was one of his guarantors when he got absolution for his part in the Becket affair, and in the last years of Roger's life he was frequently employed as a papal judge delegate. The second phase begins with Roger's death. After this date, his responsibilities as canon of Southwell and parson of Norwell,[2] which must always have occupied part of his time, became his main preoccupation. The existing evidence shows a marked restriction of his activity to places within about twenty miles of his parsonage at Norwell. He witnessed charters with his fellow canons of Southwell; he intervened in the local affairs of the abbeys of Welbeck and Rufford; he concerned himself with the future of his nephew Reginald, to whom he ceded part of the revenues of his church at Norwell. It is noticeable that the only charters of Roger's successor, Geoffrey, archbishop of York, in which he appears, were concerned either with guaranteeing the future of his nephew or with the affairs of Welbeck. He seems no longer to have been a member of the archbishop's household, but to have acted as a local official or agent of the archbishop in Nottinghamshire—hence the letter which he wrote testifying to the action taken to put the canons of Welbeck in possession of the church of Whatton.[3] Even the last incident of his life, which seems at first sight to have a very large background, may be explained by its local context. In 1198 Innocent III made him a preacher of the crusade in the province of York. It was a strange appointment for a man of eighty or thereabouts, but when we notice that his companion was the prior of the near-by monastery of Thurgarton, we may see the appointment as a task for a local dignitary rather than a tribute to the international reputation of a famous scholar.

---

[1] See below, pp. 282–5.

[2] The evidence for Vacarius himself acting as parson of Norwell is found in Archbishop Geoffrey's confirmation of Vacarius's gift of half the church to his nephew Reginald in 1191–4. The parish church belonged to Vacarius's prebend, which he had held for over twenty-five years, and the archbishop thought it necessary to take evidence that Vacarius's predecessors had been accustomed to give the church to vicars: Vacarius must therefore have broken the custom by holding it himself. (*Liber Albus* of Southwell, pp. 49–50: Professor Holt kindly supplied me with photographs of a transcript in Reading University Library.)

[3] For the text of this letter see below, p. 286, 1; and for the position of a bishop's official at this time see C. R. Cheney, *English Bishops' Chanceries, 1100–1250*, Manchester, 1950, pp. 20–1, and *From Becket to Langton*, 1956, pp. 147–8.

During this half-century of activity in the northern province, there is only one occasion on which we hear of him in connection with the schools, and this was not as a teacher but as a student, not at Oxford but at Northampton. In one of his later works, of which I shall say more in a minute, he lets drop quite accidentally that while he was studying at Northampton he had replied to an objection to the Christian faith which had been raised by some Jews in controversy with their Christian neighbours.[1] The passage tells us nothing about the subject of his studies, but it is perhaps relevant that the Southwell statutes of 1225 allowed a period of study of theology in the schools as a valid ground for non-residence.[2] As we shall see, Vacarius's later works show clear traces of theological study, and there would be nothing unusual in a parson or canon of mature years returning to the schools for this purpose. A much more ambitious contemporary of Vacarius, Gerald of Wales, did precisely this: after he had studied law in Paris as a young man, he went, when he was already an archdeacon, and about fifty years old, to study theology at Lincoln. Such cases could be multiplied without difficulty; they do not exclude a combination of study and teaching, but they certainly do not require it.

If we turn from official documents to Vacarius's writings, we must begin with the most famous of his works, the *Liber Pauperum*. This work is an efficient and reasonably well organized collection of extracts from the *corpus* of Roman Law with explanatory glosses, designed as a brief and inexpensive compendium of those parts of Roman Law which were most valuable for a working knowledge of the subject. It is certainly an early work. No doubt the materials were collected, and for all we know to the contrary, the work may have been compiled in its totality, while he was still a master in the schools of Bologna. In its scholarship and in the opinions it reports it is entirely a product of the teaching of the first generation of Bolognese masters after Irnerius. There is very little in it of

---

[1] For this work see below pp. 264–5. The essential words are: 'O stulta et imperita cogitatio, sicut Iudei apud Norhamptoniam, ubi degebam causa studendi, christianis vicinis meis obiecerunt quod Dominus noster Ihesus Christus turpiter in visceribus matris sue includebatur circa pudenda, per que de ventre eius exivit. Ego autem inductus fui ad respondendum Iudeis, et quesivi a quodam eorum...' (P. Ilarino da Milano, *L'eresia di Ugo Speroni nella confutazione del Maestro Vacario, Studi e Testi*, cxv, 1945, 527). This passage was first noticed by Kuttner and Rathbone, *Traditio*, vii (1949–50), 322, but they drew the (as I think) unacceptable conclusion that 'we must probably interpret *causa studendi* as meaning, to teach'.

[2] *V.C.H. Nottinghamshire*, ii. 152–61.

Vacarius's own opinions, and it could well have been the compilation of a young man following in the footsteps of his great masters. It is certain that he either brought the work to England from Bologna or that he brought with him the materials from which he compiled it during his early years in Theobald's service. All the existing manuscripts seem ultimately to derive from England, and it could only have achieved the success to which these manuscripts bear witness in an environment in which the study of Roman Law had reached no high level of sophistication. We have Vacarius's word for it that he made his compilation to meet the need of those who wanted a brief compendium of Roman Law; but whether these men were in the ordinary sense of the word students, or practitioners in ecclesiastical courts, or both, he does not say.

Zulueta thought it was certain that many of the opinions ascribed to Vacarius in glosses of the work came from his lectures in Oxford. The sources of these opinions are a more complicated question than can be discussed here, or than I am capable of discussing, but I can find no evidence for the connection which Zulueta postulates. In the first place, Vacarius certainly taught at Bologna and the few references to him in continental sources almost certainly derive from his Bolognese days.[1] As for the references to Vacarius in the glosses of the *Liber Pauperum*, it would be a gross simplification to suppose that they must come from formal lectures. It is indeed very likely that during his fifty years in England Vacarius had pupils whom he guided through the contents of his book; but to judge from what we know of his life, they are more likely to have been pupils of a country parson than students of a university lecturer. In the last resort, Zulueta's picture of Vacarius as a scholastic lecturer was based on the general consideration that the only opening in England for a 'pure civilian' like Vacarius was academic. So far as general considerations have any weight, this one appears to me the precise opposite of the truth. For reasons which I explain shortly, academic opportunities in England in the middle years of the twelfth century were extremely

---

[1] Zulueta noted two opinions of Vacarius quoted in Bulgarus's *De regulis iuris* and three in Hugolinus's *Dissensiones* (pp. xxii–xxiii). He thought that 'they may well have been derived from some copy of the *Liber Pauperum*', but in the absence of any trace of its use abroad or of any evidence that the opinions were drawn from the *Liber Pauperum*, and in view of the common connection of all three men with Bologna, it seems much more likely that the opinions go back to Vacarius's days as a master at Bologna.

limited; but there was a growing demand for Roman Law as a support for the practice of Canon Law. Besides, it is not true to say that Vacarius was a 'pure civilian'. His later writings, which have been too much neglected, show a wide range of interests, and it is to these that we must turn in the first place if we are to understand his later career.

The first of these works, which was probably written in the 1160s, is a short treatise on a theological problem which aroused bitter controversy in the second half of the twelfth century, namely the manner of the union between the divine and human natures of Christ. This controversy, which had been given its first impetus by Gilbert de la Porrée, obtained a wide diffusion through the work of Peter Lombard. Vacarius, however, did not learn of it in a scholastic context. His interest in the subject was aroused by a conversation with a friend who had adopted the new-fangled views of Gilbert de la Porrée and Peter Lombard.[1] Vacarius himself does not seem to have known anything about the scholastic sources of the controversy; he only knew that the new views 'had been invented by certain modern masters' and that they had been very widely adopted. After the conversation which had aroused his interest, he discussed the question with others and learned from them the main arguments in favour of the new opinions. His purpose in writing was to convince his friend of the error of these views, and in order to do so he used arguments drawn from Boethius and supported by the authority of Augustine on the Psalms and Claudianus Mamertus on the Soul. This last work was a book which so far as I know had no currency in scholastic debate, and Vacarius's arguments do not seem to be connected with any tradition in the schools. He wrote as an independent observer of the

---

[1] From the abundant literature on this subject, the following may be cited for the continuing controversy in the late twelfth century: G. Morin, 'Lettre inédite d'un étudiant en théologie de l'université de Paris vers la fin du XIIe siècle', *Recherches de théologie ancienne et médiévale*, vi (1934), 412–16; N. M. Haring, 'A Latin Dialogue on the Doctrine of Gilbert of Poitiers', *Mediaeval Studies*, xv (1953), 243–89; xvii (1955), 143–72; 'Two Austrian Tractates against the Doctrine of Gilbert of Poitiers', *Archives*, xxxii (1965), 127–67; P. Classen, 'Aus der Werkstatt Gerhochs v. Reichersberg', *Deutsches Archiv*, xxiii (1967), 31–92, where much of the earlier literature is cited. Vacarius's treatise has been edited by N. M. Haring in *Mediaeval Studies*, xxi (1959), 147–75: but it should be noted that the date *c.* 1150–5 which the editor adopts on the basis of Maitland's conjectural date '1156 or shortly after' for the *De Matrimonio* is almost certainly too early. The fact is that the treatise on marriage cannot be earlier than 1156, but there are no strong grounds for any date before 1170.

vagaries of the schools, and he quoted his authorities in a long-winded discursive fashion uncharacteristic of scholastic practice.

The same spirit of detachment from a scholastic environment is to be found in the treatise on marriage which he wrote shortly afterwards.[1] In it he dealt with one of the most familiar and urgent problems of the twelfth century—what makes a marriage, and how and when can it be dissolved? In this treatise he shows a remarkable independence of contemporary opinions and disputes. In his view the subject had been greatly confused by modern writers, and it is virtually certain that he included the great canonist Gratian in this censure. He brought his Roman Law expertise to bear upon the question in the hope of providing a clear and authoritative solution. He cut right across the leading opinions of his time in suggesting that the main element in a valid marriage was the *traditio* of the woman by her family to her husband. But, though he knew something about the alternative views, he did not in any way seek to present a systematic reply to them or to meet objections in a formal scholastic way. Here, as in his earlier work, he wrote as a man of learning and experience, not as a teacher, still less as a formal expounder of Roman Law, although this was the source of most of his ideas.[2]

Finally there is the last and longest of his later works. It is a treatise addressed to a man who had been his intimate friend when they were together in the schools, presumably of Bologna. Their ways had parted long ago: the friend, Hugh Speroni, had become a man of importance in Piacenza and the founder of a heretical sect; Vacarius had sunk himself in the English countryside. Here Vacarius's nephew Leonard brought him a book as a gift from his old friend. Vacarius read it again and again: some of it he admired but he deplored its heresies, and he wrote a long treatise to persuade his friend of his errors. The letter which introduces this

[1] Edited by F. W. Maitland, *Law Quarterly Review*, xiii (1897), 133–43, 270–87.

[2] Following J. de Ghellinck, 'Magister Vacarius: un juriste théologien peu aimable pour les canonistes', *Rev. d'histoire ecclésiastique*, xliv (1949), 173–8, Kuttner and Rathbone (op. cit., p. 288 n. 25) speak, in connection with Vacarius, of 'contempt for canon law'. But this is surely too strong: Vacarius shared with other students of Roman Law a strong sense of the superiority of their materials over those of the canonists, and criticized some of the methods which canonists used to force their texts into agreement, but there is no evidence that he despised Canon Law as such: his English career would be unintelligible if he had.

work provides the best clue we have to his personality and outlook:

> I do not believe you can have forgotten the brotherly love and intimate friendship which bound us together when we were in the schools living in the same house. At that time you used to submit your affairs to my judgement. It is this that specially obliges me to sympathize with you in your tribulations. The more serious these are, the more vehemently I commiserate with you in your great misfortune. For, as I have learnt from your letter and from other reports, you have disturbed the Church of God to the danger of your own soul. In your book, which you sent me by my nephew Leonard, you have said many things against the Church. I have read it again and again and although I have found many good and true things in it finely expressed, they are corrupted and made useless by the mixture of errors and especially by the wickednesses to which they lead.[1]

The errors which Vacarius proceeds to argue against are a very mixed lot, covering most of the ground of the popular heresies of the late twelfth century: priesthood, baptism, eucharist, purification, and good works. Essentially Hugh Speroni's heresies added up to an attack on the efficacy of the whole ecclesiastical structure and discipline of the Church. Considering the gravity of his friend's errors, Vacarius's answers are forbearing and good-humoured, though not without their spice of invective. In the main, he wrote simply as an orthodox friend, without abuse and with very little apparatus of learning. His quotations are overwhelmingly biblical, but they also show some independent reading in Jerome and Augustine. In view of the common legal background which he shared with his friend, it is not surprising that he appealed several times to Roman Law, but I can detect no knowledge of modern theological works or methods of argument.[2] The general outlook of the work is similar to that which we have already found in the work on the Person of Christ; Vacarius was a thoughtful, well-read, orthodox man, who disapproved of modern novelties, so far as he knew about them, and retained, though without excessive emphasis, a predilection for Roman Law.

In the main, therefore, these works confirm the impression of the documents relating to his later career. They show him as a

---

[1] P. Ilarino da Milano, *L'eresia di Ugo Speroni nella confutazione del Maestro Vacario* (*Studi e Testi*, cxv, 1945), p. 477. The whole work is printed, pp. 477–583.

[2] The editor's reference to Peter Lombard on p. 559 is misleading.

scholarly man who had no longer any close connection with the schools—one of the many such men in the late twelfth century in England, who after a brilliant career in a foreign school, became more or less totally immersed in the practical life of government and of local affairs. There was plenty of work and adequate rewards for experts in the field of administration and law. But the demand for high-class academic teachers who hoped to make a living by teaching scarcely existed, for the simple reason that any serious and ambitious young man who wanted to have a choice of up-to-date and influential teachers went abroad. Those who remained in England were either too humble in their aspirations or too poor to create opportunities for men of high academic distinction: numerous though such students must have been, their needs did not inspire a scholastic literature until the last years of the century, nor so far as we can see did they create any institutions with a continuous academic tradition. We have only to set the small fragments of English works written in the schools beside the large body of literature inspired by the life of courts and monasteries, and contrast these fragments with the contemporary scholastic literature of France, to see how feebly the English schools emerge from the comparison. Before the last decade of the century England was a scholastically undeveloped country.

II

At this point the question must be asked whether an exception to this gloomy academic picture must not be made in favour of Oxford. Is there not here at least a story of continuous academic development from the beginning of the twelfth century to its end? This is certainly the picture which has been slowly built up during the last hundred years, and in this picture Vacarius plays an important part, for he fills a gap between two periods of notable (or at least strongly presumed) activity in the Oxford schools, of which the first occupies the reign of Henry I and the second begins in the early years of Richard I. In the intervening years we can name no master unless it be Vacarius, and it would be difficult to find a more glittering array of testimony to his place as a lecturer on Roman Law in the middle years of the century. For Zulueta, 'to doubt whether Vacarius ever taught at Oxford is to doubt against the evidence'. To Professor Kuttner and Miss Rathbone it appears certain 'that Vacarius taught there in Stephen's reign', and for Professor Le Bras, quite simply, 'Vacarius ... fonda l'école d'Oxford' and William of Drogheda, the Oxford master who died in 1245, was 'élève de Vacarius, légiste à Oxford'. Even Mr. Emden in his great *Biographical Register* appears to regard the fact of his lecturing in Oxford as beyond question. All that is in doubt is the date, and on this Mr. Emden thinks that 'the precedent of the theological lectures delivered before 1167 in Oxford by Theobald of Étampes and Robert Pullen renders the date 1149, given by Robert of Torigny, by no means untenable'.[1]

Mr. Emden's words bring us to the centre of the problem. The suggestion is that since there was an established tradition of advanced teaching in Oxford before 1167, it is not unreasonable to think that Vacarius carried on this tradition, which can be seen gathering new strength in the last years of the century. But unfortunately the main premise is based on extremely fragile foundations and, like many established views about the early history of famous schools, it is arrived at by giving a maximum content to every favourable scrap of evidence and ignoring unfavourable symptoms and general improbabilities.

The evidence for a flourishing school of theology at Oxford in the reign of Henry I hangs on the work of two men, Theobald of Étampes, who taught in Oxford between about 1100 and 1130, and Robert Pullen, who taught from about 1133 to 1137. But on a close inspection it appears likely that Theobald was no more than a schoolmaster who never taught theology at all; and Robert Pullen, who was certainly a serious teacher of theology, stayed only for a few years before going off to the richer pastures of Paris. With him advanced teaching in Oxford emerges for a dim instant only to return almost at once to total obscurity.

This picture is so unlike the one which is generally accepted that it requires a few words of explanation. We may turn first to Theobald of Étampes. It is certain that he taught at Oxford and it is generally accepted that he taught theology to classes of between sixty and a hundred students.[2] If this were true, it would be

---

[1] Zulueta, pp. xvi–xvii; S. Kuttner and E. Rathbone, 'Anglo-Norman Canonists of the Twelfth Century, *Traditio*, vii (1949–51), 323; G. le Bras, *Histoire du droit et des institutions de l'Église en Occident*, vii (1965), 33, 318; A. B. Emden, *B.R.U.O.* iii. 1939.

[2] The literature on Theobald of Étampes is summarized in Emden, *B.R.U.O.* iii. 1754. The fullest account of his career is by Professor Foreville, *Studia Anselmiana*, xli (1957), 9–19; this is a valuable contribution, though our interpretations

impressive evidence of academic activity, since sixty students in theology would argue a much larger number of students in the Arts. But our only reason for thinking that he taught theology is that four of his six surviving letters are on more or less theological subjects, and very violent, abusive and dogmatic tirades they are. The inference that he taught theology because he held violent views on the valid priesthood of sons of priests, the necessity of baptism, the lack of necessity of confession, and the superiority of secular clergy to monks, is (to say the least) extremely flimsy. Moreover, it is contradicted by the explicit statement of the writer who replied to his last letter. He characterized him as a little man who was still engaged in the study of secular subjects, and he described him as one of a vast number of masters of the liberal arts to be found in every town, city, and village. It is from this same author that the figure of sixty or a hundred students also comes. Whatever we may think of the numbers, it is certain that they were not intended as a compliment but as a jibe. Theobald had unwisely sought in his abusive letter to enhance the value of secular clerks by speaking of their scarcity, and his enemy turned on him with the retort, 'How can you speak of a *scarcity* of clerks when even you who are nobody are said to act as a master to sixty or a hundred clerks?'[1]

Numbers, of course, have no meaning in controversial writings, but even if we were to accept this figure as a guide, its significance is the very opposite of that which is generally ascribed to it. The implication is not that Theobald was the master of an impressive school, but that he was only one of an army of petty schoolmasters teaching a too large number of schoolboys, who aspired to the ranks of the secular clergy. As Theobald's enemy remarked, such

of the evidence differ on almost every important point. Five of Theobald's letters are in *P.L.* clxiii. 765–810, and a sixth in *Studia Anselmiana*, xli. 52–3; the important reply to this letter occupies pp. 54–110 of the same publication.

[1] *Studia Anselmiana*, xli (1957), 54, where the writer describes Theobald as 'tantillum clericellum litteris adhuc secularibus intentum'. For the general description of his position, see p. 65: 'Nunquid non sunt ubique terrarum liberales magistri, qui dicuntur et clerici? Tu quoque nescio quis, nonne magistri vice sexagenos aut centenos plusue minusue clericos regere diceris, quibus venditor verborum cupidus efficeris, forsitan ut eos incautos nequissime fallas, sicut et ipse falleris? Unde ergo ista tua clericorum penuria? Nam ut de ceteris provinciis sileam, fere totidem aut plures sunt per Galliam et Alemanniam, per Normanniam et Angliam, non solum in urbibus et castellis, verum etiam et in villulis peritissimi scholarum magistri quot fiscorum regalium exactores et ministri. Unde ergo clericorum penuria?'

men were to be found everywhere. They were 'as common as royal tax collectors'.

That at least is how Theobald of Étampes appeared to a contemporary. No doubt he was an unreliable contemporary, but his evidence gains some support from the notice which tells us of the arrival of Robert Pullen in Oxford in 1133 to teach the Holy Scriptures. He came, we are told, to teach a subject which had fallen into disuse in England before his day.[1] This writer, therefore, certainly did not see Robert Pullen as the inheritor of a vigorous theological tradition, and the fact that he left Oxford so quickly to go to Paris indicates that he neither found nor created a vigorous school.

This should not surprise us. It was only in very favourable conditions, such as those which Paris pre-eminently enjoyed, that twelfth-century schools could build up and maintain a consistent tradition of academic teaching. This could only be done where there were many students, a plentiful supply of lodgings and food, a permanent body of masters, and a general environment favourable to scholastic growth. Oxford met none of these conditions. It was a small town, probably incapable of housing or feeding many students, without a cathedral church or any other obvious endowment for scholarship.[2] There is no sign of any flow of able students, and even if there had been, the rising reputation of Paris and Bologna, and the civil war of Stephen's reign which disturbed the Midlands for several years, would have been sufficient to discourage them.

On a general view, therefore, there is no evidence of continuous scholastic activity on anything but the humblest level in the first half of the twelfth century. Thereafter, if for the moment we leave Vacarius on one side, there is not a single lecturer who can be named at Oxford after Robert Pullen's departure in about 1137

---

[1] Oseney Annals: 'MCXXXIII. Magister Robertus Pullein scripturas divinas quae in Anglia obsoluerant, apud Oxoniam (Oxenefordiam) legere cepit.' *Annales Monastici*, ed. H. R. Luard, iv (R.S., 1869), 19. For the reading *Oxenefordiam* see H. E. Salter, *Medieval Oxford* (O.H.S. c, 1936), p. 91 n. 3.

[2] The number of houses inside and outside the walls in 1086 was 946, of which 478 were destroyed or too poor to pay tax. Even on the assumption of a fairly rapid recovery of English town life, Paris was probably five times the size of Oxford. For the growth of Paris at this time see L. Halphen, *Paris sous les premiers Capétiens*, 1909; A. Friedmann, *Paris, ses rues et ses paroisses du Moyen Âge à la Révolution*, 1959; *Paris, croissance d'une capitale* (Colloques: Cahiers de Civilisation, Paris, 1961); A. L. Gabriel, *Garlandia*, Frankfurt a. M., 1969.

until Alexander Nequam's arrival in about 1190. No doubt schoolmasters continued to teach elementary subjects to unexacting pupils; no doubt also these lowly tasks and aims gradually opened up more specialized fields and more ambitious aims. But the process has left no names until the last decade of the century. Gerald of Wales did indeed find masters and pupils in Oxford in about 1186, but he was able to entertain all the masters and their chief pupils at a single dinner; and the remaining pupils and the leading citizens of the town at a second sitting.[1]

Then, quite suddenly, the picture changes. After the years of emptiness, the last ten years of the century are filled with the names of masters and students. We hear for the first time of students coming from abroad; we hear of lectures in theology and law as well as grammar; and there were probably also developments in Aristotelian natural science and philosophy, which put the Oxford masters on these subjects on a level with those of Paris. This is not the place to tell the story of this transformation, but simply to note its causes and its results so far as they concern the study of Roman Law.

As for the causes, the most important was probably the persistent state of war between France and England in the years after 1193. This war lasted longer, was fought more bitterly, and had wider diplomatic and economic consequences than any earlier war. We have the evidence of Gerald of Wales as proof of the impossibility which it created for students wishing to go abroad.[2] For the first time, ambitious and wealthy students were constrained to stay in England, and this gave English schools a chance to compete on favourable terms with their foreign rivals. Although Gerald of Wales himself did not choose to go to Oxford, there can be no doubt that Oxford was the chief beneficiary of this situation.

One reason for this was almost certainly the growth of Oxford as a convenient meeting place for ecclesiastical courts which had to summon litigants from several parts of the country. The central position of Oxford in the Canterbury Province had never acted as a strong inducement to scholars who were long-term travellers in search of the best masters. But it was a persuasive argument for judges, litigants, and counsel who came together for a short time, and had to count the miles and days of their journey. The growth

---

[1] Giraldus Cambrensis, *Opera Omnia* (R.S., 1861), i. 72–3.
[2] Ibid. i. 93.

in legal business no doubt helped to make it convenient for qualified lawyers to set up schools in Oxford.

There is a vivid illustration of the way in which geographical
convenience, the growth of litigation, and the teaching of law
supported each other, in an incident recorded by Jocelyn of
Brakeland. At the end of 1197, Abbot Sampson of Bury St.
Edmunds was a papal judge delegate sitting with the archbishop
of Canterbury and the bishop of Lincoln in a case concerning the
monks of Coventry. The parties had been summoned to Oxford,
and Abbot Sampson gave a dinner party for the fourteen monks
of Coventry who represented their abbey. The monks all sat at one
table, and at a second table there were the masters of the schools
who were engaged in the case.[1] We cannot say that all these
masters taught at Oxford, but the convenience of being close at
hand for such business is very evident. The outlines of the teaching
which these masters gave is only now beginning to emerge and
there is still much to be done. Yet enough is known to make it
certain that the level of professional competence and the opportunities for teachers in Oxford were rising rapidly in the last
decade of the century.[2]

In this legal teaching there seems to have been an understandable emphasis on points of procedure. England with its precocious
development of legal processes in the secular courts was well
placed to encourage an interest in the intricacies of forms of action
and niceties of procedure in ecclesiastical cases also. So far as we
can judge at present, all the ideas and all the principles of law came
from Bologna, and it is only in the study of cases and procedures
that there are signs of real intensity of thought at Oxford.[3] In this
situation, Vacarius's textbook, which was believed to provide all
the Roman Law that the student needed for practical purposes in

[1] Jocelin de Brakelonde, *Chronica*, in *Memorials of St. Edmund's Abbey*, ed.
T. Arnold, i (R.S., 1890), 295.

[2] Despite some errors and exaggerations H. G. Richardson, 'The Oxford Law
School under John', *Law Quarterly Review*, lvii (1941), 319–38, must be men-
tioned as the beginning of a new phase in discussions about legal studies in
Oxford.

[3] I make these remarks with some hesitation in view of the protest by Kuttner
and Rathbone, *Traditio*, vii. 290–2, against the exaggeration of the English
concentration on matters of practical interest. The question is clearly a matter of
degree, and all practical interests must have a foundation of theoretical structure; but when all allowances have been made, the high proportion of works on
procedure and case law, and the derivative nature of the theoretical rules, seem
to give ample justification for these generalizations.

the ecclesiastical courts, came into its own. No doubt its merits had
been gaining recognition for some time, but the evidence that the
Liber Pauperum was a central textbook in the legal teaching at
Oxford belongs to the period after 1190. Most of the evidence was
collected by Zulueta and requires no long rehearsal here. It will
suffice to mention that it was among the books which the Frisian
student Emo copied at Oxford in about 1195, while he worked
through the night to build up a small collection of essential legal
texts; and that the existence of *Pauperistae* in Oxford in the years
around 1200 testifies to the popularity of Vacarius's book in
the formative years of the Oxford schools.[1] This evidence has
recently been supplemented by the researches of Mr. Ker, whose
discoveries of scraps of manuscripts of this period in the bindings
of Oxford books, have raised the number of existing manuscripts
or fragments of the *Liber Pauperum* to about eighteen.[2] All these
manuscripts seem to belong to the last years of the twelfth century
or the first half of the thirteenth, and this distribution confirms
what we know from other sources of its relatively short-lived
popularity.

If one were to indulge in the outmoded game of finding a date
for the foundation of the University of Oxford, the year 1193,
when the war between the French and English kings entered its
longest and most embittered phase, would be as good as any; and
if one looked further for a textbook which provided one of the
foundations for the new academic tradition, the *Liber Pauperum*
would have a very high claim. The process by which books, not
always the most interesting, emerge as essential textbooks in
university disciplines is always obscure. The first requirement is
that they should meet precise and widely shared needs. Who the
author is, and whether or where he has lectured on his own book
or any other, is a matter of indifference. The *Liber Pauperum* met
the needs of law students for a generation between about 1190 and

---

[1] Zulueta, pp. xvii–xviii.

[2] The number cannot be exactly calculated since it is not always clear whether
the fragments belong to one or more MSS. The additions for which Mr. Ker is
responsible are listed in N. R. Ker, *Pastedowns in Oxford Bindings* (Oxford
Bibliographical Soc., N.S. v, 1954), items 16, 46, 133, 249, and in *Kunsthistorische
Forschungen zum 70. Geburtstag O. Pächts* (1973), p. 80 (Oxford, Bodleian MSS.
Rawlinson C. 435, and Q. b. 5, and Worcester Cathedral MS. F. 171). Despite
its fragmentary state, this large range of new material will substantially increase
our knowledge of the place of the *Liber Pauperum* in academic teaching at the
end of the 12th century.

1220. What Vacarius had been doing, or where he had done it fifty years earlier, is another matter. To this problem we must now turn, and ask whether he himself had lectured on Roman Law at Oxford in the middle years of the twelfth century.

III

To answer this question we must now finally consider the literary evidence from which the whole story of Vacarius's Oxford lectures arose. This consists of three passages in three independent sources, and I shall deal with each in turn.

1. *John of Salisbury*

The only witness who knew Vacarius, and could have told us what we want to know about him, was John of Salisbury. Unfortunately, in his only mention of Vacarius, he was not interested in telling us what we want to know. He introduced his name as an illustration of a line of thought which appeared to him more important than the trivial facts of Vacarius's career. He was discussing tyranny, and, after surveying the characteristics of various tyrants, he came to King Antiochus, the supreme expression of tyranny in the Old Testament. Antiochus was the ruler who had dared to enter into the Holy of Holies, to perform the priestly functions in person, to set up the Idol of Abomination, to burn the books of the Divine Law, and to slaughter anyone who obeyed or was found in possession of the Book of God's Law. He was not, however, simply a figure of the past. He was the type of the last and greatest Tyrant, the Antichrist who would arise in the final stage of the world's history. So, if we would look for the symptoms of the Last Days, we must look for an Antiochus in our midst. With this in mind, John of Salisbury turned to the present:

Vidi temporibus meis nonnullos sacerdotali se immiscentes officio et humeros temerarie supponentes, ut archam praeriperent ab humeris Leuitarum, loci immemores qui in praesentem diem dicitur Ozae percussio. Alios uidi qui libros legis deputant igni nec scindere uererentur, si in manus eorum iura peruenirent aut canones. Tempore regis Stephani a regno iussae sunt leges Romanae, quas in Britanniam domus uenerabilis patris Theodbaldi Britanniarum primatis asciuerat. Ne quis etiam libros retineret edicto regio prohibitum est et Vacario nostro indictum silentium; sed, Deo faciente, eo magis uirtus legis inualuit quo eam amplius nitebatur impietas infirmare.[1]

In retrospect it may seem ludicrous to detect an Antiochus in King Stephen, and perhaps even when he wrote this passage in 1159 John already knew that a greater tyrant than he had arisen in Henry II, whose name he could not mention. But in principle the two were identical in their exercise of secular power over the Church and in thwarting the course of ecclesiastical justice. It was this that made Stephen the special object, and perhaps the only mentionable object, of John's detestation. But it also meant that Stephen had to be portrayed in terms comparable to those in which he had described Antiochus. He must burn the books of the law and, if not kill their owners and servants, at least prohibit their use and silence their advocates. Whatever John of Salisbury may precisely have meant by what he said, the form of what he says is strictly determined by the context in which he says it. He is generally thought to imply that Vacarius had been lecturing on Roman Law and that King Stephen had forbidden his lectures. Lecturing suggests an institution in which lectures can take place, and so the remark has come to be associated with Oxford. And this was plausible on an already existing presumption that flourishing schools existed in Oxford in which such lectures could take place. But John of Salisbury says nothing of all this. His words might equally well mean that Vacarius advised litigants, or that he practised in the ecclesiastical courts, or simply that he was the legal authority in Theobald's household concerned with the advancement of ecclesiastical justice. If John's words mean anything precise, they should mean that Vacarius, the representative of Canon Law, was forced to go into exile for a time, and this is not impossible: at about the time when he was writing these words John of Salisbury himself was fearing a similar fate. In the end, however, nothing happened to John of Salisbury, and the incident of his much canvassed 'disgrace' suggests that he was capable of a good deal of exaggeration in speaking of the dangers and miseries of an official's life.[2] As for the burning and destruction of books, this is surely a flight of rhetoric. All that we can certainly deduce from John of Salisbury's remarks is that King Stephen obstructed the course of ecclesiastical justice, and showed his displeasure, in

---

[1] *Policraticus*, ed. C. C. J. Webb (Oxford, 1909), ii. 398–9.

[2] See *The Letters of John of Salisbury*, i. 257–8, and the texts cited there.

ways no longer ascertainable, against the chief expert in the ancillary science of Roman Law whom the archbishop had introduced into England. Why does he not speak clearly? Because he had more important things to say which could only be darkly hinted at. He was not interested in adding to our knowledge of historical facts, but in suggesting the shape of things past, present, and to come. He was thinking about the end of the world, not about the prosaic details of Vacarius's employment. For these we must look elsewhere.

2. *Robert of Torigny*

First of all we must look to the Chronicle of Robert of Torigny, monk of Bec and then abbot of Mont-St.-Michel. His work is mostly a record of miscellaneous political and local events. In its earliest form it ended in 1154, but it was continued by a contemporary hand down to 1186.[1] In the process of continuation, a number of erasures were made in the earlier part of the Chronicle to make room for new entries which seemed more interesting to the compiler than those which he erased. The final result is so disorderly and marred by so many elementary confusions that it is hard to believe that the later stages of compilation and revision were supervised by the original author. Nevertheless, the additions are some of the most interesting things in the Chronicle, and there is a special interest in the series of additions relating to incidents in the history of learning. These are found under the years 1128, 1130, 1149, and 1152. The insertions in 1128 and 1152 refer to translations from Greek into Latin by James of Venice and Burgundio of Pisa, and they are closely related to a long account of the latter which occupies most of the entry about the Lateran Council of 1179 (wrongly inserted under the year 1182). The entries which concern us here, however, are those for 1130 and 1149, and these also are closely related to each other and to the *Liber Pauperum*, as the following extracts will show.[2]

---

[1] The best account of these additions is still that by L. Delisle, *Chronique de Robert de Torigni* (Soc. de l'Hist. de Normandie, 1872–3). There is additional information in the edition by R. Howlett, *Chronicles of the Reigns of Stephen, Henry II and Richard I*, iv (R.S., 1889), but without the reliability of Delisle. The whole question of the sources, dates, and authorship of these additions requires a new study. For the present it can only be said that the additions with which we are concerned were made not later than 1182.

[2] The addition for 1130 required the deletion of some facts about Scottish history (Howlett, op. cit., p. 118), and that for 1149 the deletion of an epitaph on Letard, abbot of Bec (ibid., p. 158).

Robert of Torigny, CHRONICLE		Master Vacarius, LIBER PAUPERUM: PROLOGUS
1130	1149	
Gratianus, episcopus Clusinus, coadunavit decreta valde utilia ex decretis, canonibus, doctoribus, legibus Romanis, SUFFICIENTIA AD OMNES ECCLESIASTICAS CAUSAS DECIDENDAS, QUAE FREQUENTANTUR IN CURIA ROMANA ET IN ALIIS CURIIS ECCLESIASTICIS. Haec postmodum abbreviavit magister Omnebonum, episcopus Veronensis, qui fuerat ejus discipulus.	Magister Vacarius, gente Longobardus, vir honestus et juris peritus, cum leges Romanas anno ab incarnatione Domini M°C°XL°IX° in Anglia discipulos doceret, et multi tam *divites quam pauperes* ad eum causa discendi confluerent, *suggestione pauperum, de Codice et Digesta excerptos novem libros composuit,* QUI SUFFICIUNT AD OMNES LEGUM LITES, QUAE IN SCHOLIS FREQUENTARI SOLENT, DECIDENDAS, si quis eos perfecte noverit.	Incipit prologus libri *ex uniuerso enucleato iure excerpti et pauperibus precipue destinati* ... Quibusdam enim qui mihi *suggesserant* opus hoc faciendum ... precio leuissimo comparandum et breui tempore perlegendum et tenuioribus precipue destinatum, diuina donante liberalitate, perfeci. Sed cum EA QUE IN SCOLIS FREQUENTARI SOLENT magis elegerim, *in nouem ex iustiniano distribuitur libros* ...

The interesting thing about the two entries in the Chronicle is that, although they are separated chronologically by nineteen years, they were clearly made at the same time and come from the same source. This can be seen in several ways. Firstly, they describe a single programme of legal study in its two complementary branches: Gratian (in 1130) provides all that is necessary for settling the cases which ordinarily arise in the ecclesiastical courts, and Vacarius (in 1149) provides all that is necessary for settling the legal conflicts which ordinarily arise in the schools. And, if we were in any doubt about the unity of the two entries, the doubt would be resolved by observing the similarity of phraseology, which arises in part at least from their both borrowing from the Preface to the *Liber Pauperum*. Indeed, in the entry for 1149 the greater part and perhaps the whole could have been culled from this Preface.[1] The source of the date 1149 alone remains mysterious. Liebermann conjectured that it came from a colophon in a manuscript of the *Liber Pauperum*. It is known that a manuscript once existed with a damaged inscription in which the letters MCXL or

[1] See F. Liebermann, 'Magister Vacarius', *E.H.R.* xi (1896), 310; Zulueta, p. xv.

something like them could be faintly detected, and the reviser of Robert of Torigny's Chronicle may indeed have got the date from such a source.[1] If so, we do not know whether the date originally referred to the completion of the work itself or the copy, and in our ignorance it would be unwise to attach much importance to it.

What do these entries tell us? About the biographies of the persons mentioned, very little indeed. There is an egregious error in the description of Gratian as bishop of Chiusi—an error which no doubt arose from knowing that he was connected with this town (he seems to have been born in the neighbourhood) and imagining the rest.[2] On Vacarius, the main part of the information is built out of the hints in the Preface of his book. On Omnebonus, the abbreviator of Gratian, it is certainly right that he became bishop of Verona, and probably right that he was a pupil of Gratian; but the name Omnebonum which the chronicler gives him was the popular name, not of the author, but of his *book*.[3]

Despite this small error, the mention of Master Omnebonus has a special importance, for there is a real link between his work and that of Vacarius. They were both abbreviations of a large body of material which was new in the schools of Bologna in the 1140s: Omnebonus abbreviated the very recent work of Gratian in Canon Law; Vacarius the recently digested *corpus* of Roman Law with the recent glosses of its first commentators. They must both have been teaching in Bologna at the same time. Omnebonus was probably a somewhat older man—old enough to serve as a judge delegate in the time of Eugenius III (1145–53).[4] But scholastically

---

[1] C. F. C. Wenck, *Magister Vacarius* (Leipzig, 1820), p. 64.

[2] For Gratian's association with Chiusi see S. Kuttner in *Studia Gratiana*, i (1953), 20, and *Dictionnaire de Droit Canonique*, iv. 611.

[3] It will be convenient at this point to have the text of the only other witness to Omnebonus's career, the Chronicle attributed to Alberic of Trois-Fontaines (written *c.* 1227–51). Under the year 1156 there is the following entry: 'Item in eodem anno, quidam magister egregius Omnebonus nomine librum de concordia discordantium canonum diligentissime ordinavit in duas partes, primam partem in 26 Distinctiones, secundam in causas 37 per quaestiones diversas satis artificiose propositas. Et hic liber a nomine auctoris *Omnibonum* appellatur; et hunc secutus est tempore Alexandri pape Gratianus cardinalis, qui multa addidit, ita quod de 26 distinctionibus centum distinctiones fecit; et per ipsum ista doctrina magis facta et autentica' (*M.G.H.SS.* xxiii. 843).

[4] Jaffé–Wattenbach, *Reg. Pont. Rom.* ii, no. 9654. For his works, see F. von Schulte, *Gesch. der Quellen u. Literatur des canonischen Rechts*, i (1875), 119; Denifle, *A.L.K.G.* i (1885), 461–9; Grabmann, *Gesch. der Scholastischen Methode* (1913), ii. 227; G. le Bras, *Hist. du Droit et des Institutions de l'Église en Occident*, vii (1965), 80, 86–8, 96.

they belonged to the same generation, and they were similar in the range of their interests—Roman and Canon Law, theology and grammar and logic. Omnebonus, the pupil originally (it would seem) of Abelard, was the more sophisticated and 'advanced' theologian and canon lawyer; Vacarius the more professional civilian; but both converged on the general and theological problems of their own day. They were both essentially abbreviators of other men's work, and by the time that the notices about them were inserted in Robert of Torigny's Chronicle their works had been left behind by later scholarship. The greatest enemy to their enduring influence was their method of simplification. When they abbreviated, they rearranged their material: Omnebonus reduced the 101 Distinctiones of Gratian's *Prima Pars* to 26; Vacarius rearranged the matter of the 50 books of the Digest and the 12 books of the Code into 9 books corresponding roughly to the scheme of the Institutes. An admirable simplification for beginners in a new field, but hopelessly confusing as a basis for advanced study. So their works slipped out of the mainstream of Bolognese learning, and survived only in a less demanding environment—for example in England.[1] This was the state of affairs to which the additions in Robert of Torigny's Chronicle bear witness. Where the man who inspired these additions had learnt to admire these works we cannot tell. Probably it was in England. Wherever it was, it must have been a scholastically backward area in which Vacarius could still seem a complete foundation for a legal education.[2]

Whatever their weakness, therefore, as a biographical source these entries are not devoid of information about a phase in legal learning. Above all, they testify to a growing awareness of the progress of learning as a historical phenomenon. Everywhere in the

[1] One of the three surviving MSS. of Omnebonus (with a revised Part I) is English of the late 12th century (Bodleian Library, Tanner MS. 8, pp. 1–299). See G. le Bras in *Rev. des sciences religieuses*, vii (1927), 649–52; viii (1928), 270–3; and in *Bodl. Q.R.* v (1927), 191. The MS. gives no author's name, but begins with a rubric, 'In numero cleri quisquis probus optat haberi / Est opus ut scriptis iugiter meditetur in istis.'

[2] Writing at about the time when the additions to Robert of Torigny's Chronicle were made, Ralph Niger provides independent evidence of the enthusiasm for the *Liber Pauperum* in England among men who, in his view at least, had very little instruction in Roman Law. He writes that he has seen the process of enticing men to Roman Law 'in Italia et maxime in Anglia, ubi quidam scioli picati legibus, in libro qui dicitur "pauperum" de iure minus instructi, equitatem iuris Romani magnificabant' (H. Kantorowicz and B. Smalley, 'An English Theologian's View of Roman Law', *M.A.R.S.* i, 1941–3, pp. 237–52).

late twelfth century chroniclers were awakening to the importance of the new forms of learning and to a curiosity about the men who had brought about the change. Naturally their sources of information were very insecure, and the precise details of the lives of learned men and authors, however little removed in time, were as obscure to them as they are to us. The few facts they reported were remembered or misremembered, reported and misreported, confused and imagined, in ways that are now beyond disentangling. In notices such as these, we see Gratian, already a bishop by 1180, becoming a cardinal by 1230, while Omnebonus and Gratian reversed their roles during the same period, the disciple becoming the master and the master the pupil.[1]

Our next source will disclose an intermediate stage in Gratian's popular transformation, and will show another face of Vacarius in his journey from history to legend.

3. *Gervase of Canterbury*

We now come to the third and most important witness—the only one who connects Vacarius with Oxford. In that part of his *Acta Pontificum Cantuariensis Ecclesiae* which deals with Archbishop Theobald (1139–61) Gervase wrote words about Vacarius which have been held to clinch the argument that he lectured at Oxford in the reign of King Stephen. To assess the authority of these words, they must be considered (as I think they have not been) in their full context. This requires a somewhat long quotation, and for ease of reference I have italicized the passage about Vacarius and supplied some dates in the margin.

1139–43 Erat autem in diebus illis apostolicae sedis legatus Henricus Wintoniensis episcopus, qui erat frater regis. Hic cum de jure legati, licet privilegium suum plusquam deceret extenderet in inmensum, suumque archiepiscopum et episcopos Angliae ut sibi occurrerent quolibet evocaret, indignatus Theodbaldus, et Thomae clerici Lundoniensis industria fretus, egit apud
1143 Celestinum papam, qui Innocentio successit, ut, amoto
1143–5 Henrico, Theodbaldus in Anglia legatione fungeretur. Oriuntur hinc inde discordiae graves, lites et appellationes antea inauditae. Tunc leges et causidici in Angliam primo vocati sunt, quorum primus erat magister Vacarius. *Hic in Oxonefordia legem docuit, et apud Romam magister Gracianus et*

[1] See above, p. 277 n. 3.

Alexander, qui et Rodlandus, in proximo papa futurus, canones compilavit.

1140   Interea mortuo Turstano Eboracensi archiepiscopo, ex dono
1141   regio successit Willelmus. Cujus electioni cum non consentiret
1143   archiepiscopus Theodbaldus, sacravit eum apud Wintoniam
        Henricus ejusdem civitatis episcopus.[1]

There are several things to be said about this message. First of all, although Gervase had no personal knowledge of the period about which he is here writing, he evidently has a very good—one can almost certainly say a contemporary—domestic source.[2] He is able to describe in great detail and accurately the situation in which Archbishop Theobald found himself in the early years of his pontificate. Henry of Blois, bishop of Winchester, had been made legate by Pope Innocent II and during the lifetime of this Pope, Theobald suffered a constant series of humiliations at the legate's hands. The death of Pope Innocent II in September 1143 changed the whole prospect. Theobald at once prepared to go to Rome to stake out his claim to the legatine position with the new Pope, Celestine II. He attempted to get the man who was probably the best equipped Romanist and canonist in England, Gilbert Foliot, to accompany him, but Foliot refused.[3] There can never have been a time when Theobald felt more acutely the need for expert legal advice, and it is in this context that Gervase places his employment of Vacarius. Theobald was well received by Pope Celestine, and he seems to have been given the legatine position which he sought. But Celestine died in March 1144 and his successor, Lucius II, reverted to the policy of Innocent II. Theobald, therefore, returned to England without the legateship, but possibly with Vacarius, and there is plenty of evidence from other sources that the years 1144–5 were filled with incessant strife between the archbishop and Henry of Blois.[4] So far, therefore, Gervase presents a consistent and chronologically intelligible account, and the next event which he describes—the disagreement between Theobald and Henry of Blois over the consecration of the new

---

[1] *Historical Works of Gervase of Canterbury*, ed. W. Stubbs, ii (R.S., 1880), 384–5.

[2] For Gervase's use of earlier sources see Stubbs, op. cit. i (R.S., 1879), pp. xii–xvi; ii, pp. xli–xlii.

[3] A. Saltman, *Theobald, Archbishop of Canterbury* (London, 1956), p. 20.

[4] Ibid., pp. 20–2.

archbishop of York in September 1143—fits into the narrative without difficulty.

But what of the intervening sentence which places Vacarius in a wider setting? It breaks the narrative, and it leaps to the eye that it is a later insertion. Its reference to Gratian in Rome and to Pope Alexander III and his supposed collection of Canons could scarcely have been written before the end of the twelfth century. The sentence has all the appearance of a gloss inserted, perhaps in the first instance marginally, to explain to a later generation who Master Vacarius was. It exhibits the same mixture of knowledge eked out by imagination which we have already found in the additions to the Chronicle of Robert of Torigny. The author of this gloss knew that Gratian's work was a main prop of papal government and assumed that he had worked at Rome; we are half-way to the identification with the Cardinal Gratian of Alexander III's pontificate which we find in Alberic of Trois-Fontaines. Gervase knew also that there were collections of Alexander III's decretals in circulation, and he supposed that Alexander himself had made them. He knew that Vacarius's *Liber Pauperum* was used in connection with lectures on Canon Law at Oxford—did he also make the assumption that Vacarius had himself taught there?

All we can say in answer to this question is that the whole sentence reflects the point of view of the late twelfth or early thirteenth century, and that this was the period at which Gervase was writing.[1] The *Acta Pontificum* itself was written after 1205 and the substance of the sentence under discussion would be entirely consistent with this date. We cannot of course be sure that Gervase himself was the author of this insertion. He may have found it in the source which lay before him in 1205. It may even be an addition by a later hand, for the unique manuscript of the work was not written until 1262.[2] But whatever view we take of it, we must not be misled by the contemporary accuracy of the surrounding

---

[1] Professor Kuttner calls the sentence 'die dunkle Notiz des Gervasius' and dismisses its suggestion that there was a school of Canon Law at Rome in the time of Gratian (*Repertorium der Kanonistik, 1140–1234, Studi e Testi*, lxxi, 1937, p. 128 n.) To make sense, the sentence must either have a comma after *Gratianus*, or a plural verb instead of *compilavit*: either 'While Vacarius taught at Oxford, Gratian taught at Rome, and Roland made a collection of canons'; *or* 'While Vacarius taught at Oxford, Gratian and Roland made a collection of canons at Rome'. In either case, the Oxford–Rome nexus is fanciful. For Gervase's ignorance of events at this time, even at Canterbury, see Stubbs, op. cit. ii, p. xv. [2] For the MS. see Stubbs, ii, p. vii.

details to place this sentence about Vacarius, Gratian, and Alexander III on a similar level of historical fact. What it chiefly tells us is that at the beginning of the thirteenth century these three sources were the subject of a body of teaching at Oxford in which they were all associated in common report.

What does all this amount to? First, the literary evidence which has seemed so solid and coherent to many scholars turns out on inspection to be full of ambiguities—a patchwork of fact and fancy. From it no certain biographical conclusions, but some interesting illustrations of the history of learning, can be drawn. Secondly, there is no evidence of a continuing academic tradition at Oxford until the last years of the twelfth century. Whatever support the hypothesis of Vacarius's lectures at Oxford in the reign of King Stephen may have received from this general picture of academic activity must be discarded. Thirdly, everything we know about Vacarius suggests that he ceased to be a master of the schools in any strict sense of the term when he left Bologna. This does not mean that he never had any pupils in England, but only that there is no institutional framework within which his teaching, if it existed, can be placed.

APPENDIX

A. The Documentary evidence for the career of Master Vacarius in England[1]

Abbreviation: *w.*=witnessed

A. *Charters of Theobald, archbishop of Canterbury (1139–1162)*

i. 1150–4.   *w.* Judgement of archbishop in dispute between abbot of Battle and William, clerk of Hythe (A. Saltman, *Theobald, Archbishop of Canterbury*, p. 242).

ii. 1150–61.   [prob. March 1155]. *w.* notification of settlement of dispute between Templars and Pain, clerk of Findon (ibid., p. 496; B. A. Lees, *Records of the Templars in England in the Twelfth Century*, 1935, pp. 237–8).

---

[1] Much of the information in this Appendix was first collected by Liebermann and Zulueta in the works quoted above, but I have collected it again partly to give it a clearer arrangement, which will bring out the various aspects of Vacarius's career, and partly to add a number of new items, which help to fill in the picture. I am indebted to Professor J. C. Holt, Mrs. M. Lovatt, and Dr. D. M. Smith for their help in providing new material.

B. *Charters of Roger, archbishop of York (1154–1181)*[1]

i. 1159.   *w.* confirmation in favour of monks of Pontefract when their church was consecrated (*E.Y.C.* iii, no. 1477; W. E. Wightman, *The Lacy Family in England and Normandy*, p. 84).

ii. 1170–81.   *w.* confirmation in favour of Warter Priory (*E.Y.C.* x, no. 69).

iii. 1177–86.   *w.* grant at Rouen to royal clerk Roger of Warwick (*Lay Folks Mass Book*, ed. T. F. Simmons (E.E.T.S., 1879), pp. xlv–xlvii; *E.H.R.* xi (1896), 313 n.).

iv. 1180.   *w.* settlement of dispute between the archbishop and canons of Guisborough (*Cartularium Prioratus de Gyseburne*, ed. W. Brown, ii (Surtees Soc., 1894), 47–9).

C. *Documents concerning Roger, archbishop of York (1154–1181)*

i. 1162–7.   *w.* agreement between Archbishop Roger and Bishop of Durham (*E.Y.C.* ii. 276; *Historians of Church of York*, ed. J. Raine, iii (R.S., 1894), 79–81).

ii. 1164.   Magister V. messenger of Archbishop Roger in Paris (*Materials for History of Thomas Becket*, v (R.S., 1881), 117).

iii. 1171.   A witness for the absolution of Archbishop Roger (ibid. vii (R.S., 1885), 500).

iv. 1174–81.   *w.* gift of Nigel de Mowbray to Archbishop Roger (D. A. Greenway, *Charters of the Honour of Mowbray 1107–1191* (British Academy, 1972), p. 212).

D. *Charters of Geoffrey, archbishop of York (1189–1212)*[2]

i. 1191–3/4.   Confirmation by Archbishop Geoffrey of Vacarius's gift of one half of his prebend at Norwell to his nephew Reginald (*Liber Albus* of Southwell, transcript in Reading University Library, pp. 49–50).

ii. 1191–8.   *w.* grant of church of Whatton to canons of Welbeck (London, B.L., MS. Harl. 3640, fols. 124^r and 127^v).

iii. 1191–1205. *w.* at Southwell (?) confirmation of church of Littleborough to canons of Welbeck (B.L., MS. Harl. 3640, fol. 127^v).

---

[1] I have to thank Dr. D. M. Smith for supplying me with photographs of Archbishop Roger's charters from the collection of *Episcopal Acta* in the Borthwick Institute, York.

[2] For this section Mrs. M. Lovatt very kindly allowed me to use the material which she has collected for her work on 'The Career and Administration of Archbishop Geoffrey of York', which will contain the full texts of the archbishop's charters.

E. *Document concerning Geoffrey, archbishop of York (1189–1212)*

i.　after 1195. Letter of Vacarius to Archbishop Geoffrey reporting, as an official of the archbishop, the action taken by Radulfus dean of Croxton in putting the canons of Welbeck in possession of the church of Whatton (B.L., MS. Harl. 3640, fol. 128ᵛ; see below Text no. 1).

F. *Documents concerning the Province of York*

i.　1191–5.　　*w*. Charter of Bishop Hugh of Lincoln in favour of canons of Malton.[1] (*Registrum Antiquissimum*, ed. C. W. Foster and K. Major (Lincoln Record Soc. 1933), ii. 31.)

ii.　1198.　　Nominated, together with the prior of Thurgarton, by Innocent III as a preacher of the Crusade in the Province of York (*Chron. Rogeri de Hovedene*, ed. W. Stubbs (R.S., 1871), iv. 75).

G. *Charters witnessed with canons of Southwell*

i.　*c.* 1167–84. (*Rufford Charters*, ed. C. J. Holdsworth, 2 vols. (Thoroton Soc. xxix, 1972; xxx, 1974) i, no. 172.)

ii.　*c.* 1175–84.　(ibid. i, no. 267.)

iii.　1165–96.　(ibid. ii, no. 338.)

iv.　1196–1200.　(ibid. ii, no. 296.)

v.　　*w*. charter of Reginald son of Reginald knight of Collingham, granting land at Norwell to St. Mary of Southwell (*Liber Albus* of Southwell, p. 373; transcript in Reading University Library, p. 581).

vi.　1191–1205. see D iii above.

H. *Other documents connected with Southwell and its neighbourhood*

i.　1164–7.　　Canon of Southwell (prebendary of Norwell) (Pipe Roll, 13 Henry II, p. 138).

ii.　1184–6.　　Fined for forest offences with canons of Southwell (Pipe Roll, 31 Henry II, p. 114; 32 Henry II, p. 105).

iii.　1186–94.　　ditto (Pipe Roll, 33 Henry II, p. 169; 34 Henry II, p. 196; 6 Richard I, p. 82).

iv.　*c.* 1180–1200.　*w*. with his nephew Leonard a charter of Richard son of Kyre, sealed with the seal of St. Mary of Southwell (*Rufford Charters*, ii, no. 507).

---

[1] Although this is a charter of a Bishop of Lincoln, I am inclined to think that the Master Vacarius who witnessed it was our Master Vacarius, acting on behalf of the Yorkshire beneficiaries, and not the Vacarius who is later found as canon of Lincoln: my reasons are that the latter is never called *Master* and seems at the time of this charter not yet to have been a canon of Lincoln (see below, J iv).

v. *c*.1190.[1]   *w.* judgement of Abbot of Rufford and Master R. de
Capella, canon of Southwell, papal judges-delegate, in dispute
between R. Fitzwalter parson of Whatton and Henry *clericus*,
son of Henry *medicus* of Nottingham, about the chapel of
Aslockton in the parish of Whatton (B.L., MS. Harl. 3640,
fol. 128).

I. *Activity as Papal Judge Delegate*

.   24 March 1176; with Gregory; prior of Bridlington (*E.Y.C.* ix. 241;
see D. A. Greenway, op. cit., p. 247).

ii. 30 June 1177; with Abbot of Fountains (*J.-L.* 13937; *Papal
Decretals relating to the diocese of Lincoln*, ed. W. Holtzmann
and E. W. Kemp, Lincoln Record Soc. xlvii, 1954, pp. 20–1).

iii. 22 July 1179; with Abbot of Vaudey (W. Holtzmann, *Papsturkunden
in England*, 1931, i, no. 169).

iv. 4 Sept. 1179; acting alone in arbitration between St. Faith's,
Horsham, and Coxford, Norfolk (*E.H.R.* xi (1896), 747–8).

v.   undated (Alexander III); with Bishop of Hereford (*J.-L.* 14224;
Lat. III App. XLI. 2).

vi. undated (Alexander III); with Abbots of Rufford and Leicester
(Bodl. MS. Tanner 8, p. 595; see Kuttner and Rathbone, op.
cit., p. 287 n. 18).

vii. *c.* 1180; with Clement Abbot of St. Mary's, York in arbitration
between Bullington Priory and Welbeck Abbey regarding the
churches of Whitton (Lincolnshire) and Roston (Lincolnshire).
(B.L., MS. Harl. 3640, fol. 125; see below Text no. 2).

J. *Vacarius's nephews in England*

i.   *c.* 1170–80. His nephew Leonard brings him the book of Hugh
Speroni (see above p. 264).

ii. *c.* 1180–1200. *w.* with his nephew Leonard (see G iv above).

iii. 1191–3/4. Vacarius grants half his church at Norwell to his
nephew Reginald (see above pp. 260 n. 2, 283 (D i)).

iv. 1196–after *c.* 1212. There is a Vacarius, chaplain to the precentor
of Lincoln (1196–*c.* 1200) and canon of Lincoln (*c.* 1200–after
c. 1212) who is not our Master Vacarius but possibly a nephew.
(*Registrum Antiquissimum*, Lincoln Record Soc. ix (1958), 76;
iv (1937), 161; x (1973), 65–6).

---

[1] This document is clearly connected with a mandate of Clement III of 9
June 1189 (W. Holtzmann, *Papsturkunden in England* (1931), i, no. 26), but it is
hard to know whether it belongs to an earlier or later phase in the dispute. (See
also E i.)

B. Texts

1. See p. 284 (E i) above

Venerabili patri et domino in Christo sibi karissimo G. dei gratia Ebor' archiepiscopo et Angliae primati suus V*acarius* dictus magister, eternam in domino salutem. Noverit discretio vestra quod cum ecclesia de Whatton' auctoritate iudicum delegatorum a supremo pontifice adiudicata fuisset canonicis de Welb', Radulfus tunc decanus de Cokston', voluntate Ade tunc abbatis de Welb' et mea et mandato nostro qui eramus vestri officiales, misit ipsos canonicos in corporalem possessionem prefate ecclesie de Whatton', et hoc primati vestre scripsimus ut super hoc testimonium veritati perhiberemus. Valeat in domino excellentia vestra.

2. See p. 285 (I vii) above

Universis sancte matris ecclesie filiis prior et conventus de Bolington salutem. Noverit universitas vestra nos ratam habere compositionem factam inter nos et A. abbatem et canonicos de Welb' super controversiam quae vertebatur inter nos et Odonem clericum de Whiten' super ecclesiam de Whiten' sicut continetur in scripto iudicum nostrorum C. scilicet abbatis Ebor' et Magistri Vacarii quod in haec verba monstratur: Clemens abbas monasterii Ebor' et Magister Vacarius universis sancte matris ecclesie filiis videntibus vel audientibus literas has, salutem. Notum facimus universitati vestre quod controversia illa, quae vertebatur inter moniales de Boling' et Odonem clericum super ecclesiam de Whiten' cuius possessores extiterunt canonici de Welb', in presentia nostra tali compositione sopita fuit. Prefata ecclesia de Whiten' canonicis de Welb' cum omni integritate sua in perpetuam possessionem remanebit. Et moniales de Bulingt' ecclesiam sancte Edithe de Ristona in Lindeseia cum omnibus appendiciis suis in perpetuum possidebunt, et insuper quandam mansuram in parochia sancti Bavonis in Lincoln'. Sciendum autem quod canonici de Welb' debent warantizare monialibus prefatam ecclesiam de Ristona contra advocatos. Notandum preterea quod si canonici de Welb' prefatam ecclesiam de Ristona aliquo privilegio vel scripto confirmatam habuerint, nihil eis proderit adversus moniales. Similiter si ecclesia de Whiten' in scriptis monialium munita fuerit, non nocebit canonicis. Hanc autem compositionem (confirmavimus MS.) auctoritate apostolica et nostra confirmavimus et ratam fore decrevimus in perpetuum.

Quod autem nos scilicet prior et conventus de Bulingt' de communi consilio huic compositioni assensum prebuerimus et eam perpetuis temporibus ratam esse decrevimus, eam munimine sigilli capituli nostri corroboramus. Coram hiis (*names omitted*).

R. W. SOUTHERN

12

Peter of Corbeil in an English Setting

AMONG the letters of Senatus, prior of Worcester (1189–96), is one to Master William of Tonbridge, 'probably a master at Oxford',[1] a member of the *familiae* of three bishops of Worcester (1186–98),[2] whose progress he had observed with pleasure over the years from his early studies of the liberal arts and law to his present pursuit of theology. But, he warns his friend, the roses of the rich garden of theology have many thorns, dangerous for the unwary. A book has recently appeared in your schools, he continues, in which the unnamed author treats irreverently of the Trinity and other fundamentals, concerning which the prior cites many examples, by chapter or subject.

The incipit given by Senatus is that of the *Quinque libri sententiarum*, published before the year 1170[3] by Peter of Poitiers, the latest of the 'quatuor labyrinthe Francie' attacked by Walter of St. Victor for their outrageous innovations in theological debate.[4]

Despite the protests of the Victorine and of the heir of Saint Wulfstan the condemned volume enjoyed a wide circulation over a long period. Soon after its publication, moreover, an abbreviation was made of which four examples survive,[5] one being the present codex F. 50 in the library of Senatus's cathedral (=W), written about 1200. A scribal error[6] proves that W was copied

---

[1] Cf. R. W. Hunt, 'English Learning in the late Twelfth Century', *T.R.H.S.*, 4th ser., xix (1936), 29 and nn. 2 and 3 for references.

[2] MSS. London, British Libr., Cotton Vesp. B. xxiv, fol. 16ᵛ, Harley 3650, fols. 4 and 77ᵛ; J. H. Bloom, MS. Cat. in Worcester Cathedral Library, Class B. vol. ii, Overbury, PP314B600.

[3] Hunt, op. cit., p. 30 n. 1. For the date of publication of the *Sentences* cf. P. S. Moore, 'The Works of Peter of Poitiers', *Publications in Medieval Studies, Univ. of Notre Dame*, i (Notre Dame, Indiana, 1936), 40. The full text is in *P.L.* ccxi. 790–1280.

[4] P. Glorieux in *Archives*, xix (1952), 187–335, especially pp. 298–304, 310, 315, 327.

[5] Moore, op. cit., p. 174 n.

[6] Mlle M. Dulong, to whom I am deeply indebted for transcripts of many of

from a beautiful late twelfth-century manuscript formerly belonging to another west of England house, the Augustinian priory of Lanthony Secunda, near Gloucester, now MS. 142 of Lambeth Palace Library (=L).[1] The remaining copies are MSS. Dole 98 and Reims 509.[2]

In the Lanthony manuscript the text is not a simple abridgement of the original but includes a number of insertions, sometimes of considerable length, often preceded by the letter .A. Marginal glosses, some in the fine text hand, others in various hands difficult to date but, from their content, probably *c.* 1200, quote the opinions of twelfth-century masters: Gilbert de la Porrée and his followers, Robert Pullen, Hugh of St. Victor, Robert of Melun, John of Tours, the Lombard, Maurice, Odo, Peter Manducator, Peter the Chanter, Paganus, Simon of Tournai, Peter of Corbeil, Simon of Sywell, Baldwin of Canterbury, and three unidentified masters, R., Al., and W. Following the abbreviation in L, and written in the same hand, is a series of *Questiones* one of which has a long description of the council of Reims, part of which recurs in an insertion in the main part of the codex.[3] Again many masters are quoted both in the text and in the accompanying glosses.

The Worcester Cathedral manuscript incorporates in the text many of the marginalia of L and has in addition a number of original glosses of great interest.

On first reading MSS. L and W many years ago I was struck by the number of quotations of Peter of Corbeil in the insertions and glosses and by the frequent marginal references in L, in a very distinctive rough hand, to the *Questiones Magistri W.* Similar references in the same hand, Dr. Hunt pointed out to me at the time, occur in a copy of Peter the Chanter's commentary on the Psalter (MS. Oxford, Bodleian, e Mus. 30), while marginalia by at least one of the scribes glossing L have been added to the main gloss of Peter Lombard's *Sentences* in MS. Corpus Christi College, Oxford, 52 (=C).[4] The provenance of the two Oxford books is

---

the extracts used here, pointed out that the scribe of W col. 138c mistakenly copied two words of a gloss below L fol. 39va into the gloss below fol. 39vb.

[1] N. R. Ker, 'Archbishop Sancroft's Rearrangement of the MSS. of Lambeth Palace', in E. G. W. Bill, *A Catalogue of the MSS. in Lambeth Palace Library* (Oxford, 1972), p. 42.

[2] Cf. p. 287 n. 5 above.

[3] Fols. 117rb, 20^{ra-b}.

[4] I should like to thank Dr. Hunt for calling my attention to these and other

unknown but it is worth noting that the main gloss in C is largely identical with that in MS. O. viii. 9 in Hereford Cathedral Library described in a contemporary twelfth-century hand as the gift of Ralph the archdeacon, presumably Ralph Foliot, a royal justice and a member of the *familiae* of successive archbishops of Canterbury.[1] All four manuscripts L, W, e Mus., and C have, therefore, some connection with the western dioceses. All four have glosses by Peter of Corbeil.

Peter of Corbeil, a theologian lecturing in Paris in the 1190s, was the master of Innocent III and a favourite of Philip Augustus for his wit and his skill in diplomacy.[2] After Innocent's vain attempt to secure his promotion to the deanery of York, he became bishop of Cambrai in 1199 and in 1200, at the instance of the chapter of Sens, he was transferred by the Pope to that see, where for twenty-two years he played a leading role in the affairs of Church and State. Famous as preacher and theologian he was often quoted by Stephen Langton and his followers and contemporaries as Corbulensis and later as Senonensis.[3] He and his *sequaces* upheld one of the three 'most famous opinions' in the christological controversy[4] and he was one of the few theologians quoted by canonists of the French school.[5] But although the only modern scholar who has seriously tried to assess his importance in the development of scholasticism considers him an original thinker whose views concerning the psychology of faith were an essential link in the transition from the ideas of the twelfth century to those of the thirteenth,[6] relatively few of his opinions are in print and not one of his scholarly works has been identified.

Oxford MSS. having connections with L, and for many helpful discussions. At his suggestion I shall prepare an article on the handwriting of the glosses, with illustrations, for the *Bodleian Library Record*.

[1] Cf. A. Morey and C. N. L. Brooke, *Gilbert Foliot and his Letters* (Cambridge, 1965), pp. 45, 270.

[2] John W. Baldwin, *Masters, Princes and Merchants*, 2 vols. (Princeton, N.J., 1970), ii. 36–7, 362–9, for the life and references.

[3] A. M. Landgraf, 'Untersuchungen zur Gelehrtengeschichte des 12. Jahrhunderts', *Miscellanea Giovanni Mercati*, ii (*Studi e Testi*, cxxii, 1946), 264 ff., and *Dogmengeschichte der Frühscholastik*, 3 vols. in 6 parts (Regensburg, 1952–5); cf. also n. 6 below.

[4] O. Lottin, *Recherches de théologie ancienne et médiévale*, vii (1935), 73 f., and E. Rathbone, 'John of Cornwall: a Brief Biography', ibid. xvii (1950), 53 n. 42.

[5] S. Kuttner, *Repertorium der Kanonistik (1140–1243)* (*Studi e Testi*, lxxi, 1937), pp. 60, 64–5, 207.

[6] G. Englhardt, *Die Entwicklung der dogmatischen Glaubenspsychologie in der mittelalterlichen Scholastik*, *Beiträge*, xxx. 4–6 (1933), 37, 116 ff., 123.

The discovery, therefore, of some thirty references to his teachings in four English manuscripts[1] whose interrelations show they must have been accessible, in places not widely separated, to a group of scholars seemed highly significant and worthy of further study.

While the masters quoted Master Peter's opinions on a variety of subjects they were interested above all in his views about sin and related questions, no fewer than thirteen of the extracts, nos. 2–7, 18–22, and 35, drawn from all four manuscripts, being concerned with these matters. Other topics included christology, transubstantiation (nos. 12, 16, *26–*29, 32), justice and mercy (nos. 8 and 14), faith (nos. 30–1), *timor servilis* and *timor initialis* (nos. 9 and 10), temptation (no. 17), and marriage (nos. 13 and 34). Several of the extracts turn on points of grammar (e.g. nos. 4, 26, 27, 30, 33). Obviously the scholars handling these texts must have had, like Langton and his pupil Geoffrey of Poitiers, a high regard for the master of Innocent III with whose published works they were familiar. His *Summa* is quoted in C (nos. 19, *20, *21) and, with specific reference to the chapter on original sin, in e Mus. (no. 35). L has a brief marginal gloss, in the hand usual in such inserted references, *In Questionibus M.P. de Corb. Coitus Abrahe* (no. 13). By a fortunate chance C has a gloss in the same hand beginning *Coitus Abrahe* in which the opinion of Peter of Corbeil is cited among various anonymous arguments. These two glosses evidently refer to a discussion on marriage in a group of theological *questiones* accessible to the users of L and C. But whether Peter of Corbeil was the compiler of the whole group or merely one of the masters quoted cannot yet be determined. The possibility that Master Peter may have commented on Romans is suggested by extract no. 11, though the passage as we have it is discussing the text of Peter of Poitiers. If through these extracts modern scholars are able to trace any of the works of Peter of Corbeil, the unknown masters will have made a notable contribution to our knowledge of one of the most attractive figures in the French schools of their period.

Apart from their value for the history of the Paris schools, what

---

[1] Cf. Appendix, pp. 298 ff. below. The extracts with an asterisk are on the same page as or very close to those specifically ascribed to Peter of Corbeil. It seems probable they may also be his. I have noticed no reference to any other *Summa* but his.

can be learned from L and its associated manuscripts of the scholars who studied them so assiduously, and of the milieu in which they worked? From the wealth of material already collected certain conclusions emerge.

We may begin with the Lanthony codex of the abbreviation of Peter of Poitiers which, since it has palaeographical links with C and e Mus. and was copied by W, seems to have been the central manuscript of the group. It is probable that the insertions in the text of L, two of which quote Peter of Corbeil, may (on the analogy of the marginalia of L that are incorporated in the text of W) represent an earlier gloss stratum in the exemplar from which L was transcribed. They must therefore be early additions. Where were they made? An .A. insertion in the section on the sacraments is suggestive, in that it shows the interpolator at work building up his argument from disparate sources of English origin, especially from two collections of *questiones* of the latter half of the twelfth century in MSS. London, British Libr., Harley 3855 (= H), and Oxford, Bodleian, Rawlinson C. 161 (= R). MS. R, accepted by Dr. Hunt as English, includes two sets of *questiones* which Landgraf considered of the greatest importance;[1] these, we may add, are preceded by the *Sentences* of Peter of Poitiers. In general the insertion abridges the text found in H and R and occasionally omits essential words. For one section where the text of L and W seems hopelessly corrupt the corresponding *questio* in R is given in full for comparison (L fol. 74ra: lines 32–90 below).

L fols. 83vb–84ra, W cols. 305d–306g

.A. Virtus sacramenti inviolabilis est. Dicit enim auctoritas: Tardiores corde etiam intelligunt quod virtus sacramenti nec perversitate dantis nec accipientis violari potest.

Nota igitur quod nomina privativa in *bilis* desinentia quando privant possibilitatem, ut cum dicitur: Hoc est impossibile vel Deus est incom- 5 prehensibilis. Quandoque tollit facilitatem, ut peccatum in Spiritum Sanctum est irremissibile, id est non facile remittitur; quandoque aptitudinem, ut iste est illaudabilis, id est non aptus laudari; quandoque actum, ut iste est instabilis, non quin aliquando stet sed actum stabilitatis removet. 10

[1] A. M. Landgraf, 'Quelques collections de "Quaestiones" de la seconde moitié du XIIe siècle: premier classement', *Recherches de théologie ancienne et médiévale*, vi (1934), 368–93, especially 381, 382–3.

Ad sciendum ergo quid istorum iiiior accipitur cum dicitur: Virtus sacramenti est inviolabilis, nota quid dicatur virtus sacramenti.

Quidam dicunt quod virtus sacramenti est ipsum sacramentum, scilicet tinctio exterior. Alii quod ipse effectus sacramenti scilicet remissio
15 peccati. Alii quod sit ipsa unitas ecclesie in qua est omnis qui sincere accipit sacramentum baptismi. Et hii melius sentiunt. Hec enim nec culpa dantis vel accipientis violari potest. Hec est enim tunica Domini que scindi non potest.

Si enim dicatur secundum alios quod sit ipsum sacramentum vel
20 effectus eiusdem, dicimus quod violari potest, et tribus modis: vel iteratione ut quando scienter iteratur baptismus; vel enormitate ipsius persone ut quando ficte [quis H] accedit; vel etiam quando non fit in forma ecclesie. Si autem queritur de eo qui nesciens iterum baptizatur quid ei conferatur, nihil; sed meritum est danti. Sicut sacerdos qui
25 invenit oblatam benedictam in altari missam super eam dicens, nihil consecrat, quia ibi nihil transubstantiatur quia prius [transubstantiatum erat R]; meretur [fol. 84ra] tamen [sacerdos in R] eo ministerio ...

Dicit itaque M. Maur[itius] quod virtus sacramenti est illa prima institutio sacramenti que facta est a Christo que nullius hominis virtute
30 potest vel debet mutari. M. P. quod virtus sacramenti est unio ecclesie que similiter violari non potest.

L fol. 84ra

R fol. 153ra

L fol. 84ra	R fol. 153ra
33 Item. De ecclesia malignantium sunt qui	Ecclesia malignantium sunt qui
sunt in ecclesia numero non merito	sunt in ecclesia numero non merito, corpore non mente.
35 Sed iste puer baptizatus est in ecclesia corpore non mente; ergo est de ecclesia malignantium. Si numero et merito.	Si iste paruulus baptizatus est in ecclesia corpore non mente; ergo est de ecclesia malignantium. Similiter est in ecclesia numero non merito; ergo non est in ecclesia ut membrum Christi. Si dicas numero et merito, ergo merito suo uel alieno. Probo quod neutrum.
40 Sed ipse nihil meruit	Nullum meritum est in isto nec fuit in isto propter quod esset membrum Christi; ergo iste nullo merito suo est de ecclesia fidelium.
nec parentes eius,	Item nec merito parentum nec aliorum; ergo non merito alieno.

sint enim in
mortali peccato.

Parentes eius semper fuerunt in
mortali peccato,
ergo nec sibi nec filio meruerunt
esse membrum Christi.
Si dicas quod alii meruerint;

Si ecclesia

quia fortassis ecclesia,
sic circa ecclesia meruit isti ut   45

ergo uidetur quod possit
hec eidem demereri.

sit membrum Christi; ergo potest
eidem hoc demereri,
quod nec uidetur.

Item ponatur quod sit adultus et

Item ponatur quod iste paruulus
crescat et

peccet mortaliter.

committat aliquod mortale peccatum.

Ergo uidetur quod

Sic opponitur:
Ecclesia isti meruit ut ipse sit de
ecclesia fidelium et   50

meritum ecclesie cassatur.

meritum ecclesie non potuit cas-
sari;
ergo iste est adhuc membrum
ecclesie. Et positum est prius quod
sit in mortali peccato; ergo simul
potuit esse in mortali peccato et
esse membrum ecclesie.

R(esponsio)

Propter hec inconuenientia
uitanda, dicimus quod

Auctoritas illa

auctoritas illa—
scilicet *ecclesia malignantium sunt
qui sunt in ecclesia numero et* [fol.
153rb] *non merito, corpore non

intelligenda est de adultis qui
sunt in ecclesia numero non
merito.

mente* loquitur de discretis solummodo et adultis,
et ita nulla est obiectio de paruulis
qui licet sint membra ecclesie per
unionem caritatis, tamen non sunt
in ea mente, quia mentem non
possunt mouere ad credendum
uel diligendum.   55

Vel, ut sit generalis,
potest dici quod et pueri sunt
numero et merito, sed nec suo
nec alieno, quia hoc uocabulum
merito accipitur ibi in ui aduerbii,
non in ui nominis;

Tamen
possumus dicere quod sunt
numero et merito sed nec suo nec
alieno, quia hoc uocabulum *merito*
ibi accipitur in ui aduerbii, non in   60
ui nominis.

merito
id est *iuste*
Sicut qui cum originali decedit
merito dampnatur, sed nec suo
nec
65 alieno sed *merito*, id est *iuste*
quia decreto Dei.
Sic ergo paruulus est de ecclesia
merito quia benefitio baptismi.

Vnde quidam dicunt
70 quod sunt paruuli etiam templum
Dei, licet secundum eos non
habeant uirtutes,
et hoc solo
benefitio sacramenti.

Nos uero dicimus
75 quod eis in baptismo
conferuntur uirtutes.

Vt sit sensus:
Iste *merito* est in ecclesia,
id est iste *iuste* est in ecclesia.
Sicut dicit: Qui cum originali
decedit merito damnatur sed nec
merito suo nec
alieno sed *merito*, id est *iuste*,
quia decreto Dei.
Iste ergo paruulus est de ecclesia
merito quia beneficio baptismi;
et est notandum quod omnes
paruuli percipiunt in baptismo
sacramentum et rem sacramenti.
Rem sacramenti dico remissionem
peccatorum omnium et collatio-
nem uirtutum quas omnes habent
paruuli in habitu quidem sed non
in usu, in munere, set non in actu.
Ad quod sic opponitur: Iste
paruulus habet fidem, ergo
operantem per dilectionem uel
non. Si operantem per di(lectio-
nem), ergo habet fidem et usum
fidei, ergo discretus est. Si habet
fidem non operantem, ergo
ociosam, ergo mortuam.
Item iste paruulus habet uirtutes
et non proficit in eis, ergo potius
dicendum est retrogradi quam
stare.
Propter hec argumenta dixerunt
quidam
quod paruuli non habent uirtutes,
concesserunt tamen quod sunt
templum Dei,
et hoc solo
beneficio sacramenti
per quod consecuti sunt remissionem peccatorum sed non collatio-
nem uirtutum.
Nos uero dicimus ut supra dictum
est
quod paruuli in baptismo
conferuntur uirtutes.

Si uero queritur utrum
habeant fidem operantem
per dilectionem uel non,
neutrum concedimus.

Sed quod postea oppositum est de
fide et aliis circa illud, intelligas
dictum esse de adultis.
Si uero instet quis et dicat:
Paruulus habet fidem operantem
per dilectionem uel non,
neutrum concedimus,   80
quia illa disiunctio proponitur de
adultis habentibus fidem in
quibus aut est occiosa aut operans
per dilectionem sicut in simili-
tudine uidere potes. Iste puer
habet rationem, ergo utitur ea uel
cassa est in eo ratio. Sic uidetur
probari quod iste habeat uirtutes.
Iste paruulus est templum Dei et
innocens est ab omni peccato et est
in uia, ergo uirtutes habet. Vel
sic: Iste paruulus baptizatus est
in Christo, ergo Christum induit,
ergo nouum hominem, ergo
uirtutes.

fol. 84^{ra-b}

Quidam dicunt quod baptismus
est aque lauacrum uerbo uite
consecratum;
M. Pe. quod ipsa tinctio.

fol. 152vb

Quidam dicunt quod baptisma
est aque lauacrum uerbo uite
consecratum.
Magister P. dicit quod baptisma
est tinctio.
Sed illi et aliis multis modis potest
opponi.

Nos quod est gratia

que confertur homini quando
intingitur et immergitur in
nomine Patris et Filii et
Spiritus Sancti qua carere non
potest, quia ei inseparabiliter
adheret.

Magister dicit quod baptisma est   85
gratia
que confertur homini quando
immergitur, in
nomine Patris et Filii et
Spiritus Sancti, qua carere non
potest, que ei inseparabiliter   90
adheret.

The first part of the insertion (ll. 1–3) is found in a *questio*
peculiar to the English collections H and R[1] (H. fol. 37^{va-b}, R fols.

[1] Cf. A. M. Landgraf, 'Some Unknown Writings of the Early Scholastic
Period', *New Scholasticism*, iv (1930), 21, 22, for parts of these *questiones*.

145vb–146rb). The interpolator of L, omitting an exemplum, takes up the thread of the *questio* again in the discussion of *verba privativa in bilis desinentia* (ll. 4–24) which seems to constitute a special case of words with this ending treated in a contemporary grammatical work, the *Verba preceptiva*.[1] This treatise, a copy of which Thomas of Marlborough took with him to Evesham after leaving the schools of Exeter and Oxford, Dr. Hunt assigns to the school of Ralph of Beauvais, an English grammarian teaching in France.[2] The text of L, omitting a further discussion of the exemplum in H and R, continues (ll. 24–8) to the end of the *questio* in the Harleian manuscript and then utilizes in developing the argument (ll. 29–32, 33–80, 81–90) three *questiones* found elsewhere in the Rawlinson codex.[3] This insertion, which makes use of no fewer than four *questiones* found together only in an English collection, is lacking in the Reims copy of the abbreviation of Peter of Poitiers, and the same is true of at least one of the citations of Peter of Corbeil.[4] These additions to the original must therefore have been made by someone who had access to English sources. The impression of English orientation is strengthened by other evidence. Dr. Hunt and Miss Smalley have noted the use of *schemata* by several twelfth-century English scholars,[5] a practice Landgraf described as one of various means characteristic of English manuscripts of this period, adopted to make the text more readily usable.[6] In the margins of L, W, and C *schemata* sometimes overlap. Another such device noted by Landgraf is the numbering of columns for ease of reference. In W the columns have contemporary Arabic numerals, and, in the centre space, letters dividing the page vertically. A similar concern for the convenience of

---

[1] MS. London, British Libr., Add. 16380 fol. 122vb: 'Nomina in *bilis* desinentia frequencius dignitatem vel aptitudinem significant ut amabilis, habilis: amabilis id est dignus amari, habilis id est dignus vel aptus haberi. Aliquando autem aliam habent significationem, ut probabilis, quod facile ab auditore recipitur.' Cf. R. W. Hunt, 'Studies in Priscian in the Twelfth Century—II: School of Ralph of Beauvais', *M.A.R.S.* ii (1950), 28.

[2] Hunt, op. cit., p. 14 n. 3 and p. 28.

[3] Fols. 161^{ra-b}, 153^{ra-b}, 152vb.

[4] A comparison of selected rotographs of L with the Reims text established these two points. Later I shall make a more detailed comparison of L, Dole, and Reims.

[5] Hunt, *T.R.H.S.*, 4th ser., xix. 33–4; B. Smalley, *The Becket Conflict and the Schools* (Oxford, 1973), pp. 174, 233.

[6] Cf. A. M. Landgraf, 'Studien zur Theologie des zwölften Jahrhunderts', *Traditio*, i (1943), 213.

students is shown by the glossator who gives for the *Questiones Magistri W.* in L and e Mus., and for a collection of extracts from Augustine in L, quire and folio numbers, often a rubric, and sometimes the incipit of the relevant paragraph.

The palaeographical links between L, C, and e Mus., the references to the *Questiones Magistri W.*,[1] which have must been early additions to L since on fol. 89^{rv} a gloss with a late twelfth-century content has been written round one such reference, and the incorporation of glosses from L, including some by M. Al. and M. W., in the text of W suggest that these manuscripts were closely connected from an early date.

Turning now to the elaborate glosses in L, we find them to be markedly concentrated in certain sections, obviously reflecting the special interests of the compilers. Here, beside the citations of many well-known French and English masters, contemporary and of the previous generation, in the schools of Paris, there is a reference to the English canonist Simon of Sywell, clerk of Archbishop Hubert Walter and one of Thomas of Marlborough's teachers, while references to three unidentified masters—R., Al., and W.— of whom the third seems to be the most important, are conspicuous.

Now M. W. is on several occasions set apart from the masters of Paris—M. W. et Parisienses, M. W. et etiam Parisienses—while in the *Questiones* following the abbreviation of Peter of Poitiers is a long discussion with the rubric *Opinio Parisiensium de homine assumpto*,[2] with marginalia overflowing into the space between the columns, and including one note by Peter of Corbeil (no. 11) and at least one by M. W. This master was therefore to be distinguished from those of Paris. The same would seem to be true of M. Al. (with whom he is sometimes in disagreement), evidently a contemporary since their very frequent glosses are often written by the same scribe. Whether M. W. is identical with the author of the *Questiones M. W.* or with one or other Master W. cited in a work by Abbot Anselm of Pershore (1198–1203) in MS. Royal 2 D. IX of the British Library[3] and in *questiones* in MS. 190 of University College, Oxford,[4] cannot yet be determined. That he is not

---

[1] I hope to publish a list of the *questiones* elsewhere.

[2] Fols. 110vb–111.

[3] Fol. 113vb.

[4] R. W. Hunt, 'The MS. Collection of University College, Oxford', *Bodl.L.R.* iii (1950), 31 (fols. 116^v–118^v, 119^v–123^v).

Willelmus de Montibus seems certain.[1] Could he be Master William of Tonbridge, the friend of Prior Senatus of Worcester,[2] since his glosses in L are to the text of the abbreviation of Peter of Poitiers and sometimes consist of parts of the original text not included in the shorter version? There is so far no evidence whatever.

From this brief discussion it appears that in the last decade of the twelfth century and the years following there was keen interest in the dioceses of the west of England in the latest developments of speculative theology, especially in that of Peter of Poitiers and Peter of Corbeil, among scholars whose activities are revealed in a group of four manuscripts from that region. While these men were familiar with the doctrines of contemporary French schools and those of an earlier generation, they quote on equal terms unidentified masters, R., Al., and W., who it would seem belong nearer home. More intensive study of the glosses in L and other books from the area Lanthony–Worcester–Hereford will undoubtedly bring to light links with other manuscripts and further clues relating to the persons concerned and perhaps to the place of their teaching. Meantime there is endless scope for research and speculation.

E. RATHBONE

APPENDIX

I

From the Insertions and Glosses to the Abbreviation of Peter of Poitiers's Sentences

MSS. London, Lambeth Palace Library 142 = L Worcester Cathedral Library F. 50 = W

1. L fol. 2va margin, W col. 6de text, to an insertion following I. 4 *significationem singulare* (801B), which is in fact Peter of Poitiers's text 806C10–808A8.

Secundum M.p. de Corb. testimonio suorum (rubric L).
Quatuor sunt apud grecos vocabula quibus equipollent iiiior latina:

---

[1] Father MacKinnon found no connection between the material I had collected on M. W. and the writings of Willelmus de Montibus; cf. his thesis, 'The Life and Works of Willelmus de Montibus', MS. Oxford, Bodleian, D.Phil. d. 2214 (1959).

[2] Cf. p. 287 above.

Usia idem est quod essentia; usiosis idem quod subsistentia; ypostasis idem quod substantia; prosopon idem quod persona. Per usiam itaque res significatur secundum quod intelligitur esse. Itaque Pater est usia quia est illa essentia qua est; idem dicitur subsistentia quia autem ipse solus illam habet essentiam. . . . Item ymago est similitudo rei inanimate ad rem inanimatam; parabola facti ad factum; paradigma persone ad personam.

2. L fol. 30va, W col. 103g, an insertion after II. 12, 981A3–7.

M.P. de Curb. Tropo quodam dicitur peccatum pena peccati vel causa. Precedens enim peccatum causa est desertionis a gratia, scilicet causa quare quis deseratur a gratia. Signum autem desertionis est sequens peccatum. Ratione ergo sequele dicitur sequens peccatum esse pena prioris quia scilicet signum est.

Unde sic exponuntur auctoritates: *Omnia peccata media inter primum peccatum et ultimum* etc. Et iterum: *Crimina criminibus vindicantur,* id est, precedentia peccata vindicantur desertione gratie, cuius signa sunt sequentia peccata. Ista auctoritas sic exponitur, scilicet: Que fuerunt oblectamenta homini patienti, Deo sunt instrumenta punienti, id est, peccata in quibus delectatur homo sunt instrumenta, id est quasi documenta, qualiter debeat punire Deus, quia iuxta quantitatem peccatorum punit Deus. Quodam ergo modo instruit Deum quantitas peccati de quantitate pene. Dicimus tamen quod et peccatum recte est instrumentum puniendi quo Deus punit, quia spoliat animam gratuitis et vulnerat in naturalibus. Cum ergo Deus puniat animam, quesito quo? Recte respondetur: Pro instrumento quia peccato punit illam. Si fiat questio pro causa / fol. 30vb formali, se ipso punit illam.

Item numquid contritionem quam habet aliquis de peccato, meruit? Solutio: Contritio active intellecta, que est unum eorum que confert Deus in iustificatione, que sunt fides, motus, contritio, peccatorum remissio, ex gratia datur, et hanc non meruit; et contritio passive quam dicunt aliqui meruisse, quod non diffinio. Vere quidem dicitur quod peccato meruit desertionem gratie. (Cf. no. 23.)

3. W col. 105d margin to *Vere quidem dicitur* in extract no. 2.

M.P. d. Cor. concedat quod omne peccatum est pena. Sed quedam est pena sui ipsius, quedam est pena alterius, quamvis tamen non videatur esse pena quia statim non sentit quid agat, immo delectat eum quamdiu est in actu; sicut est de scabioso quando scalpit se delectat eum, sed cum desinit scalpere sentit amaritudinem.

4. W col. 104d margin to II. 12, 981C7 *Queritur utrum peccata in quantum sunt peccata sint pene* . . .

M.P. de Corb. Nota quod est pena puniens quale est mortale peccatum, et talis pena non habet esse suum a Deo, immo pocius ab homine vel a diabolo. Habet tamen a Deo sicut pena, et unitur peccato Deus ad puniendum tanquam instrumento, homine vero ut ministro, licet invito. Unde quociens homo peccat mortale, velit nolit se ipsum punit.

Est iterum peccatum pena affligens que iuste infligitur a Deo propter peccatum, quale est hebetudo illa que pro velut ex peccato, et illa a Deo est. Sed nonne talis corruptio parificatur peccato corrumpenti ut quanta scilicet sit culpa, tanta et sit pena? Si, inquam, est: Aliquem punit Deus ex condigno, cum soleat dici quod Deus quemcumque punit, citra merita punit. Ideo solent quidam distinguere quoniam Deus punit quandoque pena exteriori et temporali et supra merita, ut Iob, sed illud *supra* ad coronam est. Quandoque punit pena gehennali et tunc *supra* citra merita. Quandoque punit interiori de qua iam diximus, et tunc punit ex condigno. Vel forte etiam interius puniendo punit citra merita. Minor enim sequitur hebetudo ex peccato quam debeatur illi.

5. W col. 131 margin to II. 19, 1016C12 *anima peccati.*

Secundum M.P. de C[orbolio]. Originale peccatum dicitur lex membrorum quia quasi quadam lege choartamur ad veniale peccata saltem. Dicitur etiam tirannus carnis quia velimus nolimus surgunt in nobis primi motus. Dicitur et languor nature quia naturalis potentia languet a bono. Dicitur et fomes peccati quia vicia incendit in nobis. Dicitur autem originale et active, quia prestat originem viciis, et passive, quia contrahitur ab origine. Et inde, quia sicut baculus infixus luto excitat fetorem et trahit immundiciam, ita anima infusa corpori. Et sicut non sentitur fetor luti nisi moveatur, quia talis est natura immobilium, ita nec sentitur nec percipitur corruptio illa carnis donec anima infundatur. Et sicut baculus lutum olet, sic anima vim concupiscibile[m] olet, seu sapit [MS. sapit seu] carnem, sicut vinum sapit lignum vasis.

Item videtur Deo imputandum quod animam scienter infundit vasi corrupto unde scit eam contrahere immundiciam, sicut ei videtur imputandum qui scienter bonum vinum infundit vasi corrupto. Sed ad hoc respondetur quod vas ipsum Deus purum fecit et de materia incorrupta, cui disposuit infundere animam mundam et incorruptam. Sed ipse homo vas sibi a Deo traditum corrupit, nec Deus a dispositione sua ideo cessare debuit. Homo quidem quasi a Deo anime implorat infusionem quociens exercet corruptionis generacionem.

6. W col. 132 top margin to II. 19, 1018D7 *Queritur autem.*

M.P. de C[orbolio]. Ad hoc dicimus quod licet pater et mater sint, tamen dum generant caro ab eis decisa immunda est propter pruritum; ideoque anima ei infusa immundiciam a carne contrahit et efficitur immunda. (Cf. No. 20.)

7. W cols. 141–2 lower margin to an insertion, *Item queritur an primi motus prohibentur ubi dicitur: Non concupisces* between paragraphs 1 and 2, II. 21, 1029A.

Item M.P. de Corb. Primos motus habemus communes cum brutis quia surgunt ex sensualitate que est nobis communis cum illis. Quare ergo nobis imputatur primus motus ad choitum et non illis? R[esponsio] Nobis imputatur primus motus et non illis et hoc tribus de causis: tum ideo quia in nobis habet originem ex vicio sed non illis: tum quia nobis suggerit peccare quod non illis, qui autem alii suggerit peccare in hoc ipso peccat; tum eciam ideo quia nos rationales sumus et possumus per rationem chohibere ne ulterius procedat. (Cf. no. 18.)

8. L fol. 47ra W col. 164c in a long insertion before III. 9, 1058D.

M.Pe. de Curb. sic: Secundum quosdam opus iustitie dicitur ubi evidentior est iusticia, misericordie ubi evidentior est misericordia. Sed melius forte fiet distinctio per positivum quam per comparativum. Est enim idem opus iusticie et misericordie, ut *Parcere penitenti*. Hoc enim dicit auctoritas sic: *Quod Deus iustificat impium et de iusticia et de misericordia est.* (Cf. no. 14.)

9. W col. 179. *.A. Servilis timor est ex tumore ergo est malum*; cf. III. 18, 1082D8.

Magister P. de Corb. concedit quod servilis timor est malus et quoddam donum Dei est malum, sicut quoddam opus Dei scilicet malus homo. Sed licet serviliter timere sit malum non tamen est meritorium pene.

10. W col. 182 to III. 19, 1086B.

M.P. de Corb. Queritur an initialis timor sit virtus quia si est, ergo eius usus est usus meritorius. Sed eius usus est timere penam, ergo ipsum est meritorium. Solutio. Vel dicendum quod non sit virtus, dicitur tamen virtus quia numquam est in aliquo sine socia caritate. Vel, si est virtus, non tamen eius uterque usus est meritorius.

11. L fol. 79^v top margin to IV. 16, 1203C9.

M.P. de Corb. *Numquid Israel non cognovit* Gl[osa] Proprie autem omnes audisse et ita Iudeos audisse, sed quia possent audisse et non cognovisse, affirmat etiam cognovisse. Et post pauca: Israel dicitur cognovisse doctrinam evangelii et adventum Christi quia contradicere non potuerunt ratione vel auctoritate, sed non vere cognoverunt ut menti eorum bene sederet. Item: *Ceteri vero excecati sunt.* Gl[osa] Iudei in voluntate sua adiuti sunt non inmissa malitia sed deserente gratia, ut qui scientes verum dicebat esse falsum de cetero non intelligerent quod verum est, et hoc meruit invidia male voluntatis. Item consequenter ibidem: *Fiat mensa eorum etc.* Gl[osa] Iniquitatem noverunt sed tamen in ea perstiterunt; ex his patet quod sciverunt Christum esse messiam in lege promissum. Cur ergo crucifixerunt, cum scriptum sit: *Si cognovissent* etc. Responsio: Maiores cognoverunt, alii non, et pro illis oravit Dominus in cruce, pro aliis non.

12. L fol. 87ra margin W col. 318ef text in an insertion after V 12, 1247C5. *Iste panis fiet id quod est unitum corpori Christi.*

De sacramento eucharistie sic obicitur: Iste panis est et de cetero non erit. Simus in tempore transubstantiationis; ergo desinet esse; ergo adnullatur vel adnichilatur. Cantor dicit primam illationem falsam esse.

Deest enim in premissis hoc: Et non convertitur in aliud. Quod falsum est. M.P. de Curbull. concedit quod desinet esse, non tamen adnullatur quia in aliud transfertur.

13. L fol. 89ᵛᵇ to V. 17, 1261B2. *Unde cum omnis Iudei teneantur subici legibus* . . .

In margin: In Questionibus M.P. de Corb., *Coitus Abrahe.* (Cf. no. 34.

II

From a Collection of questiones *in* L (*fols. 96ᵛᵃ–123ʳᵇ*) *following the Abbreviation of Peter of Poitiers's* Sentences

14. L fol. 98ᵛᵃ.

Universe vie Domini misericordia et veritas . . . Solutio: *Universe vie etc.* dupliciter solet exponi, id est tantum misericordia et veritas sunt vie Domini; scilicet quedam est misericordia quedam iustitia. Vel sic: *Universe vie Domini.* Omnis via est misericordia et veritas, id est, in qualibet operatione sua Dominus secundum misericordiam suam et iusticiam agit.

M.P. de Curb. Vie Domini due sunt, vel qua incessit ad nos, vel qua nos incedimus ad eum. Qua incessit ad nos due, scilicet duo adventus illius, unus in carnem, alter ad iudicium; primus in misericordia, secundus in iustitia quando reddet unicuique pro meritis. Qua nos incedimus ad eum similiter due, scilicet declinare a malo in quo attenditur iustitia, et facere bonum in quo misericordia. Et hee expositiones sunt sec. Aug[ustinum]. (Cf. no. 8.)

15. L fol. 101 bottom margin.

Item. Esto quod iste simpliciter credat fornicationem esse tantum peccatum quantum adulterium, et fornicetur. Iste tantum se obligat apud Deum quantum credit esse suum peccatum. Ergo tantum peccat quantum se peccare credit. Item tantum contempnit fornicando quantum contempnit et adulterando. Ergo tantum peccat fornicando quantum peccaret adulterando. Sed tantum credit se peccare quantum si peccaret adulterando. Ergo tantum peccat quantum credit se peccare.

Dicit M. P. de Curb. quod quantum putat quis peccare tantum peccat in ascendendo, scilicet ut si committat leve peccatum in genere plurimum se putet peccare; non e contrario, quia non si parum putat peccare parum peccat; sed si multum, multum. Sed si peccaverit quis minus et putet se peccasse magis, non ideo tantum peccavit quantum putat se peccasse. Et est pius error iste et ad maiorem invitat contritionem.

16. L fol. 110ᵛᵇ bottom margin.

M.P. de Curb. non concedit quod Christus sit homo assumptus nec recipit huiusmodi locutiones: Homo assumptus est aliquid, quia hoc nomen homo supponit personam.

III

From Glosses on Peter Lombard's Sentences[1]

MS. Oxford, Corpus Christi Coll. 52 = C

17. fol. 74va (to II, d. 24 c. 3).

M.P. de Corb[olio] dicit: Sicut puer viribus suis potest stare sed non resistere impellenti, sic ipse poterat quidem stare et poterat etiam temptari; sed non poterat, manens in illo statu, temptari et stare, quia impulsus caderet, et ita status mutaretur. Sed M[agister] videtur aliter procedere. Potuit stare, suple *in temptatione,* et tunc melius inferes: ergo poterat resistere temptationi. Sed prior videtur determinanda: in temptatione potuit stare. Hec vera est; sed non potuit in temptatione stare, unde illa illatio falsa est. Et tamen videtur hanc recipere: Potuit stare in temptatione et ita temptationi resistere, sed non mereri quia nihil in eo tunc erat quod ad peccatum impelleret. Item si temptatur, stat vel cadit; sed sive stet temptatus sive cadat non manet ille status; ergo non potuit temptari in illo. R[esponsio]. Status esset in temptatione, sed non maneret. quia esse desineret; tunc puer sine robore stat, sed non resistit impellenti, sed acceptis viribus resistit. Sed hec ultima ratio non facit (74vb) contra Magistrum quia concedit quod poterat temptari in illo statu et resistere temptationi, non tamen mereri, quia illud resistere non esset ei meritorium cum non haberet bona gratuita. Facit autem contra eos qui dicunt quod resistere temptationi esset meritorium, qui forte non concedunt quod posset temptari in illo statu.

*18. fol. 75rb (to II, d. 24 c. 8).

Sicut ipse actus in bruto non est peccatum. sed est in homine, ita primus motus in nostro surgente est peccatum. quamvis non sit peccatum in bruto. Qui enim peccare suggerit, peccat. (Cf. no. 7.)

19. fol. 84ra (to II, d. 32 c. 4 *respondentes dicimus*).

Hec non est opinio M.P. de Corb. Dicit enim quod ille fomes nullo modo sive ante baptismum sive post est a Deo, et hoc probat in *Summa,* sed ab homine vel diabolo.

*20. fol. 84rb (to II, d. 32 c. 8).

Item hic queritur: Deus creavit animam mundam an immundam? M.P. dicit quod immundam, id est, quando fuit immunda; quia quam cito fuit fuit immunda. De hoc in *Summa* [M. Petri de Corbolio?]. (Cf. no. 6.)

*21. fol. 85rb (to II, d. 33 c. 9).

Videtur quod inepte redarguerit eos de intellectu illius auctoritatis: *Ego sum Deus* etc., quia non fuerunt adeo fatui ut ipsam de pena eterna intelligerent ut scilicet aliquis eternaliter puniretur pro morte alterius, si de

---

[1] Cf. p. 289 for the relationship between the main gloss in this manuscript with that in Hereford Cathedral Library O. viii. 9.

pena temporali non erant arguendi. De ea enim intelligi debet. Solutio in *Summa*.

22. fol. 86ʳᵇ (to II, d. 35 c. 1).

Hic agitur non de originali nec veniali sed mortali peccato, quia per hoc quod dicit in prima descriptione contra legem Dei excluditur veniale, quia non est prohibitum cum caveri non possit. Ex hiis tribus descriptionibus tres orte sunt opiniones. de peccato actuali: de prima, quod peccatum actuale consistit tam in voluntate quam locutione quam opere; ex secunda, quod solus actus interior peccatum est; ex tertia quod peccatum nichil est, quia ut illa asserit opinio ea que per privationem dicuntur, non sunt aliqua. Cum ergo ibi dicatur quod peccatum est inobedientia etc., nichil est. M.P. de Cor. dicit quod peccatum aliquid est et ab homine vel a diabolo, non a Deo est.

*23. fol. 87ʳᵇ top (to II, d. 35 c. 10).

In quantum peccatum est Nota cum dicit *In quantum peccatum corruptio boni est* . . . Et nota quod dicit: Que sunt homini oblectamenta faciendi sunt Deo instrumenta puniendi. Ipsis autem actionibus punit nos Deus quasi instrumentis ut ipse deformate a debito fine et virtutis informatione deforment naturalia et corrumpant et hebetent. (Cf. no. 2.)

*24. fol. 87ʳᵇ (to II, d. 35 c. 11 *abstinere*).

M.P. dubitat an hec sint verba [in] originali qũia cum abstinentia sit virtus quare abstinere a cibo nihil esset? Posset etiam aliter solui, sic.

*25. fol. 106ᵛᵃ (to III, d. 14 c. 1 *creare mundum*).

Non provenit quia *creare* cum tali adiuncto non copulat tantum actum. M.P.

26. fol. 106ᵛᵃ (to III, d. 14 c. 2).

Videtur quod conditor huius libri concederet animam Christi scire creare mundum licet non posset. A simili Filius scit generare se quia scit facere quicquid Pater scit facere. Posset dicere quod generare non est agere, et sic non sumitur sub medio, secus si diceretur: Scit creare quia creare est agere. M.P. de Corb. neutrum concedit: *anima Christi scit creare.* quia aliud copulat infinitiuum quam solum actiuum; et hec falsa: *Filius scit generare.*

*27. fol. 106ᵛᵇ top (to III, d. 14 c. 3).

Quare Deus non dedit illi potentiam omnium, ut scientiam (rubric). Cum dicitur scit facere vel creare sic copulatur non tantum scientia sed aptitudo exercicii. Unde magister P. negat hanc: Mancus citharista scit citharizare, licet habeat scientiam citha[rizandi]; et hanc: Anima Christi scit creare mundum vel se vel animam.

*28. fol. 106ᵛᵇ (to III, d. 14 c. 4).

M.P. utramque concedit: Homo habuit eam ab eterno. et idem homo accepit eam in tempore, quia hoc verbum *accepit* determinat respectum nature quia scilicet secundum humanam naturam acceperit. Eiusdem rationis videtur hic: Christus habuit inceptionem. quia incepit esse homo, et sic inceptione incipit esse homo, et sic inceptio ei infuit.

*29. fol. 110ᵛᵇ bottom margin (to III, d. 18 c. 4 *quia potuit consumpta mortalitate*).

M. videtur sibi contrarius cum supra in capitulo *Hic oritur questio ex predictis sumens originem* (III, d. 16 c. 1) dixerit: Christum habuisse necessitatem moriendi. Unde dicit M.P. quod hoc quod hic dicitur falsum est, quia ex quo semel subiectus fuit necessitati mori, non potuit non mori, et sic non potuit consumpta mortalitate supervestiri immortalitate.

30. fol. 115ᵛᵃ (to III, d. 23 c. 4).

Nota M.P. de Corb. Credere Deo vel Deum potest quis fide qualitate informi; credere in Deum, non nisi fide virtute. Cum autum dicitur: Iste credit articulos fidei, hoc verbum *credit* ibi generaliter sumitur ut complectatur et fidem informem et fidem virtutem. Secundum hoc non sequitur talis illatio: Iste credit omnes articulos fidei, ergo credit in Deum.

31. fol. 116ʳᵃ (to III, d. 23 c. 9 *tempore vel causa*).

Hoc secundum propriam assertionem dicit M.P. de Corb. Concedit quod fides virtus scilicet naturaliter precedat.

Hic secundum privatam opinionem. dicebat enim caritatem non esse nisi Spiritum Sanctum.

32. fol. 137ʳᵇ (to IV, d. 10 c. 4).

Deus dixit Verbo mentali, id est Verbum genuit, et facta sunt omnia. Sed vi verbi prolati in voce fit transubstantiatio panis in corpus Christi. Aliter ergo dicitur quod Verbo facta sunt omnia et aliter quod Verbo fit de pane corpus Christi.

Non est concedendum quod panis sit materia corporis Christi, nec quod panis transubstantietur in sanguinem et vinum in carnem, sed panis in carnem et vinum in sanguinem. Item non est admittendum quod panis erit corpus Christi nec quod corpus Christi fuit panis. Videretur enim propter verbum substantivum quod in illa transubstantiatione inveniretur materiam primordialem remanere. Cum verbis autem notantibus transubstantiationem possit competenter admitti huiusmodi: Panis fit corpus Christi; de pane fit corpus Christi; panis consecratur, transubstantiatur, transmutatur in corpus Christi. Hanc autem indiscussam relinquimus: Panis consecratur in Christum, ad quam videtur facere quedam auctoritas in canone misse ubi dicitur: *Corpus rationale.*

Immo hostia sancta ascripta rationalis, trahens nos a ritu bestiali. Et dicitur sic ab effectu quia facit nos sanctos, ascriptos in libro vite et rationales, id est ratione bene utentes. Sic ergo exposita auctoritate, non cogemur hanc admittere: Panis transubstantiatur in Christum vel in personam vel in hominem. Nec ullo modo concessit Magister P. Mand. vel Magister P. de Corb. (Cf. no. 12.)

33. fol .147vb (to IV, d. 18 c. 5 *vel per sanctos suos*).

M. hec determinabit infra sic: non dat digne. Sed non valet hec deter-minatio quia non ipsum sacramentum dat digne nisi per sanctos. Ideo M.P. de Corb. vim dicit esse faciendam in hoc verbo *dat*, ut nemo dicatur dare nisi qui habet. Mali ergo gratiam non dant quamvis illi qui ab eis sacramenta accipiunt digne gratiam consequantur.

34. fol. 162va (to IV, d. 33 c. 1).

Coitus Abrahe cum ancilla fuit legitimus; ergo fuit coniugalis; ergo coniugium fuit inter Abraham et Agar; ergo Ismael fuit de legitimo coniugio; ergo debuit venire ad successionem patris sicut Ysaac. Contra. Non erat heres filius ancille cum filio libere. Item si Agar fuit uxor legitima quare dictum est ei ut eam eiiceret?

M.P. de Corb. dicebat quod non erat matrimonium inter Abraham et Agar et tamen coitus excusabatur propter auctoritatem Spiritus Sancti et sacramentum abdite rei. Tamen aliud innuitur in decretis C. xxxii. q. iiii. Recurrat (c. 2). Ibi dicitur quod Ysmael non suscepit portionem hereditatis quia superbus fuit et sic patri ingratus, unde meruit exheredari. (Cf. no. 13.)

IV

From Glosses to Peter the Chanter's Commentary on the Psalter

35. MSS. Oxford, Bodl., e Mus. 30, p. 121b, and Oxford, Corpus Christi Coll., 49, fol. 133vb (to Ps. 50: 7 *Ecce enim in iniquitatibus conceptus sum*).[1]

Ecce quod vere vincis homines iniusticia quantumcumque iustos, quia *ecce in iniquitatibus* quantus ardor penitentis. qui non solum actualia. sed etiam originale confitetur, et ponit plurale pro singulari. Vel iniquitates pluraliter dicit quia due sunt conceptiones, prima in commixtione et concursu seminum, secunda in infusione anime. In prima contrahitur originale peccatum per causam, in secunda per effectum.

In the margin opposite *Vel iniquitates . . . effectum*: In *Summa* M.P. de C[orbolio] capitulo de originali peccato.

[1] MS. Oxford, Corpus Christi Coll. 49, s. xii^ex, has a number of the same marginalia as MS. e Mus. 30.

13

Oxford University Sermons
1290–1293

THE data collected by Little and Pelster in *Oxford Theology and Theologians c. 1282–1302*[1] have been used mainly in two ways hitherto. Their discoveries have thrown light on the careers and writings of individual masters and on university customs. The content of the *quaestiones* and sermons which they listed and analysed so carefully still remains largely unexplored. Here I shall attack the sermons. Pelster listed 128 university sermons given at Oxford during the academic years 1290–3.[2] The preachers include Dominican and Franciscan friars, seculars, and an occasional guest speaker, such as Raymond Gaufredi, Minister General of the Franciscan Order. Some names are given; other preachers are anonymous; but when a friar preached, the church, whether of the Preachers or Minors, is noted, so that we know which Order the friar belonged to. Pelster described the two manuscripts which contain records of the sermons: Worcester Cathedral Q. 46 (= W) and New College, Oxford, 92 (= N). The two collections overlap: we have two texts in some cases, but not in all. Mr. G. Mifsud has given a fuller account of N in his thesis 'John Sheppey, Bishop of Rochester, as Preacher and Collector of Sermons'.[3]

I shall take the rich information provided by Pelster for granted and also the notices in Dr. Emden's *Biographical Register of the University of Oxford to A.D. 1500*.[4] Readers can look up all the Oxford men referred to in this paper for themselves. Nor is it necessary to offer a full bibliography of recent studies on medieval preaching.[5] These Oxford texts fit into the pattern of university

[1] O.H.S. xcvi (1934), abbreviated here as LP.
[2] LP, pp. 149–215.
[3] MS. Bodleian Library, Oxford, B.Litt. d. 177 (deposited 1953).
[4] Cited in this volume as *B.R.U.O.*
[5] See J. B. Schneyer, *Wegweiser zu lateinischen Predigtreihen des Mittelalters*

sermons of the period. The preachers use the structure and techniques recommended in *Artes praedicandi*. This is clear from the
specimen sermons of Hugh of Hartlepool O.M. and Simon of
Ghent, edited by Little and Pelster from the collection.[1] My aim
is to study the Oxford theologians' interests, concerns, and attitudes as expressed in their sermons. There is room for further
inquiry. Given the number of sermons, the difficulty of the hands,
and the carelessness of the scribes, I had to limit myself to a
sketchy survey. A student who asked different questions, or even
the same, would find much that I have missed out.

The preachers spoke as academics to students and colleagues.
When preaching on saints' days, they appropriated saints who
were reputed to have taught in the schools. Saint Clement, Pope
and Martyr, studied philosophy before his conversion, according
to the *Golden Legend*.[2] 'He was a schoolman, just as we are; afterwards he became a churchman', says Thomas Sutton O.P.[3]
Saint Edmund of Abingdon, archbishop of Canterbury 1233–40,
canonized in 1246, evoked possessive pride. An anonymous
Dominican proclaims on Saint Edmund's feast day: 'He taught
Arts and theology too in this town, to the great honour of the whole
university, which nurtured and brought forth such a man. He was
also a pastor of the Church and primate of this province.'[4] The
chancellor, John Monmouth, quotes the words of 'our blessed
archbishop Saint Edmund' on receiving the viaticum.[5]
An anonymous Franciscan gives a fuller version of the saint's
exclamation on receiving Communion and relates his vision of the
Christ Child, his vision of his dead mother while he was regent in
Arts 'in this university', and his combat with the devil, whom he
mastered by making the sign of the Cross.[6] His assiduity as arch-

(Bayerische Akademie der Wissenschaften, i, 1965), especially pp. 547–55, on
sermons by scholastic preachers. On *exempla* see now C. Delcorno, 'L'exemplum nella predicazione volgare di Giordano da Pisa', *Istituto Veneto, Memorie,*
cl. di scienze morali, lettere ed arti, xxxvi (1972), 3–121.

  [1] LP, pp. 192–215.
  [2] James of Varazze, *Legenda aurea*, ed. Th. Graesse (Leipzig, 1850), p. 779.
  [3] W fol. 26ᵛ.   [4] N fol. 55ᵛ.
  [5] W fol. 195ᵛ, in a sermon preached on Septuagesima Sunday, 1292. See
C. H. Lawrence, *St. Edmund of Abingdon* (Oxford, 1960), p. 104, for the versions
of this story. John Monmouth's comes close to that in the *Life* by Eustace of
Faversham; see ibid., p. 218.
  [6] W fols. 309ᵛ–310ᵛ, preached on 16 November 1290. See Lawrence, op. cit.,

bishop in daily preaching and hearing confessions is mentioned.[1] This friar refers to a 'holy book', by which he seems to mean Saint Edmund's life and example. On clerical learning the saint says and defines in what order, by what means, and to what end one should study. First one should learn what is more efficacious for one's salvation. The pupil should study more eagerly and carefully what most enables him to acquire love and worth, since that is divine science. The purpose should be to obtain one's eternal reward. That is how Saint Edmund studied. The friar contrasts the sordid motives of 'legists and sophists' with Saint Edmund's purity.[2]

His cult was not popular in the later Middle Ages outside Salisbury and Abingdon;[3] so it is interesting to find Oxford theologians appealing to him as a paradigm of the scholar and pastor, and telling of his life and miracles some fifty years after his death. He belonged to Oxford.

We find few specific references to Oxford customs. The preachers blame masters and scholars for the standard sins. The system by which bishops granted licences to beneficed clerks to absent themselves from their cures in order to study at universities comes in for criticism. Friar Nottingham O.P. does not question the purpose of the system, the promotion of study; but he finds fault with the clerks' neglect to appoint suitable priests to take

pp. 101–4. The preacher tells the stories in his own words; it is difficult to know which *Life* he used.

[1] W fol. 310^{rv}. This item could have been taken from several of the *Lives*.

[2] W fol. 310. The preacher compares the Cross to a book, in which the cries of the wicked and the songs of the just are read, apropos the story of how Saint Edmund overthrew the devil by the sign of the Cross. This text follows immediately; but something may have dropped out: 'In sancto etiam libro est specialiter legendum quemadmodum fecit beatus Eadmundus. Bene distinxit de doctrina clericorum et dicit (et) diffinit quo ordine, quo studio, quo fine quis addiscat. Quo ordine, quoniam illud est prius addiscendum quod saluti est efficacius. Quo studio, illud ardentius et attentius est addiscendum per quod maxime amorem et honorem [*sic*, honestatem or bonitatem?] adquirit addiscens. Talis est scientia divina. *Primum* enim *querite regnum Dei* . . . Quo fine, illud principaliter est addiscendum quo adquiritur premium sine fine mansurum . . . Ideo tertio modo addiscebat beatus Eadmundus, et eo modo non addiscunt omnes sophiste nec legiste . . .'

The 'holy' book cannot refer to Saint Edmund's *Speculum Religiosorum* and *Speculum Ecclesie*, ed. H. P. Forshaw (Auctores Brit. Med. Aevi, iii, 1973). Neither version of the *Speculum* has anything resembling this passage of the sermon.

[3] Lawrence, op. cit., pp. 4–5.

charge during their absence. They bargain as to payment; the character and competence of their substitutes do not weigh with them. The incumbent hardly ever resides in his parish, spending his time elsewhere, 'now at Paris, now at Oxford, now with a king or an earl'.[1]

The most valuable item of information concerns the study and practice of medicine at Oxford. Our knowledge of these is scanty for the thirteenth century, perhaps because 'the medical school remained the smallest of the higher faculties'.[2] John Westerfeld O.P. mentions it when outlining the conduct suitable to various groups of scholars in a sermon preached 14 June 1293. Artists should avoid arts which have been banned (as magic, presumably); lawyers should avoid numerous pleas and crooked counsels; medicos should avoid rash treatment in a critical case, where carelessness involves risk. Otherwise they may kill a patient unwittingly by their extravagantly concocted doses. It is one thing to practise and another to receive authorization to do so. Medicos 'in this university' are quite well controlled; but they follow the course for a year or two, or hardly that, and immediately buy a practice on their return home. Westerfeld suggests that the Oxford faculty of medicine, however small, had a tight organization and a significant number of students, though many went down without taking a degree. His complaint against unqualified doctors agrees with evidence already available on the impossibility of restraining quackery outside universities in northern Europe until the fourteenth century. Even then, royal regulations on the expertise required of physicians and surgeons were tentative and ineffective.[3]

Do the sermons tell us anything of Oxford attitudes to politics?

---

[1] N fol. 105ᵛ, W fol. 288. See L. E. Boyle, 'The Constitution "Cum ex eo" of Boniface VIII', *Mediaeval Studies*, xxiv (1962), 263–302.

[2] V. L. Bullough, 'Medical Study at Mediaeval Oxford', *Speculum*, xxxvi (1961), 600–12.

[3] W fol. 47: 'Etiam isti medici vitent medicationes presumptuosas in casu periculoso, ubi possint de levitate incurrere periculum. Quid enim si (per) potiones suas immodeste confectas interficiant vivum hominem contra conscientiam? Possunt vel ministrare vel potestatem ministrandi accipere. Verumtamen in ista universitate satis cohibentur; sed vix audie(n)t per unum vel per duos (annos?) istam scientiam et cum venerint in partibus suis statim baliam pactizarent.'

See V. L. Bullough, 'Training of the Nonuniversity-Educated Medical Practitioners in the Later Middle Ages', *Journal of the History of Medicine and Allied Sciences*, xiv (1959), 446–58. Mrs. Susan Hall kindly helped me on this point.

The years 1290–3 marked the calm before the storms roused by the Bull *Clericis laicos* of 1296 and the baronial opposition to Edward I of 1297. Edward's war taxation fell heavily on clergy and laity alike. There was grumbling in the early 1290s, but no united stand to resist him as yet.[1] Some of our preachers, notably William Hothum O.P., worked in government service as advisers and diplomats. They would hardly have attacked the Crown on grounds of oppression of the Church or extortion from the laity.

Henry Sutton O.M. struck a belligerent note in a sermon on Saint Thomas Becket, preached on 29 December 1292. Saint Thomas exposed himself to martyrdom in defence of righteousness and of 'the liberties of the commonwealth', while his fellow bishops took cover or even opposed him. Afterwards the king, who had proscribed Saint Thomas for no lawful cause, did humble penance at his tomb.[2] Sutton substituted 'the liberties of the commonwealth' for the more usual expression 'liberties of the Church' as the reason for Becket's martyrdom. His fellow bishops, it is assumed, ought to have backed him against Henry II on the wider grounds of 'public good'. If Sutton had a modern parallel in mind, however, he left his hearers to draw it for themselves. An anonymous preacher on the text Matthew 9: 8 states that a ruler is 'good' if he does not depart from justice, and that he is 'bound' to uphold the liberties of the Church. Again the preacher stops short here.[3] Otherwise we find banalities on the difference between the good king and the tyrant with no discussion of the problem of resistance to tyranny.

It is striking from the point of view of politics that preachers on Saint Edmund's day never mention his objections to royal misrule, although he had been a noted mentor of Henry III. I have found no reference to Robert Grosseteste at all. The bishop of Lincoln had no saint's day, since attempts to procure his canonization had failed; but it seems surprising that an Oxford scholar of his status

[1] Michael Prestwich, *War, Politics and Finance under Edward I* (London, 1972).

[2] N fol. 77, W fol. 104^rv: '. . . solus in torculari militans (pro) libertatibus reipublice, ceteris coepiscopis non solum latitantibus, sed etiam ex adverso astantibus . . . ferro compressus est.

[3] W fols. 311^v–312^v. LP overlooked this sermon, which comes between numbers 6 and 7 of the list. The text is from the Gospel for the 24th Sunday after Trinity; see J. Wickham Legg, *The Sarum Missal* (Oxford, 1916), p. 195. No. 7 is for the last Sunday before Advent. Sunday sermons were normally preached by a Dominican.

should have dropped out of mind. His memory could have supplied ammunition to attack tyranny of all sorts.[1] It was not used.

These preachers show their conformity in another way. They like to draw upon the etiquette of the royal court as a source of comparisons or *exempla*. Suppose that the king has given someone the rank of shield-bearer or groom; if he associates with knights and barons instead of keeping to his rank, does he not seem to be criticizing the king, who will certainly put him down? Similarly, we must avoid the sin of pride in God's sight. A man who pushed his way into the royal presence when dirty and badly dressed, and wanted to touch the king's cup, would deserve to be put to shame. Similarly, we must lead a clean life in God's sight. These two comparisons come from sermons by Thomas Sutton O.P.[2] An anonymous secular preacher insists on the respect due to noble rank in a sermon on the feast of Saint Edmund, King and Martyr (20 November 1292). He starts from the text: *Blessed is the land whose king is noble* (Eccles. 10: 17). Men of servile origin make worse rulers than others, he says. It is right to honour nobility. Paris practice offers an example. The chancellor there made no bones about conferring the licence on nobles, whereas he subjected others, however worthy, to long examination. Nobles are an adornment to learning; others are honoured for being learned.[3] This may be an echo of the conflict between the masters and chancellor of Paris university in the years *c.* 1280–90. The masters accused the chancellor of dispensing with the conditions required by the university in favour of a princely candidate, and of withholding the licence from duly qualified men.[4] The anonymous preacher seems to approve of the chancellor's snobbery. It is interesting that he turned to Paris when he needed an example of the honour paid to noblemen. There was less noble pressure on Oxford in this period.

All in all, the preachers are 'establishment-minded'. They

[1] S. Gieben, 'Robert Grosseteste at the Papal Curia, Lyons 1250. Edition of the Documents', *Collectanea Franciscana*, xli (1971), 340–99.

[2] N fol. 100, W fol. 281ᵛ.

[3] N fol. 46, W fol. 150: 'Sicut exemplo Parisius, (ubi) cancellarius, qui ibidem, nobiles faciliter licentians, alios, quantumque valentes, diu in examine tenuit, quia illi scientiam honorant, isti per scientiam honorantur.'

[4] H. Rashdall, *The Universities of Europe in the Middle Ages*, ed. Powicke and Emden (Oxford, 1936), i. 398–400. According to Master Robert of Sorbon (d. 1274) in *De conscientia*, ed. F. Chambon (Paris, 1902), p. 2: 'Multis enim magnatibus fit aliquando gratia ut licentientur sine examinatione.'

compensate for their conformity by harping on the virtue of humility in all walks of life. Saint Thomas Becket set an example of humility to modern doctors by preferring the office of teaching to the honour of the *magisterium*, according to Friar Bothale O.M.[1] Preachers on the feasts of Saint Simon and Saint Jude, of Saint Gregory the Great, and of King Edmund all stress the humility of the saints, and contrast it with the pride shown by modern prelates and rulers.[2] But this is religious, not social, teaching.

The sermons show concern for financial obligations. It was traditional to remind prelates that they should act as stewards, not owners, of the goods of their sees, as did Friar Nottingham O.P.[3] John Westerfeld O.P. takes a more modern line when he compares bishops to salaried employees. He gives an example: 'If you agreed with someone to perform a service, for which he should receive his food and clothing, and he scorned the office he was hired to fulfil immediately on his first day, he would be despised as proud and held in contempt.' 'You prelates', says Westerfeld, 'are certainly hired to do the work of pastoral care.'[4] The chancellor Simon of Ghent applies the same principle to scholars in an Ash Wednesday sermon. He accuses clerks of being laxer than laymen in their Lenten observance and less afraid of excommunication. Clerks who have fallen under the ban do not bother to get absolution until they come to take holy orders. Only then do they remember, and may have to go to the papal Curia to straighten out their 'irregularity'. University clerks should bear in mind that their friends may be making a great effort to support them in the schools, in order that they should profit themselves and others. Now these clerks are doing neither. Indeed, they are putting their parents' help and money to bad uses. Those who have hoped for their protégés' promotion now despair of it.[5] We have moved into a society where men get paid and are held to account if they break

[1] W fol. 246, from a sermon preached on 29 December 1290. Bothale may have got the idea that Becket declined to take a degree from the *Lives*, which state that he did not stay long in the schools; see L. B. Radford, *Thomas of London before his Consecration* (Cambridge, 1894).

[2] See the sermons by Raymond Gaufredi O.M., minister general of the Order, W fols. 294–298ᵛ, Richard of Winchester, W fols. 169–171ᵛ, and an anonymous Franciscan, W fols. 310ᵛ–311.

[3] W fol. 309. The classic piece on this subject was Saint Bernard, *De considera-tione*, III, i. 2, *Opera*, ed. J. Leclercq and H. M. Rochais, iii (Rome, 1963), 432.

[4] W fol. 83ᵛ.   [5] LP, p. 212.

their side of the bargain. The preachers appeal to a cash nexus to reinforce their moral argument.

Turning to strictly academic matters, we may look for traces of two current quarrels. First, do the sermons reflect the controversy between mendicants and seculars, which raged at Paris from 1256 onwards? Here, too, we encounter a lull in the storm. No important contribution to the pamphlet warfare at Paris appeared between 1289 and 1301.[1] The quarrel did not boil up at Oxford until 1303, though it had been simmering for some years. The parties patched up a compromise, without, as far as we know, engaging in pamphlet warfare of the Paris type.[2] To find an English equivalent we have to wait for Fitz Ralph's attack on the mendicants, launched at Avignon in 1350.[3]

These sermons show that the friars made use of their opportunities to put out propaganda for their way of living. Friar Bothale O.M. preached a recruiting sermon on the feast of the Conversion of Saint Paul, telling an *exemplum* to illustrate the danger to one's soul of neglecting a religious vocation in favour of service to a wealthy patron.[4] Thomas Sutton O.P. presented 'voluntary poverty' as the only safe way to heaven. It is hardly possible for a wealthy man not to love his wealth, however much he tries: a rider on horseback cannot trample on the earth, since he is mounted, even though his feet turn downwards, as though he meant to.[5] The fiercest cry of all comes from William Leominster, regent master at Blackfriars, preaching a Lenten sermon in 1293. Certain hissers, 'not theologians, but diabologians' (because the devil speaks through them) persuade men to scorn 'our' call to despise the world. They gloss Christ's counsels of perfection to make them mean that earthly things should be put away in affection, but not in deed. Leominster compares Christ to a master,

---

[1] See Y. M.-J. Congar, 'Aspects ecclésiologiques de la querelle entre mendiants et séculiers dans la seconde moitié du xiiie siècle et le début du xive', *Archives*, xxviii (1961), 50. On the earlier stage of the conflict see M.-M. Dufeil, *Guillaume de Saint-Amour et la polémique universitaire parisienne 1250–1259*. (Paris, 1972).

[2] Rashdall, op. cit. iii. 70–4. For the Cambridge conflict, 1303–6, see M. B. Hackett, *The Original Statutes of Cambridge University. The Text and its History* (Cambridge, 1970), pp. 241–4.

[3] For a summary of the arguments put forward in this last stage of the controversy see K. Walsh, *The 'De Vita Evangelica' of Geoffrey Hardeby, O.E.S.A.* (*c. 1320–c. 1385*). *A Study in the Mendicant Controversies of the Fourteenth Century* (Rome, 1972), pp. 84–111.

[4] W fol. 256.   [5] N fol. 100^v, W fol. 282^v.

who teaches an Art, the Art of perfect living in this case. He hands down the Art to his pupils; they expound it, as he has taught them, by word and by deed, and pass it on to their followers. Then *you* (the diabologian) come along and find another way of expounding the Art. Who believes you? Some infidels![1]

Who were 'the hissers', who denied that voluntary poverty was a condition of perfection? Leominster seems to grant them academic status, since he calls them 'theologians or diabologians'. Either he refers to the secular masters at Paris or he points us to some underground current of opinion at Oxford. The seculars who preached at Oxford 1290–3 neither objected nor retaliated to the friars' arguments, and never attacked them. The sermons indicate that the friars of both Orders were mettlesome and touchy, but that the seculars minded their manners in the pulpit, whatever they may have taught in the schools.

The second quarrel concerned Thomism. Two successive archbishops, Kilwardby and Pecham, had followed the Paris precedent in condemning certain propositions as heretical. These included some which had been taught by Saint Thomas. In 1286 Pecham excommunicated Richard Knapwell O.P. for defying the ban of 1284. The ban was not lifted during Pecham's lifetime; he died on 8 December 1292. He had put the Oxford Dominicans between the hammer and the anvil, since chapters general of their Order enjoined the teaching of Thomist theology. Some of them disobeyed the ban. It failed to prevent discussion and development of Thomist doctrine at Oxford even before Pecham died. The

---

[1] N fol. 102, W fol. 284 (*bis*): 'Nescio quid est. Nos predicamus contemptum mundi et tanto magis se tenent homines ad oppositam partem, sicut quanto magis ventus flat, tanto fortius pastor pallium suum sibi retinuit (*sic*). Credo quod diabolus inmisit novam theologiam, immo diabologiam. Nos persuademus ad contemptum mundi tanquam consilium Dei. Ipsi glosant, (dicentes) quod illud consilium debet (ita) intelligi quod terrena sunt dimittenda affectu, sed non effectu, et dicunt breviter quod omnia consilia debent intelligi secundum affectum suum. Ecce argumentum contra. Ecce unus magister facit unam artem; non dico scientiam. Ipsemet exponit artem, et quia ars est, ideo exponit opere, et discipuli sui post ipsum opere eandem artem exponunt. Tu de novo venis et aliam expositionem invenis. Quis credit tibi? Immo aliqui infideles. Dominus noster Iesus Christus artem perfecte vivendi composuit et dedit totam regulam: *Si vis perfectus esse* . . . Ipse et discipuli sui artem exposuerunt opere et effectu et illud derivaverunt ad alios . . . Si ergo sint aliqui sibilatores, non theologi, sed diabologi, qui contrariam sententiam nobis proponunt, scitote non illos esse qui loquuntur, sed diabolus loquitur per eos.'

Leominster distinguishes an Art from a science because an Art can be practised, whereas a science cannot.

preachers of 1290–3 included two keen Thomists, Thomas Sutton and Robert Orford; another preacher, William Hothum O.P., had done his best to avert Pecham's action against Knapwell.[1]

We might therefore expect to hear sniping, if not gunfire, on the banned propositions in these sermons. No Dominican preacher refers to Saint Thomas or to his theology, nor do the Franciscan preachers mention him by name or criticize him. Only a secular preacher, Simon of Ghent, makes a controversial statement in the Thomist sense; the soul is the 'form and act of the body'. Simon uses it when urging scholars and clerks to behave as 'the form and act' of Christ's mystical body, the Church.[2] He was preaching on Ash Wednesday, 11 February 1293, several months after Pecham's death. Perhaps he felt that it was safe at last to pronounce on the unity versus plurality of forms question in public. Did it cause a stir in his audience, or had most Oxford scholars lost interest in the unity or plurality of forms, which had roused such passions less than ten years earlier?[3]

Feeling curious, I took soundings to see whether the Dominican preachers showed any signs of having studied Saint Thomas. Sutton and Orford obviously had, though they maintained a discreet silence when preaching. But had their confrères? Surely some hint would transpire if the works of Saint Thomas were being read at Blackfriars. It was difficult to find a test case, seeing that the preachers touch on theology mainly to reinforce their moral lessons. However, an anonymous Dominican, preaching on Saint Martin's day, 11 November 1291, raises a question discussed by Saint Thomas in *De magistro*: 'Can a man teach and be called master or is that for God only?' Our preacher does not put his subject into *quaestio* form; but he expounds it in such a way as to offer grounds for comparison with *De magistro*.

The question posed itself in the schools because Saint Augustine taught that God alone can be said to teach by his illumination of man's mind. Robert Bacon O.P., who lectured on the Psalter

---

[1] See now *Thomas von Sutton Quodlibeta*, ed. M. Schmaus (Bayerische Akademie der Wissenschaften, ii, Munich, 1969), pp. vii–xxiii.

[2] LP, p. 211: 'Ideo bene angeli scolares et clerici dici possunt; anima enim est forma et actus corporis. Sic et clerici forma et actus esse debent corporis Christi mistici.'

[3] D. A. Callus, 'The Origins of the Problem of the Unity of Form', *The Thomist*, xxiv (1961), 257–85; 'The Problem of the Unity of Form and Richard Knapwell O.P.', *Mélanges offerts à Étienne Gilson* (Paris/Toronto, 1959), pp. 123–60.

at Oxford in the 1230s, stated clearly on his text *Thou hast taught me, O God, from my youth* (Ps. 70: 17) that God alone teaches us interiorly by illumination of our intellect; human masters teach us exteriorly. Hence a man is called master only by 'indulgence'. Bacon alludes to *De anima* ii. 5 ($417^{b}21$–5), where the Philosopher says that our knowledge comes via the senses; but he falls back upon Saint Augustine, quoting the Gospel: *Be not you called masters; one is your master, who is in heaven* (from Matt. 23: 8–9). Bacon compares divine illumination of the intellect to the sun, which illumines our sight, so that the sun itself and material things become visible; similarly 'the sun of righteousness' illumines the intellect, so that spiritual things may be seen. Hence, Bacon concludes, the name of master must be ascribed to God first and foremost.[1] The discussion took a more sophisticated form after Bacon's day. It came to involve theories of cognition and the part played by the *intellectus agens* in the process of acquiring knowledge. Saint Thomas gave the question his full attention for that very reason. The master's role in imparting knowledge also impinged on the controversy on the mendicants' function in universities. To minimize the value of human endeavour in teaching would have seemed to lessen the need for friar doctors and the dignity of the *magisterium*.

To focus on passages which lend themselves to comparison: the opinion that 'God alone teaches and can be called a master' is supported by three authorities which reappear in our sermon. They are Matthew 23: 8, Saint Augustine's *De magistro*, and the *Gloss* on Romans 10: 17, *Faith cometh by hearing*: 'Although God teaches inwardly, yet his herald proclaims outwardly.' They have one authority for the contrary opinion in common: Saint Paul says: *Wherein I am appointed a preacher and an apostle and teacher* (2 Tim. 1: 11). Both compare what Aristotle says in his *Ethics* on the inculcation of virtuous habits to the acquisition of knowledge. There must be a natural inclination to the virtues as a beginning; but they must be brought to full development by exercise. Similarly, certain seeds of the sciences are already present within us, which make it possible for us to learn them. Another point of contact is their reference to Saint Augustine's *rationes seminales*. Saint Thomas, arguing for the opinion that 'a man can teach and

[1] B. Smalley, 'Robert Bacon and the Early Dominican School at Oxford', *T.R.H.S.* 4th ser. xxx (1948), 17.

be called a teacher', replies to an objection that the pupil's knowledge pre-existed according to the *rationes seminales* implanted in
man's nature by God. He explains that they serve as a starting-
point for the teacher to work upon. Finally, both Saint Thomas
and our preacher deal with the certainty which arises from principles. It is objected, to the opinion that 'a man can teach', that
one man cannot induce inner certainty in another, since he teaches
by outward signs, which cannot bring certainty. Saint Thomas
admits that certainty in a science derives from its principles.
Therefore, the fact that something is known with certainty is due
to the light of reason, by which God speaks to us inwardly, not to
a man, who teaches outwardly, except in so far as the man resolves
conclusions into principles (which alone bring certainty). He could
not do so unless the certitude of principles were already in us. It
follows from Saint Thomas's answer that, as he has explained
previously, the human master works on given material; but he
brings into act what was already present potentially in his pupil.[1]

There the resemblance ends. The anonymous preacher also
wishes to stress the role of the human master; but he sets about it
differently. His text, *I made that in the heavens there should arise
the light that never faileth* (Ecclus. 24: 6), leads him to explain that
God is the first principle, who produces and creates the others.
He then quotes the *Ethics* and applies his proposition to the
acquisition of knowledge, as Saint Thomas did. He then argues
from Saint Augustine and Matthew 23: 8 that we need a human
master to help us to make use of our knowledge, which we have
derived from our senses. Next he adduces the missions of Saint
Peter and Saint Paul, with supporting texts. Hence, he concludes,
'we are God's ministers' to our fellow men. He does not appeal to
the Thomist concept of act and potency, and he chooses a different
illustration to clarify his meaning. Saint Thomas compared the
teacher to a physician, who helps nature to function properly. The
physician is said to be the cause of health in a patient, because he
co-operates with nature to effect a cure. Similarly, a man is said to
be the cause of science in another, because he co-operates with
natural reason. The Oxford Dominican prefers to present the

---

[1] *Quaestiones disputatae. De veritate*, q. xi, a. 1, ed. R. Spiazzi, i (Turin,
1949), pp. 223–8. For the text of the Oxford sermon and references see below,
p. 325. I am most grateful to Dr. L. Minio-Paluello and to Fr. C. Ernst O.P. for
their help on this text.

human master as God's 'instrument' in teaching. Therefore, being instrumental, we need divine grace as well as our natural capacity to perform our task.

Both doctors had the same intention: they wanted to uphold the dignity of the human *magisterium*, without denying that God was the primary source of knowledge. Saint Thomas was disputing; the Oxford doctor was preaching. That would account for the difference in tone. Nevertheless, Saint Thomas's *De magistro* would have been helpful and relevant to the Oxford friar's argument. He ignored it. The likeness comes down to a few obvious *auctoritates*, some of them already known to Robert Bacon, and a comment on a passage of the *Ethics*, which derives from a Thomist milieu. This does not prove that the Oxford friar had read Saint Thomas's *De magistro* or even his commentary on the *Ethics* directly. Indeed, it seems more probable that he had not. The comparison, for what it is worth, suggests that Thomist writings were little studied at Blackfriars. Sutton and Orford may have represented a small élite. It would be misleading to take them as typical.

Sutton himself makes an un-Thomist opposition between faith and reason, when he warns scholars that their faith is likely to waver because they put everything to the test of natural reason. The intellect, by its very nature, wavers if it cannot depend upon reason. This often happens in matters of faith, for which it is impossible for us to find a certain reason in this world. Thus a man who relies on his reason begins to waver. He must resist by faith.[1]

Nor did Thomist 'naturalism' appeal to the Oxford preachers. Saint Thomas modified the traditional teaching on *contemptus mundi* by allowing more value to secular pursuits and human effort, provided that they subserved a supernatural end, than had been customary.[2] At Oxford seculars and mendicants alike kept

---

[1] N fol. 58ᵛ, W fol. 27: 'Et ista fluctuatio temptat maxime viros scholasticos, eo quod assuescunt omnia inquirere per rationem naturalem. Natura intellectus est quod hesitet, si non habet rationem. Ita contingit sepe de fide. Qui est assuetus discutere per rationem omnia, ipse hesitans movetur a vento, eo quod non habet rationem certam de fide, de qua, cum in hoc mundo impossible est certam rationem invenire, ideo innitens se penitus sue rationi incipit hesitare.'

Sutton goes on to quote St. Gregory on reliance on faith; *Moral*. X. x, *P.L.* lxxv. 931.

[2] On the opposing attitudes see R. Bultot, 'La Chartula et l'enseignement du mépris du monde dans les écoles et les universités médiévales', *Studi medievali*,

to the conventional ethics: 'Despise the world and its vanities' they cry in chorus.[1] It was uphill work. Leominster complained in a passage already quoted: 'The more we teach men to despise the world, the more they cling to the opposite side, just as the shepherd wraps his cloak more tightly round him, the harder the wind blows.'[2]

Since their message was not original, some preachers looked for new ways to put it across. Sunshine might succeed better than storm in getting the sinner to loosen his grip on his worldly affections. Leominster tried gentle encouragement instead of denunciation. Pursuit of virtue is like copying the alphabet; the master scribe will not blame a beginner who cannot do it exactly. Or take scaling a mountain: you show willing if you put your baggage down and climb as high as you can. A gardener just tries to make his plants grow as tall as possible.[3]

Other preachers resort to pagan learning as a bait for their audience. It was an old trick to make comparisons from the *Libri naturales*, helped out by bestiary and lapidary lore. The *Ethics* presented a more exciting challenge by raising the question of values. An anonymous Franciscan, preaching on Maundy Thursday, 1291, transposes the Gospel into Aristotelian terms.[4] Aristotle defines man as a rational animal, as a social animal, and as a civilized animal. To be rational means subordinating the passions to reason.[5] To be social is to love all one's fellow men and not one's kin only, as beasts do. Here the preacher quotes 'the Commentator' (Saint Thomas) on the *Ethics*.[6] To be civilized (*mansuetus*) is to 'observe a certain mean with respect to anger' and to keep one's temper, also to be humble, obedient, and tractable.[7] Our friar

ser. III, viii (1967), 784–834; R. A. Gautier, *Magnanimité l'idéal de la grandeur dans la philosophie païenne et la théologie chrétienne* (Paris, 1951), 443–66.

[1] See for instance a sermon by the secular master John Monmouth, W fols. 194–195[v].

[2] See above, p. 315 n. 1.

[3] W fol. 204, an Ash Wednesday sermon, 1292.

[4] W fol. 158[rv].   [5] *Pol.* vii. 13, 1332[b]3–5.

[6] '... est homo animal sociale, ut dicit commentator super i Ethic.: Politicum animal est homo, politicum, id est sociale et communicativum.' From Saint Thomas, *Com. in Ethic. Nicom.* i. 7, 1097[b]11, ed. R. M. Spiazzi (Turin, 1964), p. 31: 'Homo naturaliter est animal civile.' See also *De regimine principum*, i. 1, ed. J. Mathis (1948), p. 1.

[7] He quotes *Topica*, v. 1, 128[b]17–18, and alludes to *Ethic. Nicom.* iv. 5, 1125[b] 25–6, and perhaps to Saint Thomas's commentary, op. cit., p. 222: 'Mansuetudo autem est quaedam medietas circa iras ... vult mansuetus imperturbatus esse.'

explains that Jesus showed all these qualities both in life and in death. For instance, Christ's gift of his body to his disciples at the Last Supper resembled the 'social gift', which a friend makes to his friends on his departure as a memorial. Further, Christ's love for the commonwealth was great indeed, since he, so noble, exposed himself to a terrible death for its sake. Quotations from Cicero and Ecclesiasticus on friendship clinch this part of the argument.[1] The preacher has put much ingenuity into co-ordinating Aristotle and the Gospel, without sacrificing Christian doctrine and feeling. It is interesting that a Franciscan, not a Dominican, should have quoted Saint Thomas on the *Ethics*.

Another way to use pagan learning was to tell stories of 'the philosophers'. John of Wales O.M., who died probably in 1285, had promoted this method by drawing up collections of tales about the philosophers' lives and sayings. He intended them for retail in social converse and in sermons. The pagan sages set an example to Christians by their austere detachment from the world; Anaxagoras struck him as a *magnificus contemptor mundi*.[2] There were Dominican precedents too. Saint Albert told stories of pagan philosophers and expressed admiration for the Roman emperors, who were better than modern rulers, except for the one drawback of not being Christians.[3] However, John of Wales was more influential at Oxford.

John's sober tales must have whetted the appetite for more exotic fare. Pseudo-classical *exempla* came into fashion; stories are fitted into an imaginary setting with 'classical features'. An anonymous Franciscan gives us an early specimen in an Easter Week sermon of 1293 to illustrate his lesson that a wise man will accept his share of troubles, without complaining at the human lot: 'Note how the philosophers posited two jars on the threshold of the house of Jove. All who entered had to drink from both jars. According to the philosophers, Jove's house is the world; the two jars signify prosperity and adversity, which comers into the world

---

[1] *De amicitia*, iv. 15: 'ab omnibus seculis vix tres aut quatuor nominantur (paria) amicorum'; Ecclus. 6: 15, 10.

[2] *Compendiloquium* (Venice, 1496), pars iii. 1. fol. 181H. On John of Wales see now Balduinus ab Amsterdam, 'The Commentary on St. John's Gospel, etc', *Collectanea Franciscana*, xl (1970), 71–96.

[3] J. B. Schneyer, 'Alberts des Grossen Augsburger Prediktzyklus über den hl. Augustinus', *Recherches de Théologie ancienne et médiévale*, xxxvi (1969), 114. The sermons were preached in 1257 or 1263.

must taste.'[1] This pseudo-antique type of *exemplum* had a brilliant future. The tale of the two jars reappears in a more developed form in a collection probably made by an Italian Austin friar, Michele da Massa Marittima (d. 1337), who seems to have drawn on English material.[2] The Oxford Franciscan gives an early instance of its use. Two other Franciscan preachers tell the story of the philosopher who fell into a ditch while star-gazing; but that was an old favourite.[3]

John Westerfeld O.P., a lively preacher, made the most daring use of the new technique. He may have belonged to the younger age group, since he visited Bordeaux as proctor for the Cambridge Blackfriars over twenty years later in 1316.[4] His sermon for the second Sunday after Easter shows him exploiting and distorting the data on pagan religion assembled by Saint Augustine in his *City of God*. John of Wales may have suggested the idea to Westerfeld; but he carried it further. Preaching on the Resurrection, he tries to move his hearers to gratitude and pity for the death of the Saviour by stressing the point that pagans regarded life as the most precious of all good things. The Athenians believed that the sun was 'the living god'. They judged Anaxagoras guilty and stoned him for holding that the sun was merely a burning lantern.[5] Westerfeld refers to the *City of God*: but he or his secondary source (if he had one) embroidered on Saint Augustine, who told the story in order to attack pagan beliefs as self-contradictory. He did not say that Anaxagoras was 'stoned' by the Athenians either.[6] Westerfeld presents the Athenians as having an inkling of the

---

[1] W fol. 270.

[2] B. Smalley, *English Friars and Antiquity in the Early Fourteenth Century* (Oxford, 1960), pp. 265–71, 347, 377.

[3] In one sermon it is referred directly and correctly to *Ethic. Nicom.* (vi. 7, 1141[b]), W fol. 268[v]; in another it is told in the more developed form which became popular with preachers, W fol. 254[v]; see Delcorno, op. cit., p. 73. St. Peter Damian was already using it as an *exemplum c.* 1067; see *Lettre sur la toute-puissance divine*, ed. and transl. A. Cantin (Paris, 1972), pp. 460–2 and *P.L.* clxv. 615.

[4] A. B. Emden, *A Biographical Register of the University of Cambridge to 1500* (Cambridge, 1963), p. 630.

[5] W fols. 213[v]–214, N fol. 112: 'Karissimi, si respiciamus bene ad gesta et dicta antiquorum, videre poterimus quod etiam ipsi pagani vitam precipue pre aliis eligibilem poneba(n)t, in tantum ut etiam deos vivos dicerent, ut manifeste dicit Augustinus, de civitate Dei, 18, quod Anaxagoras apud Athenienses factus est reus et lapidatus est, eo quod solem posuit ardentem lampadem, quem ipsi deum vivum esse dicebant.'

[6] *De civ. Dei* xviii. 41.

truth: they ascribed life to their gods; that was not Saint Augustine's intention.

We go on to Pythagoras: he first posited the soul's immortality and taught that it would receive rewards and punishments after death.[1] Westerfeld brings out the philosophers' expectation and hope of a future life. Saint Augustine attacked the pagan attitude to suicide by citing the death of Cleombrotus, who threw himself off a wall after reading Plato's book on the immortality of the soul, in order to pass from this life to a better one.[2] John of Wales had already told the story in a corrupt form; the name of the reader of Plato's book becomes its title, *Theobrotus*! John tells it to exemplify, not pagan error, but the philosophers' yearning for blessedness hereafter. Westerfeld puts it to the same purpose, and quotes it in the same form as John of Wales, who was probably his source. His praise of the philosophers leads up to the superiority of Christian doctrine: 'But they all lacked knowledge of the true life.' Christ alone promises true blessedness.[3]

Later in the sermon Westerfeld tells another story to illustrate Aristotle's saying that life is more precious to a virtuous man than to a bad one.[4] This tale had a long pedigree. Westerfeld probably got it from John of Wales; but he tells it vividly in his own words:

Agellius tells of a Stoic philosopher called Puplius that he had to cross the sea. When they ran into danger, he turned pale and was very upset. Someone said to him: 'You're a great man indeed, and yet you show fear at so small a thing. *I'm* not afraid!' He answered and said: 'You worthless fellow! It's no wonder that I worry about a philosopher's soul, whereas you've only to worry about a rascal's.' He made a very good answer, since life is more desirable to the virtuous man, as Aristotle says, than it is to another.

---

[1] W fols. 213ᵛ–214: 'Pictagoras etiam primo (im)mortalitatem anime posuit (et) etiam ei fore premia et penas post hanc vitam.' Knowledge of the Pythagorean doctrine of the soul was common. Westerfeld could have derived it from John of Salisbury's *Policraticus* vii. 4, ed. C. C. Webb (Oxford, 1909), ii. 104.

[2] *De civ. Dei* i. 22.

[3] W fols. 213ᵛ–214: 'Omnes aliam vitam commendabant et aliam huic vite preferebant. Ideo quidam paganus, ut dicitur in libro Platonis, qui liber vocatur Teobrodus, ubi disputatur de immortalitate anime, se precipitem muro dedit, ut transierit ab hac vita ad aliam, quam credidit multo meliorem . . . Omnes isti tamen veram vitam ignoraverunt.' See *Compendiloquium* pars i, cap. 8, ed. cit., fol. 177D–E.

[4] *Ethic. Nicom.* ix. 9, 1170ᵃ25–8; 1170ᵇ1–5.

Westerfeld proceeds to apply the tale and Aristotle's dictum to Christ.[1]

Lastly, he treats us to a risky joke in a sermon preached on 14 June 1293. Exhorting prelates to fulfil their function, he quotes Christ's command to Saint Peter, thrice repeated: *Feed my sheep* (John 21: 15–17): 'Know that Christ does not say *Feed* three times to authorize you to take three meals a day or to drink between meals, but tells you to *feed* your subjects by word, example, and temporal aid.'[2] Robert Holcot makes the same crack in his Wisdom commentary, though here it is a novice who claims three meals a day on the strength of the command to Saint Peter.[3] The fourteenth-century Dominican was a master of wit and humour. The joke accords with his character. But Westerfeld stands out as exceptional for his light touch among his fellow preachers.

To sum up: these sermons give a negative impression at first sight. The preachers keep quiet on both English and local politics. We hear only faint echoes of the quarrel between mendicants and seculars, and nothing of the ban on Thomism. The silence on Saint Thomas is not surprising, given that Saint Edmund of Abingdon is the only thirteenth-century scholar to be mentioned by name. But none of the preachers, except Simon of Ghent, makes any reference to Thomist doctrine, as far as I can see. The university sermon must have been the most taxing and thankless of academic exercises. The doctors may well have found it a chore. A clerical audience did not need that basic instruction on the creed and the sacraments which was suitable for laymen. The preachers in fact say little on the sacraments, though penance may be commended

---

[1] W fol. 214ᵛ: 'Ideo narratur de philosopho stoico, qui vocabatur Puplius. Agellius de eo narrat quod debuit transire quoddam mare, qui, cum ceperunt periclitari, pallere cepit et tristari valde, cui dixit unus: tu es tantus ac talis, et pro tam modico times, et ego non timeo. Cui respondens dixit; pessime ribalde, non est mirum (quod) ego sollicitus sum circa animam unius philosophi. Tu non es sollicitus nisi circa tuam animam nebulonis. Et optime respondit, quoniam vita est eligibilior ipsi virtuoso, ut dicit Aristoteles, quam alii, quoniam plurima consequitur delectatio ipsum virtuosum. Ex quo igitur Dominus noster fuit supra virtutes omnes, eius mors et privatio (vite) maius malum fuit.'

The tale came down through Aulus Gellius, Saint Augustine, John of Salisbury, and John of Wales. Westerfeld is the first to call the philosopher 'Publius'. The next chapter in *Compendiloquium* is headed 'De Publio et eius egregiis sententiis' (pars iv, cap. 11, ed. cit., fol. 209Q.). Westerfeld may have taken the name from there. See *Noct. Attic.* xix. 1; *De civ. Dei* ix. 4; *Policr.* vii. 3.

[2] W fol. 47ᵛ.

[3] Smalley, op. cit., pp. 192, 332.

in a Lenten sermon.[1] On the other hand, the stimulus of disputation was absent. How could one hold the attention, much less move the hearts or prick the consciences of blasé clerks?

Some preachers sought new answers to the problem. Here we come to the positive side of the sermons. Previously a gap opened out in the history of classical studies at Oxford. The didactic collections of tales about ancient philosophers made by John of Wales before 1285 seemed a poor preparation for the creative scholarship which began with Nicholas Trevet at the turn of the century and continued in the works of Thomas Waleys, John Ridevall, and Robert Holcot.[2] The preachers of 1290–3 do something to close the gap. None of them were classical scholars in the strict sense or book-hunters; but some had a spark of curiosity. His admiring interest in pagan antiquities sent John Westerfeld to the *City of God* as a source of information. He both recalls John of Wales and looks forward to Trevet and Waleys. An anonymous Franciscan tells the Gospel story in terms of the *Ethics*, as Thomas Waleys would do more daringly.[3] Another Franciscan tells a pseudo-antique *exemplum* of the type which appealed to Holcot and the compilers of *Gesta Romanorum*. Further research on Oxford in the later thirteenth century may uncover more evidence on Trevet's background. Already the first medieval commentator on *De civitate Dei* and *Ab Urbe condita* rises in a less meteoric fashion than he seemed to before. The 'classicizing friars' of the early fourteenth century had their humble forerunners.

B. SMALLEY

APPENDIX
W fols. 302ᵛ–303

Ego feci in celis ut oriretur lumen indeficiens, in Ecclesiastico.[4] Karissimi, bene videtis quod quamvis lumen ad solatium hominum omnibus communicetur per illuminationem medii, est tamen a quodam principio, puta a corpore solari, et quia non solummodo ab illo producitur principio, sed etiam a Domino, ideo non solum est illud principium quod suo radio (MS. sui radii) medium illuminat, immo ipse Deus principium est, qui aliud principium producit et creat, de quo in Matheo: *Qui solem oriri facit super bonos et malos*.[5] Non igitur (solum)

---

[1] W fols. 276ᵛ–278.   [2] Smalley, op. cit., pp. 45–202.
[3] Ibid., pp. 106–7.   [4] 24: 6.   [5] 5: 45.

tales res sunt principia a quibus exeunt alie, sed etiam Deus, qui talia principia voluit rebus imprimere, de quibus principiis dicit Sapiens, 6 Moralium, quod mores (? MS. ipse res) ante complementum preexistunt in quibusdam principiis.[1] Hoc etiam apparet in adnascentibus, quorum principia consistunt in semine, et quia tales a Deo producuntur, non solum dicitur homo principium, qui tales res seminat et plantat, immo Deus ipse.

Hec autem pro tanto diceremus, quia sicut est ita in moralibus, sic erit in speculativis. Deus enim quedam principia nobis impressit, que sunt per se cognita, in quibus que ad ipsa consecuntur necessario virtualiter preexistunt. Ex quo dico quod lumen illorum principiorum in cognitionem aliorum inducit. Ipse autem superior doctor noster est, qui ista nobis inmisit, unde Matheus: *Unus est magister vester.*[2] Etiam Augustinus: Docet ipse solus in terris, qui cathedram habet in celis.[3] Sed quia nostra cognitio intellectiva ortum habet a sensu, ideo sub istis exemplaribus proponuntur nobis quedam particularia exempla.[4] [fol. 303] Hinc est quod potest dici alius noster magister, quoniam *fides est ex auditu.*[5] Ideo oportet esse alium qui exterius annuntiet; ad Romanos: Quamquam Christus veritatem interius doceat, preco tamen exterius annuntiat.[6] 2° ad Tim.: *In quo positus sum ego doctor et magister.*[7] Christus ergo doctor et magister (est).[8]

Christus ergo doctor noster est interius illuminando, homo autem exterius annuntiando. Unde Augustinus, de doctrina christiana, cap. 3°: Cognoscimus Paulum apostolum, licet a Deo consecratum, ad hominem tamen missum, ut ecclesiam Dei confortaret, (et) etiam Petrum Cornelio missum. In Petro igitur ad Cornelium misso et Paulo ad centurionem significatur quod non solum ut ecclesie Dei copulentur a Deo consecrentur, immo istos ad hominem mittuntur. Cuius rationem

---

[1] Cf. Aquinas, *De magistro*, ed. cit., p. 225: 'Similiter etiam secundum ipsius sententiam in VI Ethicorum, virtutum habitus ante earum consummationem praeexistunt in nobis in quibusdam naturalibus inclinationibus, quae sunt quaedam virtutum inchoationes, sed postea per exercitium operum adducuntur in debitam consummationem.'
The reference is to *Ethic. Nicom.* vi. 13, 1144ᵇ1–17. Aquinas uses the same terminology in commenting on the passage; cf. his commentary on the *Ethics* vi, lect. xi, ed. R. M. Spiazzi (Turin, 1964), p. 346. See also St. Albert on the same passage, ed. Borgnet, *Opera*, vii (Paris, 1891), 459*a*–460*a*.

[2] 23: 8. Gloss. Ord. ad loc.: 'Qui illuminat hominem, quod non (facit) alius homo, sed tantum exerceat docendo; non intellectum prestat.'

[3] Cf. *De magistro*, cap. xlvi.

[4] Cf. Aristotle, *De anima* ii. 5, 417ᵇ20–8.

[5] Rom. 10: 17.

[6] Cf. Peter Lombard, comm. ad loc (*P.L.* cxcii. 1479).

[7] Cf. 2 Tim. 1: 11.

[8] Peter Lombard, op. cit.: '*auditus autem per verbum Christi*, id est per gratiam Christi doctores evangelici.'

subdit: Abiecta esset humana conditio, si per homines hominibus nichil ministrari videretur, nec verificaretur quod templum sanctum Dei estis vos.[1] Quoniam sanctificamur per fidem, fides autem instituitur per auditum, auditus autem informatur per divini verbi annuntiationem, igitur a principio per annuntiationem verbi divini sancti efficimur. Igitur ad hoc quod hoc sit verum, *templum sanctum Dei quod estis vos,*[2] quia homines hominibus verba Dei annuntiant, illis hominibus delectando et difficilia exponendo, ideo, ut dicitur ad Corinthios: *Dei coadiutores sumus*[3] in dispensatione verbi Domini. Ideo sumus ministri Dei.[4]

Ministeria rationem instrumenti habent respectu principalis agentis. Instrumentum autem, ad hoc quod effectum intentum ab agente attingat, necesse (est) ut agens aliquid sibi imprimit ultra virtutem sibi ex natura propria impressam. Ideo, cum nos sumus quasi instrumenta Dei, indigemus aliqua spirituali impressione a Deo, que quidem impressio est divine gratie communicatio.

[1] *De doctr. Christ.* prol. 6.   [2] 1 Cor. 3: 17.
[3] Cf. 1 Cor. 3: 19.   [4] Cf. 2 Cor. 6: 4.

14

Nicholas Trevet, Historian[1]

IN an essay on the manuscripts of Nicholas Trevet's Anglo-Norman *Cronicles* which I dedicated to the late E. A. Lowe, dean of palaeographers, I promised to treat Trevet's three historical works in a later study.[2] Since Trevet was an Oxford scholar, it seems appropriate to offer that study to a modern Oxford scholar whom I first knew as a fellow student of Dr. Lowe's and who has contributed so much to so many studies of history and of manuscripts. The present volume must surely be one of the few Oxford medieval studies of recent years to omit from the foreword an expression of gratitude for 'the generous help of Dr. R. W. Hunt'. No doubt the other contributors feel as indebted to his learning and kindness as I do.

The fourteenth-century Oxford scholar Nicholas Trevet has been characterized by Dr. Smalley as a 'true polymath, being theologian, biblicist, hebraist, historian and classicist', and she herself has been concerned with him in three of these roles: as biblicist, hebraist, and classicist.[3] It is in a fourth role, that of historian, that he now concerns us, though my paper makes no pretensions to the scope of Dr. Smalley's studies. I shall simply present some materials that may contribute to more detailed studies by future editors.

Nicholas Trevet was born between 1258 and 1268, son of Sir Thomas Trevet, a justice in eyre under Henry III and Edward I.[4]

---

[1] An abridged form of this essay was read as the presidential address to the Mediaeval Academy of America on 10 May 1974.

[2] Ruth J. Dean, 'The Manuscripts of Nicholas Trevet's Anglo-Norman *Cronicles*', *Medievalia et Humanistica*, xiv (1962), 95–105.

[3] Beryl Smalley, *The Study of the Bible in the Middle Ages* (2nd edn., Oxford, 1952), and *English Friars and Antiquity in the Early Fourteenth Century* (Oxford, 1960); in both, see Trevet as indexed.

[4] Information about Trevet is conveniently assembled in Emden, *B.R.U.O.* iii. 1902–3. The origin of an erroneous statement about Trevet's historical works is discussed in the present paper. To Emden's work can now be added Ruth

The Trevets were (and still are) a Somerset family, but Sir Thomas acquired property in Norfolk upon his first marriage. This fact gives colour to Leland's unsupported statement that Nicholas was born in that county, and it may have contributed to Sir Thomas's being appointed in 1272 to investigate a fire started by rioters in Norwich cathedral. Contemporary records of Nicholas's early education do not survive but we know that he joined the Order of Preachers, spent some time in Italy, was a master in the schools of Oxford, and sojourned for an unspecified period in the *studium* of Paris: 'cum aliquando in studio moraremur Parisiensi'.[1] A few of his university disputations are extant but his renown in the Middle Ages, as in modern times, is based not on philosophical and theological treatises, like those of more famous masters at Oxford or Paris, but on commentaries of a severely practical, didactic nature, and on historical works.

Trevet's earliest commentary, on Boethius's *Consolation of Philosophy*, which had the widest circulation of all of his numerous and varied works, may have served as a school-text though it was written for a friend. A commentary on the *Disciplina scolarium* of Pseudo-Boethius attributed to Trevet and shorter treatises that are surely his—on the Hebrew computus, on canons of conjunctions and eclipses, on the office of the Mass—suggest schoolroom use.[2] The major part of his work falls, however, outside the normal range of medieval academic instruction.

Trevet's commentaries generally follow the usual scholastic method,[3] but his earlier Biblical commentaries and his work on the Augustinian Rule serve chiefly to bring together glosses and explanations from other commentators. This assembling of information from wide reading is a characteristic of Trevet's scholarship throughout. It reflects not only his personal interest but also his experience and that of others in the difficulty of obtaining books, a problem to which he alludes more than once. His characteristic

---

J. Dean, 'The Manuscripts' (1962); 'Nicolas Trevet', *Dictionnaire des lettres françaises: le moyen âge* (Paris, 1964), pp. 548–9; 'The Dedication of Nicholas Trevet's Commentary on Boethius', *Studies in Philology*, lxiii (1966), 593–603. Trevet's family history is traced and recorded in the first chapter of my doctoral thesis (Oxford, 1938), which may be consulted in the Bodleian Library.

[1] Introduction to *Annales*, ed. Hog, see below, p. 331 n. 1.
[2] Dean, 'The Dedication' (1966). The doubtful authenticity of the commentary on the *Disciplina scolarium* is discussed in my thesis.
[3] The method is described by Dr. Smalley in *English Friars*, p. 59.

of being encyclopedic—though not, like some of his contemporaries, an encyclopedist—was what made his work valuable to those who commissioned special studies.

The five major non-Biblical commentaries written by Trevet—on Boethius's *Consolation of Philosophy*, on Augustine's *City of God*, on the elder Seneca's *Controversies*, on the younger Seneca's *Tragedies*, and on Livy's Roman history—are grammatical and historical in nature. He explains the texts by paraphrase and definition, discusses verse-forms[1] and such technical matters as winds and theatres, cites parallel texts and analogues, recounts the histories or legends of persons, and points out agreements or differences among authorities, sometimes giving his own opinion but more often simply recording. One feels that the grammatical comments reflect his habits as a teacher, for this appears to have been his principal role in the Order rather than preaching. What seems to interest him most, and very likely his readers also, was history, social as well as dynastic, legendary as well as factual.[2] Much of his expository work is related to history, and in the closing ten or fifteen years of his life he completed three works of history, each of distinct scope and style, one different also in language. He had probably been collecting materials for these histories during much of his mature life.

The best-known of Trevet's three historical works in our day is the *Annales sex regum Angliae*, an account in Latin of the reigns of the six kings from Stephen to Edward I (1135–1307), composed probably about 1320–3. His second history in Latin, completed about 1327–8, is a universal chronicle from Creation to the birth of Christ which he had earlier been obliged to set aside unfinished. He wrote his third history not in Latin but in Anglo-Norman because he intended it for a lady, Princess Mary of Woodstock, daughter of Edward I and sister of Edward II. This is also a universal history beginning with Creation; it continues even past the death of its patroness (1332). It was probably his last work and indeed it seems unfinished, perhaps interrupted by Trevet's own death.

For some six centuries these works have been recorded under

---

[1] His commentary on the Psalter also shows his interest in verse-forms, and in musical instruments as well.

[2] Dean, 'The Earliest Known Commentary on Livy', *Medievalia et Humanistica*, iii (1945), 96; iv (1946), 110.

varying titles with resultant bibliographical confusion. The first one is properly known as *Annales*: it is set out in annual sections. It has tables of dates for parallel kingdoms since, in addition to English history, it includes running notes on continental events and personalities. The second work, dealing with the kingdoms of the ancient world, is similarly set out in the form of annals and some bibliographers have consequently called it *Annales (ab orbe condito)*. To avoid this confusion we had better call it by the other title found in some manuscripts, *Historia (ab origine mundi)*. The Anglo-Norman work, when it has a title in manuscripts, is called *Cronicles (Chroniques, Cronycles)*. No one of these works is a translation of one of the others, though a number of bibliographers have made such an assertion. The Anglo-Norman work does, of course, conflate events of several areas, as do the Latin ones, and it does include the periods covered by the other two. But the three works differ entirely in scope, aim, and style, as will appear below, and the two Latin histories between them leave untouched the Christian era before 1135.

The manuscripts of all three works are listed at the end of this paper.

Annales

As the title *Annales* suggests, this work covers its period year by year.[1] It begins with a summary of the events leading to Stephen's accession (given under 1136), introduces the Angevin dynasty with Henry II, and closes with the death of Edward I in

---

[1] Prologue: 'Atheniensium Romanorumque res gestas certissimus auctor Salustius . . . juxta morem Romani calendarii a principio Januarii exordimur.' Text: 'Ut autem juxta nostram intentionem commodius regum gesta, qui a comitibus Andegavensibus secundum lineam masculinam descenderunt . . . complevitque aetatis suae annos sexaginta octo et dies viginti.' Editions: Luc d'Achéry, *Spicilegium*, vii (Paris, 1668), pp. 411–728 (in later edition, 1723, iii. 143–231); John Leland, *Collectanea*, iii (2nd edn., London, 1774), pp. 326–8 (brief extracts); Anthony Hall, *Nicolai Triveti, Dominicani, Annales sex regum Angliae e praestantissimo codice Glastoniensi nunc primum emendate . . .* (Oxford, 1719); Thomas Hog, *F. Nicholai Triveti, de ordine fratrum praedicatorum, Annales sex regum Angliae qui a comitibus Andegavensibus originem traxerunt (A.D. M.C.XXXVI–M.CCC.VII) ad fidem codicum manuscriptorum* (English Historical Society, London, 1845; Kraus reprt., 1964). By introducing into Hall's title a relative clause based on one in Trevet's prologue, Hog's title gives the impression that Trevet was treating six Angevin kings. Trevet does in fact treat six kings, beginning with Stephen, but specifically says that Henry II is the first Angevin king.

1307. In his prologue Trevet declares that ever since the beginning of John's reign the recording of the praiseworthy deeds of the English people has been abandoned, and he attributes this neglect either to sloth or to a delight in vituperating rather than praising the rulers. His own positive approach does suppress some unpleasant details but his praise, while generous, is tempered by frank criticism. Trevet's bias toward the Angevins need not surprise us: after all, Henry III and his son and grandson were in general friends and patrons of the Dominicans.

With the account of events in England Trevet carries along summarily those of the collateral reigns of kings, emperors, and popes. He deals chiefly with political and ecclesiastical history but includes the usual passing references to natural phenomena such as earthquakes and comets. We miss any notice of Magna Carta until the confirmation of 37 Henry III[1] and the amendments and confirmations of 25 and 27 Edward I. Trevet recounts legends and anecdotes and he records epitaphs, verses, and witty remarks, but this lightening of his material does not preclude his giving accurately the full texts of many letters, documents, and treaties.[2] He tells us in the prologue that he read historical materials while he was at the Paris house of study, copying out carefully what was relevant to England, and that he gathered material on contemporary events from reliable witnesses.[3] We may presume that he worked similarly in London and Oxford as occasion offered.

Although much of Trevet's narrative can be found in other chronicles (it would be difficult in many cases to tell in which direction the borrowing took place), occasional items are unique with him or provide information that serves as control to other sources. For example, an incidental remark by Trevet in his account of Thomas of Cantilupe furnished the historian A. G. Little with a detail for his description of academic ceremonies: from Trevet he learned that it was customary for the university

---

[1] The expression here is: 'chartas duas, unam de libertatibus quae Magnae, et aliam quae de Foresta dicitur, concessit.' The words 'quae Magnae' are lacking in the Arundel and Merton manuscripts (see list below). Ed. Hog, p. 242.

[2] Ed. Hog, p. ix. It is not improbable that his connections with the royal household and with officers of Church and Crown gave him direct access to first-hand materials; see Dean, 'Cultural Relations in the Middle Ages: Nicholas Trevet and Nicholas of Prato', *Studies in Philology*, xlv (1948), 548–54.

[3] Ed. Hog, pp. 2–3. Trevet's sojourn in Paris is likely to have been for some period between 1307 and 1314, when he was absent from Oxford. There is no record of him at the University of Paris.

ceremony of *vesperies* to conclude with a speech in which the presiding master praised the candidate.[1] Moreover, Trevet's list of the works of Thomas Aquinas—which he groups as authentic, of doubtful attribution, and spurious—has been much used in studies of Aquinas's writings.[2]

Despite their wide usefulness the *Annales* are centrally concerned with Angevin history. It is tempting to think that Trevet wrote them for Edward II, as he wrote his other two histories for individuals, but his only explanation for his endeavour is that he desired to establish a judicious balance in the recording of English history. One suspects that Trevet felt close to the royal family and that personal ties as much as a sense of history motivated this work. Yet it was a forlorn hope if Trevet composed the *Annales* to bolster Edward II's family pride and show him worthy examples to follow, for Edward was not much given to serious interests. He may well have been aware, however, of Trevet's activity since (as was mentioned above) the scholar certainly had access to royal documents. Perhaps Trevet received support from the royal purse: among his patrons were John of Drokensford (Droxford), sometime Master of the Wardrobe and Chancellor of the Exchequer, and John of Lenham, confessor to Edward II.[3] Such support might, of course, have been given him by royal ministers without particular interest on the part of the king.

The date of composition of the *Annales* can be fairly closely fixed. Trevet says in the prologue that he proposes to write the history of the Angevin kings 'ad nostram aetatem'. It would be reasonable to assume that the work was composed before the death of Edward II (1327), else his reign would probably have been included, as some of it is in Trevet's *Cronicles* composed later. And there is evidence that the *Annales* were indeed written several years earlier than 1327, probably between 1320 and 1323. Thomas of Cantilupe, whom Trevet calls 'beatus Thomas, Herefordensis

---

[1] The remark is: 'in cujus [that is, of Kilwardby] commendatione, quae solet ante principium post disputationem, quae Vesperiae appellantur, de bachilariis fieri magistrandis . . .' *Annales*, s.a. 1282, ed. Hog, p. 306; see A. G. Little, *Archivum Franciscanum Historicum*, xix (1926), 829.

[2] Ed. Hog, pp. 287–90; see P. Mandonnet, 'Des écrits authentiques de Saint Thomas d'Aquin', *Revue Thomiste*, xvii (1909), 38–55, 155–81, 257–74, 441–55, 562–73, 678 ff.; xviii (1910), 62–82, 289–307; same title in book form (Fribourg, 1910). See also Martin Grabmann in Baeumker's *Beiträge*, xxii, 1–2 (1920); on Trevet's list, see especially pp. 54–5, 79–80, 86.

[3] Dean, 'Cultural Relations', pp. 549, 554.

episcopus', s.a. 1282, was canonized by 1320.[1] Thomas Aquinas, whom Trevet calls only 'frater' and 'doctor', was canonized 18 July 1323.

While manuscripts of many of Trevet's other works can be found all over Europe, the surviving manuscripts of the *Annales* are less scattered (see list A below). They seem all to have been copied in England, as was only natural in view of the work's comparatively local interest. The *Annales* were still being copied and excerpted in the sixteenth, seventeenth, and eighteenth centuries (see list B below) and editions were published in the seventeenth, eighteenth, and nineteenth (see p. 331 n. 1).

The earliest edition, that by Luc d'Achéry in his *Spicilegium*, was made from the manuscript belonging to Emery Bigot of Rouen (1626–89), now Paris, B.N. lat. 4167A.[2] In the eighteenth century Anthony Hall, a fellow of the Queen's College, Oxford, edited the *Annales* from the copy in his college (now Queen's 304), which he called the Glastonbury manuscript, corrected from the Merton College copy (now Merton 256) and the Codex Bigotianus. In his notes, Hall gave a few details from Trevet's Anglo-Norman *Cronicles* when that work supplemented the *Annales*, using the Magdalen College, Oxford, manuscript (now Magdalen 45) for this purpose. He knew also Gale's manuscript of the *Cronicles* (now Trinity College, Cambridge, O. 4. 32).[3] Hall's prefatory matter contains transcriptions of all the references to Trevet that he could find in the works of bibliographers and historians. Although he mentioned Wharton's projected edition, interrupted by death, Hall avoided any reference to that of Hearne, his rival. Hearne had planned to publish the *Annales* from a transcript made in 1651 of the Queen's College manuscript (now MS. Jones 7 in the Bodleian Library) but was 'hindred by Enemies', as he says. Hall's edition caused Hearne many pangs of jealousy, and Hearne's letters and journals frequently express his poor opinion of Hall's scholarship.[4] Hearne's resentment extended even to a

---

[1] John Le Neve, cont. by T. Duffus Hardy, *Fasti Ecclesiae Anglicanae*, i (Oxford, 1854), 460; *D.N.B.* The first letter in Rymer's *Foedera* about the canonization is dated 1305 (*Foedera*, i. 2, 1816): the last two in 1319 are still urging the canonization (*Foedera*, ii. 1, 1818). Trevet uses 'beatus' and 'sanctus' interchangeably, as for instance in referring to Jerome and Augustine.

[2] Bigot's fine library was sold in 1706. This manuscript was in the Bibliotheca Regia, Paris, when the 1744 catalogue was drawn up.

[3] Hall (cited on p. 331 n. 1), Praefatio, sig. [a 4] and n. 3.

[4] *Remarks and Collections of Thomas Hearne*, i (1884), 145; ii (1886), 269;

friend of his own who had helped Hall to have an engraving made of the opening initial of the Queen's manuscript, supposed to be a portrait of Trevet, in order to enhance Hall's forthcoming edition. In his anger Hearne could not bring himself to consider the engraving good.

For the English Historical Society edition in 1845, Thomas Hog used Hall's text as a basis, having a better opinion than Hearne of Hall's work, and he collated in addition MSS. Arundel 46, 220, and Harley 29. A twentieth-century edition using all the now known manuscripts is still needed.[1]

Historia

Although two of the historical works by Trevet—the *Historia* and the *Cronicles*—were written for patrons, only the *Historia* has a dedicatory letter.[2] Happily for us, it explains some of the circumstances of composition of the work and by its form of address sets the date. It is addressed to Master Hugh, archdeacon of Canterbury and papal nuncio in England. Hugh was already nuncio in 1324 when John XXII bade Hugh send him a copy of Trevet's commentary on the Psalter,[3] and he had ceased to hold

vi (1902), 155–7, 161, 249, 256, 257, 260, 282; vii (1906), 23–5, 31–3, 43 (O.H.S. Publications, ii, vii, xliii, xlviii, various editors).

[1] Such an edition by Mrs. Georgina R. Galbraith was unfortunately abandoned. An edition of the chapter on the reign of Edward I is in preparation by Mr. Frank Mantello of the University of Toronto.

[2] Dedicatory letter: 'Venerande (*or* Reverende) discrecionis domino magistro Hugoni Cantuariensis ecclesie archidiacono ac domini pape nuncio in Anglia, Frater Nicholaus Treveth . . . Antiquitatis mundane ponentes aliquid exordium . . . sine qua ceptum negocium aliis intentus penitus neglexissem.' Text: 'Anni primi die tercio quem scriptura sextum vocat, ut dictum est in prohemio, Deus primum hominem Adam de limo terre plasmavit . . . In hoc anno finita est etas mundi quinta, in quo promissum meum quamvis forte apud nonnullos modici valoris sed tamen apud expertos non modici laboris solutum existimo, ad honorem Domini nostri Jesu Christi regnantis in secula seculorum. Amen.' John Bale, *Index Britanniae Scriptorum*, ed. R. L. Poole and Mary Bateson (Oxford, 1902), p. 310, and Thomas Tanner, *Bibliotheca Britannico-Hibernica* (London, 1748), p. 723, give after the salutation: 'Inter eos qui mundi concedunt exordium', and refer to Leland's *Collectanea*, iii. 152. Leland saw a copy of the work dedicated to Hugh at Buckfastleigh but gives no incipit. I have not found a manuscript with this variant. The *Historia* has not been published nor, so far as I know, studied.

[3] *C.P.L.* ii. 461. The letter, dated Kal. Sept., 8 Joh. XXII (1324), was printed by Franz Ehrle, 'Nikolaus Trivet', *Festgabe Clemens Baeumker* (*Beiträge*, Suppl. ii, 1923), p. 4 n. 3.

that office, on account of ill health, in January 1328/9.[1] The earliest record of him as archdeacon of Canterbury seems to be of March 1328.[2] Apparently he did not yet hold this office in March 1327, when we find him still cited by an earlier title, sacristan of the church of Narbonne.[3] Since he was not yet archdeacon in March 1327 and had ceased to be nuncio by January 1328/9, Trevet's letter to him must have been written between those two dates. Presumably the *Historia*, which the letter accompanies, was finished at about the same time as the letter was written.

The work had not, however, been composed all in one period of his life, as Trevet explains in the letter. After recounting the first three Ages he had been interrupted by the pressure of other occupations. On a certain occasion he had presented the incomplete work to Hugh, who thereupon desired him to add a good deal more to it. This he has now done as far as possible. He has wished to please Hugh to whom he feels indebted for manifold kindnesses 'in me et meis', and he has carried the account to the beginning of the Christian era. Upon the urging of Hugh he has included considerable material from Livy concerning Roman history. He discusses at some length the sources he has used and the problems of chronology that arise from disagreements among traditional historians. He has deemed it suitable to abridge his sources to some degree but believes that he has not omitted anything that his patron's instructions required.[4]

---

[1] *The Register of John de Grandisson, Bishop of Exeter (A.D. 1327–1369)*, i (London and Exeter, 1894), 456–8: two letters in the *Registrum commune* of John, dated 26 January 1328/9; these mention Master Icherius de Concoreto, canon of Salisbury, as nuncio in succession to Hugh of Angoulême 'propter infirmitatem sui [sc. Hugonis] corporis'. The first mention of Icherius (or Itherius, Ithier) as nuncio in *C.P.L.* ii. 296 is dated 6 Id. Jul., 13 Joh. XXII (10 July 1329).

[2] *C.P.L.* ii. 268: letter from the Pope, dated at Avignon 8 Id. Mar., 12 Joh. XXII (1328); this letter addresses Hugh as archdeacon of Canterbury without using the title 'nuncio'. Both titles are used, however, in the Patent Rolls (*Calendar of Patent Rolls, 1327–1330*, p. 247, 9 March 1328) and in letters in the *Registrum commune* of John de Grandisson in 1328 (pp. 352, 360).

[3] *Calendar of Patent Rolls, 1327–1330*, p. 26, 2 March 1327.

[4] Several parts of Trevet's long letter were printed by Jacques Quétif and Jacques Echard, *Scriptores ordinis praedicatorum*, i (Paris, 1719), 564, from a Sorbonne MS. (now Paris, B.N. lat. 16018), and by Valentin Rose, *Verzeichniss der latein. HSS.* i (Berlin, 1893), 341, from a Phillipps MS. in Berlin (1846, Rose 150). The following passage about Trevet's use of his Roman sources is not included in the published excerpts save for the first sentence, which was printed by Rose. It is transcribed from B.L. Royal 13 B. xvi, fol. 2ᵛ: 'Plurima autem de gestis Romanorum extracta de Tito Livio, que ipse ab urbe condita decem libris

The *Historia* is introduced by an explanatory rubric: 'Incipit annotacio temporum ab origine mundi extracta per fratrem Nicholaum Treveth de sacra scriptura secundum translacionem Jeronimi que immediate facta est de Hebraica veritate.'[1] It is not without reason that the work has sometimes been called *Annales ab orbe condito*, for each section has a dated heading as the *Annales sex regum Angliae* have. And although Trevet cannot now deal with every year as he did in the earlier work, since there are nearly 4,000 calculated in the pre-Christian era, he does—when he is about to leave an interval of time—close the section with the statement that in the following so many years there is nothing notable to write about.

For the first two Ages—that is, from the Creation to the Flood, and from the Flood to the birth of Abraham—there is a single succession of dates, 'Ab origine mundi'. In the second Age, a reckoning from the Flood also appears in the date-heading. After the birth of Abraham each section has four date-headings adapted from Eusebius and Bede: 'Ab origine mundi, Hebreorum, Assiriorum, Tercie etatis', with appropriate changes as history advances through the succession of ages and kingdoms. After the fall of Jerusalem, which marks the end of the fourth Age, there being no longer a Hebrew kingdom, the second entry is occupied by the Roman reckoning beginning with Ab urbe condita 164 (A.O.M. 3364). The history of the Britons is introduced at A.O.M. 2815, in the time of Samson, Eli, and Samuel,[2] and paragraphs about British history occur at intervals thereafter.

For almost every paragraph, the *Historia* cites the Bible, or one of the Fathers, or a historian as a source. Quite often there is more

prosequitur, et de bello punico secundo, quod aliis libris .x. complexus est, huic operi ad vestram instanciam inserui locis suis, secundum quod annorum series requisivit. In quibus licet multa sub brevitate, ut potui, perstrinxerim tamen exceptis oracionibus persuasoriis in concionibus habitis que persepe gesta prius narrata repetunt quas aliquando totaliter omisi sequendo Trogum Pompeium qui teste abreviatore eius Justino libro .xxxviii. tam Livium quam Salustium super insercione (MS. imser/sicione) oracionum hujus modi reprehendit quod historie modum excesserint; aliquando tamen propter dicta notabilia inmixta succincte eas posui. Nichil me credo juxta verbum vestrum de contingentibus omisisse, propter quod aliorum cronographorum qui precipue brevitati annituntur in extractis de libris Titi Livii et maxime in describendo gesta belli punici secundi metas excedere compulsus sum.'

[1] The rubric is based on a sentence in the dedicatory letter.

[2] These persons appear s.a. 2818, 2858, 2870 respectively in Bede, *De ratione temporum*, cap. lxvi (*P.L.* xc. 530).

than one authority for a given event, with comment as to whether or not they agree. Sometimes Trevet prefers one version to another but as often as not he leaves the matter open. One of his most frequently cited authorities is 'Magister in historiis', that is, Petrus Comestor's *Historia scholastica*. Augustine's *De civitate Dei* also appears often, as do Eusebius and Bede. Much of English history is attributed to 'Historia Britonum', which is in fact Geoffrey of Monmouth. Suetonius, Origen, Philo, Arnobius Rhetor, and Hugh of Fleury are among the other sources. Eutropius and Solinus appear along with Livy for Roman history. In citing Livy, Trevet often makes specific reference to the number of the book. But he makes no special remark about Livy's history when he first introduces it into his text. He quotes some passages verbatim; at other times he follows Livy in a general way. Whether his wording is his own paraphrase or a conflation with other sources, or is derived from a conspicuously variant text of Livy, are questions we must leave for eventual editors to investigate. As when he made his commentaries on Augustine and Livy, Trevet still knows only two decades, which he calls 'Ab urbe condita' and 'De bello punico secundo', that is, the first and third decades.[1] He refers also to another classical work on which he had made a commentary: Seneca's *Tragedies*. Each time that the course of events brings into the *Historia* one of Seneca's protagonists, Trevet mentions that Seneca wrote a tragedy about this person. But he does not allude to his own commentaries, either the one on Seneca or those on Livy and Augustine.[2]

[1] Dean, 'The Earliest Known Commentary on Livy' (1945), pp. 86 ff. The fourth decade was probably not known anywhere until about the time that Trevet was completing the *Historia* and then only in Italy at first. See Smalley, *English Friars*, p. 92 with n. 4, and p. 93 with reference to Giuseppe Billanovich's work in n. 1. Trevet's commentary on the first decade of Livy was edited as a doctoral dissertation by L. Van Acker at the University of Ghent, but has not yet been published. Dr. Van Acker discussed some questions of Trevet's interpretation in *L'Antiquité Classique*, xxxi (Brussels, 1962), 252–7.

[2] Portions of Trevet's commentary on the *Tragedies* have been edited from time to time: Ezio Franceschini, *Il Commento di Nicola Trevet al Tieste di Seneca* (Pubbl. dell'Università Cattolica del Sacro Cuore, *Orbis Romanus*, Milan, 1938); Vincenzo Ussani, Jr., *Nicolai Treveti expositio Herculis furentis* (Biblioteca degli Scrittori Greci e Latini, Rome, 1959); Piero Meloni, *Nicolai Treveti expositio L. Annaei Senecae Agamemnonis* (Università di Cagliari, Facoltà di Lettere e di Magistero, 3 (Sassari, 1961)); idem, *Nicolai Treveti expositio L. A. Senecae Herculis Oetaei* (Univ. di Cagliari, Fac. di Lett. 7, Rome, 1962). Apart from Van Acker's work (n. 1 above) Trevet's commentary on Livy has not to my knowledge been edited. There is no modern edition of Trevet's

In the closing pages of the *Historia* there is a great deal about Julius Caesar and about the childhood of the Virgin Mary, neglecting the period of the Maccabees to which Trevet devotes considerable attention in his *Cronicles*. The account of the Nativity is drawn largely but not exclusively from the Gospels, with mention of Cymbeline as the contemporary king of Britain. Having thus reached the end of the fifth Age, Trevet feels that he has discharged what he had promised. Though some, he says, may think that his work has little value, the experienced will recognize that it has cost no little labour.[1]

Cronicles

The third historical work, Trevet's only known vernacular composition, is the *Cronicles*.[2] It was written in Anglo-Norman for Princess Mary of Woodstock, fourth daughter of Edward I and Eleanor of Castile, who was a nun of Amesbury, one of the English cells of the abbey of Fontevrault. This work summarizes what then comprised world history from the Creation to the author's lifetime, with particular but not preponderant attention to events and personalities in England. Here as in his *Historia* Trevet bases his account of the pre-Christian era on Hebrew history as recorded in the Bible and in Christian ecclesiastical writings; his method was in this respect the standard one for his age. In contrast with the *Historia*, the *Cronicles* display relatively little interest in Roman history, nor does Livy figure as a source.

commentary on the *City of God*. The portion on Books XI–XXII was printed several times in the 15th century to complete the work of Thomas Waleys O.P. on the first ten books (*Gesamtkatalog der Wiegendruck*, iii, cols. 87–96). Many continental MSS. preserve this arrangement.

[1] See the explicit transcribed on p. 335 n. 2.

[2] Rubric: 'Ci comencent les Cronicles qe frere Nichol Trivet escrit a ma dame Marie la fillie mon seignur le Roi Dengleterre Edward le filtz Henri.' Prologue: 'Purce qe nous sumes avisez de ceux qe sont per[e]ceous en estudie q'il sont enoiez de la prolixité (MS. prolixce) d'estoires . . . tanqe l'apostoil Johan vintisme secund.' Text: 'Le primer jour del siecle, a de primes, crea Dieux ciel e terre . . .' Shorter ending: '. . . maundé par cist Louuis en Lombardie, attret moultz des citeez e villes a la subjeccion Louuis.' Longer ending: '. . . devoit entrer Escoce pur sumettre la terre a sa segnurie come aunciene droit le voleit' (MS. Rawl. B. 178). The *Cronicles* have not been published. For references to an unpublished edition and other studies see Dean, 'The Manuscripts' (1962), to which add now M. Dominica Legge, *Anglo-Norman Literature and its Background* (Oxford, 1963), pp. 298–302.

Trevet draws the early history of the Britons mainly from Geoffrey of Monmouth (or his followers) and intercalates it at appropriate points in Biblical history, following Geoffrey of Monmouth's synchronization. For the Christian era, the *Cronicles* are based largely on patristic, ecclesiastical, and monastic accounts of both history and legend. In neither period does Trevet show great concern for the more respected historical sources or for the documents that he uses in his Latin histories. On the other hand, one redaction of the *Cronicles* contains near its close a list of heretical articles that appears to be translated from a contemporary official document. Here and there in the course of the whole work Trevet includes materials, more legendary than historical, which were used by later writers; for some of these—as for some of his material in the *Annales*—we do not yet know of any earlier source.[1]

The nature and purpose of the *Cronicles* are described in a short prologue. Although this introduction contains no reference to Princess Mary—and, indeed, she is not mentioned at all until the appropriate chronological section—the rubric telling that these *Cronicles* were written for her appears in four of the manuscripts, including the earliest ones. The prologue to the *Cronicles* is as brief as it promises the work itself will be and is quite unlike the lengthy rhetorical introductions to the other two histories. One imagines that Trevet found the rhetoric of his habitual Latin awkward to render in the vernacular; and he may have thought such a style likely to discourage the attention of a royal patroness whose life has not left us any evidence of intellectual interests. He professes to be responding to a complaint that most histories are too prolix, a remark characteristic of a number of the briefer chronicles of the later Middle Ages. He says he has also heard complaints of a dearth of books, a difficulty that we know he had met with earlier in his own work.[2] For these two reasons, he continues, it has pleased him to compile a brief account of the lines

---

[1] See Dean, 'The Manuscripts' (1962), p. 96 n. 4, to which add now Robert A. Pratt, 'Chaucer and *Les Cronicles* of Nicholas Trevet', *Studies in Language, Literature, and Culture of the Middle Ages and Later, in Honor of Rudolph Willard*, ed. by E. B. Atwood and A. A. Hill (Austin, University of Texas, 1969), pp. 303–11.

[2] In a letter accompanying his commentary on Leviticus, addressed to Aymeric, Master General of the Order of Preachers, shortly after 1307, Trevet explained that he had had to interrupt a projected commentary on the Pentateuch for lack of books: 'Proposueram quippe, post duos legis libros expositos, de reliquis omnino supersedere expertus originalium penuriam in bibliotecis

descended from Adam through patriarchs, judges, kings, prophets, priests, and others, to the birth of Jesus Christ, in the hope that the account itself will attract the heart and that its brevity will make it clearer to the mind and therefore more easily remembered. To this, he goes on, he has added the deeds of the apostles, emperors, and kings down to Pope John XXII.[1] Under the term 'apostles' we note that Trevet includes the popes: this is a common medieval French use of the word for apostle, although the word 'pape' is more frequently used in the *Cronicles*.[2]

With this preamble, Trevet turns at once to the Creation. It is evident from the outset that he is writing now for a person or persons whose background and interests are quite different from those of the readers for whom he composed the *Historia*. Here are no metaphysical calculations, following Bede, as to whether earthly Time began with the *Fiat lux* or with the creation of sun and moon and stars on the fourth day, such as open the *Historia*. This is a straightforward account from Genesis, somewhat coloured by the retellings of Petrus Comestor and Vincent of Beauvais. Necessarily, much of the material in the pre-Christian part of the *Cronicles* is the same as in the *Historia* but there are a good many differences in emphasis and in choice of detail. In the matter of sources, moreover, the *Historia* is meticulous, citing one or more authorities for almost every paragraph, whereas the *Cronicles* cite sources far less often (without being any the less indebted to them) and not always at the same points or necessarily with the same references.

To cover ground rapidly Trevet keeps his dating in the *Cronicles*

---

monasteriorum Anglie ac difficultatem optenendi illa quorum aliqualis copia invenitur' (MS. Merton Coll. 188, fol. 1rb). On this see also Dean, 'Cultural Relations' (1948), p. 548. On Trevet's difficulty in obtaining a copy of Boethius's *Consolation* in Italy see Dean, 'The Dedication' (1966), p. 596. He seems not to have been in a favourable position to profit by the book policy of the Order of Preachers described by W. A. Hinnebusch in a review in *Speculum*, xxxix (1964), 708; perhaps he lived too early.

[1] Those who have erroneously said, in bibliographies and catalogues of MSS., that the *Cronicles* go to 1315 have evidently based the statement on this prologue without reading the final pages where the length of John's reign is mentioned; he was elected in 1316 and died in 1334. See below, p. 346 and n. 2.

[2] In the Rawlinson MS. the words 'pape' and 'see papal' have been effaced in most places. In the first half of the MS. these words have been replaced by 'evesqe' and 'evesché', sometimes with 'de Rome' added, written in gray ink by a hand imitating 14th-century script.

to a minimum; he does not try to account for every year as he does in his Latin histories. Such occurrences as the death of a patriarch, the coronation of a king, or the election of a pope or an emperor supply the large framework of dates. Within this scheme events are synchronized by the formula 'In the time of this . . .' ('En le temps cist . . .'), repeating the name which heads the section, with occasionally an intermediate date if it is important or if the chronology becomes unwieldy.

The work is divided first of all into books entitled Genesis, Exodus, Joshua, Judges, Kings (including some material from Chronicles), Maccabees, Gospels, Acts of the Apostles, Acts or Deeds ('Gestes') of the Popes, Emperors, and Kings. Some manuscripts include one or more additional titles after Kings—Ezechiel, Daniel, Esdras, Judith—and Josephus after Maccabees; but all of the manuscripts include the same material in the same sequence whether or not they cite these titles. While this selection follows Petrus Comestor's *Historia scholastica*, it does not use all of his material, and it suggests that Trevet may also have had before him an Anglo-Norman Bible or one of the 'Bibles historiales' of the late thirteenth and early fourteenth centuries.[1]

The books are then divided into 'estoires' which are roughly regnal in their disposition. When the material is long or diversified the 'estoire' may be subdivided into three or more 'chapitres', each devoted to a different topic. Neither the 'estoires' nor the 'chapitres' are regularly marked off in the text but coloured capitals and marginal indications often occur. That the 'estoires' were intended to be numbered (as is the case with chapters in the Anglo-Norman 'Brut') is evident from the frequent references to them by number in the body of the text. The over-all chronology is governed by the traditional six Ages, but the dates used in the *Cronicles* do not in general agree with those in the *Historia*.[2] Similarly, the synchronization of British history is not always the same in the two

---

[1] Samuel Berger, *La Bible française au moyen âge* (Paris, 1884), pp. 157 ff., 231–6; Johan Vising, *Anglo-Norman Language and Literature* (London, 1923), p. 71, no. 352; Legge, *Anglo-Norman Literature*, p. 179.

[2] In the *Cronicles* British history begins with the exile of Brutus in the time of Eli, A.O.M. 3048; the beginning of the rule of Samson is given as 3022, that of Eli 3042, and that of Samuel 3082; cf. p. 337 and n. 2. In the *Historia* the beginning of the fourth Age—the reign of David—is given under A.O.M. 2890, and that of the sixth—the birth of Jesus Christ—under 3953; in the *Cronicles* the corresponding dates are 3114 and 4182.

works. It may prove interesting for future editors to trace how these divergences arose, especially in the light of Trevet's remarks about chronology in the introductory letter to the *Historia*.

Like most of Trevet's work, the *Cronicles* are didactic, but their intention is practical and moral rather than intellectual. They were written, at least ostensibly, for a lady royal by birth and religious by profession though worldly in practice. It is not recorded that she opened bazaars or new college buildings but she did go to meet state visitors and she filled other social roles appropriate at the time for a daughter or sister of the king. And like unmarried ladies in any age and country she lent a hand in households when royal babies were born. More sporty than Chaucer's prioress with her lap-dog, Princess Mary owned greyhounds, about which she corresponded with her brother, Edward of Carnarvon, who borrowed one of them for breeding. She was the 'visitor' of her Order for England, that is, the deputy of the abbess of Fonte-vrault. No doubt this office, as well as her royal rank, allowed her more freedom of movement than other nuns enjoyed. Besides frequent absences from Amesbury on visits to members of her family, at court or country seats, or to her own properties, she made a number of long trips (some perhaps on business of the Order, although the expenses are noted in the Public Records) and several pilgrimages. In spite of generous allowances from her father and his successors she was frequently in debt, sometimes as a result of gambling. Between these interests and obligations, she moved about so freely in the world that she did not entirely escape the breath of scandal.[1]

[1] Mary of Woodstock was born in 1279 and died 29 May 1332: *Calendar of Close Rolls, 1330–1333*, p. 511. For details of her life see Mary A. E. Green, *Lives of the Princesses of England*, ii (London, 1849), 404–42, and L. Guilloreau, *Marie de Woodstock, une fille d'Édouard Ier, moniale à Amesbury, 1285–1332* (Ligugé, Vienne, 1914). More of the letters to her from her brother, Edward of Carnarvon, than Dom Guilloreau had access to are available in Hilda Johnstone's edition: *Letters of Edward, Prince of Wales, 1304–05* (Roxburghe Club, 1931). The accounts by Mrs. Green and Dom Guilloreau are based on the Public Records and published chronicles; in addition Mrs. Green quotes from MSS. of Trevet's unpublished *Cronicles*. See also Mary A. E. Wood [Mrs. Green], *Letters of Royal and Illustrious Ladies of Great Britain*, i (London, 1846), 60–3; William Dugdale, *Monasticon Anglicanum*, ii (London, 1819), 333–43; Eileen Power, *Medieval English Nunneries* (Cambridge, 1922), pp. 346–60, 380–1, 455. A document of Clement VI of 1345 cites in retrospect an affair between Princess Mary and John de Warenne, earl of Surrey (see *C.P.L.* iii. 169); there was apparently opportunity for this to have taken place during one of Mary's visits to court, perhaps the one of November 1305, when she and her niece, Joan of

It cannot be supposed, however, that Trevet sought by his account of the world and her family to reform the princess while he taught her, for she was already forty or more when he was writing. We can infer something of his estimate of her capacities and at least his hopes for her character from the style of the *Cronicles* and from his choice of material. He must have judged that she had neither sufficient training in Latin, even if the books had been available to her, to read the mass of material of which they are a digest, nor the discipline in thinking necessary to fit together the course and significance of events recorded annalistically. He spared her the heavy going of political negotiations and documents, which we find in the *Annales*, but furnished her with all the particulars of marriages and offspring that were given there —perhaps even more. He devoted a good deal of attention to miracles and legends, and to ecclesiastical matters. The latter include questions of hierarchy, sanctuary, celibacy, the development of the liturgy step by step through the centuries, the history of the translation of the Bible, details of the celebration of the Mass, and proper behaviour at it. Martyrs, saints, mystics, and other religious people figure prominently, nor are famous heretics omitted. The finding and enshrinement of relics are noted, and particular attention is given to the place and date of the founding of religious houses. Omens have a large place in the chronicle as they had in the beliefs of the time. With the schoolman's love of etymology, Trevet includes the derivations of place-names, although here he is not teaching grammar as he is in his commentaries. He is careful also to explain for his royal reader, presumed to have small Latin and no Greek, the Greek and Latin phrases that he has occasion to quote, except when these are drawn from the Bible or the liturgy. Occasionally he translates even Biblical quotations, sometimes with a comment, but he evidently expected the princess, brought up from childhood in a nunnery, to understand all of the liturgy.

In the *Cronicles*, as in the *Annales*, Trevet treats the Angevin house and the Dominican Order in detail, sometimes to the exclusion of contemporaneous individuals or episodes of at least equal importance. If he has to relate conflicts of ecclesiastical interest it is clear that his sympathies are with the Church and his own

Bar, countess of Warenne, were among the companions of the queen (see Green, *Lives*, ii. 426).

Order. When he deals with the Angevin dynasty he seems to be careful of the feelings of his patroness. Although he frankly disapproves of Henry II in the conflict with Becket, he is cautious in his treatment of John's actions. He suppresses some of the criticism of Edward I that he had allowed himself to make in the *Annales* and, although he gives considerable attention to the activities and death of Piers Gaveston, he is silent concerning a number of unhappy events in the reign of Edward II. He mentions sadly the beheading of Edmund of Woodstock, the younger half-brother whom Edward II had created earl of Kent. Edmund, he tells us, was 'mauveisement et despitosement decolé a Wyncestre'.

In the 'estoire' that begins in 1287 there is a long account of the exploits and virtues of Edward I. In closing this story Trevet compliments his Angevin contemporaries by inserting a genealogy which traces the lineage of Edward I from son to father back to Adam. In two manuscripts (P and R)[1] there is an illustrative diagram of this genealogy which carries the descent from Adam down to Edward III. As a further testimony of his attention to family history, in the story beginning 1294 Trevet interrupts the narration of public events to revert to an earlier occasion, the entry of the dowager queen Eleanor, widow of Henry III, into the convent of Amesbury, accompanied by a number of ladies and girls of the royal family and household. This is the first time he refers specifically to his patroness, as he describes the ceremony of her taking the veil 'ja entraunt le septime aan de son age'. The pious tone of this account contrasts significantly with the matter-of-fact note on the subject in the *Annales*, s.a. 1284: 'Maria, regis filia Angliae, Ambresberiae sanctimonialis efficitur, parentibus assentientibus, licet cum difficultate, ad instantiam matris regis.'[2] There is tactfully no mention in the *Cronicles* of the disagreement here alluded to between Mary's parents and her grandmother over this step. Two other references in the *Cronicles* to Trevet's patroness occur in a passage called the 'engendrure le roi Edward le fitz Henri', inserted into the story beginning with the year 1306. At an earlier point Trevet had named the children of Edward I and Eleanor of Castile, saying that Edward born at Carnarvon was the only son who survived childhood and that he would treat the daughters later. He now takes each daughter in turn, and then the three children of Edward's second marriage. He identifies all

---

[1] See below, p. 352. [2] Ed. Hog, p. 310.

the spouses and children and sometimes the grandchildren. One of the latter died 'en pucelage' and was buried at Amesbury by order of the lady Mary. When he comes to Mary herself in this account he comments on her choice of vocation—if one can call the family arrangements a choice or a vocation—praising it with a quotation from the Bible.[1]

The date of composition of the *Cronicles* presents some problems. The extant manuscripts all state in the prologue that the work will recount the 'gestes des apostoiles, emperours et rois tanqe l'apostoil Johan vintisme secund'. They all mention in the 'estoire' beginning 1252 the death of Thomas Aquinas and his later canonization. In all manuscripts the penultimate 'estoire' closes with the death of Edward I. In all, the final 'estoire' has a chapter treating part of the reign of Edward II and a chapter treating part of the reign of Pope John XXII, but neither reign is carried to its close. All the manuscripts mention, however, in opening this chapter on John that he occupied the papal see for nineteen years. Since Thomas Aquinas was canonized 18 July 1323 and since John died 4 December 1334, we can infer that in writing his *Cronicles* Trevet had reached the thirteenth-century section of his narrative by the summer of 1323 and that he was still working on them at the end of 1334.[2] Inasmuch as Trevet used a system of dating in the *Cronicles* that differed from the system used in the *Historia* (see p. 342 and n. 2), it seems probable that he did not begin the Anglo-Norman work until after he had

---

[1] 'La quarte fille [i.e. of Edward I] fu dame Marie, de qi est avaunt dit qe se maria al haut Roi de Ciel, et en taunt est de li veritablement dit, "Optimam partem elegit sibi Maria que non auferetur ab ea" [Luke 10 : 42], qe fait taunt a dire "La tresbone part s'en ad eslu Marie, qar cele part, qe est Dieux meismes, jammés ne lui tollet serra" ' (MS. Rawl. B. 178, fol. 64). This is an example of Trevet's expanding a translation with comment, a frequent medieval practice.

[2] There is nothing in the datable facts of Trevet's life to make it unreasonable to accept the detail of the length of John XXII's reign as evidence that Trevet was still alive in 1334. A mid-15th-century note which refers to Trevet as being alive in 1332 has been brought to my attention by Dr. A. I. Doyle. The note, he has kindly written me, precedes a copy of the 'Bridlington prophecy' as though it were its title, but the prophecy is in a different hand and section: 'Prophecia de sexto (?) Hibernie quam Nicholaus Tryvet scripsit et habuit a quodam viro Norman' apud Parisium Anno domini Millesimo CCC^{mo} xxxij°.' It is found in Manchester, John Rylands Library MS. Lat. 228, fol. 79. If trustworthy, this note would allow us to postulate another visit to Paris late in Trevet's life. It should be cautioned, however, that one or more Nicholas Trevets appear in the records in the first half of the 14th century who are probably not to be identified with our Dominican friar.

finished the *Historia*. On this basis we would place the composition of the *Cronicles* in the period between 1328 and 1335. But four copies, including the earliest ones, have the rubric naming Princess Mary, and she died in 1332. We must therefore consider the question of successive editions.

To do this we need to examine the final 'estoire' in some detail. It opens with the accession of Henry, count of Luxemburg, as emperor in 1306, according to Trevet (Henry VII, 1308–13), and with the coronation of Robert Bruce as King of Scotland. Some details about the papacy of Clement V follow, including the dissolution of the Templars (1312), and then the account returns to England with the 'engendrure le roi Edward le fitz Henri', to which we have referred above. The next chapter of this final story takes up the reign of Edward II. The opening sentence mentions the date of his accession, the length of his reign, and his burial at Gloucester, but does not refer to the manner of his death or to his cult that developed soon after. There is a long account of the first part of the reign, as far as the defeat at Bannockburn. At this discouraging point, Trevet turns aside and opens his chapter on John XXII, with the remark on the length of his reign that we have noted above. There is a good deal of factual information about John and his papacy but no such comment on his personality or interests as one might have expected from a protégé writing about one of his patrons. Without completing the account of John, Trevet returns briefly to imperial events; he reports the disputed election of Louis, duke of Bavaria, and some of his troubles with the duke of Austria (Frederick, not named by Trevet). In five of the Anglo-Norman manuscripts (AFMST—see the list below) and in the Middle English version (E) the *Cronicles* end here with the remark that the duke of Austria was sent into Lombardy by Louis and drew a number of towns to Louis's side: 'maundé par cist Louuis en Lombardie, attret moultz des citeez e villes a la subjeccion Louuis'.

The remaining manuscripts (that is LPR, for D breaks off incomplete in the reign of Richard I) have quite a long additional passage. This continues the history of Louis, recounting now his struggle with the papacy and his condemnation, with three Franciscan associates, on charges of heresy. Here Trevet sets out a list of nine heretical articles, both doctrinal and political, and with each heresy he provides its refutation. This passage resembles several of the known documents in that famous quarrel without corresponding exactly to any that have been printed.[1] Concluding this part of John's papacy, Trevet mentions the submission and imprisonment of the anti-pope Nicholas V which he dates in 1329 (1330). A short passage on French history follows, with some details about Louis X and Philip V, but Philip's death (1322) is not mentioned.

Trevet now returns to Edward II but not to the point at which he left him, the defeat at Bannockburn. Instead, he shows Edward in a better light by telling of a Michaelmas parliament held some years later in London (1320) at which Edward conducted himself very well and was esteemed for his good sense, a remark authentically Trevetan. The parliament, he goes on, ordained that the king should enter Scotland by force 'pur sumetre la terre a sa segnurie come auncien droit le voleit'. The continuation breaks off here, leaving untouched the rest of Edward II's reign.

Except for the length of John's papacy either form of the *Cronicles* as we have them might have been presented to Princess Mary, since the latest event in any chapter is of 1330—and Mary lived until 1332. The length of John's reign could have been inserted after her death. But it seems at least possible that Trevet's first edition, composed for a lady whom he thought of as the daughter of Edward I rather than as the sister of Edward II, closed with the 'engendrure' of her father.

Whether or not such a first edition was written, the *Cronicles* as we have them appear in two editions. We have already seen that one group of manuscripts (LPR) shares a continuation beyond the close of the other group. This group shares also at several points a difference in the interpolation of British history, as well as minor textual variants; and in these differences D ranges itself with LPR. Accurate appraisal of the character of the two redactions must of course await a critical edition of the *Cronicles*.[2]

That Trevet may have had in mind a wider audience for his Anglo-Norman history than the circle of Princess Mary is suggested by his continuing to work on the *Cronicles* after her death. Indeed, the space devoted in his continuation to the conflict

---

[1] I hope to treat this matter elsewhere. For a recent study of the quarrel see Jürgen Miethke, *Ockhams Weg zur Sozialphilosophie*, chap. 3 (Berlin, 1969); I owe this reference to the kindness of Dr. Beryl Smalley.

[2] Such an edition has been undertaken by Professor R. C. Johnston.

between Louis of Bavaria and John XXII presupposes readers who were vitally interested in the conflict between pope and emperor concerning sovereignty which was at the root of that prolonged quarrel—readers who found French easier than Latin. A wider audience is shown also by the scripts and formats of the surviving manuscripts: the work was copied at a number of different centres for readers of differing demands and tastes. Two copies, M and S, look as though they may have been transcribed by the individuals who wanted to use them, whereas P must have been made by professional scribes for a library or for a reader who could afford luxurious volumes. Professor Pratt has called attention to the presence of two copies of the *Cronicles* in the library of Thomas of Woodstock, Princess Mary's great-nephew. One was appraised at 20*d.*, the other, more elegantly bound, at twice that value. In both cases the book is called 'Cronicles Trivet'.[1] The translation into Middle English, the extant copy of which is handsomely executed, may have been called for when Middle English 'Bruts' were circulating and Trevisa's voluminous translation of Higden was discouraging readers by the 'prolixité' that Trevet endeavoured to avoid.

RUTH J. DEAN

MANUSCRIPTS
Annales

List A: medieval copies

Cambridge, *England*, Corpus Christi Coll. 152, fols. 1–48ᵛ
   (to end of John's reign)   XV¹
Cambridge, Trinity Coll. O. 4. 43, fols. 46–98 (to end of
   Henry III's reign)   XVᵐ

---

[1] Pratt, 'Chaucer and *Les Cronicles*' (cited on p. 340 n. 1), p. 311. The value of the two volumes may be roughly equated to £12 and £24 (1974). A copy of the *Roman de la Rose* in the same library was listed at 6*s.* 8*d.*, twice the value of the more elegant of the two *Cronicles* manuscripts. Thomas had also owned a copy of a book about William Marshal, valued at 20*d.*, a copy of the *Livre des Seyntes Medicines* by the father of his sister-in-law, Henry, first duke of Lancaster (called in the inventory 'Tretee de mercy grant mercy' and listed at 20*d.*), and two large volumes of Livy in French, valued at 40*s.*, which was probably the translation by Pierre Bersuire who drew largely on Trevet's commentary on Livy (see Jacques Monfrin in *Histoire Littéraire de la France*, xxxix (1962), 358–414). The inventory of Thomas's extensive library of histories and romances in three languages was printed in *Transactions of the Royal Society of Literature*, 2nd series, ix (1870), 80–3, and with variant readings in *Archaeological Journal*, liv (1897), 300–2.

London, British Libr., Add. 54184, fols. 49–130^v [1] XIV^2
London, British Libr., Arundel 46, fols. 128–239^v (to A.D.
  1298) XV^1
London, British Libr., Arundel 220, fols. 55–93 (only the
  reign of Edward I, followed by a *Continuatio*)[2] XIV$^{2/4}$
London, British Libr., Cotton Otho D. VIII, fols. 174ra–
  231ra XIV^m
London, British Libr., Harley 29, fols. 1–58 (to end of
  Henry III's reign) XIV^m
London, British Libr., Harley 3899, fols. 62–107^v (only the
  reign of Edward I)[3] XIV^1
London, College of Arms, IX, fols. 60–123 XIV$^{1/3}$
Oxford, Merton Coll. 256, fols. 1–129 XIV/XV
Oxford, Queen's Coll. 304, fols. 67ra–143vb XV$^{2/4}$
Paris, Bibl. Nationale, lat. 4167A, fols. 72–192 XIV$^{3/4}$
San Marino, *California*, Huntington Libr., EL. 1121, fols.
  29–39 (to 1163) XV$^{1/4}$
Winchester, Cathedral, XII, fols. 1–43^v (to 1267; leaves are
  missing *passim*) XV^{in}

List B: later copies and extracts[4]

Caen, Bibl. Municipale, 419, fols. 1–341 XVI^2
London, British Libr., Harley 563, fols. 124–134^v (John
  Stow's notes in English from the *Annales*, for the
  reign of Henry II and the beginning of that of Ed-
  ward I) XVI^2
London, British Libr., Harley 4322, fols. 1–134 (Henry
  Wharton's autograph copy, written on the recto only of
  each leaf. Wharton planned to publish the *Annales*: see
  Hall's edition, cited on p. 331 n. 1, Praefatio, pp. 2–3) XVII^2

[1] Formerly the Brudenell MS., Deene Park D. 6. 4 and 518; described in
Sotheby's Catalogue, 12 December 1966, lot 222, with reduced plate of fol. 49.
[2] John Koch printed a detailed description of this MS., together with its
Anglo-Norman texts, in *Zeitschrift für rom. Philologie*, liv (1934), 20–56.
[3] Possibly by the same hand as Arundel 220. In both MSS. Trevet is preceded by Geoffrey of Monmouth. Cotton Julius D. VI may also be by the same
hand and was perhaps planned to continue Harley 3899, for it opens with the
same *Continuatio* as follows Trevet in Arundel 220, viz. John Pike's compilation
of English history to 1322.
[4] Under MSS. in Ireland, Clarendon MS. 76 was cited in Bernard's *Catalogi
Manuscriptorum* (Oxford, 1697), ii. 2 as containing on fols. 41–45 extracts from
Trevet's 'Annals' between 1149 and 1318. Since the *Annales* extend only to
1307, these extracts must have been made from a MS. in which a continuation
followed the *Annales*; or the MS. may have had a false ascription. Possibly the
source was the *Cronicles*. I have been unable to trace this MS.

Oxford, Bodleian, Add. C. 296 (S.C. 27610), fol. 31 (two
passages from the years 1296 and 1297 in a collection
of extracts made by Archbishop Ussher from various
sources)   XVII[1]
Oxford, Bodleian, James 22 (S.C. 3859), pp. 30 ff. (extracts
copied from Merton 256 by Richard James, Cotton's
librarian)   XVII
Oxford, Bodleian, Jones 7 (S.C. 8914), fols. 1–116ᵛ (a
transcription of Queen's 304 by E. Earbery for C. Bee,
as appears from the bill on fol. 171ᵛ for £2. 17s. 0d; the
bill was printed by Hall, cited above, p. 331 n. 1)   1651
Oxford, Bodleian, Top. gen. C. 2, C. 4 (S.C. 3118, 3120 =
5103, 5105) (extracts by Leland, printed in *Collectanea*,
cited on p. 331 n. 1)   XVI
Rouen, Bibl. Municipale, 3069 (extracts)   XVIII

Historia

Berlin (East), Deutsche Staatsbibliothek, Phillipps 1846
(Rose 150), fols. 1*–340 (German hand)   XV[2]
Florence, Bibl. Nazionale, Conventi G. 3. 451, fols. 96–131ᵛ
(Southern French hand; breaks off s.a. 3357; includes
in that section material from Livy i. 49, A.U.C. 220–44)[1]   XIV[2]
Klagenfurt, Bischöfliche Bibl., XXXI a 9, fols. 237–339ᵛ
(probably a German hand; breaks off in B.C. 445)[2]   XV, *post* 1428
London, British Libr., Royal 13 B. XVI, fols. 2–334ᵛ (French
hand, perhaps southern; leaves missing *passim*)   XIV[2]
Paris, Bibl. Nationale, lat. 4949, fols. 1–312 (Bruges)   1462
Paris, Bibl. Nationale, lat. 16018, fols. 2–268ᵛ (French hand)[3]   1367
Paris, Bibl. Nationale, lat. 16019, fols. 3–231 (Northern
French or Flemish hand; the dedicatory letter is copied
a second time on fol. 232ʳᵛ in a larger script with some
English traits)   XIV[1]

Cronicles[4]

T   Cambridge, *England*, Trinity Coll. O. 4. 32, fols. 1ʳᵃ–
    101ᵛᵃ   XIVᵐ–1360
L   Leyden, Universiteitsbibl., Voss. Gall. F. 6, fols. 1–93ᵛ   XIV⁴/⁴

---

[1] Fr. Thomas Kaeppeli O.P. kindly brought this MS. to my attention, as
well as several others containing works by Trevet.

[2] Hermann Menhardt, *Handschriften-Verzeichnisse Österreichischer Bibliotheken*, Kärnten, Bd. 1 (Vienna, 1927), p. 62. I have not seen this MS.

[3] Plate of fol. 155ᵛ in S. Harrison Thomson, *Latin Bookhands of the Later
Middle Ages, 1100–1500* (Cambridge, 1969), no. 19.

[4] The sigla are those adopted in Dean, 'The Manuscripts' (1962), where fuller
details about the dating and scripts are given.

A London, British Libr., Arundel 56, fols. 2–77   *c.* 1375
D Oxford, Bodleian, Douce 119 (S.C. 21693), fols.
   1 (= 1^a)–69^v XV$^{1/4}$
F Oxford, Bodleian, Fairfax 10 (S.C. 3890), fols. 1ra–
   106ra XIV^m
R Oxford, Bodleian, Rawlinson B. 178 (S.C. 11545), fols.
   1–66   *c.* 1335–50[1]
M Oxford, Magdalen Coll. 45 (138), fols. 1–97^v *c.* 1335–40
P Paris, Bibl. Nationale, franç. 9687, fols. 1va–114va *c.* 1340–50
S Stockholm, Kungliga Bibl., D. 1311a (III), pp. 1–276   *c.* 1400

Later copies

H Cambridge, *Massachusetts*, Harvard, Br 98.373 F*,
   fols. 406–32 (extracts from A.D. 1012 to the shorter
   ending)   XVI
J Oxford, Bodleian, James 19 (S.C. 3856), pp. 49–53
   (extracts from several periods, dealing with ecclesiastical history; Latin sentences are intercalated)   *c.* 1620–38

Middle English version

E Cambridge, *Massachusetts*, Harvard, f MS Eng 938,
   fols. 9ra–91rb XV^2

[1] In the light of M. B. Parkes's study, *English Cursive Book Hands, 1250–1500* (Oxford, 1969), this MS., which earlier I dated XIV$^{3/4}$, should probably be placed before the middle of the century; it must of course be after 1334. See also Otto Pächt and J. J. G. Alexander, *Illuminated Manuscripts of the Bodleian Library, Oxford*, i (Oxford, 1966), p. 46, no. 596.

15

Oxford Academical Halls in the Later Middle Ages

THE earliest information from University sources concerning the number of academical halls is contained in the oldest survivor of the Chancellor's Registers. Each year on the morning following the Feast of the Nativity of the Blessed Virgin (9 September) all principals of academical halls and inns were required by ancient custom of the University[1] to appear in person or by deputy before the Chancellor or his Commissary in the church of Saint Mary the Virgin for admission of their cautions (*exposicio caucionum*) if they wished to continue in office for the ensuing year. It was expected that a record of their attendance would be entered at the time in the Chancellor's Register by the Scribe of the University; but very often the Scribe seems to have failed to do so. These omissions are unfortunate, as the annual lists of halls and their principals or their representatives furnish our chief means of ascertaining the actual number of halls in existence year by year.

In Chancellor's Register Aaa, the earliest extant of the Chancellor's Registers (1434–69), the first list of halls is that of 1436, and, thereafter, lists are entered for the years 1438, 1444–6, 1450, 1451, 1453, 1457, 1458, 1461, 1462, 1468, and 1469.[2] Then comes a break of thirty years owing to the loss of the next register. In Chancellor's Register D (July 1498 to 1506) there are lists for 1499 (incomplete), 1501, 1503, and 1505;[3] in Chancellor's Register ꝗ (December 1506 to 1516) lists for 1508, 1510 (incomplete), and 1511–14;[4] and in Chancellor's Register ℨ or E E E (1527 to

---

[1] S. Gibson, *Statuta Antiqua Universitatis Oxoniensis* (1931), p. 80.

[2] *Registrum Cancellarii Oxon. 1434–1469*, ed. H. E. Salter (O.H.S. xciii–xciv, 1930–1), i. 21–2, 39–41, 123–5, 132–5, 214–16, 247–9, 284–7, 336–9, 403–6; ii. 1–4, 48–51, 85–9, 121, 291–3, 321–2.

[3] O.U.A., Reg. Cancell. D, fols. 17ᵛ, 42, 47ʳᵛ, 101ʳᵛ, 224ᵛ–225.

[4] O.U.A., Reg. Cancell. ꝗ, fols. 65ᵛ–66, 119, 147ᵛ, 168ᵛ–169ᵛ, 199, 232ᵛ, 263ᵛ.

1540) from 1527 to 1535 and for 1537.[1] For the period 1434 to 1540 there should be 106 lists, but there are only 36, of which 3 are incomplete.

In addition to these caution-lists the Chancellor's Registers contain other notices concerning the tenure of halls. In the interval between each annual review a principal who wished to relinquish his hall was expected first to intimate to the Chancellor or his Commissary his resignation of office, and an incoming principal needed to be formally admitted. These changes are recorded with some regularity. The Chancellor's Registers, of course, contain other mentions of halls and their members in various connections, such as litigation for debt, charges of disorderly conduct, permissions to migrate, etc.

An important unofficial contemporary source of evidence for the number of halls is the list of colleges and halls compiled by the antiquary, John Rous. After incepting as M.A. about 1444, Rous became chaplain of the chantry of Guy's Cliffe, near Warwick, and there engaged in various historical and heraldic projects until his death in 1491. The original of Rous's list is not known to have survived, but a copy was made of it by Miles Windsor, fellow of Corpus Christi College (1561–1624).[2] The halls are grouped according to the part of Oxford in which they lay, and against each hall Rous notes whether it was frequented in his time by students of Arts, Theology, Law, or Grammar, and also indicates those in which Irishmen and Welshmen resided. As regards these distinctions it is perhaps as well to remark that the halls that Rous signifies as halls for Artists or halls for Legists did not always remain so, but sometimes varied on a change of principals. And so, too, as regards the residence of Irishmen and Welshmen.

Rous's list ranges in its dating from 1438, since it groups separately the halls that gave place to All Souls College on its foundation, to about 1476, since Rous notes that Trillock's Inn was now known as New Inn, presumably after its reconstruction *c.* 1476–9.[3]

[1] O.U.A., Reg. Cancell. 𝕳, fols. 332ᵛ, 335ᵛ, 337ᵛ, 339ᵛ, 341, 342, 373, 376ᵛ, 378.
[2] Corpus Christi Coll. MS. 280, fol. 51ᵛ; *Wood's City of Oxford*, ed. A. Clark, i (O.H.S. xv, 1889), 638–41. Another version of this list, from Bodl. Libr., MS. Bodley 353, was printed by Th. Hearne as an appendix to vol. iv of his edition of Jo. Leland's *Itinerary* (Oxford, 1764), but it is judged by Andrew Clark to be a later and less correct copy than that of Miles Windsor.
[3] On Trillock's Inn see W. A. Pantin, 'The Halls and Schools of Medieval Oxford: An Attempt at Reconstruction', *Oxford Studies presented to Daniel Callus* (O.H.S., N.S. xvi, 1964 for 1959–60), p. 74.

Andrew Clark also printed two lists of halls made a century later, but neither of them is helpful; the one by Simon Perrott, fellow of Magdalen (1533–50), derived from a rental of the Hospital of St. John the Baptist for 1390; the other by William Standish, also a fellow of Magdalen (1538–52) and Registrar of the University (1552–79).[1]

Other additional sources of information about the halls are the surviving fifteenth- and sixteenth-century rentals of Oseney Abbey and St. John's Hospital (and its supplanter Magdalen College), and the bursarial accounts of the older colleges, all of whom, save the Queen's College, owned halls. Oseney Abbey and St. John's Hospital were particularly notable landlords of halls, the abbey owning twenty, and the hospital ten.[2] None of the rentals of St. Frideswide's Priory, which owned nine halls, has survived, nor have those of the abbeys of Eynsham, Abingdon, and Godstow, and the priories of Littlemore and Studley, each of whom owned from one to three halls. The University, owner of four halls, has left no record of its lettings, nor have the four private landlords who each owned a hall.[3]

The following table sets out the total number of halls entered in each list in the Chancellor's Registers between 1436 and 1537 and in that of John Rous.

1436	1438	1444	1445	1446	1450	1451	1452	1453	1457
55	64	69	67	60	49	55	61	59	32*

1458	1461	1462	1463	1468	1469	Rous	1499	1501	1503
63	60	55	5*	47	50	67	24	54	53

1505	1508	1510	1511	1512	1513	1514	1527	1528	1529
52	45	10*	25	16	18	13	13	12	15

1530	1531	1532	1533	1534	1535	1537
8	11	12	9	9	7	8

* incomplete

[1] *Wood's City of Oxford*, i. 635–8.

[2] *Cartulary of Oseney Abbey*, ed. H. E. Salter, iii (O.H.S. xci, 1929), *passim*; *Cartulary of the Hospital of St. John the Baptist*, ed. H. E. Salter, ii (O.H.S. lxviii, 1915), *passim*.

[3] The ownership of halls and also their whereabouts are indicated by Dr. H. E. Salter in the list of halls that forms Appendix iii to his edition of *Registrum Cancellarii Oxon. 1434–1469*, ii. 357–67. See also the map in *V.C.H. Oxford*, iii, after p. 36.

In some lists the names of certain halls are missing, but reappear in the list for the following year. These omissions may be due to oversight on the part of the principals concerned. In 1503, Richard FitzJames, bishop of Rochester and 'Cancellarius natus' of the University, threatened to suspend all principals who had failed to appear at the annual review of cautions on 9 September.[1] Again, a blank space after the name of a hall in a list does not necessarily signify that that hall was defunct and without a principal. In Chancellor's Register D the scribe or Registrar wrote out in advance each year an identical list of halls preparatory for the review in September, with the intention of filling in the names of the principals or their representatives as each appeared. Sometimes it may be discovered on other evidence that a hall with a blank space left against it was still functioning. On the other hand, a hall may continue to be entered in these lists when, in fact, it had become ruinous and its site reverted to use as a garden, such, for instance, as St. Christopher Hall and Shield Hall.

Not all halls were self-sufficient. Some were small establishments, not served by a cook or a manciple, but formed annexes to larger halls whither their inmates resorted for their meals and lectures.[2] Although an old University ordinance disallowed tenure of two principalships by one principal, this restriction was later overcome by a principal's obtaining control over additional halls by arranging with graduate colleagues acting on his behalf to tender cautions for them in their names.[3] But in the lists of halls in the Chancellor's Registers it is seldom possible to determine which halls were grouped in this way. For instance, it is to be inferred from the wording of their entries in the list of 1457 that Great White Hall and Hawk Hall in Chainey Lane (now Market Street), Little White Hall in Ship Street, and Little St. Martin Hall at the corner of Merton Street and Grove Street were under one principal, Master Walter Bate, but it is not evident from the wording in the same list that White Hall and St. Hugh Hall in the High Street were annexed to St. Edmund Hall: this is only known on other authority.[4] It follows, therefore, that, as regards the number of halls in existence in any one year, the figures obtainable

---

[1] O.U.A., Reg. Cancell. D, fol. 47ᵛ.

[2] A. B. Emden, *An Oxford Hall in Medieval Times* (Oxford, 1927; reprint, 1968), pp. 209–10.   [3] Ibid., pp. 27, 120.

[4] *Registrum Cancellarii Oxon. 1434–1469*, i. 404, 405; A. B. Emden, op. cit., pp. 167, 168.

from the lists in the Chancellor's Register must be interpreted with caution.

With these reservations in mind, it may be concluded that John Rous may be relied on in his naming of sixty-seven halls, large and small, as known to him during his lifetime; but that, before the gap in the Chancellor's Registers between 1469 and 1499, there was a slight decrease among the smaller halls. Even so, the presence of newcomers among the halls must still be allowed for. Plummer Hall, at the corner of Ship Street and Turl Street, appears for the first time in the list of 1451 and continues until the break in the Chancellor's Registers in 1469. Burnell's Inn alias London College, after it ceased to be occupied by Benedictine monks, probably of St. Mary's Abbey, York, continued as an academical hall until its absorption by Cardinal College.[1] Magdalen Hall on its first foundation by Bishop Waynflete in 1448 had a temporary home in Bostar Hall and Hare Hall at the lower end of the High Street on the south side.[2]

After the resumption of the Chancellor's Registers in 1499 the state of the halls is more difficult to estimate, as counting the blank spaces against the entries in the lists in Chancellor's Register D gives a deceptive impression of the rate of decline. At least fourteen halls out of the thirty-three with blank spaces against them are shown from subsequent occurrences in the register to have still been in occupation. Probably the total of fifty-two in the list of 1505, the last in that register, is near the mark.[3] But it appears that during the next twenty years a much more serious drop in numbers occurred. This was in part due to the foundation of two new colleges, Brasenose in 1512, and Corpus Christi in 1517, which accounted for the appropriation of fourteen halls or former hall sites. But that was not the only cause of decrease, for in the list of 1513 the number of halls had shrunk to eighteen.[4] In Dr. H. E. Salter's view 'it was not so much the growth of colleges that caused the halls to disappear, as the decrease in the numbers of the University', which he attributes to the 'almost continuous plague' which afflicted Oxford between 1440 and 1520.[5]

---

[1] *Balliol Oxford Deeds*, ed. H. E. Salter (O.H.S. lxiv, 1913), p. 95. W. A. Pantin, 'Before Wolsey', *Essays in British History presented to Sir Keith Feiling*, ed. H. R. Trevor-Roper (1964), pp. 45–7.   [2] *V.C.H. Oxford*, iii. 193.
[3] O.U.A., Reg. Cancell. D, fols. 224ᵛ–225.
[4] O.U.A., Reg. Cancell. ꟻ, fol. 199.
[5] *Registrum Cancellarii Oxon. 1434–1469*, ii. 358.

Another explanation of some weight was put forward by the notorious Dr. John London, Warden of New College, who had known Oxford since he entered the college as a scholar from Winchester in 1503. He attributed the decrease in the number of halls to the rise of prices in Oxford. In a letter, dated 13 April 1526, to Thomas Wriothesley, subsequently Clerk to the Signet and Lord Chancellor, he complains that 'The commyns in our colledges and hallys by thes incorporations do notably increase in price and be lesse in quantitie', and goes on to remark that in his own college, 'every yere our commyns amownteth above the old rate to the somme of £60'. In support of his contention he encloses a memorandum drawn up by the Commissary 'upon thexamination of the manciples', and asks that it may be looked into. He concludes his letter with the statement that 'ther be decayed xvj hallys in Oxford wᵗin thes few yeris and now in all our hallys be nott left 70 scolers', and forecasts that 'unles thes incorporations be layd down and indifferent order taken for vitelles mo will decay shortly and the towne will decay as well as the universytie'.[1] It would seem from Dr. London's representation of the state of affairs in Oxford that the University in the reign of Henry VIII was being confronted once again with the old bogy of prices which had threatened it in the reign of Henry III. London could speak from experience on the subject of halls, for he had been Principal of Hincksey Hall in 1513 and 1514. If his account of the plight of the halls was well founded, it was to be expected that they would be more vulnerable than the colleges as they were unendowed and, having no estates, had to rely entirely on members of local trade guilds for their supply of victuals.[2]

The decline in the number of halls was not averted. In 1537, the last year in which an annual list of halls is recorded in a Chancellor's Register, the names of only 8 are entered. When, in August 1552, Dr. Owen Oglethorpe, as Vice-Chancellor, caused a census of the colleges and halls to be taken, the 8 remaining halls mustered 260 members.[3] The survivors were Broad Gates (later Pembroke College), 41 names; St. Mary Hall (later incorporated in Oriel

---

[1] London B. L., MS. Cotton Titus B. I, fol. 100ᵛ (old foliation); *Letters and Papers Foreign and Domestic, Henry VIII*, iv, pt. ii, 1220.

[2] O.U.A., Reg. Cancell. 𝔥, fol. 373. See also R. Fasnacht, *A History of the City of Oxford* (1954), pp. 77–9.

[3] *Register of the Univ. of Oxford*, vol. i, ed. C. W. Boase (O.H.S. i., 1884), pp. xxiv–xxv.

College), 23 names; St. Alban Hall (later incorporated in Merton College), 38 names; Magdalen Hall (later, after migration, appropriated by Hertford College of the second foundation), 35 names; Hart Hall (later converted into Hertford College of the first foundation), 45 names; White Hall (later Jesus College), 20 names; New Inn (later appropriated by Balliol College), 49 names; and St. Edmund Hall, 9 names.

During the interval of thirty-six years which elapsed between Dr. London's pessimistic letter and Dr. Oglethorpe's census some evidence for the numbers of members of individual halls can be obtained from a practice that first becomes apparent at the beginning of the sixteenth century. A graduate needed to have the consent of the community of the hall concerned before the Vice-Chancellor would admit him as principal. On 10 February 1508, Master John Orton was admitted principal of Great and Little White Halls and Pery Hall 'ex consensu omnium scolarium aulae'.[1] Thereafter the Chancellor's Registers contain several notices confirming this practice. Apparently all the members of a hall accompanied their principal-elect when he proceeded to the Vice-Chancellor for admission. The number of members of Hincksey Hall who took part in the election of a new principal in October 1534 was entered in the Chancellor's Register as about 20 ('circiter viginti scolares').[2] In June 1536 the number of electors to the principalship of the same hall was about 12.[3]

In September 1535 Master Robert Huick was suspended from the principalship of St. Alban Hall by the Vice-Chancellor for expressing his radical views on the 'Arts' curriculum. Eighteen members of the hall petitioned Thomas Cromwell that he might be reinstated, as 'he is a man of substantial learning, who inveighs against Dunce, Antonie, and other barbarous authors, calling them the destruction of good wits'. They won their suit.[4] A disputed election to the principalship of Great and Little White Halls and St. Laurence Hall occurred in June 1536: 14 members supported one candidate, and 9 another.[5] The members of Hart Hall who took the Oath of Supremacy in 1534 numbered 29 (26 undergraduates and 3 B.A.s):[6] it is the only hall whose numbers

[1] O.U.A., Reg. Cancell. ꓶ, fol. 46.
[2] O.U.A., Reg. Cancell. ꓶ, fol. 279.   [3] Ibid., fol. 386.
[4] *Letters and Papers Foreign and Domestic, Henry VIII*, ix. 122.
[5] O.U.A., Reg. Cancell. ꓶ, fol. 404ᵛ.
[6] Ibid., fol. 376.

on the occasion of this round of statutory oath-taking is known. These totals of membership in individual halls between 1526 and 1552 show an appreciable rise in numbers; but the rise came too late for the resuscitation of halls already defunct. By then the newer colleges were opening their doors for the admission of undergraduates, and the older colleges were shortly to follow.

Certain aspects of the halls, their administration and their buildings, during the later medieval period have been illuminated by Dr. H. E. Salter and Dr. W. A. Pantin.[1] But some reference may be in place here concerning their principals and their general position in the University.

The importance of the Oxford halls as the chief places of residence for the medieval undergraduate has come to be recognized, but the calibre of their succession of principals is also worthy of notice. An examination of the academical careers of the principals of halls, whether for Artists or for Legists, shows that they were largely drawn from the more prominent masters in the University. During the period 1434 to 1518, despite the gap of thirty years in the Chancellor's Registers, it may be reckoned that seventy-seven principals of 'Arts' halls, or their graduate colleagues, held the office of University proctor. They also figure frequently among the regent masters who held other University offices, such as the keepers of loan chests, collectors of University rents, collators of University sermons, and clerks of the market, etc. The principals of the 'Law' halls were notably active as ecclesiastical lawyers, some practising in the Chancellor's Court, some acting as officials or commissaries of bishops and archdeacons.[2] Many principals, too, availed themselves of the opportunity that their office gave them to extend their own studies with the object of adding a higher degree in theology or law to their qualifications.

Principalships evidently proved attractive to fellows of colleges, as, apparently, they were not required to resign their fellowships. It was to be expected that the principalships of halls that were owned by colleges, as St. Alban Hall and other halls in Merton Street, owned by Merton College, St. Mary Hall and, after 1451, Great Bedell Hall by Oriel College, Great Black Hall and Hart

[1] *Registrum Cancell. Oxon. 1434–1469*, i. xxvii–xxxi, ii. 357–9; W. A. Pantin, 'The Halls and Schools of Medieval Oxford', pp. 31–100.

[2] See W. A. Pantin, 'Before Wolsey', *Essays in British History presented to Sir Keith Feiling*, pp. 48–9.

Hall by Exeter College, Burnell's Inn by Balliol College, and Vine Hall and Trillock's Inn by New College, would often be sought after by fellows of their parent colleges. But other halls proved no less attractive. For instance,[1] Master Edward Trowbridge, fellow of Oriel, on resigning the principalship of Beam Hall, opposite to Merton College, in 1507, was succeeded by Master Hugh Pole, fellow of All Souls, to be followed in 1511 by Master John Gold, an expelled fellow of Magdalen and, in 1513, by Master John Blysse, fellow of Merton. Again between 1438 and 1469 Staple Hall in Schools Street had among its principals two fellows of Balliol, two fellows of Lincoln, a fellow of Queen's, and a graduate of Durham College.[2]

Besides the extra emoluments which fellows of colleges might hope to derive from the office, a principalship had a further attraction for graduates without college ties. Not a few principals coupled with the charge of a hall a cure of souls as the incumbent of a parish. Several of the benefices held by principals were in Oxford and its vicinity, but by no means all. There follow here a few examples to illustrate this practice.

Master Richard Andrewe, principal of Aristotle Hall by 1457, was at the same time vicar of St. Giles, Oxford.[3] Master Robert Lawles, principal of Haberdash Hall with Little St. Edmund Hall, had been instituted vicar of Cuddesdon, Oxon., in 1466, a year previous to his admission as principal.[4] Master Stephen Tyler, principal of Beam Hall from 1457 to 1466, was already rector of Checkendon, Oxon. Master John Fisher, B.Cn.L., principal of Beef Hall in 1457, was rector of Marston Trussell, Northants., from 1442 to 1470, and was succeeded in 1463 as principal by Master Laurence Cokkes, B.Cn. and C.L., fellow of New College, who, while qualifying for a doctorate in Canon Law, alternated in the principalship with Master John Obyn or Hobyn, B.Cn. and C.L., rector of Morcott, Rutland, and Master Thomas Reynolds, B.Cn. and C.L., rector of Warmington, Warwickshire. Master Thomas Saunders, as B.A., in 1436 obtained the principalship of Greek Hall and continued in office until he incepted as D.Cn.L.

---

[1] *B.R.U.O.* ii. 790; iii. 1490, 1909–10; O.U.A. Reg. Cancell. ꟻ, fols. 139, 147ᵛ, 199.

[2] *Registrum Cancellarii Oxon. 1434–1469*, i. 21, 39, 47, 340; ii. 2, 94, 321.

[3] *B.R.U.O.* i. 35–6.

[4] For this and subsequent biographical references see *B.R.U.O.* under name mentioned.

in 1453. Meanwhile he was instituted rector of Shellingford, Berks., in 1449, and rector of St. Martin's, Oxford, in 1452.

Peckwater Inn, one of the chief 'Law' halls, furnishes a particularly good example of the prevalence of this practice. In 1436 and still in 1438, Master Walter Sandwich, B.Cn.L., was principal, during which time he exchanged the rectory of Kingsnorth, Kent, for that of St. Michael's Southgate, Oxford. His successor, Master Luke Langcok, B.Cn. and C.L., while principal, exchanged the rectory of Chinnor, Oxon., for the same rectory of St. Michael's, Southgate. The next principal, Master John Morton, D.C.L., later archbishop of Canterbury and cardinal, who had been a fellow of the inn since 1448, combined the rectory of Shellingford, Berks., and a canonry of Wells with the post of official of the Chancellor of the University. Master William Dayfot, B.Cn.L. and also official of the Chancellor, had been vicar of Headington and Marston, Oxon., for two years before his resignation in February 1462. It is not known that his successor, Master John Cooke, B.Cn.L., who was to become a distinguished diplomat, held any benefice with the principalship, but Master William Shirwood, admitted principal in 1467, had been rector of St. Michael's, Southgate, for nearly ten years, and vicar of St. Paul's, Malmesbury, Wilts., since 1462. Master William Horsey, B.Cn. and C.L., principal by 1499, was already rector of Wootton Courtenay, Somerset, and of the free chapel of Clifton Maybank, Dorset; and the next principal but one, Master William Chichester, B.C.L., admitted in 1505, was already rector of the free chapel of Athelhampton, Dorset, and rector of Arlington, Devon. Lastly, Master Peter Lygham, B.C.L., who held two benefices with the principalship, the rectory of St. Michael's, Southgate, as had three of his predecessors, and the vicarage of St. Gulval, Cornwall, nearly forfeited the principalship owing to his absences.

To hold a benefice with the principalship of a hall required a bishop's licence or a papal indult, but records of such permission being granted are exceptional. In 1448 Master Robert Halle, D.Cn.L., on institution as rector of Mixbury, Oxon., received licence from Bishop Alnwick to hold this benefice with the principalship of Beef Hall, to which he had been admitted in 1444. Master Geoffrey Langbroke, B.Cn.L., principal of Beke's Inn by 1446, was granted a papal indult in 1443 for seven years to study at the University while rector of Manaton, Devon. Master John

Carkeke, B.Cn. and C.L., principal of Broadgates Hall by All Saints Church from 1438 to 1445, was at the same time chaplain of St. Anne's Chantry in that church, until his appointment as vicar of St. Gorran, Cornwall, in 1442, when he obtained a papal indult for four years to study at the University. It must be presumed that the many other principals of halls who held benefices were duly authorized to do so, notwithstanding the apparent lack of evidence.[1]

A review of the subsequent careers of the graduates who became principals during the course of the century covered by this article would confirm the favourable impression given by their academical record. This may be corroborated here by noting the names of twelve principals who rose to be diocesan bishops. Robert Stillington, bishop of Bath and Wells (1466–91), had been principal of Deep Hall in 1442. He incepted as D.C.L. in the following year, and probably continued as principal until his appointment as rector of Beverston, Glos., in 1443. James Goldwell, bishop of Norwich (1472–99), had been principal of St. George Hall in 1450, being at the time a fellow of All Souls, and continued as principal and fellow until after his inception as D.C.L. in March 1452. John Marshall, bishop of Llandaff (1478–96), had been admitted principal of Coleshill Hall in 1448, being at the same time a fellow of Merton, and was still principal in 1453. As has been already mentioned, John Morton, successively bishop of Ely and archbishop of Canterbury (1479–1500), had been admitted principal of Peckwater Inn in 1452 during his regency as D.C.L. John Arundel, successively bishop of Coventry and Lichfield, and bishop of Exeter (1496–1504), had been principal of Great Black Hall in 1461 and was still so in 1469, being at the same time rector of Kibworth Beauchamp, Leics. John Morgan alias Yong, bishop of St. Davids (1496–1504), had been principal of Solar Hall in 1469. Richard FitzJames, successively bishop of Rochester, Chichester, and London (1497–1522), had been principal of Urban Hall with Corner Hall and St. Christopher Hall, while at the same time a fellow of Merton, and on resignation of his fellowship in 1477 became principal of St. Alban Hall, being also canon of Wells. Richard Mayew, bishop of Hereford (1504–16), had been admitted principal of Great Black Hall in 1468, while

[1] See M. Bowker, *The Secular Clergy in the Diocese of Lincoln 1495–1520* (1968), pp. 93–8.

still fellow of New College. John Longland, bishop of Lincoln (1521–47), had been principal of Magdalen Hall from 1506 to 1507, while rector of Woodham Ferrers, Essex. John Stokesley, bishop of London (1530–9), had preceded Bishop Longland as principal of Magdalen Hall. Henry Morgan, bishop of St. Davids (1554–9), had resigned the principalship of St. Edward Hall in 1528, having held the office for at least one year.[1] And lastly, Thomas Young, successively bishop of St. Davids and archbishop of York (1560–8), had been principal of Broadgates Hall from 1542 to 1546.[2] To these may be added for good measure Edmund Bonner, Stokesley's successor as bishop of London, who had been an undergraduate of Broadgates Hall.[3] During the same period only seven heads of colleges, three of whom had been principals of halls, became diocesan bishops. The academical halls had good cause to be proud of their *alumni*.

Although much reduced in numbers, academical halls just managed to survive to take their place in Oxford of the post-Reformation era; but there was one type of hall that succumbed with notable suddennness in the face of changing times. The grammar-halls of medieval Oxford had made a distinguished educational contribution of their own. John Leland the elder, an outstanding grammarian, died in 1428, but the tradition that he had upheld was carried on by his disciple and son-in-law, John Cobbow of Lion Hall, by Richard Bulkley of Tackley's Inn, and by John Russell of Yng Hall. Cobbow closed his establishment about 1465. Bulkley was still in harness in 1458, at which date he had control of Plummer Hall and St. Laurence Hall, presumably as extra boarding-houses. He, too, had probably retired by 1465. Russell was renting St. Edward Hall, opposite Oriel College, in 1455, as a dependent hall, but how long after that he continued schoolmastering is not known. Rous mentions a fourth grammar-hall, St. Cuthbert Hall, but this appears from the list of halls for 1453 to have been one of Bulkley's secondary halls.[4]

The retirement of Cobbow and Bulkley removed the last of the Oxford grammarians of the old school. Cobbow's long-familiar occupancy of Lion Hall and Bulkley's of Tackley's Inn were

[1] O.U.A., Reg. Cancell. ♁, fols. 332ᵛ, 335bᵛ.
[2] D. Macleane, *History of Pembroke College* (O.H.S. xxxiii, 1897), pp. 78–9.
[3] Ibid., pp. 83–7.
[4] *Registrum Cancellarii Oxon. 1434–1469*, i. 339; ii. 3.

commemorated in popular usage by their two halls' becoming known as Cob Hall and Bulkley Hall respectively. In concern at the gap created by the loss of the grammar-halls the University addressed a letter in 1466 to John Chedworth, bishop of Lincoln, asking for his help, but, as Anthony Wood remarks, 'what good these letters produced I find not'.[1] The principals of St. Edmund Hall since the middle of the century had made the experiment of attaching to it St. Hugh Hall in the High Street to serve as a grammar-hall, but it was in a ruinous condition by 1487, probably owing to the rapid success of the free grammar-school erected by Bishop Waynflete, himself a former schoolmaster, in connection with his new foundation of Magdalen College.[2]

There was still room in the University, as time has proved, for new academical societies, but they have needed to be endowed and incorporated colleges. The uncertainties of the Reformation years and competition from the colleges, added to continuing economic pressures, militated against the establishment of more unendowed halls dependent upon voluntary graduate enterprise.

A. B. EMDEN

[1] *Epistolae Academicae Oxon.*, ed. H. Anstey, ii (O.H.S. xxxvi, 1898), p. 381; A. Wood, *The History and Antiquities of the Univ. of Oxford*, ed. Gutch (Oxford, 1792), i. 627.
[2] A. B. Emden, *An Oxford Hall* . . . , pp. 168–9, 173–5.

16

An Unnoticed Letter from Bessarion to Lorenzo Valla

AMONG the books and papers left to the Biblioteca Marciana at Venice by Jacopo Morelli[1] is his working copy of A. Bandini, *De vita et gestis Bessarionis* (Florence, 1777).[2] Between the leaves of this book there are preserved several loose sheets and scraps of paper (numbered fols. 1–25), covered with notes in Morelli's hand. Most of these notes are references to other books concerning matters mentioned by Bandini, but there is one exception: On fol. 19^{rv} Morelli has transcribed a letter from Bessarion to Lorenzo Valla, under the heading 'da cod. Ms sec. XV presso il cav⟨aliere⟩ Cicognara'. The letter is otherwise unknown and was never published by Morelli.

It has been, of course, our first concern after coming across this text to find the manuscript from which Morelli, according to his note, copied it, and which at that time apparently belonged to Count Leopoldo Cicognara, a distinguished collector and historian of art, who was president of the Accademia di Belle Arti at Venice from 1808 to his death in 1834. His library, consisting mainly of printed books, but containing also some manuscripts, was in Cicognara's lifetime acquired by Pope Leo XII and later incorporated in the Vatican Library.[3] However, a search at the Vaticana

---

[1] Concerning the Abbé Jacopo Morelli (1745–1819), librarian of the Biblioteca Marciana from 1778, see C. Frati, *Dizionario bio-bibliografico dei bibliotecari e bibliofili italiani dal sec. XIV al XIX*, ed. A. Sorbelli (Florence, 1913), pp. 379–84, and M. Parenti, *Aggiunte al Dizionario bio-bibliografico . . .*, i. 264–7.

[2] Shelfmark: MS. Marcian. lat., cl. XIV, 324 (collocazione 4072) olim Riserv. 123; see G. Valentinelli, *Bibliotheca Manuscripta ad S. Marcum Venetiarum*, vi. 218 (cl. XXII, no. 254).

[3] Concerning Count Leopoldo Cicognara (1767–1834) see Frati, op. cit., pp. 165–7, and Parenti, op. cit., pp. 262–3. The information in Frati, p. 166, under no. 19, that a catalogue of Cicognara's MSS. in his own hand was preserved at Florence, Bibl. Nazionale, raccolta Gonnelli, cartella 25, is erroneous. No catalogue of Cicognara MSS. can be found among the MSS. of the Biblioteca

for Morelli's source has remained without any result. The Cicognara manuscripts are in the Archives of the Vatican Library, but not at present accessible to the reader, and there is no list or catalogue available with the help of which it might be possible to trace the 'codice manoscritto del sec. XV' which Morelli saw. In any case, Morelli's indications are too vague to provide a basis for a systematic search. However, on the authority of the great scholar and librarian of the Biblioteca Marciana, and on the internal evidence of the letter itself, we can accept this text as an authentic document of the fifteenth century, although it is at present known only in this early nineteenth-century copy.

MS. Marcianus latinus cl. XIV, 324 (coll. 4072), fol. 19^{rv}

'Da cod. MS. s. XV presso il cavaliere Cicognara'
Bessario Card. Tusculanus Laurentio Vallensi s. p. d.
Fabium Quintilianum unum ex praecipuis Latinae linguae auctoribus semper putavimus: quam opinionem nostram sententia tua non solum confirmavit, verum etiam ita auxit, ut neminem iam huic in arte rhetorica praeponendum existimemus. Fecimus proximis diebus eum librum transcribi, tantum inter ceteros libros pulcritudine ac decore praestantem, quantum sol ceteris sideribus lucidior est. Verum idem, ut alii fere omnes, mendosus est, indigna sane res, ut homo facie tam liberalis, multo sanguine, multo rubore suffusa, cui ingenua totius corporis pulcritudo et regius quidam decor inest, adeo imbecillis viribus, adeo nervis infirmus sit. Quare nos quidem statuimus quam maxime fieri poterit diligentia eum librum curari, quo talis sit qualem pulcritudo eius meretur. Ad hoc vero non medici nobis desunt, sed instrumenta ad medendum. Petimus igitur abs te per humanitatem tuam, per mutuum amorem nostrum, ea instrumenta, id est Quintilianum tuum, qui solus in orbe terrarum correctus est, ad nos mittas. Tamdiu hospitabitur nobiscum quoad recte convaluerit. Postea ad te statim integer revertetur; nec parvam sibi laudem ex hac peregrinatione adeptam putabit, qui talem virum ex valetudinario bene valere fecerit. Nos vero una cum Quintiliano nostro tibi perpetuo divincti erimus. Sed haec hactenus.

Hippocratem tuum, si adhuc tuus est, aut nobis dones oportet, tantundem aut plus muneris a nobis accepturus, aut vendas tanti quanti tibi steterit, aut eius loco alium[1] a nobis librum requiras. Si vero

Nazionale either in the Gonnelli collection or in any other fonds. The raccolta Gonnelli, which is arranged alphabetically, does contain a number of letters from Count Cicognara, but not in cartella 25.

[1] The manuscript has 'aliud', an obvious mistake in transcription, which we have corrected.

abs te capite diminutus, alienaeque potestatis effectus est, quo pacto illum comparare possimus, ad nos scribas. Vale.

Bessarion writes that, mainly thanks to Valla, he has learnt fully to appreciate the pre-eminence of Quintilian among writers on the art of rhetoric. He had commissioned a copy of the *Institutio oratoria* and recently received the completed codex. This was a volume of great magnificence, but its text—just like that of practically all existing manuscripts of this work—was sadly corrupt. Therefore Bessarion begs Valla to lend him his emended manuscript of the *Institutio*, 'the only corrected copy in the world',[1] and thus to provide the 'doctors' in the Cardinal's entourage with the means of healing the diseased text, and of making the book as sound intrinsically as it was splendid in outward appearance. Immediately after the completion of the cure, so the Cardinal assures Valla, the manuscript will be returned.

Bessarion's second request concerns a manuscript of Hippocrates owned by Valla. The Cardinal seems to have reason to believe that his friend is about to part with this book, if he has not already done so, and he is determined to secure it for himself. Therefore he urges Valla to state the terms—giving him a choice of attractive propositions—on which he, or whoever was the present owner, might be willing to hand over the codex to Bessarion.

The opening words of the letter allude to Valla's early, now lost, treatise *De comparatione Ciceronis Quintilianique*[2], and imply that the Cardinal was familiar with this work—they may, of course, also allude to conversations about this subject, which had taken place at some time between Bessarion and Valla. While this part of the letter, in which the Cardinal defers in a flattering way to Valla's competence as a critic of Latin authors, is written in a relaxed and playful style, the passage concerning the Hippocrates has a greater urgency, revealing the collector's passionate wish not to let a desired object slip out of his reach.

As transmitted by Morelli, our document does not have any indication of the place where it was written, nor does it bear a date,

---

[1] Concerning the ambiguity in the humanist use of 'correctus' (= 'correct' and = 'corrected') see Silvia Rizzo, *Il lessico filologico degli umanisti* (Rome, 1973), p. 215 and pp. 268–76. There cannot be any doubt but that Bessarion uses the term here in the sense of 'emended', but he was probably not at all times very conscious of the distinction.

[2] See R. Sabbadini, *Cronologia della vita del Valla*, in L. Barozzi and R. Sabbadini, *Studi sul Panormita e sul Valla* (Florence, 1891), pp. 38 f.

but this can be fixed approximately by reference to a letter from
Valla to Tortelli from Naples, last published by R. Sabbadini and
convincingly dated by him to 1447.[1]

Valla's letter mentions the same manuscripts as the document
with which we are dealing. The passage in question runs as follows:

> Quintilianum quem poscis (habeo enim duo) iuberem tibi tradere...,
> tametsi nollem glosas quas illi feci ab aliis transcribi prius quam recog-
> noverim et alias adhuc addiderim. Nam ut scias quo studio glosas
> eas facturus sim, certum est mihi omnes libros qui supersunt legendo
> evolvere, eos presertim qui ante Quintilianum extiterunt. Quid queris?
> Emi Hypocratem qui fuit Roberti, legi fere omnia illius opera. Ubi
> aliquod ad ornamentum glosarum inveni, ut est παιδομαθεῖς vocari
> qui in sua quique arte prestantissimi sunt. Cuius hominis in hac re
> auctoritas maior est quam aut Aristotelis aut Platonis quia prior fuit.
> Tamen ut Quintilianum ad transcribendum legendumve emendatissi-
> mum habeas, enixius laborarem ut meus in tuas manus perveniret, nisi
> potius crederem me istuc venturum, presertim rege tam Rome vicino.

Evidently Tortelli has asked for the loan of Valla's corrected copy
of Quintilian but is, for the time being, put off by his friend,
because Valla wishes to revise his annotations to the *Institutio* and
to add to them further ones. His exacting ideal of scholarship
demands that a knowledge of the whole of ancient literature, at
least of all the authors prior in time to Quintilian, should be
brought to bear on the explanation of his text. Thus, when reading the works of Hippocrates, of which he had recently bought
a codex, he had found something useful for his purpose, i.e. a confirmation of the definition of παιδομαθής given by Quintilian in
Book I. 12. 10.[2]

Clearly, Valla's letter to Tortelli and our letter from Bessarion
to Valla cannot be separated by a great interval in time. Though it
is impossible to fix the date of the latter exactly, we will try to
narrow the span of time within which it was probably written, on
the understanding that this can be done only conjecturally.

We may exclude the two years when Bessarion and Valla were

---

[1] See Sabbadini, *Cronologia*, pp. 114–15, letter no. 63, of 1 January 1447, from
the autograph in MS. Vat. lat. 4053, fol. 147.

[2] See Hippocrates, *Νόμος*, ed. and tr. W. H. S. Jones (London, 1932), ii.
262–4, where παιδομαθία is named among the qualities necessary for anyone
wanting to become a doctor.

both living in Rome. Therefore the letter was written either before 1448 when Valla returned to Rome, or after 16 March 1450, when Bessarion took up his post as papal legate at Bologna.[1]

In solving this question of the date, we do not get any help from Bessarion's codex of the *Institutio oratoria*, MS. Marcian. lat. 435 (coll. 1965), which in every way corresponds to the Cardinal's description. It is a parchment codex (257 × 365 mm.), comprising ii+171 folios, written throughout in the same hand. On fol. 1 it bears the usual ex-libris and the shelfmarks in Greek and in Latin written by the Cardinal himself: 'Quintiliani institutiones. .b. Caᴸᵣ Tusculani. locus 41.' The book is lavishly produced and richly decorated in gold, red, and blue. The title-page, fol. 1, is framed on three sides by garlands, the right-hand margin showing also the miniature of a pelican. At the top of the page, the garland is interrupted by the inscription BISSARO̅. CA̅. TUSCUŁ. The bottom of the page shows the arms of Bessarion flanked by vases filled with flowers, behind which a walled town can be discerned in the distance. The incipits of individual books have elaborate initials, the beginnings of chapters are rubricated, and so are the Greek terms occurring in the text. According to the judgement of Miss de la Mare who has kindly examined my photographic copies of the manuscript, the decorations and the script are in the style characteristic of Bolognese workshops in the middle of the fifteenth century, but it is possible that the manuscript is the work of a Roman scribe imitating the style of Bologna.

However, while the evidence of the manuscript does not exclude the possibility that Bessarion's letter referring to it was written from Rome in 1447, it seems more probable that it was in fact written from Bologna, after Bessarion had taken up his residence there as papal legate. If we assume that he commissioned the work soon after his arrival and allow about six months for its completion, the letter could have been written towards the end of 1450 or early in 1451.[2] The following considerations lead to this conclusion.

---

[1] Several of Bessarion's dated Latin MSS. were written during this period at Bologna, e.g. in 1450 the Marcian. lat. 50 (coll. 1499) = Hieronymus, *Epistolae*; in 1454 the following three codices: Marcian. lat. 40 (coll. 1926) = Lactantius, *Sermones*; Marcian. lat. 381 (coll. 1847) = Tacitus, *Historiae*; MS. Oxford, Bodl. Canon. Class. Lat. 131 = Xenophon, *Memorabilia interprete Bessarione*, Aurelius Victor, *Origo gentis romanae*.

[2] See Bessarion's letter to Valla thanking him for the first two parts of the

1. The general tone of the letter expresses a degree of familiarity which seems to presuppose a period during which Bessarion and Valla had met frequently and had collaborated on various subjects, as they did in Rome during the years 1448–9. The friendship between the two men which had developed during this period and the mutual desire for each other's company are evident also from other communications sent to Valla from Bologna by the Cardinal himself, as well as by Niccolò Perotti on his master's behalf.[1]

2. When Bessarion calls Valla's Quintilian 'the only corrected copy in the world', he seems to refer to something quite widely known in the world of scholars, as if Valla's occupation with the *Institutio* had reached a stage somewhat beyond that described in 1447 in his letter to Tortelli, when he was still reluctant to allow his annotations to be used.[2] As we know that it was during the

Antidotum, in L. Mohler, *Kardinal Bessarion als Theologe, Humanist und Staats-mann*, iii, *Aus Bessarions Gelehrtenkreis* (Paderborn, 1942), p. 471, letter 24.

[1] See the letter from Niccolò Perotti to Valla, inviting him to come to Bologna: '. . . Que res clementissimo principi meo maximam voluptatem afferret', dated to the middle of 1451 by Sabbadini, *Cronologia*, p. 130, letter 79. Concerning collaboration between Bessarion and Valla during 1448 and 1449, see ibid., Valla's letter to Perotti of 17 November 1449, pp. 125–6. See also A. Perosa in his edition of L. Valla, *Collatio Novi Testamenti* (Florence, 1970), Introduzione, pp. xxxiv, xliv. Alluding to this work, Georgius Trapezuntius, in an unpublished letter, accuses Bessarion of having given his support to Valla: 'Omnes . . . dominatio tua etiam ignorantissimos et quidem coram mihi preferebat, Vallam quoque hominem penitus indoctum, theologia credo eius delectatus, quam domi tue conscripsit ac edidit.'—Mr. John Monfasani, who is editing this and other documents concerning Georgius Trapezuntius discovered by him, has kindly shown me this text in manuscript. Bessarion's joke about the 'doctors' who would be competent to cure his Quintilian if provided with the proper instruments may be an allusion to Niccolò Perotti, who had joined his *familia* in 1450, and who had become very friendly with Valla.

[2] M. Winterbottom, 'Fifteenth-century Manuscripts of Quintilian', *Classical Quarterly*, N.S. xvii (1967), 356–63, concludes, on the basis of textual collation, that a group of codices enumerated by him on p. 362 are descended from MS. Paris. B.N. lat. 7723 (*P*) which is emended by Valla, through a fair copy authorized by Valla himself. It remains to fit in his results with the external evidence concerning the different stages in Valla's work on Quintilian, but this evidence is in part doubtful and seemingly contradictory within itself. The colophon of *P*, which is not in Valla's hand, nor worded in his style (see Sabbadini, *Storia e critica di testi latini*[2] (Padua, 1971), p. 405), dates Valla's corrections to 1444, but we know from Valla's letter to Tortelli that (*a*) in 1447 he still intended to revise his annotations, and (*b*) that he had two MSS. of the *Institutio oratoria*. (Had they both been corrected by him at different times? Did he amalgamate their readings and his corrections?) It would be idle to try out the various possible hypotheses which might be made to account for all these data, given Valla's known habit of taking up finished works again and again in order to make alterations and additions; see A. Perosa, op. cit., p. xlvii and note 95.

reign of Pope Nicholas V (1447–55) that one of Valla's corrected Quintilians, or an authorized fair copy of it, served as exemplar for transcription, as well as for correction of other codices, it may be that Bessarion is asking for this particular manuscript.

3. Finally, the passage concerning Valla's Hippocrates sounds as if Bessarion was acquainted with this manuscript, which would be most likely to have happened in Rome when it was in Valla's possession. What caused him to make his urgent appeal to Valla at the particular moment was evidently that he had been alarmed by the news that the book which he coveted was going to be 'alienated'.[1]

We are thus inclined to place Bessarion's letter in 1450–1, i.e. the first years of his residence in Bologna, though the arguments for dating it in this way are admittedly speculative. One objection against this relatively late date for both the letter and the Cardinal's codex of Quintilian might be that it is difficult to understand why Bessarion, who must have been fully aware of the fact that Valla had been working for years on his emendations of the *Institutio oratoria*, should in 1450 still have commissioned a costly *codex pulcherrimus* of an unsatisfactory text, instead of waiting for the corrected exemplar. This behaviour seems to be at variance with his methods in dealing with Greek authors, where the *pulcherrimus* was usually produced only at the end of a process of collation and emendation carried out on intermediary copies.[2] The explanation might simply be that the Cardinal's special care and attention was always concentrated on the Greek section of his library, especially on the philosophical works, and that he was more likely to commit an error of judgement where the Latin side was concerned.

In any case, whatever the date of Bessarion's letter may have been, it certainly failed of its purpose, for Valla does not seem to have complied with either of the Cardinal's requests.

The text of Bessarion's Quintilian, MS. Marcian. lat. 435 (coll. 1965) has been characterized as belonging to a type based on 'private conflation' of the mutilated tradition of the *Institutio* with

---

[1] See *Institutiones*, I. 16. 1–3: 'Maxima est capitis deminutio cum aliquis simul et civitatem et libertatem amittit ... Minor ... est ... cum civitas quidem amittitur, libertas vero retinetur ... Minima est ... cum et civitas et libertas retinetur sed status hominis commutatur, quod accidit in his qui cum sui iuris fuerunt, coeperunt alieno iuri subiecti esse.'

[2] Concerning Bessarion's methods of work see E. Mioni, 'Bessarione bibliofilo e filologo', *Rivista di studi bizantini e neoellenistici*, N.S. 5 (xv), 1968, pp. 61–83.

supplements from Poggio's discovery and from medieval excerpts.[1] It is a thoroughly contaminated text which does not show any sign of having been collated with Valla's emended one, or indeed of having been subjected to any thorough revision at all. It has hardly any corrections, marginal or otherwise, the two exceptions being Book II. 15. 4, where 'opificem' had been omitted and was supplied in the margin (fol. 18), and Book IV. 2. 42, where the words 'natum filium sustuli educavi', omitted in the text, are added in the margin (fol. 51). In both cases the corrections are in the hand of Bessarion—a sign that he did sporadically collate this codex with another copy of the work (perhaps the exemplar from which it had been transcribed), and that he based his judgement concerning the corruption of the text on having examined it himself.

As to the manuscript of Hippocrates, Bessarion certainly did not succeed in obtaining it during Valla's lifetime, nor even at his death in 1465. Valla's codex contained, as we know from the letter to Tortelli, what he supposed to be Hippocrates' *Omnia opera*, but the only Hippocratean work which the Cardinal owned in 1468, when the Act of Donation of his library to Venice was drawn up, was the *Aphorisms*. We know this from the Inventory attached to this document which contained all the books owned by the Cardinal at the time;[2] though not all of them went to Venice in the first consignment which he sent in the following year.

However, the inventory of 1474, which covers both the consignment of 1469 and the books which arrived in Venice after the Cardinal's death,[3] lists an item 'Hypocrates totus, in pergameno'; and the catalogue of 1554,[4] in a section 'Libri graeci qui inveniuntur

---

[1] M. Winterbottom, art. cit., pp. 364–5. The checking of his test passages against the text of MS. Marcian. lat. 435 (coll. 1965) at the beginning of Book I (up to I. 2. 6) and Book X (up to X. 6. 2) has only yielded negative results, i.e. it was not possible to accommodate the manuscript in any of the pre-Valla classes distinguished by Winterbottom in his article, owing to the high degree of contamination of the text.

[2] Published by H. Omont, 'Inventaire des manuscrits grecs et latins donnés à Saint-Marc de Venise par le Cardinal Bessarion en 1468', *Revue des bibliothèques*, iv, no. 5 (Paris, 1894), 129–87, and again by T. Gasparrini Leporace and E. Mioni, in *Cento codici bessarionei* (Venice, 1968), pp. 97–149. The items in question are no. 182 = MS. Marcian. graec. 506 (coll. 768); no. 208 = MS. Marcian. graec. 278 (coll. 873); no. 209 = MS. Marcian. graec. 277 (coll. 630).

[3] The inventory is preserved in MSS. Vat. lat. 3960 and Vat. Reg. lat. 2099. For an edition of the 15th- and 16th-century inventories of Bessarion's library, see my forthcoming *The Library of Cardinal Bessarion*.

[4] MS. Marcian. lat. cl. xiv, 16 (coll. 4053) and MS. Marcian. lat. cl. xiv, 111 (coll. 4057).

in bibliotheca et tamen non sunt in indice Reverendissimi Cardinalis Niceni', has an entry 'Hippocratis omnia opera, et illius genus et vita, in pergameno'. This is the present MS. Marcian. graec. 269 (coll. 533), s. XI, which has in fact, on fol. 1ᵛ, in a fifteenth-century hand a Latin description of contents literally correspond-ing to the catalogue entry quoted above. It originally contained sixty Hippocratean works enumerated in a table of contents at the beginning of the volume, but it is now defective, owing to the loss of folios at the end and in the middle. It is one of the most famous of the *libri Nicaeni*, and has always been recognized as the most valuable manuscript for the history of the text of Hippocratean works; according to a recent study it is in fact the source of all surviving manuscripts containing this particular collection.[1] Obviously, it was not among the books which the Cardinal possessed when he first arrived from Greece to settle in Italy, but was acquired by him quite late in his life, between 1468 and his death in November 1472. For some reason, he did not furnish the codex with the usual full ex-libris, naming himself as possessor, but only inserted on fol. 1, both in Greek and in Latin, a brief title and the shelfmark: 'Ippocrates. locus 43.'

The question remains whether the MS. Marcian. graec. 269 could still be the same one as that once owned by Valla. Could Bessarion in the end have succeeded in acquiring it from whoever had obtained it from Valla or from Valla's heirs? There is no evidence to support a hypothesis of this kind, but neither is there any which makes it quite impossible to entertain it.

What makes it difficult to maintain that the MS. Marcian. graec. 269 could be Valla's Hippocrates is his remark that he had bought the codex 'qui fuit Roberti'. Sabbadini's interpretation of these words, viz. that this book came from the library of King Robert of Anjou, has never been contradicted. In fact, this is certainly the meaning of Valla's words and, though we do not know on what evidence his statement was based, it is quite possible

---

[1] See Th. Gomperz, 'Die Apologie der Heilkunst', *Sitzungsberichte der K. K. Akademie der Wissenschaften zu Wien*, Phil.-hist. Cl., cxx (1889), Abhand. ix, pp. 67 ff. For a new evaluation of the textual tradition see A. Rivier, *Recherches sur la tradition manuscrite du traité hippocratique 'De morbo sacro'*, Berne, 1962, *passim*. For a description of the codex see I. L. Heiberg, in Hippocrates, *Opera*, vol. i, 1, *Corpus Medicorum Graecorum*, ii (Leipzig and Berlin, 1927), Praef., pp. v–vi. Facsimile in W. Wattenbach and A. v. Velsen, *Exempla codicum graeco-rum litteris minusculis scriptorum* (Heidelberg, 1878), Tab. XXXX, XXXXI.

that it is correct. However, there is nothing in the Marcianus which points to any connection with the Angevin library. The codex has, on fol. 3ʳ, a note showing that it once belonged to a Syrian physician Georgios, but this does not absolutely exclude the possibility that it had at some other time been owned by the Angevin King.[1]

Valla's codex, as far as the contents are concerned, must have belonged to the class of which the MS. Marcian. graec. 269 is the prototype. It evidently was a large collection of Hippocratean writings purporting to be *Hippocratis opera omnia*, or *Totus Hippocrates*, and it was the collection including the *Nomos* where Valla found the confirmation of Quintilian's definition of the term παιδομαθής. This work is contained in Bessarion's Hippocrates, on fol. 3ᵛ.[2] The MS. Marcian. graec. 269 would certainly have been a prize for which the Cardinal might have hunted for a long time, and it is tempting to think that it was this invaluable codex which he had in mind when pleading with Valla to state the terms on which it could be acquired. However, this remains a hypothesis which cannot be proved.

L. LABOWSKY

---

[1] R. Sabbadini, *Le scoperte dei codici latini e greci ne' secoli XIV e XV*, anastatic reprint with author's additions and corrections, ed. E. Garin (Florence, 1967), p. 71. See also Tammaro de' Marinis, *La biblioteca napoletana dei re d'Aragon*, i (Milan, 1952), 2. Concerning the dispersal of the Angevin library see R. Sabbadini, *Giovanni da Ravenna* (Como, 1924), pp. 8 ff.; Cornelia C. Coulter, 'The Library of the Angevin Kings', *Transactions and Proceedings of the American Philological Association*, lxxv (1944), 141–55; R. Weiss, 'Il codice oxoniense e altri codici delle opere di Giovanni da Ravenna', *Giornale storico della letteratura italiana*, cxxx (1948), 133; F. Avril, 'Trois manuscrits napolitains des collections de Charles V et de Jean de Berry', *Bibliothèque de l'École des Chartes*, cxxvii (1969), 191–328.—Valla seems to have had some knowledge about the library of King Robert of Anjou; see his *De falso credita et ementita Constantini donatione*, ed. W. Schwahn (Leipzig, 1928), ch. xxiii, 72, where he says of a Bible exhibited by the Roman authorities as an autograph of St. Jerome: '. . . Illum [*sc.* codicem] ego diligentius inspectum comperi . . . scriptum esse iussu regis Roberti chirographo hominis imperiti.'

[2] According to H. Diels, 'Die Handschriften der griechischen Ärzte', part I, *Abhandlungen der K. Preuss. Akademie der Wissenschaften zu Berlin* (1905), p. 18, there are eight other MSS., predating the 15th century, which contain the Νόμος. They are Milan, Ambros. B 113 sup., s. xiv; Paris B.N. graec. 2140, s. xii–xiii; 2142, s. xiii–xiv; 2143, s. xiv; 2144, s. xiv; Vatican, Urb. graec. 68, s. xiv; Vat. graec. 276, s. xii; Vat. graec. 277, s. xiv. None of them seems to bear any signs of provenance from the Angevin library or that of Valla, but a further examination might reveal traces in one of them which have been hitherto overlooked.

IV

THE LAITY

17

E cathena et carcere: *The Imprisonment of Amaury de Montfort, 1276*

SOME time around Christmas 1275 and some ten years after the defeat and death of Simon de Montfort, earl of Leicester, at the battle of Evesham, a French ship was stopped and boarded off the coast of Cornwall or perhaps close to the mouth of Bristol Channel by four ships out of Bristol.[1] Discovering that it carried, among others, two outlawed cousins of King Edward I, Amaury de Montfort, the younger son of Simon, and his sister Eleanor, the sailors forced the ship into Bristol, where Eleanor and Amaury and all on the ship were handed over with much rejoicing to agents of Edward.[2]

Edward, in turn, as he explained to Pope Hadrian V in a letter on 8 August 1276, looked upon the 'chance capture' as an act of divine providence,[3] and he rewarded the various sailors who had seized the ship with royal protection and safe-conducts for three years.[4] For he was at war with Llywelyn of Wales, to whom he now discovered his cousin Eleanor to be betrothed; what was more, the de Montfort party was actually on its way from Normandy to Wales for her marriage to Llywelyn when the ship was intercepted. Edward therefore placed Eleanor in detention at Windsor Castle,[5] and the two Welsh Dominicans who were found on the

[1] The account followed here is that of W. Rishanger, *Chronica et Annales*, ed. H. T. Riley (R.S., 1865), p. 87.

[2] *Annales monastici*, ed. H. R. Luard, iv (R.S., 1869), p. 267, according to which the ship was becalmed outside Bristol Channel and excited the curiosity of the locals, who handed over the de Montfort party to the king, 'triumphali laetitia'.

[3] *The Liber epistolaris of Richard of Bury*, ed. N. Denholm-Young (Roxburghe Club, 1950), pp. 14–17 (n. 23).

[4] *Calendar of Patent Rolls, 1272–1281*, p. 161.

[5] *Annales monastici*, iv. 266–7.

ship with the de Montforts were released from jail in Bristol into the hands of the Dominican archbishop of Canterbury, Robert Kilwardby, who was instructed to question them closely in order to find out who had arranged or connived at the marriage.[1]

What to do about Amaury de Montfort was quite another thing. If he was a son of Simon de Montfort, the discredited baron, and a brother of Guy,[2] the author of the recent murder at Viterbo of Henry of Almaine (a cousin of both Edward and the de Montforts) he was also a cleric, and a papal chaplain at that, as well as a respected intellectual.[3] To proceed against him with any severity would brand Edward as vindictive and would certainly rouse the bishops and the papacy to anger. To release him unconditionally, as Edward told Hadrian he was quite prepared to do if the Pope insisted, would surely draw the fire of many who had suffered at the hands of his father.

Shortly after Amaury's arrest, indeed, the bishops of England had proposed that Amaury should be released into their custody, but when they found themselves unprepared to guarantee a firm watch over Amaury, as Edward demanded, both the king and the bishops decided to refer the matter to Pope Hadrian. Edward wrote him to that effect on 8 August, but Hadrian died some ten days later, and it was only in the following January of 1277 that his successor, John XXI, produced an acceptable solution.

By then, Amaury had been for the best part of a year in Corfe Castle in Dorset, where, as Edward delicately put it to Hadrian, he had been placed in 'private custody', probably on 1 February 1276. And while all the diplomatic activity was going on, probably without his knowledge, he had been far from idle. By the time Edward was writing to Hadrian in August, Amaury in fact had put together a couple of treatises on theology. He had always

---

[1] *The Liber epistolaris of Richard of Bury*, p. 46.

[2] For Guy, the Almaine murder, and its consequences see F. M. Powicke, *Ways of Medieval Life and Thought* (London, [1950]), pp. 69–83.

[3] When Amaury became a papal chaplain is not certain, but he is so described by John XXI in his mandate of 28 January 1277 to the English bishops; *C.P.L.* i. 452. Although, as C. Bémont, *Simon de Montfort, Comte de Leicester* (Paris, 1884), p. 255, has shown, he was given a licence by Archbishop Rigaud of Rouen to be ordained to major orders (subdeacon, deacon, priest) by any bishop anywhere, there is nothing to support Bémont's conclusion that he took these orders in 1268 or at any other time. There is nothing in his general confession (Appendix B) to suggest that he was anything other than a cleric in minor orders.

been studious and had had one of the best mathematicians in Europe as his tutor.[1] A bare five years before, he had completed the last of his three or four years in the Faculty of Arts in the University of Padua.[2] He was not yet stale. His training and habit of study now stood him in good stead. He read much, took careful notes, meditated on what he read, prepared drafts of his treatises on bits of parchment, and finally wrote fair copies in a clear, assured hand.

For all his scholarly industry, there were moments, in the summer months in particular, when he brooded a little over his position, and this finds expression here and there in his pages. In that summer of 1276 he was in his thirty-fourth year of age, and perhaps for the first time in his life he felt isolated if not rejected. He had been born into a large family, the fourth child, and the youngest son, of the six children of Simon de Montfort and Eleanor, the sister of Henry III.[3] He had had many honours, not least a canonry at the age of eighteen from the distinguished and zealous prelate Eudes Rigaud, archbishop of Rouen. He had been, though only because of his father's pressure on Henry III while Henry was a prisoner of his, treasurer and canon of York. But now his father's memory was execrated, his mother had died at Montargis shortly before the bridal party set out for Wales, his brother Guy was still an outcast in Tuscany because of the Almaine murder, he and his sister were in prison in England.

Above all else he felt that he had been let down badly by a close friend, possibly one of the two French knights who were on the ship with him. In the opening phrases of some fascinating pages (here printed in Appendix A) on his methodology, his fears and hopes, towards the end of the volume he composed at Corfe

---

[1] Roger Bacon, writing in 1267: *Opus tertium*, ed. J. S. Brewer (R.S., 1859), p. 35.

[2] See Bémont, *Simon de Montfort*, pp. 365–7, who cites an attestation by the University of Padua and other notables to the presence of Amaury ('quasi a triennio citra in studio Paduano laudabiliter conversatus') at Padua, where he was at death's door with fever, on the day Henry of Almaine was assassinated at Viterbo by Amaury's brother Guy. Amaury is listed as having studied at Bologna in 1269 by M. Sarti and M. Fattorini, *De claris archigymnasii Bononiensis professoribus*, ed. C. A. Albicini and C. Malagola (Bologna, 1888–96), ii. 309.

[3] Details of Amaury's life will be found in the entry in *D.N.B.*, in Bémont's *Simon de Montfort*, or in Margaret Wade Labarge, *Simon de Montfort* (London, 1962). The 1884 edition of Bémont is to be preferred to that upon which the English translation by E. F. Jacob (London, 1930) is based since Bémont prints many valuable documents there which were later dropped.

Castle, he complains bitterly, in a nice concatenation of verses from different psalms, about his betrayal by someone who clearly was an intimate of his: 'Traditus sum et non egrediebar [Ps. 87: 10] . . . etenim homo pacis mee in quo speraui, qui edebat panes meos, magnificauit super me supplantacionem [Ps. 40: 11], tradens me fallaciter et nefande in manus querencium animam meam [Ps. 34: 4].' Whoever this monstrous friend was, he was not rewarded as he had expected to be but rejected ignominiously by Amaury's captors, and Amaury gloats biblically over his fate: 'Cuius tradicionis supplicium ab hiis quibus me tradidit iusto dei iudicio reportauit, proiectus in tenebras exteriores [Matt. 8: 12]: in lacu miserie et in luto fecis [Ps. 39: 3].'

The autograph of the works that Amaury de Montfort put together at Corfe Castle in the spring and summer of 1276 survives today as part of a codex from Cerne Abbas, also in Dorset, which is now in the Bodleian Library as MS. Auct. D. 4. 13. The codex itself is bulky and ungainly. It measures 232 × 155 mm. and contains 225 folios. There are three separate works in the codex, one in a later twelfth-century hand, the other two in hands of the second half of the thirteenth century. These works were bound together and given continuous pagination in the fourteenth or fifteenth century, probably at the Benedictine monastery of the Blessed Virgin Mary, Saint Peter, and Saint Ethelwold at Cerne Abbas, to which the codex certainly belonged in the fifteenth century (ex-libris, fol. 225). According to the *Summary Catalogue* of the Bodleian Library (2571), the codex was probably acquired by the Bodleian Library between 1605 and 1611.

The first work in the codex (fols. 1–62)[1] is a pastoral manual in Latin, 'Signaculum apostolatus mei', composed in England in the second half of the thirteenth century;[2] the second (fols. 63–128) is a glossed Canticle of Canticles which was written out about 1200; the third (fols. 129–224) is what is described by the *Summary Catalogue* as 'works by Amalricus (Aimeric), probably the writer's autograph, who may have been a monk of Cerne'.[3]

---

[1] Three half-sheets at the beginning, foliated in Roman numerals, form a separate gathering. They carry a late 12th-century copy of Macrobius on the *Somnium Scipionis*.

[2] See L. E. Boyle, 'Three English Pastoral *Summae* and a Magister Galienus', *Studia Gratiana*, xi (*Collectanea S. Kuttner*, i, 1967), 138–9.

[3] The name 'Almaricus' also occurs on the spine of the codex, where there is

This last is in fact the autograph of Amaury de Montfort and is the only part of the codex that concerns us here. Nowhere in this autograph, of course, does Amaury describe himself plainly as 'Amalricus de Monteforti' or state that the place of composition is Corfe Castle. But the evidence for his authorship is well-nigh watertight. The writer is a cleric, though not a priest (fol. 218). He is in prison (fol. 136ᵛ, etc.), and he began to write there 'in carcere et cathena' at Easter 1276 (fols. 136ᵛ, 213ᵛᵃ). His sister (unnamed) is also in detention somewhere (fol. 213ʳᵃ). Their mother (equally unnamed) has died recently (fol. 131). He claims to have placed his name on the opening page of his treatises (fol. 214ʳᵃ), and the name that appears at the beginning of two of these treatises (fols. 129, 137) is 'Amalrici' (Amalricus or Amaury).

If the make-up of the autograph does not at once bring to mind a castle or a prison, it does at least suggest that the author had not a ready supply of regular parchment to hand. For although the sheets are pricked and ruled, they are of varying sizes. The gatherings, likewise, are not at all uniform, and there are bits and pieces of parchment, some foliated, some not, in between some of the gatherings:

1^8	fols.	129–136	*De principiis et partibus theologie.*
2^5		137–141	*Distinctiones ewangeliorum.* Fol. 137 is a half-sheet which overlaps the fold of sheet 138/141 and binds the gathering.
3^8		142–149	*Tabulae,* embracing gatherings 3–9 (fols. 142–211).
4^6		150–155	Continuation of *Tabulae.*
5^{11}		156–166	Continuation of *Tabulae.* Fol. 156 is a long, uneven piece with notes towards an index (*Abbas–Ordo*), strips of which overlap the fold of sheet 157/166. Fols. 157–166 are very scrappy and much indented.
6^8		167–174	Continuation of *Tabulae.* Between fols. 167ᵛ and 168 there is a jagged, unfoliated piece of vellum with notes towards an index (*Pacificus–Xtus*), tags of which peep out between fols. 173ᵛ and 174.
7^{11}		175–85	Continuation of *Tabulae.* Fol. 185 is a

a cryptic list of contents, and on the inside of the front cover, on the parchment binding (over boards).

		half-sheet, with a fold overlapping that of sheet 175/184.
8[17]	186–202	Continuation of *Tabulae*.
9[9]	203–211	End of *Tabulae*. Two unfoliated strips, carrying medical prescriptions, act as binders of the gathering. There is a rough 'file-card', with Biblical references to *Peccatum*, between sheets 206/209 and 207/208.
10[6]	212–218	Fol. 212: blank; 212[v]: note on use of concordance; 213–214: *De composicione, diuisione, et ordine tabularum*, printed below as Appendix A; 214–215: Table of chapters; 215[v]–216[v]: Index: *Abissus–Zelus*. Fol. 218 is an irregular quarter-sheet, the recto containing Amaury's '*Confessio*' (Appendix B), the verso being blank. Three side-tags, which are to be seen at the beginning of the gathering, keep it in place as the outer sheet of the gathering.
11[6]	219–224	A later index, but not in the same hand as the other gatherings.

Although these gatherings have an adventitious look about them, the sheets, half-sheets, and scraps were gathered together with patience and care. And they were the result of months of devoted, tenacious work. Conscious of the fact that he had no theological training, Amaury resolved shortly after his removal from Bristol to Corfe Castle to comb the Bible for the themes of classical theology and, as well, to attempt to compose for himself an introduction to the subject. As he informs us in the colophon (fol. 136[v]) to his first treatise, *De principiis et partibus theologie*, (fols. 129–136[v]), this work was begun and completed in the Easter season (5 April–24 May) of 1276, 'in carcere et cathena':

Hoc opus ad memoriam et inuencionem facilem scripturarum infra quadraginta dies resurectionis dominice, ex solo textu biblie, sine copia scripture alterius, breuiter compilaui anno incarnacionis dominice M.CC.LXXVI, uite mee XXXIIII in carcere et cathena. Peto autem errata corrigi, omissa suppleri, et michi ueniam indulgeri, quia nec theologie studium attigi nec scholas intraui, licet a puericia legerim sacras literas inter sciencias seculares.

Amaury is probably not exaggerating when he says that the only book he had to study was the Bible, though he is surely drawing a long bow when he states some months later that his jailors were reluctant to allow him even a Bible: 'magna precum instancia, textu biblie michi uix concesso, legi continue in sacra pagina . . .' (fol. 213va: Appendix A, lines 71–2). The imprisonment seems to have been quite mild (with eight grooms, four valets, and a single guard),[1] so any delay he experienced was probably due to a dearth of Bibles at Corfe Castle and not to stringencies of discipline.

Clearly the provision of a Bible stretched the Castle to its limits, for Amaury on occasion laments the fact that no other books are available to him (fol. 213va: 'nec scripturam aliquam habere potui preter textum biblie'), and, when writing out his *Tabulae* (fols. 142–211^{v}), he leaves blanks against the day when he would be able to consult other books: 'In tabulis spacia relinquuntur, ut plures forsitan auctoritates addantur ex libris . . .' (fol. 142).

For the moment, however, he had to make do with the Bible and with a memory now and then of what he had been taught by his tutors or in the schools at Padua (Avicenna: fol. 129^{v}; Cicero: 129; Seneca: 212ra, 213ra). And it must be admitted that he did not do too badly. The opening treatise (fols. 129–136^{v}) on the principles and divisions of theology may not be a masterpiece, but it does suggest a man who knew now to organize his materials and to deploy with some success the techniques of exposition that he had learned at Padua and elsewhere.

The very first chapter, on the insufficiency of secular sciences, shows that Amaury, for all his protestations, must have picked up a fair amount of incidental theology in his thirty-four years. Some of what he has to say is, no doubt, elementary, but there are moments when he rises above this. Commenting, with a reasonably controlled style, on the limitations of natural philosophy, he writes that even the greatest and most perceptive of the natural philosophers did not, in the long run, achieve anything more than the application of their science to ethical problems:

fol. 129

Quoniam autem omnis humana sciencia et doctrina ortum habet a sensu, et a prioribus causis quoque ad posteriora et causata procedit,

---

[1] *The Liber epistolaris of Richard of Bury*, ed. N. Denholm-Young, p. 14 n., citing P.R.O. Exchequer Accounts, 505/16, where the expenses of his imprisonment were assessed at 4s. 5½d. a day, beginning from 1 February 1276.

huius cause omnium prime, quoniam sub sensu non cadit, nullam scienciam uel certam doctrinam habuerunt, via sensus, racionis aut experimenti, quibus naturaliter utebantur. Quamuis enim de ipsa raciocinarentur quedam uera, ab effectibus posterioribus, et causatis, tamen nullatenus attigerunt misteria trinitatis, creacionis, redemcionis, et glorificacionis eterne. Que suis fidelibus ipse deus misericorditer reuelauit. Horum tamen periciores plusque sensati omnem humanam scienciam adaptarunt moribus informandis. Quoniam omnis sciencia manca quodammodo uidetur et inutilis, si non applicetur ad mores, ut ait tullius.

Having thus, to his own satisfaction, shown the inadequacy of the 'mundane particulares sciencie', as he terms them, Amaury goes on in the second chapter to a discussion of theology: 'De sufficiencia et principiis theologie'. Revelation, for Amaury, is an expression of God's compassion. And the divine knowledge God communicated in revelation in order to relieve human ignorance is only and wholly to be found in the Bible, the book of divine science: 'Hic liber diuine sciencie qui uulgariter biblia nominatur, in se continet scienciam uerissimam, que non fallit, completissimam, que omnia comprehendit, et uiuificam, que mortem excludit' (fol. 130). This science of God thus enshrined in the Bible is truly a demonstrative one: 'per discreeciones, supposiciones, et principia demonstratiue procedens' (ibid.). Beginning from the first (but now called 'per descripciones', not 'per discreeciones'), each of these ways of demonstration is now outlined in turn (e.g. 'Deus est prima causa omnium causatorum et omnium causa causarum . . . , Sapiencie xiiii capitulo; . . . Deus est qui est, id est, ens per se. Exodi iii capitulo'), covering the whole of theology from God, creation, and the Trinity, to the soul, sin, and the sacraments (fols. 129ᵛ–132).

The remaining eight chapters (fols. 132–136ᵛ) are given over to the 'seven walls' of theology ('Ueritas historiarum . . . Prophecia futurorum . . . Regula mandatorum . . . Figura sacramentorum . . . Informacio morum . . . Discreccio consiliorum . . . Spes futurorum'). The whole work ends with the colophon already cited above.

The second treatise, 'Distinctiones ewangeliorum' (fols. 137–141), is a mass of schematic divisions and scriptural references to document three headings which, he says, embrace the whole teaching of the Gospels: 'Primo, distinctiones ueritatis historice. Secundo, sermones domini et parabole. Tercio, questiones ewangelice' (fol. 137ᵛ). And it winds up with a splendidly devised schema to illustrate Christ's words in Matthew 5, 'Non ueni soluere legem sed adimplere', the basic division being, 'Impleuit corporaliter—Suppleuit spiritualiter—Finiuit temporaliter'. This schema occupies all of fol. 141.

Schemata, indeed, seem to have been Amaury's strong point. As he notes on fol. 131, when speaking of the place of imagination in the science of theology, he had already written a 'Figura et tractatus speculi et mundi' that very same year, and this included an 'imaginative schema' of the Trinity:

> Et hoc quod de trinitate de qua in supposicionibus tangitur et minus forsitan ab aliquibus intelligitur ingenio racionis, ymaginabiliter declaraui et quasi sensibiliter in ymagine et figura in qua trinitatem personarum et coequalitatem ipsarum in substancie unitate depinxi, ymaginacione sensibili circulorum, corporum et colorum, et insuper trium dimensionum intelligibili racione, in figura et tractatu speculi celi et mundi . . . (fol. 131).

This 'three-dimensional' drawing was obviously a very elaborate affair, depicting everything from the 'orders of the heavenly spirits' (each distinguished from the other by the special insignia of office) to the fall of Lucifer. One wonders what impression this feat of imaginative theology made on his sister Eleanor, for whom it was composed, probably towards the end of the voyage from France, to alleviate her sadness at their mother's death; 'Que quidem simplicibus inspicienda composui in solacium sororis mee de transitu matris nostre' (ibid.).[1]

The most interesting and perhaps original part of Amaury's work in prison is, however, the third and the longest treatise, where, from fols. 142 to 211, he has a well-conceived concordance of biblical quotations relating to Christian behaviour. There are ninety-one chapters in all in this 'Tabula' (or 'Tabule'), and they are, as he explains in his 'De composicione, diuisione, et ordine tabularum' (fols. 213–214: Appendix A, lines 85–95), divided into ten main headings, five dealing with the good and with virtue,

---

[1] On fol. 131 he states that this work was composed 'ipso anno quo presens opusculum compilaui', i.e. 1276, but on fol. 214ʳᵃ he specifies that this was 'inmediate ante ingressum carceris'. If by 'prison' he means his present prison in Corfe Castle, then this puts the date of composition as late January 1276, while still at Bristol. But since he was also a prisoner at Bristol, the phrase could refer to a period before his capture, probably while at sea (though this would put the date in late 1275, around Christmas).

five with evil and vice (hence the alternative title, 'Arbor boni et mali', on fol. 214ra). For reasons given in the 'De composicione ... tabularum', Amaury draws heavily on the Parables, Ecclesiastes, the Book of Wisdom, Ecclesiasticus, and the Psalms. The layout of the concordance is crisp and economical, with the subjects (*Deus, Fides, Mansuetudo*, etc.) and quotations neatly and clearly written in two columns.

.   .   .

If Amaury de Montfort was a splendid organizer of his materials, he was equally a careful and conscientious writer with a good sense of style and, as may be seen in some abundance in Appendix A, with an unflagging devotion to the cursus and its rhythmic endings, not to speak of the niceties of medieval punctuation. And what he devised and drafted with so much patience and professionalism was just as stylishly copied into his patchwork of quires 'manu mea' (fol. 214ra).

With the exception of the 'Confessio' (fol. 218 and Appendix B), which appears to be an unrevised draft marred by numerous cancellations and changes of direction, most of Amaury's autograph volume is probably a fair copy of rough drafts on odd scraps of parchment such as those which now serve as clamps or backings in some gatherings. Yet there are moments when Amaury seems to be composing directly on the spot. There are corrections, cancellations, afterthoughts, and, on occasion, revisions. The handwriting, however, is always firm and controlled and never fuzzy. Amaury wrote a steady notular hand which even in the 'Confessio', where it is minute and hurried, never poses any problems.

The great care that Amaury took, in spite of material difficulties, to produce a finished, legible text, was as much due to a certain ambition as to a desire to provide himself with a useful and usable instrument. True, as he reiterates, he was writing primarily for his own benefit, but there also glowed a hope that the work might be copied by others like himself who had little or no training in theology: '. . . nescio enim utrum hec noua sint uel antiqua, quoniam omnes scripture theologice preter textum biblie michi totaliter sunt ignote, sed causa memorie scripturarum incoans laborem, michi forsitan et aliis simplicibus theologiam aggredientibus profuturum' (fol. 214ra: Appendix A, lines 110–15).

But this was not all. At root the purpose was therapeutic, and the ambition morbid: 'Primo tamen et principaliter ut meipsum per scripturas instruam ad agonem et futura michi, humanitus que ignoro . . .' (ibid., lines 117–19). In most of the tormented pages in which these words occur towards the end of his volume, Amaury genuinely seems to have doubted the chances of his personal survival. By this time he had been eight months in prison, and in that August or September of 1276 the outlook seemed very bleak indeed: 'Utrum enim post hunc carcerem in quo ago presenciali-ter mensem octauum michi sit aliquid humanitus profuturum, nescio, deus scit' (ibid., lines 114–15). He and his sister had been detained on 'bare suspicion'. Both were being held without trial and without a chance to defend themselves. His frequent appeals for a hearing were ignored. Justice had fallen on bad days.

At one point, indeed, he was so convinced that his end was near that he composed a general confession in which he went through the commandments, the seven deadly sins, the corporal works of mercy, etc., accusing himself of everything from liturgical indif-ference to lasciviousness. He felt doomed; and this gave an edge of urgency to all his studying and writing: 'Laboro tamen instan-ter.' He had to make sure that something of him should survive and that his memory at least would not perish; this was why he placed his name at the beginning of each of his compositions: 'Tercio, ut si forte in hoc carcere faciam finem uite, saltem relin-quam mei memoriam, hec duo opuscula in biblia et arborem sciencie boni et mali, que omnia scripsi in carcere manu mea, cum speculo celi et mundi quod inmediate ante ingressum carceris cum tractatu suo breuiter compilaui' (fol. 214ra: Appendix A, lines 119–23).

By the very end of these pages, however, the mood has passed. He straightens his shoulders and begins to hope again. Having prayed God to look after his sister and family, with whose fate he was warmly preoccupied ('nam pro ipsis concaluit cor meum intra me'), he emphatically professes his boundless and unqualified hope in God: 'Scio enim et indubitanter scio quod ipse exaudiet preces meas, et educet me de isto carcere, in corpore aut in anima, quod multo melius est . . . Ipse autem euellet de laqueo pedes meos qui est spes mea a iuuentute mea, et de uentre matris mee fuit protector meus, et erit in secula seculorum propter nomen suum' (fol. 214rb: Appendix A, lines 137–42).

. . .

Amaury's hopes did not go unfulfilled, though some six years were to pass before he was finally set free. His cousin the king was taking no chances and would not hear of releasing him unconditionally and without the highest of guarantees.

Pope John XXI, who succeeded Hadrian V in September 1276, had a partial success when, as a result of a mandate of John's in January 1277,[1] Amaury was released into the custody of the bishops in January 1278 and was moved from Corfe to Sherborne in the same county of Dorset.[2]

The cessation of the war between Llywelyn of Wales and Edward in November 1277, and an appeal by Eleanor to Edward I in her brother's behalf just after her release and marriage to Llywelyn in October 1278,[3] saw no change in Amaury's condition. An offer by Pope Nicholas III that the papacy would hold itself responsible for Amaury's good behaviour were he allowed to depart England[4] met with Edward's favour, but the Pope died in August 1280 before negotiations had gone very far.[5] In the following year, however, a similar settlement was quickly reached under Pope Martin IV, and Amaury, who had been lodged since the previous November in the castle of the bishop of Winchester at Taunton, Somerset,[6] was finally set free on 23 April 1281, after a formal process in London at which he took an oath to depart the realm and never again return unless with papal permission. After his arrival in France, he repeated this oath before the papal representative at Arras on the following 6 May.[7]

Amaury never returned to England again, nor, so far as we know, did he ever take up again the theological writing which he had practised at Corfe Castle. The volume written so painstakingly there seems to have been left behind in Dorset, probably in the safe keeping of a monk of Cerne Abbas.

His only known literary effort afterwards is a will and last

---

[1] *C.P.L.* i. 452.

[2] *Calendar of Patent Rolls, 1272–1281*, p. 253.

[3] J. G. Edwards, *Calendar of Ancient Correspondence concerning Wales* (Cardiff, 1955), p. 76.

[4] *C.P.L.* i. 461: mandate of Nicholas to the English bishops, 17 February 1280.

[5] See the letter of Martin IV to Edward, 20 September 1281, *C.P.L.* i. 463; *in toto* in T. Rymer, *Foedera*, ii (London, 1705), 178–9.

[6] *Calendar of Patent Rolls, 1272–1281*, p. 403.

[7] See Rymer, *Foedera*, ii. 185–7, 192–4, and the documentation, with excellent notes, in F. M. Powicke and C. R. Cheney, *Councils and Synods with Other Documents relating to the English Church*, ii: *A.D. 1205–1313* (Oxford, 1964), pp. 822–3, 918–21, 977.

testament written in his own hand in November 1289 in the Dominican convent at Montargis, a little south of Paris, where his mother had died fourteen years before.

Among the many detailed bequests (e.g. his books and *instrumenta* to the Dominicans of Paris) made by Amaury, who describes himself as earl of Leicester and of Chester 'iure hereditario',[1] there is one unusual provision in which Amaury grants his hereditary rights in England to the Pope and the Cardinals, and, as well, places on them the responsibility both for the execution of the testament and for the restoration of the hereditary rights of the de Montforts in England:

> Iura et acciones michi competentes in bonis hereditariis regni anglie, sancte romane ecclesie, summo pontifici et cardinalibus lego, eorum fidei tanquam dominis foedi capitalis committentes hereditatem restituere heredibus masculinis uel aliis patris mei . . . Horum autem execucionem pronus in terram committo humilitate deuota ipsius sancte romane ecclesie disposicione complendam tenore scripture presentis quam manu mea propria scripsi et sigilli mei karactere communiui . . .

Thirteen years later, presumably not very long after the death of Amaury,[2] the papacy in the person of Boniface VIII obtained a certified notarial copy of the will, which is still in the Vatican Archives.[3] How seriously the provisions of the document were taken in 1302 is not ascertainable at present, but there is no doubt that the papacy made a careful note of Amaury's donation to itself. For as late as the time of Urban V (1362–70), the 'favourable' part of the will was still being listed, with bureaucratic optimism, among debts owed by England to the papal treasury.[4]

L. E. BOYLE O.P.

---

[1] Amaury probably drew up the will as soon as he heard of the death of his elder brother Guy in a Sicilian prison. It has not been possible to document the statement in the early 14th-century *Flores Historiarum*, ed. H. R. Luard (R.S., 1890), iii. 67, that on Guy's death, 'Emericus, frater eius, clericus eminentis litteraturae, qui ultimus fuit de progenie Guenelonis [Simon de Montfort], factus est miles, abjecto habitu clericali.'

[2] The date of Amaury's death is at present unknown. It may have been shortly before 1302, the date of the papal copy of the will.

[3] AA. Arm. I–XVIII, 123, from which the quotation above is taken. It is not a flawless copy.

[4] Archivio Segreto Vaticano, Instrumenta Miscellanea 2592, fol. 22ᵛ (new fol. 23ᵛ): 'Item transumptum testamenti deffuncti domini Amalrici de Montfort

APPENDIX A

Oxford, Bodleian Library, MS. Auct. D. 4. 13, fols. 213ra–214rb

De composicione, diuisione, et ordine tabularum[1]

Traditus sum et non egrediebar. Oculi mei languerunt pre inopia.[2] Traditus quidem: etenim *homo pacis mee in quo speraui, qui edebat panes meos, magnificauit super me supplantacionem:*[3] tradens me fallaciter et nefande
5   *in manus querencium animam meam.*[4] Cuius tradicionis supplicium ab hiis quibus me tradidit iusto Dei iudicio reportauit, *proiectus in tenebras exteriores:*[5] *in lacu miserie, et in luto fecis.*[6] Qui autem sibi *mercedem iniquitatis*[7] iustissime exsoluerunt pro premio ad quod nefandis uisceribus hanelabat, me et meos sine causa iniustissime detruserunt in
10 carcerem et cathenam, insuper et sororem meam detinent contra iura omnia consuetudinesque regnorum, cum impio iniusto et nocente iustissime operantes zelo tradicionis admisse. Cum innocentibus uero ex causa suspicionis nude tam iniuste agentes ut in iuris iniuriam teneant ferro uinctos,[8] iuris instancia et defensionis copia interdictis. In quo
15 nullo accusante, nec criminis evidencia suadente, iniuste proceditur contra iura diuina, ecclesiastica et mundana. Innocentes autem dico non quidem coram deo, cum nec infans cuius est unius diei uita super terram sit absque peccato, teste scriptura:[9] set coram hominibus a crimine suspicionis ipsius. Nec mirum si iuste procedatur cum impio,
20 et iniuste cum iustis. Iusticia enim quamuis non tota simul per omnia obseruetur, ab omnibus tamen et singulis hominibus corde diligitur, ore laudatur et opere seruatur in parte. Quippe, sine qua nec hominum societas esse potest. Unde seneca, Iusticia est tantum bonum quod ab iniustissimis et nefandissimis latronibus obseruatur.[10] Aliter enim eorum
25 societas non constaret, nisi et spolia iuste diuiderent et suis ipsorum legibus inuiolabiliter tenerentur astricti. Ceterum, nomen iusticie totam

domini pape capellani, dicentis se iure hereditario comitatus Leycestrie et Cestrie palatinum senescallumque Anglie, in quo legavit ecclesie romane et summo pontifici omnes actiones et iura hereditaria in dictis bonis in regno Anglie existentibus sive competencia. Datum Parisius anno domini millesimo CCLXXXIX XII Kal. decembris de tempore domini G. pape X.' (The Pope at the time of the will was Nicholas IV not Gregory X, who was Pope from 1271 to 1276.)

[1] In this transcription of a passage that is a little contorted in places, Amaury's final periods, capitalization, and spelling have been preserved, but not his general punctuation. Since his prose is full of Scriptural quotations or phrases these have been identified wherever possible. Corrections, additions, and insertions are also noted.

[2] Ps. 87: 10. The word 'mei' is an insertion above the line.

[3] Ps. 40: 9–10.   [4] Ps. 34: 4.   [5] Matt. 8: 12.
[6] Ps. 39: 3.   [7] 2 Pet. 2: 13.   [8] Insertion above line.
[9] Cf. Gal. 3: 22.   [10] *Locum non inueni.*

legem diuinam et humanam simul complectitur in seipso, que [fol. 213rb] et ius naturale continent et eciam positiuum. Quorum quod naturale est non tantum homines uerum eciam animalia bruta sectantur, instinctu nature, quem heu hodie plures hominum imitantur quam 30 iudicium racionis. Iuris eciam positiui, diuini pariter et humani quod quisque sibi utile estimauerit: hoc heu hodie imitatur et seruat. Nec uoluntas legi subicitur siue iuri: sed uoluntati ius. Quandoque uerba iuris applicantur utcumque, sicque iuris uelamen in uerbis queritur, dum in factis plerumque iuris contrarium inuenitur. Cuius nomen 35 infame quia displicet et notatur ad placendum hominibus: nomen iuris et colorem accomodat sibi penitus aliena.

Icirco, *oculi mei languerunt pre inopia*,[1] iudicii scilicet siue iuris, cuius instancia seu prosecucio necdum michi impetrari, quamuis in forma iuris et in iure hoc iam frequenter fuerit postulatum. *Clamaui* autem ab 40 inicio huius tribulacionis et angustie *ad deum* altissimum, deum *qui benefecit mihi*,[2] et *exaudiuit uocem meam ab hiis qui appropinquant mihi*:[3] sic eorum corda demulcens, ut non *effunderent sanguinem innocentem*[4] quem quesierant effundendum, quinimmo ut mecum in carcere agerent graciose, curialiter, et benigne. 45

Clausus ergo in carcere et cathena, instanter cum fiducia petens a domino liberari, memini uerbi Iacobi dicentis, *Petitis et non accipitis eo quod male petatis*,[5] uel non recte, ut alibi inuenitur; illius eciam ewangelici, *Nolite petere* agros etcetera,[6] et post pauca, *primum querite regnum dei et iusticiam eius et hec omnia adicientur vobis*,[7] et tercium, *Nescitis* 50 *quid petatis*;[8] et sermonis christi ad patrem, *Non mea voluntas set tua fiat*.[9] Ne igitur presumpcionis inmerite uel simplicitatis nimis indiscrete merito[10] [fol. 213va] culpandus inueniar petendo ad libitum uoluntatis humane, reuoluens in animo constanciam sare filie raguel et iudith et uerba ipsarum in tribulacionibus suis, flagella domini *quasi serui qui* 55 *corripimur ad emendacionem non ad perdicionem nostram*, credens firmiter *euenisse*,[11] ut uerbis iudith utar, ipsius agonem tribulacionis mee carceris et cathene domino deo omnipotenti tota fiducia precibus commendaui et disposicioni ipsius, sperans me aliquid accepturum ab eo qui *dat*

---

[1] Ps. 87: 10. [2] Ps. 56: 3. [3] Cf. Ps. 54: 19.
[4] Cf. Ps. 105: 38. [5] Jas. 4: 3. [6] Cf. Matt. 6: 25–7.
[7] Matt. 6: 33. [8] Matt. 20: 22. [9] Luke 22: 12.
[10] At the foot of fol. 213 there is a chronological jingle (after a false start: 'Annis ducentis'):

> Annis quingentis decies iterumque ducentis
> Unus defuerat: cum deus ortus erat.

> Ab orbe condito usque ad romam conditam, anni iiii ccc lx.
> Ab urbe condita usque ad natiuitatem christi, anni D cc xv.

The word 'urbe' has 'roma' written above it.
[11] Judith 8: 27.

60 *omnibus affluenter*[1] et non improperat pro iniuria calamitatis istius, qua
patior innocens ut predixi.

Hiis eciam animatus ad tribulacionis examen, destiti a peticionibus
cordis mei occasione predictorum, adherens precibus sancte matris
ecclesie, scilicet, horis canonicis, quibus dominum generaliter depreca-
65 tur, et oracioni dominice qua leuiora peccata soluuntur, qui utinam
dignus efficiar deuote exsoluere tam bene obsequium officii clericalis
atque id consequi, quod uerbis oracionis dominice ipse qui condidit
intellexit, et iniuste paciencium pro iusticia numero et meritis agregari,
pro eo quod iniuste pacior vincula et carceres contra ecclesiasticas
70 libertates et sacrorum canonum instituta sacrilegis manibus laicorum.

Hiis igitur in corde firmatis, magna precum instancia textu biblie
michi uix concesso, legi continue in sacra pagina, cuius habueram a
puericia exercicium literale, et sic transacta quadragesima sacro pa-
schali tempore, breuem tractatum de principiis et partibus theologie
75 breuiter compilaui ad inuencionem facilem scripturarum, sciensque
quod *nemo mittens manum ad aratrum et respiciens retro aptus est regno
dei*[2] processi ad tabulas de moribus componendas, eo quod nec doctorum tabulas nec scripturam aliquam habere potui preter textum, tum
quia aliarum materiarum loca in predicto tractatu estimo satis [fol.
80 213ᵛᵇ] esse notata ad inuencionem facilem scripturarum. Quia uero de
moribus plures sunt materie de quibus mixtim agitur et confuse, ipsas
in tabulis ordinaui, illas potissime que tanguntur in parabolis salamonis,
eo quod datam sibi a domino prerogatiuam sapiencie scriptura testatur
et omnium librorum moralium hic plures materias continere uidetur.
85 Ordinantur autem modo subscripto, et denario numerantur. Primo
quidem ea que sunt a deo et de ipso faciunt mencionem expressam.
Secundo uita et boni mores ad uitam et mutuam hominum conuersaci-
onem. Tercio status hominum, iuuentutis, senectutis, et ceteri status.
Quarto fortitudo, iusticia, et mores alii, specialiter pertinentes ad
90 status. Quinto fama, et alia que sunt ad finem uite temporalis et eterne.
Deinde de contrariis predictorum. Primo quidem auersio a deo, et mala
consequencia auersionem inmediate. Secundo septem uicia principalia: superbia etcetera. Tercio status noxii, ut malum coniugium etcetera.
Quarto rixa cum uiciis consequentibus. Quinto miseria et cetera que
95 sunt ad finem mali temporalis et eterni.

Quamuis autem alia sint nomina bonorum et malorum morum, istis
tamen solis utitur salomon in parabolis. Et reuera alia sunt hiis synonima,
et continentur in istis, ideoque hec in tabulis ordinaui. Et primo quidem
aggregaui uerba salomonis in parabolis, Ecclesiasten, et sapiencia
100 ipsius, propter prerogatiuam sapiencie quam pre cunctis hominibus a
domino meruit optinere. Quibus uerba ecclesiastici conuenienter ad-

---

[1] Jas. 1: 5.　　　　[2] Luke 9: 26.

iunxi, quia et modum loquendi et materias sequitur salomonis. Secundo uerba psalmiste Dauid regis, qui magnitudine fidei firmissime ceteros antecessit, propter quod de ipso dictum est, *Inueni uirum secundum cor meum.*[1] Post hec autem concordancias aliorum, ut sicut hii in terris 105 prefulserunt regia dignitate et gracia scripturarum sic eciam merito proponantur in ordine tabularum. In aliis uero ordo temporum obseruatur.

Hec presumpsi scribere cum fiducia omnipotentis dei non causa alicuius nouitatis edende, nescio [fol. 214ra] enim utrum hec noua sint 110 uel antiqua, quoniam omnes scripture theologice preter textum biblie michi totaliter sunt ignote, set causa memorie scripturarum incoans laborem, michi forsitan et aliis simplicibus theologiam aggredientibus profuturum. Utrum enim post hunc carcerem in quo ago presencialiter mensem octauum michi sit aliquid humanitus[2] profuturum, *nescio, deus* 115 *scit.*[3] Nescio enim quamdiu subsistam, et si post modicum tollat me factor meus. Laboro tamen instanter. Primo tamen et principaliter ut meipsum per scripturas instruam ad agonem et futura michi, humanitus que ignoro. Secundo ut prosit aliis forsitan labor meus. Tercio ut si forte in hoc carcere faciam finem uite, saltem relinquam mei memoriam: 120 hec duo opuscula in biblia, et arborem sciencie boni et mali,[4] que omnia scripsi in carcere manu mea, cum speculo celi et mundi quod inmediate ante ingressum carceris cum tractatu suo breuiter compilaui. Propter quod ipsis tractatibus preposui in titulis nomen meum. Quarto quoniam, ut ait seneca, Nunquam[5] usque adeo interclusa sunt omnia ut 125 nulli accioni locus honeste sit.[6] Idcirco ceteris accionibus michi nunc penitus interclusis, hanc studii accionem exerceo diligenter, ad exercitacionem et solacium interioris hominis et exterioris.

Deus autem tocius pacience et solacii det sorori et familie mee idipsum *sapere* consolacionis et paciencie *in alterutrum, ut unanimes uno ore* 130 *glorificent deum.*[7] Nam pro ipsis *concaluit cor meum intra me et in meditacione mea exardescit ignis,*[8] angustie, scilicet, et doloris. Set consolatus sum uerbo[9] psalmiste dicentis, *Quoniam in me sperauit, liberabo eum. Clamauit ad me et ego exaudiam eum, cum ipso sum in tribulacione, eripiam eum et glorificabo eum.*[10] *Ego* enim *semper sperabo,*[11] et *memorabor iusticie* 135 *dei solius.*[12] *Expectans expectabo dominum* donec *intendat michi.*[13] [fol. 214rb] Scio enim et indubitanter *scio quod ipse exaudiet preces meas,*[14] et educet me de isto carcere, in corpore aut in anima, quod multo melius

---

[1] Cf. Ps. 88: 21; 1 Kings 11: 4.   [2] Inserted from margin.
[3] 2 Cor. 12: 3.   [4] The 'Tabulae', Amaury's third work at Corfe.
[5] 'Nusquam' expunged before 'Nunquam'.
[6] Seneca, *De tranquillitate animi* 4. 8.   [7] Rom. 15: 5.
[8] Ps. 38: 4.   [9] Corrected by expunction from 'verbis'.
[10] Ps. 90: 14–15.   [11] Ps. 70: 14.
[12] Ps. 70: 16.   [13] Ps. 39: 2.
[14] Judith 4: 12: 'Scitote quoniam exaudiet Deus preces vestras.'

est. Quoniam *innocens sanguis*[1] noster sine causa dampnatur. *Ipse* autem
140 *euellet de laqueo pedes*[2] nostros qui est *spes mea a iuuentute mea,* et *de*
uentre matris mee fuit *protector meus,*[3] et erit in secula seculorum *propter*
nomen suum.[4]

APPENDIX B

Oxford, Bodleian Library, MS. Auct. D. 4. 13, fol. 218 (see pl. XVII)

[Confessio Amalrici]

Confiteor tibi Domine pater celi et terre[5] tibique bone et benignissime
ihesu una cum sancto spiritu coram sanctis angelis tuis et omnibus sanctis[6]
quia in peccatis conceptus, natus et nutritus, et in peccatis post baptisma
5 usque ad hanc horam sum conuersatus. Confiteor eciam quia peccaui
nimis in superbia tam uisibili quam inuisibili et inmani gloria. In
extollencia tam oculorum quam uestium et omnium actuum meorum.
In inuidia. In odio. In auaricia tam honoris quam pecunie. In ira. In
tristicia. In accidia. In commessacionibus. In ebrietatibus. In fabulis
10 ociosis. In osculis et amplexionibus inmundis. In luxuria et omni
genere fornicacionis que et ipse feci et aliis faciendo consensi. In sacrile-
giis et periuriis. In furtis. In rapinis. In accipiendo corpus et sanguinem
domini indigne. In exhortacionibus et adulacionibus malignis. In sub-
trahendo elemosinas. In pauperibus exasperando. In hospitibus non
15 recipiendo. In pauperum despeccionibus.[7] In non uisitando infirmos et
carcere positos. In non sepeliendo mortuos. In non uestiendo pauperes.
In non pascendo esurientes. In non potando sicientes.[8] In sollempnitati-
bus sanctorum et dominicis diebus ac festis, debitum non impendendo
honorem nec sobrie nec caste in eis uiuendo. Consenciendo suadentibus
20 michi in malum, nocendo[9] pocius quam adiuuando me petentes, cla-
mores pauperum non libenter neque misericorditer audiendo. In pro-
pinquis meis ac prelatis detrahendo et blasphemando. Amicis meis et
benefactoribus meis fidem rectam non seruando, debita obsequia non
rependendo. In ecclesiam dei superbe intrando et in ea stando vel
25 sedendo et egrediendo et ociosis fabulis ac turpibus colloquiis in ea cum
aliis insistendo. Vasa sancta et ministerium sanctum polluto corde vel
manibus inmundis tangendo. Oracionem et psalmodiam atque officium
diuinum[10] negligenter in ecclesia dei faciendo et audiendo. In cogitaci-
onibus eciam pessimis. In meditacionibus peruersis. In suspicionibus

---

[1] Cf. Ps. 43: 21, etc.   [2] Ps. 24: 15.   [3] Ps. 70: 5–6.
[4] Ezek. 36: 22.   [5] Matt. 11: 25.   [6] 'tuis' expunged.
[7] 'In pauperibus, pauperum despiciendo' deleted before 'In pauperum despeccionibus'.
[8] For all the statements beginning 'In non . . .' see Matt. 25: 36–43 (corporal
works of mercy).   [9] Pen changes or is sharpened at this point.
[10] 'in ecclesia dei fac' deleted after 'diuinum'.

falsis. In iudiciis temerariis. In consensu malo. In consilio iniquo. In 30
concupiscencia carnali. In delitacione et pollucione inmunda. In uerbis
ociosis et superfluis, luxuriosis atque contumeliosis. In mendaciis et
falsitatibus. In iuramentis multimodis et diuersis. In detraccionibus
assiduis. In rixis. In discordiis seminandis. In irrisionibus et falsitatibus.[1] In transgressione propositi mei. In uisu, auditu, gustu, odoratu, 35
et tactu. In superflua et uana[2] et omnimodis boni omissionibus. In
inmunda cogitacione, locucione, uoluntate, et accione.

Quia ergo in hiis et in aliis omnibus peccatis quibuscumque humana
fragilitas contra deum creatorem suum aut cogitando aut operando
peccare potest, me peccasse et reum in conspectu dei super omnes 40
homines esse cognosco et confiteor. Ideo precor uos omnes sanctos dei
in quorum conspectu hec omnia confessus sum: ut testes michi sitis in
die iudicii contra diabolum hostem et inimicum humani generis, me
ex hiis omnibus confessum fuisse, quatinus *non gaudeat de me inimicus
meus*[3] et glorietur dicens me scelera mea tacuisse et non confessum fuisse, 45
verum sit *in celo gaudium* quod solet fieri *de peccatore* conuerso et
penitente.[4] Ipso prestante et adiuuante qui uiuit et regnat deus per
omnia secula seculorum.

---

[1] 'In transgressionibus' deleted after 'falsitatibus'.
[2] Blank space after 'uana'.
[3] Cf. Ps. 40: 12.   [4] Cf. Luke 15: 7.

18

Instructions for a Devout and Literate Layman[1]

THE purpose of this essay is to examine a short but extremely interesting document containing some instructions for a devout and literate layman about his daily life, and to compare this with similar records. This document is among the Throckmorton muniments at Coughton Court, Warwickshire; it is written in Latin, in an early fifteenth-century hand, on both sides of a narrow strip of parchment, measuring 11¾ in. long by 3¾ in. wide, which was intended to be carried about in a purse;[2] it was probably rolled up into a small roll. The Latin text is printed at the end of this essay; it may be translated as follows:

Always carry this about in your purse.

Remember to take holy water every day.

You should get up out of bed with all swiftness.

Make the sign of the cross at the head, at the feet, at the hands, and at the side.

'In the name of the Father and of the Son and of the Holy Ghost may we be delivered from pains and sins, Amen.'

Concerning Saint Godric, who did not at once sign himself.

Say: 'Into thy hands, Lord Jesus Christ'; 'Our Father'; 'Hail Mary'; 'I believe in God'; immediately afterwards: 'Thou who hast made me, have mercy upon us and upon me.'

At the door when you go out say: 'All the men of this city or town from the greater [or the mayor?] to the less are pleasing to God, and

[1] My thanks are due to Sir Robert Throckmorton, Bart., of Coughton Court, Alcester, for permission to print the document, to Miss M. Thompson, custodian at Coughton Court, to Mr. M. W. Farr, County Archivist of Warwick, who has helped particularly over the history of the Throckmorton family and their muniments, and to Dr. David Rogers, for bibliographical help. [The Editors are much indebted to Dr. Rogers for further assistance given after the death of Mr. Pantin.]

[2] The kind of purse, suspended from a belt, together with a 'pair of beads', is illustrated on many monumental brasses of fifteenth-century civilians.

only I am worthy of hell. Woe is me. Welawey'; let this be said from all your heart so that the tears run; you need not always say it with your mouth; it is sufficient to say it with a groan.

As far as the church, say no other word except: 'Thou who hast made me [etc.]'. Yet sometimes if you meet a dog or other beast, you may say: 'Lord, let it bite me, let it kill me; this beast is much better than I; it has never sinned. I after so much grace have provoked you; I have turned my back to you and not my face, and I have done nothing good, but all ill. Woe is me. Welawey.'

On entering the church say: 'Lord, it is as a dog and not as a man that I presume to enter your sanctuary. Woe is me. Welawey.'

Then, plucking up some confidence, with Mary Magdalene throw yourself at the feet of the most sweet Jesus, and wash them with your tears and anoint them and kiss them; and if not with your eyes and mouth, at least do this in your heart. Do not climb up to the cross, but in your heart say with the publican: 'Lord, be merciful to me a sinner.'

Afterwards say matins of the Blessed Virgin, reverently and not too fast.

When you hear Mass, do not by any means engage in talk with other people; but while the clerks are singing, look at the books of the church; and on every feast day, look at the Gospel and the exposition of it and at the Epistle. There is a certain *Legenda Sanctorum* which is very old; look at that and especially at the Common of Saints at the end of the book.

I do not counsel you to go up to the altars, as we used to do; but be afraid, and say what you have to say in a side chapel with the Lord Jesus [?].

On weekdays, after the others have gone, say one fifty of the Psalter of the Blessed Virgin [= five decades of the rosary]; and then going back to your house [or lodging : *hospicium*] have nothing else in your heart or your mouth except 'Hail Mary full of grace the Lord is with thee'; sometimes the whole of it, sometimes only 'Hail Mary'. When you sit at table, ruminate in your mind those two words, or as far as the middle, or sometimes to the end. And every time when you drink at table, say in your heart: 'In the name of the Father', as above; make the sign (of the cross) with your hand outside the table.

If dinner is not ready when you get home, go to that room (*casam*?) and say another fifty of Our Lady [rosary].

When you dine, and also after dinner, say grace standing.

Let the book be brought to the table as readily as the bread.

And lest the tongue speak vain or hurtful things, let there be reading, now by one, now by another, and by your children as soon as they can read; and think of the wicked Dives, tormented in hell in his tongue more than in any other members.

Let the family be silent at table, and always, as far as is possible.

Expound something in the vernacular which may edify your wife and others.

When there is no reading, have your meditations; and let there be these three at least this year [?], that is to say: 'Hail Mary', 'Thou who hast made me, have mercy upon us and upon me', 'In the name of the Father and of the Son and of the Holy Ghost may we be delivered Amen.'

You can make a cross on the table out of five bread-crumbs; but do not let anyone see this, except your wife; and the more silent and virtuous she is, the more heartily you should love her in Christ.

After grace, said standing, go to that secret place, and send for William Bonet or Sir William Trimenel or others as you please, and confer with them there until vespers.

Drink once, or twice at most, and that in summer. By no means let anyone spend anything, not even one farthing, but let all be done for God's sake.

I forbid you for ever all spectacles, that is to say, dances (*choreas*), buckler-play, dicing, wrestling, and the like.

Look back, like blessed Anselm, and see how your whole life has been barren or wicked.

Let your supper be brief, lest you ingurgitate, and let all be done as above at dinner.

After supper or before, sometimes before as well, go up into your cell and pray.

As the determiners at Oxford do:

When you are in bed, go back to the beginning of the day, and look diligently in your heart: if you have done any evil, and there be sorry; if any good, and there give thanks to God, always in fear and trembling, and do not think it certain that you will survive till the morrow.

It is clear that this document does not belong to that genre of spiritual writing which is addressed to the devout reader in general, like the *Imitation of Christ* or the *Introduction à la vie dévote*. It is addressed to one particular person, in a tone which is at once intimate and authoritative; *interdico vobis* . . . It mentions one or two of the recipient's friends by name. It is very pithy, and contains some allusions which, it seems to me, would hardly be intelligible except by reference to some previous instruction or conversation, as in the reference to St. Godric. It is an *aide-mémoire*, probably intended partly to sum up, partly to supplement some previous oral instructions. The name of neither the writer nor the recipient is given; that would have been unnecessary. But we can make some conjectures about what sort of persons they were. The writer was presumably the confessor or spiritual director of the recipient; he was probably either a secular priest (perhaps the 'curate' of the local parish church) or a friar. Other possibilities might be an anchorite or a Carthusian, both types of men to whom a late medieval layman might go for spiritual direction; but these may perhaps be ruled out by the phrase about going up to the altars, 'as we used to do', which seems to imply someone free to wander about. The phrase about the 'clerks singing' suggests that the church attended was not a friars' church, even if the director was himself a friar.

Whether he was a secular or a regular, the writer was probably an Oxford graduate; this would explain his ingenious simile, comparing the nightly examination of conscience to the 'determination' which summed up a disputation at the university. And we can get some idea of the kind of books he read. Thus he refers rather cryptically to an episode about Saint Godric of Finchale, who was attacked by the devil on his sick-bed, before he had time to protect himself with the sign of the cross; he must have come across this in a life of Godric, perhaps in some collection like the *Sanctilogium* of John of Tynemouth rather than in the full-length biography by Reginald of Durham.[1] Again, he had evidently read the meditations, genuine or pseudonymous, attributed to Saint Anselm; it is interesting (though hardly surprising) to find these traditional works of three centuries before still popular. And he recommends as an ejaculatory prayer or theme for meditation the phrase: *Qui plasmasti me, miserere nostri et mei.* This was the prayer which the desert father, Saint Paphnutius, enjoined upon the converted harlot, Saint Thais, she being unworthy even to use the name of God;[2] one would like to think that the writer was a reader of the *Vitae Patrum*, but he may have come across the story second-hand in the life of Saint Thais in the *Legenda Aurea*. But at any rate these quotations seem to show someone who stands upon the ancient ways.

The recipient was clearly a layman, married, with a wife and children. He may perhaps have been a member of the Throckmorton family, since the document survives among the Coughton

---

[1] Reginald of Durham, *Libellus de vita et miraculis S. Godrici*, ed. J. Stevenson (Surtees Soc. xx, 1845), pp. 313–14; for John of Tynemouth cf. *Nova Legenda Angliae*, ed. C. Horstmann (Oxford, 1901), i. 499; Roger Wendover, *Flores Historiarum*, ed. H. G. Howlett (R.S., 1886), 77.

[2] *Vitae Patrum*, P.L. lxxiii. 662 (*Vita Sanctae Thaidis*).

muniments; at the beginning of the fifteenth century the family was connected with Fladbury, in Worcestershire, and had not yet moved to Coughton. But he was clearly a town-dweller, not a countryman; he had to walk to church, and had no private chapel, or domestic oratory, as the lord of a manor, or even a very prosperous citizen, might have. There is a reference to the men 'of this city or town'; and his house is described as 'hospicium', which means a town house, probably of some size (cf. the French 'hôtel'). Two possible members of the Throckmorton family are Thomas Throckmorton (d. 1414), retainer of Thomas Beauchamp, earl of Warwick; and John Throckmorton (d. 1445), retainer of Richard Beauchamp, earl of Warwick.[1] Both might have spent quite a lot of time in London, where they might have had a *hospitium*; it is clear that the recipient of our document had a house of his own, and not just a lodging-chamber in his lord's house. A magnate of this period might be a *dévot*; in the fourteenth century, Henry, duke of Lancaster, had written a spiritual treatise, the *Livre de seyntz medicines*,[2] and the Pageant of the life of Richard Beauchamp, earl of Warwick, shows him to be a man of some piety;[3] so that the retainer of such a man might share this piety. The so-called 'lollard knights' are also examples of genteel lay piety of a more unorthodox complexion.[4] Or again, the recipient of our document might have been a member of the Olney family of Weston Underwood (where another *dévot*, the poet Cowper, was to settle and make friends with the Throckmortons some centuries later). Quite a number of Olney records are incorporated in the Throckmorton muniments, including a mid-fifteenth-century letter of Sir Robert Olney to his daughter Dame Margaret Throckmorton in

[1] Cf. the genealogy in G. Andrews Moriarty, 'The Early Throckmortons of Throckmorton and Fladbury', *Miscellanea Genealogica et Historica*, 5th ser. VI, vi (1927). John Throckmorton (*c.* 1390–1445) was a prominent and active member of the Earl of Warwick's council who spent his life in the Beauchamp service and was evidently a trusted confidant of his master; he was one of the Earl's executors: C. Ross, *The Estates and Finances of Richard Beauchamp, Earl of Warwick* (Dugdale Soc. Occasional Papers, no. 12, 1956), pp. 11–12; see also K. B. McFarlane, *The Nobility of Later Medieval England* (Oxford, 1973), pp. 140 n. 2, 187 ff.

[2] Cf. W. A. Pantin, *The English Church in the Fourteenth Century* (Cambridge, 1955), pp. 231–3.

[3] *Pageant of the Birth, Life and Death of Richard Beauchamp Earl of Warwick K.G. 1389–1439*, ed. Viscount Dillon and W. H. St. John Hope (London, 1914), e.g. his pilgrimage to Jerusalem (pls. XVI ff.).

[4] K. B. McFarlane, *Lancastrian Kings and Lollard Knights* (Oxford, 1972).

fairly pious terms;[1] 'Your participation ys com from beyond the se, whych ys a gret tresour to you[r] soule . . .' (this probably refers to a letter of confraternity from a foreign monastery or religious order such as the Carthusians). Some of the manuscript books at Coughton may be of Olney provenance; one of these contains a number of vernacular religious treatises, including the Mirror of Sinners, the Treatise of Ghostly Battle, the Cleansing of Man's Soul, the Mirror of Saint Edmund; this is the kind of literature that would have appealed to the recipient of our document.[2]

If the recipient was of the middle class rather than of the gentry, he may have been a well-to-do merchant, like the Merchant of Prato, or the men who flocked to hear San Bernardino of Siena, or to come nearer home, a masculine and (one hopes) more balanced equivalent of Margery Kempe. Or, perhaps more likely still, he may have been a lawyer, like Sir Thomas More a century later. The reference to Sir William Trimenel as one of his personal friends (discussed below) suggests London as a setting; otherwise one might think of a country town like Worcester or Warwick, Evesham or Bedford.

Above all, the most remarkable thing we know about the recipient is that he was well educated, and could read Latin. These instructions could very well have been written in the vernacular, if that had been thought necessary; for there had been a growing body of spiritual literature in Middle English during the previous century. But the writer prefers to address the recipient in Latin; no doubt that made for conciseness and privacy. Here then is a most useful glimpse of two types of medieval men about whom we should like to know much more: the devout layman and the educated layman.[3]

The recipient is told what prayers to say on rising, as he walks to church and at the church door; on entering the church, he is to

---

[1] Throckmorton Muniments, Box 61, folder 1, item 1; see Warwick County Record Office, *Catalogue of the Throckmorton Manuscripts at Coughton Court* (n.d.), p. 14.

[2] For these treatises see J. E. Wells, *Manual of the Writings in Middle English 1050–1400* (London and New Haven, 1916), pp. 458, 372, 346; cf. Pantin, *English Church*, pp. 220 ff.

[3] For the devout and literate layman cf. Pantin, *English Church*, pp. 253 ff.; R. W. Chambers, *On the Continuity of English Prose* (E.E.T.S. o.s. clxxxvi, 1932), *passim*; K. B. McFarlane, *The Nobility of Later Medieval England*, pp. 228 ff.; Sylvia L. Thrupp, *The Merchant Class of Medieval London* (Chicago, 1948), pp. 155 ff.

throw himself at Christ's feet, like Saint Mary Magdalene. This idea would be suggested or underlined by the fact that the most prominent object to be seen on entering a medieval church would be the great rood standing above the rood-screen. Perhaps the injunction that follows: 'do not go up (*non ascendes*) to the cross' was meant literally; was the man being dissuaded from some pious practice of climbing up to the rood-loft to kiss the feet of the rood? In the instructions on how to hear Mass, it is revealing that it was necessary to forbid conversation; this must have been a tempting opportunity for meeting friends and transacting business. While the clerks are singing, the recipient is told to 'look at the books of the church'—rather an ambiguous phrase; it may mean that there were liturgical books, a missal or gradual, chained in the church for public use, as we know there were psalters and breviaries chained for public use in some churches, as at Exeter and elsewhere.[1] As the recipient could read Latin, he could have followed the Mass in the liturgical books, as a man might do now; was this what he was being encouraged to do?[2] Or was he expected to use non-liturgical devotions during Mass? We know that Saint Thomas of Canterbury used to read the prayers of Saint Anselm during the singing of the gradual at Mass; and Wolsey's statutes for the Augustinian canons speak of them as hearing Mass 'orationibus aut contemplationibus . . . intendentes'.[3] The growth of individualistic and non-liturgical devotions—the liturgical movement in reverse, so to speak—is an interesting but baffling subject. Certainly, when the recipient is told on feast days to 'look at the gospel and its exposition', this looks like using some series of homilies, rather like Mirk's *Festiall*, except that this man could use a Latin one.

[1] The inventory of Exeter cathedral in 1506 gives lists of books chained at the high altar and between the choir and the high altar; they included psalters and collections of prayers and meditations, as well as reference books like the *Summa confessorum*, the *Pupilla Oculi*, Lyndwood, etc.: G. Oliver, *Lives of the Bishops of Exeter* (Exeter, 1859), pp. 331, 334. For chained books in other churches see C. Wordsworth and H. Littlehales, *The Old Service-Books of the English Church* (Antiquaries Books, 1910), pp. 65, 134, 139, 266, and plate after p. 48.

[2] For an example of a literate layman, at Lydden, Kent, who left money in 1474 for making a window in the chapel where he and the 'curate' used to recite Office together, see *Archaeologia Cantiana*, xliii (1931), 14; this was probably a 'low side window'; but the growing use of large glazed windows in the Perpendicular period must also have helped the use of prayer-books by laymen.

[3] *Materials . . . Thomas Becket*, ed. J. C. Robertson, iii (R.S., 1877), 210; D. Wilkins, *Concilia* (1737), iii. 686.

The recommendation to read the *Legenda Sanctorum* during Mass seems at first sight surprising; the probable explanation is that the *Legenda* had appended to it (*in fine libri*) an 'exposition of the Mass', as was sometimes done, e.g. in the version used by Caxton for his English translation of the *Legenda Aurea*. This would mean that the man would follow the Mass with a paraphrase and a devotional commentary rather than a liturgical text.

Another puzzling phrase is the advice not to 'ascend to the altars, as we used to do'. This may mean that the recipient and his director had been accustomed to sit in the stalls in the chancel, and so nearer to the altar; this was normally forbidden to laymen, except for patrons and other 'sublime' persons, and perhaps our man was 'sublime' enough for that.[1] Instead, the recipient is now encouraged to retire to say his prayers in a 'chapel' (side-chapel?). One of the advantages of the ever-multiplying side-chapels and pews would be to provide privacy and recollection for the devout; and the internal 'squints' which are to be found in some churches, carefully trained upon the high altar, would enable a man to hear Mass from a side-chapel without being seen. It looks as if a love of privacy was gaining ground in churches as well as in domestic architecture. The instructions, in dealing with Mass, say nothing about going to communion; at this date even a devout layman would probably not communicate more than three or four times a year. It is in this absence of frequent communion that there is the greatest contrast with recent practice.

The recipient of these instructions is evidently expected to recite the Little Office of Our Lady, and the rosary (or psalter of Our Lady); but there is no explicit mention of the other offices that figure in books of hours and primers, such as the Office of the Dead, the Hours of the Cross and of the Holy Ghost. It would seem that our man's liturgical burden was rather less than that prescribed by John Quentin, in the late fifteenth century, where the devout layman is recommended to add the Office of the Dead, at least on holy days; and it is a great deal less than the rather formidable list of offices and Masses which great ladies like Princess Cicely and Lady Margaret recited or attended. This may partly be because our man had daily work to do, as a lawyer, say, or

---

[1] Cf. *Councils and Synods*, ii, 1205–1313, ed. F. M. Powicke and C. R. Cheney (Oxford, 1964), p. 297 (Worcester 1240): laymen are not to sit in chancels, except patrons and 'sublime persons'.

merchant, which left him less free time. But the general impression is that these instructions lay less stress on vocal than on mental prayer; what they seem to desiderate is a constant state of recollection and meditation on certain suggested themes, such as the Hail Mary, *Qui plasmasti me, In nomine Patris*. It may be noted that these themes are recommended *isto anno*, as though different or additional ones would be suggested in succeeding years. The instructions recommend our man to retire for prayer and private talk to a certain place described as 'that little house' (*casa illa*), 'that secret place', 'the cell'; this would probably be a small private room or closet, opening off a larger chamber, rather like the small studies that opened off college chambers.[1] Such a room might be about eight feet square, and would contain such books and papers as the man possessed, and could be locked up. One of the most marked features of late medieval domestic architecture was the growing desire for privacy; men withdrew from the great hall and preferred a 'privy parlour or a chamber with a chimney'.[2] As is well known, this was condemned by conservative moralists like William Langland as anti-social; but here we can see that there might be a more respectable, religious motive for privacy, namely for reading, meditation, and prayer. Men wanted privacy, as they became more literate and devout. And indeed, lack of privacy could be a severe handicap to devout practice. When Richard Whitford, in his *Werke for Housholders* (1530) recommends a life of prayer to laymen, he at once has to meet a practical objection:

But yet some of you will say: Sir, this work is good for religious persons and for such persons as be solitary and do lie alone by themselves, but we do lie two or three sometimes together and yet in one chamber divers beds and so many in company; if we should use these things in presence of our fellows, some would laugh us to scorn and mock us.[3]

---

[1] Cf. R. Willis and J. W. Clark, *Architectural History of the University of Cambridge* (Cambridge, 1886), iii. 297 ff.; *Medieval Archaeology*, iii (1959), 243 ff.

[2] *The Vision of William concerning Piers the Plowman*, ed. W. W. Skeat (Oxford, 1886), i. 293 (= B. Passus X, 94); cf. M. E. Wood, *The Medieval English House* (London, 1965), pp. 91 ff.

[3] Richard Whytford, *A Werke for Housholders* (London, Wynkyn de Worde, 1530), fol. iᵛ; cf. H. C. White, *The Tudor Books of Private Devotion* (Wisconsin, 1951), p. 157.

When real privacy was not available, as for a courtier, even a bay window would serve; we read of Thomas Cromwell in Wolsey's great chamber at Esher, 'leaning in the great window with a primer in his hand saying Our Lady Matins'.[1] And at the beginning of the seventeenth century John Gerard describes how a courtier 'read devotional books eagerly, and always carried one in his pocket. You might see him in the Court or in the Presence Chamber, as it is called, turning aside to a window and reading a chapter of Thomas A Kempis' *Imitation of Christ* . . . and after reading a little he would turn to the company, but his mind was elsewhere.'[2]

We can follow the recipient home to dinner with his family, and here an interesting picture emerges. Our man had no chaplain or Bible-clerk to read at meals, as would happen in a religious community or college or a pious magnate's household. Instead, a book is promptly produced and passed round to be read by the diners in turn; the children are to take their part as soon as they learn to read. One would very much like to know what kind of books were read at this table. We know the books that Cicely, duchess of York, had read at her table: Hilton on Active and Contemplative Life, Bonaventure, *De infancia Salvatoris*, the Golden Legend, Saint Mechtild, Saint Catherine of Siena, the Revelations of Saint Brigit; and at supper she rehearsed what had been read at dinner.[3] This is rather a highbrow collection, which may not have been available to our householder; he probably used collections of saints' lives and homilies, like Mirk's *Festiall*. Since it seems unlikely that his wife and children could understand Latin, his choice of books must have been confined to those available in translation; or conceivably if a Latin book was used, he translated it sentence by sentence. This may be what the instructions mean when they say: 'expound something in the vernacular which may

[1] George Cavendish, *The Life and Death of Cardinal Wolsey*, ed. R. S. Silvester (E.E.T.S., o.s. ccxliii, 1959), p. 104; Cavendish comments: 'which had been since a very strange sight'.

[2] John Gerard, *The Autobiography of an Elizabethan*, ed. P. Caraman (London, 1951), p. 186. It is said that the minute Elzevir editions served the occasional reading of courtiers.

[3] *A Collection of Ordinances and Regulations for the Government of the Royal Household* (published by the Society of Antiquaries, London, 1790), p. *37; Pantin, *The English Church*, p. 254; C. A. J. Armstrong, 'The Piety of Cicely, Duchess of York: a Study in Late Medieval Culture', *For Hilaire Belloc*, ed. Douglas Woodruff (New York, 1942), pp. 68 ff., esp. p. 75.

edify your wife and others.' Or it may be that a running commentary was being recommended. Reading at table might merge
imperceptibly into edifying table-talk, which was a feature of late
medieval lay piety. Already in the thirteenth century John of
Wales had written his *Summa collationum*, a systematic manual
of edifying conversation on all topics, though this was probably
intended for clerical use.[1] But we know how Margery Kempe told
edifying stories and talked about Heaven at the dinner table, to
the annoyance of her companions.[2] Edifying conversation might
come dangerously near to lay preaching; a century later, Saint
Ignatius Loyola got into trouble over this in the early days of his
conversion. It was one of the virtues of a book like Whytforde's
Werke for Housholders that it provided a safe alternative.[3] One of
the purposes of this informal reading at table, as with the more
formal reading by Bible-clerks in colleges, was to prevent idle or
vicious conversation (as college statutes make clear);[4] hence the
reference here to the sins of the tongue and their punishment.

One practice here recommended is to make (without being
noticed) a cross of five bread-crumbs on the table, presumably to
remind one of the Five Wounds; this, in a simple fashion, resembles the practice of Henry VI (as recorded by his chaplain, John
Blacman) of having 'a certain dish which represented the five
wounds of Christ as it were red with blood' set on his table by his
almoner before any other course.[5] But the idea goes back much
earlier; in a thirteenth-century monastic treatise, the monk is
recommended, when at meal-time in the refectory, to 'make a
cross of five crumbs, and say to yourself: Here the feet, there
the hands were fastened; here lay the head; here from the side
in blood flowed mercy and plentiful redemption.'[6] It would be

[1] W. A. Pantin, 'John of Wales and Medieval Humanism', *Medieval Studies
presented to Aubrey Gwynn S.J.*, ed. J. A. Watt, J. B. Morall, F. X. Martin
(Dublin, 1961), pp. 297 ff., esp. pp. 299 ff., 312 ff.

[2] *The Book of Margery Kempe*, ed. S. B. Meech and H. E. Allen (E.E.T.S.,
o.s. ccxii, 1939), pp. 11, 133–4.

[3] Whytforde (op. cit., fol. B iᵛ ff.; H. C. White, op. cit., pp. 157 ff.) recommends domestic catechizing.

[4] *Statutes of the Colleges of Oxford* (Royal Commissioners, 1853), i. 43
(Merton), 7 (Oriel).

[5] John Blacman, *Henry the Sixth*, ed. M. R. James (Cambridge, 1919), pp. 13,
35.

[6] Bodleian, MS. Laud Misc. 8, fol. 73ᵛ; this is a treatise, beginning 'Do me
totum. Nichil dixi et totum dixi', apparently to be identified with the meditations of a 13th-century Cistercian, Thomas of Wobourn; cf. J. Bale, *Index Britan-*

interesting to know by what stages this idea reached the writer of the Throckmorton manuscript.

After dinner, until vespers—it is not clear whether public or private recitation is meant—the recipient is to go to 'that secret place', the small private room already referred to, and send for his particular friends to confer with. Of the friends mentioned by name, William Bonet seems hard to identify; but Sir[1] William Trimenel may be a member of the Trimenel family which occurs in London at the end of the fourteenth and beginning of the fifteenth century; a William Trimenel is mentioned in 1386, and another William Trimenel (or perhaps the same one) occurs as a mercer and warden of London Bridge in 1425 and 1435; and in 1426 William Trimenel, citizen of London, and Idonia his wife receive a papal indult for a portable altar. John Trimenel, mercer and warden of London Bridge, 1421, 1422, was probably another member of the same family.[2] This seems to make London a likely milieu for the recipient of the Throckmorton manuscript, and an important mercer with a private oratory seems a likely confidant. The advice to confer with a good and reliable friend may have been a feature of fifteenth-century spiritual direction, for it occurs elsewhere; thus master John Quentin says; 'Seke a good and faythfull frend of good conversatyon, to whome ye may dyscover your mynde secretes. Enquere and prove hym well or ye trust in hym. And whan ye have well proved hym, do all by his counsell.'[3] One thinks of Ser Lapo Mazzei, the family friend on whom the Merchant of Prato relied so much;[4] and the type occurs in the Paston letters, this time in the form of clerical friends.[5] One

niae Scriptorum, ed. R. L. Poole and M. Bateson (Oxford, 1902), p. 450; cf. M. R. James, *Ancient Libraries of Canterbury and Dover* (Cambridge, 1903), pp. 278 (782), 280 (798, 799), 348 (1593, 1594). It has a certain anti-scholastic bias, e.g. 'Si hiis et similibus . . . diligenter intenderis, peryarmenias non curabis' (fol. 71); 'Argumenta sophisticata dampnabis omnino, sive de libris secularibus sint, sive de divinis' (fol. 74ᵛ).

[1] The epithet 'Sir' or 'Dominus' is too general to help in identifiying; it certainly does not necessarily imply a knight or lord; it might mean a secular priest.

[2] *C.P.L.* vii. 430; *Calendar of Letter Books . . . London*, ed. R. R. Sharpe (1912), i. 261, 275; *Calendar of Select Pleas and Memoranda of the City of London* (ed. A. H. Thomas), *1381–1412* (1932), p. 64; *1413–1437* (1943), pp. 176, 284.

[3] *Prymer of Salysbury Use*, Paris, F. Regnault, 1531 (*S.T.C.* 15970; Hoskins 96), fol. xxiiii.

[4] Cf. Iris Origo, *The Merchant of Prato* (London, 1957), pp. 202 ff.

[5] e.g. Sir James Gloys, Sir Thomas Howes, and Friar Brackley; cf. H. S.

could look to such a man for all kinds of advice, personal, spiritual, and temporal, over a business deal, a political affiliation, the endowment of a chantry or a hospital. In a humble, informal way, there is some analogy here with the councils of magnates.[1]

The writer shows a certain preoccupation with dogs, which was perhaps already a trait of the British character: 'Lord let it bite me!' The man's wife is to be prized for her silence; it is not clear whether he expects a general taciturnity, or merely a tactful concealment of her husband's pious eccentricities like the cross of bread-crumbs. The day concludes with a light supper and an examination of conscience, which is compared, as we have seen, to an academic 'determination'.

All amusements, or at any rate public amusements, are barred —dancing, buckler-play, dicing, wrestling are forbidden; one thinks of similar prohibitions in university and college statutes. The strictest economy and control of expenditure, down to the last farthing, are enjoined; 'let all be done for God's sake.' It is all very reasonable, but one cannot help wondering what the man's wife and children and servants felt about it.

There is a certain rather grim and rigorist air about it all, which makes one think of the Puritans and the Jansenists. The loving warmth which even poor Margery Kempe, with all her faults, showed seems lacking. But, in all fairness, we should remember two things. First there was a robustly coarse and licentious Brueghelesque element in medieval life, which inevitably provoked what seems to us excessive severity; so one has a constant alternation of rigorism and laxity. Secondly, one must remember that we do not seem to have the whole picture here. As has been suggested, these notes are probably only a summary or supplement to oral instructions already given, and we cannot tell how much they may have been tempered in fact by the more genial and humane personality of the director or the recipient. One knows, from the example of Sir Thomas More and his household, how the most heroic and uncompromising piety could be transformed by wit and affection.

It is interesting to try to put this Throckmorton document in its

Bennett, *The Pastons and their England* (Cambridge, 1932), pp. 227 ff., 231 ff., 246 ff.

[1] Cf. A. E. Levett, *Studies in Manorial History* (Oxford, 1938), pp. 21 ff.; Pantin, *The English Church*, p. 33.

place in the series of such devotional instructions for the pious layman. A few generations earlier we have, in a funeral sermon, an almost casual description of the daily regime of a devout lay-woman, Lady Cobham (1344); how she recited the Little Office of Our Lady, the seven penitential psalms, and the Litany, 'almost every day', besides attending Mass.[1] The Throckmorton manu-script is the earliest example known to me of a set of formal instructions for a layman, though something else may well turn up; we only have this through the chance survival of a few square inches of parchment. From about the middle of the fifteenth century such instructions or descriptions become rather more frequent. Master John Quentin graduated Doctor of Theology at Paris in 1473; he was canon and penitentiary of Paris.[2] He wrote a set of sermons which were printed and became quite popular; there was a copy in the Syon library, and the Oxford bookseller John Dorne (1510) sold a number of copies. But he probably became best known, in this country at least, through writing a short treatise which was subsequently translated into English in the early sixteenth century by the London printer Robert Copland, under the title *The Maner to Lyve Well, Devoutly and Salutarily Every Day for all Persons of Meane Estate*; this we find prefixed to the Primer of Salisbury use, e.g. in the edition of Paris (Re-gnault), 1531.[3] The day's plan is set out as follows: Rise at 6 a.m., dress, 'say in your chamber or lodging matins, prime and hours [presumably of Our Lady], if you can; then go to church, before you do any worldly works, if you have no needful business; and abide in the church the space of a low mass while.' Subjects for meditation are given: 'When you come from church, take heed to your household or occupation till dinner time . . . Rest after dinner an hour or half an hour . . . As touching your service, say unto terce before dinner, and make an end of all before supper; and when ye may, say *Dirige*[4] and Commendations for all Christen souls, at least on holy days . . . Shrive you every week to your

---

[1] Pantin, *The English Church*, pp. 255–6.

[2] P. Feret, *La Faculté de Théologie à Paris: Moyen Âge* (Paris, 1897), iv. 165; *Auctarium Chartularii Universitatis Parisiensis*, ed. C. Samaran and H. van Moe (Paris, 1928), iv. 41; H. C. White, *The Tudor Books of Private Devotion*, pp. 150 ff.

[3] See p. 409 n. 3 above. The spelling in the passages quoted (fols. xxi^v–xxiiii^v) has been modernized.

[4] *Dirige* is the opening word of Matins of the Dead, but it is perhaps used here and elsewhere for the whole Office of the Dead.

curate . . . Confess you every day to God . . . Consider often either by day or night, when you do awake, what Our Lord did at that hour of his blessed Passion, and where he was at that hour . . . And in going to your bed, have some good thought either of the Passion of Our Lord, or of your sins, or of the pains that souls have in purgatory or some other good spiritual thought.' It will be noted that here, as in the Throckmorton manuscript, there is no advice on how often to communicate; that would be left to the man's confessor. It will also be noted that the man envisaged was of middling rank, and therefore likely to have business occupation, or at least to be his own housekeeper, unlike the examples that follow.

Towards the end of the fifteenth century we move into the upper ranks of society, with the well-known description (it is not a set of instructions) of the daily life of Cicely, Duchess of York, the mother of Edward IV and Richard III; she died in 1495.[1] She rises at 7 a.m., recites matins of the day and of Our Lady with her chaplain; hears a low Mass in her chamber, and then breakfasts; then goes to the chapel to hear 'divine service' (the little hours?) and two low Masses; then to dinner (where spiritual books are read). After dinner she gives audience for one hour, then sleeps for a quarter of an hour, then continues in prayer till the first peal of evensong, when she takes a drink of wine or ale; then her chaplain recites with her both vespers (of the day and of Our Lady), and after the last peal she goes to chapel for sung evensong. Then supper, at which she 'recites' the reading at dinner with those present; after supper, recreation; an hour before bedtime, a cup of wine; 'and after that goeth to her pryvie closette, and taketh her leave of God for all nighte, makinge an ende of her prayers for that daye'; and by 8 p.m. is in bed. Since the Duchess was technically a lady of leisure (if such a full programme can be called leisure), and had at least one chaplain, and a chapel, furnished with a choir, her liturgical programme is much more elaborate than the previous examples; one curious feature is that while she hears three low Masses and sung vespers, there is no mention of a sung Mass, unless that is included in 'divine service'. Since she recites the office of the day as well as the Office of Our Lady, she presumably possessed a breviary as well as a book of hours or primer. There is no mention of the Office of the Dead.

---

[1] See references given on p. 407 n. 3 above.

A little later, we have the daily regime of Lady Margaret Beaufort, mother of Henry VII, as described by her confessor, Saint John Fisher; she died in 1509.[1] She rose soon after 5 a.m., and after certain devotions recited matins of Our Lady with one of her gentlewomen; then recited matins of the day with her chaplain, in her closet; then she heard four or five Masses (presumably in her chapel); then followed prayers and devotions until dinner, which was at 10 a.m. on 'eating days' and 11 a.m. on fasting days. After dinner she would go to her 'stations' to three altars daily. She recited daily 'her dyryges & commendacyons' (the Office of the Dead); 'and her evensonges before souper, bothe of the daye and of our Lady, besyde many other prayers and psalters of Davyd thrugh out the yere. And at nyght before she wente to bedde, she faylled not to resorte unto her chapell, and there a large quarter of an hour to occupye her in devocyons.' And yet nevertheless 'dayly whan she was in health she faylled not to say the crowne of our Lady, whiche after the manere of Rome conteyneth .lx. and thre [63] Aves, and at every Ave to make knelynge. As for medytacyon, she had divers bokes in Frensshe, wherewith she wolde occupy herselfe whan she was wery of prayer.'

We can picture the daily routine of these great ladies set against the framework of the grander domestic architecture of the period, moving between the chamber and the private closet, the chapel and the hall (or perhaps dining-chamber). The chapel was probably attended from a first-floor pew, as was very general with domestic chapels, connected if necessary by a gallery with the private apartments (as at Thornbury and Richmond). This would provide the seclusion or privacy which the Throckmorton man seems to have sought in a side-chapel; and in the days of infrequent communion, remoteness from the altar would not matter. Lady Margaret's visits to the altars would, however, demand, literally, some 'condescension', that is, descending to the ground floor. This type of seigneurial pew was at once part of the house and of the church.

A century later we find much the same daily routine of domestic piety among the Recusants; and here of course the domestic setting was all the more important, since they were necessarily cut off from access to the parish church. The life of Anne Dacre, Countess of Arundel (wife of Saint Philip Howard), gives the following

[1] *Works of John Fisher*, ed. J. E. B. Mayor (E.E.T.S., E.S. xxvii, 1876), i. 294 f.

account of her daily life (*c.* 1595):[1] as soon as she awoke, about 6 a.m., she said certain vocal prayers which she knew by heart, while her maids rose and dressed; then when she was dressed, she went to the chapel and recited some part of the Office of Our Lady and other prayers out of the Primer, the Manual, and other pious books; Mass followed at 8 a.m.; every day she heard two Masses, and more if possible. After Mass she remained a good space in the chapel, reciting the rest of her vocal prayers appointed for the morning of that day; and a little before dinner, if business did not hinder her, she would come thither to recollect herself. About 5 p.m. she usually went to evensong, spending in that and other prayers, together with her beads, nearly one hour. Before supper she recited her matins and lauds (of the Office of Our Lady?); and at 9 p.m. she was present at Litanies. The rest of the time till going to bed (seldom before 11 p.m.) 'she spent for the most part in Prayer, hearing or reading some spiritual book and concluded all with a most diligent examin of conscience'. She commonly received communion twice a week.

Another example of about the same date comes from the Life of the Lady Magdalen, Viscountess Montague, who died at Battle in 1608.[2] She rose 'early' (the hour not specified), and spent most of the time before dinner in prayer. She was present every day at the morning and evening service (the office of the day?) which was daily said by her priests in her chapel. For the most part she heard every day three Masses, and would have heard more if she might. In her private devotions, she said every day three offices, of Our Lady, of the Holy Ghost, and of the Holy Cross, and at least three rosaries, the Jesus Psalter, the fifteen prayers of Saint Brigit (the 'fifteen Oes'), and the common litanies, and finally sometimes the Office of the Dead. She would sometimes retire alone after dinner to the chapel to pray, as also before supper she spent an hour or often two hours in prayer, and before she went to bed she omitted not the litanies and examen of her conscience.

At a higher social level, the chapels and communities of chaplains or religious attached to the households of the Catholic Queens, Henrietta Maria, Catherine of Braganza, and Mary of

---

[1] *The Lives of Philip Howard, Earl of Arundel, and of Anne Dacres, his Wife,* ed. The Duke of Norfolk (London, 1857), pp. 203 ff., 297.

[2] Richard Smith, *The Life of the Lady Magdalen Viscountess Montague,* ed. A. C. Southern (London, 1954), p. 47.

Modena (which have left their architectural monument in the Inigo Jones chapel at St. James's) seem to presume a similar liturgical daily round.

There is evidence of a similar, if simpler, daily routine in Recusant households lower down in the social scale. A remarkable example of this was at Osgodby Hall, in Yorkshire, in the 1620s.[1] Here lived three knights and their families, under Jesuit direction. There were from two to four chaplains resident, partly for the families and household, partly for the neighbouring Catholics. On Sundays and holy days there was Mass, sermon, catechism, and spiritual reading. On weekdays there was Mass at 6 a.m. for the servants, the gentlemen, and for some of the ladies, and at 8 a.m. another Mass for the rest. At 4 p.m. vespers and matins (of Our Lady or of the day?) were said by the chaplains, with the gentlemen and ladies present; most made daily some meditation and mental prayer. After supper there were litanies at 9 p.m. and then bed. There was confession and communion at least every fortnight. Another similar example of about the same period is given in the Life of Mrs. Dorothy Lawson (d. 1632), of St. Anthony's near Newcastle upon Tyne:[2]

Her chappell was neat and rich; the altar stood vested with various habiliments, according to the fashion in Catholick countrys. Mass in the morning; Evensong in the afternoon, about four of the clock, with the Littanies of Loretto ... and a De-profundis for the faithful departed; between eight and nine att night Littanies of the Saints, att which all her servants were present. On festivall days, they allso heard Mass and Evensong, and when there was not a Sermon in the morning, there was usually a Catechisme in the afternoon, to which her neighbours children were call'd with her own household and herself never absent, delighting much to hear them examin'd, and distributing meddalls and Agnus Dei's to those that answer'd best.

It is noticeable throughout these Recusant examples how much the devotions correspond with the semi-liturgical contents of the Primer or Books of Hours, such as the various offices of Our Lady,

---

[1] J. Morris, *Troubles of Our Catholic Forefathers* (London, 1876), iii. 467 ff.; H. Aveling, *Post-Reformation Catholicism in East Yorkshire* (East Yorkshire Local History Society, 1960), pp. 33–4.

[2] William Palmes, *The Life of Mrs. Dorothy Lawson, of St. Anthony's, near Newcastle-on-Tyne*, ed. G. B. Richardson (London, 1855), p. 43. For the simpler regime of a busy housewife, Saint Margaret Clitherow (d. 1588), see J. Morris, op. cit. iii. 390 ff.; but even this included about two hours of private prayer, Mass when available, and evensong at 4 p.m.

of the Dead, and so forth, even down to the Fifteen Oes. It is not surprising therefore that many manuscript and early printed Books of Hours and Primers were preserved in Recusant households,[1] as the supporting literature, so to speak, of these devotional daily rounds; and the supply of Primers, in Latin and English, was kept up from the Recusant presses abroad; between *c.* 1571 and 1800 there were nearly fifty editions, and they were especially frequent in the early seventeenth century; there were no fewer than seven editions in the years 1631–3 alone.[2] Supplementing the Primer, less liturgical and more systematic, was the *Manual of Prayers* (referred to in the Countess of Arundel's Life); this was compiled by an English Catholic layman, George Flinton, and first printed by Father Parsons's press at Rouen in 1583; it was based on an earlier collection in Latin, made by a Fleming, Simon Verrepaens, in 1565. The prayers were taken from patristic and medieval sources, coming down to More and Fisher; some of the prayers were grouped into chapters for each day of the week (as is again suggested in the Countess of Arundel's Life—the 'vocal prayers appointed for the morning of that day'). There were many editions of the Manual, e.g. twenty-six editions between 1583 and 1640; it was only replaced much later by Bishop Challoner's *Garden of the Soul.* It will be seen from these Recusant accounts how the medieval liturgical elements were being increasingly supplemented by sermons, catechizing, and spiritual reading, as one might expect in the Tridentine period.

Can we say anything about the architectural setting of the domestic piety of these Recusant households, such as the kind of private chapel they would have used? Lady Arundel presumably lived some of the time in Arundel Castle, with access to a private chapel there; but as the domestic quarters of the Castle were ruined in 1643–4 and rebuilt more than once subsequently, there seems little hope of conjecturing what the chapel was like. She probably spent more of her time at Arundel House in London, of which we have some descriptions and illustrations;[3] it was a large, rambling house, like a country manor transplanted into town, but here again, it is not possible to identify the chapel.

---

[1] There are for instance several such books preserved at Coughton Court.

[2] I have to thank Dr. David Rogers for these and the following bibliographical details.

[3] *Archaeologia*, lxxii (1921–2), 243 ff.

Lady Montague lived for the most part at Battle Abbey, where the abbot's house had been adapted and extensively added to by Sir Anthony Browne, father of the first Viscount Montague. Her biographer[1] tells us that she kept here a small establishment of three priests, and

> built a chapell in her house (which in such a persecution was to be admired), and there placed a very fair altar of stone, whereto she made an ascent with steps and enclosed it with rails; and, to have everything conformable, she built a choir for singers [choir-stalls, or a choir-loft?], and set up a pulpit for the priests, which perhaps is not to be seen in all England besides. Here almost every week was a sermon made, and on solemne feasts the sacrifice of the mass was celebrated with singing and musicall instruments, and sometimes also with deacon and subdeacon.

The chapel must have been fairly large, since it sometimes contained 120 people. It seems impossible to tell whereabouts in the domestic buildings at Battle it was; possibly one of the larger rooms in the medieval abbot's house was adapted for the purpose.[2] We can get in some ways a clearer picture of the architectural setting of domestic worship at another house belonging to the Montagues, at Cowdray (Sussex), where Lady Montague presumably spent some of her time. Cowdray is now gutted by fire, but it is possible to trace the imposing domestic chapel, built and enlarged *c.* 1530–40; it was two storeys high, measured 50 feet by 24 feet, with a polygonal east end, an organ loft, and a western gallery for the family, communicating directly with the private apartments on the first floor.[3] It may well have served as a model for Lady Montague's chapel at Battle. Two well-known Recusant houses, Stonor (Oxon.) and East Hendred (Berks.), incorporated medieval domestic chapels, which presumably were used regularly when circumstances allowed. On a smaller scale, Harvington Hall (Worcs.) is a remarkably unspoilt example of a Recusant manor house; it has several hiding-places, and two small chapels on an upper floor, one of them with its walls strikingly decorated with red and white drops, no doubt representing the blood and tears of the Passion; a suitable background for Recusant domestic worship, with the Mass, the Jesus Psalter, and the rest. No doubt in most

---

[1] Richard Smith, op. cit., p. 43.
[2] For the abbot's house at Battle see *Archaeologia*, lxxxiii (1933), 139 ff.
[3] W. H. St. John Hope, *Cowdray and Easebourne* (London, 1919), pp. 78 ff.

Recusant houses the chapel was made so as to be indistinguishable from an ordinary room, when not in actual use. With easier times in the eighteenth century, the domestic chapels become more elegant, sometimes following the contemporary taste for the 'gothick', as at Mapledurham (Oxon.) and Milton (Berks.), while the chapel at Cowdray was redecorated with baroque stucco work.

There were of course analogies to this Recusant piety, *mutatis mutandis*, outside the Roman communion, rather in the same way as Roman spiritual books were often adapted for Protestant use. We have a good picture of a devout Puritan household, with a daily round of prayer, meditation, spiritual reading, sermons, and discussions with the chaplain, in the diary of Lady Hoby, at Hackness in Yorkshire at the end of the sixteenth century.[1] And a little later, for a devout, highly organized Anglican household, of a Laudian type of spirituality, we have of course the very well-known picture of the 'Arminian nunnery' at Little Gidding. Higher up in society, devout Anglicans, especially women at the Court, became aware of the need for some equivalent of the Catholic Books of Hours or Primers; and it was for these that John Cosin (later Bishop of Durham) compiled his well-known *Collection of Private Devotions, in the Practice of the Ancient Church, called the Hours of Prayer*, based on an Elizabethan Primer, and published in 1627.[2]

In 1696–7 Mrs. Mary Astell published *A Serious Proposal to the Ladies for the Advancement of their True and Greatest Interest*, in which she advocated the setting up of what she called a 'Monastery or . . . a Religious Retirement', in which ladies could devote themselves to a life of prayer and study. She does not set out a detailed horarium, beyond recommending 'the daily performance of the Publick Offices after the Cathedral manner, in the most affecting and elevating way, the celebration of the Holy Eucharist every Lord's Day and Holy-day, and a course of solid and instructive Preaching and Catechizing'; the ladies might also undertake the education of the daughters of gentlemen. While this perhaps represents a logical development of earlier experiments like Little Gidding, it is clearly less domestic amd more institutional than

---

[1] *The Diary of Lady Margaret Hoby, 1599–1605*, ed. D. M. Meads (London, 1930).

[2] *Diary of John Evelyn*, ed. E. S. de Beer (Oxford, 1955), iii. 45–6; C. J. Stranks, *Anglican Devotion* (London, 1961), pp. 66 ff.

anything we have so far been considering. Not surprisingly Mrs. Astell ran into opposition, and her projected community was never realized. If it had been, it would have resembled the communities of pious, well-born ladies, the *Damenstiften*, that existed (and still exist) in Lutheran countries like Germany and Scandinavia, taking the place of the pre-Reformation convents. It is remarkable that the social and religious need for such institutions was not more strongly felt in England.[1]

In the eighteenth century we find William Law (author of the *Serious Call*, 1728), in retirement at Kings Cliffe, following and recommending a regime in some ways resembling that of the medieval and Recusant households we have been considering.[2] Law rose at 5 a.m. and began the day with private prayer and study; but the characteristic feature of his regime was that the day was punctuated by periods of household prayer at three-hour intervals—at 9 a.m., at noon, at 3 p.m., and at 6 p.m. This reminds one of the original *raison d'être* of the Little Hours of the Roman Breviary; and it was perhaps a familiarity with Law that helped to make some of the early Tractarians find the Breviary congenial. Law concluded the day, as one might expect, with an examination of conscience, which he likens to the way in which a business man makes up his accounts every night—this may be compared with the simile of the 'determination' in the Throckmorton manuscript. On certain days of the week Law and his companions attended morning prayer in the adjacent parish church. It is important to remember that, as has already been pointed out, the domestic oratory was less important to Anglicans than to the Recusants, since Anglicans had access to the parish churches, and were encouraged to use them. Similarly every cathedral close must have had a circle of pious lay people who would make the cathedral services the centre of their devotional life; and at watering-places too, like Bath or Tunbridge Wells, the public church service played a more important part in the daily routine than one might expect. We can see a last example of the daily routine of domestic

---

[1] Stranks, op. cit., pp. 174 ff.

[2] For other examples of proposed Anglican communities, both male and female, in this period see J. Wickham Legg, *English Church Life from the Restoration to the Tractarian Movement* (London, 1914), pp. 281 ff.; in 1659 John Evelyn proposed a community 'to preserve science and cultivate themselves' which would have included a laboratory as well as a chapel. I am indebted to Dr. R. A. Beddard for drawing my attention to Mrs. Astell.

devotion in the formal family prayers, for family, guests, and servants, that survived in some households until within living memory, as described for instance by Augustus Hare at Hickleton and Powderham and by Percy Lubbock at Earlham. But that is a far cry from the Throckmorton manuscript from which we started.

W. A. PANTIN†

APPENDIX

Throckmorton Muniments (Coughton Court), 76 (box 30)

Parchment strip: 11¾ in. by 3¾ in. The words printed within pointed brackets ⟨ ⟩ are interlined in the original hand.

recto

Deferatur in bursa semper.

Memorandum de aqua benedicta omni die sumenda.

Quod omni velocitate surgendum sit de lecto.

De signo crucis ad capud, ad pedes manus et latus:

In nomine Patris et Filii et Spiritus Sancti liberemur a penis et peccatis ⟨Amen⟩.

De sancto Godrico, qui non statim signavit se.

Dicatur ⟨In manus tuas Domine Ihesu Christe⟩. Pater noster. Ave Maria. Credo in Deum. ⟨statim post⟩

Qui plasmasti me miserere nostri et mei.

Ad hostium ⟨exeundo dicatur⟩: Omnes homines huius civitatis ⟨vel ville⟩ a maiori ad minorem placent Deo, et ego solus dignus sum inferno. Ve michi. Welawey: dicatur ex toto corde, ita ut lacrime currant; non semper proferatur ore: sufficit quod gemendo.

Usque ad ecclesiam nullum aliud verbum nisi: Qui plasmasti. Aliquando tamen si obviaveritis cani, vel alteri bestie dicas: Domine laceret me, interficiat me; multo melior me est ista bestia; ipsa nunquam peccavit. Ego post tantam graciam provocavi te. Verti ad te tergum et non faciem, et nichil boni feci, set omnia mala. Ve michi, Welawey.

Intrando ecclesiam dicas: Domine, ut canis, non ut homo, presumo ingredi sanctuarium tuum. Ve michi, Welawey.

Deinde accepta aliquali fiducia, cum Maria Magdalena prosternas te ad pedes dulcissimi Ihesu et lacrimis lava et unge et osculare; et si non oculis et ore, saltim in corde fiant. Non ascendes supra ad crucem, set in corde dicas cum publicano: Deus propicius esto michi peccatori.

Postmodum dicatis matutinas de beata Virgine reverenter, non nimis festinanter.

Cum vero missam audieri⟨ti⟩s nullo modo faciatis colloquium cum aliis, set dum cantant clerici, respiciatis in libris ecclesie, et omni die festo videatis evangelium et exposicionem ipsius et epistolam. Est quedam legenda sanctorum antiqua valde; in illa videatis et maxime in communi sanctorum in fine libri. Non consulerem quod ascenderetis ad altaria, sicut solebamus, set time⟨atis⟩, et dicatis in capella cum Domino Ihesu [?] dicenda vestra. In ferialibus diebus post recessum aliorum dicatis unam quinquagenam psalterii beate Virginis, et tunc eundo ad hospicium nichil aliud in corde nec in ore nisi: Ave Maria gracia plena Dominus tecum; aliquando totum, aliquando tantum: Ave Maria. Illa duo verba vel usque ad medium, aliquando in finem, ruminetis in mente, cum sedetis in mensa. Et omni vice quando potabitis in mensa, dicatis in corde: In nomine Patris, ut supra. Extra mensam faciatis signum cum manu.

verso

Si prandium non sit paratum cum veneritis domi, eatis in casam illam et dicatis aliam quinquagenam de Domina.

Cum prandendum fuerit ⟨et eciam post prandium⟩ dicatis gracias stando.

Eque cito deferatur liber ad mensam sicut panis.

Et ne lingua proferat vana seu nociva, legatur nunc ab uno, nunc ab alio, et a filiis statim cum sciant legere, et cogitetis de divite nebulone cruciato apud inferos in lingua magis quam in aliis membris.

Sileat familia in mensa et semper, quatenus est possibile.

Aliquando exponatis in vulgari quod edificet uxorem et alios.

Quando non legitur, habeatis meditaciones vestras, et sint ille tres sole saltim isto anno, scilicet: Ave Maria; Qui plasmasti me miserere nostri et mei; In nomine Patris et Filii et Spiritus Sancti liberemur. Amen.

Poteritis facere crucem ⟨in mensa⟩ de quinque micis, set nullus hoc videat excepta uxore; que quanto magis silens et virtuosa; tanto cordialius in Christo diligenda.

Post gracias stando dictas, adeatis locum illum secretum et mittatis pro Willelmo Bonet [?] et ⟨domino⟩ Willelmo Trimenel vel aliis quibus placet, et conferatis ibi usque ad vesperas.

Semel vel bis ad plus bibatis ⟨hoc in estate⟩ nullo modo permittatis aliquem expendere nec unum quadrantem, set omnia propter Deum ⟨fiant⟩.

Interdico vobis ⟨perpetuo⟩ omnia spectacula, scilicet choreas, lusum bokelarie, aleas, luctamina, et huiusmodo.

Respice a retro ⟨cum beato Anselmo⟩ qualiter tota vita sterilis vel ⟨nepharia⟩.

Sit cena brevis, ne ingurgiteris, et fiat ut supra ⟨in prandio⟩.

Post cenam vel ante ⟨aliquando et ante⟩ ascendatis in cellam et oretis.

Sicut faciunt determinatores Oxonie, in lecto redeatis ad principium diei et videatis ⟨diligenter⟩ in corde quid mali fecistis et ibi dole, quid boni et ibi Deo gracias age, semper in timore et tremore, ne consideres pro certo ⟨te⟩ supervicturum in crastinum.

A BIBLIOGRAPHY OF THE PUBLISHED WRITINGS OF R. W. HUNT

R. W. Hunt has been an editor of *Mediaeval and Renaissance Studies* since its inception in 1938. He is one of the General Editors of *Oxford Palaeographical Handbooks*, and he has been a member of the editorial committee of the series *Auctores Britannici Medii Aevi* since the beginning. He contributed to the bibliographies of the *Oxford Dictionary of the Christian Church*, 1st edn. (London, 1957) and 2nd edn. (London, 1974), and wrote articles for the second edition.

1936

'English learning in the late twelfth century', *T.R.H.S.*, 4th ser. xix. 19–42. (Reprinted 1968.)

1939

Reviews:

Classical and Mediaeval Studies in honor of Edward Kennard Rand, ed. L. W. Jones (New York, 1938), in *Medium Aevum*, viii. 62–5.

Dom Adrian Morey, *Bartholomew of Exeter, Bishop and Canonist: a Study in the Twelfth Century* (Cambridge, 1937), in *Medium Aevum*, viii. 65–7.

1941

Review:

J. W. Thompson, *The Medieval Library* (Chicago, 1939), in *Medium Aevum*, x. 107–13.

1942

Review:

S. Harrison Thomson, *The Writings of Robert Grosseteste, Bishop of Lincoln 1235–1253* (Cambridge, 1940), in *Medium Aevum*, xi. 107–10.

1943

'Alberic of Monte Cassino and Reginald of Canterbury', *M.A.R.S.* i. 39–40.

'Studies on Priscian in the eleventh and twelfth centuries, I: Petrus Helias and his predecessors', *M.A.R.S.* i. 194–231. (To be reprinted in *Collected Papers*.)

1946

'Gift of Shelley manuscripts', *Bodl. L.R.* ii. 144–5.

1947

'The collection of mediaeval Latin verse in MS. Cotton Titus D. xxiv: supplementary notes', *Medium Aevum*, xvi. 6–8.

'The cataloguing of the Rawlinson manuscripts, 1771–1844', *Bodl. L.R.* ii. 190–5.

With J. Dover Wilson, 'The authenticity of Simon Forman's Bocke of Plaies', *Review of English Studies*, xxiii. 197–200.

Review:

Bedae *Opera de Temporibus*, ed. C. W. Jones (Mediaeval Academy of America, 1943) and *Bedae Pseudepigrapha: Scientific Writings falsely attributed to Bede*, ed. C. W. Jones (Cornell University Press, 1939), in *Medium Aevum*, xvi. 62–4.

1948

With W. A. Pantin and R. W. Southern, ed. *Studies in Medieval History presented to Frederick Maurice Powicke* (Oxford).

'The disputation of Peter of Cornwall against Symon the Jew', ibid., pp. 143–56.

'The introductions to the "Artes" in the twelfth century', *Studia Mediaevalia in honorem R. J. Martin O.P.* (Bruges, 1948), pp. 85–112. (To be reprinted in *Collected Papers*.)

Additional note to D. A. Winstanley, 'Halliwell Phillipps and Trinity College Library', *The Library*, 5th ser. ii. 277–82.

1949

'The Abbot and Convent of Merevale v. the Rector of Halsall', *Transactions of the Historic Society of Lancashire and Cheshire*, ci. 47–61.

'Tanner's *Bibliotheca Britannico-Hibernica*', *Bodl. L.R.* ii. 249–56.

1950

'Studies on Priscian in the twelfth century, II: the school of Ralph of Beauvais', *M.A.R.S.* ii. 1–56. (To be reprinted in *Collected Papers*.)

'Stephen of Antioch', *M.A.R.S.* ii. 172–3.

'Hugutio and Petrus Helias', *M.A.R.S.* ii. 174–8. (To be reprinted in *Collected Papers*.)

'The manuscript collection of University College, Oxford: origins and growth', *Bodl. L.R.* iii. 13–34.

'The Lyell Bequest', *Bodl. L.R.* iii. 68–82.

'Medieval inventories of Clare College Library', *Transactions of the Cambridge Bibliographical Society*, ii. 105–25.

'Notes on the Distinctiones monasticae et morales', *Liber floridus Paul Lehmann gewidmet*, ed. B. Bischoff and S. Brechter (St. Ottilien), pp. 355–62.

Article on 'Palaeography (Latin)' in *Chambers's Encyclopaedia*, new edn., vol. x. (Reprinted 1966.)

1951

Review:
British Museum: Catalogue of Additions to the Manuscripts, 1921–1925
(London, 1950), in *The Library*, 5th ser. v. 207–9.

1952

'A fragment of a manuscript from the Abbey of Saint Victor at Paris',
Bodl. L.R. iv. 124–6.
'The cataloguing of Ashmolean collections of books and manuscripts',
Bodl. L.R. iv. 161–70.

1953

'Manuscripts containing the indexing symbols of Robert Grosseteste',
Bodl. L.R. iv. 241–55.
A Summary of Western Manuscripts in the Bodleian Library at Oxford,
vol. i: *Historical Introduction and Conspectus of Shelf-marks* (Oxford).

1954

'Balliol College, History', *V.C.H. Oxfordshire*, vol. iii: *The University of
Oxford* (London), pp. 82–9.
'Chapter headings of Augustine *De trinitate* ascribed to Adam Marsh',
Bodl. L.R. v. 63–8.
With S. G. Gillam, 'The curators of the Library and Humphrey Wanley'
Bodl. L.R. v. 85–98.

1955

'The Library of Robert Grosseteste', *Robert Grosseteste: Scholar and
Bishop*, Essays in Commemoration, ed. D. A. Callus O.P. (Oxford),
pp. 121–45.

1957

'List of Phillipps manuscripts in the Bodleian Library', *Bodl. L.R.* vi.
348–69.

1958

'Appendix to R. Loewe, 'Alexander Neckham's knowledge of Hebrew',
M.A.R.S. iv. 29–34.
'The "lost" preface to the *Liber Derivationum* of Osbern of Gloucester',
M.A.R.S. iv. 267–82. (To be reprinted in *Collected Papers*.)

1959

Reviews:
The Oxford Book of Medieval Latin Verse, newly selected and edited
by F. J. E. Raby (Oxford, 1959), in *Medium Aevum*, xxviii. 189–94.
The English Library before 1700, ed. F. Wormald and C. E. Wright
(London, 1958), in *Archives* (Journal of the British Records Associa-
tion), iv. 49–50.

1960

'A manuscript belonging to Konrad Peutinger', *Bodl. L.R.* vi. 578–9.
'A manuscript from the library of Petrarch', *The Times Literary Supplement*, 23 September, p. 619.

Reviews:

H. Walther, *Initia Carminum ac Versuum Medii Aevi Posterioris Latinorum. Alphabetisches Verzeichnis der Versanfänge mittellateinischer Dichtungen* (Göttingen, 1959), in *Medium Aevum*, xxix. 130–2.

Mittellateinisches Wörterbuch, Bd. I, Lief. 1 (Munich, 1959), in *Journal of Theological Studies*, N.S. xi. 205–6.

1961

Saint Dunstan's Classbook from Glastonbury, Bodleian MS. Auct. F. 4. 32 (Umbrae Codicum Occidentalium, IV, Amsterdam).

'The collections of a monk of Bardney: a dismembered Rawlinson manuscript', *M.A.R.S.* v. 28–42.

Reviews:

Mittellateinisches Wörterbuch, Bd. I, Lief. 2–3 (Munich, 1960), in *Journal of Theological Studies*, N.S. xii. 372–4.

A. N. L. Munby, *The Dispersal of the Phillipps Library* (Cambridge, 1960), in *The Library*, 5th ser. xvi. 154–5.

K. M. W. Strecker, *Introduction to Medieval Latin*, transl. R. B. Palmer (Berlin, 1957), in *Medium Aevum*, xxx. 49–51.

1962

'A manuscript belonging to Robert Wivill, bishop of Salisbury', *Bodl. L.R.* vii. 23–7.

'The medieval home of the Bologna manuscript of Lactantius', *Studia in honorem E. A. Lowe* (*Medievalia et Humanistica*, xiv), pp. 3–6.

'William Pownall antiquarian', *Lincolnshire Architectural and Archaeological Society Reports and Papers*, IX. ii. 158–63.

Reviews:

E. A. Lowe, *English Uncial* (Oxford, 1960), in *Medium Aevum*, xxxi. 45–6.

Die mittelalterlichen Handschriften der Universitätsbibliothek Basel: Beschreibendes Verzeichnis, Abt. B, Bd. I. Bearbeitet von G. Meyer und M. Burckhardt (Basle, 1960), in *Journal of Theological Studies*, N.S. xiii. 205–8.

1963

With R. H. C. Davis, 2nd edn. of H. W. C. Davis, *A History of Balliol College* (Oxford).

'Humanistic script in Florence in the early fifteenth century', *Journal of the Society for Italic Handwriting*, no. 37, pp. 6–11. (Reprinted 1965.)

Review:

The Didascalicon of Hugh of St. Victor, transl. with introduction and notes by Jerome Taylor (New York, 1961), in *Modern Philology*, lxi. 310–12.

1964

'Oxford grammar masters in the Middle Ages', *Oxford Studies presented to Daniel Callus* (O.H.S., N.S. xvi), pp. 163–93. (To be reprinted in *Collected Papers*.)

Review:

J. Wardrop, *The Script of Humanism: Some Aspects of Humanistic Script, 1460–1560* (Oxford, 1963), in *The Library*, 5th ser. xix. 283–4.

1965

'A manuscript from the library of Coluccio Salutati', *Calligraphy and Palaeography, essays presented to Alfred Fairbank on his seventieth birthday*, ed. A. S. Osley (London), pp. 75–9.

'Humanistic script in Florence in the early fifteenth century', ibid., pp. 272–4. (Reprint, see under 1963.)

1966

'A dismembered manuscript: Bodleian MS. Lat. th. e. 32 and British Museum Add. MS. 17376', *Bodl. L.R.* vii. 271–5.

'An opportunity missed: the Didot manuscript of Cicero, *De Amicitia*', *Bodl. L.R.* vii. 275–80.

'Greek manuscripts in the Bodleian Library from the collection of John Stojković of Ragusa', *Studia Patristica*, vii. 75–82.

'The Sum of Knowledge: universities and learning', *The Flowering of the Middle Ages*, ed. J. Evans (London), pp. 180–202.

'Illuminated manuscripts at Cambridge', *The Times Literary Supplement*, 14 April, p. 336.

Preface to photographic reprint of *Catalogi Codicum Manuscriptorum Bibliothecae Bodleianae Pars Quarta: Codices Thomae Tanneri* (Oxford, Clarendon Press).

Article on 'Palaeography (Latin)' in *Chambers's Encyclopaedia*, new revised edn., vol. x. (Reprint with corrections, see under 1950.)

1968

'English learning in the late twelfth century', *Essays in Medieval History* selected from *T.R.H.S.*, ed. R. W. Southern (London), pp. 106–28. (Reprint with corrections; see under 1936.)

Reviews:

The Diary of Humfrey Wanley, 1715–1726, ed. C. E. Wright and Ruth Wright (London, 1966), in *E.H.R.* lxxxiii. 186–7.

Catalogue of Manuscripts in the Libraries of the University of Pennsylvania to 1800, compiled by N. P. Zacour and R. Hirsch (Philadelphia, 1966), in *E.H.R.* lxxxiii. 197.

1969

'Newman's notes on Dean Church's Oxford Movement', *Bodl. L.R.* viii. 135–7.
Preface to photographic reprint of *Bodleian Library Quarto Catalogues*, I: *Greek Manuscripts* (Oxford, Bodleian Library).

1970

With D. A. Callus O.P., ed. *Iohannes Blund, Tractatus de Anima* (Auctores Britannici Medii Aevi, II, London).
'Verses on the Life of Robert Grosseteste', *Studies in Medieval and Renaissance Culture . . . In Honor of S. Harrison Thomson* (*Medievalia et Humanistica*, N.S. i), pp. 241–51.
Duke Humfrey and English Humanism in the Fifteenth Century (Bodleian Library Exhibition Catalogue).

1971

'The deposit of Latin classics in the twelfth-century renaissance', *Classical Influences on European Culture, A.D. 500–1500*, ed. R. R. Bolgar (Cambridge), pp. 51–5.
Review:
Supplement to reprint of H. Walther, *Initia Carminum ac Versuum Medii Aevi Posterioris Latinorum* (Göttingen, 1969; see under 1960), in *Medium Aevum*, xl. 64–6.

1973

'Pietro da Montagnana; a donor of books to San Giovanni di Verdara in Padua', *Bodl. L.R.* ix. 17–22.
Introduction and additions to photographic reprint of *Bodleian Library Quarto Catalogues*, II: *Laudian Manuscripts* (Oxford, Bodleian Library).
An Exhibition of Manuscripts to Commemorate the 400th Anniversary of the Birth of Archbishop Laud, 7 October 1573–10 January 1643 (Oxford, Bodleian Library).

1974

'Note on the history of the collections of papyri', *An Exhibition of Papyri, mainly in Greek, at the Bodleian Library and at the Ashmolean Museum, for the XIV International Congress of Papyrologists, Oxford, 24–31 July 1974* (Bodleian Library Exhibition Catalogue), pp. 7–8.

1975

'Absoluta: the Summa of Petrus Hispanus on Priscianus Minor', *Historiographia Linguistica* (Amsterdam), II. i. 1–23. (To be reprinted in *Collected Papers*.)
'A manuscript containing extracts from the Distinctiones Monasticae', *Medium Aevum*, xliv. 238–9.

John Benjamins B.V. of Amsterdam have in hand a project to publish,
as vol. v. in *Studies in the History of Linguistics*, R. W. Hunt's
Collected Papers on the History of Grammar in the Middle Ages.
Contents:

'Studies on Priscian in the eleventh and twelfth centuries, I: Petrus
Helias and his predecessors.' (See under 1943.)

'Studies on Priscian in the twelfth century, II: the school of Ralph
of Beauvais.' (See under 1950.)

'Hugutio and Petrus Helias.' (See under 1950.)

'The "lost" preface to the *Liber Derivationum* of Osbern of Gloucester.'
(See under 1958.)

'The introductions to the "Artes" in the twelfth century.' (See under
1948.)

'Oxford grammar masters in the Middle Ages.' (See under 1964.)

'Absoluta: the Summa of Petrus Hispanus on Priscianus Minor.'
(See under 1975.)

INDEX OF MANUSCRIPTS

Aberdeen, University Library
216: pp. 24, 30, 41, 45, 49; plate VI*a*
Autun, Bibliothèque Municipale
5: p. 62 n.
19: p. 62 n.
Auxerre, Bibliothèque Municipale
234: pp. 67, 68, 70, 71, 72, 73, 99,
100, 101
Avranches, Bibliothèque Municipale
221: p. 126

Bamberg, Staatsbibliothek
Bibl. 95: p. 12 n.
Class. 42 (M.V.10): pp. 17, 19;
plate II
Class. 46 (M.V. 14): p. 15; plate I
Patr. 113 (B. IV. 27): pp. 17, 19
Belluno, Biblioteca del Seminario
Gregoriano
Lolli 25: pp. 223 n., 225–6, 232–6,
252
Berlin, East, Deutsche Staatsbibliothek
Diez. B 148e: p. 148
    B Sant. 66: pp. 3 n., 80–1
Phillipps 1651 (Rose 24): pp. 18, 19
    1684 (Rose 15): p. 20
    1715 (Rose 172): p. 83
    1833 (Rose 138): p. 156
    1846 (Rose 150): pp.
    336 n., 351
Berlin, West, Staatsbibliothek der
Stiftung Preussischer Kulturbesitz
lat. fol. 252: pp. 75–6, 81
Berne, Burgerbibliothek
104: p. 146 n.
136: pp. 72–3, 74–6, 78–80, 86, 96–7
250: p. 8 n.
330: pp. 161, 163–4, 221 n.
347: pp. 161, 163–4
357: pp. 161, 163–4, 221 n., 233 nn.,
235 n.
395: p. 75 n.
633: p. 79
A 91: p. 150

Bordeaux, Bibliothèque Municipale
421: p. 124
Bourges, Bibliothèque Municipale
400: p. 83
Bristol, City Library
4: p. 118 n.
Brussels: Bibliothèque Royale
5345: pp. 75–6
9845–8 (Van den Gheyn 1218): p. 82
10030–2 (Van den Gheyn 1508):
    p. 92
10054–6: p. 21
10098–10105 (Van den Gheyn 1334):
    pp. 67, 75 n., 82 n., 100, 102
II 1635: p. 86

Caen, Bibliothèque Municipale
419: p. 350
Cambrai, Bibliothèque Municipale
164: p. 13 n.
Cambridge, University Library
Ee. 2. 31: pp. 124, 126
Ii. 3. 12: p. 157 n.
— Corpus Christi College
9: p. 36 n.
34: p. 124 n.
49: p. 62 n.
152: p. 349
267: pp. 30–1
281: pp. 187, 189, 194, 195–7
371: pp. 187, 194
— Gonville and Caius College
6: p. 119 n.
100: p. 124 n.
108: pp. 124, 136–7
— Pembroke College
12: p. 60
15: p. 60
61: p. 59 n.
100: p. 59 n.
308: p. 116 n.
— Peterhouse
56: p. 127
89: p. 135
147: p. 131
184: p. 132

Cambridge (*cont.*):
— Queens' College
5: p. 58 n.
6: p. 58 n.
— St. John's College
97: p. 455
— Trinity College
241 (B. 11. 2): p. 30
405 (B. 16. 44): pp. 27 n., 30
895 (R. 14. 22): pp. 187, 194, 196–7
982 (R. 16. 34): p. 24
1262 (O. 4. 32): pp. 334, 347, 351
1273 (O. 4. 43): p. 349
Cambridge, Massachusetts, Harvard University Library
Br 98. 373 F*: p. 352
fMS Eng 938: pp. 347, 352
Cesena, Biblioteca Malatestiana
cod. lato destro xxiii. 6: p. 126 n.
Cologne, Dombibliothek
186: p. 163
— Erzbischöfliches Archiv, Pfarrarchiv S. Maria im Capitol
Capsula 34, 1: p. 20
Conches, Bibliothèque Municipale
7: p. 42
Cortona, Biblioteca Comunale e dell'Accademia Etrusca
78: p. 250 n.
Coughton Court, Warwickshire
Throckmorton Muniments
76 (box 30): pp. 398–411, 412, 420–2
Box 61, Folder 1, item 1: pp. 402–403

Darmstadt, Hessische Landes- und Hochschulbibliothek
1957: p. 12 n.
Dijon, Bibliothèque Municipale
568 (329): pp. 128 n., 129 n., 133, 139
Dole, Bibliothèque Municipale
98: pp. 288, 296 n.
Douai, Bibliothèque Municipale
392: p. 42
698: p. 126
Dublin, Trinity College
174: p. 24
Durham, Cathedral Library
B. 11. 22: pp. 135–6
B. 11. 23: p. 136
B. 11. 24: p. 136
B. 111. 10: p. 27 n.
B. 111. 27: pp. 131–2
B. 111. 28: pp. 131–2
B. 111. 29: p. 137
B. 1v. 19: p. 130
C. 111. 15: pp. 209, 219
— Dean and Chapter Muniments
Loc. i:2: p. 136 n.

Erlangen, Universitätsbibliothek
2112: pp. 19–20
Évreux, Bibliothèque Municipale
1: pp. 67, 69, 70, 71, 91, 100, 102–4
Exeter, Cathedral Library
3500: pp. 24, 35, 49; plate IIIa
3507: p. 38
3525: p. 46 n.

Florence, Biblioteca Laurenziana
Ashb. 876: p. 252
1702: p. 242 n.
Fiesole 28: p. 227 n.
pl. 36, 49: p. 243 n.
pl. 37, 25: pp. 222 n., 223 n., 226, 231, 232–9, 247, 249, 250–1, 252, 253; plates XXIV, XXV
pl. 38, 25: p. 236 n.
pl. 47, 31: pp. 222 n., 223 n., 227–8, 232–5, 252, 253; plate XXII
pl. 48, 29: p. 80 n.
pl. 49, 9: p. 21
pl. 63, 20: p. 160 n.
pl. 68, 5: p. 227 n.
pl. 76, 40: p. 20
pl. 97, 31: p. 227 n.
S. Croce 20 sin. 7: p. 228 n.
S. Marco 264: pp. 250 n., 251 n.
284: pp. 74–5, 80
Strozzi 42: p. 235 n.
75: pp. 66, 68–9, 70, 71–2, 75, 99, 100, 104–5
— Biblioteca Nazionale Centrale
Conventi G. 3. 451: p. 351
Magliabecch. VII. 1158: p. 242 n.
— Biblioteca Riccardiana
153: pp. 232 n., 234 n.

Geneva, Bibliothèque Publique et Universitaire
lat. 169: p. 81
Graz, Universitätsbibliothek
482: pp. 202, 203 n., 205 n., 207–9, 211, 212, 213, 215, 218
856: pp. 167, 168, 169, 170, 174–7

Hamburg, Staats- und Universitäts-
bibliothek
53c in scrin.: p. 84 n.
Hereford, Cathedral Library
O. iii. 2: p. 30
O. viii. 9: pp. 59, 289
P. ii. 13: p. 61 and n.

Karlsruhe, Badische Landesbiblio-
thek
Aug. LXXIII: p. 21
Klagenfurt, Bischöfliche Bibliothek
XXXI a 9: p. 351

Laon, Bibliothèque Municipale
141: p. 123 n.
412: pp. 205 n., 206 n., 207, 209,
214, 215, 216, 217, 218
Leipzig, Universitätsbibliothek
lat. 1291: p. 120 n.
Leyden, Universiteitsbibliotheek
B.P.L. 191 B: pp. 67, 69, 100, 105
199: p. 80 n.
Burm. Q. 13: p. 148
Voss. Gal. Fol. 6: pp. 347, 348, 351
Voss. Lat. Fol. 12β (+Voss. Lat.
Fol. 122+London B.L.
Royal 15 B. XII): pp. 146,
149, 151, 156, 157–9, 163–
164, 165
Fol. 67: p. 75 n.
Fol. 70. 1: p. 156
Fol. 122: *see* Voss. Lat.
Fol. 12β
Lat. Qu. 2: p. 84 n.
Qu. 30: pp. 161, 163–4,
221 n., 233 nn., 235 n.
Qu. 83: p. 77
Qu. 106: pp. 157–8
Lat. O. 81: pp. 222 n., 223–4,
232–5
Lincoln, Cathedral Library
31: p. 58 n.
113 (A. 5. 3): pp. 209, 213, 218–19
174: p. 53
London, British Library
Additional 11983: pp. 185, 187,
189, 193, 195–7
16380: p. 296 n.
17376: p. 427
23944: p. 30

25104: pp. 67, 69, 70,
71–2, 99, 100, 106
37517: p. 55
40165A: p. 47 n.
47678: p. 81
54184: p. 350
Arundel 46: pp. 332 n., 335, 350
56: pp. 347, 352
220: pp. 335, 350 and n.
Burney 213: p. 232 n.
Cotton Julius A. VIII: p. 189
Julius D. VI: p. 350 n.
Nero E. I: p. 36 n.
Otho D. VIII: p. 350
Tiberius C. I: pp. 25, 34, 35,
36, 41, 44, 45, 49; plate
IIIb
Titus B. I: p. 358 n.
Titus D. XXIV: p. 424
Vespasian B. XXIV: p. 287 n.
Vitellius A. XII: pp. 24, 25,
30, 38–9
Harley 29: pp. 335, 350
563: p. 350
2682: p. 81
2687: p. 80 n.
3024: p. 5 n.
3080: p. 44 n.
3640: pp. 283–4, 285, 286
3650: p. 287 n.
3855: pp. 291, 292, 295–6
3899: p. 350
4322: p. 350
4927: p. 75
4995: p. 252
Royal 2 D. IX: p. 297
5 E. XVI: pp. 25, 30, 47
5 E. XIX: pp. 25, 26 n., 36, 40,
42, 45
5 F. XIII: p. 44 n.
6 B. XV: pp. 24, 25, 26 n., 47
7 E. VII: p. 130 n.
8 E. IV: p. 83
8 F. V: p. 42
11 A. V: pp. 67, 100, 105–6
12 C. XV: pp. 205–7, 209, 213,
214–18
13 B. XVI: pp. 336 n., 351
15 B. XII: *see* Leyden, Voss.
Lat. Fol. 12β
15 B. XIX: p. 25
15 C. II: p. 25
Appendix 1: pp. 25, 32, 48

London (*cont.*):
— College of Arms
IX: p. 350
— Lambeth Palace Library
56: p. 27 n.
142: pp. 287 n., 288–9, 290–7, 298–
299, 301–2
149: pp. 30, 35
325: p. 83
Longleat, Library of Marquess of
Bath
27: pp. 187, 189, 192, 193 n., 194,
195–7

Madrid, Biblioteca Nacional
8514 (X. 81): pp. 238 n., 239 n.
Manchester, John Rylands Library
Lat. 9: p. 12 n.
228: p. 346 n.
Marburg, Staatsarchiv
Hr 4, 15: p. 20
Metz, Bibliothèque Municipale
223: p. 42
Milan, Biblioteca Ambrosiana
B. 113 sup.: p. 375 n.
H. 14 inf.: p. 72 n.
H. 46 sup.: p. 242 n.
Q. 35 sup.: p. 250 n.
R. 26 sup.: p. 243 n.
— Biblioteca Trivulziana
789: p. 242 n.
2151: p. 228 n.
Modena, Biblioteca Estense
γ. D. 66 (Campori 41): p. 223 n.
Mons, Bibliothèque Publique
219 (109): p. 243 n.
Monte Cassino, Biblioteca Monastica
361 P: p. 80 n.
Munich, Bayerische Staatsbibliothek
cod. lat. 822: p. 229 n.
3824: p. 18
6364: pp. 161 n., 162
6369: pp. 151, 160–1, 162,
165
6929: p. 85 n.
14353: p. 161 n.
14436: pp. 161–2
14460: p. 121 n.
15738: p. 229 n.
29020: p. 161 n.

New Jersey, Princeton University
Library
Scheide 22: p. 59

New York, Library of H. P. Kraus
Gospels (formerly Bodmer; Phillipps 3015): pp. 12–13
Nijmegen, Universiteitsbibliotheek
61: p. 123 n.

Orléans, Bibliothèque Municipale
20 (17): p. 12 n.
267 (223): p. 156
277 (233): p. 156
306 (259): pp. 150, 156
Oxford, Bodleian Library
Add. C. 296 (S.C. 27610): p. 351
Auct. D. 1. 19. (S.C. 2335): p. 56 n.
D. 2. 8 (S.C. 2337): pp. 116,
138, 139; plate IX
D. 4. 13 (S.C. 2571): pp. 382–
389, 392–7; plate XVII
F. 1. 15 (S.C. 2455): p. 55
F. 4. 32 (S.C. 2176): p. 426
Barlow 15 (S.C. 6422): p. 126 n.
Bodley 52 (S.C. 1969): p. 61
86 (S.C. 1894): p. 59 n.
94 (S.C. 1904): p. 136
97 (S.C. 1928): p. 55
132 (S.C. 1893): p. 136
230 (S.C. 2123*): p. 136
250 (S.C. 2503): p. 56
287 (S.C. 2435): pp. 133,
139; plate XII
319 (S.C. 2226): p. 30
353 (S.C. 2495): p. 354 n.
377 (S.C. 2745): p. 136
392 (S.C. 2223): pp. 25, 26,
29, 48
444 (S.C. 2385): pp. 25, 26
477 (S.C. 2005): p. 61
496 (S.C. 2159): p. 194
568 (S.C. 2008): pp. 122,
124, 127, 140–1; plate
XVI
672 (S.C. 3005): p. 60
691 (S.C. 2740): p. 136
698 (S.C. 2521): pp. 25,
26 n., 28, 29 n.
732 (S.C. 2711): p. 136
756 (S.C. 2526): pp. 25,
26 n., 29, 40, 42, 45, 49;
plate VI*b*
765 (S.C. 2544): pp. 25, 29,
32–3, 34, 36, 38, 39, 45,
49; plate IV

768 (S.C. 2550): pp. 25, 28, 29 n., 45
775 (S.C. 2558): p. 55
785 (S.C. 2624): p. 135 n.
835 (S.C. 2545): pp. 25, 45, 58, 60
Canon. Class. Lat. 131: p. 370 n.
   224: p. 246
   254: p. 247 n.
Canon. Misc. 106: p. 246 n.
   217: p. 238 n.
Canon. Pat. Lat. 186: p. 118 n.
   223: p. 245 n.
Digby 104: pp. 186–7, 194, 195–7
  153: pp. 211, 213
  166: p. 193 n.
  225: p. 130 n.
D'Orville 77+95 (S.C. 16955+ 16973): pp. 160–1, 162, 164, 165
  302 (S.C. 17180): p. 160 n.
Douce 119 (S.C. 21693): pp. 347, 348, 352
  366 (S.C. 21941): p. 59
Fairfax 10 (S.C. 3890): pp. 347, 352
Fell 1 (S.C. 8688): pp. 25, 26 n., 27, 36, 45
  3 (S.C. 8687): pp. 25, 26 n.
  4 (S.C. 8689): pp. 25, 26 n., 27, 29 and n., 36–7, 42, 45
Holkham Misc. 36: p. 244 n.
James 19 (S.C. 3856): p. 352
  22 (S.C. 3859): p. 351
Jones 7 (S.C. 8914): pp. 334, 351
Lat. th. e. 32: p. 427
Laud Lat. 86: pp. 187, 194, 197
  104: pp. 19–20
Laud Misc. 8: p. 408 n.
  105: pp. 17–18, 19
  118: p. 60
  371: p. 59 n.
  460: p. 61 n.
  546: p. 60
  695: p. 126 n.
  746: p. 126 n.
Lyell 2: p. 63 n.
  3: p. 56 n.
e Mus. 30 (S.C. 3580): pp. 288–9, 290–1, 297, 303 n., 306
  153 (S.C. 3672): p. 60
Rawlinson B. 178: pp. 339 n., 341 n., 345, 346 n., 347, 348, 352

C. 161: pp. 291, 292–6
C. 435: p. 272 n.
C. 723: pp. 25, 40, 45
G. 109: p. 190
Q. b. 5 (S.C. 16019): p. 272 n.
Tanner 8: pp. 278 n., 285
Top. gen. C. 2 (S.C. 3118 = 5103): p. 351
  C. 4 (S.C. 3120 = 5105): p. 351
— Corpus Christi College
 49: pp. 303 n., 306
 52: pp. 288–9, 290–1, 296, 297, 303–6
 119: p. 121 n.
 209: p. 58 n.
 220: p. 53 n.
 232: pp. 187, 194
 280: p. 354 n.
— Jesus College
 3: p. 60
 93: p. 62
— Keble College
 22: pp. 24, 25, 30, 38, 39, 42, 45, 49, 138; plate V
 26: pp. 126–7, 139–40; plate XIII
— Lincoln College
 Lat. 29: p. 130 n.
  42: p. 227 n.
  101: p. 61
— Magdalen College
 45 (138): pp. 334, 347, 349, 352
— Merton College
 55: p. 124 n., 131
 188: p. 340 n.
 256: pp. 332 n., 334, 350, 351
— New College
 92: pp. 307–22
 98: pp. 134, 140; plate XIV
 112: p. 136 n.
— Oriel College
 31: p. 136
 43: p. 131
 77: p. 126 n.
— The Queen's College
 304: pp. 334, 350, 351
— St. John's College
 49: pp. 117, 126, 139; plate X
— Trinity College
 18: p. 455
 28: p. 30

Oxford (*cont.*):
39: p. 27 n.
— University College
67: pp. 134, 140; plate XV
190: p. 297
191: p. 26 n.
— University Archives
Reg. Cancell. Ꮜ: pp. 353–4, 358 n.,
  359 nn., 364 n.
Reg. Cancell. D: pp. 353, 356 n.,
  357 n.
Reg. Cancell. Ꮖ: pp. 353, 357 n.,
  359 n., 361 n.

Paris, Bibliothèque de l'Arsenal
711: p. 84
720: p. 251
1116E: pp. 66–7, 68, 70, 71, 75,
  100, 107
— Bibliothèque Mazarine
3473: pp. 210–11, 213
— Bibliothèque Nationale
français 9687: pp. 345, 347, 348,
  349, 352
grec 2140: p. 375 n.
  2142: p. 375 n.
  2143: p. 375 n.
  2144: p. 375 n.
latin 943: p. 30
  1860: pp. 67, 72, 93, 100, 107–8
  1912: p. 19 n.
  3050: pp. 121, 122, 139; plate
    XI
  4167A: pp. 334, 350
  4418: pp. 14–15
  4588A: p. 80 n.
  4949: p. 351
  5001: p. 159 n.
  5014: pp. 182, 184
  5730: p. 160 n.
  6106: pp. 245, 254; plate
    XXVII
  6332: p. 158 n.
  6365: pp. 150, 155
  6370: p. 163
  6510: p. 205 n.
  6620: p. 156
  6842D: pp. 220–2, 233–5,
    240 n., 253; plate XX
  7156: pp. 211–12
  7158: pp. 211–12
  7299: pp. 150, 152–5, 165;
    plate XIX

7400B: p. 159 n.
7647: p. 84
7665: p. 161 n.
7723: pp. 252, 371 n.
7774A: pp. 81, 82
7775: pp. 81, 82, 85 n.
7776: p. 80 n.
7794: pp. 75–6, 80
7823: p. 81
7989: pp. 222 n., 223, 231,
  232–5, 239–47, 248–50, 251,
  254; plates XXVI, XXVIII
8049: pp. 221 n., 233 nn.,
  235 nn.
8663: pp. 151, 155
9575: p. 116 n.
13076: p. 147 n.
13108: p. 163 n.
14749: p. 78
15172: pp. 67, 72, 73, 99, 100,
  108–9
16018: pp. 336 n., 351
16019: p. 351
16089: pp. 200–2, 205, 207,
  213
16110: p. 205 n.
16159: p. 212
16221: p. 121 n.
16677: *see* Vatican, Reg. lat.
  1587
16678: p. 156
17903: p. 91 n.
18104: p. 80 n.
nouv. acq. lat. 137: p. 150 n.
  340: p. 75 n.
  454: pp. 151, 159–
    160, 161, 163–4,
    165
  1611: p. 156
  1630: p. 156

Reims, Bibliothèque Municipale
509: pp. 288, 296
680: p. 123
864: pp. 122, 124
Rome, Biblioteca Angelica
720: pp. 67, 75, 93, 100, 109
1895: pp. 66, 67–71, 85–6, 88, 94–5,
  100, 109–10; plate VIII
— Santa Sabina
XIV L 1: p. 128 n.
Rouen, Bibliothèque Municipale
488: p. 42

1040: p. 75 n.
1111: p. 80 n.
3069: p. 351

St. Gallen, Stiftsbibliothek
546: p. 187
904: p. 251 n.
919: p. 168 n.
972b: p. 168 n.
1012: p. 167 n.
1050: p. 167 n.
Salisbury, Cathedral Library
4: pp. 25, 48
5: pp. 25, 31, 49
6: pp. 25, 45
7: pp. 25, 47
9: pp. 25, 29, 47
10: pp. 25, 29 and n., 37, 39, 42, 45
11: p. 25
12: pp. 25, 28 n., 48
14: pp. 31–2
22: pp. 31–2
24: pp. 25, 40
25: pp. 25, 28 n., 29 n., 39 and n., 45
33: pp. 25, 26 n., 29 and n., 31, 37, 40
35: pp. 25, 26 n., 28 n., 32, 33, 47
37: pp. 25, 28 n., 32 n., 46
57: pp. 25, 26 n., 29 nn., 32
58: pp. 25, 26 n., 32
59: pp. 25, 26 n., 28 n.
61: pp. 25, 29 n., 32, 47–8
63: pp. 25, 28 n., 32, 33, 37, 40, 42–3, 46
64: pp. 25, 29 n., 48
65: pp. 25, 26, 29 n., 32, 49
67: pp. 25, 26 n., 31, 40, 46
78: pp. 25, 28 n., 29 nn., 30, 44 n., 46
88: pp. 25, 30, 40, 41, 46
100: p. 33
106: pp. 25, 29, 30 n., 32, 33, 37, 44 n., 46
109: pp. 25, 28 n., 32 n., 43, 48
110: pp. 25, 29 n.
112: pp. 25, 26, 33
114: pp. 25, 32 and n., 37, 43
115: pp. 25, 33, 47
116: pp. 25, 29 nn., 48
117: p. 33
118: p. 25
119: pp. 25, 31, 32, 43, 46

120: pp. 25, 28 n., 31, 32
124: p. 25
125: p. 25
128: pp. 25, 29, 30, 32 n., 37–8, 39, 43, 46
129: pp. 25, 32 and n., 46
130: pp. 25, 47
131: pp. 25, 29 nn., 48
135: pp. 25, 28 n., 34 n., 46
136: pp. 25, 48
137: pp. 25, 26 n.
138: pp. 25, 26 and n., 28 n., 30, 32, 38, 40, 43
139: pp. 25, 28 n., 29 nn., 48
140: pp. 25, 28 n., 29, 38, 43, 46
142: p. 33
154: pp. 25, 29, 30, 34 n., 38, 43, 46–7
157: p. 24
159: pp. 25, 47
160: p. 25
162: p. 25
164: pp. 25, 33
165: pp. 25, 28 n., 30, 33, 43–4, 44 n., 47
168: pp. 25, 28 n., 44
169: pp. 25, 28 n., 29, 32–3, 48
179: pp. 25, 26 n., 27, 28 n., 32, 44 and n.
197: pp. 25, 28 n., 32, 48
198: pp. 24, 25, 26 and n., 48
San Marino, California, Huntington Library
EL. 1121: p. 350
HM. 132: p. 52 n.
HM. 19915: p. 63 n.
Seville, Biblioteca Colombina
5. 6. 14: pp. 208–9, 213, 215, 218
Stockholm, Kungliga Biblioteket
D. 1311a (III): pp. 347, 349, 352
Sydney, University Library
Nicholson 2: pp. 66, 69–70, 71–2, 99, 100, 110–11

Troyes, Bibliothèque Municipale
161: p. 123
187: p. 123
239: p. 42
461: p. 83
469: p. 83
480: p. 122 n.
504: p. 123 n.
624: p. 123

Troyes, Bibliothèque Municipale
(*cont.*)
658: p. 83
710: p. 42
718: p. 135
820: p. 123
860: p. 124 n.
982: pp. 122, 123 n.
1046: p. 125
1519: p. 122 n.

Vatican City, Archivio Segreto Vaticano
AA. Arm. I–XVIII, 123: p. 391 n.
Instrumenta Miscellanea 2592: p. 391 n.
— Biblioteca Apostolica Vaticana
Barb. lat. 4: pp. 223 n., 225, 226 n., 231, 232–6
Ottobon. lat. 750: p. 184 nn.
1829: p. 243 n.
1870: pp. 209–10
Pal. lat. 189: p. 6 n.
210: p. 6 n.
957: pp. 66, 67–71, 73, 74, 85–6, 99, 100, 111–12; plate VII
1564: pp. 20–1
1577: p. 161 n.
1631: p. 6 n.
Reg. lat. 54: pp. 147, 149
118: p. 17
200: p. 5 n.
314: p. 72 n.
358: pp. 67, 100, 112
520: p. 159 n.
762: p. 160 n.
1561: pp. 77, 148, 149
1575: pp. 66, 68–9, 70, 71, 72, 75, 91, 99, 100, 112–13
1587 (+Paris B.N. lat. 16677): pp. 145–65; plate XVIII
1709: p. 147
1762: p. 160
1911: pp. 185, 190 n.
2099: p. 373 n.
2120: pp. 147, 148, 149
Urb. graec. 68: p. 375 n.
Urb. lat. 45: p. 228 n.
64: p. 230
391: p. 228 n.
442: p. 228 n.

462: p. 228 n.
670: pp. 222 n., 223 n., 228–9, 232–5, 252
890: p. 228 n.
1342: p. 228 n.
1345: p. 228 n.
Vat. graec. 276: p. 375 n.
277: p. 375 n.
Vat. lat. 1671: pp. 222 n., 223 n., 224, 231, 232–5
2794: p. 242 n.
3087: pp. 66, 68–9, 70, 71–2, 75, 99, 100, 113–14
3403: pp. 222 n., 223 n., 226–7, 232–5, 252, 253; plate XXIa
3803: pp. 82–3
3960: p. 373 n.
4053: p. 369 n.
4929: pp. 72–4, 77–8, 79, 84–5, 99
8171: p. 148 n.
Vendôme, Bibliothèque Municipale
189: p. 84 n.
Venice, Biblioteca Nazionale Marciana
graec. 269 (coll. 533): pp. 374–5
277 (coll. 630): p. 373 n.
278 (coll. 873): p. 373 n.
506 (coll. 768): p. 373 n.
lat. 40 (coll. 1926): p. 370 n.
50 (coll. 1499): p. 370 n.
381 (coll. 1847): p. 370 n.
435 (coll. 1965): pp. 370, 372–3
cl. II, 40 (coll. 2195): p. 455
cl. XII, 80 (coll. 4167): p. 237 n.
cl. XIV, 16 (coll. 4053): p. 373 n.
cl. XIV, 111 (coll. 4057): p. 373 n.
cl. XIV, 124 (coll. 4044): p. 246
cl. XIV, 324 (coll. 4072): pp. 366, 367–8
Vienna, Österreichische Nationalbibliothek
179: pp. 222 n., 223 n., 225 n., 229–30, 232–6, 252
362: pp. 168, 169 n., 170
2302: p. 205
3198: pp. 222 n., 223 n., 230, 232–6, 253; plate XXIb
s.n. 338: p. 169 n.
s.n. 4755: pp. 223 n., 229, 233–5, 252, 253; plate XXIII

Washington, Library of Otto H. F.
Vollbehr (formerly)
Rutilius: pp. 232 n., 252
Winchester, Cathedral Library
XII: p. 350
Wisbech, Museum
5: p. 62
Wolfenbüttel, Herzog-August-
Bibliothek
Gud. lat. 224: pp. 243–4
Guelf. 299 Extrav.: pp. 222 n.,
223 n., 226 n., 227, 231 n., 232–5,
252

Worcester, Cathedral Library
F. 50: pp. 287–9, 290–2, 296, 297,
298–302
F. 171: p. 272 n.
Q. 46: pp. 307–27
Würzburg, Universitätsbibliothek
Mp. Med. f. 3: p. 205 n.

Zürich, Zentralbibliothek
A 135: p. 168 n.
C 49: p. 21
C 101: pp. 167–9, 170, 174–7

INDEX OF PERSONAL NAMES

Abbo of Fleury, *St.*, 39, 152–3, 154, 155–6, 162, 164
Abelard, Peter, 106, 113, 115 n., 184, 190, 278
Achéry, Luc d', 331 n., 334
Adam of St. Victor, 113
Adrian IV, *pope*, 86
Aimeric, 382, *and see* Montfort, Amaury de
Alan of Lille, 107
Albaldus, Demetrius, 232 n.
Alban, *St.*, 152
Alberic of Monte Cassino, 423
Alberic of Trois-Fontaines, 277 n., 281
Albert the Great (Albertus Magnus), *St.*, 126 n., 200, 201–2, 204, 205, 213, 321, 326 n.
Alcuin (Albinus), 5 n., 40, 45, 147, 148
Aldhelm, *St.*, *bishop of Sherborne*, 158
Alexander III (Roland Bandinelli), *pope*, 86, 277 n., 280, 281 & n., 282, 285
Alexander of Aphrodisias, 205–6, 208
Alexander of Hales, 119, 121 n., 125, 126, 129
Alexander, *dean of Wells*, 193 n.
Alfarabi, 205–6, 208, 212, 219
Alfred of Sareshel (Alfredus Anglicus), 209, 210, 219
Algazel, 202, 207, 208
Alkindi, 206, 207, 210, 217
Almansor, *see* Razes
Alnwick, William, *bishop of Lincoln*, 362
Amalarius of Metz, 25, 30, 33, 38, 46
Amalricus, 382–3, *and see* Montfort, Amaury de
Ambrose, *St.*, *bishop of Milan*, 36, 38, 43 & n., 45, 48, 107, 111
'Ambrosiaster', 31, 40
Amman, Jost, 61
Anaxagoras, 217, 321, 322
Andrew, *prior of Fleury*, 155
Andrewe, *master* Richard, 361
Angilbert of Saint-Riquier, 5
Anselm, *St.*, *archbishop of Canterbury*, 131, 132, 194, 400, 401, 404, 421

Anselm, *abbot of Pershore*, 297
Antiochus, *king*, 273–4
Appleby, William, 136
Apuleius, 21, 70, 74–5, 76, 80, 96, 100, 104, 106, 107, 109, 110, 111, 113, 114, 208, 226, 231, 232, 455
Aquila Romanus, 226, 227, 228, 229, 231–2, 235, 237, 238, 250, 252, 253
Aquinas, Thomas, *St.*, 120 n., 122, 123, 137, 201, 315–16, 317–19, 320–1, 324, 326 n., 333, 334, 346
Aristotle, 111, 119, 120, 121 & n., 122, 123–4, 125, 126, 132, 201, 202, 203, 205, 206, 207, 208, 210, 212, 213 n., 215, 216, 217, 218, 219, 270, 317, 318, 319, 320–1, 323–4, 325, 326 nn., 369, *and see* Pseudo-
Arnobius Rhetor, 338
Arnulf, *bishop of Orléans*, 77–8
Arnulfus, *monk of Bohéries*, 105
Arnulph of Liège, 132, 134, 140
Arundel, John, *bishop of Coventry & Lichfield, bishop of Exeter*, 363
Arundel, *countess of*, *see* Dacre, Anne
Arundel, *earl of*, *see* Howard, Philip
Asconius Pedianus, 238 n., 248–9, 251
Ashenden, John, 130
Astell, *mrs.* Mary, 418–19
Athanasius, *St.*, 43
Augustine, *St.*, *archbishop of Canterbury*, 152
Augustine, *St.*, *bishop of Hippo*, 5, 6 n., 18, 19 & n., 25, 26, 27, 30, 31, 32, 33, 36, 37–8, 39, 40, 43 & n., 44, 45, 46, 47, 48, 49, 73 n., 105, 107, 112, 124, 127, 131, 132, 136, 140, 169, 175, 263, 265, 297, 302, 316–18, 322–3, 324 n., 325, 326–7, 330, 334 n., 338, 425, *and see* Pseudo-
Aurelius Victor, 370 n.
Averroes, 125, 126, 201, 203, 204–5, 206, 207, 208, 209, 210, 212, 213, 214, 216, 217, 218, 219
Avicenna, 126 n., 202, 203, 204, 206, 207, 208, 209, 210–11, 212, 215, 385
Aymeric, *master-general O.P.*, 340 n.

Bacon, Robert, 316–17, 319
Bacon, Roger, 60, 210, 381 n.
Baldwin, *archbishop of Canterbury*, 288
Bale, John, 186–7, 188, 189, 192, 194, 335 n., 408 n.
Barbaro, Francesco, 221–2, 233 n., 240 n., 253
Bartholomaeus Anglicus, 129, 189
Bartholomaeus de Ledula, 126 n.
Bartholomew of Bruges, 200
Bartholomew, *bishop of Exeter*, 423
Barzizza, Gasparino, 250 n.
Bate, *master* Walter, 356
Beauchamp, Richard, *earl of Warwick*, 402
Beauchamp, Thomas, *earl of Warwick*, 402
Beaufort, *lady* Margaret, 405, 413
Beccaria, Antonio, 232 n.
Becket, Thomas, *St.*, *archbishop of Canterbury*, 185, 260, 311, 313, 345, 404
Bede, 30, 41, 44, 46, 48, 136, 147, 148, 163, 190, 337, 338, 341, 424
Bee, C., 351
Begna, Georgius, 240 n., 245–7, 254
Belvantessis, Johannes, 114
Bembo, Bernardo, 246, 247 n.
Benedict, *St.*, 5 n., 150 n.
Berengaudus, 43
Bernard, *St.*, *abbot of Clairvaux*, 86, 106, 130, 132, 313 n.
Bernardino of Siena, *St.*, 403
Bersuire, Pierre, 349 n.
Bertcaudus, 8 n.
Bessarion, *cardinal*, 366–75
Bigot, Emery, 334
Blacman, John, 408
Blund, *master* John, 428
Blysse, *master* John, 361
Boethius, 55, 93, 110, 147, 156, 263, 329, 330, 340 n., *and see* Pseudo-
Bonaventura, *St.*, 119–20, 121 n., 123, 127–8, 407
Bonet, William, 400, 409, 421
Bongars, Jacques, 149, 157
Boniface VIII, *pope*, 391
Bonner, Edmund, *bishop of London*, 364
Bothale, *fr. O.F.M.*, 313, 314
Bracciolini, *see* Poggio
Brackley, *friar*, 409 n.
Bréquigny, L. G. O. de, 159

Brigit, *St.*, 407, 414
Browne, *sir* Anthony, 417, *and see* Montague
Brunetti, Elias, 121 n.
Bruni, Leonardo, 227
Brutus of Troy, 342 n.
Bruyll, John, *bishop of Annaghdown*, 211, 213
Bulgarus, 262 n.
Bulkley, Richard, 364–5
Burgundio of Pisa, 275
Burleigh, Walter, 111
Bury, Richard of, *bishop of Durham*, 138

Caecilius Balbus, 87, 95, 97
Caesar, C. Julius, 245, 254, 339
Caesarius of Heisterbach, 169
Calpurnius Siculus, 221 n., 248
Cantilupe, Thomas, *St.*, *bishop of Hereford*, 332–3, 333–4
Capgrave, John, 138 n.
Capioni, Pietro, *see* Cippico, Pietro
Carkeke, *master* John, 362–3
Cassian, John, *St.*, 25, 37
Cassiodorus, 25, 26 n., 27, 41, 103, 147, 148
Catherine of Braganza, *wife of Charles II, king of England*, 414–15
Catherine of Siena, *St.*, 407
Catullus, 224, 230, 231 n., 237 n., 239, 241, 242, 243, 247, 248, 249
Caxton, William, 405
Celestine II, *pope*, 279, 280
Censorinus, 70, 71–2, 73, 74, 86–7, 99, 100, 101, 104, 106, 108, 110, 113, 114
Challoner, Richard, *bishop in partibus*, 416
Charlemagne, *emperor*, 3, 4, 5, 12, 22, 80–1
Charles the Bald, *emperor*, 15, 17
Chaucer, Geoffrey, 130–1, 343
Chedworth, John, *bishop of Lincoln*, 365
Chichester, *master* William, 362
Christina, *queen of Sweden*, 147, 148
Christina of Markyate, 115 n.
Chrysostom, John, *St.*, 131
Cicely, *duchess of York*, 405, 407, 412
Cicero, 21, 66, 70, 74, 75–6, 78, 80–2, 82 n., 87, 90, 91, 93, 96–7, 98, 100, 101, 102, 103, 104, 105, 106, 107, 110, 111, 113, 114, 145, 146, 147,

149, 150–2, 153, 156, 157–64, 221 n., 227 n., 232 n., 237–8, 246, 248, 253, 321, 368, 385, 427, 455, *and see* Pseudo-
Cicognara, *count* Leopoldo, 366–7
Cippico, *family*, 239–40, 242, 244
Cippico, Alvise, 247
Cippico, Coriolano, 246, 247 n.
Cippico, Pietro, 245–7
Ciriaco of Ancona, 245–6
Cittadini, Celso, 80 n.
Claudian(us), 102, 241–2, 254
Claudianus Mamertus, 263
Claudius, *bishop of Turin*, 5 n.
Clémanges, Nicolas de, 78, 81
Clement I, *St., pope*, 308
Clement III, *pope*, 285 n.
Clement V, *pope*, 347
Clement VI, *pope*, 343 n.
Clement XI, *pope*, 147
Clement, *abbot of St. Mary's, York*, 285, 286
Cleombrotus, 323
Clitherow, Margaret, *St.*, 415 n.
Cobbow, John, 364–5
Cobham, Thomas of, 64
Cobham, *lady*, 411
Coignet de la Thuilerie, Gaspard, 221 n.
Cokkes, *master* Laurence, 361
Colete, Thomas, 111
Colocci, Angelo, 224
Colon, Fernand, 208
Constantinus Africanus, 205, 209, 218
Constantius III, *emperor*, 178
Contugi, *ser* Francesco di *ser* Bonfiglio de', 228
Contugi, Matteo de', 228
Cooke, *master* John, 362
Copland, Robert, 411
Cornaro, Giovanni, 250 n.
Cosin, John, *bishop of Durham*, 418
Costa ben Luca, 209
Cotton, *sir* Robert, 351
Cromwell, Thomas, 359, 407
Cunibert, *archbishop of Cologne*, 39
Curlo, Giacomo, 235 n.
Cuspinianus, Johannes, 230
Cuthbert, *St., bishop of Lindisfarne*, 152
Cymbeline, *king of Britain*, 339
Cyprian, *St., bishop of Carthage*, 17–18, 19, 47, 103

Cyril, *St., patriarch of Alexandria*, 43 n., 169

Dacre, Anne, *countess of Arundel*, 413–414, 416
Dagulf, 6, 12
Damascenus, John, *St.*, 86 n.
Damian, Peter, *St., cardinal-bishop of Ostia*, 322 n.
Daniel, François, 157, 158
Daniel, Pierre, 77, 78–9, 84, 146–7, 148–52, 155, 157, 158–9
Dayfot, *master* William, 362
Demetrios, *presbyter*, 4 n.
Dio Chrysostomus, 222 n.
Dionysius, *see* Pseudo-
Dorne, John, 411
Drogo, *son of Charlemagne*, 21
Dungal, 5 n.
Dunstan, *St., archbishop of Canterbury*, 426

Earbery, E., 351
Edmund the Martyr, *St., king of East Anglia*, 312, 313
Edmund (Rich) of Abingdon, *St., archbishop of Canterbury*, 308–9, 311, 324
Edmund of Woodstock, *earl of Kent*, 345
Edward I, *king of England*, 311, 328, 330, 331–2, 335 n., 339, 345, 346, 347, 348, 350, 379–80, 390
Edward II, *king of England*, 330, 332, 333, 343, 345, 346, 347, 348
Edward III, *king of England*, 345
Edward IV, *king of England*, 412
Einhard, 3, 6, 7, 17, 20
Eleanor of Castile, *wife of Edward I, king of England*, 339, 345
Eleanor of Provence, *wife of Henry III, king of England*, 345
Emo (of Frisia), 272
Ennodius, 66, 69, 70, 80, 82–4, 85, 93, 98, 100, 101, 102, 103, 104, 105, 106, 107, 110, 111, 112, 114, 455
Eugenius III, *pope*, 86, 277
Eugenius IV, *pope*, 245 n.
Eusebius, *bishop of Caesarea*, 48, 337, 338
Eustace of Faversham, 308 n.
Eustratius, 210–11

Eutropius, 338
Evelyn, John, 419 n.
Evortius, *bishop of Orléans*, 39

Faber, Johann, *bishop of Vienna*, 230
Festus, Pompeius, 246 n.
Filelfo, Francesco, 252, 253
Fiocchi, Andrea, 229 n.
Firmicus Maternus, 78
Fishacre, Richard, 131
Fisher, John, *St.*, *bishop of Rochester*, 413, 416
Fisher, *master* John, 361
FitzJames, Richard, *bishop of Rochester, Chichester, London*, 356, 363
FitzRalph, Richard, *archbishop of Armagh*, 314
Flemmyng, Robert, 227 n.
Flinton, George, 416
Folcwich, *bishop of Worms*, 12
Foliot, Gilbert, *bishop of Hereford, London*, 280
Foliot, Ralph, *archdeacon of Hereford*, 289
Fonzio, Bartolomeo, 229, 232 n., 234, 253
Forman, Simon, 424
Fosco, Palladio, 242, 247
Fournival, Richard de, 67, 71, 72, 81, 85, 86-7, 93, 100, 114
Freculphus, *bishop of Lisieux*, 30, 32, 43
Frederick I, *emperor*, 168
Frederick II, *emperor*, 204
Frederick, *duke of Austria*, 347
Frontinus, 245
Fulbert, *St.*, *bishop of Chartres*, 161
Fulgentius, 43 n., 78, 102, 220 n., 228

Gale, Roger, 334
Galen, 203
Garazda, Petrus, 229 n.
Gaufredi, Raymond, *minister general O.F.M.*, 307, 313 n.
Gaveston, Piers, 345
Gellius, Aulus, 70, 79, 91, 98, 100, 101, 104, 106, 107, 110, 111, 113, 114, 323-4, 455
Geoffrey of Monmouth, 194, 338, 340, 350 n.
Geoffrey of Poitiers, 290
Geoffrey of Vinsauf, 76

Geoffrey, *archbishop of York*, 260, 283-4, 286
George of Trebizond, 371 n.
Georgios, *physician*, 375
Gerald of Wales, 89-92, 261, 270
Gerard of Abbeville, 81
Gerard of Cremona, 203, 208
Gerard, John, 407
Gervase of Canterbury, 279-82
Gerward, *monk of Lorsch*, 6, 17
Gilbert de la Porrée, *bishop of Poitiers*, 263, 288
Gilbertus Anglicus, 204, 205
Gildas, 190
Giles of Rome, 101
Giovanni (Gherardi?) of Prato, 242 n.
Glaber, Radulfus, 181
Gloys, *sir* James, 409 n.
Godescalc, *monk of Orbais*, 4, 9, 10, 12
Godric of Finchale, *St.*, 398, 400, 401, 420
Gold, *master* John, 361
Goldwell, James, *bishop of Norwich*, 363
Grandisson, John de, *bishop of Exeter*, 136, 336 nn.
Grandrue, Claude de, 81 n., 84 n., 107, 109
Gratian, 117, 118-19, 122, 123, 127, 133, 264, 276-7, 278, 279-80, 281 & n., 282
Gregory I (the Great), *St.*, *pope*, 25, 27, 37, 43 n., 68, 69, 70, 71, 74, 93, 96, 100, 101, 103, 107, 109, 111, 112, 123 n., 132, 135, 313, 319 n., 455
Gregory X, *pope*, 391 n.
Gregory, *prior of Bridlington*, 285
Gregory of Tours, 190
Grillius, 75 n.
Grosseteste, Robert, *bishop of Lincoln*, 62, 125, 135, 210, 311-12, 423, 425, 428
Guido Aretinus, 111
Guillelmus de Boldensele, 105
Gundissalinus, 210
Gundulf, *bishop of Utrecht*, 39

Hadoardus, *monk of Corbie*, 87, 160
Hadrian V, *pope*, 379, 380, 390
Hall, Anthony, 331 n., 334-5, 350, 351
Halle, *master* Robert, 362

Hartwic, *monk of St. Emmeram*, 161–2
Hatfield, Thomas, *bishop of Durham*, 136
Hearne, Thomas, 189, 334–5, 354 n.
Hegesippus, *see* Pseudo-
Heinsius, Nicholas, 148, 149
Heiric of Auxerre, 72, 78
Helias, Petrus, 423, 424, 429
Helinand of Froidmont, 76
Helpericus, 153
Henri d'Andeli, 77
Henrietta Maria, *wife of Charles I, king of England*, 414–15
Henry VII, *emperor*, 347
Henry I, *king of England*, 191, 266, 267
Henry II, *king of England*, 274, 311, 331, 345, 350
Henry III, *king of England*, 311, 328, 332, 345, 349, 350, 358, 381
Henry VI, *king of England*, 408
Henry VII, *king of England*, 413
Henry VIII, *king of England*, 358
Henry of Almaine (Cornwall), 380, 381 n.
Henry, *1st duke of Lancaster*, 349 n,. 402
Henry of Blois, *bishop of Winchester*, 187–8, 258, 279–81
Henry of Charwelton, 206
Henry of Ghent, 136
Henry of Huntingdon, 189
Higden, Ranulf, 51 n., 189, 349
Hilary, *bishop of Chichester*, 139
Hilary of Poitiers, *St.*, *bishop*, 43 n., 48, 84 n.
Hildebert, *bishop of Le Mans*, *archbishop of Tours*, 91 n., 190–2, 194
Hildoard, *bishop of Cambrai*, 13 n.
Hilduin, *abbot of St. Denis*, 21
Hilton, Walter, 407
Hincmar, *archbishop of Reims*, 116 n.
Hippocrates, 367–8, 369, 372, 373–5
Hoby, *lady*, 418
Hog, Thomas, 331 n., 335
Holcot, Robert, 324, 325
Horace, 93, 102, 110, 147
Hormisdas, *St.*, *pope*, 43 n.
Horsey, *master* William, 362
Hothum, William, 311, 316
Howard, Philip, *earl of Arundel*, 413
Howes, *sir* Thomas, 409 n.
Hrabanus Maurus *abbot of Fulda*,

archbishop of Mainz, 5–6, 21, 38–9, 107
Hugh of Angoulême, *archdeacon of Canterbury*, 335–6
Hugh of Fleury, 338
Hugh of Hartlepool, 308
Hugh, *St.*, *bishop of Lincoln*, 284
Hugh, *prior of Montacute*, *abbot of Muchelney*, 189, 192–3, 194, 195 n.
Hugh de Noyen, *prior of Montacute*, 193
Hugh of St. Cher, 128 n., 138
Hugh of St. Victor, 105, 117, 119–20, 190, 288, 426
Hugo III, *abbot of Cluny*, 163
Hugolinus, 262 n.
Hugutio of Pisa, 64, 116 n., 424, 429
Huick, *master* Robert, 359
Humbert of Romans, 141
Humfrey, *duke of Gloucester*, 232 n., 428
Hyginus, 160 n.

Iacobus de Guisia, 189
Icherius (Itherius, Ithier) de Concoreto, *canon of Salisbury*, 336 n.
Ignatius Loyola, *St.*, 408
Innocent II, *pope*, 279, 280
Innocent III, *pope*, 86, 260, 284, 289, 290
Irnerius, 261
Isidore of Seville, 25, 30, 33, 40, 43 n., 102, 106, 132, 161 n., *and see* Pseudo-
Itier, Bernard, 80 n., 84 n.
Ivo, *St.*, *bishop of Chartres*, 33, 113, 122

James of Varazze, 308 n.
James of Venice, 275
James, Richard, 351
Jerome, *St.*, 25, 27, 39, 40, 41, 43 n., 48, 68, 69, 70, 71, 82 n., 90, 93, 95, 100, 101, 102, 103, 104, 105, 106, 107, 108, 109, 110, 111, 112, 113, 114, 161 n., 227 n., 265, 334 n., 337, 370 n., 375 n., 455
Joan of Bar, *countess of Surrey or Warenne*, 343 n.
Jocelin, *bishop of Salisbury*, 31
Jocelyn of Brakeland, 271
Johannes Ariminensis, 242 n.
John XXI, *pope*, 380, 390

John XXII, *pope*, 335, 336 nn., 339 n.,
341, 346, 347, 348, 349
John, *king of England*, 332, 345, 349
John of Cornwall, 86 n.
John of Drokensford (Droxford), 333
John of Garland, 76–7
John of Lenham, 333
John of London, 455
John of Orléans, 86 n.
John of Salisbury, 112, 258–9, 273–5,
323 n., 324 n.
John of Secheville, 204, 213
John Sichardus, 20
John of Tours, 288
John of Tynemouth, 401
John of Wales, 321, 322, 323, 324 n.,
325, 408
Jones, Inigo, 415
Jordan of Saxony, 120–1
Josephus, Flavius, 190, 342
Judith, *wife of Charlemagne*, 5–6
Julius Paris, 68, 70, 71, 72, 73, 74, 99,
100, 101, 111
Julius Valerius, 72, 99, 104, 106
Justinian, *emperor*, 78
Justinus, 6 n., 336 n.
Juvenal, 93, 157

Kemly, *fr.* Gallus, 167–9, 170, 174
Kempe, Margery, 403, 408, 410
Kempis, Thomas À, 407
Kenelm, *St.*, 152
Kilwardby, Robert, *archbishop of Can-
terbury*, 120–1, 125, 126, 127, 131,
132 n., 136, 140, 315, 333 n., 380
Kirkstede, Henry, 136
Knapwell, Richard, 315–16
Kuenburg, *count* Franz Joseph, 229

Lactantius, 370 n., 426
Lampugnano, Andrea, 226
Lancaster, *duke of, see* Henry
Lanfranc, *archbishop of Canterbury*,
25, 30, 36
Langbroke, *master* Geoffrey, 362
Langcok, *master* Luke, 362
Langland, William, 406
Langton, Stephen, *archbishop of Can-
terbury*, 118 n., 125, 128 n., 289,
290
Latini, Brunetto, 130
Laud, William, *archbishop of Canter-
bury*, 428

Law, William, 419
Lawles, *master* Robert, 361
Lawson, *mrs.* Dorothy, 415
Leland, John, the elder, 364
Leland, John, 39, 329, 331 n., 335 n.,
351, 354 n.
Leo I (the Great), *St.*, *pope*, 43 n.
Leo XII, *pope*, 366
Leo, *bishop of Vercelli*, 21
Leo Hebraeus, 242 n.
Leofric, *bishop of Exeter*, 30, 35, 55
Leominster, William, 314–15, 320
Leonard, *nephew of Vacarius*, 264–5,
284, 285
Leoni, Pier, 209–10
Letard, *abbot of Bec*, 275 n.
Leto, Pomponio, 224
Libri, Guglielmo, 145–6
Lindenbrog, Friedrich, 84 n.
Livy, 160 n., 190, 330, 336, 338, 339,
349 n., 351
Llywelyn, *prince of Wales*, 379, 390
Lombard, *see* Peter Lombard
London, John, *warden of New College*,
358, 359
Longland, John, *bishop of Lincoln*, 364
Lothar I, *emperor*, 16
Louis the Pious, *emperor*, 4, 5, 6,
9 n., 13, 14, 15, 16, 21–2
Louis VII, *king of France*, 184
Louis IX, *St.*, *king of France*, 133, 139
Louis X, *king of France*, 348
Louis, *duke of Bavaria*, 339 n., 347–8,
349
Lucio, G., 240 n.
Lucius II, *pope*, 280
Lucretius, 248
Lupus, *abbot of Ferrières*, 9 n., 81,
158 n., 163
Lygham, *master* Peter, 362

Mabillon, Jean, 80 n.
Macrobius, 67 n., 70, 91, 95, 100, 104,
106, 107, 109, 110, 111, 113, 114,
145, 146, 149, 150–2, 153–4, 155–
164, 229 n., 247, 382 n., 455
Maimonides, 208
Mainsforth, John, 61
Malberthorp, John, 61
Manegold of Lautenbach, 190
Manuel, '*king of Greece*', 168
Map, Walter, 90, 92
Marbod of Rennes, 193

Mareste, M. de, 108
Marsh, Adam, 425
Marshal, William, 349 n.
Marshall, John, *bishop of Llandaff*, 363
Martial, 147, 148, 241
Martianus Capella, 21
Martin IV, *pope*, 390
Martin of Braga, *St.*, 70, 98–9, 100, 101, 104, 105, 106, 107, 108, 110, 113, 114, 455
Mary of Modena, *wife of James II, king of England*, 414–15
Mary of Woodstock, *daughter of Edward I*, 330, 339, 340, 343–4, 345–6, 347, 348, 349
Matthew of Vendôme, 76, 147, 194
Maurice, *master*, 288, 292
Mayew, Richard, *bishop of Hereford*, 363–4
Mazzei, *ser* Lapo, 409
Mechtild, *St.*, 407
Medici, Cosimo de', 243 n.
Medici, Giovanni di Cosimo de', 228, 234, 253
Medici, Lorenzo de' (the Magnificent), 209
Mesue, 218
Methodius, 113
Michael II, *emperor*, 5
Michael Scot, 200, 201–2, 204, 206, 215
Michele da Massa Marittima, 322
Michon-Bourdelot, P., 224
Middelburch, *see* Petrus de
Middleburch, Jacobus, 230
Mirk, John, 404, 407
Monmouth, John, *chancellor of Oxford*, 308, 320 n.
Montague, Anthony Browne, *1st viscount*, 417
Montague, *lady* Magdalen, *viscountess*, 414, 417
Montefeltro, Federigo da, *duke of Urbino*, 229, 234
Montfaucon, Bernard de, 147, 159
Montfort, Amaury de, 379–97
Montfort, Eleanor, *daughter of Simon*, 379–80, 381, 387, 389, 390
Montfort, Eleanor de, *wife of Simon, sister of Henry III*, 381, 391
Montfort, Guy de, 380, 381, 391 n.
Montfort, Simon de, *earl of Leicester*, 379, 380, 381, 391 n.

Monulf, *bishop of Utrecht*, 39
More, Thomas, *St.*, 403, 410, 416
Morelli, *abbé* Jacopo, 366–7, 368
Morgan, Henry, *bishop of St. Davids*, 364
Morgan (Yong), John, *bishop of St. Davids*, 363
Morton, John, *bishop of Ely, archbishop of Canterbury*, 362, 363
Mowbray, Nigel de, 283
'Moyses Egyptius', 206, 208–9, 215

Naplave, Jacobus, 247 n.
Neckham (Nequam), Alexander, 76, 270, 425
Niccoli, Niccolò, 221, 226, 227 n., 231, 232, 236, 242 n., 243, 244, 247–51
Nicetas, 6 n.
Nicholas III, *pope*, 390
Nicholas IV, *pope*, 392 n.
Nicholas V, *anti-pope*, 348
Nicholas V, *pope*, 371–2
Nicholas of Cues, *bishop of Brixen*, 210
Nicholas of Lyra, 128 n.
Nicholas of Paris, 121
Nicholas de Waldey, 193 n., 194
Nicolaus Damascenus, 205
Nicolaus Peripateticus, 200–19
Niger, Ralph, 278 n.
Nogarola, Isotta, 225, 231
Nonius Marcellus, 248
Noris, Enrico, 147
Nottingham, *fr.* O.P., 309–10, 313

Obyn (Hobyn), *master* John, 361
Ockham, William of, 135
Odo, *master*, 288
Oglethorpe, Owen, 358–9
Olney, *sir* Robert, 402–3
Omnebonus, *bishop of Verona*, 276–8, 279
Orderic Vitalis, 181
Orford, Robert, 316, 319
Origen, 17, 19, 25, 47, 338
Orosius, 190
Orsini, Fulvio, 227
Orton, *master* John, 359
Osbern of Gloucester, 425, 429
Osmund, *St.*, *bishop of Salisbury*, 31, 33–4
Oswald, *St.*, *king of Northumbria*, 152
Otmar, *abbot of St. Gallen*, 39
Ovid, 147, 148, 191, 239, 241, 243

Paganus, 288
Pain, *clerk of Findon*, 282
Palladius, 147, 220 n., 221, 222, 253
Paphnutius, *St.*, 401
Papias, 64
Paschalis Romanus, 210
Paul, *St.* (*Apocalypse*), 166–80
Paul the Deacon, 32, 44, 190
Pecham (Peckham), John, *archbishop of Canterbury*, 64, 315–16
Pelagius, 31, 49
Perion, *fr.* Joachim, 75 n.
Perotti, Niccolò, 227, 371
Perrott, Simon, 355
Persicini, Giovanni, 226
Persius, 93
Petau, Alexander, 112, 113
Petau, Paul, 72 n., 84 n., 112, 149, 158, 221 n.
Peter of Blois, 92
Peter the Chanter, *see* Petrus Cantor
Peter of Corbeil, *bishop of Cambrai & Sens*, 287–306
Peter of Cornwall, 424
Peter Damian, *see* Damian, Peter
Peter Lombard, 116–18, 125, 126, 127, 133, 138, 139, 263, 265 n., 288, 303–6, 326 nn.
Peter the Manducator, *see* Petrus Comestor
Peter of Poitiers, 287, 290, 291, 296, 297, 298–302
Peter of Saintes, 190
Peter of Tarentaise, 127, 139, 140
Peter the Venerable, *abbot of Cluny*, 181, 182
Petrarch, 72 n., 220 n., 426
Petronius, 149, 161 n., 220–54, *and see* Pseudo-
Petrus Cantor, 91 n., 125, 288, 306
Petrus Comestor, 125, 128 n., 288, 305, 338, 341, 342
Petrus Helias, *see* Helias, Petrus
Petrus Hispanus, 428, 429
Petrus de Middelburch, 227 n.
Philip II (Augustus), *king of France*, 289
Philip V, *king of France*, 348
Philip, *bishop of Bayeux*, 80 n., 83–4, 84 n., 85
Philip of St. Edward, *canon of Salisbury*, 31
Philo Judaeus, 338

Pierre de Joigny, *canon of Rouen*, 67 n.
Pietro da Montagnana, 428
Pike, John, 350 n.
Pithou, Pierre, 79
Plato, 201, 217, 323, 369
Plautus, *see* Pseudo-
Pliny, the elder, 17, 19, 20, 21, 80 n., 160 n., 161 n., *and see* Pseudo-
Pliny, the younger, 66, 67–8, 69, 70, 74–5, 76, 80, 84 n., 85, 89, 90–1, 96, 100, 103, 104, 105, 106, 107, 110, 111, 112, 113, 114, 227–8, 253, 455
Plumetot, Simon de, 81
Poggio Bracciolini, 81 n., 220, 221, 223, 231, 236, 237 n., 238–9, 244, 247–51, 253, 373
Pole, *master* Hugh, 361
Poliziano, Angelo, 244 n.
Pompeius, *see* Festus, Trogus
Pomponius Mela, 72, 73 n., 84, 85, 232 n.
Pontano, Gioviano, 229 n.
Prester John, 168
Primas, Hugh, 190
Priscian, 21, 120–1, 232 n., 237, 250–1, 253, 423, 424, 429
Propertius, 224, 239, 241, 243–4
Prosper of Aquitaine, *St.*, 43 n.
Prudentius, 55, 93, 110
Pseudo-Aristotle, 227
Pseudo-Augustine, 31, 32, 44, 46, 219
Pseudo-Boethius, 329
Pseudo-Cicero, 74, 75 n., 85
Pseudo-Dionysius, 5
Pseudo-Hegesippus, 101
Pseudo-Isidore, 83
Pseudo-Petronius, 223 n.
Pseudo-Plautus (*Querolus*), 66, 70, 72–4, 77–8, 87, 99, 100, 101, 104, 106, 108, 110, 113, 114
Pseudo-Pliny, 246
Pseudo-Quintilian, 72, 99
Pseudo-Seneca, 98, 108, 114
Publilius Syrus, 87, 103
Pullen, Robert, *cardinal*, 267, 269–70, 288
Pusculus, Ubertinus, 225
Puteanus, 146 n.
Puteolanus, Franciscus, 222 n.
Pythagoras, 323

Quentin, *master* John, 405, 409, 411–412

Quintilian, 72, 88, 94 n., 100, 101, 108, 113, 238 n., 252, 367, 368, 369, 370, 371–2, 375, *and see* Pseudo-

Quintus Curtius Rufus, 71–2, 99, 100, 104, 106, 110, 113, 114, 455

Rabanus, *see* Hrabanus

Radbert (Paschasius Radbertus), *abbot of Corbie*, 82

Radulphus, *dean of Croxton*, 284, 286

Radulphus Glaber, *see* Glaber

Ralph of Beauvais, 296, 424, 429

Ralph, *archdeacon of Hereford*, 289

Raymond of Antioch, 183

Razes, 203, 210

Reginald FitzJoceline, *bishop of Bath & Wells*, 193

Reginald of Canterbury, 423

Reginald of Durham, 401

Reginald, *son of Reginald, knight of Collingham*, 284

Reginald, *nephew of Vacarius*, 260, 283, 285

Regnault, F., 409 n., 411

Revius, Jacobus, 148, 149

Reynolds, *master* Thomas, 361

Richard I, *king of England*, 266, 347

Richard III, *king of England*, 412

Richard of Cluny (& Poitou), 181–3, 184–6, 187–8, 189–90, 191–2

Richard, *son of Kyre*, 284

Richard, *dean of Wells*, 193 n.

Richard of Winchester, 313 n.

Richarius, *St.*, 36

Richelieu, *cardinal*, 149, 152

Ridevall, John, 325

Riga, Petrus, 194

Rigaud, Eudes, *archbishop of Rouen*, 380 n., 381

Rinuccini, Alamanno, 228 n.

Rishanger, William, 379 n.

Robert of Anjou, *king of Naples*, 369, 374–5

Robert Bruce, *king of Scotland*, 347

Robert of Lewes, *bishop of Bath & Wells*, 192

Robert of Melun, 288

Robert of Orléans, 86 n.

Robert of Sorbon, *master*, 312 n.

Robert of Torigny, *abbot of Mont-Saint-Michel*, 267, 275–7, 278, 281

Roger, *archbishop of York*, 259–60, 283

Roger de Mandeville, 192

Roger of Waltham, 130

Roger of Warwick, 283

Roland Bandinelli, *see* Alexander III, *pope*

Rous, John, 354, 355, 357, 364

Rufinus, 17

Russell, John, 364

Rusticius Helpidius Domnulus, 72

Rutilius Lupus, 226, 227, 228, 229, 231–2, 234 n., 235, 237, 238, 250, 252, 253

Sallust, 93, 105, 160 n., 331 n., 336 n.

Salutati, Coluccio, 243, 245 n., 250–1, 427

Sambucus, Johannes, 230

Sampson, *abbot of Bury St. Edmunds*, 271

Sandwich, *master* Walter, 362

Sassetti, Francesco, 229 n.

Saunders, *master* Thomas, 361–2

Scalamonti, F., 245 n.

Schäbel, Henricus, 169

Scipio Aemilianus, 164

Sedulius, 147

Senatus, *prior of Worcester*, 287, 298

Seneca, the elder, 330

Seneca, the younger, 14 n., 15, 20, 67–8, 70, 88, 91, 94 n., 97, 98, 100, 101, 102, 103, 104, 105, 106, 107, 108, 110, 111, 112, 114, 227, 242 n., 330, 338, 385, 392, 395, 455

Seneca, Thomas, 242, 243, *and see* Pseudo-

Serafino of Urbino, 242 n.

Sergius, 147, 148

Seton, William, 137

Sforza, Galeazzo Maria, *duke of Milan*, 226

Sheppey, John, *bishop of Rochester*, 307

Shirwood, *master* William, 362

Sichardus, *see* John

Sidonius Apollinaris, 19, 20, 69, 70, 87, 90, 91, 97, 100, 103, 104, 105, 106, 107, 110, 111, 112, 114, 224, 455

Simon of Ghent, *chancellor of Oxford* 308, 313, 316, 324

Simon of Sywell, 288, 297

Simon of Tournai, 288

Simone della Tenca, *ser*, 220 n.

Smaragdus, *abbot of St. Mihiel*, 48
Smith, Richard, 414 n., 417 n.
Solinus, 102, 103, 232 n., 338
Sozomeno of Pistoia, 251
Speroni, Ugo, 264–5, 285
Standish, William, 355
Statileo, Marino, 242
Stephen, *king of England*, 266–7, 269, 273–5, 279, 282, 330, 331
Stephen of Antioch, 424
Stephen of Tournai, 86 n.
Stillington, Robert, *bishop of Bath & Wells*, 363
Stojković, John, 427
Stokesley, John, *bishop of London*, 364
Stow, John, 350
Strabo, *see* Walafrid
Suetonius, 190, 338
Surrey, *countess of, see* Joan of Bar
Surrey, *earl of, see* Warenne, John de
Sutton, Henry, 311
Sutton, Thomas, 308, 312, 314, 316, 319
Symmachus, Aurelius Memmius, 162 n.
Symmachus, Quintus Aurelius, 91, 103, 112
Symon the Jew, 424
Symphosius, 158

Tacitus, 222 n., 227 n., 370 n.
Tanner, Thomas, *bishop of St. Asaph*, 335 n., 424
Terence, 16, 93
Thais, *St.*, 401
Thegan, 4 n., 15
Theobald, 111
Theobald, *archbishop of Canterbury*, 258–9, 262, 273–5, 279–81, 282
Theobald of Étampes, 267–9
Theodosius II, *emperor*, 178
Theodulf, *bishop of Orléans*, 5
Thomas, *St., apostle of India*, 168
Thomas Aquinas, *see* Aquinas
Thomas Becket, *see* Becket
Thomas of Cantilupe, *see* Cantilupe
Thomas of Ireland, 93, 132
Thomas, *clerk of London*, 279
Thomas of Marlborough, 296, 297
Thomas of Otterbourne, 189
Thomas of Wobourn, 408 n.
Thomas of Woodstock, 349
Throckmorton, John, 402

Throckmorton, *dame* Margaret, 402–3
Throckmorton, Thomas, 402
Thurstan, *archbishop of York*, 280
Tibullus, 78, 85, 147, 224, 239, 241, 242, 243
Tideus, 208
Tillet, Jean de, 159 n.
Tinti, *ser* Giovanni, 245 n.
Tortelli, Giovanni, 369, 371, 373
Trapezuntius, *see* George of Trebizond
Traversari, Ambrogio, 231, 252
Trevet, Nicholas, *O.P.*, 325, 328–52
Trevet, Nicholas, 346 n.
Trevet, *sir* Thomas, 328–9
Trevisa, John, 349
Trimenel, Idonia, 409
Trimenel, John, 409
Trimenel, *sir* William, 400, 403, 409, 421
Trithemius, *abbot of Spondheim*, 186, 189
Trogus, Pompeius, 336 n.
Trowbridge, *master* Edward, 361
Tyler, *master* Stephen, 361

Urban V, *pope*, 391
Urso, 211
Ussher, James, *archbishop of Armagh*, 351

Vacarius, *master*, 257–86
Vacarius, *canon of Lincoln* (? *nephew of master Vacarius*), 284 n., 285
Valerius Maximus, 70, 72, 73 n., 74, 99, 104, *and see* Julius Paris
Valla, Bernardino, 244 n.
Valla, Lorenzo, 252, 366–75
Vegetius, 109, 245
Verburg, Isaac, 160 n.
Verrepaens, Simon, 416
Vespasiano da Bisticci, 227–8, 234
Vespucci, Giorgio Antonio, 227 n., 230, 235–6, 250 n., 253
Veterano, Federico, 229
Vibius Sequester, 72, 73 n., 77, 148
Victor IV, *anti-pope*, 182
Victorinus, *St., bishop of Pettau*, 41
Victorinus, Marius, 20
Victorinus, Maximus, 147, 148
Victorius of Aquitaine, 153
Vincent of Beauvais, 128–9, 131, 133, 138, 139, 341
Virgil, 6 n., 93, 224, 240, 241, 243

Vitalibus, Bernardus Venetus de, 222 n.

Walafrid Strabo, 5 n., 15, 16 n.
Waleys, Thomas, 325, 338 n.
Walter, Hubert, *archbishop of Canterbury*, 297
Walter of St. Victor, 287
Wanley, Humphrey, 425, 427
Warenne, John de, *earl of Surrey*, 343 n.
Warwick, *earls of, see* Beauchamp
Waynflete, William, *bishop of Winchester*, 357, 365
Wendover, Roger, 401 n.
Westerfeld, John, 310, 313, 322–4, 325
Wharton, Henry, 334, 350
Whitford, Richard, 406, 408
Wibald of Corvey, 75, 81
Willelmus de Montibus, 132, 134, 297–8
William II (Rufus), *king of England*, 191
William, *duke of Aquitaine*, 184–5
William of Auxerre, 121 n.
William of Drogheda, 267

William, *clerk of Hythe*, 282
William of Malmesbury, 23, 33, 34
William of Ockham, *see* Ockham
William of Orléans, 86 n.
William of St. Carilef, *bishop of Durham*, 60
William de Tatewic, 135
William of Tonbridge, 287, 298
William, *archbishop of York*, 280
Windsor, Miles, 354
Wivill, Robert, *bishop of Salisbury*, 426
Wolsey, Thomas, *archbishop of York, cardinal*, 404, 407
Wood, Anthony, 365
Wriothesley, Thomas, 358
Wulfran, *St.*, 33, 39
Wulfstan, *St.*, *bishop of Worcester*, 287
Wurth, Richard, 61
Wynkyn de Worde, 406 n.

Xenophon, 370 n.

York, *duchess of, see* Cicely
Young, Thomas, *bishop of St. Davids, archbishop of York*, 364

Zarotus, Antonius, 222 n.

INDEX OF PLACE-NAMES[1]

Aachen, 3–22
Abingdon, 308–9
Aix (Poitou), 182
Alet, 211 n., 212
Amesbury, 339, 343, 345, 346
Angers, *see* St. Aubin
Arezzo, 220 n.
Ashridge, 455
Augsburg, 18
Autun, 62
Auxerre, 161, 221 n.
Avignon, 72 n., 220 n., 221, 314, 336 n.

Bamberg, 17
Basle, 232 n.
Beauvais, 296
Bec, 27 n., 80 n., 83, 84 n., 85, 275
Belluno, 226
Beverley, 140
Blois, 60
Bologna, 119 n., 127 n., 222 n., 257,
   258, 261–2, 264, 269, 271, 277–8,
   282, 370–2, 381 n., 426
Bourges, 83
Brescia, 7–8, 9, 10, 11, 13, 14, 16–17,
   20, 225
Brixen (*now* Bressanone), 210
Bruges, 250 n., 351
Buckfastleigh, 335 n.
Burton-upon-Trent, 194
Bury St. Edmunds, 60, 63, 136

Cambridge, 136, 314 n., 322, 406 n.
Canterbury, 30, 55, 56, 211, 259, 281 n.,
   and see Christ Church, St. Augus-
   tine's
Capo d'Istria, 247 n.
Casentino, 232 n.
Cerne Abbas, 382, 390
Chester, 60, *and see* St. Werburg's
Christ Church (Canterbury), 30, 55,
   156–7
Cirencester, 28, 60

Clairvaux, 83
Cluny, 67 n., 75 n., 81, 163, 164, 181–
   192, 194, 248
Cologne, 81, 213 n., 244 n.
Constance, 251
Corbie, 82–3, 159–60, 164
Corvey, 75, 81

Durham, 27, 60, 83, 136, 137

Eberbach, 17, 19
Ely, 140
Evesham, 62, 296
Évreux, 126 n.
Exeter, 30, 35, 55, 136, 138, 296, 404

Ferrara, 225
Fiesole, 228, 253
Fleury (Saint-Benoît)-sur-Loire, 77,
   78, 79, 145–6, 149–56, 158–9, 162,
   163, 164
Florence, 226–7, 227–8, 229, 230,
   231–2, 234, 235, 240, 242 n., 243–6,
   247–50, 252, 253–4, 366 n., 426, 427,
   and see San Marco
Fountains, 58, 83
Freising, 85 n., 160, 161 n., 162
Fulda, 6, 20–1

Gannita (Nijmegen), 6 n.
Gembloux, 75
Glastonbury, 30, 39, 334, 426

Heidelberg, 111
Holkham, 81, 244 n.
Holme Cultram, 63

Lanthony (Secunda), 27, 288
Laon, 207
Liège, 102, 105
Limoges, *see* St. Martial
Lincoln, 58, 261
Little Gidding, 418

[1] This is restricted to places which are accepted or suggested in this volume as significant in the writing, transmission, and study of classical and medieval literature.

London, 61, 64, 211, 332, 406 n., 411
Lorsch, 4, 6 & n., 7, 8, 9, 10, 12–13, 17–18, 19, 82
Lyre, 67, 75 n., 80 n., 104

Mainz, 18, 21
Malmesbury, 30
Merton, 105
Messina, *see* San Placidio
Metz, *see* St. Vincent
Micy St. Mesmin, 72 n.
Milan, 222 n., 227
Montacute, 192–3
Montargis, 381, 391
Mont-Saint-Michel, 80 n., 84 n., 275
Monte Cassino, 85 n.
Montecatini, 228 n.
Mortemer (Rouen), 108
Muchelney, 192–3

Naples, 225 n., 235 n., 369
Neuberg, 169
Nijmegen, *see* Gannita
Northampton, 261, *and see* St. Andrew's
Notre-Dame (Paris), 67 n.

Old Sarum, 23 n.
Orléans, 5 n., 76–80, 82, 84–5, 86, 146, 149
Oseney (Oxford), 61, 355
Oxford, 61, 64, 126 n., 206, 257–8, 261, 262, 266–74, 279–82, 287, 296, 307–27, 328, 329, 332–3, 353–65, 408 n., 411, 427, 429, *and see* Oseney, St. John's Hospital

Padua, 240, 244 n., 247, 381, 385, *and see* San Giovanni di Verdara
Paris, 64, 67 n., 75 n., 80 n., 84 n., 92, 126 n., 139, 211, 213, 258, 261, 267, 269, 270, 289, 290, 297, 310, 312, 314, 315, 329, 332, 346 n., 391, 409 n., 411, *and see* Notre-Dame, St. Denis, St. Germain-des-Prés, St. Jacques, St. Sulpice, St. Victor, Sorbonne
Piacenza, 264
Peniscola, 455
Poitou, *see* Aix
Pontigny, 101
Prato, 242 n., 403, 409

Ramsey, 62
Ravenna, 72
Regensburg, *see* St. Emmeram
Reims, 83, *and see* St. Remi
Rievaulx, 83
Rome, 92, 123 n., 147, 188, 224, 231, 243, 244, 247 n., 248–50, 280, 281 n., 369, 370–2, 375 n.
Rouen, 416, *and see* Mortemer, St. Wandrille

St. Albans, 193 n., 194
St. Andrew's (Northampton), 194
St. Aubin (Angers), 80 n.
St. Augustine's (Canterbury), 30, 55, 455
St. Denis (Paris), 20, 75 n.
St. Emmeram (Regensburg), 161 & n.
St. Evroul, 181
St. Gallen, 167, 251
St. Germain-des-Prés (Paris), 150
St. Jacques (Paris), 125–6, 210
St. John's Hospital (Oxford), 355
St. Martial (Limoges), 80 n., 84 n.
St. Martin's (Tours), 159–60
St. Mary's (York), 357
St. Médard (Soissons), 6, 7
St. Nicholas (Vienna), 230
St. Remi (Reims), 116 n.
St. Sulpice (Paris), 83
St. Victor (Paris), 67, 79, 81, 84, 107, 108–9, 149, 425
St. Vincent (Metz), 18
St. Wandrille (Rouen), 33
St. Werburg's (Chester), 52 n.
Saints-Gervais-et-Protais, 84 n.
Salisbury, 23–49, 58, 60, 61, 309
San Giovanni di Verdara (Padua), 428
San Marco (Florence), 226–7, 231, 232, 250 n., 252
San Placidio (Messina), 224
Sherborne, 30, 36
Soissons, 6, 8, 10, 12, 13 n., *and see* St. Médard
Sorbonne (Paris), 81, 93, 149, 152, 200, 212, 336 n.
Southwell, 259–60, 261
Speyer, 232 n.
Syon, 411

Toledo, 203
Tours, 67, 75 n., 81, 82, 112

Traù (Trogir), 239–40, 241 n., 242, 244, 245–6
Trier, 7

Urbino, 229, 242 n.

Venice, 128 n., 221, 222 n., 240, 242, 245 n., 246 n., 250 n., 252, 366, 373
Verona, 225, 231, 233 n.
Vienna, 4, 7–8, 9, 19, *and see* St. Nicholas

Villers-en-Brabant, 92
Volterra, 228

Wells, 30
Wimborne, 64
Winchester, 30, 55, 358
Worcester, 36 n., 287

York, 259–60, *and see* St. Mary's

Zara, 245–6, 247 n., 254

ADDENDA TO PAGES 66-114

The *Florilegium Angelicum* also appears in:

Cambridge, St. John's College MS. 97, fols. 214–229ᵛ (s. xiv; John of London, fl. 1364; St. Augustine's, Canterbury). Apuleius, Pliny, Cicero Orat., Sidonius, Seneca *de Ben.*, Cicero Tusc., A. Gellius, Ennodius.

Oxford, Trinity College MS. 18, fols. 181–185ᵛ (s. xiv; Bonshommes of BMV, Ashridge, s. xv). Ennodius, Pliny, Seneca epp., *Proverbia*, Cicero Tusc.

Venice, Biblioteca Nazionale Marciana MS. lat. cl. II, 40 (coll. 2195), fols. 1–12ᵛ (s. xiv, Italy). Gregory, Jerome, Macrobius, Seneca *de Ben.*, Martin of Braga, Sidonius, Ennodius, Q. Curtius, Seneca epp.

Catalogue of the Papal library at Peniscola, ed. M. Faucon, *La Librairie des Papes d'Avignon*, vol. ii (Paris, 1882), p. 140, no. 933. Macrobius, Apuleius, Pliny, Ennodius, Seneca.

tem fecit spem abstulit ceterum uerbis abundabat sine com
mendatione partium singularum in uniuersum magnificus
uale. L. ANNAEI SENECAE LIB XVI EXPLICIT
INCIPIT EIUSDEM LIBER XVII SENECA LUCILIO SS
Omnis dies omnis hora quam nihil sumus ostendit & aliquo ar
gumento recenti admonet fragilitatis obliuos aeterna
meditatos respicere e cogit ad mortem quid si bi iussd princip
um uelit quaeris senecionem cornelium equitem r. splendi
dum & officiosum noueras & tenui principio se ipse promo
uerat & iam illi decliuis erat cursus ad cetera facilius enim
crescit dignitas quam incipit. pecunia quoq. circa pauper
tatem plurimum amorem habet dum ex illa eropat hae
etiam senescio diutius imminebat ad quas illum duae res
ducebant efficacissimae & quaerendi & custodiendi scientia
quarum uel altera locupletem facere potuisset & hic homo sum
mae frugalitatis non minus patrimonii quam corporis dili
gens. cum ex consuetudine mane uidisset & cum per totum diem
amico grauiter adfecto & sine spe iacenti usq. in noctem adse
disset & cum hilaris cenasset & genere ualitudinis praecipiti arrep
tus angina uix con praessum aetatis faucibus spiritum traxit
in lucem. intra paucissimas ergo horas quam omnib. erat fan
acua lentur officiis functus decessisse qui & mari & terra pecu

Bamberg, Staatsbibliothek, Class. 46, fol. 64. (*Scale* 9 : 10)

candidus· pretia eius xx in
libras caerulei xviii
usus increta calcis inpatiens.
nuper accessit & uestorianū.
ab auctore appellatum·
& ex aegypti leuissima par
te· pretium eius in libras xi·
ideo & puteo lani usus· prae
terq̄· adfenestras cylon uo
cant· nonpridem adpostari
& indicum coeptum est· cu
ius pretium x vii· Ratio
inpictura· adincisura· hoc
est umbras diuidendas· ab
lumine est & uilissimum
genus lomenti quod tritum
uocant· quinis assibus aesti
matum caerulei sinceri.
experimentum incarbone
ut flagret fraus· uiola arida
decocta in aqua· succoq̄ per
linteum expresso· increta
ere iriam uis in mediana·
ut purget ulcerattaque &
emplastris adiciunt item
caustics· teritur autem diffi

cillime fril· inmedendo len
ter mordet· adstringitq̄· & ex
plet ulcera· uritur inficilib.
ut prosit· pretia rerum quae
usquam posuimus· non ignora
mus alia aliis locis esse & om
nibus paene mutari annis· pro
ut nauigatione constiterint
aut utquisq̄· mergatus sit· aut
aliquis praeualens man cipes
annonam flagellet. non obliti
demetrium atota se plasia
neronis principatu accusa
tum apudconsules· poni ta
men necessarium fuit quae
plerumque erat romae· ut
exprimeretur auctoritas
rerum·

C·PLINI SICVNDI

NATVRALIS· HISTOR̄

LIBER·XXXIIII·INCIP̄

IDITVS POST MORTEM·

Bamberg, Staatsbibliothek, Class. 42, fol. 49ᵛ. (*Scale* 5:6)

a. Exeter Cathedral 3500. Exon Domesday, fol. 9. (*Natural size*)

b. London, British Library, Cotton Tiberius C. I, fol. 112ᵛ. (*Scale* 7 : 10)

IV

a. fol. 1

b. fol. 18

c. fol. 51

Oxford, Bodleian Library, MS. Bodley 765. (*Natural size*)

Reuelatur enim ira di de celo super omne im-
pietatem & iniustitiam hominum eorum qui
ueritatem dei in iniustitia detinent quia
qd notum est di manifestum e illis. D[eus]
enim illis manifestauit. Inuisibilia enim
ipsius a creatura mundi p ea que facta
sunt intellecta conspiciuntur Sempiterna qq
ei uirt ac diuinitas ita ut sint inexcusabi-
les quia cum cognouissent dm n sicut dm
glorificauerunt aut gras egerunt sed eua-
nuerunt in cogitationibus suis & obscuratum
est insipiens cor eorum Dicentes enim se esse
sapientes stulti facti sunt Et mutauer-
glam incorruptibilis di in similitudinem
imaginis corruptibilis hominis & uolucrum
& quadrupedum & serpentium Propter qd tradidit illos ds in desideria cordis eorum in immundiciam ut contumeliis afficiant corpor su-
in semet ipsis. Qui comutauerunt ueritate
di in mendacium & coluerunt & seruier-

Oxford, Keble College, MS. 22, fol. 6. (*Natural size*)

a. Aberdeen, University Library, MS. 216, fol. 36. (*Scale* 6:7)

b. Oxford, Bodleian Library, MS. Bodley 756, fol. 1. (*Natural size*)

EXCERPTA DE LIBRO MACROBII SATURNALIORVM.

A nimo medius districta servanī. ¶Oporter ūsari
incontinuo sermones. ut castitate integros: ita
appetibiles venustate. ¶Sapiente ñ convenit lu-
do. ſ: serio fertari. ¶Nō nulla dere alia q̃ dedocē
q̃ t homib; colloq; p ēe iocundius. ¶Supfluum. ē. int sciences nota pferre. ¶Oar̄ papiriī puer q̄ cum parente suom in curia fuerat: pcunctat filium. qonam in senatu agissent patres. Puer
respondit tacendum ēe. neq; id dici licere. Omnibus fit avidi-
or audiendi secretum rei: & silentium pueri, animūq; ead
inq̃ rendum ēubat. Unū puer urgētur matre lepidō atq; festi-
vi mendacij consilium capit. Actum dicere in senatu. utrum
videt utilius ēe m̄ reip; ut duas uxores fieret: an ut una ap d'duos nu-
pta ēt. Hoc illa ū audivit: ad ceteras in mensa as affert. pdieq;
ad senatu confluunt. orant ut una poti duob; nī pta fieret.
Senatores q̃ illa ēt mulierū intempies. & q̃ d
sibi postulatio istec vellet. mirabantur. & nīt paris rei pdi
q̃ tilla verecundi secus impudicā in sariu pavescebant.
Puer nī medius pgres: metū dom̄t. & q̃ d sī mat̄ audire insti-
tisset. & q̃ o mat̄ ipse simulasset enarrat. Senat̄ fide atq;
ingenium pueri exosculat. consultumq; fact. ne pē illū
puer cū parib; p h in curiā removere. ſ Amat̄ cuidam
antiq̃ uba & venustate oblitterata pferenda ēe dicentia
respondit. Antani moribus; pteritus. & ubis pteritis; loq̃ m.
¶A multas voluptas nos amovet. qb; fortuna fecit ut viveri.
ſ Sic loq̃ ndum ē cū hominib; q̃ si d̄s audiat. sic loq̃ ndū ē
cū d̄o. tanq̃ homines audiant. ſ Nichil a d̄o petam? qd vel
te ros indecor sit hominib; confiteri. ſ Religiosus hovor

VO:DÑO: fuuſ ſer
uuſ. ſedulam in oīnibʒ ſer
uitutem. Et hunc librū t
offero ſediſ apłicę glā. qui
ex ſententiarū maieſtate
ſcintillet. et eloquii pfulge
at claritate. Clauſule bre
ueſ ſunt. et uerbiſ memoabi
libuſ inſignite. Edidert eaſ ueteriſ eloquentie uiri.
et cū ſūmo eloquutioniſ ornatu poſteriſ reliquerunt.
In unū corpuſ meo labore liber iſte opactuſ eſt. et redac
tuſ in formā. Et qa omſ mittere ñ potui. elegi et collegi
de oīnibʒ: in qbʒ letaretur et delectaret aīa tua. Et ut nīi
dem miniſtrii meū in hac parte: ñ partiū puteſ uł reputeſ
hc labore. Vigilanti qippe op̄ fuit. ad cernendū et diſcernen
dū. tot et tantoʒ ſententiaſ oratoʒ: cū philoſophʒ dicat. Non
habet admirationem una arbor: ſi in eandē altitudinē tota
ſilua ſurrexr. Totuſ next illoʒ uirtuſ eſt. et emineront ſin
gula. ñ ſint paria legerentr. Defloraui tariū floſculoſ digno
reſ. et candidioreſ manipuloſ turſ ocłiſ pſentaui. Patet ibi tā
philoſophoʒ quia diuinoʒ numeroſa facundia: et pfūdir ſen
ſuſ uenuſtiſſimiſ ſermonibʒ ueſtiunt. Et hoc multū credidi
illi tue ſingulari excellentie ſueuire: ut ſ̄ep ad manū habeaſ.
unde poſſiſ et pſonaſ et locoſ et teporibʒ aptare ſermoneſ. Hicł

Rome, Biblioteca Angelica, MS. 1895, fol. 1. (*Natural size*)

Oxford, Bodleian Library, MS. Auct. D. 2. 8, fol. 105. (*Scale* 2:3, *see p.* 138)

X

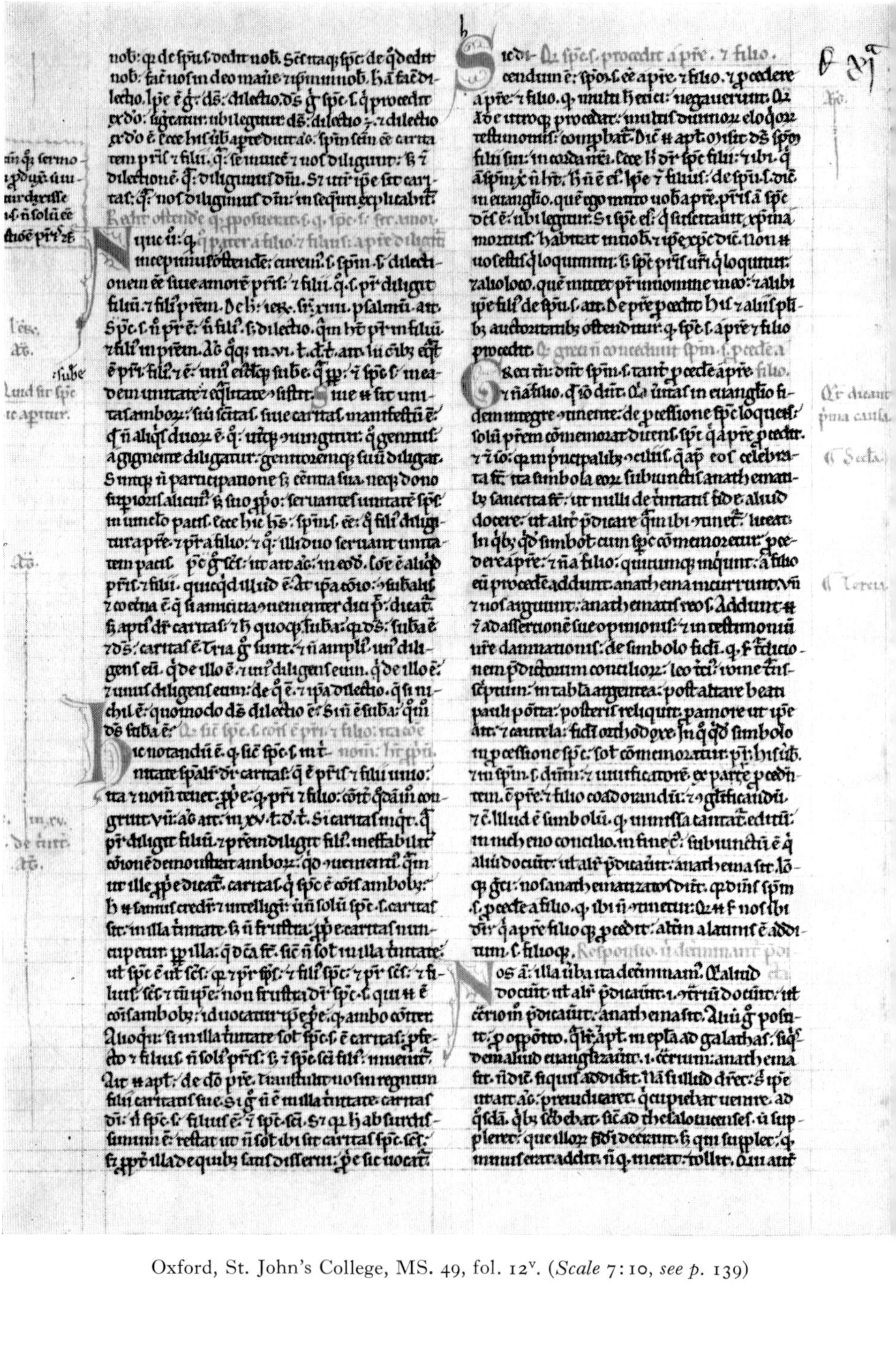

Oxford, St. John's College, MS. 49, fol. 12v. (*Scale* 7:10, *see p.* 139)

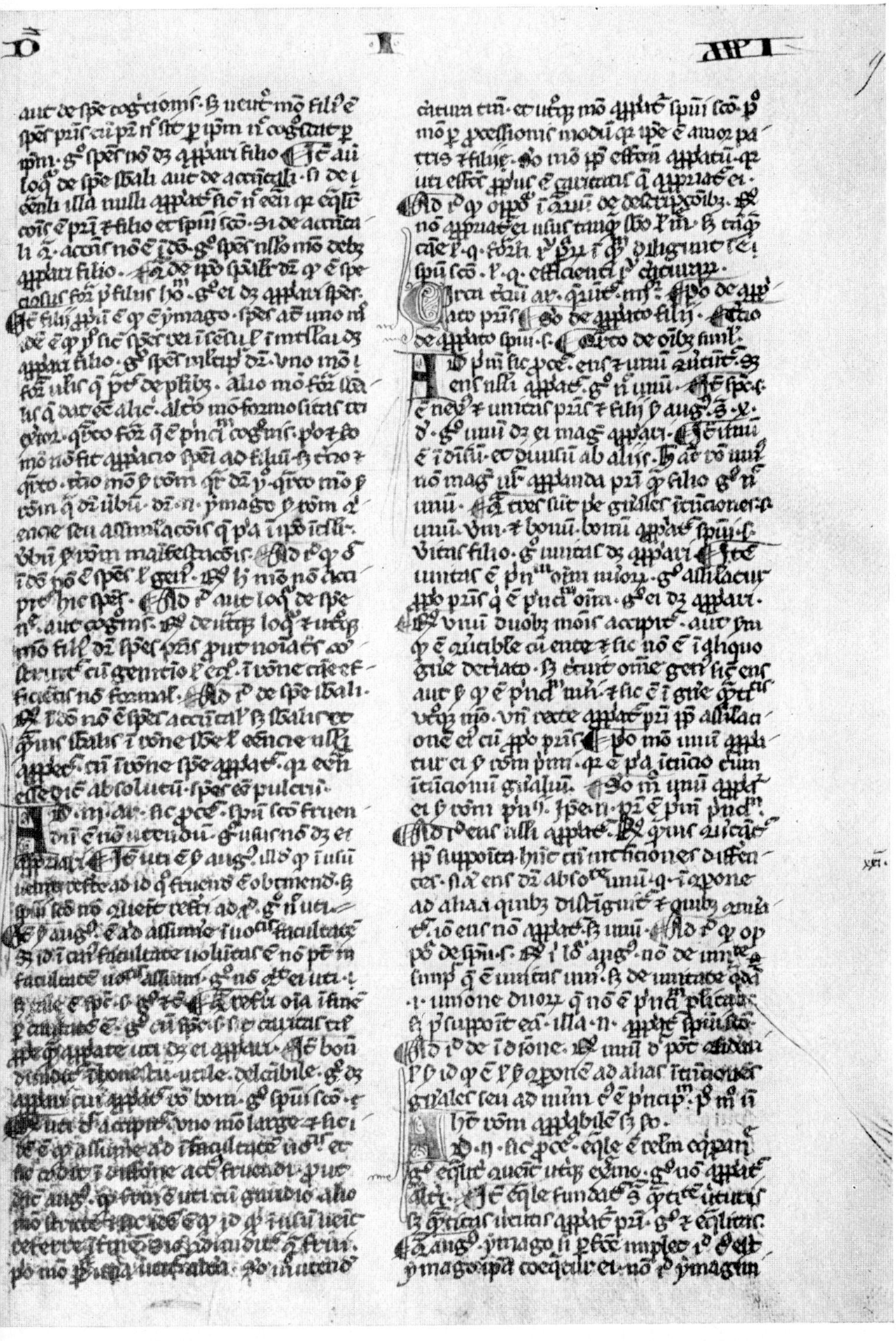

Paris, Bibliothèque Nationale, lat. 3050, fol. 76. (*Scale* 2 : 3, *see p.* 139)

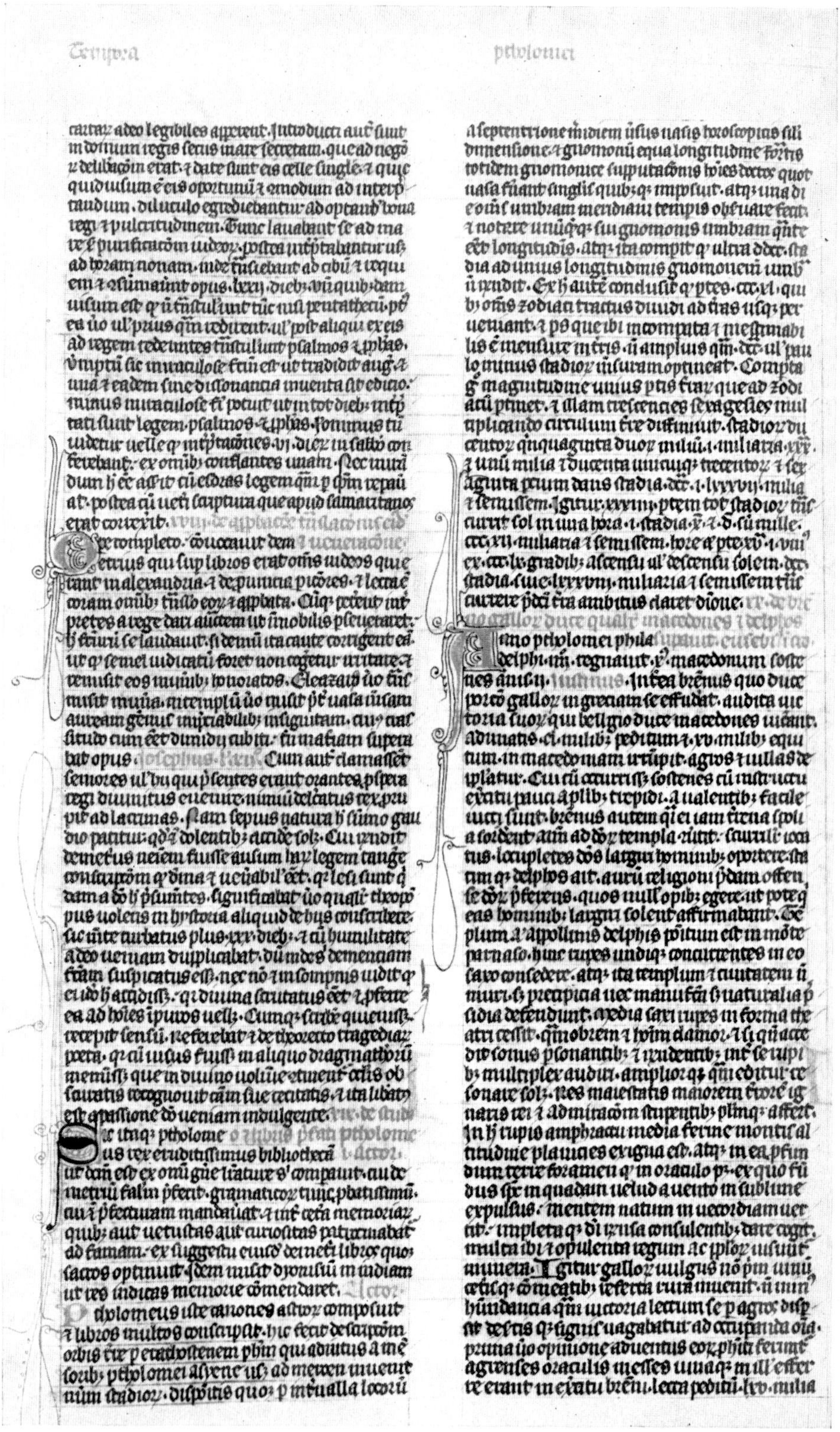
Tempora
ptholomei

Oxford, Keble College, MS. 26, fol. 17ᵛ. (*Scale* 2:3, *see p.* 139)

eft) Oxford, Bodleian Library, MS. Bodley 287, fol. 74ᵛ. (*Scale* 9:16, *see p.* 139)

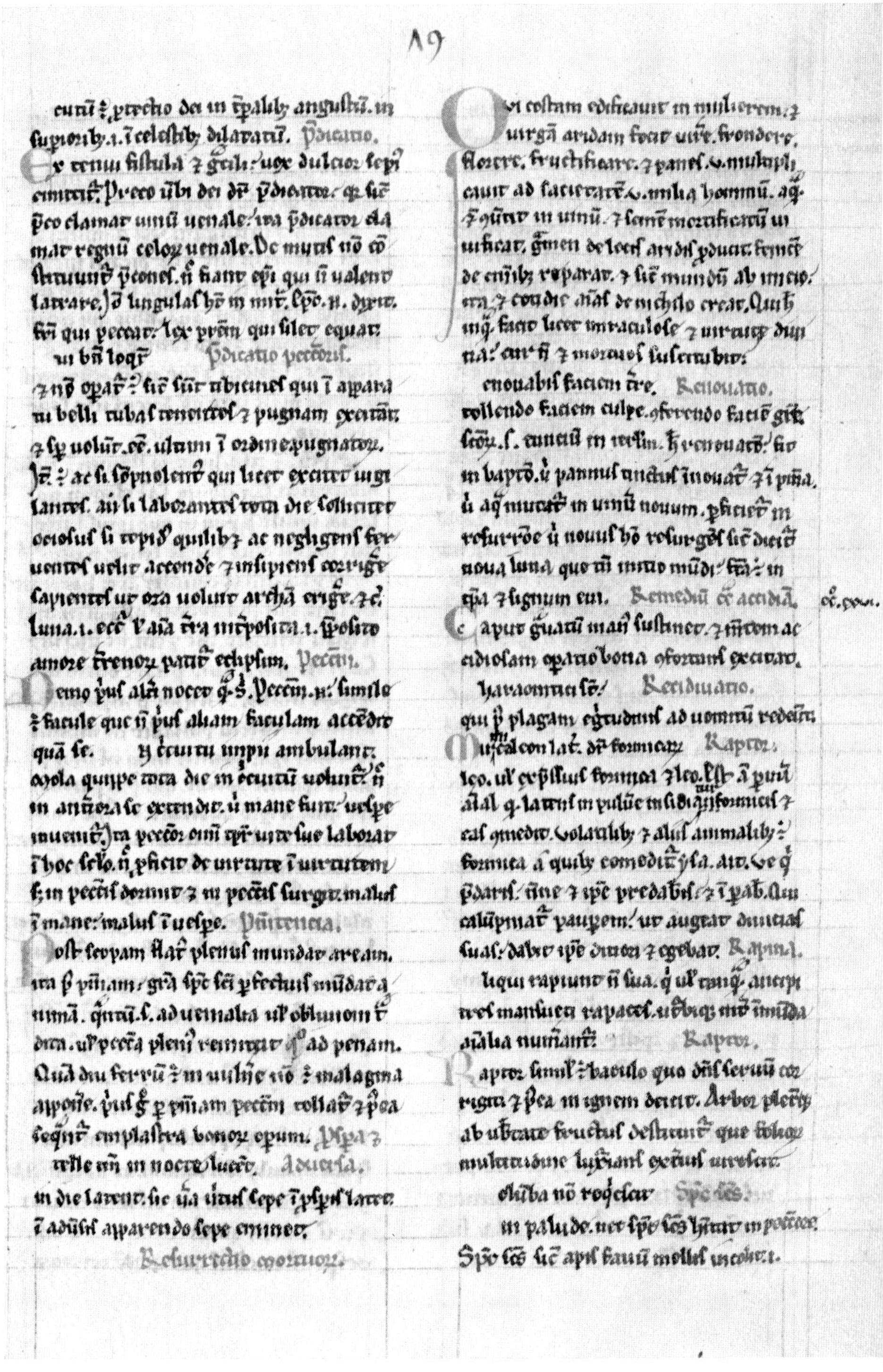

Oxford, New College, MS. 98, fol. 138. (*Scale* 7:8, *see p.* 140)

(*right*) Oxford, University College, MS. 67, fol. 52^{v}. (*Natural size, see p.* 140)

ff.

fius n̄ q̄feat nūfſa e t aliq̄ nunoꝛis bꝛate q̄ uteꝛ nartatoꝛibus
t exᵖo i pmonibꝛ fius pene tota anglia cōtitt. Qh' uꝛ ad pꝛeſi
cationem et conuerſionem.

Exēplo om̅ꝰ ꝙ aliꝰ edoceri. infra ſe uidr̄.
Exēplū bonū cōtitt aliū pꝛodr̄. ꝙ ſe abbe.
Exemplū malū multis nocet. infra ſe mōcho.

Exēplū a melioꝛi e ſūndū. Ex untis pꝛm fruit duo. ꝙ
Aur t tulle. uiꝛ ſūt ste uite ſꝫ nifoꝛtunate. i mūdanis
i tru ꝙ i die ſepulte ſue tāta ſūt pluuie i mūdacō ꝙ ni
pliꝫ diebꝫ n̄ potuit ſepeliri. uxoꝛ aꝰ peſſime uite ſꝫ foꝛtu
nata. p̄ moꝛte uēuſꝫ filia eoꝛ cōgitare cepit aiꝰ uita uim
tayetuꝛ. fta i extaſi indr̄ locū amenisſimū i q̄ pꝛeꝫ uidr̄
rint i ampleyꝰ ei ꝉogaꝰ ut eā ſecū retiuet. illo reſpon
dente n̄ poteꝝ in h' iemāe. Si duxis uita q̄ duxi huc
uenieꝝ. moꝛ ꝛ——ꝛ ab eo ducta e ad aliū locū de q̄ deoꝛſū
reſpicienꝝ uidit uirtū i hoꝛribili toꝛuito. Que cuilas t cla
mans filie dixit. filia inte q̄ pateoꝛ ꝝ tu mea uita mea
illa redies ad ſe t teſtiaꝝ ꝙꝰ ſi huius que uidat cōſmata e
ad ſe q̄ꝙꝰ uita pꝛio t fta ꝙ tule ſta. Qh' uꝛ ad gaudia padi
ſi et penas miſerū.

Eloquncia ntūalia e elito ualis q̄u demoſtenes q̄ſpā
bras comode ꝓferre n̄ poſſi uitiū oꝛis ſui tanto
ſtudio expugnauit ut illeꝰ exꝓſſio ꝙ uolebat
ꝓꝓter denīꝙ ad h' puenit ut uadoſis liutoꝛibꝫ in
ſiſtens declamatoꝛes fluctuū ſtrigoꝛ i buſꝙā eſſet oꝛe ꝙ
calculis inſertis iſtitu t diu loq̄ ſoliꝰ ejat ꝙ uacuū pꝛipꝝ
eet atꝙ ſoluē. Qh' uꝛ ad aſſuefactioē t uſi ſu cōſuetudi
nem et eleriauit.

ffallacia mulieris infra ſe muliere.
ffalſitas teſtiū nocet. infra ſe teſtimonio.
ffalſū iuraꝝ punit. infra ſe iuramento.

Falſū nipoꝛtū ꝙ demūdari. Ex uita pꝛm i rau—t. Euge
nia filia philiꝑ ꝓfecti alexādꝛie xv. anoꝛū retu
laus nobili uiro nubē fugiens t ſe uirū filāns h—tū
religionis i quādā moſtio ſuſtepit ſeꝙ fratem eugeniū
uocauit. ꝙ moꝛtuo moſtij ꝓpoſito ꝑpoſitꝰ e fribꝫ. Quedā a
matrona diues t nobilioꝛ de alexandria eſtimaꝰ eū uirū
i amoꝛe ipſi uehemēt exarſit i tm̄ ut infua ſe filāns
et pꝛo eo mandaꝰ. tm̄ aū lectū eiꝰ ſoliꝰ eet tꝑe ſiui ei expo
ſui eūꝙ aꝑhendes amplectit t deoſtulat. et carnale
copulā muitat. Qꝛ ille abhoꝛres t illā arguens timis
illa ne foꝛte ſtelus ꝑplicitet clamare cepit ꝙ eugenius
uolint eā uiolare. coꝛeit ꝙꝰ tota familia t h—iꝰ rei coꝛā
philippo ꝓfecto ducti teſtes ſiit. ayclācia eugeniū foꝛtū

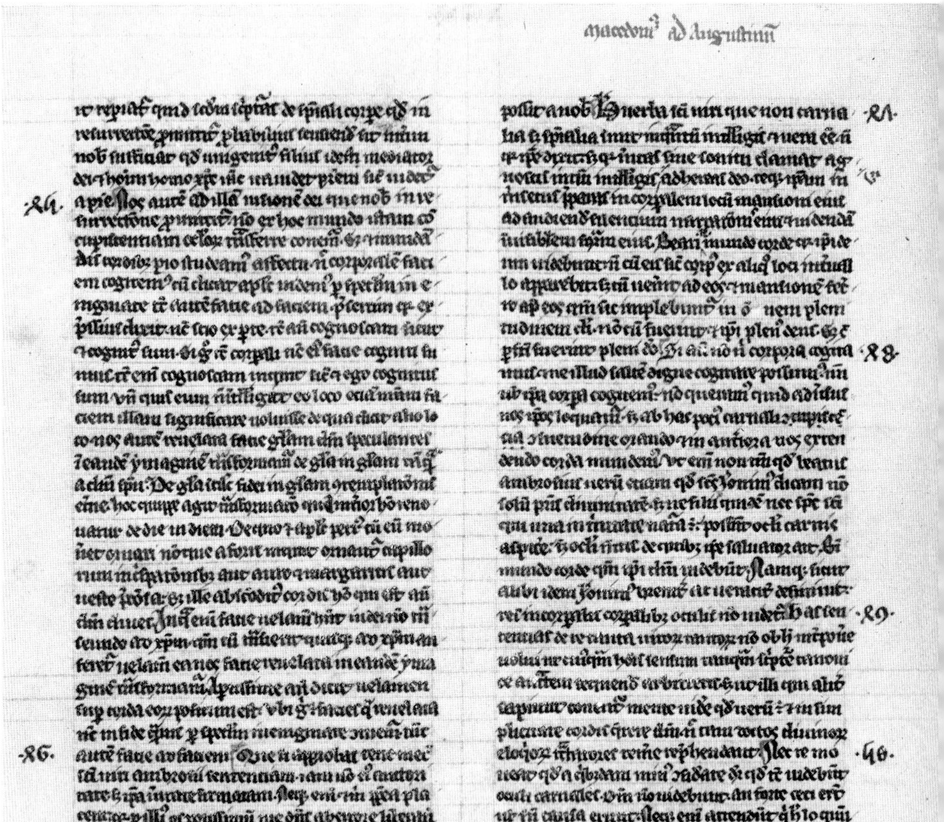

Oxford, Bodleian Library, MS. Bodley 568, fol. 242v. (*Scale* 13:20, *see p.* 140)

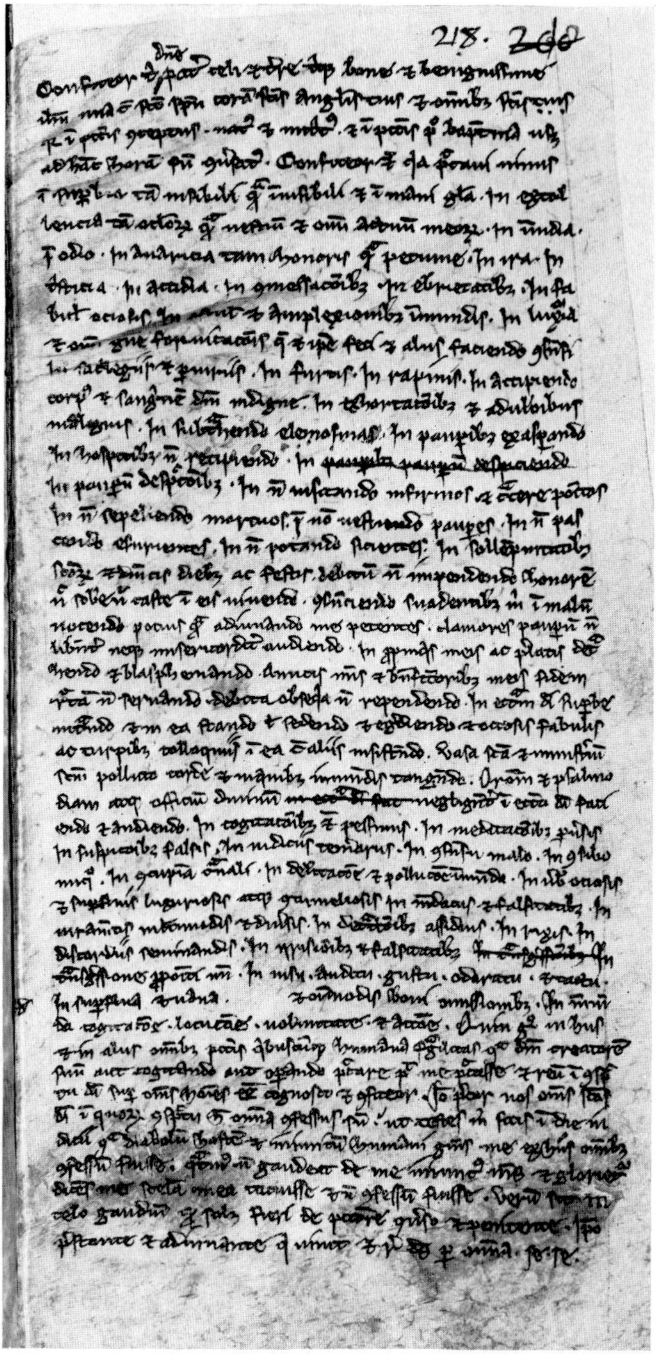

Oxford, Bodleian Library, MS. Auct. D. 4. 13, fol. 218. (*Scale* 19:20)

cuiq; de duabus altera dedit ut in eo cui adheret cognata sibi & simile sen re pe

rire; terra e sicca & frigida aqua vero frigida & humecta e; haec duo elementa

licet sibi psiccu humectuq; contraria sint p frigidum tam comune unig; ut aer

humectus & calidus e; & cu aque frigidus contrarius sit calori conciliatione tamen

focu copulat humoris; Sup hunc ignis cu sit calidus & siccus humore quidem

aeris respuit siccitate: sed conectit psocietate caloris; Et rsit ut singula

queq; li mentoru duos sibi hinc inde vicina singulis qualitatibus vel ut quibusdam

amplectat ulnis; A qua terra frigore: aer e a sibi nectit humore; Aer que

humecto simile & igni calore sociatur; Ignis aeri miscetur ut callidiq; rursum

qt siccitate; Terra igne sico pact a qua rigore non respuit; haec tamen

quaria elas vinculorum si elementa duo fore nihil int ipsa firmitatis habuisse;

Sit ia minus quidem valido aliquo tamen nexu vincienda nodat; int quat

tuor vero insolubilis conligatio e cu duesum mitates duabus interiectionib;

vinciunt; Qd erit manifestius si in medio posuerim ipsam contrarietatem fa

sus de timeo platonis exceptam; Divin decoris in quit ratio post plabat talem

fieri mundum quid & visum pat & tactu; Constabat aut neq; uideri ali

quid posse sine igni beneficio; neq; tangi sine solido; Et solidum nihil e sine

terra; Unde omnem mundi corpus designat; ut in struere fabricator incipi

ens ui dr duo conuenire sine medio conligante non posse & hoc e optimu

vinculum qd & separata & aseliganda deuinceat; unam vero int

iectione tunc solum posse sufficere cu superficies sine altitudine

uicienda e; at ubi artanda vinculis e alta dimensionum nisi ge

mina interiectione cognecta; Inde aer e & aqua int igne ter raq;

contexuit & ita poma una & sibi conuentis ugabilis compagin

ta cucurrit elementoru diuersitate ipsa differentiaru ae qua li

Paris, Bibliothèque Nationale, lat. 16677, fol. 9ᵛ. (*Scale* 4:5)

incorporis intelligibilis lineā pmā defluxe· Ideo & aduagas stell· if cælumpui spemir
refero· qc heqq abilla qappl· uner dr· innumeris scisse· & inuariā mor ceuariscacere
tority· Hic ergo numeror cuiquario aptissime ungue· cu hic ad err· ncer ut dixim° ad
cælizonus ille refer'tae· Sed ille ratione scisso part· hic numero· Illa u qnario numero
appicas excepta· potenne ultra celras eminenris euenit· qd solus omia quqq·fqq· induit
& explexus e· Esse aut dicim° intelligibilis· Videri ceo corporulis omia seu dimepicap
habeant seu caducu· Hic ergo numeror simul omia & sup & sub iecta designar· Aur
ceu deus sum'e· aur mens excoe nata· in rerū speciei conanence· Aut mundi anima
qanimaru omiu fons e· Aut cælestia suq·ad nos·aut crena piacurae· ce sicqnari°
rerū omiū numeror ipse· Deseda septenarii numeris eunctione dicta hac passacbica
preuicacus per efficace sufficiant· Terciae deterib· eo quare qqneu uilear reuoluam°
Gæometrici corpeus ab impari pmā planiciei interib· linee estar· Hise ni ergo nar forma
concludit· Car u pmā inqrua· Inuenit· Jce seim sedm platone id sedm ipsi ueritacis arcanu
illa sua in se uinculo colligari qb· quiectra media cus pscat uiuculi firmitate· Cu u medi
& cas ipsa geminat· eaq· extimas in renacui tantu sacetia ipsolubilu uinciunt· Pmo erg
cnario co ungit numero· ut int duas sum'af mediū quo uincnqrae acciperxe· Quatnariu
u duas medicares pm omiu u nact° est quas ab hoc numero· di mundane mor as rifex
editorq· muciat insolubili in se uinculo elementa de quinx· sic inme a plaronis ad ser
tum est· Non aluica ce crouersa sibi ac repugnantia & nature cōmune in abnuenra ne
pmiscet· Terra dico & igne potuisse pra iugabile copia· ceneta federari nisi duob·
medusaeris & aque nexib· uincerentur· Jraeni elemenca ip se duersissima opifex
cam dscordinis opor tunitate cnexuit· ut facile ungere· Nā cu bingessent in singu
lis qualitares· tale unicuiq· dedit uthi neo cui adherere·& cognata
sibi & simile repperiret· Terra e sicca i frigida· Aquero frigida & umer caes
Haec duo elemenca & sibi psic & umer·diq· ceraliasint· p frigidu tam cōmunice
ungunt· Aer umectus & calidus e· Et cu aque frigide e cerali sit calor
cali arione cam socu copulat umoris· Suphune ignis cu sit cali & sicc·umorem
quidē aeris respuit siccirare· sed & necte pci & care caloris· Et terra sic ut singu
la queq· elemen coru duo sibi bin e inde u uicina· singulis qualicatib·tue qb·dā amplec
cant ulnis· Aqua craris sibi necte humore· Erigine aerem· Aer·aque humore·simile
& igni calore sociat· Ignis aeri miscet ut calido·erie ungit siccicate· Terra igni siccu·
Aqua rigore nrespue· Hec cum uariciat uinculois sielemca duo forent· nihil in ipsa
firmicaris habuisse· Sicra mip· quide ualido·ali q cam nexu un ciencia poclure·
Inte quacuor u insolubit collagacio e·cuidus sumicares· duab· inte cionib·· unciantur·
At eric manifestu si immedio posuerim' ipsa continencia sens· de Tymeo plato pf excerpta·

a. fol. 1

b. fol. 12ᵛ

c. fol. 4

d. fol. 75ᵛ

Paris, Bibliothèque Nationale, lat. 6842D. (*Scale: a,* 9:10; *b, c & d, natural size*)

. PETRONIVS .

. ARBITER .

VM. alio genere furiarū declamatores inquietantur· qui clamant· hæc uulnera pro libertate excæpi· hūc oculū pro uobis impendi· date mihi ducem qui me ducat ad liberos meos· Nam succisi poplites membra nō subtinent· hæc ipa tollerabilia essent· si ad eloquentiā ituris uia facerent· Nūc & rerū tumore· & sententiarū uanissimo strepitu· hoc tm proficiūt· ut cū in forū uenerūt·

a. Vatican City, Biblioteca Apostolica Vaticana, Vat. lat. 3403, fol. 31ᵛ. (*Natural size*)

hoc faciet· ibis in crucem· polluisti sanguine domicilium meum inuiolatum· fecistiq; ut me quisquis uoluerit, inimicus sacerdotio pollat·

Quisquis habet nummos secura nauiget aura
Fortunamq; suo temperet arbitrio·
Vxorem ducat daphnen· ipsumq; licebit
Acrisium iubeat credere quod daphnen.
Carmina componat· declamet· concrepet· omnes
Et pagat causas· sitq; Catone prior.
Iurisconsultus paret· non paret habento
Atq; esto quicquid seruius et Labeo.
Multa loquor· quid uis nummis presentibus opta tat
Et ueniet· clausum possidet archa iouem :— θεῶ δδξα
PETRonius ARbiter satyricon lib feliciter explicit :—

MCCCXL· Georgij Antonij vespucij :—

b. Vienna, Nationalbibliothek, 3198, fol. 63ᵛ. (*Natural size*)

Plinius s̄. Secundo suo salutem

REQVENTER HORTATVS
es ut epistolas quas paulo accura
tius scripsissem colligerem publi
caremq̄. Collegi non seruato tem
poris ordine. neq̄ enim historiam
componebam. sed ut quęq̄ in ma
nus uenerat. Superest ut nec te
consilii. nec me peniteat obsequii. Ita enim fiet ut
eas quę adhuc neclectę iacent requiram. et si quas
addidero non supprimam. Vale. Plinius s̄. Adri
ano suo salutem.
Via tardiorem aduentum tuum prospicio. librum quem prioribus epi
stolis promiseram exhibeo. Hunc rogo ex consuetu
dine tua et legas et emendes. eo magis q̄ nihil ante
peręque eodem stilo scripsisse uideor. Temptaui N
imitari Demosthenem semper tuum caluum. nup
meum figuris duntaxat orationis. Tantorum ui
rorum pauci equitius adsequi possunt. Nec mate
ria ipsa huic uereor ne improbe dicam emulationi
repugnauit. Erat enim prope tota in contentione
dicendi. Q̄d me longe desidię indormientem exci
tauit si modo istum ego qui excitari possim. Non
tamen omnino marci nostri ΛΗΚΥΘΟΥϹ fugimus. q̄
tiens paulum itinere decedere non intempestiuis a
menitatibus admonebamur. Acres N non tristes ęę

publicare

† neglide

Senecae Rhetoris declamationes

VM ALIO GENERE furia
declamatores inquietantur : qui cla
mant hęc uulnera pro libertate publica
excipi : hunc oculum pro uobis impendi · Date
mihi ducem qui me ducat ad liberos meos · Nam
succisi poplites membra non sustinent · Haec
ipsa tolerabilia essent si ad eloquentiam ituris
uiam facerent · Nunc et rerum tumore et sen
tentiae uanissimo strepitu : hoc tantum profi
ciunt : ut cum in forum uenerint : putent se
in alium terrarum orbem delatos · Et ideo
ego adolescentulos existimo in scholis stultissi
mos fieri : quia nihil ex iis quae in usu habemus :
aut audiunt : aut uident · Sed pyratas cum
cathenis in litore stantes : et tyrannos edicta
scribentes : quibus imperent filiis ut patrum
suorum capita precidant · sed responsa in pestilen
tiam data : ut uirgines tres aut plures immo
lentur · Sed mellitos uerborum globulos : et
omnia dicta factaq̃ quasi papauere & se sanxo
sparsa · Qui inter haec nutriuntur non magis

Vienna, Nationalbibliothek, s.n. 4755, fol. I. (*Scale* 5:6)

Phebo pulcrior et sorore phebi
horti tubere quod creauit ~~uidi~~ uuida
Vt mortem nauis uenire ardas
Sato iam capias perisse partem

Plura nolebat proferre credo et ineptiam preterito cuian
alia tryphene gytona in partem nauis inferiore diunt co
rimbiaq; domine pueri adornat caput immo superuilia
etiam profert depixide. sateq; iacture linia meta scisa
totam illi formam suam reddidit. Agnouit tryphena neq;
gytona lacrimisq; turbata tunc primu bona fide puero basiu
dedit. Coeterum eumolpos et periclitantiu aduocatius et
p(re)sentis concordie auctor ne sileret sine fabulis. hilaritas
multa in muliebrem leuitatem cepit iactare qua facile
adamar ent q(u)ato etiam filiorum obliuiscerentur nullamq;
ce femina tam pudicam que non peregrina libidine usq;

a. fol. 8

amoui nec uenit in mentem quoq; consederis aruis. Quid
diutius moror ne hanc quidem partem corporis mulier ab
sonuit uictorq; miles utrumq; persuasit. Iacuerunter
go una non tantum illa nocte qua nuptias fecerunt sed
postero etiam ac tertio die p(er)clusis uidelicet conditorij fonb;
ut si quis ex ignotis cognitisq; ad monumentum uenisset
putasset expirasse super corpus uiri pudicissima uxorem
Coetero delectatus miles et forma et secreto quicq; boni per
facultates poterat coemebat et prima statim nocte in mo
numentu ferebat. Itaq; cruciumd; arie parentis ut ui
derunt laxata custodiam detraxere nocte pendente supimaq;
mandauerunt officio. At miles circumscriptus dum resi
det ut postero die uidit una sine cadauere crucem neritus
supplicium mulier quod audisset exponit nec se expectaturp
iudicas sententia sed gladio ius diture ignauie siue commenda
ret modo comedet ergo illa perituro locum et fatale con
ditorium familiari ac uiro faceret. Mulier non minus
misericors q(uam) pudica nec istud dij sinant ut eadem tem-

cruciarij
uiius

b. fol. 9

Florence, Biblioteca Laurenziana, 37, 25. (*Natural size*)

P. RVTILII LVPI SCEMATA DIANOEAS EX
GRECO VORSA. GORGIA.

Rosapodosis. Hoc schema duobus modis fieri et tractari
potest. Nam sententiis duabus aut pluribus propositis, sua
cuiusq; ratio uel posterius reddetur, uel statim sub una quaq;
sententia subiungetur. quibus posteris ratio subinferetur. huius

c hanc a cicerone
apptri diffinitio
nes

a. fol. 35

quendum accommodatus. Dissolutum autem perorationib;
siue conclusionibus. est enim passiuu. 1. affectus animi
comouens

DE VSV.

Vsus est quam greci XPTIAN uocant. comemoratio oratio
nis alicuius uel facti uel utriusq; simul celerem habens de
mostrationem. que utilitatis alicuius plerumq; causa pro
fertur. Vsuu autem alii sunt orationales alii actuu
Orationales sunt quibus oratio inest sola: Vt plato di
cebat, musas in animis esse ingeniosor. Actiui uero in
quibus actus inest solus: Vt diogenes, cum uidisset pue
rum indecenter agentem pedisecu uirga percussit. Vel
mixte, si addas percussit dicens quare sic erudisti. Inter
est autem inter usum et comemorationes hoc, quod usus
breuiter profertur comemorationes uero quas ATTOMNH

b. fol. 24

M.T.C. AD. h. LIBER. V. EXPLICIT. INCIPIT LIBER. VI.
8 ISTRIBVTIO e ai i plures res aut psonae negotia qda
certa dispartiut hoc mo. Qui uiru iudices nome diligit se
natus. hunc odit necesse. Petulantissime enis semp iste oppugnauit
senatu. qui equestre loca spledidissimu cupit ee i ciuitate is oportet
istu maximas penas dedisse uelit. ne ista sua turpitudie ordmi hones
tissimo macule atq; decori sit. qui paretes habetis ostendite istius sup
plicio uob impios hoies no place. Quib; liberi st statute exemplu. quare
pene sint i ciuitate hoib; istusmodi comparate. Ite SENATVS e
officiu. cosilio ciuitate iuuare. Magistratus o officiu. opera idilige

faurie
v. gb libius ostē
rie gorgli

c. fol. 62ᵛ

Florence, Biblioteca Laurenziana, 37, 25. (*Scale: a, b, natural size: c* 9:10)

a. p. 188

c. p. 188

b. p. 193

d. p. 193

Paris, Bibliothèque Nationale, lat. 7989. (*Natural size*)

al. regibus

imperatas atqz syriæ regionibusqz oīb; et dīuītib; et liberis achaiæ populis pecuniaz exigeret mag
nitudē exercituum quas ipse obtinebat sibi nume
rat. Legiones effecerat cuiuz romanoz nouaz quarū
unaz traduxerat unaz ex sicilia ueterānaz quā ge
mellaz appellabat. unaz ex creta et macedonia ex
militib; quæ dimissi a superiorib; imperatorib; i[...]
cōsederāt. duas ex asia quas Lentulus consul cōscribē
Præterea magnum numeruz ex thesalia. boecia. achaia
supplemēti noīe i legiones distribuerat. his antoni
legiones duas sagitarios
ex creta lacedemone
exponto atqz siria
liter admiscuerat. preter has expectabat cuz Sci[...]
syriā reliquisqz ciuitatib; tria milia numō habebat
cohortes sexcenarias / delectos equites septē mi[...]
sexcentos gallos deuoturus adduxerat / quingetos [...]
al. VI.
al. delectoz equiz

a. fol. 102[^v]

cuz, de loco et de tpre eius rei cōtrouisia inferet / & uoce & manibus
uniusi ex uallo ubi cōstiterat significare cępit. ut statū, dimitteret
neqz oī interposita fide firmiū, esse posse si i aliud tpus differetur.
Paucis cū, esset i utraqz parte, uerbis disputatū, res huc deducitur,
ut ii q brevent domicilium; aut possessiōes i hispania statū, reliq ad uaru
flume dimittaū nequid eis noceat neu quis inuitū sacrāmto dicere
cogat a Cæsare cauet. Cæsar ex eo tpre diū, ad flume uaru uenuit
se frumentū, datuz pollicet. Addit etiā, ut quid qsqz eozū i bello ami
serit quæ sint penes milites suos ut qui amiserat restituat / militib;
equa facta extimatioē pecuniæ, p ut dissoluit rebz Quascūqz postea
cōtrouisias milites int se habuerit sua spote ad Cæsarē, introdu
xerūt. Petreius atqz Afranius cū, stipediū, a legionib; pęne seditioe
facta flagitaret / au illi dies, noctū, ueisse diceret Cæsar ut cogn
osceret postulat. eoqz utriqz quod statuit cotenti fuerūt. Circit
tertia parte exercitus eo biduo dimissa duas legioes suas ante
cedere / reliquas subsequi iussit. ut no longo int se spatio ca
stra faceret / eiqz negotio. Q. Fusius; Calenū; leg.tiū; prefecit.
hoc eius pscripto ex hispania ad uariū flumen est iter factū;
atqz ibi reliqua pars exercitus dimissa.

Commentarioruz belli ciuilis pompeiani ac iuli[...]
Cesaris gesta et tēpus libeat. primusq; expli[...]
corcirā regnū iacit arq; exercepsit sibi et eius fore dubi[...]
florentibz cui idus. augustus. ex xxv. beneime[...]

b. fol. 93

Paris, Bibliothèque Nationale, lat. 6106. (*Natural size*)

.CLAVDIANI POETAE DE PHONICE
.CARMEN INCIPIT.

OCEANI summo circusfluus aequore lucus.
Trans Indos Eurumque nitet: qui primus anhelis
Sollicitatur equis: uicinaque uerbera sentit
Humida roranti resonant cui lumina cursu
Vnde rubet uentura dies longeque coruscis
Nox afflata rotis refugo pallescit amictu.
Hic fortunatus nimium Titanius Ales
Regna colit solusque plaga defensus iniqua
Possidet intactas egris animalibus oras.
Seua nec humani patitur contagia mundi.
Par uolucer superis. stellas qui uiuidus aequat
Durando membrisque terit redeuntibus aeuum.
Non epulis saturare famem. no fontibus ullis
Assuetus prohibere sitim. sed purior alti
Solis feruor alit uentosaque pabula potat
Tethyos innocui carpens alimenta uaporis.
Arcanum radiant oculi iubar. igneus ora
Cingit honos. rutilo cognatum uertice sydus.
Attollit cristatus apex. tenebrasque serena
Luce secat. tyrio pinguntur crura ueneno.
Ante uolant Zephiros penne. quas credulus ambit
Flore color. sparsos super arefacit in auro.
Hic neque concepto foetu. neque semine surgit.
Sed pater est prolesque sibi. nulloque creante